The Blackwell Guide to Aristotle's *Nicomachean Ethics*

Blackwell Guides to Great Works

A proper understanding of philosophy requires engagement with the foundational texts that have shaped the development of the discipline and which have an abiding relevance to contemporary discussions. Each volume in this series provides guidance to those coming to the great works of the philosophical canon, whether for the first time or to gain new insight. Comprising specially commissioned contributions from the finest scholars, each book offers a clear and authoritative account of the context, arguments, and impact of the work at hand. Where possible the original text is reproduced alongside the essays.

Published

1   The Blackwell Guide to Plato's *Republic,* edited by Gerasimos Santas
2   The Blackwell Guide to Descartes' *Meditations,* edited by Stephen Gaukroger
3   The Blackwell Guide to Mill's *Utilitarianism,* edited by Henry R. West
4   The Blackwell Guide to Aristotle's *Nicomachean Ethics,* edited by Richard Kraut
5   The Blackwell Guide to Hume's *Treatise,* edited by Saul Traiger

Forthcoming

The Blackwell Guide to Kant's Ethics, edited by Thomas E. Hill, Jr
The Blackwell Guide to Hegel's *Phenomenology of Spirit,* edited by Kenneth Westphal
The Blackwell Guide to Heidegger's *Being and Time,* edited by Robert Scharff

THE BLACKWELL GUIDE TO

ARISTOTLE'S
Nicomachean Ethics

EDITED BY RICHARD KRAUT

Blackwell
Publishing

© 2006 by Blackwell Publishing Ltd

BLACKWELL PUBLISHING
350 Main Street, Malden, MA 02148–5020, USA
9600 Garsington Road, Oxford OX4 2DQ, UK
550 Swanston Street, Carlton, Victoria 3053, Australia

The right of Richard Kraut to be identified as the Author of the Editorial Material in this Work has
been asserted in accordance with the UK Copyright, Designs, and Patents Act 1988.

First published 2006 by Blackwell Publishing Ltd

1   2006

Library of Congress Cataloging-in-Publication Data

The Blackwell guide to Aristotle's Nicomachean ethics / edited by
Richard Kraut.
    p.   cm.—(Blackwell guides to great works)
    Includes bibliographical references and indexes.
    ISBN-13: 978-1-4051-2020-3 (hardcover : alk. paper)
    ISBN-10: 1-4051-2020-7 (hardcover : alk. paper)
    ISBN-13: 978-1-4051-2021-0 (pbk. : alk. paper)
    ISBN-10: 1-4051-2021-5 (pbk. : alk. paper)
  1. Aristotle. Nicomachean ethics.   2. Ethics.   I. Kraut, Richard, 1944– .   II. Series.

B430.B53 2005
171'.3—dc22
2005014101

A catalogue record for this title is available from the British Library.

Set in 10 on 13 pt Galliard
by SNP Best-set Typesetter Ltd, Hong Kong

For further information on
Blackwell Publishing, visit our website:
www.blackwellpublishing.com

Contents

Notes on Contributors

Chris Bobonich is Associate Professor of Philosophy at Stanford University. He has written a number of articles on Greek ethical, psychological, and political philosophy, and is the author of *Plato's Utopia Recast* (2002).

Sarah Broadie is a Wardlaw Professor at the University of St Andrews. She is the author of *Nature, Change and Agency in Aristotle's Physics* (1984), *Passage and Possibility: A Study of Aristotle's Modal Concepts* (1984), *Ethics with Aristotle* (1991), and the introduction and commentary to *Aristotle, Nicomachean Ethics*, translated by Christopher Rowe (2002).

Roger Crisp is Uehiro Fellow and Tutor in Philosophy at St Anne's College, Oxford. He is the author of *Mill on Utilitarianism* (1997), and has translated Aristotle's *Nicomachean Ethics* (2000).

Dorothea Frede is Professor of Philosophy at Hamburg University. She is currently working on a new German translation of and commentary on the *Nicomachean Ethics* for the Berlin Academy series.

Paula Gottlieb is Professor of Philosophy and Affiliate Professor of Classics at the University of Wisconsin–Madison. She has analyzed *Nicomachean Ethics* Books I and II for the Project Archelogos, and is writing a book on Aristotle's ethics.

Rosalind Hursthouse is Professor of Philosophy at the University of Auckland, New Zealand. She is the author of *On Virtue Ethics* (1999) and various articles in the same area, including some on Aristotle's ethics.

T. H. Irwin is Susan Linn Sage Professor of Philosophy and Humane Letters at Cornell University. He is the author of *Plato's Gorgias* (translation and notes, 1979), *Aristotle's First Principles* (1988), *Classical Thought* (1989), *Plato's Ethics*

(1995), and *Aristotle's Nicomachean Ethics* (translation and notes, 2nd edn, 1999).

Richard Kraut is Professor of Philosophy and Classics, and the Charles E. and Emma H. Morrison Professor in the Humanities, at Northwestern University. He is the author of *Socrates and the State* (1984), *Aristotle on the Human Good* (1989), and *Aristotle: Political Philosophy* (2002).

Gavin Lawrence is Professor of Philosophy at the University of California, Los Angeles. He is the author of a number of articles on Aristotle's ethics and on modern ethics.

Gabriel Richardson Lear is Assistant Professor of Philosophy at the University of Chicago. She is the author of *Happy Lives and the Highest Good: An Essay on Aristotle's Nicomachean Ethics* (2004).

Susan Sauvé Meyer is Associate Professor of Philosophy at the University of Pennsylvania. Her current work focuses on Greek and Roman ethics, and she is the author of the forthcoming *Ancient Ethics*.

A. W. Price is Reader in the School of Philosophy at Birkbeck College, University of London. His work focuses on ancient Greek ethics and moral psychology, and he is the author of *Mental Conflict* (1995) and *Love and Friendship in Plato and Aristotle* (extended edn, 1997).

C. D. C. Reeve is Delta Kappa Epsilon Professor of Philosophy at the University of North Carolina at Chapel Hill. He has translated Plato's *Republic* (2004), and is the author, most recently, of *Love's Confusions* (2005).

Malcolm Schofield is Professor of Ancient Philosophy at the University of Cambridge. His books include *Saving the City* (1999) and *The Stoic Idea of the City* (expanded edn, 1999). He is co-editor (with Christopher Rowe) of *The Cambridge History of Greek and Roman Political Thought* (2000).

Jennifer Whiting is Chancellor Jackman Professor of Philosophy at the University of Toronto. She works primarily on moral psychology (both ancient and modern), and has published various articles on Aristotle's metaphysics, psychology, and ethics.

Charles M. Young is Professor of Philosophy at Claremont Graduate University. He is currently completing a monograph on Aristotle's accounts of the virtues of character, as well as the module on Book V of the *Nicomachean Ethics* for Project Archelogos.

Acknowledgment

By permission of Cambridge University Press, section 1 of chapter 14 by Malcolm Schofield, "Aristotle's Political Ethics," incorporates and expands material from chapter 14 of *The Cambridge History of Greek and Roman Political Thought*, edited by Christopher Rowe and Malcolm Schofield (Cambridge: Cambridge University Press, 2000).

Abbreviations

An. Post.	*Posterior Analytics*
An. Pr.	*Prior Analytics*
Cael.	*On the Heavens*
Cat.	*Categories*
De An.	*De Anima (On the Soul)*
EE	*Eudemian Ethics*
Gen. An.	*Generation of Animals*
Gen. et Corr.	*On Generation and Corruption*
Hist. An.	*History of Animals*
Meta.	*Metaphysics*
MM	*Magna Moralia*
Mot. An.	*Movement of Animals*
NE	*Nicomachean Ethics*
Part. An.	*Parts of Animals*
Phys.	*Physics*
Pol.	*Politics*
Rhet.	*Rhetoric*

Introduction

Richard Kraut

Aristotle currently occupies a privileged position in the study of moral philosophy. Along with a handful of other historical figures – Hume, Kant, Mill, and perhaps several others – he is regarded as someone whose approach to the philosophical study of ethics must be learned (though not necessarily accepted) by any serious student of the subject. More than any other philosopher from antiquity or the medieval period, he is read as someone whose framework for ethics might still be viable, or at any rate might be incorporated or transformed into a larger scheme that combines his insights with those of others. It would be foolish to think that he deserves to have the last word about any matter that he discussed, that he had no blind spots or limitations, or that he can help with every aspect of ethical inquiry. Nonetheless, in moral philosophy, he is someone with whom one must come to terms, even if one decides to become anti-Aristotelian.

Philosophical discussions of practical questions were at the center of the Academy, the school of research that Plato established in Athens in the early fourth century BC, and at which Aristotle (born in Stagira, and therefore never an Athenian citizen) arrived in 367, when he was seventeen years old. There he remained as an active participant in discussions until Plato's death twenty years later. He then left Athens and continued his philosophical and scientific studies in other parts of the Greek world. It is generally accepted that the treatise in moral philosophy for which Aristotle is best known – the *Nicomachean Ethics* – was written not during these earlier periods of his life, but some time after he returned to Athens in 334 and established his own research center in the Lyceum, just outside Athens.

There he wrote and lectured until the year before his death in 322. It is often assumed that some – perhaps many – of his philosophical treatises were delivered as lectures, or at any rate that those lectures were drawn from material that has been preserved in his written works. It is not likely that Aristotle himself was the one who gave the word "Nicomachean" to this ethical treatise. Nicomachus was the name of his father and of his son; perhaps the son had something to do with the arrangement of the treatise named after him, but this is a matter of speculation. When Aristotle refers, in the political essays that were collected together to form his *Politics*, to points already made about ethical subjects, he calls those writings *ta ēthika* – the writings that have to do with character (*ēthos*). He does not call them *Nicomachean* – or for that matter *Eudemian* (the name of his other major work about ethical matters) – but simply *ta ēthika*, "the ethical things." "Ethical" is, of course, the word that we now use to refer to *anything* having to do with right and wrong, good and bad, obligation and duty, and what ought to be done. When Aristotle speaks of *ta ēthika*, by contrast, he and his readers hear the root term *ēthos*, and thus they take those compositions to have states of character as their principal concern. It is easy to see why both the *Eudemian Ethics* (Eudemus was a student of Aristotle, and perhaps therefore also an editor of this work) and the *Nicomachean Ethics* should be called studies of character: the topics to which they are principally devoted are the qualities of mind that we should cultivate and praise, or avoid and blame.

It is now so widely taken for granted that "ethics" (or "moral philosophy" as it is sometimes called) is the name of a distinct branch of philosophy that we must constantly force ourselves to remember that this way of carving up the subject had to be invented, and that Aristotle was one of its inventors. Plato does not divide philosophy into ethics, political theory, epistemology, and so on. On the contrary, it is reasonable to take him to believe that philosophy is a single and unified subject, no part of which can profitably be investigated in isolation from the others – that, for example, the study of the visible cosmos in the *Timaeus* must be combined with the study of pleasure in the *Philebus*, legislation in the *Laws*, knowledge in the *Theaetetus*, and so on. Aristotle, by contrast, assumes, in writing his ethical works, that the subject under investigation has its own distinctive subject matter, that it employs a methodology peculiarly appropriate to that subject matter, and that its students need not pursue philosophical questions that lie outside the realm of ethics. In the opening pages of the *Nicomachean Ethics*, he calls the kind of expertise that he takes his readers to be acquiring "political" expertise, indicating that (unlike many philosophers of our time) he does not think of political theory and ethics as two separate and autonomous parts of philosophy. The *Nicomachean Ethics*, then, is conceived as the first volume of a two-volume study. If Aristotle had to give a single title to that entire two-volume work, it would be *politikē*, the study of political matters, though (to render a phrase he employs at X.9.1181b15) "the philosophy of human affairs" might better convey the scope of his inquiry. But he clearly thinks that *politikē* can also properly serve as the name of the second volume of that study, and that *ta ēthika* is a suitable name for its first volume.

Although *ta ēthika* is what he (in the *Politics*) calls his study, because so large a portion of its contents is devoted to an examination of character, he does not announce, in the opening lines of the *Nicomachean Ethics*, that this will be the principal topic, or even one of the topics, to be discussed. Instead, he works his way toward this topic. We are already well into the material of Book I before we get an indication that the study of character will occupy an important place in the rest of the work. What Aristotle begins with, instead, is the phenomenon of human striving, and the object of all of that striving: "every craft and inquiry, and likewise every action and decision, seems to aim at something good" (*NE* I.1.1094a1–2). That initial observation is then used to build a case that good ought to be the ultimate topic of our investigation: this is what we are aiming at in all that we do, and so we will profit by having a better understanding of what it is. We are led to a study of states of character only because of the connection Aristotle seeks to establish between what is ultimately good and certain states of character. Some of those character states – the ones that are widely recognized as virtues – are good to cultivate and exercise, and deserve to be praised; others, widely recognized as defects or vices, must be avoided and blamed.

In placing what is good at the center of his ethical theory, Aristotle is following the lead of Plato, who has Socrates declare in Book VI of the *Republic* that everything we do is undertaken for the sake of the good, and that good must therefore be the highest object of philosophical study. But although Aristotle's thinking is heavily indebted to Plato in this way, there is nonetheless a remarkable difference – one that Aristotle is eager to emphasize, in Book I, chapter 6 of the *Nicomachean Ethics*. He takes Plato and his followers to be advocating the study of a completely general study of goodness – so general that it would apply equally to anything in the universe whatsoever. The Platonist wants to know what is being said about any *X* when it is called good, or good for someone, or a good something or other. Aristotle thinks that is a pseudo-study because it seeks to bring together things that ought to be considered separately. What he proposes is that there is a single study of the *human* good. If one refuses to pay attention to features of human beings that are distinctive of them, and proceeds instead to speculate at a more abstract level, so that what one says about goodness applies no less to plants, animals, gods, good times, good places, and so on, there will be nothing worthwhile to discover. But when we pay attention to the psychology of human beings – particularly to the fact that we are capable of reasoning and responding, in our emotional life, to reasons – then we will be able to make good use of our study of what is good.

This focus on the good of *human beings* – based on the idea that our daily lives can be improved through a better understanding of *human* well-being – is precisely what gives Aristotle's moral philosophy its distinctive character. It is a remarkably bold philosophical enterprise because it is (for all of its antipathy to Platonic abstraction) an attempt to find a theory of great generality – one that applies not just to fourth-century Greek males, but to all members of the human species – that will at the same time help us shape our political institutions and guide our political and individual decisions. It is a theory that in some way is anchored in our knowledge of the empirical world; that is, in highly general long-term facts about the sorts of creatures that human beings are. There are all sorts of good reasons for being skeptical about whether this sort of project can succeed. One can reasonably ask whether Aristotle is guilty of making the same sort of error that he believes his Platonist friends have made: seeking too high a level of generality. Can one, in other words, discover significant truths (truths that are useful in guiding our actions) about what is good for every single human being? Why should the fact that one is a human being play a role in one's thinking about how to live one's life? Is the notion of what is good for a human being robust enough to serve as the basis for practical reasoning or does deliberation need to be guided by a much richer palate of concepts (such notions, for example, as rights, duties, and obligations) than the ones that Aristotle studies? He is the inventor of a philosophical program whose merits and deficiencies are extremely difficult to assess. That is precisely what makes him an exciting author to read. An open-minded, careful, and intelligent reader who engages with Aristotle's "philosophy of human affairs" will inevitably be confronted with some of the deepest foundational questions of ethical life.

The essays collected in this volume are published here for the first time, and collectively they present a portrait of the interpretive and philosophical issues that any serious reader of Aristotle's *Nicomachean Ethics* must confront. Chris Bobonich's essay (chapter 1) emphasizes the value of also paying careful attention to Aristotle's other ethical writings, particularly his early dialogue, *Protrepticus*, and his other major ethical treatise, the *Eudemian Ethics*. Although the *Nicomachean Ethics* has long been regarded as the final and definitive statement of Aristotle's moral philosophy, and the *Eudemian Ethics* (which shares three books with its *Nicomachean* counterpart) has been neglected by all but a few specialists, there is no good reason for the radical imbalance in the attention they receive. Aristotle thought about practical problems for his whole philosophical career, and what he says about them in one work sometimes differs in important ways from what he says about them elsewhere. One cannot but have a deeper understanding of the *Nicomachean Ethics* if one goes beyond it and pays attention to Aristotle's less-studied ethical works.

Gavin Lawrence's essay (chapter 2) assesses the strengths and weaknesses of Aristotle's theory of human well-being, as that theory is expounded in Books I and X (chapters 6–8) of the *Nicomachean Ethics*. He is particularly concerned with two questions. First, when Aristotle asks his audience to consider whether human beings have an *ergon* (often translated "function"), and goes on to argue that they do – namely, to exercise the reasoning and reason-responsive parts of the soul – is he committing a fundamental error by leaping over a gap that can never legitimately be crossed: a gap between facts and values, or between what is prudentially valuable and what is morally admirable? Second, when Aristotle returns to the topic of well-being in Book X of the *Nicomachean Ethics*, and gives a series of arguments designed to show that the happiest life (that is, the most *eudaimon* life) belongs to someone who spends much time exercising theoretical excellence, is he bringing himself into conflict with the main lines of his ethical theory? There would be no conflict if Aristotle were merely saying that contemplation (the exercise of theoretical reason) is one among many worthwhile reasoning or reason-governed activities; but in Book X, chapters 7–8 he seems to be giving it a special, indeed an exalted, position, making it somehow the pinnacle of a well-lived life. Lawrence finds that ideal problematic, but argues that this does not reveal any flaw in Aristotle's fundamental starting-point: to find out what counts as living well, we must "look to basic facts about the kind of creatures we are and the sort of world we live in."

Book I of the *Nicomachean Ethics* moves back and forth between a first-order inquiry into the nature of the human good and second-order reflections on the proper method for carrying out such an inquiry. Aristotle warns his audience not to expect more from his arguments than his subject matter allows: he cannot give them mathematical precision, and he expects his arguments to be acceptable only to those who have already been brought up in good habits. Yet he does take himself to be answerable to appropriate standards of good reasoning. Many of these standards are set forth in Book I, but an extremely important component of Aristotle's methodology is not made explicit until a much later point in his treatise (Book VII, chapter 1). That "endoxic" or "dialectical" method is the subject of my contribution to this volume (chapter 3).

The principal thesis of Book I is that since the human good, *eudaimonia*, consists in excellent or virtuous exercises of our powers as creatures who reason and respond to reasons, a more concrete specification of what that good is requires an examination of what those excellent or virtuous qualities of mind are. It is to that more concrete specification of the human good that Aristotle turns in the closing chapter of Book I, which serves as an introduction to the discussion of virtues that occupies Books II–VI. Aristotle has both a general theory about what sorts of states of mind the virtues are and a more detailed account of particular qualities of mind that he takes to be virtues – such qualities as courage, generosity, justice, and so on. But both the general theory of virtue and the concrete portraits of particular virtues are informed by something that has come to be called "the doctrine of the mean" (though Aristotle simply refers to virtues as states that lie in and aim at a mean – "*doctrine* of the mean" does not correspond to any phrase he uses). He claims that it is of practical value to recognize the intermediacy of the virtues, but it is far from clear what he has in mind. Rosalind Hursthouse's essay (chapter 4) argues that there is no truth in this "doctrine" as it is ordinarily understood, but that nonetheless we should recognize several great insights within Aristotle's discussion. Properly understood, Aristotle's principal contribution, in his treatment of the virtues, is to describe the many ways in which we can go astray in our efforts to do the right thing, and of the role played by the emotions in guiding or misguiding our deliberations. To go astray in life is to fail to acquire the skills we need to keep our emotional and cognitive resources in balance.

Although anyone who is familiar with Aristotle's moral philosophy recognizes how important it is to him that the virtues are intermediate states, there is another recurring theme in his discussion of the virtues that can easily be overlooked, partly because he does so little to explain the significance of that theme. The term *kalon*, which can be translated "beautiful," "fine," or "noble," depending on the context, pervades Aristotle's practical philosophy, and has an especially important role to play in his discussion of the virtues. What is *kalon* is, in some way, the aim of every virtuous action (*NE* III.7.1115b12); this is a point that is made throughout Aristotle's discussion of individual virtues, but it is difficult to know what it means. Gabriel Richardson Lear (chapter 5) proposes that Aristotle conceives of virtuous actions as possessing a special kind of beauty. People of excellent character take pleasure in the public performance of fine deeds because these acts exhibit a kind of proportionality, just as the beautiful works of certain craftsmen are so well balanced that nothing can properly be added to or taken away from them. The fineness of virtuous activity, then, is of a piece with the intermediacy of virtue.

It should be clear that for Aristotle praiseworthiness and blameworthiness are important categories of practical thought, and enter into the outlook of any mature human being. Human beings of good character do not act well merely in order to be praised, and do not refrain from wrongdoing merely in order to avoid blame; nonetheless they are not indifferent to praise, and they know when praise and blame are deserved – not just in their own case, but in general. Blame and culpability are especially important to an ethical theory as deeply implicated in politics as Aristotle's, and so it is not surprising – given the overt political orientation of the *Nicomachean Ethics* – that he pays so much attention, in Book III, to working out a theory of praiseworthiness and blameworthiness. As Susan Sauvé Meyer emphasizes in chapter 6, our understanding of this aspect of Aristotle's moral philosophy is greatly enhanced when we compare the *Eudemian* and *Nicomachean* treatments of it. Reading the two discussions together helps us see that Aristotle does not embrace the thesis that one is responsible for one's actions only if one is responsible for one's character. Her analysis should be compared with Chris Bobonich's discussion of the relationship between Aristotle's two major ethical treatises.

It would be difficult to appreciate Aristotle's conception of ethical virtue without absorbing oneself in the details of his discussion of particular virtues, and certainly none of his little essays on those individual character traits creates as much difficulty for a modern reader as does his discussion of *megalopsuchia* (literally "greatness of soul," but also translated as "magnanimity" or "pride"). Aristotle describes this virtue as an "adornment" of the other virtues, in that it makes all of them greater (*NE* IV.3.1124a1): here, once again, the aesthetic aspect of Aristotelian virtue comes to the fore. And yet, what are we to make of someone who takes himself to be worthy of great things, who is ashamed when he receives benefits from others, and wishes to be superior to others? Roger Crisp's essay (chapter 7) surveys the many and seemingly disparate characteristics that Aristotle attributes to the great-souled person, and considers whether we have good reason to object to any of them. Like Gabriel Richardson Lear, he finds in Aristotle an ideal of moral beauty – or, as he puts it, "nobility" – that fits uncomfortably with modern moral sensibilities. But that seemingly alien aspect of Aristotle's ethics makes reading him all the more worthwhile; it forces us to ask whether we can justifiably have disdain for greatness of soul.

No virtue receives greater attention from Aristotle than justice. He devotes the whole of Book V of the *Nicomachean Ethics* to it, and justifies assigning it so large a space by citing the proverb "in justice is the sum of all virtue" (V.1.1129b29–30). Without calling attention to his disagreement with Plato, who proposes in the *Republic* that *dikaiosunē* can be given a single definition, Aristotle takes it for granted that this is really the name for two virtues: by calling someone "just," we may mean either that he is lawful or that he is fair and equal (both "fair" and "equal" are used as translations of *isos*). The first half of Aristotle's analysis – *dikaiosunē* as lawfulness – invites the question of whether he is talking about our virtue of *justice*, and the further question of whether he has a greater respect for law than he should. But the second half – *dikaiosunē* as equality or fairness – should assure us that his discussion of at least this aspect of *dikaiosunē* has as its topic the virtue that we call justice. Charles Young (chapter 8) proposes, in fact, that we can find some striking similarities between Aristotelian justice as equality and some familiar ideas of contemporary political philosophy. There is, he argues, a notion of impartiality built into Aristotle's conception of justice. It "invites us, in conducting our relations with others, to assume a perspective from which we view ourselves and . . . others as members of a community of free and equal human beings, and to decide what to do from that perspective."

In Book VI, Aristotle, having completed his discussion of the virtues of character, carries out a survey of the virtues of thought – technical skill (*technē*), scientific knowledge (*epistēmē*), practical wisdom (*phronēsis*), theoretical wisdom (*sophia*), and understanding (*nous*). One of the principal goals of this book, as Aristotle indicates in its opening chapter, is to give his audience a firmer grip on the kind of person one should aim to become, as one avoids the extremes of excess and deficiency in one's actions and emotions. What sort of person is that? Someone who has practical wisdom, and ideally someone whose practical wisdom is used in the service of philosophy – the activity that gives fullest expression to the virtues of theoretical inquiry. Aristotle discusses technical skill here only in order to emphasize the ways in which the other virtues of thought are superior to it. The center of his attention in Book VI is the virtue of practical wisdom, a quality of mind that governs the emotions by making use of clever instrumental reasoning, excellent non-routinized deliberation about the proper and ultimate ends of life, and perception of particular facts that play a telling role in decision-making. C. D. C. Reeve (chapter 9) emphasizes the striking difference between this approach to reasoned practical thought and one that seeks a single dominant value that must, in every circumstance, be maximized.

Several of the themes explored in this essay – the apparently limited scope of deliberation, the interdependence of ethical virtue and practical wisdom, and the dependency of action upon perception (and of good action on perception informed by virtue) – are also investigated in the essay of Paula Gottlieb (chapter 10). She places special emphasis, however, on what she takes to be one of Aristotle's best discoveries: that just as we can study the elements of good theoretical reasoning (the theoretical syllogism), so too we can investigate the ingredients that lead to good action by way of a *practical* syllogism. One of the premises of such a syllogism, she argues, must refer to the character of the agent. So a practical syllogism, properly formulated, will reveal how this kind of person, using both an assumption about some end to be sought, and further assumptions about what someone of this type should do in these circumstances to achieve that end, was led to perform this concrete act. Practical thinking, so conceived, is shot through with particularities and generalities of various kinds. "A practical syllogism with all general terms," as Gottlieb points out, "could not be practical, and it is no small achievement on Aristotle's part to grasp this point."

Book VII of the *Nicomachean Ethics* is devoted to two independent topics. Its last four chapters (11–14) ask about the nature and value of pleasure, a topic that is then taken up once again in Book X, chapters 1–5. (The treatment of pleasure in Book VII belongs as well to the *Eudemian Ethics*. So one can say either that the editorial process that led to the *Nicomachean Ethics* was sloppy, because of this inelegant repetition; or wise, because the treatise is enhanced by including two discussions of pleasure.) But the bulk of this book (chapters 1–10) is devoted to states of character that deviate from virtue, though not in the same way as the defects of character studied in Books II–V. The most important of these deviations are *akrasia* ("incontinence," "lack of self-control," "weakness of will," or sometimes left untranslated and Latinized: acrasia) and *enkrateia* ("continence," "self-control," "strength of will"). The *akratēs* (who suffers from *akrasia*) and the *enkratēs* (who possesses *enkrateia*) see, in some way or other, what they should aim at and what they should do here and now. They are therefore better human beings than those who are in error about what their ends should be. But, at the same time, there is something in them, caused by a desire or emotion, that opposes their recognition of what they should do here and now; and, in the case of the *akratēs*, this opposing factor leads all the way to action. One of the puzzles about Aristotle's examination of these states of minds, as A. W. Price emphasizes in chapter 11, is whether he acknowledges the existence of what Price calls "hard acrasia," that is, a clear-eyed recognition, undiminished by any cognitive weakness, that one should not now be doing what one is in fact doing. Does the *akratēs* really recognize that what he is doing right now is not what he should do, or is his thinking in some way dimmed because of his desires or emotions? The traditional interpretation, which Price discusses and compares with various alternatives, holds that, according to Aristotle, some intellectual failure accompanies every case in which someone acts against his better judgment.

The second main topic of Book VII – pleasure – is one that occupies Plato in several dialogues (it is the principal topic of his *Philebus*, but also plays an important role in *Protagoras*, *Gorgias*, and *Republic*). But a thesis to which he gives voice in the *Protagoras*, and combats in all of his other works – that pleasure is the proper and sole ultimate end of human beings – gathered strength in spite of his opposition to it, and became the guiding ethical principle of the Epicurean school, which was established in Athens one generation after the death of Aristotle. Hedonism was revived in the modern era, and the leading utilitarians of the eighteenth and nineteenth centuries (Jeremy Bentham and John Stuart Mill) embraced it. But there is now a consensus among philosophers that the equation of good and pleasure is too simple. What role, then, should pleasure play in our lives? As Dorothea Frede (chapter 12) argues, if we want to acknowledge the great value of pleasure and its strength as a psychological factor, but also want to deny that it should be the ultimate aim of all that we do, we can do no better than look to Aristotle's discussion in Books VII and X for help. Aristotle looks for a way of showing that although pleasure is *a* good – that in fact it should be woven into everything of value – it is not *the* good, because it is by its very nature not suited to be a goal. As Frede says, "That our actions should be done *with* inclination rather than *because* of inclination is an insight that should never have dropped out of moral discourse."

It is a remarkable feature of the *Nicomachean Ethics* that such a large part of it – two of its ten books – is devoted to *philia* (friendship). Plato treats this subject in one of his short dialogues (*Lysis*), but his fuller discussions of social affiliation are about erotically charged relationships (*Symposium* and *Phaedrus*). Aristotle, by contrast, has little interest in *erōs*. He assumes that nearly all of our interactions with other human beings are not erotic, but that many of the people we encounter – all but those whom we actively dislike – are, in some way and to some degree, dear (*philos*) to us. To study *philia*, then, is to study an extremely wide variety of human relationships, ranging from the intimacy of family relationships and close comrades, to the cooler ties of fellow citizens, friendly strangers, and business associates. One of the remarkable features of Aristotle's discussion of *philia* is that he is able to use his theory of virtue, and his conception of its centrality to a well-lived life, to classify and understand the value of this wide variety of human relationships. Jennifer Whiting (chapter 13) calls our attention to the many ways in which Aristotle's discussion of friendship extends and complicates his moral psychology. He emphasizes the importance of not treating other human beings as mere instruments – for one should benefit one's friends for *their* sake – but at the same time seems to find a kind of self-love behind every virtuous action. Whiting's goal is to find the coherence in Aristotle's blending of apparent egoism and altruism.

Aristotle's examination of friendship is followed by a second discussion of pleasure. (It is noteworthy that it does not refer to Book VII's discussion.) He then returns, in Book X, chapter 6, to the unfinished business of the whole treatise. Although he noted, in Book I, that three kinds of lives are thought especially attractive – a life of pleasure, a political life, and a life devoted to philosophical study and contemplation – he has not yet compared the merits of these last two kinds of lives. We know, from his discussions of pleasure, why this should not be our goal, and he downgrades pleasure (or, at any rate, a certain kind of pleasure) once again, in Book X, chapter 6, by arguing that amusement should always be subordinate to more serious matters. In the next two chapters, he turns to the comparison of two kinds of lives – one philosophical, the other political – and affirms the superiority of the life of philosophical contemplation. And yet the final chapter of his treatise insists that we must continue this study of ethical virtues by seeing how these qualities of mind can be sustained and enhanced through legislation. Having affirmed the inferiority of the political life to that of the philosopher, Aristotle nonetheless urges the members of his audience to acquire a detailed understanding of the varieties of political systems and the various factors that preserve and destroy them. But as Malcolm Schofield (chapter 14) points out, the *Nicomachean Ethics* is shot through with the idea that ethics and politics are inseparable. From the very start, Aristotle takes himself to be addressing people who want to take part in politics. He several times affirms the political nature of human beings, and repeatedly emphasizes the political dimensions of many of the virtues (courage is primarily a military quality, justice is lawfulness, and the virtues that have to do with wealth and honor are exercised primarily in the civic arena). The *Nicomachean Ethics*, unlike its *Eudemian* counterpart, is framed by its political orientation.

One of the many ways in which we can try to learn from Aristotle's moral philosophy is to locate him in a narrative about the history of ethics – a story that might involve decline, or progress, or both, depending on how it is told. We can ask, for example: are the concepts that play an important role in modern moral philosophy ones that have exact or close parallels in ancient ethics? If Aristotle thinks about ethics in a way that differs markedly from the way in which we do, is that because we have lost touch with certain insights, or is it because he lived in a social world that we are well rid of? T. H. Irwin's essay (chapter 15) reminds us, however, that we must not impoverish our understanding of the history of ethics by thinking only in terms of an ancient/modern contrast: that would omit the richness of moral philosophy in the medieval period, and in particular it would lose sight of the ways in which Aquinas appropriates and develops Aristotle's ideas. By showing how Aquinas places Aristotle's conception of well-being into a framework of natural law, the validity of which is independent of divine or human will, Irwin challenges the thesis, endorsed by G. E. M. Anscombe, that in Aristotle we find no notion of moral requirement because that concept makes sense only if there is a legislator, divine or human, who determines what is required. According to Irwin, the common view that the Greeks lack a juridical conception of ethics, and that Christianity laid the groundwork for a radically different philosophical framework, should be rejected in favor of a more complex narrative that emphasizes continuity and development.

Sarah Broadie (chapter 16) brings this volume to a close with a salutary warning: because so much of what Aristotle says is "extraordinarily sensible as well as illuminating," and so much of it rightly shapes our thinking today, we can all too easily slip into thinking that "in this or that important modern debate there is a theory of which Aristotle holds a version, or a side which he is recognizably on." On the contrary, she insists: "Many of our own central preoccupations in ethics are with questions on which, for one or another reason, Aristotle has little or nothing to say." In particular, she argues, we must not look to the *Nicomachean Ethics* for a justification for doing what is right, or for a method – conveyed by a formula or a series of rules – for making better day-to-day decisions. She also notes that, although much that Aristotle wrote about continues to provoke debate, there are other topics that preoccupied him but have, for no good reason, disappeared from our intellectual agenda. The proper use of leisure, for example, is no longer a subject of philosophical inquiry, though Aristotle considered it a topic of great importance. Several other contributors to this volume – for example, Gavin Lawrence and Dorothea Frede – come to the same conclusion in their essays. We should look to Aristotle not only for tools that help with current ethical problems, but also for a framework that unsettles our all-too-familiar philosophical agenda. He can change our conception of what the study of ethics should be.

1

Aristotle's Ethical Treatises

Chris Bobonich

The *Nicomachean Ethics* is by far the best known of Aristotle's ethical works, but it is not the only one that has come down to us. We also have the *Eudemian Ethics*, the *Magna Moralia* (the *Great Ethics*), and fragments of the *Protrepticus* (*Exhortative*). Before turning to their philosophic contents and the controversies that have arisen about them, however, we must consider some important philological questions concerning their authenticity, their chronology, and the relations of dependence among these texts.

Background

Roughly speaking, we can divide Aristotle's writings into two main groups: the "school-writings" and the more popular writings. The school-writings include all the texts that are commonly studied by scholars and students today, such as the *Categories*, *De Anima*, the *Metaphysics*, the *Physics*, and the *Politics*, as well as the *Eudemian Ethics*, the *Magna Moralia*, and the *Nicomachean Ethics*. (They include everything in the Revised Oxford Translation of Aristotle except for the *Constitution of the Athenians* and the Fragments which include parts of the *Protrepticus*.) These texts, in general, lack the polish that we would expect from works intended for an audience outside Aristotle's school, the Lyceum. They are usually thought to be the notes from which Aristotle himself lectured or which he circulated in the Lyceum (or, less plausibly, students' notes of Aristotle's lectures). Scholars have staked out the possible extreme positions; that is, that all these texts are by Aristotle, or that none is, as well as a variety of positions in between. Nevertheless, there is a fairly solid consensus that most of these are by Aristotle, and a similar consensus about which of the transmitted texts are inauthentic.[1] Unfortunately for us, there are serious doubts about the *Magna Moralia* and the *Protrepticus*, and, to a much lesser extent, the *Eudemian Ethics*.

From references in Cicero, and many other Greek and Roman sources, we know that Aristotle also wrote works, many of them dialogues, intended for a broader audience outside the Lyceum. They include several that share their name with a Platonic dialogue; for example, the *Sophist*, the *Statesman*, and the *Symposium*. The *Protrepticus* falls into this more popular category, although it is not clear whether it was a dialogue. Unfortunately, it is the only one of these works of which we have substantial portions.[2]

There are ancient stories in Strabo (64 BC–c.21 AD) and Plutarch (c.50–c.120 AD) that Aristotle's school-writings were not available even to the Lyceum from the time of the death of Theophrastus around 285 BC (Aristotle's successor as head of the Lyceum) until some time in the first century BC. They were then edited and published in Rome by Andronicus of Rhodes, perhaps after various losses and dislocations of the text, and it is from this edition that our present corpus of Aristotle derives. Scholarly opinion is divided on the accuracy of this story, although few think it is entirely without basis. There is also a growing inclination to think that some of the school-writings were known between Theophrastus and Andronicus and that the sources of Andronicus' edition were more complex than Strabo and Plutarch suggest (see Düring 1957; Moraux 1973–2001; Sandbach 1985; Barnes and Griffin 1997; Frede 1997; Long 1998). These difficulties in the history of Aristotle's texts help explain the transmission of some inauthentic works as well as the loss of some authentic ones. But they also help explain another noteworthy feature of Aristotle's corpus: a number of what we now treat as single works were not put together in their present form by Aristotle (this is clearly true of the *Metaphysics* and may be true of the *Politics*) and any part of them may have undergone repeated revision by Aristotle.

Protrepticus

We have three ancient catalogues of Aristotle's writings: that in Diogenes Laertius (probably third century AD), that in the "Anonymus Menagii" (probably Hesychius of Miletus, fifth century AD), and that in two thirteenth-century Arab writers which is attributed to a certain "Ptolemy" (whose identification remains disputed). In all of these, there is a reference to a work called the *Protrepticus* which is no longer extant. A *protrepticus logos* (of which we have other ancient examples) is a speech or discourse (*logos*) which aims at turning (*trepō*) the reader toward (*pro*) a certain way of living. There are explicit references to it in Stobaeus (latter half of the fifth century AD) and in several Aristotelian commentators. From these, we learn that the *Protrepticus* was directed to Themison, a king of the Cypriots, and encouraged him to pursue philosophy. Our sources also report an argument from it roughly of the form that to settle rationally the question of whether one ought to philosophize one must investigate whether philosophy exists and whether it should be pursued. But this inquiry is itself a form of philosophizing so that one is rationally required to philosophize.

There was relatively little else to go on in establishing the text of the *Protrepticus*. In 1869, however, Ingram Bywater made the crucial suggestion that chapters 5–12 of the *Protrepticus* of the Neo-Platonist Iamblichus (c.250–330 AD) contain extensive excerpts from Aristotle's own *Protrepticus*.[3] In 1961, Ingemar Düring published a reconstruction of the text of Aristotle's *Protrepticus* based over-whelmingly on Iamblichus. Düring isolates from Iamblichus over 5,000 words that he argues can be accepted as probably genuine fragments of Aristotle's *Protrepticus*. Scholars have disagreed over how secure the attribution of these texts to Aristotle is, but there is considerable agreement that Iamblichus preserves much authentic material.[4] Scholars also generally agree that the *Protrepticus* is an earlier work of Aristotle's, and some reasonable grounds have been given for dating it to around 350 BC. (Aristotle was born in 384 BC, came to Athens at around the age of seventeen to study at Plato's Academy, and remained there until Plato's death in 347 BC.) In my discussion of the *Protrepticus* below, I shall accept the fragments from chapters 6–12 of Iamblichus as containing much genuine Aristotle, even if the debate has not yet been conclusively settled. Since the case for the authenticity of these fragments is strong enough to persuade many good scholars and since the *Protrepticus* has received little discussion in the past forty years, it seems worthwhile to try to bring it into dialogue with Aristotle's other ethical writings.

Eudemian Ethics and *Nicomachean Ethics*

The *Nicomachean Ethics* exists in ten books, the *Eudemian Ethics* in eight (some editors combine what others treat as Books VII and VIII to make seven books in total). There are three shared or "common books": *EE* IV = *NE* V (on justice), *EE* V = *NE* VI (on intellectual virtue), and *EE* VI = *NE* VII (on pleasure). The common books thus include two of the most discussed books in Aristotle's ethical thought: that on intellectual virtue, including its discussion of "practical wisdom" (*phronēsis*), and that on pleasure, including its discussion of incontinence or *akrasia*. From the time of Aspasius (the author of the first surviving commentary on Aristotle's ethics, written in the first half of the second century AD), the *Nicomachean Ethics* with the common books has attracted the lion's share of attention. (The situation before Aspasius is more controversial.) As Anthony Kenny (1978: 1) points out: "since the Middle Ages commentaries on the *Nicomachean Ethics* have appeared about once a decade; the *Eudemian Ethics* has received only four commentaries in its whole history."[5] Indeed, the *Nicomachean Ethics* with the common books might well be the most analyzed text in the history of Western philosophy. The *Eudemian Ethics*, despite some recent work, remains comparatively neglected. There are, for example, few, if any, modern editions of the *Eudemian Ethics* that print its full text along with the common books.

In the nineteenth century, under the influence of Schleiermacher and Spengel, scholars generally held that the *Eudemian Ethics* was inauthentic. But in the twentieth century, its authenticity was defended by Case and, most influentially, in 1923 by Werner Jaeger in *Aristotle: Fundamentals of the History of his Development*. (This was the seminal work for the study of Aristotle's development and I shall discuss some of Jaeger's views below.)

Yet even among those who accepted the authenticity of the *Eudemian Ethics*, it was generally held that: (a) it is earlier than the *Nicomachean Ethics*; (b) the *Nicomachean Ethics* is by far the philosophically superior work; and (c) the common books had their original and proper home in the *Nicomachean Ethics* (although there was more disagreement over this point than the first two). But, in 1978, Anthony Kenny challenged all three claims drawing on internal evidence, evidence about the knowledge of these works by other writers, stylometric analysis (the quantitative study of features of style), and arguments about their philosophical content. Kenny suggested that the *Eudemian Ethics* with the common books was the canonical work by Aristotle on ethics. The *Nicomachean Ethics* was formed by transferring the common books from the *Eudemian Ethics* to fill out a truncated text or incomplete set of lectures that constituted the *Nicomachean Ethics* without the common books.

Scholarly reaction to Kenny's work has been mixed: he has persuaded few that the *Nicomachean Ethics* is earlier than the *Eudemian Ethics*, but a majority may now think that the common books were originally part of the *Eudemian Ethics*.[6] Nevertheless, philosophers and scholars still overwhelmingly take the *Nicomachean Ethics* as their focus. In my discussion below, I shall assume that the *Eudemian Ethics* is genuine and consider some of the issues that arise from reading its five books together with the three common books.

Magna Moralia

Finally, let us turn to the *Magna Moralia*. It consists of two long books (the first has thirty-four chapters, the second has seventeen) and is roughly the size of the *Eudemian Ethics* without the common books. Its structure and contents bear a close resemblance to the *Nicomachean Ethics*, but especially to the *Eudemian Ethics*. There are no known ancient or medieval commentaries on it and the *Magna Moralia* has suffered from even greater neglect than the *Eudemian Ethics*.

There is also considerably more doubt about its authenticity. In the nineteenth century, Schleiermacher, somewhat eccentrically, held that it was the only genuine ethical work by Aristotle. Its authenticity was rejected by Jaeger, Walzer, Brink and, more recently, by Kenny and Rowe. It has been accepted as genuine, at least in important parts, by von Arnim, Dirlmeier (in a change of mind), and, more recently, by Düring and Cooper.[7]

The critics have especially pointed to: (a) features of style that seem unAristotelian and in some case indicative of late origin (for example, terminology claimed to derive from Theophrastus or the Stoics); (b) internal references inconsistent with Aristotle's authorship; (c) inconsistencies with Aristotle's other views, espe-cially the theology of *Metaphysics* Book XII; and (d) such a close resemblance to parts of the texts of, especially, the *Eudemian Ethics* and the *Nicomachean Ethics* (including some quotation) as to suggest that the author of the *Magna Moralia* is summarizing and condensing them.

Counter-arguments have been mounted by the defenders of the *Magna Moralia*, and perhaps the plausible defense of it suggests that it is only in part Aristotelian. John Cooper, for example, suggests that the *Magna Moralia* may well be a student's revised notes from a set of lectures given by Aristotle perhaps prior to the *Eudemian Ethics* and the *Nicomachean Ethics* (other defenders of the *Magna Moralia* think that it is based on an incomplete written text of Aristotle that has been edited and added to, perhaps heavily at times, by a later Peripatetic). There is, at this point, I think, insufficient evidence to decide definitively between some such view and the suggestion of the critics that the *Magna Moralia* is an epitome of Aristotle's ethics produced by a later Peripatetic, at any time from Theophrastus' term as head of the Lyceum (322–285 BC) to the second half of the second century BC.

Whether or not we accept, at least in part, the authenticity of the *Magna Moralia*, it seems to be a work with an independent, cohesive point of view to a lesser degree than the *Eudemian Ethics*, the *Nicomachean Ethics*, or the *Protrepticus*. At any rate, the most interesting recent work on the *Magna Moralia* consists in painstaking analyses of the fairly subtle ways in which its treatment of various ethical issues is thought to differ from that of the *Eudemian Ethics* and the *Nicomachean Ethics*. For this reason, and because it is more difficult to say with confidence what differences embody Aristotle's own views, I shall focus my discussion in the rest of this chapter on the *Eudemian Ethics* and the *Protrepticus*.[8]

Jaeger's developmentalism

Jaeger's 1923 book was a milestone in Aristotle studies. Previously, it was over-whelmingly the case that Aristotle's works were read as forming a single, elaborate system. Jaeger argued that, instead, we can trace a development or evolution in Aristotle's thought. In particular, Jaeger finds three stages with a trajectory of increasing distance from Plato. With respect to metaphysics, in the first, chrono-logically earliest stage, Aristotle accepted Plato's metaphysics, including transcen-dental Platonic Forms and the immortality of the soul understood in a strongly dualist way. At the same time, Aristotle did independent work in logic, broadly speaking, that was in tension with this Platonic metaphysics. In the second, more critical, stage, Aristotle rejects the existence of Platonic Forms, but still sees himself as "the renovator of Plato's supersensible philosophy." First philosophy now studies not the Forms, but the separate, non-sensible, unchanging and eternal substance that is god or the unmoved mover of *Metaphysics* Book Lambda. In the final stage, Aristotle broadens his conception of first philosophy to include the study of sensible substances as part of the study of being as such. In this stage, Aristotle's interest in empirical research, such as the compilation of the constitutions of Greek cities and the lists of Olympic victors, occupies an increasingly large part of his work.

Similarly, Jaeger finds three stages in Aristotle's ethical thought and these stages are marked by his changing conception of *phronēsis*. (This is usually rendered as "practical wisdom" in translations of the *Nicomachean Ethics*. Since it is an important question whether Aristotle's understanding of what *phronēsis* is changed during his career, I shall leave it untranslated.) The *Protrepticus* is Aristotle's "later Platonic period," in the *Eudemian Ethics* we find "reformed Platonism," and in the *Nicomachean Ethics* "late Aristotelianism" (Jaeger 1962: 231). According to Jaeger, in the *Protrepticus* Aristotle accepts the existence of Platonic Forms, and *phronēsis* here is the sole intellectual faculty relevant to practical conduct. It is understood in the "purely Platonic" way as "philosophical knowledge as such" (1962: 81–2). *Phronēsis* is a distinct faculty that grasps the eternal norms or standards provided by the Forms. The branch of knowledge concerned with practice and conduct is thus a species of theoretical science, that is, political science, and it can be as exact as geometry. In the second period, that of the *Eudemian Ethics*, Aristotle has abandoned Platonic Forms. *Phronēsis* still grasps the highest reality and value, but this is now god in the form of the supersensible unmoved mover (1962: 239). It is this knowledge of god that provides the norm for conduct. And although Aristotle here has a more favorable view of the role of experience in thinking about matters of conduct, there is no contrast drawn between such knowledge or understanding and the exact sciences.

Such a contrast is the leitmotif of the last stage of Aristotle's ethical thought in the *Nicomachean Ethics*, which makes thematic its rejection of the central ideas of the *Protrepticus*. The *Nicomachean Ethics* is a "public recantation" of the *Protrepticus*' views. In the *Nicomachean Ethics*, Aristotle distinguishes *phronēsis* from the theoretical faculties; here it is a practical faculty concerned with what is ethically desirable and what is advantageous for the agent. It does not have "the highest and most valuable things in the universe for [its] object and . . . is not a science at all" (1962: 83). Political "science" is thus sharply opposed to the exact sciences; its propositions cannot be both universal and informative, its inferences are not exceptionless (1962: 85).

Jaeger's picture has been widely criticized: G. E. L. Owen offered an influential account in the 1960s depicting an Aristotle who moves from early radical opposition to Plato to later views that have deep Platonic affinities. Others have sketched distinct developmental views and some have suggested that Aristotle's habits of revising earlier material repeatedly throughout his career makes any developmental hypothesis precarious.[9] Regardless of one's final evaluation of the details of Jaeger's work, it has, I think, at least two aspects of lasting significance for the study of Aristotle's ethics. First, it encourages us to be alive to the possibility that there are distinct – and perhaps fundamentally different and inconsistent – views in Aristotle's ethical writings. Second, Jaeger rightly focuses on Aristotle's conception of the kind of knowledge possible in matters of conduct, including the faculty that attains it and its exactness, and the place of such knowledge in a good or happy life. I shall focus on these issues in the rest of this chapter.

Protrepticus

I shall not here attempt to sketch even in rough outline the contents or arguments of the *Protrepticus* and I shall focus on points of possible divergence from Aristotle's other writings rather than on the many points of overlap and continuity. Even if we ultimately reject it, Jaeger's interpretation of the *Protrepticus* remains a good way in to some of its central issues. According to Jaeger, Aristotle in the *Protrepticus* still adheres to the Platonic understanding of *phronēsis*. On this conception, *phronēsis* is "theoretical knowledge of supersensible being and practical moral insight"; it is "knowledge of true being [that] was in fact a knowledge of the pure Norms by reference to which a man should order his life" (Jaeger 1962: 239, 83). The *Protrepticus* agrees with Plato in "bas[ing] ethical action entirely on the knowledge of being" (Jaeger 1962: 84). It is not entirely clear how strong a claim Jaeger intends to make here. But let us consider a particularly robust version of this claim: the entire intellectual state sufficient for acting virtuously or correctly is constituted by the best sort of grasp or understanding of universals.[10]

We might well wonder whether Plato himself in fact held such a view. If Plato holds, as Aristotle typically does, that different faculties are correlated with different objects, then it seems hard to see how he could hold the robust version of this thesis. Actions and the things they involve – for example, this man, that sword – are particulars rather than universals and as such seem to require a faculty capable of grasping particulars. Even if these particulars have non-sensible properties, such as being just, they also have sensible properties that seem central to their identification and individuation. So there seems to be a need for perceptually based judgments to enter, in some way, into decisions about what to do, and this requires some perceptually based way of grasping the truth in addition to a theoretical understanding of universals.

Now, it is the case that, at least in some dialogues, Plato seems to think that once a person grasps the relevant ethical first principles, he will easily and without exception get particular judgments right. In the *Euthyphro*, for example, once a good definition of piety is in hand, Socrates will be able to "say that any action of yours or another's that is of that kind is pious; and if it is not of that kind, that it is not" (6E6–7). In the *Protagoras*, the possession of the measuring art, which is a kind of knowledge, would "by showing us the truth, bring peace to our soul basing it on the truth and would save our life" (356D8–E2). This art, by allowing us to measure the good and bad attaching to different courses of action, allows us to come to the right decisions, even in difficult or confusing cases.[11] In the *Republic*, however, Plato seems to be less confident that knowledge of universals, that is knowledge of Forms, will guarantee correct particular judgments, and seems more inclined to think that such knowledge will require supplementation in order to produce particular judgments that can, perhaps at best, be such that they typically have a high degree of accuracy (for example, *Republic* 472–3B, 500B–501C, 516–20C, 539E–540A, and 592AB).

Nevertheless, it is true that Aristotle devoted great energy in *Eudemian Ethics* Book V = *Nicomachean Ethics* Book VI to distinguishing *phronēsis*, characterized as the virtue that brings it about that one deliberates well concerning what is good (*NE* VI.5.1140a24–8, 1140b20–30) from theoretical understanding, that is, from knowledge or understanding (*epistēmē*) and wisdom (*sophia*).[12] Jaeger makes the important suggestion that the most significant ethical difference between the mature work of Aristotle and the work of Plato, as well as the earlier Aristotle, is that Aristotle eventually comes to separate *phronēsis* from theoretical or philosophical understanding and to establish the independence of each. It is this idea and some related issues that I shall focus on in the rest of my discussion of the *Protrepticus*. Although Jaeger's own views may be unsatisfactory, the issues themselves remain important and require, I think, considerably more research.[13]

It is one of the most striking features of the *Protrepticus* that such separation and independence of theoretical understanding and the virtue that is responsible for good deliberation seem to be lacking. Consider the following passage (since the *Protrepticus* remains little read I shall quote from it extensively):

> Those who are to be good doctors or trainers must have a general knowledge of nature, so good lawmakers too must be experienced about nature – and indeed much more than the former . . . For just as in the productive arts the best tools were discovered from nature, as, for instance in the builder's art the plumb line, the ruler, and the compasses – for some come from water, others from light and the rays of the sun . . . in the same way the statesman must have certain boundary-markers taken from nature itself and from truth, by reference to which he will judge what is just, what is fine, and what is beneficial . . . Nobody, however, who has not practiced philosophy [*philosophēsanta*] and known the truth is able to do this. Furthermore, in the other arts and crafts people do not take their tools and their most exact reasonings from primary things themselves and so attain something approaching knowledge: they take them from what is second or third hand or at a distant remove, and base their reasonings on experience. The philosopher alone imitates exact things themselves [*autōn tōn akribōn*], for he is a spectator of them, not of imitations . . . But it is clear that to the philosopher alone among craftsmen belong laws that are stable and actions that are right and fine [*orthai kai kalai*]. For he alone lives by looking at nature and the divine. Like a good helmsman, he moors the principles of his life to that which is eternal and unchanging, makes fast there, and lives as his own master.[14]

There are two especially striking features of the passage.[15] First, Aristotle seems to hold that only a philosopher can be a good lawmaker or statesman. Further, the reason for this is that good lawmaking and statesmanship must be based on philosophy (*philosophia*, 84.18–19, cf. 85.1–2), that is, on theoretical understanding (*epistēmē theōrētikē*) of "exact things themselves" (74.1–2 [B69], 85.8–9). Second, for similar reasons, only a philosopher performs actions that are right and fine. Upon first examination, these claims seem to be in deep tension with Aristotle's views in, for example, the *Eudemian Ethics*, the *Nicomachean Ethics*, and the *Politics* as well.

On a connected point, a second passage shows that the value and importance accorded to philosophy by the *Protrepticus* is strikingly high and, correspondingly, the evaluation of non-philosophical lives and activities is very low:

> For one will find that all the things that seem great to men are merely a façade; hence it is finely said that man is nothing and that nothing human is stable. Strength, size, and beauty are laughable and of no worth . . . Honors and reputation, things envied more than other things, are full of indescribable nonsense; for to him who catches a glimpse of things eternal it seems foolish to take these things seriously. What is there among human things that is great or long-lasting? It is owing to our weakness, I think, and the shortness of our life that even this appears great. Who, looking to these facts, would think himself happy and blessed, if, from the very beginning, all of us (as they say in the initiation rites), are shaped by nature as though for punishment? . . . Nothing divine or blessed belongs to humans, except that one thing alone which is worth taking seriously – as much as there is in us of intellect [*nou*] and *phronēsis*: this alone of our possessions seems to be immortal, this alone divine . . . For intellect is the god in us – whether it was Hermotimus or Anaxagoras who said so – and mortal life contains a portion of some god. We must, therefore, either philosophize or say farewell to life and depart hence, since all other things seem to be great nonsense and frivolousness. (77.13–79.2, B104–10)[16]

This, too, seems to be in tension with Aristotle's other ethical and political works.

It is not my purpose to try to settle here how far there are actual conflicts in Aristotle's thought, but I shall discuss some points of apparent tension. This is all that can be done because interpretive controversy surrounds both sides of the comparison. To the extent that we offer a "deflationary" reading of the *Protrepticus* passages, it is easier to bring them into agreement with Aristotle's other writings and these other writings can themselves also be interpreted in such a way as to bring them closer to the *Protrepticus* understood in a stronger way. These difficulties are especially pressing, since, on the issues of the nature of *phronēsis*, and the place of philosophy in the good or happy life in the *Eudemian* and the *Nicomachean Ethics*, there is widespread and deep disagreement among scholars. Thus any remarks can only be quite preliminary.

But to begin with the *Protrepticus*, we might first wonder how much weight these passages can bear. The *Protrepticus* is a work intended for a more general audience than the school-writings, and it also has the explicit intention of persuading readers toward leading a philosophical (or, at any rate, more philosophical) life. So one might expect some degree of rhetorical exaggeration and that the advantages of philosophy should be painted in bright colors. The danger of such an interpretive strategy is that it makes it all too easy to read away Aristotle's apparent claims in favor of what we think he should, according to our own judgments of plausibility, say or what he says elsewhere. In any case, even if such adjustments must be made at the end of the day, we should begin with a straightforward reading of the text.

(1)   To begin, Aristotle in the first passage claims that only the philosopher's actions are "correct [*orthai*] and fine [*kalai*]."[17] Since being fine is a necessary condition of being virtuous, only the philosopher acts virtuously and is virtuous, or acts justly and is just. Aristotle also makes clear the reason for this surprising restriction. The agent must know the truth about the just (*dikaion*), the fine (*kalon*), and the good or beneficial (*sumpheron*, 84.24–85.2), and must know these eternal and unchanging things (85.22) in the best kind of way, that is, in a philosophic, accurate way.[18] In the *Eudemian* and *Nicomachean Ethics*, the virtues are divided into those of character (*ēthikai*) and the intellectual (*dianoētikai*) virtues (*EE* II.1.1220a4–5; *NE* I.13.1103a3–7). In chapter 1 of the common book *EE* V = *NE* VI, Aristotle divides the rational part of the soul into two subparts: one that reflects upon things that cannot be otherwise and one that reflects upon variable things. The former is the scientific or understanding (*epistēmikon*) part, the latter the calculative part (*logistikon*), that is, the one concerned with deliberation (*bouleusis*) (*NE* VI.1.1139a1–16). The virtue of the former is wisdom (*sophia*), while *phronēsis* is the virtue of the latter. Wisdom and its component, understanding (*epistēmē*) are not required for the virtues of character or *phronēsis*, while *phronēsis* and the virtues of character mutually require each other. The possession of *phronēsis* and the virtues of character is sufficient for being virtuous and just.

This picture is complicated by the fact that Aristotle seems to recognize two different kinds (or employments) of one important state by virtue of which the soul grasps the truth, that is, intellect (*nous*). There is a theoretical kind or employment of intellect that consists in the proper grasp of the first principles of the sciences, that is, a grasp of them as first principles. But there is also a practical kind or employment of intellect that is at least intimately related to *phronēsis* understood as the virtue of the deliberative part. Some scholars think that practical intellect functions so as to derive a grasp of ethical universals starting from particulars. Others hold that the function of practical intellect is to recognize the particulars relevant to deliberation as being of a certain kind. But even on the former interpretation, the way in which a person with *phronēsis* grasps ethical universals may fall far short of the grasp of universals had by one who possesses wisdom (*sophia*): it may, for example, lack the structure and organization of a proper Aristotelian science. Few scholars think that either the *Eudemian Ethics* or the *Nicomachean Ethics* requires that one have the intellectual virtues of a philosopher in order to be virtuous or just or to act virtuously or finely.[19]

(2)   This first passage also claims that a person cannot be a good lawmaker (84.13) without possessing the same kind of philosophic knowledge of what is just, fine, and good. This, too, seems to be in deep tension with Aristotle's views elsewhere. First, in the common book, *EE* V = *NE* VI, Aristotle claims that *phronēsis* and political expertise or statesmanship (the knowledge possessed by the good statesman) are the same psychic state, but differ in their being or their definition (*NE* VI.8.1141b23–1142a11). Roughly, *phronēsis* is concerned primarily with the goods available through action for the individual himself, while political expertise is concerned primarily with the goods available through action for the city as a whole. Although political expertise may thus have a certain kind of generality not found in *phronēsis*, Aristotle does not say that it has, or more nearly approximates, the structure of a proper Aristotelian science or that it involves a better grasp of the relevant first principles. So similar sorts of considerations to those noted in (1) about *phronēsis* in the common books might seem to apply to political expertise.[20]

Second, in the ideal city of the *Politics*, all citizens share in ruling on equal terms and this equality in political power is justified by the fact that all these citizens will be equally virtuous. But few of the citizens will be philosophers and Aristotle does not suggest that those among them who are philosophers should possess extra political authority. Doing the best job of ruling in a city requires nothing more than *phronēsis* and the virtues of character: in particular, it does not require philosophical education.[21]

Finally, in a related point, Aristotle in the *Nicomachean Ethics* and the *Politics* not infrequently excludes various kinds of theoretical knowledge as something that the statesman does not need to have. For example, with respect to the study of psychology, Aristotle remarks "the student of politics, then, must study the soul, and must study it with these objects in view [questions about happiness insofar as it is an activity of the soul], and do so just to the extent that is sufficient for the questions we are discussing; for further precision [*exakriboun*] is perhaps something more laborious than our purposes require" (*NE* I.12.1102a23–6).[22]

(3)   Our second passage from Iamblichus gives a remarkably pessimistic account of the goodness of a non-philosophic life and of the worth of non-philosophic activities and goods simply. The only thing in human life that is an important good is intellect and *phronēsis* (78.13–14). In the context, it seems clear that this cognitive state is the same sort of grasp of unchanging and eternal things referred to in the previous passage.

Given the strong contrast in value between intellect and *phronēsis* and "all other things," this passage may suggest that the sole component of complete happiness or the happiest life is this sort of theoretical understanding. But this is not the respect in which the *Protrepticus* passage differs most sharply from Aristotle's views elsewhere. Aristotle does not explicitly say here that just and virtuous actions are not part of the happiest life. His position, however, seems to have the consequence that a life without philosophy is of little worth. This does not commit him to the idea that a life of virtuous action is worth little, since, as we have seen, the *Protrepticus* seems to hold that virtuous action requires philosophic understanding. But the claim that any life without philosophic understanding is of little value to its possessor is in deep tension with Aristotle's views elsewhere. In the *Nicomachean Ethics*, he holds that a life of practical virtue without theoretical virtue is happy in a "secondary kind of way" (*NE* X.8.1178a9–10). It is also the view of the *Politics* that such a life of practical virtue, even if not the best life, is at least a very good one. The *Protrepticus* passage might also suggest an even stronger claim; that is, that actions expressing practical virtue, even if they occur in the life of the philosopher and even if they do have positive value, do not have a prominent place in that life or contribute significantly to its happiness.[23]

This brief survey leaves us with pressing questions that need answers. First, are these apparent differences really genuine? Even if we accept that the *Protrepticus* fragments (or at least the ones referred to here) are by Aristotle, we might think that more extensive investigation will show that there is really no serious disagreement between them and the later works we have considered.

Second, if we do find that at least some of these differences are genuine, we need an explanation of them: we need a philosophical account of why Aristotle might prefer one to the other (and preferably one that does not make the earlier view a simple mistake to be outgrown). In particular, if we accept these differences, we must try to read *Eudemian Ethics* Book V = *Nicomachean Ethics* Book VI in light of the *Protrepticus* passages. Why does Aristotle need to develop an account of a faculty of *phronēsis* that is neither a species of nor the genus for wisdom? What work does this do for him that was not done before? In light of the value that the *Protrepticus* gives to theoretical understanding as a good to possess, what accounts for, or grounds, the value of *phronēsis* once it is a separate faculty? Finally, why does Aristotle come to think that theoretical understanding is not necessary for a life of practical virtue? Does *phronēsis* in his later conception of it do the same work as the theoretical understanding required in the *Protrepticus* or does Aristotle come to think that such work is no longer necessary for a life of practical virtue or of happiness? These questions still require answers, even if we reject Jaeger's developmentalism in its entirety. Such an inquiry is both of considerable importance and still in its beginning stages.

Eudemian Ethics

It is also true, I think, that serious philosophical investigation of the *Eudemian Ethics* is in its beginning stages. Although many passages have been discussed in the literature, these discussions are usually only a supplement to the analysis of the passages from the *Nicomachean Ethics* and few have attempted to read the *Eudemian Ethics* with the common books as a whole work. Here I shall only mention a few of the most discussed apparent differences between the unique books of the *Eudemian Ethics* and those of the *Nicomachean Ethics*.

(1)   It is controversial whether Aristotle holds a monistic or a pluralistic conception of happiness in the *Nicomachean Ethics*; that is, whether he thinks that happiness consists in just one good or more than one kind of good. In particular, some have thought, especially in light of Aristotle's praise of the contemplative life in *NE* Book X, chapters 7–8, that he holds that the happiest life consists in as much contemplation as possible. It is also disputed, if Aristotle does endorse a contemplative understanding of happiness in Book X, whether this is his position throughout the *Nicomachean Ethics* or whether he holds a pluralistic account elsewhere in that work.[24]

But it has been somewhat less controversial (although not unanimously accepted) that in the *Eudemian Ethics* Aristotle holds a pluralistic conception of happiness that includes all the virtues, both intellectual and those of character, and within the former, both practical as well as theoretical virtues. At the end of the function argument in the *Eudemian Ethics* Book II, chapter 1, Aristotle concludes:

> now since happiness was agreed to be something complete, and a life may be complete or incomplete – and this holds with virtue also (in the one case, it is the whole; in the other, a part) – and the activity of what is incomplete is itself incomplete, happiness must be activity of a complete life in accordance with complete virtue. (1219a35–9)

And later in this chapter Aristotle appears to suggest that complete virtue includes both the practical as well as the theoretical ones:

> And as physical well-being is made up of the virtues of the several parts, so is the virtue of the soul, insofar as it is a complete whole. Virtue is of two forms, virtue of character, and intellectual virtue. For we praise not only the just, but also the intelligent and the wise [*sophous*]. (II.1.1220a2–6)[25]

Moreover, there may well be nothing in the *Eudemian Ethics* that corresponds to the claim in Book X of the *Nicomachean Ethics* (at least as understood by some interpreters) that the happiest life consists in as much contemplation as possible.

It has sometimes been thought that the closing chapter of the *Eudemian Ethics*, VIII.3, makes a similar claim on the strength of the following passage:

> What choice, then, and possession of natural goods – whether bodily goods, wealth, friends, or other things – will most produce the contemplation of god, that choice or possession is best; this is the finest standard, but any that through deficiency or excess hinders one from contemplation and service of god is bad; this a man possesses in his soul, and this is the best standard for the soul – to perceive the irrational part of the soul, as such, as little as possible. (1249b16–23)

But on one prominent and plausible interpretation of this passage, it is only discussing the choices of goods in cases when the demands of the practical virtues of justice, courage, moderation, and so on have already been met. On this reading, the passage advises maximizing contemplation only after these demands have been satisfied. It is not clear how much time ethical requirements absorb, but this does not seem to give contemplation a dominating role.

If we accept the chronology *Protrepticus – Eudemian Ethics – Nicomachean Ethics* and also think that both the *Protrepticus* and the *Nicomachean Ethics* give a considerably more prominent role to contemplation, then we seem to have Aristotle changing his mind twice. If we add to this the idea I shall turn to next, that is, that the *Eudemian Ethics* is more confident than the *Nicomachean* that ethical inquiry can resemble rigorous theoretical inquiry, matters might seem only to get worse. The more akin ethical inquiry is to theoretical inquiry, is it not natural to expect that greater value is attached to contemplation? But perhaps if ethical reflection is less sharply distinguished from theoretical inquiry, then there is less pressure to see a purely contemplative life as a candidate for the best possible life. Yet if this is so, we shall especially need an interpretation of *phronēsis* in the common book *EE* V = *NE* VI, the role that it plays, the need for it, and its value. Getting clear on these issues remains one of the most important tasks in understanding the relations among these three works.[26]

(2)   A second set of issues concerns the epistemology and methodology of the *Eudemian Ethics* and the *Nicomachean Ethics*. Jaeger and others have found significant differences, but this claim has also been sharply resisted.[27] As a way into these issues, consider the initial parts of both works. There is at least a loose correspondence between the order of topics in the unique books of the *Eudemian* and the *Nicomachean Ethics* and remarks on methodology come early in both: *EE* Book I, chapter 6 (1216b26–1217a17) and *NE* Book I, chapter 3 (1094b11–1095a13). First, two well-known passages from the first book of the *Nicomachean Ethics*:

> Our account would be adequate if it has as much clearness [*diasaphētheiē*] as the subject-matter admits of; for exactness [*to . . . akribes*] is not to be sought for alike in all accounts, any more than in all the products of the crafts . . . We must be content,

then, in speaking of such subjects and starting from them to indicate the truth roughly and in outline [*tupōi*], and in speaking about things that are only for the most part true [*hōs epi to polu*] and starting from them to reach conclusions that are of the same sort . . . it is the mark of an educated person to look for exactness in each class of things just so far as the nature of the subject allows: for it seems to be pretty much the same thing to accept a merely persuasive account from a mathematician and to demand from a rhetorician demonstrative proofs. (*NE* I.3.1094b11–27)

Hence anyone who is to listen adequately to lectures about what is fine and just and, generally, about the subjects of political expertise must have been brought up in fine habits. For the that [*to hoti*] is the starting-point, and if this were sufficiently plain to us, there will be no need for the why [*tou dioti*] in addition; and the person who has been well brought up has or can easily get the starting-points. (*NE* I.4.1095b4–8)

From the first book of the *Eudemian Ethics*:

For by advancing from things said truly but not clearly [*ou saphōs*], one will arrive at what is said clearly, always exchanging the usual confused statement for what is better known [*gnōrimōtera*]. Now in every discipline there is a difference between what is said in a philosophic manner and a nonphilosophic one. Therefore statesmen too should not think that the sort of study [*theōrian*] that not only makes the that [*to ti*] evident, but also the why [*to dia ti*] is not part of their job. For it is the mark of a philosopher to proceed in that way in every inquiry. (I.6.1216b32–9)

It is certainly not obvious that the passages are irreconcilably contradictory. But they are quite different in tone and, at least on first inspection, seem to be in tension with each other. One important task for further work is to better understand what their relations are.

The *Nicomachean Ethics* claims that the subject matter of ethics limits the exactness that can be attained in its accounts, and that ethics will indicate its truths only roughly and in outline. Its premises and conclusions will hold only for the most part. Its lack of exactness is thus not simply a matter of the practical purpose of the inquiry, but is owed to the nature of human actions and values themselves.[28] In the *Eudemian Ethics*, the task of ethics is to move from obscure or confused claims to those that are clear and better known (and presumably this is better known by nature). This is Aristotle's standard description of rigorous investigation and learning (for example, *Meta.* VII.3.1029b3–12; *Phys.* I.1; *Topics* VI.4) and the *Eudemian Ethics* stresses that its inquiry will be treated in a "philosophical" manner.[29] In particular, this inquiry will reveal not just the fact but also the reason why. This is a normal task in a demonstrative science as well as in certain uses of dialectic, and getting to the reason why is a difficult and challenging endeavor. The second passage from the *Nicomachean Ethics* dismisses this as something either superfluous or easy.

There are, of course, ways in which we can try to bring these passages closer together so that they differ more in emphasis than in overall view.[30] Nevertheless, it is true that there are no passages in the *Eudemian Ethics* (or the common books) in which Aristotle claims that ethics lacks exactness because of its subject matter. The explicit distinction that Aristotle draws in the programmatic first book of the *Eudemian Ethics* contrasts productive sciences, which include political science, with theoretical science. In a productive science, Aristotle says that understanding is not the most important aim, although he does not deny that it is to be sought or is feasible. He does not, however, as he does in the *Nicomachean Ethics*, contrast political science with theoretical science with respect to exactness.

[Socrates] inquired what virtue is, not how it arises or from what. This is correct with respect to the theoretical sciences [*tōn epistēmōn . . . tōn theōrētikōn*], for nothing belongs to astronomy or physics or geometry except knowing and contemplating the nature of things that are the subjects of those sciences; though nothing prevents them from being useful in a coincidental way to us for much that we need. But the end [*telos*] of the productive sciences is different from understanding and knowing [*tēs epistēmēs kai gnōseōs*], e.g. health is different from medical science, good political order (or something of the sort) is different from political science. Now to know anything that is fine is itself fine; but regarding virtue, at least, not to know what it is, but to know out of what it arises is most precious. For we do not wish to know what courage is but to be courageous . . . (*EE* I.5.1216b9–22)[31]

These differences are especially interesting if the consensus opinion that the common books originally belonged to the *Eudemian Ethics* is correct. It is in the common books that we find both (a) the account of *phronēsis*, in *NE* Book VI = *EE* Book V, and (b) one of the classic places in which Aristotle advocates a method of appealing to "reputable opinions" (*endoxa*). This method starts from reputable opinions and reformulates and reworks them in order to arrive at the truth.[32] Both (a) and (b) have been sometimes thought to bear significant relations to Aristotle's claims about the lack of exactness in ethics, either as their grounds or their results. If we accept that the common books had their original home in the *Eudemian Ethics*, then either Aristotle has not yet worked out the full implications of his view or (a) and (b) are detachable from his claims about exactness.

In order to advance our understanding of what Aristotle has to say about the place of reason in practical reflection, we would need an account of at least the following topics and of their interrelations:

1   Most obviously, we would need an account of the nature of *phronēsis* in the *NE* Book VI = *EE* Book V, of the functions it performs, and of how it grasps and deals with the relevant particulars and universals.
2   Aristotle strongly links virtuous action with hitting the mean point on continua of actions and affections (for example, *EE* II.6 and *NE* II.3) and with aiming

at the fine (*kalon*) which he sometimes gives a theoretically rich specification (*EE* VIII.3.1248b8–1249a17; *NE* III.7.1115b7–24; *Meta.* XIII.3.1078a31–b6). We need to explain in more detail what sorts of intellectual operations are involved in both of these tasks, what faculties are involved, and how articulate (and articulable) these goals are.

3   *Phronēsis* is only half of what is needed for full practical virtue: a virtuous person also requires the proper disposition of the non-rational part of the soul, that is, the virtues of character, and a person cannot have either *phronēsis* or the virtues of character without possessing the other. In order to understand the cognitive structure of *phronēsis*, we also need to understand the conceptual resources and structure of the properly trained non-rational part of the soul.

4   We need an account of the role of principles in practical reflection: how they function both in the psychological reality of deliberation and in its justification or explanation as well as in ethical education. Are informative "for the most part" principles possible in ethics (or even the occasional exceptionless principle) and what faculty achieves and possesses them? What sort of cognitive grasp can we have of them?

5   Both the *Eudemian* and the *Nicomachean Ethics* are treatises with a practical intention: in both the inquiry aims at leading a better life. What is the relation of the "philosophical ethics" of the sort actually presented in the *Eudemian* and the *Nicomachean Ethics* to the virtuous person? What, if anything, is lacking from the virtue of someone who is not familiar with such works? What faculty or faculties are employed in using such discussions and how is this knowledge articulated and deployed?

I have focused on issues surrounding the place of reason in practical reflection and in the happy life for two reasons. First, these are important themes running throughout all of Aristotle's ethical writings, and it thus provides one way of surveying the *Protrepticus* and the *Eudemian Ethics* and their relation to the *Nicomachean Ethics* that I hope is informative even in such a brief space. Second, I think that the sets of problems discussed here remain central to understanding Aristotle's ethical thought, as well as its relation to that of Plato, and that we do not yet have good answers to all the questions raised. These are not, however, the only dimensions along which these works can be usefully compared and there are, for example, interesting apparent differences between the *Eudemian Ethics* and the *Nicomachean Ethics* on the use of a function argument to help specify the content of happiness, on the conception of friendship, and the analysis of voluntary action.[33]

Nevertheless, it remains true that the amount of work devoted to the *Protrepticus* and the *Eudemian Ethics* over the past century (not just in books and articles, but in teaching and scholarly discussion) is several orders of magnitude smaller than the corresponding work on the *Nicomachean Ethics*. In particular, two of the philosophically most important books of Aristotle's ethics, *EE* V = *NE* VI (on intellectual virtue), and *EE* VI = *NE* VII (on pleasure and *akrasia*), have been interpreted primarily or exclusively as part of the *Nicomachean Ethics* and in the context of the rest of the unique books of the *Nicomachean Ethics*. To echo a justly famous remark by Anthony Kenny, we do not yet know what we can discover by reading the common books in a corresponding way in the context of the unique books of the *Eudemian Ethics*.

Acknowledgments

I would like to thank Kellie Brownell, Emily Fletcher, Corinne Gartner, and Richard Kraut for their comments on this chapter.

Notes

1 Among the works universally agreed to be spurious is a brief ethical treatise, *Virtues and Vices*. With respect to the names of the treatises, Nicomachus was Aristotle's son (Aristotle's father had the same name) and Eudemus of Rhodes was Aristotle's student; the works bearing their names may have been edited by or dedicated to them. On the transmission of Aristotle's writings, see Düring (1950, 1957) and Moraux (1951, 1973–2001). Older, but still useful, is Zeller (1962: 48–160).

2 Cicero refers to Aristotle's "golden river of speech" (*Academica* 38), an unlikely description of the school-writings. For a good brief overview of these topics, see Guthrie (1981: 49–88). For a text of the fragments, see Ross (1955); for a discussion of previous editions, see Wilpert (1960).

3 For an overview of information about the *Protrepticus* until the time of his writing, see Rabinowitz (1957: 1–22).

4 Rabinowitz (1957) is a radically skeptical attack on efforts to reconstruct Aristotle's *Protrepticus*. For correctives, see the introduction to Düring's edition (1961: 9–39); its bibliography also contains references to critical reviews of Rabinowitz (1957). There are a number of valuable papers in Düring and Owen (1960). More recently, the Iamblichus material has been accepted, at least in large part, by Monan (1968), Guthrie (1981), and Nightingale (2004). Since Rabinowitz, there has been no sustained argument for its rejection. Rabinowitz is most persuasive when criticizing the use of material from sources other than Iamblichus. Düring's own edition is controversial, since it extensively reorders the material in Iamblichus to produce a text. Hutchinson and Johnson (forthcoming) provide a new and detailed case for accepting the authenticity of much of the material in Iamblichus based on a comparison with his use of Platonic texts in the same work.

5 See Kenny (1978: 1–50) and Rowe (1971: 9–60) for a discussion of the text's history and its reception.

6 See, for example, Rowe (1983). The question is complicated by the possibility that Aristotle, at different times, revised any or all of the books comprising these works and that he himself joined the common books to the *Nicomachean Ethics*.

7   For a beginning, see Dirlmeier (1958), Düring (1966: 438–44), Rowe (1975), Kenny (1978: 215–39), and Cooper (1999: 195–211).

8   For more on the *Magna Moralia*, see Rowe (1975), Cooper (1999: 195–211, 336–55), and Natali (2001: 6–10).

9   For discussions, see Owen and Nussbaum (1986: 180–99, 200–20), Graham (1987), Rist (1989), Barnes (1995: 1–26), Code (1996), and Wians (1996).

10   It is consistent with this to allow that an appropriate desiderative or emotional state is necessary for acting virtuously or that such states are (causally) necessary for acquiring or sustaining the appropriate grasp of universals. It would rule out, however, that an appropriate desiderative or emotional state is in itself a necessary constituent of the required cognitive state.

11   My translations. *Euthyphro* 7B6–C9 suggests that what is desired is a definition that would allow automatic application in the way that we make judgments in counting, measuring, and weighing; cf. *Protagoras* 356C4–357C1. In the *Euthyphro*, knowledge of a definition is knowledge of a universal. It is less clear exactly what the knowledge of the measuring art consists of in the *Protagoras*, but it is a form of knowledge (*epistēmē*, 357B6). My views have been influenced by both my discussions with David Johnson and his PhD dissertation (Stanford University, 2002).

12   *NE* VI.3–5. On intellect (*nous*) and practical intellect, see below n. 19.

13   We might well, for instance, reject the idea that Aristotle becomes a radical empiricist in his last period. Further, disputes over whether the *Protrepticus* (and other fragmentary works of Aristotle) accept transcendental Platonic Forms and personal immortality have, I think, distracted attention from some fundamental issues. Further, if we accept that the common books had their original home in the *Eudemian Ethics*, Jaeger's interpretation of that work becomes problematic.

14   Translations of the *Protrepticus* are based on Düring (1961) and Hutchinson and Johnson (forthcoming). I cite the page and line numbers in des Places' (1989) edition of Iamblichus, in this case, 84.9–85.23, for each reference. In the first reference to a passage, I also cite the fragment numbers in Düring (1961), in this case B46–50, which are also used in Barnes (1995).

15   It is sometimes suggested that since Aristotle's popular writings are in dialogue form, we cannot assume that the point of view of any excerpt is Aristotle's, without knowing the speaker and context (see Düring 1961: 29–32). In the case of the *Protrepticus*, however, whether or not it is a dialogue, the fragments are sufficiently long and consistent with each other that it is reasonable to take them as expressing Aristotle's views. Second, there are arguments in the *Protrepticus* that establish only weaker conclusions about the need for philosophy and we might think that in some places Aristotle uses "philosophy" in a non-technical sense. But the presence of weaker arguments need not undermine Aristotle's commitment to the conclusions of stronger ones and the context makes it clear that to philosophize here means more than just to think in an intellectually serious way. (It might have only the weaker sense in the famous argument attributed to the *Protrepticus* that to settle the question of whether to philosophize, one must philosophize. But this argument is not found in Iamblichus and its form is quite uncertain; cf. Düring 1961: 25, 178–9 and Rabinowitz 1957: 34–41).

16   Some have thought that this passage is from another of Aristotle's lost works, the *Eudemus*; on these issues, see Bos (1984, 2003). On Anaxagoras, cf. *EE* I.5.1216a10–

27 and *Meta*. I.3.984b15–20, which also help make it clear that the *Protrepticus* is referring to theoretical understanding in this passage; see also Nightingale (2004: 22–3). For related passages, see Iamblichus 71.13–74.7 [B41, 59–70] and 79.9–84.2 [B10–21, 42–4]. The passage 71.16–18 suggests that nothing benefits a person unless it is accomplished by reasoning and in accordance with *phronēsis*. The passage 72.22–74.7 may come close to suggesting that happiness consists in "possessing the most accurate truth" (72.24–5, *hē akribestatē alētheia*) or a kind of theoretical understanding (74.1–2, *theōrētikēn . . . epistēmēn*). In the latter passage, we find that human beings have come to be for the sake of "exercising *phronēsis* and learning" and that the ultimate end (*telos*) for human beings is to exercise *phronēsis* (82.7–9).

17 Passage 85.20–23 shows that this is a general claim about virtuous actions, not just those concerned with lawmaking.

18 "Exact" (*akribēs*) characterizes reasonings at 85.4, and the things themselves that the reasonings concern at 85.7. The *Protrepticus* is not fully specific about what is required for such understanding, but it is only available after philosophizing (85.1–2).

19 The literature on *phronēsis* and practical intellect is vast. For starting-points with further references, see Monan (1968), Cooper (1975, 2004: 270–308), Irwin (1975), Kenny (1978, 1979), McDowell (1979, 1980, 1998), Sorabji (1980), Wiggins (1980a, b), Engberg-Pedersen (1983), Dahl (1984), Whiting (1986), Broadie (1987, 1991), Kraut (1989, 1993), Annas (1993: 66–84), and Bostock (2000). For an account that is especially optimistic that ethics can be a "for the most part" science, see Reeve (1992) and comments in Bobonich (1994).

20 Interestingly, Iamblichus 85.16–17 suggests that laws made by non-philosophers cannot be fine (*kalon*); 85.19 only explicitly says they cannot be secure or stable (*bebaios*). For discussion of political expertise, see Miller (1997: 5–14) and Kraut (2002: 92–3). Stewart's (1892) notes on *NE* VI.7.1141b23–5 are useful. One might think that, for example, *NE* I.2.1094a18–3.1095a13 and X.9.1180b28–1181b15 suggest that a course of study comparable to reading the *Nicomachean Ethics* is required for the good statesman. But although such study is intended to be practical and thus improve practice in some way, it is not clear that philosophical reflection is any the more necessary for being a good lawmaker than it is for the task of the *Nicomachean Ethics* itself, which is to become a virtuous person.

21 *Politics* VII.9, VII.14–15. For discussion, see Kraut (1997: 133–48; 2002: 192–239) and Miller (1997: 191–251).

22 Cf. *Politics* VII.1–2, Broadie (1991: 62–3), and Kraut (1997: 59–63, 138–9). I discuss exactness in the section on the *Eudemian Ethics* below.

23 The interpretation of *NE* X.8.1178a9–10 and, more generally, of *NE* Book X, chapters 7–8, are highly controversial. For a start, see Whiting (1986), Kraut (1989), Broadie (1991: 366–438), and Cooper (1999: 212–36; 2004: 270–308). On the *Politics*, see Book VII, chapters 1–3, Kraut (1997 *ad loc.*), and Miller (1997: 346–57). I discuss the conception of happiness in the *Eudemian Ethics* below.

24 I leave aside refinements here; for example, a basically contemplative view might require optimizing contemplation, but allow other goods to count as tiebreakers (see n. 23 for further references).

25 Cf. *EE* II.4.1221b28–30. Translations of the *Eudemian Ethics* draw on Woods (1982); of the *Nicomachean Ethics* on Broadie and Rowe (2002). For analysis, see Cooper

(1975: 115–33) and Kenny (1978: 190–214); for dissenting views, see Rowe (1971: 33–8) and Kraut (1989: 169–70).

26 The puzzles of *EE* VIII.3 have not yet, I think, been resolved. Jaeger (1962: 228–58) sees the contemplation of god as providing a standard for all choices and the basis of a "theonomic ethics." Other discussions include Monan (1968), Cooper (1975: 133–43), Broadie (1991: 383–8), and Whiting (1996). On the conception of happiness in the *Magna Moralia*, see, on opposite sides, Cooper (1975: 121–4) and Kraut (1989: 287–91).

27 For yes, see Jaeger ([1923] 1962), Allan (1961), Rowe (1971: 63–72), Devereux (1986), and, with qualifications, Anagnostopoulos (1994: 61–4); for no, see Monan (1968: 116–48). For persuasive criticism of Jaeger, see Kenny (1978: 161–89); for an aporetic discussion, see Jost (1991).

28 For a useful survey of Aristotle's use of exactness and related notions, see Anagnostopoulos (1994). For the notion of being for the most part and its cognitive implications, see the works in n. 19, especially Reeve (1992). On Aristotle's attitude toward general principles in ethics, see McDowell (1979, 1980, 1998), Nussbaum (1990: 54–105), and Irwin (2000); on particularism as an ethical view, see Dancy (1993) and Hooker and Little (2000).

29 On being better known by nature, see Burnyeat (1981) and Scott (1995: 91–156). Since Owen's classic (1986), first published in 1961, interest in Aristotle's appeal to "appearances" (*phainomena*) and "reputable opinions" (*endoxa*), and in his conception of the nature of dialectic and its role in discovering truth, has generated an enormous literature. For a recent discussion with useful references, see Wlodarczyk (2000), which also notes the role of dialectic in moving to what is better known by nature (2000: 180–210).

30 *EE* I.6.1216b40–1217a17 qualifies in some ways the requirement to proceed in a philosophic way. The passage warns against bringing in non-germane arguments and stresses the importance, at least in some cases, of relying on appearances (*phainomena*) rather than arguments, but Aristotle does not link either of these concerns to a lack of exactness in ethics. The *Eudemian Ethics* (I.7.1217a18–21) says that it aims to discover "clearly [*saphōs*] what happiness is [*ti estin*]"; the *Nicomachean Ethics* says that it will provide an "outline" of happiness (I.7.1098a20–22, cf. X.9.1179a33–5) and connects this to the lack of exactness possible in ethics (I.7.1098a26–1098b2).

31 Cf. *EE* I.1.1214a8–14 and note the "not only . . . but also" phrasing and see Devereux (1986). *NE* II.2.1103b26–9 makes the point about the practical aim of its inquiry, but immediately connects this with its lack of exactness, II.2.1103b34–1104a11.

32 This is also found in unique books of the *EE*, e.g., VII.2.1235b13–18 and outside ethics, e.g., *Phys.* IV.4.211a7–11. Some useful discussions are Barnes (1980), Owen and Nussbaum (1986: 240–63), and Cooper (1999: 281–91); also see Wlodarczyk (2000).

33 For the function arguments, see *EE* II.1 and *NE* I.7; on friendship, see Cooper (1999: 312–55); on voluntary action, see Heinaman (1988) and Meyer (1993). It is sometimes thought that the *EE*'s account of the voluntary and the involuntary differs from that of the *NE* and that the *EE*'s account is radically defective because it cannot show that force (*bia*) can make an action involuntary. Although there may be significant differences between the *EE* and the *NE* accounts of voluntary action, an interpretation

that sees the earlier work as making crudely obvious and elementary mistakes is not inherently attractive (even if we are ultimately led to accept it). In this case, we need not see the *Eudemian Ethics* as just a gross mistake. We should not see *EE* II.9.1225b8–10 as presenting twin full definitions of voluntary and involuntary action. Note that at *EE* II.9.1225b1–8, Aristotle characterizes the voluntary only in terms of knowledge, but he adds to this at 1225b8–10 to cater for the lack of force in his definition of the voluntary. He then says that "this is what the voluntary is" (b9–10). He does not say anything so strong about "the involuntary" at 1225b10; there he states only a sufficient condition of being involuntary that must be supplemented in a way corresponding to the definition of the voluntary in order to get a definition of the involuntary.

References

Algra, K., Barnes, J., Mansfeld, J., and Schofield, M. (eds) 1999: *The Cambridge History of Hellenistic Philosophy*. Cambridge: Cambridge University Press.

Allan, D. J. 1961: "Quasi-mathematical Method in the *Eudemian Ethics*." In S. Mansion (ed.), *Aristote et les problemes de methode*, pp. 303–18. Louvain: Publications Universitaires.

Anagnostopoulos, G. 1994: *Aristotle on the Goals and Exactness of Ethics*. Berkeley, CA: University of California Press.

Annas, J. 1993: *The Morality of Happiness*. Oxford: Oxford University Press.

Barnes, J. 1980: "Aristotle and the Methods of Ethics," *Revue Internationale de Philosophie* 31: 490–511.

—(ed.) 1985: *The Complete Works of Aristotle*, 2 vols. Princeton, NJ: Princeton University Press.

—(ed.) 1995: *The Cambridge Companion to Aristotle*. Cambridge: Cambridge University Press.

—1997: "Roman Aristotle." In J. Barnes and M. Griffin (eds), *Philosophia Togata. II: Plato and Aristotle at Rome*, pp. 1–69. Oxford: Oxford University Press.

—2003: "Aristotle and the Methods of Ethics," *Revue Internationale de Philosophie* 34: 490–511. Ouagadougou: Presses Universitaires de Ouagadougou.

—and Griffin, M. 1997: *Philosophia Togata. II: Plato and Aristotle at Rome*. Oxford: Oxford University Press.

Bobonich, C. 1994: "Review of C. D. C. Reeve," *Practices of Reason: The Philosophical Review* 103: 567–9.

Bos, A. 1984: "Aristotle's *Eudemus* and *Protrepticus*: Are They Really Two Different Works?," *Dionysius* 8: 19–51.

—2003: "Aristotle on the Etruscan Robbers: A Core Text of 'Aristotelian Dualism,'" *Journal of the History of Philosophy* 41: 289–306.

Bostock, D. 2000: *Aristotle's Ethics*. Oxford: Oxford University Press.

Broadie, S. 1987: "The Problem of Practical Intellect in Aristotle's *Ethics*," *Proceedings of the Boston Area Colloquium in Ancient Philosophy* 3: 229–52.

—1991: *Ethics with Aristotle*. Oxford: Oxford University Press.

—and Rowe C. 2002: *Aristotle's Nicomachean Ethics*. Oxford: Oxford University Press.

Burnyeat, M. 1981: "Aristotle on Understanding Knowledge." In E. Berti (ed.), *Aristotle on Science*, pp. 97–139. Padua: Editrice Antenore.

Bywater, I. 1869: "On a Lost Dialogue of Aristotle," *Journal of Philology* 2: 55–69.

Code, A. 1996: "Owen on the Development of Aristotle's Metaphysics." In William Wians (ed.), *Aristotle's Philosophical Development: Problems and Prospects*, pp. 303–25. Lanham: Rowman and Littlefield.

Cooper, J. 1975: *Reason and Human Good in Aristotle*. Cambridge, MA: Harvard University Press.

—1999: *Reason and Emotion*. Princeton, NJ: Princeton University Press.

—2004: *Knowledge, Nature, and the Good*. Princeton, NJ: Princeton University Press.

Dahl, N. 1984: *Practical Reason, Aristotle, and Weakness of the Will*. Minneapolis, MN: University of Minnesota Press.

Dancy, J. 1993: *Moral Reasons*. Oxford: Oxford University Press.

Devereux, D. 1986: "Particular and Universal in Aristotle's Conception of Practical Knowledge," *Review of Metaphysics* 39: 483–504.

Dirlmeier, F. (ed. and trans.) 1958: *Aristoteles, Magna Moralia*. Berlin: Akademie-Verlag.

Düring, I. 1950: *Notes on the Transmission of Aristotle's Writings*. Stockholm: Almqvist and Wiksell.

—1957: *Aristotle in the Ancient Biographical Tradition*. Stockholm: Almqvist and Wiksell.

—1961: *Aristotle's Protrepticus*. Stockholm: Almqvist and Wiksell.

—1966: *Aristotelis*. Heidelberg: Carl Winter.

—and Owen, G. E. L. (eds) 1960: *Aristotle and Plato in the Mid-fourth Century*. Sweden: Göteborg.

Engberg-Pedersen, T. 1983: *Aristotle's Theory of Moral Insight*. Oxford: Oxford University Press.

Everson, S. (ed.) 1998: *Companions to Ancient Thought, IV: Ethics*. Cambridge: Cambridge University Press.

Frede, M. 1997: "Epilogue." In K. A. Algra, M. H. Koenen, and P. H. Schrijvers (eds), *Lucretius and his Intellectual Background*, pp. 771–97. Amsterdam: Koninklijke Nederlandse Academie van Wetenschappen.

Graham, D. 1987: *Aristotle's Two Systems*. Oxford: Oxford University Press.

Guthrie, W. K. C. 1981: *A History of Greek Philosophy*, vol. 6: *Aristotle: An Encounter*. Cambridge: Cambridge University Press.

Heinaman, R. 1988: "Compulsion and Voluntary Action in the *Eudemian Ethics*," *Nous* 22: 253–81.

Hooker, B. and Little, M. 2000: *Moral Particularism*. Oxford: Oxford University Press.

Hutchinson, D. and Johnson, M. (forthcoming): *Aristotle Protrepticus*. Indianapolis, IN: Hackett.

Irwin, T. H. 1975: "Aristotle on Reason, Desire and Virtue," *Journal of Philosophy* 72: 567–78.

—1990: *Aristotle's First Principles*. Oxford: Oxford University Press.

—2000: "Ethics as an Inexact Science: Aristotle's Ambitions for Moral Theory." In B. Hooker and M. Little (eds), *Moral Particularism*, pp. 100–29. Oxford: Oxford University Press.

Jaeger, W. [1923] 1962: *Aristotle: Fundamentals of the History of his Development*, trans. R. Robinson, 2nd edn. Oxford: Oxford University Press.

Jost, L. 1991: "Eudemian Ethical Method." In J. Anton and G. Kustas (eds), *Essays in Ancient Greek Philosophy*, vol. 4, pp. 29–40. Albany, NY: State University of New York Press.

Kenny, A. 1978: *The Aristotelian Ethics*. Oxford: Oxford University Press.

—1979: *Aristotle's Theory of the Will*. Oxford: Oxford University Press.

Kraut, R. 1989: *Aristotle on the Human Good*. Princeton, NJ: Princeton University Press.

—1990: "Review of Reeve (1988), *Practices of Reason*," *Political Theory* 18: 492–6.

—1993: "In Defense of the Grand End," *Ethics* 103: 361–74.

—1997: *Aristotle Politics Books VII and VIII*. Oxford: Oxford University Press.

—2002: *Aristotle: Political Philosophy*. Oxford: Oxford University Press.

Long, A. 1998: "Theophrastus and the Stoa". In J. M. van Ophuijsen and M. van Raalte (eds), *Theophrastus: Reappraising the Sources*, pp. 355–83. New Brunswick: Rutgers University Press.

McDowell, J. 1979: "Virtue and Reason," *The Monist* 62: 330–50.

—1980: "The Rôle of Eudaimonia in Aristotle's Ethics." In Amelie Rorty (ed.), *Essays on Aristotle's Ethics*, pp. 359–76. Berkeley, CA: University of California Press.

—1998: "Some Issues in Aristotle's Moral Psychology." In S. Everson (ed.), *Ethics*, pp. 107–28. Cambridge: Cambridge University Press.

Meyer, S. 1993: *Aristotle on Moral Responsibility*. Oxford: Blackwell.

Miller, F. 1997: *Nature, Justice, and Rights in Aristotle's Politics*. Oxford: Oxford University Press.

Monan, J. 1968: *Moral Knowledge and its Methodology in Aristotle*. Oxford: Oxford University Press.

Moraux, Paul. 1951: *Les listes anciennes des ouvrages d'Aristote*. Louvain: Éditions Universitaires de Louvain.

—1973–2001: *Der Aristotelismus bei den Griechen: von Andronikos bis Alexander von Aphrodisias*, 3 vols. Berlin: de Gruyter.

Natali, C. 2001: *The Wisdom of Aristotle*, trans. G. Parks. Albany, NY: State University of New York Press.

Nightingale, A. 2004: *Spectacles of Truth in Classical Greek Philosophy*. Cambridge: Cambridge University Press.

Nussbaum, M. 1990: *Love's Knowledge*. Oxford: Oxford University Press.

Owen, G. E. L. 1986: "*Tithenai ta phainomena*." In G. E. L. Owen and M. Nussbaum (eds), *Logic, Science, and Dialectic*, pp. 239–51. Cambridge: Cambridge University Press.

—and Nussbaum, M (eds.) 1986: *Logic, Science, and Dialectic*. Cambridge: Cambridge University Press.

des Places, É. (ed. and trans.) 1989: *Jamblique Protreptique*. Paris: Les Belles Lettres.

Rabinowitz, W. 1957: *Aristotle's Protrepticus and the Sources of its Reconstruction*. Berkeley, CA: University of California Press.

Reeve, C. D. C. 1992: *Practices of Reason*. Oxford: Oxford University Press.

Rist, J. 1989: *The Mind of Aristotle: A Study in Philosophical Growth*. Buffalo: University of Toronto Press.

Rorty, A. (ed.) 1980: *Essays on Aristotle's Ethics*. Berkeley, CA: University of California Press.

Ross, D. 1955: *Aristotelis Fragmenta Selecta*. Oxford: Oxford University Press.

Rowe, C. J. 1971: *The Eudemian and Nicomachean Ethics: A Study in the Development of Aristotle's Thought*. Cambridge: Cambridge Philological Society.

—1975: "A Reply to John Cooper on the *Magna Moralia*," *American Journal of Philology* 96: 160–72.

—1983: "*De Aristotelis in tribus libris Ethicorum dicendi ratione*: Particles, Connectives and Style in Three Books from the Aristotelian Ethical Treatises," *Liverpool Classical Monthly* 8: 4–11, 37–40, 54–7, 70–4.

Sandbach, F. 1985: *Aristotle and the Stoics*. Cambridge: Cambridge Philological Society.

Scott, D. 1995: *Recollection and Experience*. Cambridge: Cambridge University Press.

Sorabji, R. 1980: "Aristotle on the Rôle of Intellect in Virtue." In Amélie Rorty (ed.), *Essays on Aristotle's Ethics*, pp. 201–19. Berkeley, CA: University of California Press.

Stewart, J. 1892: *Notes on the Nicomachean Ethics of Aristotle*, vol. 2. Oxford: Oxford University Press.

van Ophuijsen, J. and van Raalte, M. 1998: *Theophrastus: Reappraising the Sources*. New Brunswick: Transaction.

Walzer, R. and Mingay, J. 1991: *Aristotelis Ethica Eudemia*. Oxford: Oxford University Press.

Whiting, J. 1986: "Human Nature and Intellectualism in Aristotle," *Archiv für Geschichte der Philosophie* 68: 70–95.

—1996: "Self-love and Authoritative Virtue: Prolegomenon to a Kantian Reading of *Eudemian Ethics* VIII. 3." In J. Whiting and S. Engstrom (eds), *Aristotle, Kant and the Stoics: Rethinking Happiness and Duty*, pp. 162–99. Cambridge: Cambridge University Press.

Wians, W. (ed.) 1996: *Aristotle's Philosophical Development: Problems and Prospects*. Lanham: Rowman and Littlefield.

Wiggins, D. 1980a: "Deliberation and Practical Reason." In Amélie Rorty (ed.), *Essays on Aristotle's Ethics*, pp. 221–40. Berkeley, CA: University of California Press.

—1980b: "Weakness of Will, Commensurability and the Objects of Deliberation and Desire." In Amélie Rorty (ed.), *Essays on Aristotle's Ethics*, pp. 41–65. Berkeley, CA: University of California Press.

Wilpert, P. 1960: "The Fragments of Aristotle's Lost Writings." In I. Düring and G. E. L. Owen (eds), *Aristotle and Plato in the Mid-Fourth Century*, pp. 257–64. Sweden: Göteborg.

Wlodarczyk, M. 2000: "Aristotelian Dialectic and the Discovery of Truth," *Oxford Studies in Ancient Philosophy* 18: 153–210.

Woods, M. 1982: *Aristotle Eudemian Ethics Books I, II and VIII*. Oxford: Oxford University Press.

Zeller, E. 1962: *Aristotle and the Earlier Peripatetics*, trans. B. Costelloe and J. Muirhead. New York: Russell and Russell.

2

Human Good and Human Function

Gavin Lawrence

Talk of "the human good" is apt to mystify us – and even more so talk of "the human function." Yet in a way nothing could be more ordinary. It seems we can ask: what is *the best thing we can get* in our lives as human beings? And surely we have most reason to aim at that: why go for any lesser good than the greatest available? *That* would be irrational. So somewhere here is a constitutive principle of practical rationality. Not only *can* we ask after the practicable best, but so asking and aiming is *what it is to be* practically rational. "The human good," then, so far conceived, is simply the (formal) object of rational endeavor. But *what* actually is it? Indeed, why suppose there is any answer to this question? Yet, actually an answer of sorts is not so hard (should we be surprised?). For, if asked such a question, what better thing can we, as humans, seek than a *wonderful*, or *successful*, life? What better thing can we do in our lives than do well? That is something worth having, and worth having *entirely for itself* – it is not sought as a means to something else that we would rather have, or that we could get in addition. And if we get that, it is *enough* – what more could we want than a great life? There is nothing more that, added, would make up some good greater than that, and so a good that was more an object of rational choice (although perhaps a successful life might be made still more successful).

So, as rational agents, we aim at the best we can get, and this looks to be a wonderful life. Thus conceived, reason's task is now correctly to work out both what counts as, or constitutes, such a life, and how to secure it: a matter of goal-internal and of goal-external deliberation. As Aristotle says at *Politics* VII.13.1331b26–38:

> Since there are *two things* in which success [*to eu*] comes about in all things, and of these two *one* lies in the target and the end of actions being posited correctly, and *one* is to find out the actions bearing on the end (for it is possible for these both to disaccord and to accord with each other: for sometimes while the target is proposed finely, in acting to hit on it people go wrong; and sometimes they hit on all the things

towards the end, but have posited an end that is bad; and sometimes they go wrong in each: for example, in medicine: for sometimes neither do they discern finely what kind of condition the body ought to be in to be healthy, nor do they, in regard to the definition [*horos*] posited by them, hit on the things productive [of it]: but it is necessary in arts and disciplines [*epistēmai*] for both these things to be mastered [*krateisthai*], viz. the end and the actions to the end.[1]

These twin tasks are the proper object or target of our practical reason, whether as individuals working out our own best lives, or as parents or elders in more familial communities, or as local or international politicians seeking to create societies whose citizens are positioned to enjoy wonderful lives.

But where is reason to look for an answer? Suppose it is rational – as it surely is, at least qualifiedly or defensibly – to aim at a *physically healthy* lifestyle. What do we look to in order to specify this? We look to what the human body *does* – at how it works or functions – and at the facts of our world, at the impact of different environmental conditions on the body, and of available diets and forms of exercise, and so on. Where else would it make *sense* to look? So, too, with specifying a wonderful, or successful, human life. We look to facts about what it is to be alive as a human, at what it is for a human to *do* – at how the human functions – and at the facts of our world, at how situated we are, both in general, and in our particular geographical and cultural–historical location. Where else would reason *sensefully* look for an answer? And if one does well (*eu*) what it is for a human to do, will that not precisely be doing well as a human?[2]

We have already started in a way – a rather abstract way – to reason about how to specify the best achievable good. But thus far there seems an ordinariness and obviousness about the approach – an approach that we can characterize in three claims:

1 *Human good – practical reason*   The best thing we can get, the human good or practicable good, is the (formal) object, or target, of practical reason – both to determine and to attain.
2 *Human good – best life*   The best thing we can get is the best, or most successful, life.
3 *Best life – living as a human, and doing it well*   A successful life is a matter of living as it is for a human to live, and doing that well or successfully.

Now doing something well is doing it *excellently*; that is, in accord with, or in the manner of, the excellences (or virtues: *aretai*) proper to it: these are the criteria of its success. And so we need to consider human living and its excellences. Yet this can all appear terribly problematic. A first line of concern is that one or all of (1) – (3) are just false, or at least lack justification. So, for example, the idea that "goal-internal deliberation" is really a rational task has notoriously been challenged, both in itself and in its attribution to Aristotle. Again, it may be queried whether it is not after all human to do all sorts of nasty things. Are we then to say that doing these well constitutes a successful life? A second concern is that, even if (1) – (3) were fine, they do not actually get us anywhere substantial. They leave the human good radically under-determined. Even a subjectivist could accept them, suitably interpreted. And so, if we eventually come up with some determinate objective result, it will seem that this can only be because at some point along the road we have helped ourselves to further resources – in the shape of an implausibly rigid, and possibly metaphysical, conception of human nature (a Nietzschean suspicion).

I think Aristotle himself ends in a position which we should not – or should not rush to – accept. But all too often this is taken as a *modus tollens* of his starting-point. I hope to suggest that so easy a *bouleversement* of Aristotelianism is misconceived, that Aristotle's starting-point is as intuitive and vivid as ever, and that we can disembarrass ourselves of his substantial answer. True, the position, even when so stripped down, may not be correct – but, if so, it is not as obviously wrong as some suppose. And there is much to learn from it.

1 The Teleological Conception of the Practicable Good

1.1 The opening move

The *Eudemian Ethics* starts straightaway by asking what living well or successfully (*to eu zēn*) consists in and how it is obtained (I.1.1214a14–b6, I.3.1215a4–5; cf. *to eudaimonein kai to zēn makariōs kai kalōs*. I.1.1214a30–31). But the *Nicomachean Ethics* starts further back, with a *teleological* conception of the good: that is, the good in some object or systematic area or realm is the end, or *that for the sake of which* the other things in the object or area are. It is thus the principle of being and of organization of everything else in that object or area: that something belongs in the area, and what place it then has, are settled by its relation to the end.

Here in the first step of the *NE*, Aristotle's concern is with the good in two rational realms: those of production (*poiēsis*) and of chosen action (*praxis*); and he illuminates the latter via the former.

S1 (I.1.1094a1–3): *The conception of the good as end*: "Every art and every systematic enquiry [*methodos*], and similarly both action and choice, are held to aim at some particular good" (cf. I.7.1097a15–22).

Chosen action, like an art, is aimed at some good that is its end – which is "the good of it."

Of course, there is also a difference between these two realms, as Aristotle immediately notes (S2: I.1.1094a3–6): the ends of the one are simply activities, the ends of the other are products over and above its activities.[3] But this difference is irrelevant to the main point at issue (cf. S5: I.1.1094a16–18). He notes also that where there are ends, or products, beyond the activities, they are better than their activities. This I understand as an instance of a general "*finality*" value principle: if X is for the sake of Y, Y is better or more worthy of rational choice than X.

Now evidently:

S3 (I.1.1094a6–8): *Multiplicity of ends* There are many actions, arts, and disciplines, and so, by (S1), there are many ends (cf. I.7.1097a16–18, 1097a25–6).

But within this multiplicity of rationally organized activities, there is also very evidently further rational structure. This is particularly clear in the case of skills:

S4 (I.1.1094a9–16): *Principles of hierarchy and of comparative value*:

1 *Hierarchy of arts* Many arts are hierarchically ordered, some being "under," or subordinate to, another. This principle of rational structure is iteratable both *vertically* (a12–13), into "trees" or "pyramids," and *horizontally* (a13–14) – there are other "trees" or "pyramids."
2 *Correlative hierarchy of ends* One art is subordinate to another when the ends of the one are pursued *for the sake* also of the ends of the other, and thus superordinate (or "architectonic"), one.[4]
3 *Comparative value* The ends of the superordinate arts are more worthy of rational choice than the ends of the subordinate, i.e. if end E is pursued *in order to* attain end F, then F is more worthy of choice than E (another instance of the general *finality* value principle above).

So within the multiplicity of ends there is a principle of rational construction or organization: the ends of some arts are pursued for the sake of, or in order to attain, the ends of others, and this is iteratable; and the higher, more final, end is ever the better (cf. I.7.1097a25–34). This rational structure, though illustrated by productive disciplines and their products, is not confined to them, but applies equally to chosen action: the two realms are in effect treated here as one large one – call it "rational endeavor" (**S5**: I.1.1094a16–18).

Now clearly these principles yield a "definition" of *the* good of *all* rational endeavor (**S6**: I.2.1094a18–22). For if all the horizontal pyramids of rational endeavors were to unite in a single vertical, or overarching, one, then the end of the most superordinate or architectonic endeavor would be the very top end, that for whose sake all the ends below it are also worth choosing; and this would – by the principle of comparative value – be "*the* good, i.e. the very best," the most worthy of rational choice. And as Aristotle then remarks:

S7 (I.2.1094a22–4): "Won't knowledge of this [*the* good, i.e. the best] have a great impact actually on our life, and just as archers who have a target we would better hit on what we should [*to deon*]?"

We have then a *formal* account of *the* practicable good: what we now want to know is its *matter*, its content. Aristotle goes on to pose two questions (1094a24–6):

Q1: What is this ultimately final good?
Q2: Which discipline (*epistēmē*) or ability (*dunamis*) has it as its proper object?

The second he addresses immediately (I.2.1094a26–b11). For it will be the job of this discipline not only to attain or realize but also to determine what materially its good is – as it is the job of medicine to say what counts as health. His argument, influenced by Plato's *Statesman*, is by formal criteria. Given the correlative hierarchy principles, the top good is the end of the top rational endeavor, where this is marked by two criteria: architectonicity and authoritativeness. *Politikē* satisfies these, and so its end, whatever that is, is the topmost one, viz. "the human good." Armed with the correct "method" (1094b11), we can turn back to the first question, and re-frame it as asking what good it is that *politikē* has as its end (I.4.1095a14–17). This, *Q1*, is *the* question of the *Nicomachean Ethics*. It gets an answer by *NE* VI.12–13, and a fuller consideration and defense in *NE* X.6–8.

In short, Aristotle's opening move in the *NE* consists in introducing a teleological concept of *the* practicable good – or the human good – as the final end or object of rational endeavor, as that for whose sake all other ends are. We are shown how to keep the idea of the good as the end, despite the multiplicity of ends, by uncovering a hierarchical rational order. This order is equally one among the corresponding rational endeavors (arts and chosen actions). Clearly, the highest good is the object of the highest of these, both to determine and to attain. And this endeavor, Aristotle argues, is *politikē* (cf. VII.11.1152b1–3).

1.2 Three remarks

This passage in *NE* I.1–2 raises many questions. I shall remark on three.

(**R1**) *Practical philosophy: the subject matter* In *Metaphysics* VI.1.1025b18–25, Aristotle claims that all rational thought (*dianoia*) is "either practical or productive or theoretical." The *Nicomachean Ethics* and *Eudemian Ethics* are works whose concern is primarily with the "practical." They are practical in one familiar sense – they are pragmatic, or aimed at action ("we are investigating what excellence is not in order [simply] to know it, but in order to become good" Aristotle says at *NE* II.2.1103b27–9). And they are practical also in being concerned with action and not production. But their concern is with *action* in a sense unfamiliar to the modern ear. The primary topic is not any intentional action, but *praxis* in a very delimited sense, of what Aristotle calls *prohairetic* or "preferentially chosen" action. As he says in the *Metaphysics* passage above, "of things produced, their starting-point is in the producer – either intelligence [*nous*] or skill [*technē*] or ability [*dunamis*]; of things done [*ta prakta*], it is in the doer – preferential choice [*prohairesis*]: for the thing done and the thing chosen are the same." Such "chosen" action is action that agents take to be fully rational. This is action that agents take *as* what, given their values, their views of how best to live, is *the best* or *the wise* thing for them to do, if they are to be living well in general (cf. *NE* VI.5.1140a25–8): it is what they take it they *should* do (*dei haplōs*), where this is the un-subscripted, or unqualified, "should" of practical reason, equivalent to "should, if I am to be living or acting well," the maximally unqualified perspective of practical reason.

So Aristotle is not claiming that just any intentional action aims at some good (or something thought good by the agent). His primary focus is restricted to fully rational action in the sense above – action taken by the agent to be constitutive of living well. Getting this correct is the subject matter of *Practical Philosophy* (cf. McDowell 1980: esp ss. 1–6; Lawrence 2004a).

Aristotle here envisages a possible overarching structure to all practical and productive rationality. At this point he is not much interested in their differentiation, but later he will make even more explicit the subordinate role of productive to practical thought (*NE* VI.2.1139b1–4, VI.5 *init.*, and compare I.2.1094a28–b6). But what of the *third* realm of rationality, theoretical thought? In working out the best human life, the political inquiry of the *Nicomachean Ethics* can be viewed as aiming to place each of these three realms of human rationality – of which it is itself one – in their correct position in human life. Crudely, the picture will be this: practical or political reason utilizes all the productive uses of reason, and its own practical capacities, with a view to determining and realizing its end, the end that its citizens live the best possible human life: and this turns out to be a matter of organizing our human lives – at social, domestic and individual levels – to open up, and prepare us to enjoy, free time in which to engage in theoretical thought (cf. *Pol.* VII.14.1333a16–15.1334b5): for that is the best human living. (We shall see reason to wonder whether this picture misconstrues the nature both of theoretical and of practical thought.)

(R2) *Politike: the "architectonic endeavor"* Politikē, the most architectonic endeavor, seems somewhat ambiguous in status. *Politikē* is presumably to be complimented by *epistēmē* or *dunamis* (*NE* I.2.1094a26). One might suppose it an (architectonic) art, a *technē* (*epistēmē* here being used in a Platonic way that does not strongly contrast with *technē*). It is called a *methodos* in 1094b11, and *methodos* was aligned with *technē* in 1094a1. And, indeed, it has productive aspects: it is compared to medicine, which gives orders not to health, but for the sake of ensuring health (VI.13.1145a6–11; cf.1144a3–6); its function is in part to make the citizens good people, ones with the excellences or correct values, and so capable of fine actions (I.13.1102a7–10, I.9.1099b29–32, II.1.1103b2–5), to make laws – which are likened to its "products" (X.9.1181a23), to bring about *eudaimonia* (I.4.1095a15–20), and to do so as an end different from itself and its own activities (X.7.1177b2–18). One might suppose it also something that, like any craft, is open to abuse – that it can be exploited by an expert to achieve its counter end, say the interests of the ruling class rather than the good of the whole citizenry (cf. VI.5.1140b21–5). Aristotle, however, would have us conceive of it as what I will call "public wisdom" – the same state as *phronēsis*, practical wisdom, but practical wisdom writ large; that is, deployed on a larger stage (*NE* VI.7–8). And, as such, it is a disposition, not a capacity, and cannot be used badly. (This is not to say that practical or political thought [*dianoia*] itself may not be mistaken, whether in the specific determination of the end it posits, or in the means that it reckons appropriate.)

The status of *politikē* requires its own discussion. That it is not a *technē* has, I suspect, at least in part to do with the unqualified rational status of its end. The ends of arts are particular (*kata meros*), and there is a larger practical perspective available on them; we can stand back and ask: is it good to pursue this end (now or in general or up to what point: cf. *NE* I.2.1094a28–b2)? But with "living well in general" – the end of *phronēsis* and *politikē* – there is no further rational perspective to which to retreat. *Qua* rational such is one's end, and so *qua* rational one must pursue what one takes to constitute it – *must* on pain of irrationality (of going *against* reason).

Thus, the formal end of *politikē* "embraces the ends of the others" (I.2.1094b6), "with the consequence that this [the end of *politikē*] would be the human good." The phrase "the human good" occurs here for the first time. Yet clearly Aristotle takes himself to have introduced the idea already: it is simply the notion of that topmost end which would be "the good," i.e. the best thing that humans can get through rational endeavor: *to prakton agathon*. If, as he argues, *politikē* is the topmost endeavor, then its end – *whatever that is* – is this human good.

This end, Aristotle says, is the same for an individual as for a society (I.2.1094b7–8; cf. *Pol.* VII.2–3, VII.15.1334a11–14). As a *politikos*, one aims to make one's society attain the best end; as a *phronimos*, one aims for oneself to attain it. But now one might wonder whether these aims could not conflict. For example, might one not be needed in political office by one's country, yet have personal reasons not to? Or might not one as a *politikos* have reason to enact some measure which, while for the common good, results in harm to oneself or one's family? This, I think, is mistaken. The first quandary is not a political question but a private one: for one's sphere as a private person covers also one's duties as a citizen of one's society. In the second, if the measure is just, then as a private person one has nothing to complain of – and indeed should stand fully behind such a measure.

(Castro's early land reforms took property away also from his own family.) So I suspect there is not room for conflict between the deliverances of the two, although of course there are problems of adjudicating public and private pressures (cf. *Pol.* VII.2–3).

But there is another, trickier, issue. Aristotle here envisages a hierarchy of ends and rational endeavors, some of which have ends that are products over and above the activities of the endeavor, some that are not. In the latter case, presumably the relevant activity constitutes the immediate end.

	Endeavor	*Activity*	*End*
Form 1	*Technē*	*T*'ing	*T* product
	Sculptor	Sculpting	Sculpture
Form 2	*Phronēsis/politikē*	*P*'ing	*P*'ing

Now it seems:

(Product end): Where rational endeavor (RE) has a *product* as its end, over and above its RE'ing activity, there must be a higher rational endeavor that *uses* that product.

(Action end): Where rational endeavor (RE) has its RE'ing *activity* as its end, and no separate product, that activity may be pursued for a further end, or it may not; if it is not, then such RE'ing action would constitute a final end – or *the* final end (if there is, or can only be, one).

If so, where does *politikē* stand?

1 As the topmost endeavor, it seemingly cannot have a product; for then there would be a still higher endeavor that would be a consumer or user of its product.
2 As the topmost endeavor, its actions then are its end (these are political, or practically rational, actions). As actions exemplifying or realizing the topmost highest endeavor, they cannot be pursued also for the end of any higher endeavor. So seemingly they must be the final end.
3 The topmost end turns out to consist in contemplative actions – the activity of the theoretical part of the soul (*nous*).
4 Either these are political actions or they are not:
    (a) If they are, then must they not be the exercise of the same ability? But Aristotle says not (he separates *to epistēmonikon* and *to logistikon*, e.g. in VI.1).
    (b) If they are not, then *politikē* does not seem to be the highest rational endeavor after all! But Aristotle says it is.

Aristotle is aware of something of this tension (*NE* VI.12.1143b33–5). In VI.13 he tells us that *politikē*, although the most authoritative art, is not authoritative over *sophiai*, nor the better part of the soul (i.e. *nous*): it issues commands for its sake but not to it. The activity of *sophia* is the content of the highest end. The best end – contemplating – is the *formal* and/or *final* target of theoretical wisdom; and it is the *efficient* target of *politikē*, i.e. the end to bring about (cf. VI.12.1144a3–6). But this still leaves us with the following tension. On the one hand, we want to say that contemplative activity is not political action – it is what political action strives to bring about the opportunity to engage in ("it sees how it may come about"; VI.13.1145a8–9). On the other hand, we want to say that "yes, that piece of contemplation is a *practically wise* action, a well-chosen use of free-time." We shall come across this problem again.

(**R3**) *Existence of such a good* Yet why suppose there is any such "highest good" in the first place? This has caused much controversy. Some interpret Aristotle here (I.2.1094a18–22) as arguing for its existence, albeit fallaciously; others take him in this remark only to be hypothesizing its existence.

Two brief remarks. First, the main thrust is simply *definitional*: an account of what *the* practicable good is follows quite straightforwardly from the preceding principles. This is an account of what it is *formally speaking*: as such it has "formal existence." And as such it is the proper object of *politikē* to work out what, if anything, *it* is "materially" (and attain it). It is not immediately clear that there *has* to be a material answer. Perhaps it is intelligible that *politikē* might conclude that nothing "materially" fits the formal bill. (And in *thus* losing its object, *politikē* might efface itself, at least as a useful endeavor.)

Second, it turns out to be virtually non-controversial that there is such a good and that, nominally, it is *eudaimonia* (I.4.1095a17–20; cf. I.7.1097b22–3); controversy arises over what constitutes this. But even here it does not seem ruled out *ab initio* that *politikē* might determine that there was no coherent resolution to such controversies about *eudaimonia* (cf. VII.1.1145b4–6).

We may say: *politikē*, in investigating what *eudaimonia* is, assumes that there is an answer, but its investigations may bring us to question whether its object has anything more than formal existence.

1.3 *NE* I and its four moves: the RRCC structure

The introduction of this teleological notion of the human good as *the* final end, and as the formal object of practical reason or *politikē*, is the *first* of four main argumentative moves in *NE* Book I. The *second* move offers an initial elucidation of this good by specifying it, at least *nominally*, as *eudaimonia*, or synonymously as living well or successfully (*eu-zōia*) or as doing well or successfully (*eu-praxia*) (I.4.1095a17–20).

Later, in I.7.1097a25–b21, Aristotle produces a justification even for this nominal specification, again by appeal to formal criteria. The practicable good is *unqualifiedly final* – an object of choice for itself and never on account of something else. And it is *by-itself-sufficient* (*autarkes*). If you have the good, then this "makes life choice-worthy and lacking in nothing." (And so it is non-aggregatable – you cannot add a further good to it to improve on it, to make a good greater than it is by itself; cf. *Philebus* 20E–21A.) *Eudaimonia* is held evidently to satisfy these criteria (cf. p. 37).

The point, in any case, is one of quite general agreement (I.7.1097b22–3 echo I.4.1095a17–20). Where controversy gets going, Aristotle thinks, is over what more substantially *eudaimonia* consists in: for here ordinary people have disparate views, as do the wise (I.4.1095a18–30). Aristotle – following his usual "endoxastic" methodology[5] – considers these various views, or at least those that are prevalent or seem to have something to them, and raises problems (*NE* I.4–6).

So the nominal specification of the highest good, the object of *politikē*, as *eudaimonia* is, while hardly controversial, equally not very illuminating. Add to this the controversy and puzzles surrounding the various views offered of it, and it is unsurprising that "it is desired that it still be said more clearly what [the best thing] is" (I.7.1097b22–4). The Function Argument – the *third* move – is offered as a more substantial way to elucidate the human good by consideration of human function (I.7.1097b22–1098a20). Its main conclusion is that the human good, *eudaimonia*, is an activity of soul – a rational life-activity – in accord with its proper excellence over a complete life time. This, Aristotle says, is an "outline of the good" (I.7.1098a20–26). He then tests it by considering how well it enables us to make sense of the various opinions, *endoxa*, resolve tensions between them, and give each a proper place (I.8); and again how well it can deal with various further puzzles over *eudaimonia* (I.9–12).

The *fourth* move picks up this conclusion and suggests a natural way to fill in the outline: "Since happiness is a kind of activity of soul in accord with perfect excellence, one ought to examine in detail about excellence: for perhaps in that way we would come to a better understanding also about happiness" (*NE* I.13.1102a5–7). This sets the agenda for the detailed study of the human excellences of character and of intellect, and of their inter-relation, which occupies the books that immediately follow, viz. *NE* II–VI. The study culminates in Book VI (especially chapters 1, 7, 12–13), where it is argued that there are basically two excellences: practical wisdom, together with all the excellences of character, and then theoretical wisdom; and that theoretical wisdom is the more final of the two and the excellence of the better part, while practical wisdom looks to see how to arrange things so as to secure free time in which to contemplate. This view is echoed in *NE* X.6–8 (for example, 1177a12–18, 1177b1–15), where its implications for *eudaimonia* are drawn out, and some six arguments given for the superiority of the contemplative life over the merely practical or political.

Crudely, we can represent the overall strategy of the *NE* as one of *role–role–content–content* (RRCC). Once the central question of the practicable, or human, good has been posed and articulated, Aristotle addresses this question first by clarifying the *role* of *eudaimonia*, or living well; then by clarifying the *role* that excellence or virtue plays within that; this in turn leads to an investigation of the *content* of human excellence and of the relation between the two principal virtues (and their respective activities), in order finally to deliver a specification of the *content* of human *eudaimonia*.

The main links in the chain of Aristotle's inquiry can be laid out as follows:

Link 0 — Link 1 — Link 2 — Link 3
The Human Good is The Good Life is The Excellent Life is The Virtuous Life is
   The Life of this and that
Living *successfully* — Living *excellently* — Living *justly* etc. — Doing *this* and
   that
eudaimonia — energeia kat'aretēn — kat'andreian etc.

That is, Living well-*S* consists in Living well-*E* consists in Living well-*V* consists in Living well-*P*, in the following sense. (Link 0) The practicable good, the aim of *politikē*, is generally conceded to be, nominally, *eudaimonia* – living *successfully*, the life that is most choiceworthy (*hairetōtatos*, I.4; justified in I.7). (Link 1) The Function Argument then suggests that this consists in reason-involving life-activity in accord with its proper excellence(s). What these are is not yet specified. Later, Link 2 (I.13), Aristotle makes clear that nominally at least these are the *virtues* as ordinarily recognized (i.e. justice, courage, temperance, wisdom) – for these are just the ordinarily acknowledged names of the *good states* with respect to their various reasoning-involving activities (actions and emotions). But this too does not by itself generate a specific conception of what in particular is the wise or courageous act to choose (Link 3). Even those who are wicked will consider themselves as having the best states by name (cf. II.8.1108b23–6). To get these *particulars* correct, humans need, generally speaking, to be well brought up in the practices of virtue and in the liberal occupations – those befitting a free human in free-time. What is missing in this portrayal is the strand that leads Aristotle to distinguish *within* living well between the two principal excellences, and the lives typified by them, the political and the contemplative.

1.4 Ambiguities in Aristotle's target

It is virtually non-controversial that the highest practicable good is *eudaimonia*. Controversy breaks out over what constitutes it. Yet actually there is a lack of clarity in Aristotle's very target. First, is he seeking the single best good in a competition between goods one on one, and so where any addition to the singly best good would result in a greater good than it, taken by itself? Or is he seeking *the* practicable good, where this is understood as non-aggregatable – as such that nothing *could* be added to it to make a good that is greater than it is by itself? I believe it is the second of these competitions. It is, for instance, hard to see what the interest of the first competition would be; and the criterion of unconditional finality looks to be motivated by a concern with the non-aggregatable good, and not obviously relevant in the first competition (cf. Lawrence 1997).

Second, when he asks what living well is, is he asking after the best kind of life-activity, or after the best life? On one line, the latter falls out simply as a function of the former: the best life is simply that with the maximum amount of the best life-activity over a complete life-time (a best activity to best life value transfer principle): "the activities are authoritative over the life" (I.10.1100b33, 1100b9–11). This seems plausible at a certain level of specificity. Thus, in the case of the human being, reason-involving life-activity is better and more final than the life-activities of nutrition or perception. But if one then redeploys the move *within* rational life-activities, to suggest that the best human life would consist in a maximal amount of some one rational activity, this does not have the same immediate plausibility. Here one may start to wonder whether there are not facts about the general shape of human life and its seasons that equally impact on the evaluation of best or appropriate life-activity (for example, the four stages of life on the Hindu pattern, or Aristotle's own series of seven-year stages); and again such facts as those about human need for variety, and about relations of fertility and enhancement between various activities.

But, even more important, there is the following lack of clarity in the target of "the greatest good obtainable," or the best or perfect human life. In one sense, a person lives a perfect life – makes a success of their life – if they have the correct values and correctly bring them to bear so as to do what is called for, or best, in their situation. So doing, they will do nothing they regret doing. But the situations they face may be defective, even tragic, ones, involving circumstances which rightly they would rather had not arisen in the first place. In another sense, a person lives a perfect life only if they do the above *and* the situations that arise for them are not defective but the *optimal* ones for a human being – that in this sense bring out the best in a human: for perhaps some excellences are better than others, and some exercises of the same excellence better than others. The target here is the best life a human can enjoy in the optimal circumstances for a human – the best that is ever available. As practically rational agents, we have *both* targets or ideals. We aim to live the best life we can in the circumstances that life presents us, *whatever* these are (and they may involve our choosing to die), and we aim that life should present us with the *best possible* circumstances. Call this the Utopian target. And this latter constitutes the norm, or measure, of unqualified success and defect in human life.

It is, I have argued, this Utopian target that is Aristotle's principal aim in the *Nicomachean Ethics* (Lawrence 1993a). But this, in its turn, is not straightforward. For how are we to set about working out what is the best possible human life and what are to count as defects in the human situation? This can be developed in at least two ways, "theological" and "species-contextual." In the former, the best possible human life is measured against the very best possible life in the sense of the life of the best substance: for theology here is not the study of, for example, the Christian God, but the highest branch of ontology, whose basic topic is the notion of success, or perfection, in the category of substance (a metaphysical subject indeed – and still so even if it were claimed that the human is the best substance; cf. VI.7.1141a20–22). In the other perspective we remain within the frame of the human form of life in working out what is optimal, with no measuring against the forms of life of other species or beings. There is here no sense to such interspecies evaluations. The principal difference in perspectives is that on the former, but not on the latter, it makes sense to suppose that the condition of being human is itself a possible defect an individual can suffer. We shall return to these ambiguities in sections 2 and 3 below.

1.5 Overview: three aspects of Aristotle's approach

Aristotle's practical philosophy can be viewed broadly as a version of a practical reason approach to ethics.

(1) *The teleological good and practical reason*   It is one that puts a certain teleological conception of the good center stage, together with a correlative conception of practical reason. This practicable good – the good of action – characterized in terms of finality, is "pure" in this sense: it is thus far uncommitted as regards the notion of benefit, or of what is in the agent's own interests.

Consider the example of health. Health is the good of – or success in – medicine. But attaining it is not of benefit to its practitioner, the doctor, *as such*: in fact, it is of benefit, but of benefit to the patient (who may, *incidentally*, be the doctor). The *technē* and the technist *as such* – i.e. *qua* having the skill – are perfect (cf. *Republic* I.341d–342b). So the teleological good in an area certainly does not have to benefit the kind of agent whose success as such it is. And viewed as the exercise of perfection, it could not benefit them: for the *technē* and technist *as such* are perfect and cannot be benefited *as such*. (Set complexities about despotic rule aside.) Similarly, a human agent with all the correct values and dispositions – *a perfect agent* – who attains the success of agency, i.e. does well – is not thereby benefited by their success: it *is* their success as an agent. You can benefit an agent by helping them attain their success; and harm them by impeding them, but their success itself, their doing well, *is* their good – it does not *do* them good (except incidentally).

It is part of our function as practically rational agents to *care about* our success (we do not rely on nature here): it is part of our job to determine it and to pursue it (the two tasks mentioned in the introduction). So we would not be succeeding as practically rational agents unless we took ourselves to be succeeding – it is a condition on our success, on doing well, that we *take* what we do to constitute doing well or living successfully. It is thus something in which we could take a proper pride and feel a certain sense of satisfaction.

(2) *Eudaimonism* The approach is, as generally with the Greeks, *eudaimonist*. That is, it is accepted as a common starting-point that the greatest good we can get is a successful life. Controversy is then located over what constitutes this. Aristotle moves to resolve such controversy by a careful clarification of the logical category of the correct answer, and by bringing out the Utopian nature of the target that this makes available.

Some scholars are tempted to divide the argument of *NE* I into an analytic part, of conceptual analysis, followed by a synthetic part that draws on empirical information, starting in the Function Argument. In my view, the Function Argument would belong to the former rather than the latter, but I think the imposition of this distinction unhelpful. Aristotle's strategy is better viewed as a continuous one, of "formal squeeze." Each of the four main "moves" Aristotle makes is not impossible to resist, just difficult: the objector has to make the running, and motivate the rejection. This is hard, since each move forward seems almost just a clarification of the preceding one – like tacking where there is virtually no wind.

(3) *"Virtue theory"* Whether one should regard Aristotle's view as a "virtue theory" depends on how one takes that term of art. Certainly he gives a place to virtue. But so do the positions he opposes. There is the popular view that allows the virtues of character to be goods –goods of soul – but views the external goods, of wealth and so on, as primary: goods of soul are fine provided they do not interfere too far with prudential business. Here Aristotle aligns himself with the Democritean/Socratic program of *the revaluation of value*, and objects that this view gets values upside down: it is goods of soul – of life – which are primary and which set limits on the goodness of external goods. However, this can suggest that the be-all-and-end-all of life is *being* a good person, *having* all the correct values – that the excellences or virtues of soul are the human good. But to this Aristotle objects that the human good is not *being* a good person, but *actually living* the life of a good person, of *realizing* one's values and excellences *in actions and feelings*. Indeed, as we shall see, one of Aristotle's main aims is to make clear the correct logical location of virtue in an account of the human good.

The most common error in recent so-called "virtue theory" is to set the virtuous person up as the criterion, or canon, of virtuous action. The view that "the virtuous/wise thing to do is what the virtuous/wise person does" is either trivially true or false. It is trivially true that the wise and virtuous do wise and virtuous acts: for so acting is criterial of being wise and virtuous – otherwise, special stories apart, you will not count as virtuous or wise. But taken as the criterion for *what it is for* an act to be wise or virtuous – viz. that the wise or virtuous would do it – it is false. That is not what it is for an act to be wise or virtuous. The virtuous or wise do not, after all, in their deliberations to determine what is the virtuous or wise thing to do, proceed *by* asking themselves what the virtuous and wise would do. There is, of course, taking advice, and deferring to authority: "I did it because he said it was the thing to do, and he is wise" (cf. *NE* I.4.1095b9–13). There are, admittedly, particular heuristic techniques, such as when I take someone I know and believe to be wise – say Philippa Foot – and ask myself what *she* would think or do in this situation and try to, as it were, "hear her voice" on the topic. But this is simply one among many imaginative techniques of addressing the question *what it is best to do* – the direct question, and one where appeal to the question "what would the practically wise do here?" has in general no independent help to offer in answering it. It is certainly not the criterion of its being wise. Aristotle's view then is one that puts practical rationality center stage, not "virtue theory," if envisaged in the way that, say, Louden (1984) attributes to him.

2 Human Function

2.1 Aim, rationale, and structure

The aim in the Function Argument is to make *clearer* what the human good is – clearer than the uncontroversial "nominal" claim that it is *eudaimonia* or living well or doing well. Even so, the argument yields only an outline, something that in turn needs filling in (I.7.1098a20–26). It is not, I believe, intended to stand alone. Its conclusion has to be tested by its adequacy in enabling us to make sense of the many things people say about living well or success (cf. I.8.1098b9–12, and *passim*). For these locate our topic.

In it Aristotle suggests that we can illuminate the practicable best, or *eudaimonia*, by considering human function – viz. what it is proper or peculiar for a human as such to do. The *rationale* for this is that generally with functional items their good and their success is a matter of their function (i.e. of their functioning well). So the good of a flautist, or success as one, is a matter of playing well. And doing something *well* is equivalent to doing it in *accord with the excellence or virtue proper to the activity*. So, if it is the particular, or peculiar, function of the human to be alive in a certain way, then our good or success will be a matter of our engaging in this human kind of life-activity, and doing it well, i.e. in accord with its proper excellence(s).

It is taken as obvious that if the human has a function it must be a way of being alive – and not just any way of being alive but one peculiar to humans. Aristotle argues by elimination that since it is not the life of growth and nutrition (shared by plants) nor the life of perception (shared with animals), it must be "some kind of practical life of the part that has reason" (*praktikē tis [zoē] tou logon echontos*). He then clarifies this in two important ways. First (I.7.1098a4–5), the kind of reason-involving activity at issue covers a wide range, one that includes the emotions which can follow and respond to reason, as well as more strictly intellectual or "dianoetic" activities (I.13 and VI.1.1138b35–1139a15 make this clear). Second (I.7.1098a5–7), the practical life at issue is living in the strict sense of "second actuality": this is a matter of actually exercising life-faculties, not merely possessing them ("Gavin sees" said of me when asleep is true in the latter sense, but not the former). Aristotle concludes that our good or success is actually engaging in such life-activity and doing it well, i.e. in accord with the excellence proper to it. He then adds: "if the excellences are several, then in accord with the best and most perfect [*teleiotatēn*]" (I.7.1098a17–18). We will come back to this addition (section 2.5).

2.2 Problems and the upshot of the argument

This, somewhat simplified, is the gist of the argument. It is notoriously problematic. It demands peculiarity of function, but does not Aristotle's god also engage in rational activity? And how plausible is it, in the first place, to ascribe a function to human beings – does talk of function not require a designer, and Aristotle's god is no creator? Moreover, the argument seems to many fallacious, in various ways. We want to know the greatest good a human can get; and now we are told it consists in functioning or living as a good human specimen. But why should living like that get us what we want? Why should that be the object of our rational desire? Simply to assert it seemingly leaves a huge gap in the argument. Now, these and their like are, I believe, by and large, misunderstandings. But they require much careful discussion. Here I shall merely indicate some lines of response.

It helps to start by asking what Aristotle is aiming to achieve. The argument is obviously rather formal, in the sense that it aims only to provide an "outline of the good," and does not aim to derive a specification of the human excellences. Thus, an immoralist like Thrasymachus in Plato's *Republic*, who takes injustice to be human excellence, can agree with its conclusion. But if its conclusion can be so widely agreed, that must make us wonder what clarification of the human good the argument really achieves.

The question we need to ask is: what do we learn from the argument that was not clear before? These are, I think, the following points (cf. Lawrence 2001):

(**P1**) *Life and living: the correct logical category of answer* In learning that the human good is an activity according to excellence, we learn about the correct category of answer to our question. Specifically, we learn that: (**P1A**) the human good is a good of soul – of life – and not of body (like health or beauty), nor an external good (like wealth and power). The ordinary view is that what matters most in life is money, power, and status, or one's beauty and health, and that ethical respectability is a nice extra (*Pol.* VII.1.1323a25–7, 1323a34–8). Aristotle takes this view to put values or goods upside down (cf. section 1.5). What matters most is one's soul – being a person of a certain sort, one with correct values (for only so will one be in a position, say, to use wealth properly). However, Aristotle goes further. (**P1B**) It is not just that the goods of soul have this priority. We need to be careful about the kind of good of soul. For the end of human life is not becoming a good human, one with all the correct values. (If it were, then if I put you – good person that you are – into a dreamless sleep for the rest of your life, I will not have harmed you.) It is rather a matter of realizing those values, or excellences, in actually living well, over a full life-time. In effect, Aristotle takes the synonymy of *eudaimonia* with *euzōia*, living well, very seriously. And this in two respects: *eudaimonia* is primarily a matter of a good of soul or life (P1A), and the sense of life at issue is *exercise* of life-faculty (P1B).

(**P2**) *Human living* It is not just any being alive that matters, or is proper, to us, but being alive as humans. This is a matter of rational life-activity broadly speaking, and not our merely nutritive or bestial lives. No one says that someone had a wonderful or successful life, and then offers as grounds that "they had 20/20 vision all their lives" or that "they digested well." These are enabling conditions: defects here can impede, even prevent, the kind of living that matters to us – it is hard to lecture on Aristotle if bent double with a stomach ulcer. Enabling then, but not constitutive. For us, the distinctive way of being alive is properly rational action (feeling and thought) – *praxis*: that is, proper human living exhibits rational choice, and the excellences of such choice. It is this that differentiates us from other living things. In effect, Aristotle takes the synonymy of *eudaimonia* with *eupraxia* very seriously.

(**P3**) *The logical role of excellence* Aristotle denies that our good consists in being a good person, or having the human excellences. But equally his answer does make clear that the excellences have a central role in the account of human good, and what that role is. Our good consists in activity that *accords with*, or *realizes*, them (cf. *NE* VI.13.1144b24–30). What is clarified is the *logical* place or role of the human excellences.

These are the main points that, I believe, Aristotle is after in the Function Argument. They may seem formal, yet they are sufficiently contentful and informative to count as an outline of the human good. For they suffice to rule out many contemporaneous accounts of the human good simply on the grounds of offering as answers things of the wrong logical category. But Aristotle is less interested in refuting a view than in releasing the truth there is in it. And, as he tries to show in I.8., the account he has given provides a frame in terms of which we can make sense of the many things that are generally said (the *legomena*) about the human good or success, and reveal their proper place and contribution. In giving this outline, Aristotle is not trying to argue against an immoralist or to provide any Archimedean justification for his favored view. The "opposition," so to speak, is rather the logical mess of ordinary and reflective views about the human good, or at least those of them that are prevalent or seem to have something to them (I.4.1095a29–30). Aristotle's task is to provide a focal account that allows us to see and retrieve such truth as there is in these views – to sort out their various contributions into their proper logical place. In particular, these views, when offered as *complete* accounts of *eudaimonia*, go wrong in one of two ways.

Many ordinary views tend not to appreciate that *eudaimonia* must centrally be a good of soul. More philosophical or reflective views appreciate this, but fail to see that it is a matter of actually living a life of a certain sort, not merely being a person of a certain sort; and, in so failing, they fail to specify the very kind of human activity of which the human excellences are the proper excellences. His own account that "the *eudaimōn* is he who is active in accord with perfect excellence and sufficiently equipped with external goods not for any chance length of time but for a perfect life time" (I.10.1101a14–16; cf. *Pol.* VII.1.1323b40–1324a2) makes clear the focal place of (rational) activity, the way excellence comes in, and the place that external goods have – their "sufficiency" being determined by the needs of rational life-activity if it is to be well done (cf. VII.13.1153b21–5). Even so, it is only an outline of the good. But it also points the way forward, in suggesting an obvious way to start filling it in – by examining the excellences that are proper to human action (cf. I.13, move 4).

2.3 Two problems: (1) Fallacy and gap

If the Function Argument is aimed at the above points, (P1) – (P3), they are, I think, not easy to resist. Yet the argument strikes many as suspect and problematic. Two (interconnected) kinds of worry perhaps stand out.

First, our central question is that of the greatest good a human can obtain. The Function Argument seems to offer an answer in terms of "living the life of a good human specimen." But to many it seems odd to suppose our greatest good – our happiness or success, what is most in our interest, the object of rational choice – is to live the life of a good human specimen. Is there not at least some gap here between the good whose specification we are seeking and the answer provided by the appeal to human function?

Well, what sort of gap? Various charges of fallacy have been leveled at the argument – and often run together – and various kinds of "gap" may be alleged here. Thus, some suppose a *fact–value* gap: does the Function Argument not deliver a factual biological conclusion about human flourishing, whereas are we not seeking something evaluative – a conclusion about what we *should* pursue, and one cannot move from an "is" to an "ought"?[6] Or a *nature–reason* gap: does human reason not yield a vantage point that transcends our nature, leaving us free to invent ourselves (at least within the broad constraints of our nature)? Or a *species–individual* gap: the good of the species is perhaps served or constituted by humans living excellently, but may not this suppress and alienate each of us from our own individual good? Or, analogously, a gap between the *common* or *public* good and our *private* good. Or a *moral–prudential* gap: is Aristotle's question not a prudential one – asking after our best interests – but his answer a moral one – a life of virtuous activity, even if initially it is conceived only formally? Yet a life of virtuous activity seems neither necessary nor sufficient for the prudentially best life, or at least not without further argument. We are here peering into the cauldron of modern moral philosophy. This requires painstaking exorcism. But we can start a response.

Our target is the practicable good, characterized as unqualifiedly final and as the object of practical reason (or *politikē*). We can think of this formal target as an empty box, and our question as one of how properly to fill it. True, we have learnt something: the box is *labeled* "great life" – "*eudaimonia*" or "living well" or "doing well." This is not nothing. It is some constraint on possible answers that they must be viewable as falling under such descriptions, and, in fact, I have suggested above (section 2.2) that Aristotle takes this very seriously (cf. I.8.1098b20–22). But initially it is not very illuminating. For it is common ground between those who have enormously divergent views about what substantially the good in question is, even what type or category of good it is. And we face a plethora of such opinions: everyone has a view. On the one hand, we face a range of more ordinary views, which prima facie advance items that surely have something to do with the good in question, but which are offered as rivals to each other, and where even the most plausible prove inadequate when taken as constitutive of it, and in particular to lack that finality we are seeking (I.5.1095b23–4, 1095b31–2). On the other hand, there are high-flown sophisticated philosophical accounts, which impress many (I.4.1095a25–6), but which are open to sophisticated objections, and which in any case seem fairly clearly not to talk about the kind of good that is the object of inquiry (I.6, esp. 1096b31–1097a13). So, more ordinary views are all over the place, and, individually investigated, problematic; the main philosophical type of account (Platonism and its variations) is, sophisticated as it is, basically empty and going nowhere. Where then can we look for a more helpful account of the human good, or success? That is our problem.

Aristotle offers a suggestion (*tacha*). Take the notion of the good or success in things more generally. Where the items have a function, that is, have something that it is proper for them as such to do – like the car, the heart, the flautist – their good or success consists in their actually performing their function well. (Everything about them is organized around that.) So *if* the human can be so viewed, as having something proper for it as such to do, then we could hope to illuminate the human good or success by appeal to this.

So far, it is just a suggestion, with a rationale. Even if misguided, it does not seem very mysterious. Suppose, for instance, we were inquiring after bodily success. There is general agreement that we can label it "health." But what really is that? There are many divergent ordinary views, and more philosophical or theoretical ones that define it as, for example, the balance of the four elements or humors, or of Yin and Yang. A sensible suggestion would be to consider the function of the human body, what it is proper for it to do: for doing that well will be bodily success. The idea then has an intuitive appeal – and one can indeed wonder where else to look. Yet equally one may be suspicious: might not such an appeal to human function be just another piece of philosophical make-believe, on a par with the Platonic view Aristotle himself has dismantled in the preceding chapter, thus forewarning us against philosophy?

A certain caution is indeed in order. And all the more so in the light of Aristotle's own presentation of the difficulty of our position. Such caution should make us wary of the size or type of results; of the sensitivity of a candidate account to ordinary, and other, opinions generally; of the space an account leaves open for challenge and dispute. Yet in these respects at least, Aristotle's account should be reassuring.

1 The results of the argument are in a way modest and formal – so much so that recent scholarly opinion has worried whether the argument really achieves anything very much. Yet, I have suggested, it is not without power; it was just not quite where the reader expected progress to be made.

2 As we have said, the Function Argument is not intended to stand alone, as I.8 makes clear. Its specification – and even the general style of answer – is tested in the light of the sense it allows us to make of the *legomena* – opinions to which it must be responsive (section 2.2).

3 The argument still leaves room for disagreement over the specification of the human excellences – both in general and in detail or both in name and in substance. True, Aristotle has views about the nature of such disputes: if you think injustice is the human excellence, you probably do not need argument but chastisement (cf. *Topics* I.11.105a3–8). But his argument here is not aimed at resolving any such disputes; it is not trying to provide some independent biological or scientistic grounding for the ethical life, as ordinarily conceived, being the best. So Aristotle is not illicitly cutting off the possibility of certain disputes.

Let us consider, as an example, one way that gives rise to a charge of a gap or a mismatch. This stems from presupposing a certain "prudentialist" interpretation of "the highest good" that is the object of inquiry. It can seem that this good *must* be something of benefit to the agent (for example, their welfare), must be their greatest interest, where this is heard prudentially. (The view goes hand in hand with a certain prudentialist conception of practical reason: that the formal object of practical reason is an individual's "*own* best interest," heard in this prudential tone or emphasis.) So understood, there seems an evident gap between this and the life of virtuous activity: the latter appears neither obviously necessary nor sufficient for the former. To connect them would require further argument, to the effect, for example, that living virtuously, as things are, leads to more of what each agent wants for themselves (cf. Wilkes 1978).

This misconstrues Aristotle's strategy. His concept of the highest practicable good is more formal, introduced as it is in terms simply of finality (cf. sections 1.1, 1.5). It does not already assume that the good of an X – or the success of an *X* – must benefit an *X*. (The highest good of medicine is the health of the patient – something of benefit, but not to the doctor.) In terms of Aristotle's frame, someone with such worries – who feels that they already have an independent hold on the human good as evidently, to an extent, prudentialist – needs to make their case at a different juncture. They should make it part of the *answer*, and not try to build it into the very question. That is, they should, for example, try to argue that selfishness is an excellence or virtue (shades of Ayn Rand). Or else, if they accept Aristotle's nominal list of excellences, they may argue that, when we get to particulars, what the practically wise will determine as the wise action will turn out a lot more prudentially slanted than Aristotle apparently envisages. That is, when we come to specify the contents of living well, or excellently, as a human being, the correct answer is a prudential one.

In short, the kind of specificity that such prudential thoughts bring is not *written in* to the concept of highest good that is in question (as a constraint on answers); but neither, on the other hand, is it *written out* of the answer (in terms of what actually constitutes excellent human living). The problem can be raised – it has not been illicitly dismissed. So this reply is more one about re-siting such a dispute than resolving it.

"But surely we *do* have an independent line on what the human good can be? And does it not include much that is prudential?" This is in a way correct, except it is unclear what leverage is being sought from "independent." It is correct in that we can make a list of ordinary good and bad things in human life, a list that will include many "prudential" items; and any attempted specification of the human good would have to show how it took these into account, and, if it controverted any, would need to explain why they did not have the place or role or importance we had thought (cf. *NE* VII.14.1154a22–5; and the diagnosis offered by the revaluation of value). If "independent" points just to that – that an account must acknowledge and address our ordinary views, and if it ignored them would thus far undermine its claim to be giving an account of the human good – well, this is Aristotle's own view and what he takes himself to be doing in *NE* I.8.

2.4 Problem (2): Talk of function

There are, however, challenges which stem from more than the kind of caution instanced above, and which introduce larger philosophical themes. Many turn on the notion of "function," and query whether the attribution of a function, or of proper function, to a human is not really rather mysterious – as is talk of *what it is for a human as such to do*.

The idea of function in question is a normative one in the following way. Very briefly, to say that "the *X* φs" in this functional sense of "do," implies that an individual *X* *ought to* φ, and is *defective* in some way if it does not. For example, "the swallow migrates" implies that this individual swallow ought to; and that if it does not, there is something wrong, some failure – whether "internal" to the swallow (it has, say, a broken wing), or "external," in its environment (it is, say, in a cage or the mouth of a cat). This talk is normative in that it supports such "*oughts*" and claims of imperfection, defect, mistake, and failure. In this sense it offers a *norm*, in no mere statistical sense of the "typical." This is a grammatical point, characterizing a way of talking (cf. Anscombe 1958; Lawrence 1993b; Thompson 1993).

Now various challenges can be made to it. (1) It may be claimed to be a non-sensical way of talking, reaching for some bogus metaphysical "glue"; or one that is nonsensical outside the realm of artifacts – and its application to natural objects a mere *façon de parler*, or an historical-cum-folk-psychological hangover from a theistic view of the natural world as a divine artifact. Alternatively, it may be allowed to have *some* place as a way of talking, just not the one here envisaged. In this vein it may be claimed: (2) there are such natural, or "biological," norms, but these are of a different order from, and can be at odds with, rational ones. Thus it may be suggested that it is *for a human* to feel such emotions as envy, spite, and jealousy – such is within the range of what it is natural for a human as such to feel; yet from the perspective of a rational norm it may be that we ought never to entertain such feelings. (And if there are natural norms of reason too, well, why should natural norms form a consistent set?) Or (3) the objection may rather be about distance than conflict. That is, it may be conceded that there are such natural norms, but they fall far short of delivering anything like a determinate view of the human good of the sort we are seeking. Such facts about human nature are sufficiently indeterminate to be quite consistent with *rival* specifications of this good, and where the facts run out relativism steps in. If we do appeal to them to ground a determinate answer, we will be relying on some overly rigid and likely metaphysical conception of human nature. And is this not just what Aristotle ends up doing, in his appeal to the divine nature of intuitive intellect (*nous*) and its activity, contemplation?

This last is an objection put forcefully by Bernard Williams (1985). However, on the one hand it is debatable whether the kind of relativism Williams envisages is really intelligible (cf. Wiggins 1976; McDowell 1986). On the other hand, the criticism of Aristotle's account as "super-objective," as dependent on metaphysics for its alleged objectivity, has some grounding. *Yet* there is nothing essentially metaphysical about Aristotle's *project*. Filling in the outline of the good is a matter of our appealing to our best thoughts about the excellences, our nature, and the world we live in. That Aristotle's own best thoughts on these topics should strike us as in part "metaphysical" does nothing to unseat the project and stop us using it to deliver a quite ordinarily objective answer about how best to live, neither too indeterminate nor too specific.

This does not speak to those who already find something objectionably meta-physical even in the very talk of proper function. This requires its own discussion. But I think our ordinary talk is "Aristotelian," and it is not so easy to suppose it can be displaced or viewed as erroneous.

2.5 A further difficulty: the additional conclusion and defective circumstances

I turn now to a rather different worry. The Function Argument suggests that the practicable good, successful human living, is a life of reason-involving activity done well. But this is in tension with my claim that Aristotle's target is the Utopian good. For reason-involving activity done well occurs also in defective circumstances – the life of the perfect person who fights the just war, or who has to cope with health problems, their own or others, and so on. And the activity of one excellence may be better than another. So the general category of such activity done well is, it appears, a necessary but not a sufficient condition of the Utopian good. We need some further distinction here, a fault-line *within* the category of reason-involving activity well done.

Now this, I think, is at least part of what motivates the addition of the further clause in the conclusion: "and if the excellences are several, in accord with the best and most perfect [*teleiotatēn*]." Unfortunately, it is controversial whether this should be understood *comprehensively* or *selectively*. That is, is Aristotle saying that, if there are several excellences, the human good would be rational activity that (a) accords with the most complete set of the excellences, or (b) that accords with the single best, or most perfect or final, excellence? Scholars are much divided, and not without reason. After all, in favor of the comprehensive, one might compare eyesight: the good of the eye, or success in an eye, consists in its performing its function, seeing, well, i.e. in accord with the excellence proper to seeing; and if there are several, then surely in accord with the best, i.e. most complete, set. There are various defects of sight, and various aspects to its correctness – and one needs all of them to enjoy perfect seeing.

Yet I favor the selective reading. "Best" sounds selective, and this initial interpretation seems reinforced by the subsequent "tactical" passages, where Aristotle temporizes on whether in the end *eudaimonia* will consist in several best activities, or in one, the very best, here transparently selecting one from among others: I.8.1099a29–31, VII.13.1153b9–12, X.5.1176a26–9. Moreover, the selective reading opens up the formal possibility of a further structure, or focality, within human excellences, where one excellence is for the sake of another – *a possibility that is then realized*. For, according to Aristotle, there do turn out to be several – in fact, two – excellences, one the combination of practical wisdom with the excellences of character, and the other theoretical wisdom; and the latter is better and more final in relation to the former (VI.12–13; cf. X.7.1177a12–18).

But if we now bring the Utopian point to bear, it may suggest the following. Suppose there are two values, one better than the other. In order to be living the best possible human life I will need my activities *at least* to realize the higher value; otherwise, while they may be good in that they realize the lower value, they will not be the best living a human can achieve. Yet in *at least* realizing the higher, it does not immediately follow that they cannot *also* be exhibiting the lower value;

and, indeed, possibly they must do so. Such issues are not yet settled insofar as the exact relations between the excellences (and between their respective activities) is not settled (for example, perhaps the activity is to be assessed under descriptions or aspects).

So if theoretical wisdom is the best excellence, then for my life to be perfect, my activities must realize, or accord with, it. While an act that exhibits generosity may be fine and the best action in the circumstances, it would not be the finest living. Yet in saying this, it seems left unsettled whether action that realizes this best or most final excellence could, or could thereby, also realize the less final or subordinate excellence. That is, on this kind of selective reading, a certain kind of comprehensivist thesis, although perhaps not quite what comprehensivists envisaged, is not ruled out: it is just that it is not being explicitly propounded here.

At this point it may be protested that we do know the relation between the excellences – it is that of finality – and this itself settles our issue. For it belongs to a "more final" excellence to *include*, or *embrace* (*periechein*), any less final ones. However, this may mean only that where a lower excellence is needed, it and its activity are for the sake of the higher and do not thereby add something of independent value that would produce some greater value than the best by itself: rather, they simply ameliorate some defective or impedimental condition. If so, this is not enough to settle whether an activity that actually realizes the higher excellence one was or was not thereby also realizing the lower – not enough, that is, to decide between the following two models.

Model 1: the "exclusive-cum-productive" model   The possibility that Aristotle entertains here, and affirms later, is that there may be two (or more) excellences, each the excellence proper to its own rational activity, and the excellences and activities may be so related that the one is for the sake of the other. Aristotle's position turns out to be that the best activity is contemplation in accord with theoretical wisdom; whereas action in accord with "the other excellence" (X.8.1178a9), viz. practical wisdom, is, while good in a secondary way, also for the sake of the best activity. The activities of practical wisdom free up the stage of life so that the activity of *nous* can walk unimpeded: so that we are free to engage in the activity that is most truly the realization of ourselves. The task of practical wisdom is, in effect, to remove the impediments to such realization. With the impediments to our living as our true selves removed, we do not have to choose to be ourselves. We are like gods who are mired in defective circumstances: once practical reason removes the impediments, then like gods – or elements (*Phys.* VIII.4.255b2–13) – we simply actualize ourselves, in contemplation. Herein we act well – achieve *eupraxia* – like a god (*Pol.* VII.3.1325b14–30), *without choice.*

Model 2: the "two dimensions of assessment"   Humans have to *choose* to contemplate – and so, for them, contemplating is an action in a way that it never is for a god. *We* may contemplate when we should not; and *we* may fail to contemplate when we should. So when we contemplate, we are, unlike a god, open to two different ranges of assessment as to whether in so doing we are doing well:

1 It can be asked whether we are contemplating well; that is, are we realizing the excellence proper to that (viz. *sophia*).
2 It can be asked whether in contemplating (whether well or badly) we are thereby acting well; that is, wisely, i.e. in accord with the excellence of practical wisdom (and the rest).

If so, then the activity of contemplating can be the material content of acting with practical wisdom. And for my life to be perfect human living, I must pass on *all* fronts of assessment to which I am vulnerable. So I need the full or perfect set of excellences – and perfect human living is living that realizes all, or both, of them: it must be wise in both theoretical and practical ways. That is the practical form of our human life.

Which model is Aristotle's? That is one problem, and it is one we have come across already in connection with *politikē* (section 1.2, R2; it arises also in the notion of *eupraxia*). Now I have suggested that the Function Argument takes what is distinctive of humans as the life of *praxis* in the sense of chosen action. This may seem to favor the latter model. Yet even so, it would still be uncomfortable that *our* best activity is such that it exhibits an excellence of a different order – one of theoretical, not practical, wisdom. That is, the excellence in question is *not* an excellence of choice, of specifically human action. That is a second problem. It is not clear to me that Aristotle squarely faces up to either problem, but this is a matter for investigation elsewhere.

3 The Final Account of Human Good

3.1 The life of perfect success

I claimed that the second clause of the Function Argument's conclusion introduces a further focality as a formal possibility, a possibility that is subsequently realized. In *NE* VI.1.1138b35–1139a17 Aristotle says that, just as earlier in I.13 he had distinguished two parts of the rational soul, the rational and (potentially) irrational, so now in the same way he needs to distinguish two parts within the strictly rational soul, viz. the scientific (*epistēmonikon*) and the calculative (*logistikon*) (cf. *Pol.* VII.14.1333a16–30). They concern different kinds of object, the former things whose first principles cannot be otherwise, the latter things whose principles can be: "for relative to things that are different in kind, so is the part of the soul naturally aligned with each also different in kind, since it is in virtue of a certain similarity and kinship/propriety (*oikeiotēs*) that knowledge belongs to them" (VI.1.1139a8–11).

There is a suggestive correlativity here between eternal and contingent truths and parts of the rational, or dianoetic, soul with corresponding properties (cf. X.7 *init.*). Each of these parts of soul is then said to have a best state or excellence (relative to its proper function); and our task is to determine what these are (VI.1.1139a15–17; cf.VI.2.1139b12–13). It is this further distinction introduced in VI.1 that lays the ground for the reconfiguration of the topography of the excellences in VI.12–13: no longer are the excellences of character contrasted with those of intellect as in I.13, but now the intellectual excellence of *phronēsis together with* the excellences of character is contrasted with the excellence of *sophia*. And they are so related as to instantiate I.7's formal possibility of a second focality, one excellence being for the sake of the other.

So Aristotle's final position on the central question of the best possible human life (*Q1*) is already clear in outline by the end of *NE* VI (cf. VI.7.1141a18–b8). It is a life of contemplation in accord with its proper excellence, theoretical wisdom – an answer in the tradition of the *sophoi* like Thales and Anaxagoras: "To contemplate whatever pertains to the heavens and to the stars and the moon and the sun in the heavens, as though everything else was of no worth" (*Protrepticus* fr.11W; *EE* I.5.1216a10–16; cf. also *NE* VI.7.1141b2–8, X.8.1179a13–16; *EE* I.4.1215b6–14; Plato, *Timaeus* 47Aff). A kind of half Kant. Its objects are of divine and incomparable value (cf. *peritta . . . kai thaumasta kai chalepa kai daimonia*; VI.7.1141b6–7). It is correlatively the activity of the most divine part of the soul, *nous*. It is a life that to the many would likely seem ridiculous (*NE* X.8.1179a13–16; *EE* I.4.1215b6–14). For it, unlike practical wisdom, does not have any explicit concern with human *eudaimonia* as part of its content – indeed, it seems useless, humanly speaking. But, as Aristotle argues, it can nonetheless itself constitute human *eudaimonia*; it can be the activity that well done constitutes our final goal, the finest human living (*NE* VI.12.1144a3–6, VI.13). Its very uselessness is a mark of its perfection; were it useful, it would point to the existence of other goods beyond itself (cf. VI.7.1141b3–8; cf. *Meta.* I.1.981b17–23).

In *NE* X.6–8 Aristotle returns to the discussion of *eudaimonia*, and considers again the *topos* of the three main candidate lives (cf. *NE* I.5). In X.6 he argues against the life of physical pleasure; in X.7–8 he allows that both the other candidates are successful lives, but argues that the life in accord with theoretical wisdom is best, while the life "in accord with the other excellence" (X.8.1178a9), the political life, is *eudaimōn* only to a secondary degree. The first of these arguments, the "direct argument" (X.7.1177a12–18), runs:

1   *Formal claim*   If there are several excellences, then *eudaimonia* would be constituted by activity according to the best (*kratistē*) excellence, which would be the excellence of the best part of the soul, if there were one part better than the others (cf. the second clause of the Function Argument as interpreted above).

2 *Existential claim* There is indeed such a best part of the soul – whether *nous* or something like it, whether it is actually divine or the most divine-like thing in us (cf. X.7.1177a19–21).

3 *Conclusion* Therefore perfect *eudaimonia* would be the activity of this part (*nous*) in accordance with its proper (*oikeia*) excellence – and this activity is, as has been said, a *theoretical* one.

This is followed by a series of other arguments, one way of dividing which is as follows: (2) the Criteria Argument (X.7.1177a18–b26); (3) the Defensive Argument (X.7.1177b26–8.1178a23); (4) the Argument from "the Activity of the Gods" (X.8.1178b7–23); (5) the Animal Evidence Argument (X.8.1178b24–32); (6) the Argument from "What Pleases the Gods" (X.8.1179a22–32).

3.2 Contemplative and political lives

Aristotle's exact position over the two successful lives has occasioned much controversy. My own view is that the difference between these lives is not one between people who have different values, one *devoted* to contemplation, the other to political action. Aristotle is not advocating *a value monism*. Rather, it is the same person in both cases, the *phronimos*, the practically wise person who has *all* the correct values and excellences. The difference between the two lives lies in their circumstances. So, as I understand Aristotle:

1 The life of perfect success in the case of a human would be a life whose circumstances left one free to engage entirely in the best activity, contemplation – that is, a life whose circumstances were such that it was *always best to do the best activity*. This is thus an *activity, or life, monism*.

2 But this is not to say that a life whose circumstances were such that it was never best to do the very best activity – that did not leave one free to contemplate at all – could not be a *eudaimōn* one; no, if filled with political activity well done, it would be a successful life, albeit only to a secondary degree.

Clearly, if we take the latter as our base line, then lives whose circumstances leave the agent free-er, and free-er to engage in the best activity of contemplation, will thereby be ever more unqualifiedly successful ones. And the former is explicitly an ideal that is out of our reach: for it is the life of a god, and what a god obtains for all time, we can at best attain only for some of our life-time (*NE* X.7.1177b26–34; *Meta.* XII.7.1072b14–15, 1072b24–5; cf. *Cael.* II.12.292a22–b5). For we have inevitable human needs – physical, emotional, and social – so that, even in optimal circumstances, it will sometimes be best to address these, and not best to contemplate (cf. *NE* X.8.1178b3–7). But that it is out of our reach does not mean it should not function as a regulative ideal. We should strive to arrange our lives and circumstances, individually and socially, so as to create as much free time in which to contemplate as is ever possible given the human condition even at its optimal.

This is no silly maximization thesis. We must always do what is best in the situation, but it is part of so doing to have an eye on bringing about situations in which it is best to do the unqualifiedly best activity. The real problem Aristotle faces here is that, insofar as contemplation appears to us as a mysterious activity, we have no real practical understanding of how to deliberate about when it is best to contemplate and when it is best to forgo it (cf. Lawrence 1993a: 31–2).

3.3 Determining the best life: the need for a fault-line

Aristotle, then, holds out as ideal an activity monism, not a value monism. The Function Argument is concerned with life-activities at a fairly general level – with different basic ways of being alive. What is distinctive about the human way of being alive is, roughly, our capacity for reason-involving activity very broadly construed (so that it includes our emotional lives). Now to say that the human good consists in a life-time of this activity, done well, has a certain plausibility. Without it – and left only as a mere vegetable or dumb beast or sunk in dreamless sleep – our life does not seem worth continuing; and done badly, we could end up wasting our life or worse – we could ruin our own lives and those of others.

Yet clearly, as we said, such an *undifferentiated* notion of rational activity well done *cannot* itself figure as the specification of the perfect life *sans phrase*, the Utopian goal – because of the point about defective circumstances and possible superiorities within excellences. We must, it seems, find a *fault-line* to mark off the favored subset.

The fault-line Aristotle offers, formally, in the Function Argument is the possibility of there being more than one excellence and one being more final, and so better, than another, and correlatively with their activities (cf. *Pol.* VII.14.1333a25–30). This possibility is realized in the shape of the two excellences of theoretical and practical wisdom and their respective activities. The human good then is a life entirely consisting of theoretical activity well done – albeit as regulative ideal.

But *this* strikes us as much less plausible. In one direction, our task is to try to understand both what Aristotle's suggestion amounts to, and how he got there. In another, our task is to emend it while trying to preserve what truth it has. These are large tasks. What follows is perforce perfunctory, a mere *tour d' horizon*.

3.4 Upping the human condition: the theistic ideal

That the fault-line should be between practical and theoretical wisdom, and their respective activities, can seem reasonable. For considerations are not hard to find that apparently reveal the unsuitability of the one, and the suitability of the other, to be the perfect activity.

(1) *The apparent unsuitability of practical reason*   As we have seen (section 1.2, R2; section 2.5, model 1), practical reason has a productive aspect: it looks to determine and bring about an end that is not simply its own activity – it looks by its own nature beyond itself. Its function is to determine and bring about *eudaimonia*, as an end other than its own operation and activities. As productive in this way its activities are relatively un-final (cf. X.7.1177b1–4, 1177b18) and unsuited to occupy free time (1177b4–15, 1177b17–18: "unleisurely").

Admittedly, its operations and activities *can* themselves constitute living well, for they may be what constitutes living well and wisely *in the circumstances*. But this is so only to a secondary or qualified degree – imperfectly. For the circumstances in which such activity is best are defective ones: if they were perfect, we would *already* be enjoying that living well which practical activity seeks to secure for us (cf. *Cael*. II.12.292b4–7). So part of its point and value lies in its helping to bring about the enjoyment of free time, or prevent impediments to that – whether for the agent themselves or for others. But our very need for such practical activity – the fact that this can, for us, be the best and wisest thing to do – reveals a defect, something less than perfect, in the human situation.

The activities of *politikē* and *phronēsis* are thus concerned with securing human living well in such a way that they themselves *cannot* unqualifiedly, or perfectly, constitute it. Their activities are humanly *useful,* whereas it appears that the perfect activity not only can be, but *must* be, *useless,* on pain of pointing to some further good outside itself. The perfect activity is thus *autotelēs*: self-ended. Indeed, part of the worth of our practical activity is dependent, or conditional, on there being some seriously good activity to occupy free time and constitute unqualified living well: if all we were up to were idle amusements, natural Disney-landers, then part of what makes humans worth bothering about, worth all the pain and fuss, would disappear (cf. X.6.1176b27–33). The *Politics*, which makes "free time" the "single *archē* of all things" (VIII.3.1337b32), offers at least four criteria for an activity's being appropriate to occupy free time: it must be (1) seriously good (*spoudaios*), not trivial; (2) final, and not merely recuperative or relaxing (VIII.5.1339a26–31); (3) noble, and not merely necessary (VIII.3.1338a14, 1338a30–22); and (4) worthy of a free person's engaging in, and not useful (1338a15, 1338a30–22).

Practical activities are admittedly seriously good (some even pre-eminent in nobility and grandeur, *NE* X.7.1177b16–17); but they are in certain ways productive and useful. And, from a different direction, we can worry also about their relative lack of self-sufficiency (X.7.1177a27–34): acting generously requires something to be generous with, and a suitable recipient or occasion. Such dependencies threaten the *supply* of these activities. Will there be an adequate sufficiency of them to fill up a life-time with worthy activity? And such a shortage is, seemingly, exacerbated by their very success. (You comfort a crying child; if you succeed, you must find something else to do.) In more optimal circumstances, there will be a dwindling prospect of just wars to fight, charitable works to engage in, and so on: doctors will find themselves hanging around the surgery like Maytag repairmen, rationing out the occasional patient. Moreover, such a shortage is desirable. One can hardly attempt to restore the supply by doing injustice in order to give oneself and others the chance of worthwhile lives rectifying it (à la Jason of Thessaly; *Rhet.* I.12.1373a24–7).

(2) *The apparent suitability of contemplation* Given such a view of the function of practical reason, it is natural, as we said (section 1.2, R2), to look to the third realm – that of theoretical *dianoia* – for the ideal activity. This seems to promise activities that meet the criteria for the proper occupancy of free time: they are serious and concern things of the greatest value (cf. *Part An.* I.5.644b22–645a4); they are fully final – our interest in them is pure in that we seek nothing from them beyond understanding or appreciating them for what they are (*NE* X.7.1177b1–4; cf. *Meta.* I.1.981b13–982a1). Thus theoretical activity, contemplation, has that uselessness that marks perfection.

This is reinforced by a complex web of influences: the tradition of "the wise"; a certain consonance with ordinary ideas of how perfect beings would live (*NE* X.8.1178b7–23). If that were not enough, it chimes with Aristotle's own views of the nature and "metaphysical status" of theoretical intellect (*nous*) and its contemplative activity. *Nous*, or theoretical intellect, is clearly something very special for Aristotle. Since it is not "bound up with matter," it is not studied by the *phusikos* (*Meta.* VI.1.1026a5–6; cf. *Part An.* I.1.641a33–b10; *De An.* I.1.403a28), and it "seems like a different genus of soul" (*De An.* II.2.413b24–7; cf. II.3.415a11–12). It is by far and away the most valuable and best part of the human soul – either itself divine or the most divine of things in us (*NE* X.7.1177a12–18, 1177b6–1178a8; cf. VI.13.1145a6–8). And its value lies in part in the supreme value of its objects (cf. *EE* I.5.1216b19–20; *NE* VI.7.1141a19–20, 1141a34–b8, X.7.1177a20–21); it is valuable by itself for itself (*NE* X.8.1178b31). (Whether, and in what sense, it is, in act, the same as its objects – as is the case with the perfect substance – are questions we must set aside.)

Aligned with this is the background of Aristotle's own "first philosophy," or "theology." As we said, this is not the study of some god or of religion, but of ontology, the study of being *qua* being, and in particular the study of success or perfection in the focal category of being, viz. substance (cf. Ackrill 1972; Lawrence 1997, 2004b). Such a perfect substance presents the measure of success in substance and so a measure of inter-species evaluation of the success of all other substances – and the closer we approximate to it, the better our life (cf. X.8.1178b21–3, 1178b24–32; *Cael.* II.12.292a22–b5). The influence of such a theology is present here, even if Aristotle ducks full discussion of it (cf. X.8.1178a22–3).

3.5 Puzzles over theoretical reason and contemplation

This ideal looks somewhat overly intellectual, yet it is even stranger than it may initially seem. (a) The theoretical activity, contemplation, is not an activity of inquiry or research, but a supposed exercise of understanding already achieved (cf. X.7.1177a26–7). Theoretical *inquiry* would run afoul of the "*X* for the sake of *Y*" *finality* value principle (cf. section 1.1), its end – the possession of understanding – being more valuable than the process to it. It would also be vulnerable to shortage of supply, if sciences are supposed completable (as I suspect Aristotle envisages: certainly the perfect substance is not going to be incomplete in any way). (b) Its value seems to be a function of the value of its objects – rather than the human understanding of them (VI.7.1141a20–22, 1141a33–b3, X.7.1177a20–21): a difficult topic. (c) In any case, it seems curiously detached from human life (cf. Clark 1975: 183). Aristotle allows that it may be better with "co-workers" (X.7.1177a34–b1), but insofar as the activity, the "work," is not clear, it is not clear what role fellow workers play. Again, regardless of whether we are talking about intellectual discovery or intellectual appreciation, this is, for us, *embedded* in a huge range of human attitude and emotion – joy and delight, surprise, wonder, excitement, pride, relief, challenge, and curiosity – not to mention frustration, disappointment, and anxiety *et al.* – a messy emotional interweave and dynamic unsuited to the quietly perfect being. Aristotle talks mostly of a pure and lasting pleasure here (cf. VII.12.1153a1, X.7.1177a22–7), and even so the details of its conversation are left fairly blank: it seems largely cut off from anything but an incidental involvement with the range of human emotions that are bound up with practical wisdom.

Let us take just the first of these, (a), the idea that the (or the best) exercise of theoretical reason is contemplation, where this is envisaged as an exercise of the understanding – an actualization of already possessed knowledge of a certain systematic field. Some do not find this particularly puzzling. Thus Kraut (1989: 73) suggests it is "a process of reflection on a system of truths already discovered . . . an activity that goes on whenever one brings certain truths to mind: it occurs not only when one silently reflects, but also when one lectures or writes about a certain subject . . ." It is a matter of "consciously considering truths," "a state of mind" that is "the activation of the understanding one has achieved . . ." By contrast, I find it problematic whether there is any such activity as Kraut here discerns. One could push in several directions.

(1) *Grammatical error* It is perennially tempting to take thought or thinking – or understanding or knowing – as a process ("silent speech"), or even as an activity, in the sense of something that occupies time, but which because it is something complete in itself, unlike a process, is extendable infinitely in time. And so it is tempting to take "exercising one's understanding" as such an activity: to suppose that we can ask "are you understanding at the moment?" in a *sense* that parallels asking "are you seeing – or jogging – at the moment?" (or "how long did you . . .?"). But as Hardie (1968: 344) succinctly remarked: "knowing is not a way of passing the time." In this direction one suspects a grammatical error at the heart of Aristotle's view (cf. Wittgenstein 1953: 139–204).

(2) "*Intellectual appreciation*" We could perhaps look in an aesthetic direction. Aristotle himself suggests some analogy with music (*Pol.* VIII.3, VIII.5); and in the *De Partibus Animalium* I.5.645a8–37, again with an aesthetic parallel, this time with painting and sculpture, contemplation seems an intellectual appreciation of an organism as a wondrously ordered and working whole – an appreciation of its structure of "this for the sake of that," of final causality, a structure that is an analog to beauty. Obviously this requires understanding how the organism and its parts work, but the activity is one of appreciative intellectual wonder, even joy, something akin to the intellectual appreciation of a work of art. At its core, it is the appreciation of order (of the relevant causes) – cf. *Phys.* VIII.1.252a12 – and the principle of order (that notion of *taxis* that is perhaps a ground or principle of goodness: cf. *EE* I.8.1218a21–4). This could be extended to mathematics, and then perhaps also to the order of the cosmos itself (*EE* I.5.1216a13–14, Anaxagoras' view) and thence perhaps to its first principle – where the surrounding system disappears, leaving one in a perhaps mystic admiration and unity with the One, in an active enlightenment – the very principle of order without the order that is dependent on it (the general *sans* army). But although such contemplation may be pushed eventually into some such quasi-mystic direction, one can stick at the more aesthetic level – at the intellectual appreciation of natural and mathematical structures. Now, there may be such doings, and they may be ways of occupying time (*diagōgai*). But it is not clear that there is some "straightforward" basic life-activity here, a distinct form of living, rather than a sophisticated mixture of many aspects of our humanity. Nor would it plausibly have the be-all-and-end-all status in human life that Aristotle accords contemplation – at least not if shorn of its mystic extensions. In short, I do not think that we should rush to suppose that we understand what contemplation is, or even what theoretical reason and reasoning is, for Aristotle.

3.6 Free time, the secular ideal, and practical reason

But if this contemplative conception of the ideal life seems thus problematic, it also seems easy to emend. Can we not just drop anything that smacks of the absolute or metaphysical and keep the focus on free time (*Freizeit*)? It is free time that we need to supply to citizens and to ourselves as individuals; and we need to have some idea of the sort of activities that properly fill it (*Pol.* VIII.3.1337b33–5); and to provide, and be provided with, the proper education to equip us to engage in such activities. Echoing Plato's *Laws*, Aristotle criticizes the Spartans for failing in this critical aspect of education: "That is why the Spartans were preserved while they made war, but when they ruled, perished, because they did not understand how to occupy free time [*scholazein*], and never engaged in any other kind of training [*askēsis*] more fundamental [*kuriōtera*] than military [*polemikē*]" (*Pol.* II.9.1271b3–6; cf. VII.14.1333b5–1334a10 etc.). In our search for activities or occupations suitable for free time, we can broaden the intake to cover scientific and mathematical *research* – and why not the fine arts, and their creation as well as appreciation? Indeed, we can appeal to the role that Marx and Mill give to the individual's *self-development*.

This "secular" revision keeps Aristotle's focus on the notion of free time, while challenging whether theoretical thought or contemplation is intelligible as an occupant of it, or plausible as the sole one. But in challenging one arm of Aristotle's contrast, it seems to acquiesce in its second half, in the supposed unsuitability of practical reason's activities. And indeed there is, even from a "secular" perspective, a temptation to a *constraint* view of ethics – roughly of the sort "first clear the moral decks, then you are free to do as you like, to develop as you wish." Quite what this amounts to is not transparent. But, sidestepping this, we may say that Aristotle's apparent demotion of the activities of practical reason is – at least shorn of its metaphysical backdrop – prima facie absurd.

For a start, there are all sorts of activities "in accord with the other excellence" that belong as constituents in an ideal human life, in human life at its best: giving birth or watching the birth of your child, giving your child a much-desired bicycle on his or her birthday, for example. And, more generally: domestic bliss, time to cement and enjoy friendships, time to bring up and enjoy the company of one's children, time to look after the elderly and enjoy their company, to play a role in one's community, to sing in a chorus – all the human richness of a life.

The extent of such activities is wider than may at first appear. It includes also such things as time for a naturally placed grief – having the free time (cf. compassionate leave) in which to grieve for those who have lived full lives and are passing with their generation (one's parents, not one's children). Or again, we should not be led to suppose that comforting a child that has fallen over is not properly an ideal activity, on the grounds that it would have been better if it had not happened and we could have gone on with something else (gardening, reading, and so on). Are we to hope that such accidents happen as little as possible – and to do what we can to prevent them? Are we then to dress up children like the Michelin Man? Now, it is not that there are not proper concerns about the supervision of play and the design of playgrounds, but something about the very texture and parameters of human life would be being distorted by such a view of the ideal human life. This is the sort of thing we do as humans, and that happens to us given what we do: knocks and bruises, physical, emotional, and intellectual, are part of human living going well, even at its very best.

And is not *work* – if one can talk so abstractly about it – part of this too, part of what it is human to do even "ideally"? One might begin here with various practices of hunting – say, a practice among a group of tribal hunters of running down large prey over several days of pursuit – or certain practices of cooking, building, cloth-making, or of gardening in the sense of primitive agriculture. These are social, cooperative, practices – part of second, not first, nature, yet which, as such, form the very fabric of human life; such practices are open to improvement, and involve skills that are passed from generation to generation, the passing itself being also a practice or aspect of the practice. In modern society, the practices, and traditions, of work, and the possibilities of their social position, are obviously more complex – both in their pluses, by way of the kind, variety, and interweave of their place and contribution, and in their minuses, by way of the kind and variety of vulnerability and exploitation to which they open us (cf. Engels 1845).

Now it seems that Aristotle demotes work, or at least productive activity, as not being appropriate for a free human. One major element controlling this line of thought "intellectually" (as against, for example, social prejudice) is the *finality* principle of value (cf. section 1.1): that where one thing is for the sake of another, it would be more ideal, where possible, to have the latter without the bother of the former – to eat the deer rather than to have to hunt it. But the ideal this holds out distorts the nature and fabric of human life and activity: perhaps it fails to register the creative, open-ended aspect of human activities (individually and as practices), and the role of such practices as constituting the substance of human life at a historical juncture, the frame of basic possibilities in whose terms individuals largely compose their life, or have their life composed. Crudely, you might think of the position of work in life as more like that of language. Admittedly, Aristotle is not without responses. He has his own historico-genetic story leading to "Egypt," an ideal of free time and its activities (*Meta.* I.1.981b13–982a1) – a "work-less" ideal implicit in the etymologies of *a-scholia* and *neg-otium*. He can claim he is uncovering a structure within what humans do – their general functioning or work-1; there is a focality such that activities of work-2 are for the sake of the activities or doings of free time. This topic of work and business and free time has an intricacy we cannot do justice to here.

But it is not merely that there is *some* room for some practical activities as ideal constituents of the ideal life. *All* human doings are assessable as practical or ethical (cf. section 2.5, model 2). For the most fundamental criteria of success in living as a human are those of "the other excellence," practical wisdom and the excellences of character: these are the basic ways of humanly going right and wrong. There are other criteria of success to do with the specific actions we choose – like making a nice cup of tea. And it may or may not matter that we do those well by their criteria: that is, playing the violin badly rather than well might be living well or wisely. So, being a worthwhile activity – something worth a human being's spending life time engaged in – is an ethical assessment; it is part of something's counting as a wise thing to do; and it is part of being judged or appreciated as such that it constitutes good human living. Much more needs to be said. My worry is that the second arm of Aristotle's contrast is also problematic.

3.7 Re-thinking the fault-line?

There are many ways to contrast practical with theoretical thought (*dianoia*), and indeed Aristotle employs several.[7] But it is a dangerous place to draw the fault-line.

I find the ease with which we talk of practical and theoretical reason – our sus-
ceptibility to the grip of certain pictures of what these are – rather alarming. And
moreover, on one view at least (model 2), all our rational actions are ones of
practical reason, so that we would have to be looking for a fault-line *within* the
actions of practical reason.

Yet, whatever the difficulties with drawing it, the distinction of Utopian and
non-Utopian targets in living well seems intuitive and inescapable. It is a fact of
human life that, *even for the good*, there are better and worse ways for human life to
go; and that many of these are ones that humans can do something about, individually, socially, and politically. And they should, as a matter of practical wisdom, do
something about these – and part of this very doing is getting clearer about what
these ways are. So the discussion itself is something wise to engage in.

We may look to other ways of drawing the fault-line, and perhaps come to think
of it as a matter not of a single fault-line but a network of considerations. With
an eye still on Aristotle, we may distinguish between the *defect-remedying* and the
good-enjoying exercises of an excellence (cf. *Pol.* VII.13.1332a7–27), where this is
not simply a distinction like the Platonic one between instrumental and final (cf.
NE I.6.1096b1–13). The defect-remedying actions we do for themselves because
it is what is just or courageous – we, say, try to rescue the drowning person – but
this is not an episode one would ideally wish to be part of one's life (*Pol.*
VII.13.1332a14–15). Yet there are other just and generous actions we naturally
would, and would hope to, have the opportunity to engage in during our lives.
Or again (and relatedly) we may distinguish between the *necessary* and the *noble*
(cf. *Pol.* VII.14.1333a30–b5).

Taking another tack, we can suggest that it is not so much the activity itself –
what we do in one sense – but the spirit we do it in, or with what attitude, or
what role we conceive of, or find, it playing in our life, and in our intellectual and
emotional economy and development: a matter of how it is chosen, or for what,
and, in particular, for whom. The suggestion again is one not entirely foreign to
Aristotle:

> That is why it is noble also for those among the young who are free persons to dis-
> charge many of the jobs that are held to be servile; for with regard to being noble
> and not noble, actions differ not so much with respect to themselves as by way of
> their end and for whose sake they are done. (*Pol.* VII.14.1333a7–11, diverging from
> Kraut (1997) over *heneka tinos*: see VIII.2.1337b17–21)

The *Politics*, simply by putting the focus on the idea of free time, sets us several
themes for further investigation: (a) the notion of free time itself (for surely
bringing up children should not be excluded); (b) the temptation to a constraint
view of morality which is not quite right (especially if all our fully rational actions
are ones of practical reason); (c) the possibility of wasting one's life – frittering it
away on trivia – and the need to do something with it, to make something of it,

which leads into the neglected topic of distinguishing the serious and deep from the light-minded and trivial; and (d) the need for appropriate education to equip one to fill free time fruitfully.

4 Conclusions

The account of the ideal human life that Aristotle ends up offering is seriously problematic. Even if we dispense with contemplation as he conceives it, and replace it with a more secular alternative, this can still implicate us in a problematic understanding of practical reason. These and other general difficulties about practical and theoretical reason may encourage us to look for the needed Utopian fault-line elsewhere. That said, Aristotle is, I believe, correct – or, if wrong, then interestingly wrong – in the following respects.

(1) *Practical philosophy* The ideas that there is a greatest good we can get, that this is a wise and wonderful life, and that it is the object of practical reason to work out more specifically what constitutes this in the circumstances of our lives, both individually and socially, and then to attain it.

(2) *Human function* In determining what counts as living well and doing well, we perforce look to basic facts about the kind of creatures we are and the sort of world we live in. Among these are the very general facts Aristotle points to in his Function Argument: about the correct category of human success being a matter of actual living; about the central importance of reason-involving life-activities; and about the logical role of the excellences. These provide an outline of the good, and point to an obvious way to fill it in.

(3) *Utopian target* Aristotle is also, I believe, correct in seeing the importance of what I have termed the Utopian target. It is a fact of human life that, even for the good, there are better and worse ways for life to go – some of which we can, and should, do something about. We need to be clear about what these are: for only thus will we be able to deliberate aright about what we should do, and demand aright from those who are supposed to be organizing our society aright.

(4) *Role of free time* There are admittedly difficulties in elucidating the notion of free time and its proper activities. But Aristotle is correct in emphasizing its centrality. Our modern *Weltanschauung* is dominated by a work "ethic" that invites us to view "normal" life as a matter of five days labor and two days R&R – itself increasingly viewed as an opportunity for business to recoup its outlay on the workforce. And, correspondingly, we are increasingly encouraged to view education as education for gainful employment, not as the requisite preparation for a truly rich life (cf. *Pol.* VIII.3.1338a9–22, 1338a30–32). But there is *all* the difference between vacation and free time. In the blurring of this distinction, we lose nothing less than our lives in the most important sense. That this is the proper end for human beings is something we cannot afford to lose sight of, individually

and, even more so, politically: at the lighter end of examples, just think of the number of human life hours spent in line at the DMV or playing a slot machine.

As Marx – in Aristotelian rather than Atomist mood – says: "Beyond the realm of necessity begins that development of human energy which is an end in itself, the true realm of freedom, which, however, can blossom forth only with the realm of necessity as its basis. The shortening of the working day is its basic prerequisite" (Marx 1894: 959). To which he could have added "and a liberal education, a Harvard for all."

Acknowledgments

Many thanks to Catherine Atherton, Richard Kraut, Calvin Normore, the UCLA History Group, and, especially, Hans Lottenbach.

Notes

1   Compare *EE* II.11.1227b19–22, I.1.1214a14–15 (and the rest of I.1 and I.2); *NE* VI.9.1142b22–33; *Cael.* II.12.292b5–7. See Broadie (1987: s.20) and Kraut (1997: 123–5).
2   In the goal-internal task of determining what constitutes the best life, practical reason as conceived here does not operate *in vacuo* – as it were from pure reason, analyzing out the relevant concepts. Nor does it operate, Humean-style, as a mere orchestrator or scheduler of desire satisfaction (or of desires we desire to have, etc.). Much enters here: being brought up in the standards and ways of the virtues – to have the correct criteria of success in action – and general experience of human life.
3   It is natural to take this "difference" in ends as correlative to the "similarity" of the preceding sentence, and so as a distinction between the ends of skill (and *methodos*), on the one hand, and those of chosen action, on the other, rather than as a new distinction orthogonal to that between production and action.
4   I do not think that the "also" (*NE* I.1.1094a16) should be taken to imply that the ends in question are sought for themselves as well as for further ends. I think it covers simple instrumental ends as well (cf. I.7.1097a25–7).
5   This methodology consists in: (a) collecting the opinions (*endoxa, legomena*) on a topic – at least those that are prevalent or seem to have something to them; (b) generating puzzles (*aporiai*) between them, as to how they can all be true; (c) where possible providing resolutions (*luseis*), often in terms of a grammatical distinction, revealing an ambiguity ("Gavin sees" and "Gavin does not see" can both be true, said of me when asleep). So doing allows us to preserve both, and refines the truth there is in them (*NE* VII.1.1145b2–7). (d) Failing that, if one rejects an opinion, one owes an explanation of why it at least seemed true (VII.14.1154a22–6). Two comments. First, the method is, I think, in part Aristotle's response to the *Meno*'s challenge of the paradox of inquiry.

Second, the background thought is that people on the whole do not say things without reason; and so one's default position should be that there is something in what they say – however confused and jumbled it might be (cf. *EE* I.6.1216b26–35): if so, one's basic target is not to refute people, but to refine and release the truth there is in what they say.

6 One way this comes up is in the contrast between indicative and gerundive readings: cf. Kenny (1965–6) and Mackie (1977: ch.1, s.11).

7 The difference between eternal and contingent (VI.1); the absoluteness of the one versus the species-specificity of the other (cf. VI.7); the aim of truth versus truth in conjunction with correct desire: VI.2; cf. *De An.* III.10.433a14–15.

References

Ackrill, J. L. 1972: "Aristotle on 'Good' and the Categories." In S. M. Stern, A. Hourani, and V. Brown (eds), *Islamic Philosophy and the Classical Tradition*, pp. 17–25. Oxford: Oxford University Press; reprinted in J. Barnes, M. Schofield, and R. Sorabji (eds), *Articles on Aristotle*, vol. 2, pp. 17–24. London: Duckworth, 1977.

Anscombe, G. E. M. 1958: "Modern Moral Philosophy," *Philosophy* 33: 1–19; reprinted in *Collected Papers*, vol. 3, pp. 26–42. Oxford: Blackwell, 1981.

Broadie, S. 1987: "The Problem of Practical Intellect in Aristotle's Ethics," *Proceedings of the Boston Area Colloquium in Ancient Philosophy* 3: 229–52.

Clark, S. 1975: *Aristotle's Man*. Oxford: Oxford University Press.

Engels, F. 1845: *The Condition of the Working Class in England in 1844*. Oxford: Oxford University Press, 1999.

Hardie, W. F. R. 1968: *Aristotle's Ethical Theory*. Oxford: Oxford University Press.

Kenny, A. 1965–6: "Aristotle on Happiness," *Proceedings of the Aristotelian Society* 66: 51–61; reprinted in J. Barnes, M. Schofield, and R. Sorabji (eds), *Articles on Aristotle*, vol. 2, 25–32. London: Duckworth, 1977.

Kraut, R. 1989: *Aristotle on the Human Good*. Princeton, NJ: Princeton University Press.

—1997: *Aristotle, Politics Books VII and VIII*. Oxford: Oxford University Press.

Lawrence, G. 1993a: "Aristotle and the Ideal Life," *Philosophical Review* 102: 1–34.

—1993b: "Reflection, Practice, and Ethical Skepticism," *Pacific Philosophical Quarterly* 74: 289–361.

—1997: "Nonaggregatability, Inclusiveness, and the Theory of Focal Value: *Nicomachean Ethics* 1.7.1097b16–20," *Phronesis* 42: 32–76.

—2001: "The Function of the Function Argument," *Ancient Philosophy* 21: 445–75.

—2004a: "Reason, Intention, and Choice." In A. O'Hear (ed.), *Modern Moral Philosophy*, pp. 265–300. Cambridge: Cambridge University Press.

—2004b: "Snakes in Paradise: Problems in the Ideal Life," *Southern Journal of Philosophy* 43: 126–65.

Louden, R. 1984: "On Some Vices of Virtue Ethics," *American Philosophical Quarterly* 21: 227–36.

McDowell, J. 1980: "The Role of *Eudaimonia* in Aristotle's Ethics," *Proceedings of the African Association* 15; reprinted in A. O. Rorty (ed.), *Essays on Aristotle's Ethics*, pp. 359–76. Berkeley, CA: University of California Press, 1980.

—1986: "Critical Notice of *Ethics and the Limits of Philosophy*, by B. Williams," *Mind* 95: 377–86.

Mackie, J. L. 1977: *Ethics: Inventing Right and Wrong*. Harmondsworth: Penguin.

Marx, K. 1894: *Capital*, volume 3. Harmondsworth: Penguin, 1991.

Thompson, M. 1993: "The Representation of Life." In R. Hursthouse, G. Lawrence, and W. Quinn (eds), *Virtues and Reasons*, pp. 247–96. Oxford: Oxford University Press.

Wiggins, D. 1976: "Truth, Invention and the Meaning of Life," *Proceedings of the British Academy* 62: 331–78; reprinted in *Needs, Values, Truth*, 3rd edn, pp. 87–138. Oxford: Oxford University Press, 1998.

Wilkes, K. 1978: "The Good Man and the Good for Man in Aristotle's Ethics," *Mind* 87: 553–71; reprinted in A. O. Rorty (ed.), *Essays on Aristotle's Ethics*, pp. 341–58. Berkeley, CA: University of California Press, 1980.

Williams, B. 1985: *Ethics and the Limits of Philosophy*. Cambridge, MA: Harvard University Press.

Wittgenstein, L. 1953: *Philosophical Investigations*. Oxford: Blackwell.

Further reading

Annas, J. 1993: *The Morality of Happiness*. Oxford: Oxford University Press.

Broadie, S. 1991: *Ethics with Aristotle*. Oxford: Oxford University Press.

Cooper, J. 1975: *Reason and Human Good in Aristotle*. Cambridge, MA: Harvard University Press.

—1999: *Reason and Emotion*. Princeton, NJ: Princeton University Press.

Foot, P. 2001: *Natural Goodness*. Oxford: Oxford University Press.

Reeve, C. D. C. 1992: *The Practices of Reason*. Oxford: Oxford University Press.

—2000: *Substantial Knowledge: Aristotle's Metaphysics*. Indianapolis, IN: Hackett.

Santas, G. 2001: *Goodness and Justice*. Oxford: Blackwell.

White, N. 2002: *Individual and Conflict in Greek Ethics*. Oxford: Oxford University Press.

3

How to Justify Ethical Propositions: Aristotle's Method

Richard Kraut

The Nature of Aristotelian Justification

When we reflect about how we should lead our lives – the undertaking for which the *Nicomachean Ethics* is meant as a guide – our reflections can easily turn on themselves, leading us to raise questions about the nature of the very process we are going through. We will want to know, for example, not only what is good, but how we can know what is good, how we can find out more about it, and how we can identify defects in our current notions and practices. It is not surprising, then, that the opening chapters of Aristotle's treatise are filled with remarks about the proper ambitions of ethical inquiry, the shape an ethical theory should take, and how the success of such an enterprise should be evaluated. Aristotle and his audience seek not only first-order truths about practical matters, but also a second-order account of how first-order ethical propositions are to be justified.

Justification, as it is sometimes conceived, is an attempt to find common ground with a real or imagined intellectual opponent, and to derive the proposition whose justification is in question from that real or hypothetical consensus.[1] Whether or not someone else is actually convinced by the justification one constructs, the person who possesses such an argument can reasonably say that the selected target audience *ought* to be convinced because anyone who starts from the common core of accepted beliefs ought to arrive at the disputed conclusion one is attempting to prove. But Aristotle is not seeking that kind of justification for his ethical theory. What he looks for, instead, is a way we can assure *ourselves* (not someone who might or does disagree with us) that whatever changes we make in our practical beliefs, as a result of inquiry, are changes for the better. Ethical inquiry is an attempt to become wiser about practical matters, not to convince a real or hypothetical opponent. It is part of one's own intellectual and moral development, not an attempt to convince a hypothetical skeptic or to bring it about that more people think and act as one does.

The *Endoxa*

We will begin our discussion of Aristotle's proposed method for testing the truth of ethical propositions with a remark he makes, in *NE* VII.1, about the procedure to be used for investigating the phenomenon of *akrasia* (reason's lack of self-control):

> One should, as one does in other cases, set out what seems to be the case [*ta phainomena*] and, by first going through the puzzles [*diaporēsantes*], in this way prove, first and foremost, all of the reputable opinions [*endoxa*] about these ways of being affected [that is, about *akrasia* and other conditions of the soul], but if not all, then most, and the most authoritative; for if the difficulties are solved and the reputable opinions [*endoxa*] remain, adequate proof has been given. (VII.1.1145b2–7)

In studying *any* subject, practical or theoretical, the first step must be to set out – that is, to take careful notice of – "what seems to be the case" (*ta phainomena*) in the area under investigation. But what seems to be the case *to whom?* Only to the person who is conducting the inquiry, whether or not anyone else agrees? That would be a precarious position from which to begin. Why suppose that one has an exclusive monopoly on the truth? At the other extreme, it would be preposterous to begin by paying careful attention *only* to what seems to be the case to *everyone*. Why should disputed opinions receive no attention?

Something between these extremes is what Aristotle has in mind, as we can see by turning to a term that occurs twice in this passage: *endoxa* (the singular is *endoxon*). Aristotle says that if the *endoxa* (translated "reputable opinions")[2] remain – that is, if they survive the tests that are applied to them – then they have been adequately proved. But what are *endoxa?*

The Greek term, as its translation suggests, refers to what is thought by certain people who actually exist. *Endoxa*, in other words, are not mere hypotheses invented by some investigator. (A *doxa* is someone's opinion, and so *endoxa* are opinions of a certain kind.) They are opinions accepted by certain people – but by whom? Translating *endoxa* as "reputable opinions" implies that they are reputable people – but who are they, and what confers their reputability on them?

Aristotle answers these questions at the beginning of his *Topics*. "*Endoxa* are what appears [*dokounta*] to all or to most or to the wise, and in these cases [i.e. the wise], to all of them, or most, or the ones who are most notable and reputable [*endoxois*]" (I.1.100b21–3). If a view is held by everyone, or most people, or a small number – namely those who have a deserved reputation for wisdom (regardless of whether all such people agree, or whether a view is in the minority) – then it will, according to *Topics* I.1, qualify as an *endoxon*; and, according to *NE* VII.1, it should therefore be given some attention at the beginning of an investigation.

We can safely assume that in our *NE* VII.1 passage Aristotle uses his terms *phainomena* and *endoxa* to refer to the same things. In effect, then, his idea is that the first thing we must do, when we investigate a subject, is to pay careful attention to what seems to be the case either to everyone, or to most people, or to a special and much smaller group – those who have already studied the subject. Furthermore, as our *Topics* I.1 passage indicates, when we take into account the views of "the wise" – those who have gone before us in the study of our subject – we should certainly pay attention to views held by all of them. But if they disagree (as often happens), we are not to dismiss them all. Rather, we should attend to both quantitative and qualitative factors: what do most of them say? What is believed by those of them who, though in the minority, have the greatest renown and reputation?

Aristotle does not say *why* we should begin an inquiry with a survey of these opinions, but we can make a good guess about what he has in mind. Throughout his writings, he upholds the idea that the human mind, when properly oriented, is apt to find the truth, or something close to it. "One should pay attention to the undemonstrated sayings and opinions of those who have experience and are old, or to those who have practical wisdom, no less than to demonstrations. For, because they have an eye that derives from their experience, they see rightly" (*NE* VI.11.1143b11–14). Certain insights come to people as a matter of course, as they accumulate experience; they may not have made a philosophical study of ethics, but we should pay careful attention to what they say and think.

That does not require an ethical investigator to consider everything that has been thought by anyone at all. The opinions of those who are mad, or of mere children, will not qualify as *endoxa*, since they lack the basic reasonableness of normal adults and are severely limited in their experience (*EE* I.3.1214b28–9). But when a view is held by a large number of ordinary adults, who have some experience of a certain matter, then a student of ethics must consider the possibility that they may be right.

The same respect is due to those who have made a special study of a subject, and are not merely relying on their untutored impressions: even if these theorists disagree, as often happens, it is unlikely that each of them is completely mistaken. Rather, we should expect each to have achieved some grasp, however partial, of the truth (*Meta.* II.1.993a30–b4).

At *Rhetoric* I.1.1355a15–18, Aristotle says: "Human beings have a nature that is sufficient for the truth, and for the most part they arrive at the truth. That is why someone who is good at hitting upon the *endoxa* is equally good at hitting upon the truth." This confirms our conjecture that what lies behind his insistence that intellectual investigations begin with *endoxa* is his confidence in the adequacy of ordinary human faculties and truth-gathering processes – reason, perception, experience, science – for getting at the truth or what is not too great a deviation from the truth.

Although everything that is an *endoxon* has something to recommend it, because it is something that seems to be the case to some possessor of truths who has at least minimal competence, that does not guarantee that all of the *endoxa* are error-free. Aristotle's idea is that if one collects enough of them carefully, omitting the opinions of those who are in no position to grasp the truth, and casting a wide net that includes the views of those who have made a special study of the subject under investigation, as well as ordinary people who have some experience of it, then one will have enough material to make further progress. The task of the theoretician is to turn that mixed bag of truths, near-truths, and falsehoods – all of them deriving from "reputable" sources (that is, from people who have some claim to credibility) – into something that meets higher intellectual standards.

It is remarkable that Aristotle takes the views of those who are not wise – that is, those who have not systematically investigated a subject – to be no less worthy of attention than those who are wise. Why not instead give greater weight to the views of those who have studied a subject than to those who have not? In fact, why pay any attention at all to the views of the many, when the subject under investigation has been given a more thorough examination by others?

Aristotle gives us a clue about how he would answer this question when he denies that great misfortunes are compatible with happiness. He says: "No one would consider happy a person living in that way – unless he were defending a thesis at all costs" (*NE* I.5.1096a2). The term Aristotle uses here (*thesis*: matching precisely our English term) has a technical sense: it is the paradoxical supposition of a well-known philosopher (*Topics* I.11.104b18). When arguing with each other, philosophers have been known to persist in defending, at great length, propositions that, to most people, lack all plausibility. (Socrates and some of his followers really did believe that one could be happy in the midst of misfortunes; see *Gorgias* 470e, 507c.) Perhaps it really appears, to some of those who spend their lives philosophizing, that these propositions are true. But if so, they appear true only because the philosophers defending themselves in debate want them to be true; and they want this because they want to win arguments. There is, in other words, a danger that those who specialize in a subject will become so eager to win points over other specialists, or to achieve prominence, that they will lose their ability to tell what is reasonable to believe. That is perhaps why Aristotle's method requires the student of a subject to pay attention not only to what seems to be the case to specialists in a field, but also to what seems to be the case to ordinary people. Doing so serves as a safeguard against the possibility that a subject has been badly distorted by the professional ambitions of those who specialize in it. Philosophers *can* be right when they hold views that conflict with common opinion (that is why Aristotle's method requires us to consult their opinions), but they can also be wrong. And so it is part of proper method to pay attention to the views of both specialists and non-specialists.

We should remind ourselves that for Aristotle consulting *endoxa* is a general method, not one to be used solely for investigating ethical topics: "One should, *as one does in other cases*, set out what seems to be the case . . ." (*NE* VII.1.1145b2–3, emphasis added). He employs it repeatedly in his investigations of theoretical matters (see, for example, his discussion of place at *Physics* IV.1–5). That sets Aristotle's conception of methodology apart from many epistemologies of the modern era, for it has become a prevalent belief, in educated circles, that when a discipline takes the form of a science, then those who are learning that subject should pay attention only to the ideas of those who have distinguished themselves as specialists, and can ignore whatever views ordinary people have about the matter. Even so, in many areas of intellectual inquiry, we heed Aristotle's requirement that students of a subject look both to the wise and to the many. In particular, when we study moral philosophy, it is reasonable to throw into the mixture of opinions that we take seriously not only the theories of those who have spent their lives studying the subject, but also the common moral consciousness, not only of our time and place, but of other times and places as well. If we have Aristotle's motives, our purpose, in casting such a wide net, will not be to construct arguments that should be found convincing to all those who differ from us, but to borrow material from them that might be useful in improving our conception of how we should live.

Aporia

We should turn now to the second stage of the endoxic method (as I shall call it – sometimes it is called Aristotle's "dialectical" method): "going through the puzzles" (*diaporēsantes*). That verb is cognate to a noun occurring frequently in Aristotle's writings: *aporia*, which means "without a way of passing through." In common parlance, a person who encounters an *aporia* is in difficult straits or lacks the resources (often monetary) needed to achieve his aims. What Aristotle means, then, is that, after we have set out the *phainomena* – what seems to be the case to the many or the wise – we will notice that we are in intellectual straits: it will not be immediately apparent to us how we are to proceed. Why so? When we look at the passages in which Aristotle lays out the *aporiai* (plural of *aporia*) for his audience (for example: *NE* I.10–11, II.4, III.4, V.9–11, VI.12–13, VII.2, VIII.1, IX.8–9, and X.2–3), it becomes evident that he thinks that a survey of the *endoxa* yields many apparent contradictions. Those who have made a special study of a subject do not agree among themselves; or there are apparent conflicts between what most ordinary people think and the opinions held by those who have a reputation for wisdom. So, "going through the puzzles" is a process of taking note of all the apparent conflicts thrown up by a survey of the *endoxa*.

This is a process that Aristotle describes most fully at *Metaphysics* III.1. He says there that intellectual progress is never a smooth and unproblematic accumulation of beliefs, but rather resembles a process of finding oneself tied up; in order to see how to escape and go forward, one must take a careful look at what is holding one back (III.1.995b24–33). The student must be genuinely puzzled, for otherwise he will not know what the goal of his inquiry is (995a34–995b2). The difficulties can be solved only by someone who understands them, and this involves seeing what is meant by each of the conflicting opinions, and looking for reasons for each of them. Aristotle likens the process to that of rendering a judgment in a law court after listening to each of the contending parties (995b2–4). But of course there is this difference between the role of the juror and that of the student investigating a subject: the student must regard the intellectual puzzles of his subject as his own, not someone else's. The parties whose views are examined by the endoxic method may or may not be aware of the fact that their beliefs are in conflict with those of others. They themselves may not be puzzled at all. But the student who is learning a subject *is* aware of these conflicts, and (as the legal analogy implies) must study, with an open mind and some degree of sympathy, the point of view of each party. If a student does not feel, at this initial stage of his inquiry, that there is no way out – that he is tied down – then he will not subsequently do a good job of studying the puzzles with a view to solving them. Accordingly, the most accomplished statement of the puzzles, on the part of a teacher, would be one that induces a student to be genuinely perplexed.

How are these puzzles, created by the apparent conflict among *endoxa*, to be resolved? If there were a mechanical method for doing so, the study of ethics and all of the other branches of philosophy would long ago have become a routine of little interest. We must instead fall back on trial and error, and there is no guarantee that, with sufficient effort, we will be able to see our way through the difficulties. Yet Aristotle does try to offer some help: he advises us to look for a particular kind of deficiency in the *endoxa*, namely, their ambiguity. It is built into the nature of language that what we say can be construed in different ways, and yet it is all too easy (especially if one has no special training) to overlook this fact. Because of the multivocity of our terms, what we say can be both true and false: true, when construed in one way; false, when construed differently. And that provides the best way of showing that seemingly opposed *endoxa* are not really in conflict, when properly construed. This is presumably what Aristotle has in mind when he says that, after one sets out the *phainomena*, one's first priority should be to prove *all* of the *endoxa*; but that, if one cannot do so, then one must settle for proving most of them (*NE* VII.1.1145b2–7). One can prove that all of the *endoxa* are correct by showing that all of the conflicts among them are merely apparent; in that case, what each party holds to be true really is true, when interpreted in the right way. But Aristotle warns us in this same passage that it is not always possible for all of the *endoxa* to survive examination. What appears true to some people may simply be false, even though these people have some credibility in the area under investigation.

It might seem that there is a tension in Aristotle's description of the endoxic method. As we have seen, he holds that students of a subject must be genuinely puzzled by the difficulties of their subject before they can make progress (*Meta.* III.1.995a34–b2). But, on the other hand, he thinks that a good way to solve these problems is to recognize that words are said in many ways. There would indeed be a conflict between these two aspects of the endoxic method if the several different ways in which a word is used were immediately apparent to anyone who uses it. For then every linguistically competent student of a subject would immediately see how to resolve the apparent conflicts among the *endoxa*; there would be no sense of puzzlement, and no need to search for a solution. What Aristotle must be assuming, then, is that there is no way of detecting the multivocity of our words prior to engaging in the endoxic method. It is by noticing apparent conflicts among the *endoxa*, and looking for a way in which all of them can be construed as true, that we recognize the many different ways in which words are used.

Finding and Explaining Errors

Aristotle says that our first priority should be to preserve *all* of the *endoxa*; that is, to find a way to show that apparently conflicting views are really in agreement, when their ambiguities are recognized. But he realizes that a search for ambiguity may properly come to the conclusion that there is none, and in that case, at least one of two conflicting reputable opinions must be false. (Aristotle allows for this possibility when he says, at *NE* VII.1.1145b5: "if not all, then most." That is, if we cannot prove that all of the *endoxa* are true, then our second-best alternative is to prove that most of them are true.) In these cases, we have to make a decision: which of the two contradictory *endoxa* are we to accept? How does Aristotle think we should go about answering that question?

He says: "if not all, then most, and the most authoritative" (VII.1.1145b5–6), but what makes certain reputable opinions most authoritative (*kuriōtata*)? When we look at what Aristotle's writings do, when they encounter conflicting reputable opinions that cannot be reconciled by the recognition of ambiguities, what we find is that he evaluates the strength of the arguments that can be found for and against the conflicting options. For example: some say that pleasure is the good, but the arguments they use merely show that it is a good, not the good (*NE* X.2.1172b23–8). Aristotle does not say "this reputable should be accepted and that one rejected because the first seems more plausible than the second." He does not appeal to some notion of intuitive plausibility. Rather, he argues for one position and against the other. So, for an *endoxon* to be "most authoritative" is simply for it to be the one that is best supported by argument. Its authority comes from the fact that it wins us over.

But Aristotle thinks there is more for us to do, after we have decided which of two conflicting appearances to accept as true. For even if we have made the correct decision about where the strongest argument lies, it may reasonably be asked why those whose views we reject have gone wrong about this matter. After all, they have some claim to credibility – otherwise what they think would not have been counted as an *endoxon*. And so, if we want to be completely confident that we are right to reject their view, we should find a good explanation of what has led them astray. As Aristotle says: "One should not only say what is true but also what causes error. For this contributes to confidence. For when it becomes apparent why something that is not true seems true, that makes one all the more confident . . ." (*NE* VII.14.1154a22–5). He then continues with an explanation of why it appears to certain people that the pleasures of the body are the ones that are always to be chosen over all others. Such pleasures, he says, are over-valued because they drive out pain, and those who over-estimate their worth cannot experience different kinds of pleasures (VII.12.1153a26–13.1153b21). It is common for mistakes to be made by those who concentrate on too limited a range of cases; that often leads them to accept a generalization that does not in fact hold true of other sorts of cases. People have mistaken views about friendship, for example, because they are most familiar with only one of its kinds (IX.9.1169b22–8). Or their experience of good and bad fortune makes them assume that this is precisely what happiness and unhappiness are. They overlook the possibility that although good fortune is needed for happiness and misfortune can undermine happiness, these are not themselves the same thing as happiness (I.8.1099b6–8). Those who have some minimal degree of familiarity with a subject are very unlikely to be entirely mistaken about it (*Meta.* II.1.993a30–b7), and when they do make mistakes, something is distorting their judgment or preventing them from seeing the truth. A student of a subject should be able to give a good explanation of what is misleading those who are the victims of false appearances. He should be able to say not only "they give bad arguments" or "they give no arguments," but also "here is what they are right about" and "here is why they have not been convinced by the arguments that lead to the right conclusions."

When each conflicting appearance can be accepted as in a way correct, though in a way incorrect, we already have an explanation of why there is disagreement and error: the conflicting parties have not recognized the ambiguity of the terms they use. But, as we have seen, Aristotle thinks that sometimes one of two conflicting appearances is true and the other false. In these cases, ambiguity is not the cause of error, but it will turn out that there is some other explanation of why what seems to be the case to a competent adult who has some experience of a subject is not the case.

None of this commits Aristotle to saying that those whose views are mistaken can or should be led by students of a subject to acknowledge their errors. It is one thing for A to have a good explanation about why B's views are defective; another for A to change B's mind, or to be able to do so. B may stubbornly insist that he is right and refuse to re-think the matter with an open mind; or his experience may be too limited, and he may resist recognizing that fact; or he may lack the mental acuity needed to recognize a point of view superior to his own. Someone who uses a term that is said in many ways may fail to recognize the ambiguity, even after it is pointed out to him; he might insist that what he says is unequivocally true and that what his opponent says has no merit. Aristotle's method requires students of a subject to investigate that subject with an open mind, and to give a fair hearing to different points of view, but that does not mean that they must convince everyone else who has a view about the matter, or that those others be persuadable.

Can There be Proof in Ethics?

One other term that Aristotle uses in *NE* VII.1.1145b2–7 calls for comment: the goal of his method is to *prove* that something is the case. "One should . . . set out what seems to be the case [*ta phainomena*] and, in this way, prove . . . the reputable opinions . . . for if the difficulties are solved and the reputable opinions remain, adequate proof has been given" (1145b2–7). The goal of his method is to bring about a transformation in one's mind: one starts entirely with what merely appears to be the case (*ta phainomena*), but in the end the propositions one is left with have all been proven (*deiknunai* and *dedigmenon* are Aristotle's words here) to be so.

The Greek words Aristotle uses here, an infinitive and participle derived from *deiknumi*, are not technical terms of logic or philosophy. When I *deiknumi* a proposition, I show that it is true. This showing or proving is the payoff of all inquiry: investigation is a goal-directed process that aims at transforming appearances into propositions that have earned greater confidence because they – at any rate, the ones that have made it through the process – have been proven. The fact that what students of a subject begin with has, at that stage, the status of an appearance does not mean that, at that point, those students are or should be in doubt about whether those appearances are true. Some appearances may be universally accepted and utterly plausible; even so, at the beginning of the process of inquiry, they have not yet been shown to be the case. They acquire that status only when one's inquiry has come to a successful conclusion, and all of the puzzles of a field have been resolved.

We can see why Aristotle thinks that someone who has inquired in the way he recommends has made considerable intellectual progress. Such a student has consulted a wide range of opinions, and has sought conflicting points of view. From all of this diverse and sometimes conflicting material, he has constructed a consistent body of beliefs. He now has a better understanding of the truth than he had before because he has detected ambiguities that are hidden below the surface of language. Because of his open-minded encounter with conflicting beliefs, he has been forced to sort out truth from error by evaluating the merits of conflicting arguments. And when he comes to the conclusion that some people are mistaken, he has arrived at an explanation of why they have failed to arrive at the truth, as he has.

But has anything been *proved*? It might be thought that in ethics proof (as we use that notion) is simply not possible, and that moral philosophy is never entitled to use that word about what can be achieved by even the best of methods. According to this way of thinking, beliefs about ethical matters may be justified to a degree, and some people's beliefs might be more justified than others. But in order to *prove* anything in ethics, one would have to do more than what Aristotle's endoxic method can do – and, it might be claimed, ethics is not a field in which more can be accomplished.

Someone who thinks that ethics is circumscribed in this way will find some support for this view in a well-known passage near the end of the first chapter of John Stuart Mill's *Utilitarianism*. Speaking of his "Utilitarian or Happiness theory," he says that he will give "such proof as it is susceptible of," but then adds immediately: "It is evident that this cannot be proof in the ordinary and popular meaning of the term. Questions of ultimate ends are not amenable to direct proof. Whatever can be proved to be good, must be so by being shown to be a means to something admitted to be good without proof." Later in the paragraph, he softens his stance:

> There is a larger meaning of the word proof, in which this question is as amenable to it as any other of the disputed questions of philosophy. The subject is within the cognisance of the rational faculty; and neither does that faculty deal with it solely in the way of intuition. Considerations may be presented capable of determining the intellect either to give or withhold its assent to the doctrine; and this is equivalent to proof. (Mill 2002: 236–7)

In saying this, Mill is conceding that although it is possible to have some degree of justification for one's beliefs about practical matters (which inevitably turn on "questions of ultimate ends"), that level of justification is lower than is available in other matters. After all, "proof" would be a useless term if we never allowed ourselves to use it on the grounds that *no* proposition is susceptible of proof. In the "ordinary popular meaning of the term," we can prove many things: for example, I can prove to you that I am wearing a wrist watch by rolling up my sleeve and showing it to you. Perhaps Mill's idea is that a proof must be not merely persuasive to some degree, but so persuasive as to be compelling and conclusive. And, Mill might hold, in practical matters, that standard of argumentation can be achieved only when one is selecting the best means to an end, but never when one is deciding among ends. He thinks he can offer some plausible considerations about what our highest end should be, but that the nature of his subject matter makes it impossible for argumentation, his own or anyone else's, to do better than that.

That puts Mill in a precarious position. He is not merely conceding that the arguments *he* will be using are not compelling; rather, his claim is that there can be no compelling arguments here – even though there can be (and he will himself offer) arguments that are sufficiently persuasive. But if, as Mill insists, it is possible to give good arguments about what one's ultimate end should be, then how do we know, in advance, that there can be no arguments about this topic that are conclusive and compelling – arguments that anyone would call a "proof" in the "ordinary popular meaning of the term"?

It is important, in any case, to see that Aristotle does not downgrade the intellectual credentials of ethical inquiry, as Mill does. He takes himself to have a *general* method of establishing what is true – general in that it applies to many subjects, not just to ethics – and believes that there is nothing about ethics that makes it a subject in which argumentation, by its very nature, has a lower claim to acceptability than argumentation in other areas. He concedes that there are many who cannot be persuaded by ethical arguments (*NE* X.9.1179b4–20); but that, he thinks, shows the defects of the audience, not of ethical theory itself. Whatever he means by saying that the goal of the endoxic method is to prove (*deiknunai*) that something is the case, he believes that such an achievement is no less possible in practical philosophy than it is in other intellectual endeavors. Mill's "proof" of his principle is achievable only by lowering the standards of what can be expected of a proof. Aristotle, by contrast, sees no reason to admit that in ethics we must work with a lower standard of justification than is used in other fields of inquiry.

He is well aware that others disagree. "Fine and just things, which are what political science studies, have much variety and variation, and so they seem to exist only by convention, and not by nature" (*NE* I.3.1094b16–17). Aristotle accepts the premise – there is considerable variation among fine and just things – but rejects the conclusion, drawn by others, that all such matters are arbitrary human inventions that lack a grounding in anything that exists independently of our customs, beliefs, and feelings. (That is what it would mean for them to exist by convention alone, and not by nature.) The claim that ethics rests on convention alone is nonetheless an *endoxon*: this is the way it seems to some people, including those who have a reputation for wisdom. (A sophist of the fifth century, Antiphon, took the demands of justice to be merely conventional, and contrasted them with the urgent demands of nature.) And so it is not a view that Aristotle can or wishes to dismiss without a hearing. But to show that conventionalism in ethics is mistaken, and why it is mistaken, requires the whole of his ethical theory. We will come to see, when we study this subject, just what sort of variation there is in this field. And, if Aristotle's treatment of the subject is successful, we will come to the conclusion that, in spite of this variation, we are no less able to establish ethical truths than we are able to establish truths in other fields of inquiry. The test of a claim made about "fine and just things" is not whether it accords with the laws or the accepted customs of this or that community (as we would have to agree, if these things exist only by convention), but whether it can survive the same intellectual tests that the endoxic method prescribes for every inquiry. Ethical beliefs can be proven, no less than can mathematical, biological, or astronomical beliefs.

It might nonetheless seem that Aristotle is, after all, downgrading the level of justification achievable by ethical inquiry because, soon after he notes that such matters seem to rest on convention alone, he insists that "we must be satisfied, in speaking about such matters and proceeding from them, to show [*endeiknusthai*] what is true roughly and in outline, and when discussing matters that hold for the most part, and proceeding from them, to arrive at conclusions of the same sort" (*NE* I.3.1094b19–22). He goes on to say that it is the mark of an educated person to seek as much precision in each field as the nature of the field allows: we should not accept mere persuasiveness from a mathematician nor demand demonstrations from an orator (b24–8).

That might make it sound as though Aristotle, like Mill, is asking his audience to place lower intellectual demands on the arguments of ethical inquiry than those of other studies. But we should be careful here. Aristotle is not judging the credentials of ethics and other fields by applying to them all a single kind of measure or standard. On the contrary, he is asking us to have different expectations of different fields: not *higher* standards for some fields and *lower* for others, but *different* standards. An orator who addressed his audience by putting everything into the form of deductive arguments would fail miserably – he would be a worse orator, not a better one – but this does not mean that the intellectual standards by which oratory is to be assessed result from a lowering of the standards used elsewhere. Similarly, although ethics must be judged by the same endoxic method used to prove truths in every other field, we should recognize that it is a field in which some of what is shown to be true holds only for the most part. Aristotle has already given two examples in *NE* I.3: to show his agreement with the thesis that political science studies a subject in which there is great variation, he notes that "some have been destroyed by their wealth, and others by their courage" (1094b18–19). Wealth and courage do not generally result in death – but they sometimes do. Ethics is a field in which we must expect to find many generalizations of that sort, but Aristotle's point is not that we must therefore think the less of the power of ethical argumentation. Ethics, when it is assessed by the endoxic method, is not made inferior to other subjects by the fact that many of its statements exhibit this kind of imprecision.

Foundationalism

When Aristotle describes the endoxic method, in *NE* VII.1, he mentions only some of the procedures that he thinks intellectual investigations should follow. We have already considered one of his omissions: when an inquirer thinks that an *endoxon* is false, he should explain how it happened that a competent thinker went astray. Now let us consider another omission: Aristotle believes that an ethical inquiry, like any other methodical intellectual investigation, should impose a hierarchical order on the propositions it studies. That requirement is imposed in the following terms:

> Let it not escape our notice that arguments from starting-points differ from those that are towards starting-points . . . For one should start from things that are known, but things are known in two ways: for some are known to us, others known without qualification. Presumably, then, we should start with what is known to us. (*NE* I.4.1095a30–b4)

When Aristotle says here that "we should start with what is known to us," he is presumably referring to the first stage of the endoxic method, in which an inquirer sets out what seems to be the case by taking careful note of the reputable opinions. To say that these things are "known to us" is to give them a low cognitive status – one that is compatible with their being false. Aristotle simply means that we are familiar with or can easily become familiar with these sorts of starting-points; that is precisely why this is the best place to start an inquiry. Our passage then says that we should proceed from these humble beginnings to something else that also deserves to be called a starting-point (*archē*: "principle" is an alternative translation). That second starting-point – the one toward which we proceed – will be something that has higher credentials, as an object of cognition, than the lowly appearances with which we began. If someone acquires knowledge of that higher starting-point, his state of mind counts as knowledge in the strict sense. (Here again we should draw a contrast with Mill: in saying that the principle of utility cannot be proved, he is implying that it cannot be known in the strictest sense.) That highest starting-point, toward which inquiry moves from its humble origins, is the sort of thing that can shed light on all of the other parts of our inquiry. It is precisely because it has this great power to illuminate that an inquirer who comes to understand it must be credited as having knowledge in the strict sense.

This is what Aristotle is getting at when he calls our attention to the difference between proceeding toward and proceeding from a starting-point: after we use our initial starting-points to arrive at the highest principle, we do not stop there, but proceed in the opposite direction, using our understanding of the highest principle as a way of acquiring a better understanding of those initial assumptions from which we began. The analogy Aristotle uses in this passage (omitted from the quotation above) confirms that this is what he has in mind: "just as the path on a race course goes from the starting line to the far end, or back again" (I.4.1095a33–b2). Here he is referring to the fact that races were run up and down a linear path, the "far end" being the place at which the competitors would reverse course and race back to their initial starting-point. This implies that after an inquirer reaches the starting-point that is knowable without qualification, his next step is to return to the material with which he started. There would be no point in doing that unless his understanding of the starting-point that is unqualifiedly knowable can give him a better grasp than he once had of the humble starting-points of his inquiry.

It is understandable that Aristotle's statement of the endoxic method in *NE* VII.1 omits this fundamental aspect of his conception of how ethics should be studied. For, at that point in his treatise, he wants to alert his audience only to those points about method that will guide his discussion of *akrasia*. The proper understanding of *akrasia* merely has to reconcile the conflicting appearances and solve the puzzles that have been raised about this mental phenomenon. Not every aspect of ethics that requires study (virtue, responsibility, *akrasia*, pleasure, friendship) has its own special starting-point, and so the treatment of *akrasia* in Book VII does not look for one. Rather, Aristotle's idea is that ethics as a whole does have a fundamental starting-point, the understanding of which will illuminate the entire subject. It is not enough for students of ethics (or any other subject) to iron out inconsistencies and decide which among conflicting opinions is better supported by argument. They must also arrange their beliefs in an architectonic order: lower-order beliefs must be supported by their relationship to the fundamental principle of the entire subject.

There is no mystery about what Aristotle has in mind: the fundamental starting-point that must be understood by the student of ethics, the concept on which all others depend, is the good of human beings. In order to understand the linchpin of the whole subject, the student must make his way through the *endoxa* and *aporiai*. He must show how the *aporiai* can be solved by a proper understanding of the human good, and how most, if not all, of the *endoxa* can be preserved; but, in addition, he must return to the starting-points of his inquiry – the *endoxa* he used as stepping stones on his path to the good – and come to a better understanding of them.

This is the program carried out throughout the *Nicomachean Ethics*. Aristotle begins with one of the *phainomena*, that is, with what seems, or is thought, to be the case: "every craft and inquiry, and similarly every action and decision, seems [*dokei*; "is thought" is an alternative translation] to aim at some good" (I.1.1094a1–2); and he soon adds many more. He notes that the widely accepted opinion that happiness (*eudaimonia*) is the highest good leaves unresolved the conflict between different ideas about what happiness is (I.4); and he then surveys some of the most prevalent conceptions of happiness (I.5), giving considerable attention to the view, held by some of those who have a reputation for wisdom, that the good is what all good things have in common (I.6). He uses some of the *phainomena* as premises in an argument for the conclusion that excellent activity of the rational soul is what happiness is (I.7). And, in the chapters that follow, he claims that by upholding this conception of the human good, much of what is said about happiness can be preserved (I.8), several *aporiai* can be solved (I.10–11), and explanations for erroneous views can be found (I.8).

But Aristotle does not think that the task of defending a conception of the good has been completed by the end of Book I, for the systematic ordering that he thinks any legitimate subject must exhibit has not yet been achieved. The student of ethics, having moved from humble starting-points to the grand principle of the subject, and having seen that principle pass several important tests, now has to reverse direction, and undertake an elaborate investigation of the things that were taken for granted but not well understood at the beginning of the inquiry. It was assumed, in Book I, that such things as virtue, pleasure, friendship, and the like, were good, but at that point there was only a partial understanding of what these things are, and therefore only a partial understanding of why they are good. Aristotle's project, in the rest of the *Nicomachean Ethics*, beyond Book I, is to use his conception of happiness as virtuous activity supported by adequate resources to illuminate all of the other topics that belong to the subject. It is only when that elaborate project comes to an end that the full merits of its foundational premise – the thesis that the human good is virtuous activity – can be fully appreciated, and it is only then that the student of ethics can be said to have knowledge in the strict sense.

The Test of Experience

In fact, Aristotle claims that even after students of ethics have moved from the foundational premise of the subject back through all of the assumptions from which they began their inquiry, they must subject the whole theory to one further test. Surveying it as a whole, they must be confident that it is not merely satisfactory as a theory, but also satisfactory when assessed against their experience of life. After pointing out that his conception of happiness corresponds to the ideas proposed by wise men – Solon and Anaxagoras, for example – he adds:

> But although these things too instill some confidence, the truth in practical matters is judged on the basis of the facts and of life. For they are authoritative in these matters. One should examine what was said earlier by bringing it up against the facts [*erga*] and life, and if they harmonize with the facts, one must accept it, but if they are out of harmony, then one must reject one's statements. (*NE* X.8.1179a17–22)

This is a point Aristotle made earlier, in his discussion of pleasure: no argument that condemns all pleasure as evil will carry conviction, he says, because "arguments about what has to do with feelings and actions are less persuasive than facts." Accordingly, when arguments conflict with what we perceive or feel (*aisthēsis*), we should reject the arguments as unsound (X.1.1172a34–b1). We noted earlier (in the second section) that the endoxic method requires a student to pay serious attention not only to the arguments of those who have a reputation for wisdom, but also to what seems to be the case to a large number of non-specialists. Arguments can lead us astray, and so we should ask ourselves whether they clash with widely held views of those who are guided not by theory but by their everyday perceptions and experience. Similarly, Aristotle holds that even after a theory has been shown to preserve a large number of reputable opinions – those of the wise as well as the many – it needs to correspond to something that lies outside of theory and argumentation. Even if it passes the many intellectual tests to which it is put, an ethical theory must fit with the way we experience our lives. For ethics has to do not merely with the way we should think, but the way we should feel.

Accordingly, if on certain occasions we cannot but feel pleasure, or anger, or fear, then we are right to reject a theory, however well supported, that tells us that we must never have such feelings. Here we have a test of an ethical theory that is specific to ethics, and does not apply to all systematic intellectual undertakings. A theory about plants does not have to be lived – it only has to be believed – and so the only tests it must pass are intellectual tests. A theory about how human life should be lived has to pass those same kinds of tests, but must do more: it has to be something we can live with.

Is Aristotle's Method too Conservative?

The endoxic method, as we have been using the term, is a procedure that includes not only the tests mentioned in *NE* VII.1 (setting out the *endoxa*, going through the *aporiai*, saving as many *endoxa* as possible by finding ambiguities or assessing competing arguments, solving the puzzles), but all of the others that we have noted: explaining falsehood, moving toward a foundational starting-point and then returning to one's initial assumptions, and (a procedure peculiar to practical subjects) confirming one's results by seeing how well they match felt experience. It may seem that such a method, however valuable it may be in expunging false-hoods, is unduly conservative because it restricts one's study of a subject to options that have already been surveyed by other people. One collects the views of others, including the many and the wise; when apparent conflicts among them are noticed, one decides among them, or shows that the conflicts are merely apparent; and one puts the surviving *endoxa* into a certain order of explanation, making sure that the whole fits with one's feelings. But all that can emerge from this process, it might be said, are the views of others: nothing new can be discovered. Of course, in order to decide between conflicting beliefs, one must search for arguments. But presumably those arguments must rely on premises that are themselves reputable opinions; that is, opinions already held by someone or other. It might seem that the student of ethics cannot bring to bear on the subject any new ideas, however plausible they may seem to him. He might fail to find the foundational principle that illuminates all other aspects of the subject because he is not allowed to bring into his collection of *endoxa* ideas that occur to him alone.

But this charge of conservatism overlooks the fact that Aristotle himself – or anyone else who is studying ethics and proposing an ethical theory – has standing as someone whose views are reputable and should therefore be included among the *endoxa*. He is someone who is making a special study of ethics, and so he is a member of the class of those who are wise. (We have all along been assuming that what the wise think may turn out to be false, without it ceasing to be the case that they are wise. It is their study of a subject that makes them wise, not the acceptability of their views.) What seems true to anyone who is undertaking a serious investigation of a subject thereby becomes a candidate for consideration by the endoxic method. For example, when Aristotle opens the *Nicomachean Ethics* with the observation that every craft, inquiry, action, and decision seems to aim at what is good, he makes an observation that perhaps no one else had previously formulated, but the novelty of that observation would not disqualify it from counting as an appearance that plays an important theoretical role. Because it is an *endoxon*, it can be used as a premise in arguments for or against some other *endoxon*. An ethical theorist guided by the endoxic method can be as inventive as he likes: he can discover ideas no one has ever had before, and he can use these to reach conclusions that no one has ever reached before. Aristotle's own theory certainly does not confine itself to working with premises that had already been stated by others. His foundational premise – that the human good consists in excellent activity of the rational soul, adequately supplied by resources, over a sufficient length of time – had never been formulated before, and the arguments for it rely on premises that are original to Aristotle.

Accordingly, when ethical inquiry gives itself the task of setting out, as an initial step, what seems to be the case, there will be two different ways for an investigator to assure himself that a proposition falls into this category. One is partly sociological: one looks not at the credibility of the proposition that is held to be true, but rather at the credentials of those who hold it to be true. Here the questions to be asked are: do those who believe this proposition have some credibility? Are they in any position to assess the truth about this matter? However, as we have just seen, there is a second way in which an investigator can assure himself that a proposition should be included among the *endoxa*: he may rightly take himself to be someone who has some access to what is true in this area of investigation, and the proposition under consideration may strike him as having some claim to credibility. He considers what seems true to him, and for him to do this, he must confront the proposition under consideration, and to assess its plausibility. That is quite different from what happens when he looks at the views that others hold, and asks whether those appearances should be included among the *endoxa*. When he does this, he does not ask "is this plausible?" but only "is this person someone whose views deserve consideration?" For if he were to restrict the *endoxa* to those appearances that he himself finds plausible, he would lose one of the greatest benefits of the endoxic method: he would not be forcing himself to give a fair hearing to ideas that do not represent the way things seem to him. His examination would only be self-examination – or, at any rate, it would be an examination of what he has in common with others, at the initial stage of inquiry. For the endoxic method to be a valuable tool of inquiry, it must avoid two methodological extremes: a refusal to consider what strikes one as plausible, on the grounds that no one else has ever had that thought; and a refusal to consider any idea of another person, on the grounds that it seems to one to have no initial plausibility.

Once we recognize that the endoxic method (construed broadly, to include procedures not mentioned in *NE* VII.1) allows an inquirer to introduce novel views into the class of *endoxa*, it becomes clear that Aristotle does not use or need any other method than this. He can bring to ethical theory ideas that represent his own peculiar take on the subject – ideas, for example, that stem from his theories about the soul, or the divine, or nature, or any other matter. Arguments drawn from premises peculiar to Aristotle's way of thinking should not be contrasted with his employment of the endoxic method, but should be seen as part of the material to which the method is applied.

"Brought up Well"

After Aristotle distinguishes, in *NE* I.4, between two different kinds of starting-points – those known to us, and those known without qualification (1095a30–b3) – he adds: "So, presumably we should begin with things known to us." That is why one needs to have been "brought up well in one's habits," if one is to be a good student of this subject (b4–6). For, he adds a few lines later, someone who has learned good habits at an early stage in his life "either has these starting-points, or can easily get them" (b7–8). A person who has developed bad habits will not be able to acquire a satisfactory ethical theory.

This is not a statement about the method to be used in ethical theory – proper habituation when one is a child is *not* part of the endoxic method – but it implies that certain people will never be able to use the method successfully. There will be something missing from what they bring to the method: they will not have all of the starting-points on which a justified ethical theory rests. But why not? Why cannot they do as well as others at making a survey of the reputable opinions? After all, someone who has received a poor moral education as a child is able to determine what seems to be the case to the many and to the wise, and to look for ambiguities or arguments that would resolve or adjudicate the differences between competing *endoxa*.

Aristotle must be assuming here that the materials with which the endoxic method works include how things appear *to oneself* – not merely how they seem to the many and to the wise. If someone has been brought up badly, and does not recognize this fact about himself, many propositions will strike him as being true, and will be included among the data of his ethical theory, even though they do not deserve serious consideration. The very fact that he has been badly raised means that he does not have sufficient competence, in the study of ethics, to be counted among those whose opinions merit careful scrutiny. And so, even if he tries to make progress in his study of ethics, by paying attention to what others think, he will be handicapped by his attention to data that ought to be excluded.

Aristotle is perhaps also assuming that part of what it is to be brought up in bad habits is to give little or no weight to the way things seem to others but not to oneself. If a child is allowed to treat others as inferior to himself – as people to be manipulated but not loved, honored, or respected – he will not want to acquire, and perhaps cannot acquire, the intellectual habits needed for the successful use of the endoxic method. There will be very few, if any, opinions besides his own that he will think deserve a hearing, and when the opinions of others conflict with what immediately strikes him as being the case, he is likely to dismiss them. If he comes to the study of ethics with the fixed view that any sacrifice he makes in his power, wealth, and status is inherently a loss in his well-being, or if he finds nothing appealing and pleasant about doing well at a task undertaken for the sake of others, then his ears will be closed to the suggestion that there are other things, beyond his ken, that are no less valuable, perhaps more valuable, than what strikes him as good. His ethical views might be internally consistent. But he lacks the breadth of ethical experience and intellectual objectivity that are needed, if one is to employ the endoxic method successfully and arrive at a genuine proof of what one believes.

Aristotle's thesis that a student of ethics must have been brought up in good habits is an application of a more general thesis that he insists upon. In any subject that we successfully study, we must bring to it more than the minimal mental skills that are needed to be counted as a person engaged in the process of thinking. We must also have a proper exposure to the phenomena under investigation: we must go beyond surveying what others think, and must become familiar with the realities that constitute the subject matter of those opinions. The foundational principles of every science are derived from what we learn through experience (*An. Pr.* I.30.46a17–21; cf. *Gen. An.* III.10.760b27–33; *Cael.* III.7.306a7–17). Every inquiry, not just ethical inquiry, will properly refuse to give credence to the views of those who have too little acquaintance with the phenomena under investigation. It is not unique to ethical theory that the propositions it contains would not be accepted by all rational human beings.

It would be a mistake to think that it is a defect in an ethical theory if it does not offer arguments about good and bad that ought to be accepted by any thinking person on the basis of propositions that that person already accepts. That would be a defect if the only reason to look for justification is to change the mind of someone with whom one disagrees. But Aristotelian justification, we noted from the start, is not an attempt to persuade others with whom one disagrees, or to transform imaginary ethical skeptics into good people. It is an attempt to get outside oneself and to learn from others, but its goal is to achieve justified *self*-assurance, not consensus.

Notes

1 "[J]ustification is addressed to others who disagree with us, and therefore it must always proceed from some consensus, that is, from premises that we and others publicly recognize as true . . ." (Rawls 1999: 394).
2 Alternative translations: "common opinions," "received opinions," "the views people hold." But, as we will see, an opinion can be included among the *endoxa* even if it is not widely accepted (therefore not "common"), and even if it is unique to the inquirer (therefore not "received" or something "people hold"). "Reputable opinions" is defended in Barnes (1980: 498–500).

References

Barnes, J. 1980: "Aristotle and the Methods of Ethics," *Revue Internationale de Philosophie* 37: 490–511.
Mill, J. S. 2002: *The Basic Writings of John Stuart Mill.* New York: Random House.
Rawls, J. 1999: "Justice as Fairness: Political not Metaphysical." In S. Freeman (ed.), *Collected Papers*, pp. 388–414. Cambridge, MA: Harvard University Press.

Further reading

Irwin, T. H. 1981: "Aristotle's Methods of Ethics". In D. J. O'Meara (ed.), *Studies in Aristotle*, pp. 193–223. Washington, DC: Catholic University of America Press.
—1988: *Aristotle's First Principles.* Oxford: Clarendon Press.
Kraut, R. 1998: "Aristotle on Method and Moral Education." In Jyl Gentzler (ed.), *Method in Ancient Philosophy*, pp. 271–90. Oxford: Clarendon Press.
Reeve, C. D. C. 1992: *Practices of Reason.* Oxford: Clarendon Press.

4

The Central Doctrine of the Mean

Rosalind Hursthouse

I shall claim that there is no truth in the doctrine of the mean as ordinarily understood, and that we see this quite clearly when we look at it outside the context of Aristotle's ethical works. The latter contain, however, at least two great insights expressed in its terms which I aim to extract from the distorting influence of Aristotle's use of the doctrine. One may even be called "the central doctrine of the mean" when that is understood in a certain way – hence the title of this chapter.

The Doctrine of the Mean outside Aristotle's Ethical Works

Intimations of the doctrine of the mean – in literature, medicine, mathematics, and philosophy – seem to have been around well before Aristotle, but, for the purposes of this chapter, I will go no further back than Plato, beginning with the *Statesman* at 283c–284e. Here "length and brevity, and excess and deficiency in general" are said to be the things to which the art of measurement relates (283c), and a distinction is drawn between measuring things that are large and small relative to each other, and things that exceed and fall short of "the due measure" (*metrion*) (283e). Later on, this is filled out as measuring the "lengths, depths, breadths, and speeds of things in relation to what is opposed to them" and measuring "in relation to what is in due measure/moderate [*metrion*], what is proper/ fitting/appropriate [*prepon*], what is fitting/ appropriate/timely/ [*kairon*], what is as it ought to be/fitting/necessary [*deon*] and whatever avoids the extremes for the mean [*meson*]" (284e). (Note that, although some translators render the verb not as "measuring" but as "assessing," and "the due measure" in a variety of ways, including "the mean," it is the same root all the way through.) Plato also claims that exceeding and falling short of due measure is what differentiates bad and good people (283e), and that, quite generally, all skills produce all the good and fine things they do produce by avoiding the more and the less than what is in due measure and by preserving measure (284a–b).

As features of the doctrine of the mean here we might note: (1) the casual alignment of the large and the small, or the more and the less, with excess and deficiency (note that the ambiguity of the Greek comparative, which can mean both "more" and "too much," makes the transition much easier than it is in English); (2) the assumption that the mean (what is in due measure) is, or is what produces, what is good or best; (3) the assumption that all the skills, including virtue, aim at the mean; and (4) the plethora of terms – *metrion, prepon, kairon,* which in different contexts are more or less interchangeable – with which it is associated.

In the *Statesman,* where he is discussing the art of statesmanship, Plato does not extend the scope of the doctrine beyond the skills. But in the *Timaeus* (for example, at 31b–32b, 35a, 36a, 43d) it acquires the status of a general explanatory principle, shaping the account of the creation of the cosmic body and the cosmic soul, the human soul, the human body, the physiology of sensation, and the nature of disease. As Tracy (1969) and Hutchinson (1988) note, in the latter area at least, Plato is in close accord with prevailing medical theory, which held (roughly, with many variations) that health depended on the due measure/proportion/balance/ moderate blending of opposites, and that illness came about through their excess and deficiency. So, as further features of the doctrine of the mean, we might note: (5) its status as a principle in medical theory; and, more generally; (6) its status as a quite general explanatory or "scientific" principle.

Aristotle, of course, does not share Plato's passion for the mathematical knowledge that the latter no doubt has in mind when he speaks of the mean in relation to the art of measurement in the *Statesman;* nor will he be so inclined to think of *metrion* and *to mesotēs* as mathematical proportion as Plato is clearly doing in the *Timaeus.* Indeed, translators note that Aristotle uses *to meson* and *to mesotēs* indifferently in the ethical works. But he takes over from Plato all the features of the doctrine identified above.

Here he is, for example, confidently employing it as a general explanatory principle in *De Generatione et Corruptione:*

> [so that] hot and cold, unless they are equally balanced, are transformed into one another [and all other contraries behave in a similar way]. It is thus, then, that in the first place the elements are transformed; and that out of the elements there come to be flesh and bones and the like – the hot becoming cold and the cold becoming hot when they have been brought to the mean . . . Similarly, it is in virtue of a mean condition that the dry and the moist and the rest produce flesh and bone and the remaining compounds. (*Gen. et Corr.* II.7.334b22–30)

And in *De Anima:* "the sense itself is a mean [*mesotēs*] between any two opposite qualities" (II.11.424a2). And in *De Generatione Animalium:*

for all things that come into being as products of art or nature exist in virtue of a certain proportion [*logō tini*]. Now if the hot preponderates too much [is excessive?] it dries up the liquid; and if it is very deficient it does not solidify it; whereas for the artistic or natural product it is necessary to have this proportion – the proportion of the mean. (*Gen. An.* IV.2.767a16–20)

And in *De Partibus Animalium,* where the general principle "now everything has need of an opposite as counterbalance in order that they may achieve moderation/due measure and a mean [*metrion kai ton meson*]; for it is the mean that contains the substance and proper proportion and not either of the extremes apart from it" (II.13.652b17–20), leads him to his unfortunate conclusions about the three cavities or chambers in the heart:

Of these three cavities it is the right that has the most abundant and the hottest blood . . . the left cavity has the least blood of all and the coldest; while in the middle [*meson*] cavity the blood, as regards quantity and heat, is intermediate [*mesai*] between the other two, being however of purer quality than either. (*Part. An.* III.4.667a1–4)

In fact, it has a big influence on Aristotle's views on the heart, with respect to the three cavities in *Historia Animalium*: "the right-hand one the largest of the three, the left-hand one the smallest and the middle one [*mesen*] intermediate in size [*meson*]" (*Hist. An.* I.17.496a20–22), and its being the most important organ of the body, in *Parva Naturalia*: "this [the common organ] must be situated midway [*meson*] between what is called 'before' and 'behind' . . . further, since in all living beings the body is divided into upper and lower . . . clearly the nutritive principle must be situated midway [*en mesō*] between these regions" (467b28–468a1), and on his views on blood in *Historia Animalium*: "In very young animals it resembles ichor and is abundant; in the old it is thick and black and scarce; and in middle-aged animals its qualities are intermediate [*mesos*]" (*Hist. An.* III.19.521a32–b4).

What should our reaction be to Aristotle's use of the doctrine of the mean in his ethical works once we have noted the way it operates in his "scientific" works? (The passages above are not the only examples.) Urmson (1973) defended what, following Curzer (1996), we may call a "quantitative" interpretation of the doctrine of the mean. Aristotle says that our target is to act and feel "on the right occasions, about/with respect to the right people, for the right reasons, in the right way or manner [which] is the mean and best" (*NE* II.6.1106b21–2). According to the quantitative interpretation, we read this as claiming that our target is to act and feel on neither too many nor too few occasions, about or toward neither too many nor too few things, with respect to neither too many nor too few people, for neither too many nor too few reasons (or "with neither too many nor too few ends"). The quantitative match for "in the right way or manner" has to be varied from case to case rather than having a general statement. We may have, for example, "neither a too great (strong/intense) nor a too small (weak) an extent/amount" or "neither too quickly nor too slowly" or "for neither too long nor too short a time" and so on.

Urmson also claimed that the doctrine thus interpreted was by and large true and "at the very least . . . a substantial doctrine worthy of Aristotle's genius." I claimed (Hursthouse 1980–81) that, on the contrary, thus interpreted it was not only a false doctrine but a silly one and hence should not be ascribed to Aristotle. And, more recently, Curzer, defending an "Urmsonian" interpretation, claims that it is a plausible view and hence that (given the textual support) there is no reason not to ascribe it to Aristotle.

Claiming that (under a certain interpretation) the doctrine is true, or at least plausible, is, for Urmson and Curzer, obviously important. Most of us who work on Aristotle's ethics do so in the belief that he is one of the greatest moral philosophers of all time and that (almost) everything he says about ethics is either true or worth taking very seriously indeed. So we are reluctant to attribute implausible views to him, and that was why I was so puzzled, in the earlier article, by the prevalence in the ethical works of the implausible (in my view) talk about excess and deficiency, and Aristotle's commitment to the mysterious mathematical symmetry of there being precisely two, opposed, vices corresponding to each virtue (Hursthouse 1980–81: 59–60). But that was before I became aware of the use of the doctrine of the mean as a general explanatory principle in Aristotle's predecessors and in his other works. This casts it in an entirely different light.

If we regard it as peculiar to the ethical works, we are bound to take it seriously, to work on the assumption that there must be something right about *it*, just as we assume that there must be something right about the idea that we have a final end, or that *megalopsuchia* is a virtue. (Of course, we may try our hardest and still fail to find anything, but we remain open to the possibility that someone else will do better.) But if it is not peculiar to the ethical works, the principle of charity does not apply to it in the same way. We do not work on the assumption that there must always be something right in what Aristotle says in his "scientific" works, and we assess the doctrine of the mean as it appears there on its own merits.

When we do, it stands revealed as, to be blunt, simply whacky, emphatically not a principle "worthy of his genius" (in contrast, say, to his hylomorphism) but a bit of completely misguided science-cum-metaphysics that appears to have been generally accepted in his day. Thereby we lose any reason to try to find something right about *it* in the ethical works, for its presence there, notwithstanding its implausibility, is no longer puzzling. Suppose we think we have, as a general principle that can be fruitfully employed in physiology, physics, and astronomy, in medicine and other *technai*, the view that what is "intermediate" – a *meson*, a mean, a midpoint – is appropriate, fitting, in due measure, right, correct, best, a stable mode of being. Suppose further that we have a tradition of seeing some version of this principle as obviously applicable in ethics. Then nothing could be more natural than to apply it there.

However, the fact that the doctrine is simply whacky, that there is no truth in it whatsoever, does not entail that its application in ethics will always have the factitious effect it has when Aristotle so hilariously applies it to the heart. If you lack knowledge in a particular area, the doctrine will be no aid in discovering the truth. But if you already know a lot about an area, as we assume Aristotle does about ethics, its effect may be fairly harmless. What you know may sometimes be expressed in slightly distorting terms but its truth should still be discernible. And it is the true things Aristotle has to tell us about ethics that we should be looking for, not any truth in the doctrine of the mean itself. So let us have a look.

The "Mean" in Action and Feeling

I shall begin by going through the bits of the texts where the doctrine of the mean is first introduced, being skeptical about whether it is contributing anything useful. The introduction of the doctrine of the mean in the *Eudemian Ethics* is abrupt. Although the preceding discussion has covered what virtue is produced and destroyed by, and drawn the analogy between virtue and physical well-being, it has done so with no mention at all of the mean, excess, and deficiency. These all appear for the first time at II.3.1220b21–3 in relation to "every divisible continuum." Before this, the emphasis is not on what is between excess and deficiency but on what is best: "the best disposition is produced by the best things . . . for example, the best exertions and nourishment are those from which physical well-being results" (II.1.1220a22–5).

The parallel passages in the *Nicomachean Ethics* (II.2.1104a12–26) do bring in the doctrine in relation to what virtue is produced and destroyed by and the medical analogy, where it is said that "the sorts of things we are talking about," viz. excellences of character, are destroyed by deficiency and excess, just as strength and health are. Excessive training and too little training destroy our strength; eating or drinking too much (and presumably too little) destroy our health, whereas drinking and eating "proportionate" (*symmetra*) amounts creates, increases, and preserves it. Similarly (II.2.1104a25–6), temperance and courage are destroyed by excess and deficiency and preserved by "what is intermediate" (*mesotētos*).

Is this an improvement on the *Eudemian Ethics*? Does the doctrine of the mean contribute anything true? At first sight, one might suppose so. When we first read these remarks about strength and health, they may seem obviously true and in an obviously quantitative way. We all know middle-aged people who are undermining their strength and health by taking no exercise and eating gross amounts; we have all at least heard of people who damaged their strength and health by becoming fitness or diet freaks. But a moment's thought should remind us of cases where strength and health have been harmed not by large or small quantities of exercise or food but by the wrong quality of either. This person destroyed their knee joints by jogging on hard pavements; that one undermined their health by eating only fast foods. Having the right – the best – sorts of food or exercise is at least as important as avoiding excess and deficiency; that is why we need doctors and trainers to tell us what they are.

How does the analogy work with respect to the individual virtues? The discussions in the *Nicomachean Ethics* that precede the formal introduction of the doctrine of the mean in II.6 nearly all look quantitative. But it also seems that there the examples are being only sketched in, and will be qualified later. (As he emphasizes at II.7.1107b14, "we are talking in outline, and giving the main points, contenting ourselves with just that.") So he says "Someone who runs away from everything, out of fear and withstands nothing becomes cowardly" (II.2.1104a21–2), but, as he will say later (VII.5.1149a6ff), "someone who is naturally of the sort to fear anything – even a mouse rustling – is cowardly with a brutish cowardice." Similarly, someone "who is frightened of nothing at all and advances in the face of just anything becomes rash" (II.2.1104a22–3), but he will say later (III.7.1115b25–6) that someone who fears nothing would be "some sort of madman." Again, at II.4.1105b2 he says that we are badly disposed in relation to becoming angry if we are violently or sluggishly disposed, but well disposed if we are disposed "in an intermediate way." But when he comes to discuss "mildness" in IV.5, he makes it clear that "violently" and "sluggishly" are not the only ways of being badly disposed.

So the quantitative remarks that express the doctrine of the mean are to be qualified later in non-quantitative terms. Finally, from these early passages, we should note that at II.3.1104b21 Aristotle says, in relation to pleasures and pains, that people become bad "by pursuing them and running away from them," but here he does not say "too much" or "to excess" as the doctrine of the mean would suggest. He says, rather, that we become bad "through pursuing or avoiding the wrong ones, or at the wrong time, or in the wrong manner or in any of the other ways distinguished by reason." And he will have no reason to qualify that later.

The formal introduction of the doctrine in both texts draws a distinction between one sort of mean and the mean "relative to us." This distinction is proper to the Aristotelian ethics, not a variant on the doctrine of the mean to be found in his other works, so it is worth looking carefully at what it is doing and whether the doctrine of the mean is contributing anything in this unique context.

Apart from telling us that "the mean relative to us is best" and that it also produces the best state (II.3.1220b26–30), the *Eudemian Ethics* says nothing about what either sort of mean is, but this (we assume) is made clearer in the parallel passage which begins at *NE* II.6.1106a26, where the distinction is drawn in terms of the mean "with reference to the object" and the mean relative to us. The mean "with reference to the object" is the simplest form of *meson* or *mesotes* in mathematics, the arithmetical mean. It is what is (a) equidistant from each of its two extremes, which is (b) one and (c) the same for all. The mean "relative to us" is the sort of thing that (a) neither goes to excess nor is deficient, and this is (b) not one thing, nor (c) is it the same for all.

Does this make it clear what is meant by the mean "relative to us?" And, if so, is the illumination provided by the contrast between the (a)s or the contrast between the (b)s and (c)s? According to Woods (1982), commenting on both passages, it is provided by the (a)s. "The contrast seems to be that between the midpoint ["mean," *meson*] on some scale, which is a matter of calculation" (Woods 1982: 111) and "[t]he second mean, which involves an evaluative element, since it refers to what is intermediate between excess and defect, i.e. what avoids too much and too little, and therefore cannot be determined without reference to human needs and purposes – hence the phrase "relative to us" (Woods 1982: 112). The *EE* apparently confounds the (a)s by saying that "in every divisible continuum there exists excess, deficiency and a mean," bringing in the "evaluative element" straightaway, instead of, as the *NE* has it, "in every divisible continuum one can take more, less or an equal amount." So, on this reading, the doctrine of the mean makes a significant contribution to our understanding of the mean "relative to us" by introducing "the evaluative element."

But what I noted above as a feature of Plato's discussion of the doctrine of the mean in the *Statesman* (to which Aristotle's distinction between the two sorts of mean is standardly compared), namely the "casual alignment" of the more and the less with excess and deficiency, is not peculiar to the *EE*. Aristotle does it in the *NE* too, saying of both sorts of mean that the "equal" is a kind of mean between what exceeds and what falls short (II.6.1106a29) and, with explicit reference to the *arithmetical* mean, that it exceeds and is exceeded by the same amount. So I do not think we can claim that the mean "relative to us" introduces "an evaluative element" *because* Aristotle mentions excess and deficiency in its (a), and understand it thereby.

Let us look instead at the other clauses, (b) and (c), with which he draws the distinction in relation to the Milo example. As far as weight of food to be eaten is concerned, there is just one arithmetical mean, namely 6 minae, and, given that there is just one, it is, inevitably, "the same for all." But "relative to us," this is not so. The trainer, the expert who is "looking for the mean" will choose, say, eight for Milo and four for someone else who is just beginning their training. So "the" mean is not the same for all and hence not just one thing.

But if these – (b) (not) one thing and (c) (not) the same for all – are bound to stand or fall together, why does Aristotle explicitly mention them both? This suggests that the Milo example is rather condensed, and needs to be filled out. And the various ways in which "extremes" are to be balanced (in proportion) for a healthy, "mean" diet, described in the ancient medical literature, show us how to do so.

They took the weight and age of the patient to be relevant, for example. So, we might say, the mean relative to even one of us is not one thing, because the trainer may have prescribed 8 minae for Milo at the beginning of his training to build him up and four later on when he has put on some weight, and it is not the same for all, because he may have prescribed different amounts at corresponding times for older or younger men, for bigger or smaller ones. Unsurprisingly, they also took account of different sorts of food. We may suppose the minae of food to be eaten in a week to be made up of different proportions of, say, meat, fruit, and bread. Let us say 80 percent meat is a lot, 20 percent a little. The arithmetic mean is thus 50 percent. The trainer, seeking the mean relative to us, starts Milo off on 40 percent and rapidly raises it as his training progresses. He makes corresponding adjustments to his intake of fruit and bread. They also took account of external factors which upset the internal balance. So suppose Milo gets sick, has to stop training and, following doctor's orders, eat only bread and fruit. When he comes back, the trainer starts him off on a slightly different regimen. They took account of the seasons, so the trainer prescribes in one way in winter and another in summer and so on.

This gives real point to the double insistence of "not one thing and not the same for all." But why, one might wonder, is this called the mean relative to *us*? True, it is relative to human beings, Milo, and the other people the trainer is prescribing for, but that seems to be the accidental upshot of the fact that we happen to be talking about prescribing for them. Surely a horse-trainer, responsible for choosing the diet of the horses in his care, will not choose just one diet, nor the same for all, but prescribe differently for old Bucephalus and spirited young Pegasus and pregnant Xantippe and in summer and winter, and according to how much exercise they have been getting recently and so on. And he will, thereby, be "choosing the mean, not in the object but relative to us" – to *us*, not to horses (cf. Brown 1997). For Aristotle, echoing Plato, claims quite generally that every expert "tries to avoid excess and deficiency" and seeks the mean relative to us (*NE* II.6.1106b5–7), even though not every expert is concerned with what is the mean – and best – for some of *us* in the way Milo's trainer is.

Why, for example, does Aristotle not follow Plato further, and, having said there are two standards for more and less (and hence for what is equal or intermediate), describe his second mean as "the due measure," *to metrion*? Well, no doubt, in emphasizing that the mean "relative to us" is not one thing and not the same for all, Aristotle wants to cancel any Platonic suggestion that in ethics, or medicine or the various *technai*, there are absolute standards, that could, in theory, determine what was "the due measure" with mathematical precision (cf. Hutchinson 1988). The arithmetical mean is, as Woods says, "a matter of calculation and can therefore be ascertained in abstraction from particular circumstances" (1982: 111–12); the mean "relative to us," according to Aristotle, is not and cannot.

Why, then, does he not describe his second mean as "relative to the circumstances/the situation," which seems so obviously to be what it amounts to? One reason must surely be that "relative to the circumstances/the situation" cannot be substituted for "relative to us" when Aristotle is speaking of virtue itself as a mean disposition. But, more to the point, even in the context of the mean as something that is aimed at on a particular occasion, it cannot be relativized to circumstances without the assumption of a goal or end. I cannot aim at the mean relative to "the circumstances" or even relative to my circumstances in a vacuum, for in the absence of an end, there is no answer to the question "*Which* of the circumstances are relevant?" It is Tuesday, spring, the sun is shining, I cannot swim, I owe Jake $10.00, I am in a foreign country, Bucephalus is old, Milo is a well-trained wrestler, and so on.

But if we allow any end to be assumed, we surely depart too far from Plato's absolute standard. Aristotle agrees with him that it is the experts, and the virtuous, who succeed in hitting the mean, not just anyone; and a mean that is "relative to the circumstances," where the relevant circumstances are determined simply by the agent's personal end, collapses into something that the incompetent and the vicious could hit upon equally well. I am not interested in making a good pot; I just want to have fun trying. Given my end, I will hit "the mean relative to the circumstances" if it does not take me too long to make a sort of pot (and I don't accidentally make rather a good one too quickly in which case I shall want to have another go) and I don't get too dirty or tired trying, and don't waste too much expensive clay. And, similarly, bent on deceiving my husband, I aim at "the mean relative to the circumstances," being careful to avoid appearing too eager that he should go away for a week, without annoying him by appearing too indifferent, arranging to visit some of his relatives but not so many as to leave me without enough time to spend with my lover – and may well hit upon it readily enough if I am clever. So the mean "relative to the circumstances" is either not the sort of thing that can ever be aimed at, or, if made sufficiently determinate to be a target by the individual agent's end(s), can be hit upon by the incompetent and vicious as well as by the experts and the virtuous.

So we have to find a way of reading "relative to us" that preserves the second mean as something that the experts and the virtuous hit upon and others miss. And the right place to look is surely at the beginning of Book I. The various experts, and the virtuous, all have certain ends. All of these are the sorts of goods a human being can pursue in action or possess, human goods or "goods for us." And it is these human goods, things that are good relative to us humans, that, taken as ends, determine which circumstances are relevant. In the context of the *technai*, the expert's end – about which *qua* expert he does not deliberate – is to bring about a good product, a good pot or a good (strong, healthy) wrestler or horse. Thereby, experts aim at the mean "relative to us," but the dilettante does not. In the context of ethics, our end just is *the* human good, the supreme good "relative to us"; this involves excellent activity, acting and feeling well, and it is that, assumed as an end, that determines which circumstances are relevant for the agent in a given situation.

The mean "relative to us" in the ethical context is, then, the mean relative to such relevant circumstances. (Modern philosophers might say relative to "the morally relevant circumstances" but, in practice, that phrase tends to have a much narrower extension.) Of course, such circumstances may well include facts about the agent. As Brown (1997: 86) says, "obviously whether your conduct counts as generous depends on how wealthy you are" and whether or not I am being intemperate in eating a large steak may be determined by how big I am and/or whether or not I am in training. But even if I am huge, and in training, eating the steak will fail to be a temperate act if I turn a blind eye to the fact that it was someone else's meal or that I can't afford it, disregarding the constraints of the other virtues (cf. *NE* III.11.1119a19–20). The mean "relative to us" in the ethical context can be one thing for you and another for me if (but only if) a difference between us makes for different circumstances relevant to the end of each of us acting or feeling well.

So, yes, the contrast between the arithmetical mean and the mean "relative to us" *is* a contrast between what is always the same and what varies according to the particular circumstances; and, yes, the mean "relative to us" cannot be determined without reference to human goods. But our understanding of this all-important notion of the mean "relative to us" does not come from the mention of "excess and deficiency," nor is its "evaluative element" (if that is what the reference to "human goods" is) introduced by it. So the doctrine of the mean has contributed nothing to it.

The Central Doctrine of the Mean

Whenever Milo's trainer prescribes, he is aiming at the mean "relative to us." He is thereby, on each occasion, aiming at something determined by the variety of circumstances which are relevant, given his end *qua* trainer. And, when the example is filled out, we can see that this could be summed up by saying that his target is to prescribe the right food, in the right amounts, on the right occasions, in relation to the right people, for the right reason. This is strictly parallel to the II.6.1106b21–2 passage, according to which our target is to act and feel "on the right occasions, about/with respect to the right things, with respect to the right people, for the right reasons, in the right way or manner."

For reasons that will emerge later, I shall label this passage – the above claim about our target, just as it stands with no mention of the mean, excess, or deficiency – "the central doctrine." My question now is: is anything illuminating added by *calling* this a doctrine of the mean and adding (as Aristotle does) that our target is hitting upon "what is the mean and best?"

The passage gives us what Curzer (1996) has helpfully described as five "parameters" with respect to which we can go wrong in a particular sphere. According to the Urmsonian quantitative interpretation, calling our target a mean does add something because it tells us that the "*deon*" in the various parameters (the right Xs or the Xs one should) can be captured in terms of too many/much and too few/little, and so on. In my earlier article (Hursthouse 1980–81) I argued against that view. I began by pointing out that the very idea that the concept of "for the right aim or reason" could be captured by specifying it as a mean between too many and too few aims or reasons had only to be stated to be seen as absurd. I then went on to argue, with respect to courage, temperance, and "patience," that the *qualitative* idea that there are objects or people it is right to fear or enjoy or be angry with and others it is wrong to fear or enjoy or be angry with could not be captured in such a way either. Fearing the right objects with respect to courage, for example, is not a matter of fearing, say, three, some figure in a mean between two or less and four or more. I do not count as courageous if, as a "fearless phobic," the three objects I fear are the dark, enclosed spaces, and mice, but only if they are death, pain, and physical damage – the *right* objects. I now want to pursue this line of thought.

What the quantitative version of the doctrine of the mean latches on to is that almost all the parameters seem to be straightforwardly measurable. Objects, people, and occasions are, surely, all countable, and amount, though not countable, is still measurable. (The exception is "way or manner." "How did she do it? Let me count the ways." Or should I measure them? How do I set about doing either?) And, it seems, where you can count or measure, you can mark points on a continuum from 0 to whatever, and thereby speak of the more or "too much" and the less or "too little" and the mean between them.

But this is where the talk about the mean misleads us, for counting objects is not a straightforward matter; nor, in the present context, is counting people. How both are to be counted is determined by how they are described. At the buffet, there are, let us say, six plates-of-food, but only three plates-of-healthy-food. At the bar, there are six bottles-of-wine but only two bottles-of-wine-within-my-means. At the party, there are ten people other than me, but only five men and only one unmarried one. In my city, there are, no doubt, scores of people of bad character, dozens of people I associate with, eight friends of mine, six people to whom I owe money, just one man who is my father. And right and wrong objects and people are identified as such by the way they are described.

The wrong objects enjoyed by the self-indulgent are "the pleasures of the table, wine and sex" (VII.14.1154a18) that fall under the descriptions "unhealthy," "unaffordable," or "contrary to what is fine"; the right objects fall under the contrary descriptions (III.11.1119a16–20). The wrong people to whom the wasteful give, or on whom they spend, are those who fall under the descriptions "bad character" or "acquaintance rather than friend" (or "friend rather than debtor" or "someone other than one's father" [cf. IX.2.1164b30–1165a5]). The right people with whom to get angry include those who can be described as making you or people close to you a target of abuse (IV.4.1125b8–9) (though perhaps we may infer from VII.5.1149a9–14 that one's father is usually a wrong object even if he has insulted you or those close to you). Aristotle does not give us an example of wrong people, but we all know at least some of the descriptions they fall under – people who have reminded you of your obligations, people who catch you out in making a mistake, or voice mild criticism of you, people who innocently and/or unintentionally fail to give you what you want or prevent you from getting or doing what you want.

Moreover, although we, and Aristotle, find it natural to talk about fearing things or objects, "they" are much harder to identify than the things for which most people have an appetite. When we first think of the "objects" of fear, we may think in terms of things one can name and count, and thereby in terms of someone fearing numerically more, or fewer, things than the one who is courageous. Our background assumptions save us from construing Aristotle's claim that someone who is "cowardly with a brutish cowardice" fears anything (VII.5.1149a7–8) literally. We don't suppose he is afraid of flowers or books, but imagine him to be easily frightened by large dogs, noises such as the rustling of a mouse, his own shadow, being in a boat, horses, goats – as well as a whole lot of other things which are more common amongst sane adults (poverty, disease, earthquakes, death, and pain). It is not clear whom Aristotle means by the "brutish" – if he is referring to people who we would say were mentally handicapped (and also perhaps people born deaf, and neglected?) then perhaps we would just accept that they found all these things fearsome and leave it at that. But certainly when we are training ordinarily timorous children, we talk to them as though we were assuming that mostly "what they fear" is pain or some vaguely conceived sort of harm, assuring them that the large animals will not hurt them, that they are safe in the boat, and that the noises and shadows do not mean that there is "anything" there, teaching them that the right objects of fear are what can be described truly as dangerous or fearsome things (cf. III.7.1115b15).

The importance of, as we would say, getting objects under a certain description is strikingly obvious in the case of death as a fearsome object. Someone who is the sort not to fear death at all is presumably a sort of madman (III.7.1115b26) and beyond the pale as far as courage, cowardice, or rashness is concerned. But without being any sort of madman, someone may not fear death under a certain description. Death as a way of escaping from poverty, or sexual passion, may not be something the coward fears on the battlefield but something he accepts (III.7.1116a13–14). Similarly, the courageous man does not fear a death on the battlefield that can be described as fine, though he is the sort to fear death. And what "the central doctrine" latches on to is precisely the importance of describing objects and people.

Now, the interesting thing about "the central doctrine" (II.6.1106b22–3) as quoted above (p. 105) is that it is not, as it stands, a doctrine of "the mean," as we understand that phrase in English, i.e. as something lying between excess and deficiency. Taken out of its context, which indeed bristles with references to excess and deficiency, it reads naturally as suggesting, not an image of something intermediate *between* two other things, but the very image Aristotle gives us at II.9.1109a25, namely that of the center of a circle. When we think of the center of a circular target as what we are supposed to hit, we see immediately that "there are many ways of going astray . . . whereas there is only one way of getting it right (which is exactly why the one is easy and the other difficult – missing the mark is easy, but hitting it is difficult)" (II.6.1106b29–33).

The 1106b22–3 passage gives us five parameters within which we can go wrong but, as Curzer notes, "[M]ost virtues do not involve exactly these five parameters, but instead involve fewer, more, or different parameters" (1996: 130). For example, II.9.1109a27–8 adds "to the right extent" and drops "about the right things," with respect to both anger and giving and spending. The target for feeling anger seems, uniquely, to need a further parameter – right length of time. (One might think that this fell under the very general "in the right way or manner/as one should," but Aristotle is clearly not assuming that this is so, for at IV.5.1125b32–3 we get both. Nor can it fall under "to the right extent/amount" because we get failures in both at IV.5.1126a10–11.)

So we have something like six to eight parameters within which we can go wrong. Indeed, if we add in the complication of continence in the modern (not Aristotelian) sense, we may have as many as twelve to sixteen. (In the modern sense, "continence" is not restricted to the same areas as temperance [VII.4.1148b12–13], but covers, quite generally, hitting the target in action but missing it in feeling.) Thereby we arrive at what I regard as one of Aristotle's most illuminating and profound insights – the *detailed* account of why "there are many ways of going astray . . . whereas there is only one way of getting it right."

It is not only a great insight into what is required for acting (and feeling) well, it is also one of his most practically instructive, the best corrective to our tendency to think that if we, for example, tell the truth, or give a man his due, or put ourselves out of pocket, we can congratulate ourselves on having "hit the mark." It not only tells us to examine our consciences before reaching this satisfying conclusion, but also gives us, in all the different parameters, the detailed instructions about how to do so. It is not easy to delude oneself if one goes through all of them carefully, and not often that one emerges from the process convinced that one did indeed hit the mark bang on. And it thereby shows us exactly how we can set about improving ourselves.

Having got this great insight clearly in our sights, we can discard as simply distorting effects the surrounding talk of excess and deficiency. Failures to hit the center obviously cannot be divided up into those that are excessively or deficiently off target. If you are "excessively" far to the right you are thereby "deficiently" close to the left, excessively high is deficiently low and so on. No individual miss-hit is excessive rather than deficient or vice versa; *any* miss-hit is "too far" from the center. It is part and parcel of the image of hitting the center that we attach significance to landing more or less far from it, and strongly suggests that the center itself need not be a single point but, like a bull's-eye, something that we may count as having hit even if we are not precisely in the center of it (cf.

II.9.1109b19–21 and IV.5.1126a31–b4.) We are not, after all, in an area where mathematical precision is called for.

However, we need not do such violence to the text as to discard all talk about hitting the mean. For the center – the middle – of a circle, that brilliant image, *is* "a mean," a *meson* (though for reasons best known to themselves, even the most helpfully literal translators conceal this fact). Hence we can retain "the central doctrine" as, indeed, "the central doctrine of the mean" if we remember that, *qua* the center of a circle, "the mean" does not involve excess and deficiency. (One might wonder how Aristotle could have supposed for a moment that it did. Well, distressing as it is to recognize, he was prepared to assert [*De Incessu Animalium* 4.706a20–22, 5.706b10–14] that the right is superior to the left and higher to lower, so he can attach sense to missing the *meson* of a circle by going deficiently high and excessively low, deficiently right and excessively left, deficiently NNE and excessively SSW, and so on.)

Virtue as a Mean Disposition and the Moral Education of the Passions

So much for a doctrine of the mean in action and feeling. What about virtue as a mean disposition? Aristotle says in both ethical texts that virtue is a kind of mean insofar as it is effective in hitting the mean, but there is clearly more to his thought than that. Virtue as a mean disposition unavoidably has something to do with being neither excessive nor deficient. What is it?

When Aristotle comes to telling us what virtue is (*EE* II.2.1220b6ff and *NE* II.5.1105b19ff), he does not, as a modern reader might expect, say that the virtues are dispositional states (*hexeis*) with respect to actions, but that they are states "in terms of which we are well . . . disposed in relation to passions" (II.5.1105b26–7). In both texts, when he goes on to run through the virtues and vices on his chart, he begins by bringing this feature out (though he abandons it in favor of actions such as giving and spending pretty quickly). If we are to look for truths in Aristotle in relation to virtue and vice anywhere, which he expresses in terms of a mean between excess and deficiency, we should follow Curzer in concentrating on the "passion parameters." But instead of looking, as Curzer does, for truth *in* a quantitative doctrine of the mean, we should rather be looking for truths about being well disposed in relation to the passions.

Let us return again to the medical doctrine of the mean. Plato and Aristotle both accept it, and they both see the health of the human body as obviously analogous to the health or goodness of the human soul. Thereby they see goodness – virtue – as a mean state, a *meson* or *mesotēs* between opposite extremes in the soul (or the affective soul). The medical idea is that these opposing extremes must be blended or balanced or brought closer together for health, so that there is neither excess nor deficiency in any one. But instead of being distracted by excess and deficiency, let us be struck by something else. The hot and the cold, the wet and the dry (or whatever elements your fancy lights on when you use the doctrine of the mean in medicine) are all supposed to be *there* in the human body. Disease is not conceived of as an alien something getting in to the human body (as we now know it often is) but as its natural elements getting out of balance (or harmony or due measure or proportion or symmetry).

Now that is a *wonderful* way to think about virtue and being well-disposed in relation to the passions. What it yields is the idea of the human passions as natural elements in the human *psyche*, things that are supposed to be there, which can be brought into a balance or harmony – from which virtue arises. This gives substantial content to Aristotle's view that, although we do not have the virtues by nature, they are not contrary to nature; indeed, we are fitted by nature to receive them (II.1.1103a24–5). Although there are, as he notes (II.6.1107a9–11), some passions which are singled out by name as ones we should never have, for the most part the capacities to have the passions are part of the natural endowment of a psychologically healthy human child.

What is so wonderful about it can be seen if we contrast it with the different way in which Plato regards the passions in his darker moments. In *Republic* 440C–D, 588B–591D and in the *Phaedrus*, we have what Annas nicely dubs "the suppressed-beast model" (1999, where she argues forcefully that the model is atypical in Plato). The passions, or at least some of them, especially the appetites, appear as animals to be controlled, coerced, dominated, even enslaved, by superior (and unsympathetic) reason. On this picture, the virtues *are* contrary to (our) nature – not, of course, the nature of our best part, just the dirty animal part. On the other picture, our natural passions are not, in themselves, things that virtue, in the form of knowledge, has to subdue or extirpate, but the very material from which virtue is constituted. It is their presence in us, as much as our reason, that makes us "fitted by nature to receive the virtues."

If you thought of the physical appetites as something that should not be there, then you should welcome a baby who was not eager to feed, or a toddler who early became very picky about his or her food and always had to be cajoled into eating. But such a baby or child would not have the natural virtue of temperance; it would clearly be defective. Moreover, it would not be defective because it was showing early signs of tending toward the adult human vice or defect of being "insensate," but simply because it is an unhealthy animal. (What could that adult vice or defect be? Aristotle says three times that people with that disposition hardly occur [II.7.1107b7, III.11.1119a7, 1119a11] and, in the latter two, that such people are not human. Is it the doctrine of the mean [and thereby the necessity to find a vice opposed to self-indulgence] that prevents him from saying that they could not occur because they would have died in infancy? Or has he heard tales of the Indian ascetics such as Alexander later encountered, and assumed that, having initially taken pleasure in eating, they had so perverted it by their "barbarian" beliefs as to kill it off altogether? Either way, the idea that what we call, advisedly, a "normal healthy appetite" for food is supposed to be there in the human *psyche* from birth is operative.)

So, on the medical analogy, the passions that, for the most part, small children characteristically display – and their innate capacity to display a number of others later on – are an important part of what fits us to receive the virtues. This seems to be the obvious point to read into Aristotle's claim, speaking of some (it is not quite clear which) "natural" passions, that "since they are natural, they tend to the natural virtues; for, as will be said later, each virtue is found both naturally and also otherwise, viz. as including thought" (*EE* III.7.1234a27–30) and his cryptic remark that "we are just, prone to temperance, courageous and the rest from the moment we are born" (*NE* VI.13.1144b6–7).

So the medical analogy is fruitful. It yields what I believe is the second of Aristotle's great insights in ethics, namely the idea that the capacities for various passions with which we are born are part of what fits us to receive the virtues. But, as we have seen, the relation between the medical case and the insight is fortuitous; the medical doctrine of the mean is pre-scientific nonsense.

It does not follow that we should discard everything Aristotle says in relation to virtue's being "a mean between two vices" (*NE* II.6.1107a3), for here too we may find many truths. However, rather than pursuing them, I want to concentrate on this second insight, which has nothing to do with virtue being "in a mean."

The question arises: *how* do the innate capacities for the passions fit us to receive the virtues? Well, given that all passions are accompanied by pleasure or pain (II.5.1105b22), I think we may assume that, according to Aristotle, we come into the world, for the most part, set up to enjoy and be distressed by, broadly speaking, some of the right things: for example, eating, being liked or loved, and others' enjoyment, on the one hand, and physical damage, being thwarted, and others' distress or anger, on the other. However, it is also clear that this is not enough, for, notwithstanding the VI.13.1144b6–7 passage quoted above, we know we do *not* have the virtues from birth, by nature. We must be brought up from childhood onward to delight in and be distressed by the right things (II.3.1104b11–13).

As long as we remember that the claim is that our natural passions in childhood set us up to enjoy and be distressed by just *some* of the right things, *broadly speaking*, there is no contradiction here. Certain as it is that a healthy baby enjoys eating, it is equally certain that it will stick anything it can into its mouth, and as we start teaching it language, we simultaneously start teaching it that some things it wants to eat are "nasty," "dirty," "horrid," and bad and others it is not so enthusiastic about are "yummy" and good, thereby beginning to fine-tune its healthy appetite regarding right things. Certain as it is that toddlers are distressed by pain, it is equally certain that they have no instinct for danger and we have to teach them that some things that they want to approach or touch will hurt them and are bad. But such early "correct education" (II.3.1104b13) has to have something to fine-tune; it cannot, in small children, conjure enjoyment and distress about the right things out of total indifference.

It is clear that, amongst the many "right things," it is pre-eminently important that we should come to delight in doing fine/noble actions and be distressed by doing bad/base ones. But how do we get from the early tuning of toddlers' passions to the enjoyment of fine action? Just what educational program is suggested by the second insight?

"Habituation," Aristotle tells us, but, as everyone notes, he tells us little about what this involves. Moreover, the mention of punishment at II.3.1104b16–17, his consistent coupling of children with the other *logos*-lacking animals, and the suggestion at VI.13.1144b1–11 that habituated virtue can exist without something in the faculty of reason (however we take *nous* here) tends to give the impression that habituation from childhood onward is to be conceived of as analogous to horse-breaking, that is, as a mindless process of aversion therapy. (*Politics* VII.17.1336a23–VIII.5.1340b19 goes some way to correcting this impression, but is still not much help.)

But, on Aristotle's own grounds, this cannot be right. At the very least, we need something more akin to horse-whispering to get us the beginnings of taking delight in fine actions. We also need something that reflects the fact that children are not mindless and that out of this early training, not only habituated virtue but also full virtue and hence *phronesis* must somehow eventually grow. Training children to do just, temperate, and courageous acts is not like training a horse to do trotting and cantering acts, even by the horse-whispering technique. It is all bound up with thought and talk. But how?

For an answer, we naturally turn to Burnyeat's (1980) unsurpassed account of Aristotle on moral education – but only to find that his account begins after the phase we are interested in, with young men rather than with children, leaving unexplained *how*, from "being habituated to noble and just conduct," the students in Aristotle's lecture class could have acquired "the *that*," that is the ability to know "of specific actions that they are noble or just in specific circumstances" (1980: 72). Beginning at this later stage, he also leaves unexplored why, or how, early habituation brings about "a taste for . . . the pleasure of noble and just actions." It is surely unlikely that any form of habituation will do. Do we not know that children who are forbidden all sweet foods and vilified as "greedy" and "disgusting" and "bad" when caught eating them on the sly not only fail to develop any enthusiasm for temperate actions (in this area) but dislike them increasingly?

An instructive place to look is outside academic philosophy in the Virtues Project™ books (Popov 1997, 2000). These have been designed for parents and school-teachers to use to "help children develop the virtues" and have, in a short period, proved strikingly successful. The Virtues Project™ has been recognized by the United Nations as a model program for parents in all (N.B.) cultures, is currently operating in over eighty-five countries, and is being highly praised by a wide variety of schools.

It is a grassroots movement, and no doubt philosophers would cavil at some of its details. For example, it identifies fifty-two different virtues (one for each week of the year) and we might complain that some of them are indistinguishable (trustworthiness, truthfulness, honesty) and that others (cleanliness, orderliness, enthusiasm, peacefulness, humility, modesty) are not really virtues in the full Aristotelian sense. However, unlike anything we philosophers have managed to produce, it is an extremely detailed and practical educational program and well worth our attention. Its admirable pedagogy makes it clear that the actual doing of the virtuous acts is not all there is to "helping children to develop the virtues," important as this is, and contains two features that any Aristotelian should find striking.

One is the emphasis on the use, from the earliest days, of the fifty-two virtue words, often in the context of praising a child for doing something (including reacting emotionally) which can (perhaps with a little license) be correctly described by one of them, also in the context of specifically naming a virtue which is called for in a given situation. ("Please be considerate – speak quietly"; "You need perseverance here – keep trying.") However, not all the recommended uses are confined to action-reinforcement or action-guidance. For slightly older children, at school or in the home, activities and practices are outlined which develop understanding of the words. The children are encouraged to recognize and describe their practice of named virtues, and the occasions on which others have practiced them, and to describe, or play-act, what would happen if a particular virtue was not, and then was, practiced in a particular situation. (One of many interesting examples, for courage: "You see another child being teased or hurt by other children" [Popov 2000: 151]. Another, for honesty: "You say something cruel to someone and later tell yourself he deserved it" [2000:179].) And they are also encouraged to consider and discuss what a particular virtue, say courage, is, why we practice it, and how we practice it.

So, from very early days, there is the application of the relevant words to a variety of imagined as well as real instances, and the beginning of reflection, a detailed picture of how the training is bound up with thought and talk, where the talk centers around the use of virtue words *in specific circumstances*. All of this is consistent with, but provides a much-needed supplement to, philosophers' reflections; it provides a detailed answer to the question: "How do we begin to give children the *that*?"

The other striking feature of the project is that it shares the Aristotelian premise that, in some sense, we have the virtues from the moment we are born. It claims that "all children are born with all the virtues," "in potential," "waiting to grow," and that "authentic self-esteem and real happiness come *naturally* as children experience the emergence of their virtues" (Popov 1997: 2–3, emphasis added).

This premise strongly shapes the pedagogy, which stresses, constantly, looking for something to be praised by a virtue word in a child's action (or reaction) rather than for something to be condemned. But it is not, thereby, permissive. In fact, it is markedly strict, by contemporary standards, about "setting boundaries" (obedience is one of the fifty-two virtues) and offers a number of techniques for doing so by, once again, emphasizing the virtues (and hence "Dos" rather than "Don'ts"). Naming a virtue which is called for in a given situation, which I mentioned above, is one: "Please be considerate – speak quietly" rather than "Don't shout." A related one involves offering the child a choice confined by a virtue: "Which toys are you willing to be generous with and which don't you want to share?" (to a child who keeps grabbing every one off a visiting child). And then, of course, the child is praised for doing the virtuous action. Others, for older children who are behaving badly, involve asking them what virtue is called for in the situation, or what virtue they are forgetting, or what would be the V (kind, respectful, peaceful) thing to do. The idea is that, rather than making children think of themselves as bad and lacking in virtue, the way poor Huck Finn does, they are enabled to think of themselves as potentially good, as able to recognize and practice the virtues, and find pleasure in doing so.

All very homey stuff, you may say. Well, yes. It is more impressive – very impressive I thought myself – when you read the books and see Popov handling questions, but still homey. But how could bringing up children correctly be anything other than a homey business? Moreover, it encapsulates what I have claimed in this chapter are two of the insights shrouded in the doctrine of the mean: it starts by training children, not to follow general rules but to recognize their central target in particular circumstances, and it develops their natural dispositions toward virtue.

Acknowledgments

I would like to thank Karl Steven and Frans Svensson for helpful comments on an earlier draft of this chapter.

References

Annas, J. 1999: *Platonic Ethics, Old and New*. Ithaca, NY: Cornell University Press.

Brown, L. 1997: "What is 'the Mean Relative to Us' in Aristotle's Ethics?," *Phronesis* 42: 77–93.

Burnyeat, M. F. 1980: "Aristotle on Learning to be Good." In A. O. Rorty (ed.), *Essays on Aristotle's Ethics*, pp. 69–92. Berkeley, CA: University of California Press.

Curzer, H. J. 1996: "A Defense of Aristotle's Doctrine that Virtue is a Mean," *Ancient Philosophy* 16: 129–38.

Hursthouse, R. 1980–81: "A False Doctrine of the Mean," *Proceedings of the Aristotelian Society* 81: 57–72.

Hutchinson, D. S. 1988: "Doctrines of the Mean and the Debate concerning Skills in Fourth-century Medicine, Rhetoric and Ethics." In R. J. Hankinson (ed.), *Apeiron*, vol. 4: *Method, Medicine and Metaphysics*, pp. 17–52. Edmonton, Canada: Academic.

Popov, L. K. 1997: *The Family Virtues Guide*. New York: Penguin.

—2000: *The Virtues Project™ Educator's Guide*. California: Jalmar Press.

Tracy, T. 1969: *Physiological Theory and the Doctrine of the Mean in Plato and Aristotle*. Chicago: Loyola University Press.

Urmson, J. O. 1973: "Aristotle's Doctrine of the Mean," *American Philosophical Quarterly* 10: 223–30.

Woods, M. 1982: *Aristotle's Eudemian Ethics, I, II and VIII*. Oxford: Clarendon Press.

Further reading

Bosley, R., Shiner, R. A., and Sisson, J. D. (eds) 1995: *Apeiron*, vol. 4: *Aristotle, Virtue and the Mean*. Edmonton, Canada: Academic.

Broadie, S. 1991: *Ethics with Aristotle*. New York: Oxford University Press.

Hutchinson, D. S. 1986: *The Virtues of Aristotle*. London: Routledge and Kegan Paul.

Müller, A. W. 2004: "Aristotle's Conception of Ethical and Natural Virtue: How the Unity Thesis Sheds Light on the Doctrine of the Mean." In J. Szaif and M. Lutz-Bachmann (eds), *What is Good for a Human Being?*, pp. 18–53. New York: Walter de Gruyter.

Stocks, J. L. 1969: "The Golden Mean." In D. Z. Phillips (ed.), *Morality and Purpose*, pp. 82–98. London: Routledge and Kegan Paul.

5

Aristotle on Moral Virtue and the Fine

Gabriel Richardson Lear

Aside from a few arguments about the role of the arts in moral education, beauty is a relatively neglected topic in current moral philosophy. It was not always so. Hume, for instance, modeled moral sense so closely on our aesthetic taste that he readily talks of moral beauty.[1] And, according to Aristotle, not only are virtuous actions *kalon* – beautiful, fine, noble – but the virtuous agent chooses them for this reason. Obviously, these philosophers have very different conceptions of virtue; their theories of beauty are different too, for that matter. My purpose is not to assimilate Aristotle and Hume, but rather to point out that, in spite of their great differences, they both take it for granted that virtue is fine as well as good and assume that this feature is central to what virtue is. It is curious, therefore, that modern virtue ethicists, who often trace their intellectual origins to one or other of these philosophers, have made relatively little of the beauty of virtue.

In the case of Aristotle, part of the problem is that it is not at all clear what he means by saying that virtuous action is *kalon* or what motivation he is pointing to when he says that the genuinely good person acts for the sake of the *kalon*. He sometimes contrasts acting for the sake of the fine with acting for some ulterior motive (for example, *NE* III.7.1116a12–15, IV.2.1123a24–6, VIII.13.1162b36–1163a1). This suggests that acting for the sake of the fine is somehow equivalent to choosing one's action for its own sake. And, indeed, it is notable that whereas in his general description of moral virtue he stipulates that fully virtuous actions are chosen for their own sakes (*NE* II.4.1105a31–3), in the detailed discussions of the virtues in *NE* III–V he drops any mention of this and says instead that courageous or temperate or generous actions are chosen for the sake of the *kalon*. When we recall that the *kalon* is the proper object of praise (*Rhet.* I.9.1366a33–4), it is tempting to assume that Aristotle means no more than this: the good person chooses his actions for the sake of that feature that makes them fitting objects of praise, the feature that makes them good in themselves.

As we will see below, there is truth in this assumption. What makes actions fine is also (in part) what makes them worth choosing for their own sakes. That is to say, goodness and fineness in action are in large part constituted by the same property (to anticipate: being well ordered by the human good). For this reason, we can learn a great deal about what Aristotle considers intrinsically valuable in the various virtues by examining his remarks on the specific ways in which they are fine. Indeed, "fine" is an apt translation of *kalon* precisely because being *kalon* connotes being good (although not necessarily *morally* good).[2] Nevertheless, according to Aristotle the concept of the *kalon* is not the same as the concept of the good, the *agathon*. Like our word "noble," it has connotations of being grand and open to public view. And, like our word "beauty," it promises pleasure. Thus we do not exhaust Aristotle's meaning when we interpret his phrases *tou kalou heneka* and *hoti kalon*, literally "for the sake of the fine" or "because of the fine," as "for the sake of whatever makes an action worth choosing for its own sake."

I will argue that once we understand Aristotle's notion of the fine, we may be shocked anew by the degree to which he develops his moral theory from the point of view of showing its contribution to the agent's well-being. For instance, in *NE* I.10 he argues that the virtuous person can never become wretched (although he may lose his blessedness) since the fineness of his actions will always "shine through" even in the worst of circumstances (1100b30–33). Once we appreciate the pleasantness and visibility of the fine in Aristotle's account, we realize that he is suggesting (among other things) that the fineness of virtue works as a sort of balm to the unlucky person's broken spirit. He can never become wretched because the brilliance of virtuous deeds will always give him satisfaction. (Or so I will argue.) If I am right about the way in which the notion of the fine works in this and other arguments, then there is at least some reason to suppose that when he repeats that the courageous or temperate or generous person acts for the sake of the *kalon*, he has in mind, at least in part, the peculiar delight of virtuous action.

But we must be careful to identify exactly what sort of pleasure this is. Part of the challenge of interpreting Aristotle's ethics is understanding how enjoyment and pursuit of the fine is essential to genuine virtuous activity as he conceives it and is not just an "added bonus" to being good. For, as Aristotle says, the delight the virtuous person enjoys in the fine is not "a mere ornament," but is proper to virtuous activity itself (I.8.1099a15–16). Since he conceives of virtuous action as the excellent realization of our nature as rational animals, we should expect pleasure in the fine to be in some way proper to rational activity.

In what follows, I will argue that there are three central elements of the fine or beautiful as Aristotle conceives it: effective teleological order, visibility, and pleasantness. Once this conception of the fine is in place, I will argue that he has good reason to make beauty central to his account of virtue. The experience of one's actions as beautiful is, we might say, the mode of the virtuous person's apprehension of their goodness. This awareness gratifies his spirited desire to be admirable, but more important, since virtuous action is the activity of reason, it also brings the actualization of his rational soul to its fullest completion.

I will try, insofar as possible, to make this argument without presupposing a specific account of Aristotelian *eudaimonia*. The meaning of this term, its relation to the happy life, its place in practical reasoning, not to mention Aristotle's substantive account of the good it names, are all difficult and disputed issues that cannot be fully addressed in a chapter of this scope. But since, in my view, *to kalon* is a teleological notion, and since the *telos* relevant to human action is *eudaimonia*, it will be difficult to make my argument without sometimes assuming a fixed account of happiness. I trust it will not be controversial in a discussion of Aristotle's ethics to treat *eudaimonia* as the excellent activity of reasoning. At any rate, I believe the interpretation I give of the fine can be adjusted in its details to suit a variety of readings of the *NE* without substantially altering it.

To Kalon as Effective Teleological Order

Aristotle never explains in the *NE* what *to kalon* is.[3] But it is a notion he invokes in other works of practical philosophy, such as the *Politics, Poetics,* and *Rhetoric,* and also in his discussions of biology, cosmology, and mathematics. In fact, in *Metaphysics* XIII.3 he offers what looks like a quite general account of the fine: the most important forms of the *kalon* are order (*taxis*), symmetry (*summetria*), and definiteness or boundedness (*to hōrismenon*) (1078a36–b1; cf. *EE* I.8.1218a21–3).[4] This may not seem a promising starting-point for understanding what, in particular, constitutes the beauty of virtuous actions. How exactly is keeping a promise symmetrical? And (more urgent) why should its symmetry matter from the point of view of virtue? But before trying to find these properties in human action, we should first examine more closely what they amount to in other things Aristotle calls fine.

He is explicit that in the changeable world of nature, order is the arrangement of parts with reference to, or for the sake of, a common end or good. (I'll leave aside the question of how order, symmetry, and boundedness are instantiated in unchanging things.) So, for example, the whole of nature contains the good because all its parts are ordered by reference to (*pros*) the same thing, the Prime Mover, which Aristotle likens to the general of an army or the head of a household (*Meta.* XII.10.1075a11–23). What he seems to have in mind is that in all these spheres, things are ordered (and thus good) when and to the extent that they contribute to the proper goal or activity of their "ruler." The important point for us is that not only do things manifest good order when arranged for the sake of some common good; Aristotle seems to think, given the definition of the *kalon* in *Metaphysics* XIII.3, that this arrangement makes things beautiful as well. Beauty *qua* order is not a mere formal property, then, a relation of parts *to each other*. It is (or inheres in) an effective teleological arrangement (that is, it aims at its good and succeeds in so aiming).

This interpretation is confirmed by several other passages.[5] For instance, in the *Parts of Animals*, Aristotle says that even the humblest living things reveal something beautiful, and elicit in us the pleasure felt in the presence of the beautiful, because they are all organized for the sake of an end (*Part. An.* I.5.645a21–6). And in the *Politics* (VII.4.1326a33ff) he says that a beautiful city is one whose size is limited by its proper order. It is clear that the order Aristotle has in mind is the one realized in the city's fulfilling its function (i.e. the happiness of its citizens; see Kraut 1997 not. ad 1326a5–b25). So one way things are beautiful is by being ordered with reference to their proper end or good.

The *kalon* as symmetry must also be understood in terms of teleological structure. According to *Politics* III.13.1284b8–22, something displays symmetry or proportion (*summetria*) when the size of its parts conduces to its benefit. A sculptor may create a foot that is, taken by itself, beautiful. He may model it perfectly, with instep neither too high nor too low, to be the image of a foot that could be stood upon. But if it is proportionally larger than all the other parts of the body he has sculpted, he will reject it on the grounds that it has no place in this particular sculpture. Likewise, if certain citizens acquire too much power, they should be ostracized from the city. But what determines proportionality? It is the well functioning or good of the whole. Thus, Aristotle says that a city can be well proportioned even if it has a king, provided that his extraordinary power works to the benefit of the community (*Pol.* III.13.1284b13–15; cf. VII.4.1326a37–b2). (Concentration of power in the hands of a tyrant, on the other hand, would be disproportionate since it is exercised arbitrarily and for his own advantage alone; IV.10.1295a19–22.) Symmetry, then, is very much like order. In both cases, a thing possesses it when its parts are determined in a certain way with reference to the end of the whole. But while order is concerned with the arrangement of all the parts taken together, symmetry is a matter of the relation of those parts to each other. (So, we say that a thing is unsymmetrical because one of its elements is out of proportion but that it is disordered because of the entire structure.) When each part of a thing is shaped and sized so that it can function in harmony with the other parts for their common good, then the thing as a whole has symmetry.

There is reason to think, too, that definiteness or boundedness is a teleological notion. In *Parts of Animals* I.1.641b18–19, Aristotle argues that the presence of order and boundedness in celestial bodies betrays the fact that they do not exist by chance. But since for Aristotle a chance event is one that appears to be, but is in fact not, for a genuine *telos* (*Phys.* II.5.196b17–24), we can infer that the boundedness of the celestial bodies reveals that they have a final good. The idea seems to be that when things have a boundary or limit that is a true *horos*, they are limited at *just that point* for the sake of fulfilling their function. So, in the *Politics* (VII.4.1326a5ff, cited in part above), Aristotle is concerned not just that the city be properly ordered, but that its magnitude should not exceed a certain limit in either direction (i.e., neither too large nor too small). If it is too large or too small, it will not be able to function in such a manner as to secure the citizens' happiness. Once again, this limit on magnitude is determined by the city's end or good.

We have seen that in *Metaphysics* XIII.3 Aristotle defines beauty in terms of order, symmetry, and boundedness. Study of his biological and political writings shows that these terms usually refer to some aspect of effective teleological order. The question now is whether we can apply this analysis of the fine to virtuous action. As I said earlier, the fine does not become central to Aristotle's account of virtue until his detailed discussions of the individual traits of character. (He mentions that virtue is fine only twice in *NE* II [3.1104b9–11, 9.1109a29–30] and otherwise does not mention it at all, except to say that it is an object of choice about which the good person goes right and the bad person goes wrong [3.1104b30–1105a1].) But once we appreciate that the beauty of a thing depends on its order, symmetry, and boundedness, it becomes clear that these formal properties of beauty are at the very heart of Aristotle's understanding of virtue in *NE* II.6. As is well known, he defines moral virtue as a state "effective at hitting upon what is intermediate" relative to us and falling between excess and defect (1106b28). Just like a skilled craftsman, the virtuous person takes neither too much nor too little (1106b8–14). Thus, virtuous actions display symmetry; their parts are scaled to each other proportionately to the task at hand.[6] When a just person allocates honors, for example, he balances the rewards in his gift against the merit of the citizens. Or when a good-tempered person reacts to mistreatment, he gets angry in proportion to the severity of the offense, the intention of the offender, and his own sense of dignity.

Virtuous states and, presumably, their actualizations, have the property of boundedness, too, when we think of them as intermediate. At the beginning of *NE* VI Aristotle writes:

> In all the states we have discussed [i.e., the moral virtues], just as in all the other states too, there is a certain target [*skopos*] to which the person who has reason looks when he tightens and relaxes, and there is a certain boundary [*horos*] of the intermediate states which we said are between excess and deficiency, since they are in accordance with right reason. (VI.1.1138b21–5)

Whereas no amount of consumption counts as too much to be gluttonous, nor is any gift too small to be stingy, virtuous action has determinate boundaries beyond which consumption or giving is either too much or too little. As he says in Book II, "there are many ways of missing the mark (for, as the Pythagoreans used to represent it, the bad belongs to the unlimited [*tou apeirou*], but the good belongs to the limited [*peperasmenou*]), but there is only one way of getting it right" (II.6.1106b28–31).

Notice that, in the passage from Book VI that I just quoted, the virtuous person determines the right boundary and proportion for his action by looking to a target. It is an echo of the first image in the *NE*, where Aristotle asks whether we would not be like archers with a target in view if only we had an adequate account of the human good (I.2.1094a22–4); only now, instead of an archer, the virtuous agent is imagined as a musician stringing his lyre (Broadie and Rowe 2002, not. ad VI.1.1138b23), thereby bringing to the fore the proportion and harmony characteristic of right action. But the presence of a target in both images suggests that in virtuous action, order is determined by reference to the agent's good end.

The Book VI passage also recalls Aristotle's suggestion in *NE* II.6 that we think of the virtuous intermediate as analogous to the craftsman's intermediate, for there he draws our attention to the fact that the craftsman shapes his action by looking to a goal. "Every skilled person avoids excess and deficiency, but seeks the intermediate and chooses this . . . and every skill [*epistēmē*] completes its function well in this way, by looking to the intermediate and bringing its works to this point" (II.6.1106b5–9). Aristotle's point here may not be immediately apparent since the simile may remind us of the poignant *dis*analogy between craft and virtue. In the case of the crafts, the intermediate goal is a result independent of the productive activity (*poiēsis*, VI.5.1140b6–7). Thus, it helps the craftsman to hold it in mind since he can reason backwards from it to the means that will bring it into being. So, for instance, it is plausible that it helps a cobbler decide exactly how to proceed to keep in mind that what he is making is a shoe. Because it is a shoe, and not a purse, that he is making, he will cut the leather to conform to the foot, will make it sturdier on the bottom, and so on. But since the goal at which the virtuous person's action (*praxis*) aims is the action itself, it is hard to see how looking to it could help determine how to bring it about. Once he sees his target – the virtuous action – clearly, he no longer needs the sort of practical aid focusing on a target was meant to give.[7]

But let us think about the craft side of Aristotle's analogy a moment more. What is the intermediate that guides the craftsman's actions? Presumably in the medical art it is health, or rather the health of the particular patient (I.6.1097a11–13). In the cobbler's art it is a shoe of a certain sort for a particular customer. In the sculptor's art it is a statue of (let us say) a goddess for use in the *agora*. These goals are specific, but they are not particular. That is to say, in every case the craftsman looks not to a mental image of the particular healthy condition, shoe, or statue that he will bring about by his deliberations and actions. Rather, he looks to what we may call the form of health, shoe, or statue of a goddess. His understanding of the form guides his efforts to embody it in some particular matter. Thus, by likening virtue to craft as he does, Aristotle suggests that the "craftsman of the fitting" (IV.2.1122a34–5) keeps his inner eye fixed on his understanding of what magnificent, brave, and just actions *are like*, not on the particular magnificent, brave, or just action that will be the outcome of his deliberation.[8]

But notice that in the case of the crafts, a person grasps the relevant form by knowing what the object in question is for (*Phys.* II.2.194a34–b8). A cobbler who knows only what shoes look like from the outside, and does not know that they must be useful for walking, will not be good at striking the intermediate. The good cobbler determines what counts as too much or too little by keeping in mind what a good shoe is *in a sense that includes* knowing its proper *telos* or end. So, too, it seems to me likely that when Aristotle describes the virtuous agent as looking to the intermediate in the way that craftsmen do, he means that his behavior is guided by his grasp of what brave or just or temperate actions are like in a sense that includes knowing their good or goal. This target may not be anything external to the virtuous action, *eupraxia*, itself. (Although it is worth remembering the conclusion of the *Eudemian Ethics*: truly good people [*kaloi k'agathoi*] make the contemplation of god the target [*skopos*] of all their practical choices; VIII.3.1249b16–25.) Even if the good of virtuous action is internal, we need not conceive of it as merely the act itself in all its specificity. It might instead be some property exemplified by the action, such as respectfulness of other persons, the tendency to promote the common good, or, as I believe to be Aristotle's actual view, truthfulness and rational excellence.

We can leave aside the question of what precisely the good is that guides the virtuous agent. My point for now is this: insofar as they are intermediate, virtuous actions display the sort of effective teleological order that constitutes fineness in everything. A beautiful or fine thing is one arranged and determined for the sake of its good. Thus, when Aristotle talks of the courageous or temperate or generous person as acting for the sake of the fine, he is not introducing something entirely new. For it is by being intermediate that they are fine in the way proper to human action.

The Visibility of the Fine

Defining the fine as effective teleological order does not yet distinguish it from the good, however. For anything that is well ordered by its proper good or function is, according to Aristotle, good of its kind. If we examine other of his remarks about *to kalon*, we find that visibility or "showiness" is essential to his conception as well. At *Poetics* 7.1450b34–6, he says that "to be beautiful an animal and everything made up of parts must not only be ordered but must also be of a non-arbitrary size." It turns out that the proper size depends on what can be seen or in some analogous way comprehended.[9] If something is too large, its unity and wholeness will be lost on the people contemplating it; if it is minuscule, they will not be able to see it at all (*Poet.* 7.1450b38–1451a3). But even when the eye is literally capable of seeing an object, it may still be too small to be beautiful (*NE* IV.3.1123b7). For it may be difficult to distinguish its different parts, and thus to discern their relationship to each other and to their common good (Lucas 1968, not. ad *Poet.* 7.1450b38–9). It seems, then, that in order to be beautiful or fine, a thing must not only be ordered with reference to its good, but this arrangement must also be manifest or apparent. The length of a plot, for instance, is finer "the longer it is, consistently with its being comprehensible as a whole [*sundēlos*]" (1451a9–11). Something is *kalon*, then, not simply when its arrangement is determined by its good. Its orientation to the good must be, in some relevant sense, visible.

Aristotle does not emphasize showiness or quasi-aesthetic appeal in his discussion of virtue as an intermediate in *NE* II. But even there it may not be altogether absent from his concerns. For instance, he makes a point in *NE* II.9 of how difficult striking the intermediate is. Anyone can get angry when provoked or give money to someone who asks, but not just anyone can do these things well. "Nor is it easy; for which reason it is rare, praiseworthy, and fine [*kalon*]" (1109a29–30). The difficulty of intermediate, virtuous actions makes them notable; it brings them into public view. The showiness of fine action may perhaps receive further confirmation in two other remarks: the great-souled person, who is the best and most worthy of public honor (IV.3.1123b28), acts on a grand scale specifically because beauty depends on size (IV.3.1123b5–9); similarly, actions of the *politikos* and the soldier stand out in their magnitude and also in their beauty (X.7.1177b16–17). Since, as we have seen, Aristotle makes grand size a requirement of the fine on the grounds that only then will it be visible to the appropriate audience, it is likely that he has something similar in mind when he links the fineness of magnanimous, statesman-like, and military acts to their size. Certainly, the magnificent person's great and fine deeds are a wonder to behold (*theōria*, IV.2.1122b16–18). At any rate, we can be sure that on Aristotle's account virtuous actions do have a public aspect. In *NE* X.8 he argues that the morally virtuous person needs external goods to make his virtuous intentions and character clear (*dēlos*, rather than, as we might have expected, in order to bring his intended goals into being; 1178a28–34). The implication is that unless virtuous actions are visible or intelligible as virtuous, they will be in some sense incomplete. One of the important questions for the interpretation of Aristotle's moral theory is whether the visibility of the fine is of any importance to the virtuous person. When the brave person risks his life for the sake of the *kalon*, does he choose his action because it is ordered by the human good, or does he choose it also for the visibility of that good order?

Pleasure and Praise

It is easy to interpret my question as asking whether the virtuous person wants his actions open to *public* view and thus as asking whether he chooses his actions for their praiseworthiness. But the visibility of the fine is also important as a condition of its causing (its proper) pleasure. Aristotle says that the decent person, "insofar as he is decent, delights in virtuous actions and is pained by bad ones just as a musical person delights in fine and beautiful [*kalois*] songs and is pained by bad [*phaulois*] ones" (*NE* IX.9.1170a8–11). Here I think it is clear that the pleasure comes not so much from doing what is fine as from contemplating it. And, at any rate, it is consistent with the pleasure we take in other fine things, for example poetry or perfectly ordered biological specimens, that we experience the pleasure as audience rather than as participant in the fine thing (*Part. An.* I.5.645a15ff; *Poetics* 4.1448b8–19). (Indeed, Aristotle seems to think of *all* pleasure as connected to acts of perceiving or contemplation; *NE* X.4.1174b14ff.) Thus, when I ask whether the virtuous person cares for the visibility of good order, I have in mind visibility as a condition of public praiseworthiness *and also* as a condition of the pleasure the agent himself derives from beholding the fine.

Aristotle actually defines the *kalon* in terms of pleasure and praise in the *Rhetoric*: "Whatever is praiseworthy, being chosen for its own sake, is *kalon*, or whatever, being good, is pleasant because it is good" (*Rhet.* I.9.1366a33–4). A fine action is one that is pleasant (to whom?) *because* it is good. Aristotle could mean one of two things. Either the goodness of a fine thing causes it to be pleasant; or a person takes pleasure in something fine because he is of the opinion that it is good. No doubt, Aristotle believes both. But I take it that what he wants to emphasize here, in his lectures on rhetoric, is that fine actions are pleasant because they seem, to their agents and to those assessing them, to be good. We enjoy hearing about fine actions, or witnessing them first hand precisely because they seem to us to be good. The fine in action is, we might say, the morally pleasant.

This claim needs to be qualified in two ways. First, what strikes us as *kalon* need not actually be good. We can be wrong about what really is *kalon* just as, in Aristotle's view, we can be wrong about what really is pleasant or good (*NE* II.3.1104b30–34). But here experience of the *kalon* seems more like the experience of something pleasant. The phenomenon of *akrasia* shows us that just because we find something pleasant does not mean that we have formed a reasoned judgment that it is desirable. Likewise, the shameful experience of admiring behavior even though it offends against our reasoned principles shows that our sense of the *kalon* can be independent of our rational understanding of the good. This, I believe, is part of Aristotle's point in defining the fine as what is pleasant because it is good. In describing our reaction to the fine as a species of pleasure, Aristotle is saying that the appearance of goodness we react to need not be, primarily, a matter of rational judgment. Thus, it would be more correct to say that the fine is what is pleasant because it *seems* good.

Second, I do not mean to suggest that the fine is morally pleasant in too narrow a sense. What we find to praise in action will not be limited to applications of (what we take to be) general rules of virtue or even especially to acts that benefit others or the common good. So long as an action seems excellent in some relevant respect, it will seem fine. I mention this to mark a contrast between my view and that of Terence Irwin (1985). Relying in part on the chapter of the *Rhetoric* we have been discussing and on remarks there and in the *Nicomachean Ethics* that virtue tends to benefit others (*Rhet.* I.9.1366b3–4; *NE* IV.1.1120a11–12), Irwin argues that virtuous actions are praiseworthy, and thus fine, because they aim at the good of the community. There is something curious about Irwin's thought in light of what we have already discovered. If acts are fine only when they tend to benefit the community, then the common good must be the good that determines proper order in human action. Now, no doubt for any political animal, and perhaps especially for human beings, excellence of behavior is closely connected to the happiness of others (*NE* I.7.1097b8–11). But it is odd to assume that human actions are well ordered *only* when they are arranged for the sake of the civic good. Since this is an important point, let us examine this chapter of the *Rhetoric* a bit further.

Notice that although the fine person benefits others and does not seek his own profit, his motivation does not appear to be altruistic. Rather, according to the *Rhetoric*, he benefits others for the sake of fame and honor (I.9.1366b34–1367a17). It is this regard for fame and honor over vulgar profit which appears to draw public admiration, perhaps because it reveals the person's worthier, we might almost say aristocratic, character. At least, that interpretation is supported by the following:

> And profitless possessions are fine; for they are more free [*eleutheriōtera*]. And the peculiar characteristics of a people are fine, and the signs of the things praised by them, for example wearing one's hair long in Sparta; for that's a sign of the free man, since it's not very easy for a person with long hair to do any menial [*thētikon*] work.[10] And it's fine not to do any mechanical trade; for it's characteristic of the free man not to live for another. (*Rhet.* I.9.1367a27–33)

If all fine choices have in common that they benefit other people, why is it fine to wear one's hair long? And why is there nothing in the least bit fine about menial labor? Making good horseshoes may not be as dramatic as leading an army, but surely it does an awful lot of good. This passage ought to make us reconsider Irwin's analysis of what is so noteworthy about the virtuous person's tendency to help others.[11] For here things seem to be admired just as signs of social status.

Admittedly, the *Rhetoric* is a treatise on public speaking and so we cannot assume that Aristotle himself would endorse the examples he gives of what a contemporary audience would call fine. But we need not interpret his own conception of the fine as overtly class-based (although he was evidently full of prejudice against manual laborers, cf. *Pol.* VI.4.1319a24–8, VII.9.1328b39–1329a2) in order to notice that fine things express a person's success in realizing a human ideal. So, for example, we read that the great-souled person, whose actions are the most fine, has possessions that "are fine and unprofitable rather than profitable and useful, since that is more proper to the self-sufficient person" (*NE* IV.3.1125a11–12; cf. *Rhet.* I.9.1367a27–8, quoted above). The unprofitability of his possessions is not a feature independent of their fineness. For, in general, Aristotle opposes the *kalon* and the necessary (*anankaion*). The necessary includes action that is coerced from the outside (such as by punishment, *NE* III.8.1116b2–3, X.9.1180a4–5), but it also includes any behavior (or its accompanying pleasure) that is instrumentally valuable (X.6.1176b3). This includes: converting one's wealth into a form convenient for generous giving (IV.1.1120b1); eating when hungry (VII.4.1147b24); and accepting favors from friends (VIII.1.1155a28–9, IX.11.1171a24–6). Now there is nothing surprising in thinking of instrumentally valuable actions as necessary – obviously they are necessary for achieving the relevant end. Rather, the question is why, in his view, their being necessary in this sense *precludes* their being fine. After all, in our society industriousness and efficiency are regarded as especially admirable.

But Aristotle thinks a life dominated by instrumental activity or profit-seeking is "forced" (I.5.1096a5–6), even when it is chosen by someone of his own volition. His point, I take it, is that since instrumental activity is worth choosing only for the sake of the product it creates, there is a sense in which it is onerous. The agent functions as a sort of "living tool" in the service of his needs and works "for the sake of another" – not for another person, as a slave does, but for a condition of relative leisureliness and self-sufficiency that is not, at the moment, his own (cf. X.6.1176b3–6: instrumental activities are not self-sufficient). On the other hand, people who act finely behave in a way that presupposes that they are free (enough) of the burden of meeting external demands or their own basic needs. Thus their fine action expresses their success, since, in Aristotle's considered view, leisure and self-sufficiency are necessary features of human flourishing (*NE* I.7.1097b4–6, X.7.1177b4–6).

So let us return to generosity, singled out by Aristotle as especially fine. It is clear that generosity is fine in part because it benefits others. But profligate spending, no matter how many people it benefits, is not admirable. Instead, the core of the generous personality seems to be an understanding that wealth is a useful thing, and thus that it has no value except insofar as it is put to work in promoting some good end. Unlike the profligate person, the generous person understands that giving to some people is a misuse of wealth (IV.1.1121b4–7). And unlike the stingy person, he understands that he has no need for wealth beyond a certain modest amount. (This is why it is characteristic of him not to look to his own needs when giving, IV.1.1120b6.) In fact, it is here we may find his freedom. (Quite literally, generosity – *eleutheriotēs* – is the virtue of behaving as befits a free – *eleutheros* – man.) For he is free of the fear of future need that drives at least some stingy people to hoard their wealth (IV.1.1121b24–31). Thus, his actions are fine not only because they benefit others, but also because they are shaped by his understanding of the value of money and the things it can buy. In all these ways they are ordered by the human good.

This advances our understanding of the fine in action in two ways. First, it clarifies the remark I made before about the *kalon* being the morally pleasant. I do not mean that it causes us to delight in a peculiarly moral value, such as respect for duty, altruism, or, as Irwin (1985) suggests, concern for the common good. Rather, my point is that actions strike us as fine when they seem to indicate what kind of person the agent is, that he is successful in some particular sphere or, simply, as a human being.

But, second, our discussion suggests a richer understanding of how it is that particular virtuous actions are ordered by the human good. Before, we talked of fine actions as being neither too much nor too little to bring their proper good into being. But here, in our discussion of the *Rhetoric*, we have been saying that certain actions are fine in that they show the agent to be a certain kind of person, a person with certain priorities among his values and a certain conception of human flourishing. A person may show his commitment to the good by literally bringing it into being in some partial way, but he may also express his commitment more loosely by choosing things that befit it. (The fine is also defined as the fitting, *to prepon*, *EE* VIII.3.1249a9; *Topics* V.5.135a13.) The Spartans' long braids show their love of freedom; the great-souled man does not hurry about his business and so shows that he does not take it seriously (*NE* IV.3.1125a12–16); the magnificent person buys a cheap but lovely ball as a present for a child and so shows that the value of giving is in matching the gift to the recipient, not in asserting the superiority of one's wealth (IV.2.1123a14–16). Aristotle seems to think that all these actions (or at least the last two) express the virtuous person's understanding of human good in a way that is appropriate to the occasion. Indeed, where two courses of action are equally effective in bringing about a given end, the practically wise person will choose the most fine (III.3.1112b16–17).[12] This remark suggests that, in Aristotle's view, the practicable good is grasped not only in what we bring about, but in how we bring it about.

The Value of the Fine

Let me summarize where we have come so far. We have seen that, in general, fine things exhibit the formal properties of end-directed order, symmetry, and boundedness. So, although Aristotle himself does not present it in this way, his description of virtue as a disposition to produce intermediate actions, carefully poised between too much and too little, with boundaries determined by the agent's *skopos* is, in effect, a description of the formal basis of beauty in action. But now we see that fine actions are effectively oriented to the human good not simply by being suited to bring it into being, but also by being executed in a manner that befits a person who cares about certain things above others (being a citizen, say, or having certain kinds of friendships, or knowing the truth). We could say that in showing the ordering of the bodily and emotional behavior that constitutes them, virtuous actions also show the ordering of the agent's priorities by the human good. Fine actions, therefore, are not simply performed *by* a virtuous person, they are *char-*

acteristic of a virtuous person in that they reveal his character. This, I believe, is a point of real importance.

Since the highest good qualifies as happiness only in the context of a complete life or time (I.7.1098a18–20, X.7.1177b24–6), it is questionable whether any single action could produce happiness as such. But since the virtuous person chooses his actions from a steady state of character (II.4.1105a33), each action is, at least potentially, an emblem of his life as a whole.[13] The brave commander who stays behind to help a wounded soldier to safety exemplifies a lifelong commitment to civic friendship; so too does the truthful person who nevertheless inclines to saying somewhat less than the truth on the grounds that it is more "in tune" (*emmelesteron*) to avoid irritating others (IV.7.1127b7–9); and the philosopher, who is as scrupulous in action as he is in contemplation, manifests his devotion to truthfulness in all things. At least, fine actions will manifest the agent's orientation to the good and reveal something of his life if the order of its parts can in some relevant sense be seen. But they can be seen. For I argued that according to Aristotle, all things are fine only when their effective teleological order is visible, either to the physical senses or to the mind. The sheer magnitude of the virtuous person's canvas suggests that his actions are prominent in the public eye (or at least could be, provided that his fellow citizens have had an upbringing that enables them to sense what is truly good). And when the goodness of their order becomes apparent to a person, it causes the peculiar pleasure of the fine and elicits praise.

If the fine action is one's own, it will likely inspire pride as well. Is this why, on Aristotle's account, the virtuous person aims at the *kalon* as well as the *agathon*? The image of the good person swelling with pride at the beauty of his own actions may make us uneasy. But we need not imply that he wallows in his pride if we acknowledge that acting well is a proper source of self-regarding pleasure. Indeed, the capacity of children to feel pride in their fine actions and shame in their ugly and shameful ones is crucial for the possibility of moral education as Aristotle explains it (*NE* X.9 *passim*). As children practice sharing toys with friends or dealing with disappointment, they are praised by their parents (and by people in public positions of authority who speak for society's rules) when they do these things well and reproached when they do them badly. The experience of reproach is painful and, over time, the child develops a sense of shame that holds him back from doing wrong. He also develops a corresponding sense of the fine. His parents' praise encourages him to take pleasure in having been good and, we can imagine, the older he gets, the more he is able to feel this pleasure in the fine on his own, without the prompting of external honor.

It is quite likely that Aristotle thinks it is part even of the fully mature virtuous character to enjoy the fine in what Plato would have called a *thumoeidic* or spirited way. That is to say, it seems to me likely that Aristotle follows Plato in attributing to human beings natural competitive desires to be and be recognized as "the best" which are distinct from appetitive desires for pleasure, on the one hand, and rational desires for the good, on the other. We see evidence for this in his discussion of *akrasia*. As John Cooper has argued, Aristotle's separation of weakness with respect to anger from unqualified *akrasia* depends on his distinguishing spirited non-rational desire from appetitive non-rational desire (1999b: 257–62). And it seems to me likely that he follows Plato in thinking that these spirited desires can be gratified by the beauty of virtuous action. For, like Plato, Aristotle describes moral education as being effected by the child's *spirited* concern with praise and blame and as directed toward teaching children to take pleasure in the beautiful.[14] Now it is important to see that if we human beings by nature have spirited desires, then it is part of practical wisdom to seek satisfaction for them in the *kalon*. For since the desires are inevitable, they will push us to some sort of spirited victory or other. Far better to feel pride when we manifest genuine nobility than some other way, say by subjecting fellow citizens to our political will or by dominating them physically. When spirited desires seek the fine, they "chime with reason" (I.13.1102b28) and its judgment that virtuous, intermediate action is good. Thus a wise person will take care that the beauty of his action and character is publicly visible, not all the time, but with sufficient frequency to gratify spirit. (In much the same way, reason ensures the satisfaction of appetite when it chooses food that tastes good as well as nourishes.) Here, then, is one reason that the virtuous person acts for the sake of the *kalon*, and not merely the *agathon*.

But although I believe Aristotle agrees with Plato about the relationship between spirit and the beauty of virtue, he does not in his own moral theory give it anything like the prominence it receives in the *Republic*. For the overwhelming majority of his discussion of virtue, Aristotle is content to distinguish reason from non-rational desires without making further divisions within the latter. Thus it does not seem plausible that his repeated descriptions of the virtuous person as acting for the sake of the fine are intended primarily as comments about how the virtuous person gratifies his sense of pride.[15] Nor does it seem plausible that the value of the fineness of virtue is found primarily in what it gives to spirit. Thus, if we want to understand the importance of the beauty of virtuous action in Aristotle's theory, we should look elsewhere.

There is one argument, in particular, where Aristotle appeals to the fineness of virtue to solve a problem. I refer to his argument in *NE* IX.8 that we ought to be lovers of ourselves most of all. He begins the chapter by presenting a dilemma: on the one hand, "self-lover" is a term of reproach and people think the decent person sets his own interests aside and acts for the sake of his friends; on the other hand, everyone thinks you should do most good for the person who is closest and most of all a friend and, as Aristotle argued in *NE* IX.4, that person is oneself. So should one love oneself most or not? Here is a way of describing how Aristotle resolves the dilemma that is, I believe, incomplete. Virtuous actions that benefit others typically involve delaying or denying satisfaction to the agent's appetitive (and perhaps even spirited, IX.8.1168b15–21) desires for external goods. But they gratify (*charizetai*) the most authoritative part of oneself because they gratify intelligence (*nous*). And since we are most truly our most authoritative part, that means that the virtuous person cherishes (*agapōn*, IX.8.1168b33) his true self most when he chooses to perform virtuous actions (IX.8.1168b28–34, 1169a17–18). Therefore true self-love requires that we help others. Now this argument might persuade us that genuine love of self does not require the greedy pursuit of external goods. But, so far at least, it does not show that self-love is expressed in friendship for others. Even if we grant that the good person's reason judges that he ought to help his friends, the question still remains whether in acting this way he does something good for himself, even for his true, rational self. What does reason get out of the action it orders must be done?

Aristotle has already argued (in *NE* I.7) that virtuous action in accordance with reason is the greatest human good, so in a sense the answer is obvious: "If everyone exerted himself to do the finest things . . . each individual would have the greatest good, since [the greatest good] is virtue" (IX.8.1169a8–11). But interpreting the argument solely in terms of the goodness of virtue fails to do justice to the heavy emphasis in this passage on the fineness of virtue. The vocabulary makes it clear that the fine is imagined not just as something reason chooses or does, but as a reward or benefit it assigns (*aponemei*) itself (IX.8.1168b29), on analogy with the money, honors, or pleasure that bad people assign (*aponemontas*) themselves (1168b15–21).[16] The good person is extraordinarily eager for the fine (*spoudazoi*, 1168b25, 1169a7), takes it (*hairountai*, 1169a26, 1169a32), and keeps it for himself (*peripoioito*, 1168b27, 1169a21); he competes for it (*hamillōmenōn*, 1169a8–9) and exerts himself to do the finest things (*diateinomenōn*, 1169a9). The reward appears to cause some sort of pleasure (1168b19), and talk of competing for the fine suggests that, for the virtuous person, fine actions gratify his spirited love of victory. But the overall tenor of the passage makes it clear that the fine is chosen as a gift for intellect in particular. So we should ask why the fact that virtuous actions are fine makes it especially plausible that they manifest love of the rational self.[17]

Aristotle remarks several times that in assigning the fine to himself, the virtuous person's reason is "indulged" and "gratified." In a remarkable passage, he even suggests that the pleasure and benefit of fine action so far surpass the pleasure of keeping external goods for oneself that the virtuous person will be willing to risk death for its sake:

> He will freely give up both money and honors . . . while keeping the fine for himself; for he would prefer to feel pleasure intensely for a short time than to have mild pleasure for a long time, and to live in a fine way for a year rather than to live many years in any chance way, and one fine action on a grand scale rather than many small ones. (IX.8.1169a20–25)

This reminds us of an earlier passage in which Aristotle leans heavily on the fineness of courageous actions to explain how it is that they are pleasant and voluntarily chosen. Even though the brave person suffers great physical pain and dread when he acts for the sake of the fine, to the extent that he achieves it, he achieves something pleasant (III.9.1117a35–b16).

It seems to me likely that here, too, the point of emphasizing the beauty of virtue is to show the sense in which it is delightful in itself. But now, since Aristotle has emphasized that it gratifies reason in particular, we can more narrowly identify this as an intellectual pleasure. Unlike the objects of appetite that are a pleasure to taste or to feel or to hear, fine actions are a delight for reason to contemplate or understand. We are now in a position to explain why. In general, as we have discovered, something is fine when its goodness can be seen or otherwise comprehended. Thus, it presents no impediment to reason's activity of understanding it.[18] And practicable good is, in particular, the sort of good practical reason seeks to understand. Thus the delight the decent person feels in fine action is reason's joy in its successful grasp of practical truth.

From the point of view of self-love, it is more important for the virtuous person to appreciate the fineness of his actions than we may at first recognize. On any given occasion, practical reason deliberates about how exactly to realize the practical good in the current situation, how exactly to balance each aspect of our behavior in light of our commitment to a certain conception of human flourishing. Assuming that this activity is well ordered by practical wisdom, it culminates in excellent choice and action. That is to say, it achieves whatever particular end the circumstances require and it constitutes success in living rationally. In the press of practical life, however, where a person must feed himself, engage in business with other people, and perhaps even fight battles, the virtuous agent will not have time to reflect on and delight in the excellent reasoning he knows to be the source of his happiness. Practical reason aims to get something done; so when the appropriate time arrives for action, the virtuous person must go ahead and act, and then go on to the next problem. But if practical reasoning is by nature ever sensitive to external circumstances and focused on future action, there is a risk of not fully registering in consciousness that one has already achieved the ultimate practicable good: virtuous rational activity itself. And since we rational animals only fully possess the good when we know that we do, there is a danger that the perpetual future-orientation of practical reason will impede our ability ever to have the human good in the fullest sense.

This is why it matters *to reason* that actions be fine as well as good. For when our actions are fine, their perfection is easily intelligible.[19] In fact, the grander and more beautiful they are, the more easily we know their goodness. In every intelligible nuance, they make plain the proper ordering of our priorities by the human good; that is to say, they display for us our character. In the fineness of action, reason can rest in the activity of knowing that what it has achieved is, in fact, the good it was seeking.[20] Pleasant appreciation of an action's goodness is not a dispensable moment of self-satisfaction; it completes the virtuous person's grip of the practicable good by completing the rational activity of knowing it.

Conclusion

I have argued that Aristotle conceives of virtuous actions as fine in order to emphasize the sense in which their goodness is easily intelligible and pleasant to contemplate. That is to say, in order to emphasize their value to the agent. Let us conclude by considering his discussion in *NE* I.10 of the virtuous person's resilience in the face of misfortune:

> The happy person always, or more than anyone else, does and reflects on [*theōrēsei*] actions in accordance with virtue and bears his luck in the finest way possible [*kallista*] and in a way that is harmonious in absolutely every respect . . . Many great pieces of good fortune will make his life more blessed (for these naturally help adorn it, and the use of them is fine [*kalē*] and decent). But if they happen the opposite way, they crush and maim blessedness, since they bring pains and impede many activities. But nevertheless even in these circumstances the fine [*to kalon*] shines through [*dialampei*] . . . We think the truly good and sensible person bears all chances gracefully [*euschēmonōs*] and always makes the finest things possible [*ta kallista*] from his circumstances, just as . . . a cobbler makes the finest [*kalliston*] shoe from the skins he is given. (I.10.1100b19–1101a5)

The virtuous person is musical; he is able to act with good order and grace no matter the circumstances. So even in misfortune, something of value remains in his life. But Aristotle suggests that what mitigates the misfortune of his position is not simply that his actions are as well ordered as they could possibly be given the situation, but that the beauty of these actions "shines through." To whom must this beauty be visible if it is to be of relevance in assessing the extent of his unhappiness? Other people may gaze on it, of course, but Aristotle says that it is the virtuous person, more than anyone else, who does *and reflects on* the fine. This suggests that he is making a point about the virtuous person's own state of consciousness: because he is a reliable craftsman of the fitting (IV.2.1122a34–5), something of beauty will always shine through and, given the sort of person he is, he will gaze on it. He is saved from wretchedness because the fineness of his actions ensures that he can appreciate the measure of success that *is* present in his life and thus that he can, in some meaningful sense, have it as his own.

This is not enough to make him blessed (or even happy), however, and it is a puzzle why not. One possibility is that scarcity of external goods makes it exceedingly difficult to do something fine (I.8.1099a32–3). Thus most of the unfortunate person's time will be spent wondering whether his actions, however modest, will be successful (cf. X.8.1178a34–b3). And even if he does realize some practicable good, his enjoyment of its fine good order will only be temporary, disrupted as it will be by the demands of his body. Since misfortune is likely to distract one from whatever fineness is present in life (imagine trying to keep in mind that the meal you have scraped together actually tastes good when it is not enough to quell

your hunger), it impedes, in the sense of interrupts, the virtuous person's awareness of the good order of his actions.[21] Perhaps this sort of possession of the good
is too incomplete to count as happiness, as if what must last a complete time is
not just the doing of virtuous action but also the appreciation of that activity as
pervasive and characteristic of life as a whole (cf. VII.13.1153b16–21). Be that as
it may, one thing is clear: just as in the discussion of self-love, Aristotle appeals to
the fineness of action here not to highlight its social utility, but to show its benefit
to the virtuous agent himself. Of course, to repeat, he also thinks that fine actions
tend to benefit others, but this is not his particular concern when he emphasizes
that they are fine.

As I said at the beginning, the connection between the fine and the agent's
well-being may surprise us. But its connection to intelligible order may surprise
us in another way, as well, for it reminds us that, in the first instance, Aristotle
thinks of morally virtuous action as an activity of reason (or what participates in
reason) and thus as a sort of excellent knowing (or obedience to knowledge). The
practically wise person uses his reason to figure out what careful calibration of
behavior to circumstances will be well ordered in light of his understanding of the
human good. When he succeeds, his action is fine and he can, we might say, feel
the success of his effort to know. Now even if we agree that moral virtue is a perfection of reason, we might have hoped Aristotle would value all virtuous actions,
and not only the activities of friendship, as modes of loving. But that seems to be
the part of another sort of excellent human knowing: the activity of theoretical
wisdom that contemplates a greater beauty than any to be found in human life.

Acknowledgments

I thank Sarah Broadie, Martha Nussbaum, and Richard Kraut for their helpful
comments on earlier versions of this chapter.

Notes

1 See *An Enquiry Concerning Human Understanding*, s.132; *Treatise of Human Nature*,
   II.1.8, III.3.1.
2 "Beauty" has lost even the connotation of *appearing* to be good, at least in certain
   philosophical quarters.
3 This section and the next two constitute a somewhat altered version of material from
   Lear (2004: ch. 6). Some arguments have been added, others have been condensed
   or omitted altogether to suit the different purpose of this chapter. But the basic interpretation of *to kalon* is the same.
4 Allan (1971: 67) and Cooper (1999b: 273) pointed me to this connection.
5 *Poetics* 7 supports this point (Lucas 1968: 113 not. ad 1450b37; Halliwell 1986: 98).
   Also, at *Rhet.* I.5.1361b7–14, he claims that physical beauty varies with time of life.

In youth, it is the body of an athlete; in the prime of manhood, the body of a warrior; in old age, a body capable of enduring necessary toils and otherwise free from pain. The idea seems to be that, since what counts as a well-functioning body varies with what a body is expected to do at different stages of a person's life, beauty will also vary. Beauty is, again, constituted by suitability to the end.

6 I follow Cooper (1999b) in making this connection.

7 A possible exception is the case of the generous person's accumulation of wealth for the purpose of having the means to act generously (IV.1.1120a34–b2).

8 As Broadie explains, this need not imply that "a person cannot act from virtue unless he sees himself as acting from virtue" (1991: 94) (although I am not sure how "distasteful" this view would be). Since Aristotle thinks of the virtues as highly context specific – courage is expressed on the battlefield (III.6.1115a28–31), temperance with respect to the pleasures of touch and taste (III.10), and so on – it will be sufficient for the virtuous person to recognize the sort of circumstances he is in and to aim at the sort of action appropriate under such circumstances.

9 The Greek word is *theōria*, which can mean "looking at" or "contemplation." In the biological examples here, Aristotle seems literally to mean sight. But he must be making a point about an extended sense of *theōria*, since he intends his remarks to apply to the magnitude of a plot. The right size for a plot is one whose unity can be easily grasped by memory (*Poet.* 7.1451a3–6).

10 Vernant suggests a different reason for the Spartans' admiration of long hair: it was braided and adorned before battle in the manner of Homeric warriors and so was a symbol of heroic youth and beauty (2001: 330–31). Since the Spartans seem to have thought of military prowess as the pinnacle of human excellence, my point here would be the same. They consider long hair (when it is worn in the right way) beautiful because it expresses their conception of human flourishing.

11 See Rogers (1999) for a more detailed response to Irwin's argument.

12 "If it appears that there are many ways for [the end] to come into being, [expert deliberators] look to see through which it will happen most easily and most finely [*kallista*]" (III.3.1112b14–17). (Unfortunately, *kallista* is usually translated here as "best.")

13 I thank Elizabeth Asmis for this suggestion.

14 For a full defense of this interpretation of the *Republic*, see my "Plato on Learning to Love Beauty" (Lear 2006).

15 However, Cooper makes the good point that *NE* III–V, where most of the references to *to kalon* are to be found, describe the excellence of the *irrational* part of the soul. On the other hand, he says, when Aristotle describes *rational* excellence he does so solely in relation to the good (1999b: 270–71). Although this last point is true of *NE* VI, which Cooper refers to here, it is not true of every passage of the *NE*, as I explain below.

16 Since Aristotle so emphatically uses language that suggests that reason is the beneficiary of the action it originates, I think we should at least try to avoid interpreting him as giving the familiar, very weak argument for psychological egoism: that every action is an expression of self-love since it is *my* desire that motivates it. Furthermore, this interpretation gives no role to the concept of the fine. Bostock notices this but, oddly, thinks it just goes to show that the concept of the fine is "a mere red herring" (2000: 179).

17   Much recent work on this chapter has asked whether, if virtuous actions are expressions of self-love, they can still be expressions of genuine concern for others (Annas 1988; Kraut 1989: 115–23; Pakaluk 1998: 200–202). This question is certainly important from our point of view, but notice that Aristotle takes for granted here that virtuous actions are expressions of friendship for others (IX.8.1168a33–5). His question is how actions so conceived can still be expressions of self-love. It is for *this* question that the *kalon* is relevant.

18   Notice that in *NE* X.4 Aristotle describes pleasure as an experience that completes the activity either of sensory or intellectual perception. This happens when the sensory or intellectual capacity is in the best condition *and its object is the most fine* in the relevant domain (1174b14–16).

19   Cf. *EE* VIII.3: Aristotle seems to argue that mere goodness and *kalok'agathia* issue in the same behavior, but differ in the agent's understanding of his action. Whereas the former chooses virtue for the sake of the natural goods, the latter chooses his virtuous selection of natural goods for its own sake (*NE* VII.5.1148b34–40). The fine-and-good person's more correct understanding transforms a merely good action and the good things he chooses into things that are fine (*EE* VIII.3.1249a4–11).

20   This differs from Pakaluk's interpretation (1998, not. ad IX.8.1168b25–1169a6). He suggests that since virtuous actions are intelligible, they are good for reason by being apt or appropriate to it; I suggest they are good by giving a benefit. Furthermore, I argue that *to kalon* plays an important role in the argument of IX.8 because beauty is the way in which virtuous actions are "inherently intelligible."

21   This, I suggest, is why the full exercise of virtue occurs in "primary and preferred circumstances" (Cooper 1999a: 303): these are the circumstances in which the agent most clearly understands his activity as the expression of an excellent character and as the realization of the human good. Notice that my emphasis on the way terrible luck impedes our understanding of, and delight in, virtuous action does not rest on distinguishing *eudaimonia* and virtuous action, on the one hand, from our subjective impression of such activity, on the other. (So, for somewhat different reasons, I agree with Nussbaum 2001: 327–36 that bad luck impedes activity in accordance with virtue itself.)

References

Allan, D. 1971: "The Fine and the Good in the *Eudemian Ethics*." In P. Moraux and D. Harlfinger (eds), *Untersuchungen zur "Eudemischen Ethik"*, pp. 63–71. Berlin: de Gruyter.

Annas, J. 1988: "Self-love in Aristotle," *Southern Journal of Philosophy* 27 (suppl.): 1–18.

Bostock, D. 2000: *Aristotle's Ethics*. Oxford: Oxford University Press.

Broadie, S. 1991: *Ethics with Aristotle*. Oxford: Oxford University Press.

—and Rowe, C. 2002: *Aristotle: Nicomachean Ethics*. Oxford: Oxford University Press.

Cooper, J. M. C. 1999a: "Aristotle on the Goods of Fortune." In J. M. C. Cooper, *Reason and Emotion: Essays on Ancient Moral Psychology and Ethical Theory*, pp. 292–311. Princeton, NJ: Princeton University Press (orig. pub. in *Philosophical Review* [1985], vol. 94).

—1999b: "Reason, Moral Virtue, and Moral Value." In J. M. C. Cooper, *Reason and Emotion: Essays on Ancient Moral Psychology and Ethical Theory*, pp. 253–80. Princeton, NJ: Princeton University Press (orig. pub. in M. Frede and G. Striker [eds], *Rationality in Greek Thought*, pp. 81–114. Oxford: Oxford University Press, 1996).

Halliwell, S. 1986: *Aristotle's Poetics*. Chapel Hill, NC: University of North Carolina Press.

Irwin, T. 1985: "Aristotle's Conception of Morality," *Proceedings of the Boston Area Colloquium in Ancient Philosophy* 1: 115–43.

Kraut, R. 1989: *Aristotle on the Human Good*. Princeton, NJ: Princeton University Press.

—1997: *Aristotle: Politics, Books VII and VIII*. Oxford: Clarendon Press.

Lear, G. R. 2004: *Happy Lives and the Highest Good: An Essay on Aristotle's Nicomachean Ethics*. Princeton, NJ: Princeton University Press.

—2006: "Plato on Learning to Love Beauty." In G. Santas (ed.), *The Blackwell Guide to Plato's Republic*, pp. 104–24. Oxford: Blackwell.

Lucas, D. W. 1968: *Aristotle, Poetics*. Oxford: Clarendon Press.

Nussbaum, M. 2001: *The Fragility of Goodness: Luck and Ethics in Greek Tragedy and Philosophy*, rev. edn. Cambridge: Cambridge University Press.

Pakaluk, M. 1998: *Aristotle, Nicomachean Ethics Books VIII and IX*. Oxford: Clarendon Press.

Rogers, K. 1999: "Aristotle's Conception of το καλον." In L. Gerson (ed.), *Aristotle: Critical Assessments*, pp. 337–55. London: Routledge (orig. pub. in *Ancient Philosophy*, 1993, vol. 13).

Vernant, J-P. 2001: "A 'Beautiful Death' and the Disfigured Corpse in Homeric Epic." In *Oxford Readings in Homer's Iliad*, pp. 311–41. Oxford: Oxford University Press (orig. pub. 1991).

Further reading

Broadie, S. 2005: "Virtue and Beyond in Plato and Aristotle," *Southern Journal of Philosophy* 43 (suppl.): 97–114.

Tuozzo, T. 1995: "Contemplation, the Noble, and the Mean: The Standard of Moral Virtue in Aristotle's *Ethics*." In R. Bosley, R. Shiner, and J. Sisson (eds), *Aristotle, Virtue, and the Mean*, pp. 129–54. Edmonton: Academic.

Whiting, J. 1996: "Self-love and Authoritative Virtue: A Prolegomenon to a Kantian Reading of *EE* viii.3." In S. Engstrom and J. Whiting (eds), *Aristotle, Kant, and the Stoics*, pp. 162–99. New York: Cambridge University Press.

6

Aristotle on the Voluntary

Susan Sauvé Meyer

The Significance of Voluntariness

Aristotle devotes a significant portion of the *Nicomachean Ethics* and the *Eudemian Ethics* to the topic of virtue of character (*ēthikē aretē*). In each work he precedes his detailed treatment of the particular virtues of character (courage, temperance, liberality, and so on) with a general account of ethical virtue (*NE* II–III.5; *EE* II; cf. *MM* I.5–19). The general account concludes, in both cases, with an extended discussion of voluntariness (*to hekousion*) and related notions (*NE* III.1–5; *EE* II.6–11; cf. *MM* I.9–19). In order to understand Aristotle's views on voluntariness, we must first understand why he thinks that an account of the voluntary belongs in a treatise on virtue of character.

In the *NE*, Aristotle gives two reasons for introducing the topic of voluntariness: "Since virtue concerns feelings and actions, and since praise and blame are for what is voluntary, while forgiveness and sometimes even pity are for what is involuntary, those who inquire into virtue should define the voluntary and the involuntary. This is also useful for those who legislate about fines and punishments" (*NE* III.1.1109b30–35). The second reason given here is the less important. It is elaborated on in *NE* III.5: legal sanctions are aimed at influencing behavior, and hence they are pointless if they are directed at actions that are not voluntary (1113b21–30). More important is the first reason Aristotle articulates: that voluntariness is a necessary condition of praiseworthiness and blameworthiness. The *EE* concurs in invoking praise and blame in order to explain why a discussion of voluntariness is in order in the account of character:

> Since virtue and vice and their products are praiseworthy and blameworthy, (for one is blamed and praised . . . because of those things for which we are ourselves responsible) it is clear that virtue and vice concern those actions for which one is oneself responsible [*aitios*] and the origin [*archē*]. So we must identify the sorts of actions for which a person is himself responsible and the origin. Now we all agree that he is

responsible for his voluntary actions . . . and that he is not responsible for his involuntary ones. (*EE* II.6.1223a9–18; cf. II.11.1228a9–17; *MM* I.9.1186b34–1187a4, 1187a19–21)

These and other passages indicate that Aristotle investigates voluntariness because he is interested in the causal conditions of praise and blame. It is important to understand just what kind of causal relation Aristotle takes voluntariness to be. A voluntary action, he assumes, is one whose origin (*archē*) is in the agent (*NE* III.1.1110a15–17, 1110b4, 1111a23, III.5.1113b20–21; *EE* II.8.1224b15; cf. *MM* I.11.1187b14–16), or of which the agent is the origin (*EE* II.6.1222b15–20, 1222b28–9, 1223a15; *NE* III.3.1112b31–2, III.5.1113b17–19). The *NE* favors the former locution and the *EE* the latter, but Aristotle clearly takes the two to be equivalent (*NE* III.3.1112b28–32, III.5.1113b17–21, VI.2.1139a31–b5). Such actions are according to (*kata*) the internal impulse (*hormē*) of the person (*EE* II.7.1223a23–8; cf. II.8.1224a18–25, 1224b7–15).

Aristotle regularly indicates that actions that "originate" in the agent are "up to him to do or not to do" (*NE* III.1.1110a15–18, III.5.1113b20–21, 1114a18–19; *EE* II.6.1223a2–9; cf. *MM* I.9.1187a7–24). It is important not to misinterpret this expression as attributing to agents a kind of "freedom to do otherwise." To be sure, Aristotle thinks that our actions, like much of what happens in the world, are contingent rather than necessary: they "admit of being otherwise" (*EE* II.6.1222b41–2, 1223a5–6; cf. *NE* VI.1.1139a6–14, III.3.1112a18–26). Their contingent status, however, is not a result of their being "up to us to do or not to do." On the contrary, Aristotle takes the former to be a precondition of the latter. It is because such occurrences (a) admit of being otherwise, and (b) can come about "through us," that (c) they are "up to us to do or not to do" (*NE* III.3.1112a18–26; *EE* II.6.1223a1–9, II.10.1226a26–33). Rather than attributing freedom to agents, the "up to us" locution used by Aristotle implies causal responsibility. Such agents are in control (*kurios*) of their actions (*NE* III.5.1114a2–3; *EE* II.6.1223a6–7); they are responsible (*aitioi*) for them: "A person is responsible [*aitios*] for those things that are up to him to do or not to do, and if he is responsible [*aitios*] for them, then they are up to him" (*EE* II.6.1223a7–9; cf. 1223a15–18).

Aristotle thinks such responsibility is necessary for praiseworthiness and blameworthiness (*NE* III.1.1109b30–32), and he investigates voluntariness in order to capture this causal relation (*EE* II.6.1223a9–18). But now our original question re-emerges. Why does Aristotle think that a full treatment of virtue and vice of character requires a discussion of responsibility?

A very popular answer to this question, more often assumed than stated explicitly, takes note of the fact that Aristotle thinks that our states of character, and not just our actions, are "up to us and voluntary" (*NE* III.5.1114b28–9; cf. 1114a4–31), and infers that Aristotle's main point in discussing voluntariness is to establish just this. A major difficulty for this hypothesis, however, is that the argument that character formation is voluntary occurs only in the *Nicomachean Ethics* (III.5.1114a4–13). Thus Aristotle's reasons for discussing voluntariness in his account of character cannot be exhausted by his view that we form our states of character voluntarily.

Moreover, even though Aristotle repeatedly claims that virtue is praiseworthy and vice blameworthy, he never explains this by saying that we are responsible for these states of character. Rather, his general claim is that virtue is praiseworthy because it hits the mean, and vice blameworthy because it exceeds or falls short of the mean (*NE* II.6.1106b25–8, II.7.1108a14–16). In explaining why particular states of character are praiseworthy or blameworthy, he never mentions the voluntariness of their acquisition. Rather, he points to the sorts of activities the states of character produce. For example, "mildness" is praiseworthy because it disposes us to have angry feelings and to act in anger only when we should; courage is praiseworthy because it disposes us to feel fear or confidence and to stand our ground only when it is appropriate (*NE* IV.5.1126b5–7; *EE* III.1.1228b30–31; cf. III.5.1233a4–8). Aristotle's general discussion of praise-worthiness in *NE* I.12 confirms this general pattern. The praiseworthiness of a disposition depends on the sort of activity it produces: "We praise the good person, as well as virtue, because of the actions and products . . ." (1101b14–16; cf. *EE* II.1.1219b8–9).

These remarks show that Aristotle thinks character is praiseworthy in virtue of the actions it causes, not because of anything about the process by which it comes into being. Thus the causal relation he finds essential to praiseworthiness and blameworthiness, which is what he seeks to capture in his account of voluntariness, is the one in which character produces actions. The actions that Aristotle is concerned to classify as voluntary are those produced by character.

In fact, all the topics that Aristotle discusses along with voluntariness in *NE* III.1–5 (as well as in *EE* II.6–11) concern the exercise of character. After giving his account of voluntariness and involuntariness in *NE* III.1, he proceeds to define *prohairesis* (decision, choice, intention) in III.2, deliberation in III.3, and wish (*boulēsis*) in III.4. *Prohairesis* is a feature of the exercise of character on Aristotle's view; indeed, he defines character as a "disposition that issues in *prohairesis*" (*NE* II.6.1106b36, VI.2.1139a22–3; *EE* II.10.1227b8; cf. *NE* II.4.1105a31–2, II.5.1106a3–4). A *prohairesis*, as he explains it in *NE* III.2 and VI.2, is a desire informed by deliberation (cf. *EE* II.10.1226b5–20). Deliberation, in turn, is reasoning in the light of a goal (*telos*) (*NE* III.3.1112b11–20; *EE* II.10.1226b9–13), and the goal is the object of wish (*boulēsis*), something that seems good to the deliberator (*NE* III.4.1113a22–b2). Thus all of *prohairesis*, deliberation, and wish are features of the expression of character. When Aristotle concludes his discussion of these phenomena (*NE* III.2–4) and returns to the topic of voluntariness at the beginning of *NE* III.5, he marks the transition by noting that "actions concerning these things" (presumably those involving *prohairesis*, deliberation, and wish) are "according to *prohairesis* and voluntary" (*NE* III.5.1113b3–5;

cf. *EE* II.6.1223a16–20). The actions issuing from character, Aristotle here indicates, are voluntary.

Given Aristotle's interest in actions expressive of character, one might wonder why he focuses on voluntariness rather than *prohairesis* as the relevant notion. After all, he thinks children and other animals perform voluntary actions but lack *prohairesis* (*NE* III.2.1111b8–9; *Phys.* II.6.197b6–8). Since character involves *prohairesis*, the category of voluntary activity extends more widely than that of actions produced by character. Furthermore, he regularly insists, *prohairesis* better indicates character than actions do (*NE* III.2.1111b4–6; *EE* II.11.1228a2–3). In order to see why Aristotle focuses on voluntariness, let us first identify the special significance of *prohairesis*.

A person's *prohairesis* is a better indication of his character than his actions because the same action can result from very different *prohaireseis* (plural). For example, George might give money to needy Sam in order to gain a reputation for largesse, while Sandra might do so in order to make sure that Sam does not go hungry. Or James might return what he borrowed because he has been told to do so by his parents, whom he wants to please, while John might do so because he thinks it is the right thing to do. While the first agent in each example performs the action that he should, he does not do so "*as* the virtuous person would" (*NE* II.4.1105b7–9; cf. III.7.1116a11–15). The deficiency is in his *prohairesis*, rather than in his action. Thus it is important for Aristotle, whose concern is with actions expressive of character, to have a special interest in actions done on *prohairesis*.

However, even if *prohairesis* discriminates character better than actions do, actions too discriminate character. As Aristotle says in the *EE*, one's voluntary actions as well as one's *prohairesis* "define" virtue and vice (II.7.1223a21–3). This is because it is actions, not motivations, that hit (or miss) the mean. A virtuous state of character will dispose one, for instance, to give money when, to whom, to the extent, and so on, that one should, or to stand one's ground when, against whom, in what cause, and so on, one should (*NE* II.6.1106b21–4, II.9.1109a24–30; cf. II.3.1104b22–4). Thus whether a person gives money in the circumstances in which she should (regardless of her motivation) indicates whether her character "hits the mean." If she fails to do what she should (or if she does something that she should not), then this in itself indicates a flaw in her character. Knowing her *prohairesis* would provide more detail about the flaw (this is why *prohairesis* discriminates character *better* than actions do), but the action too reflects and indicates the flaw. In extreme cases, such as those of weakness of will, the flaw will not even show up in the *prohairesis*, for the weak-willed agent is one who acts contrary to his *prohairesis* (*NE* VII.3.1146b22–3). Thus a person's actions, in addition to her motivation, express her character. This is why an account of actions expressing character will not be restricted to actions done on *prohairesis*, but will concern the wider category of voluntary actions.

Voluntariness is the relevant notion in this context because not everything someone "does" in the widest sense counts as her action in the sense relevant to praise and blame. For example, I might carry off your car keys in the mistaken belief that they are mine, or I might knock you over as a result of being pushed forcibly from behind. While taking your keys and knocking you over are arguably things that I "do," it is implausible to claim (absent additional information) that they indicate any deficiency in my character, or that I am blameworthy for them. One way of articulating this observation is to say that these actions are not voluntary (*hekousia*). Thus Aristotle, in his quest to identify the actions that are indications of character, quite reasonably resorts to the notion of voluntariness (*to hekousion*).

Ordinary and Philosophical Notions of Voluntariness

In the ordinary Greek of Plato and Aristotle's day, the distinction between voluntary (*hekousion*) and involuntary (*akousion*) serves to demarcate those actions that issue from a person from those that do not. Depending on the context, however, the implicit criteria for drawing the distinction vary greatly. According to one paradigm, the distinction between voluntary and involuntary draws the line between what we would call witting and unwitting behavior. Oedipus, who unwittingly killed his father and married his mother, acted *akōn* (Sophocles, *Oedipus at Colonus* 964ff.), as does the unwary passerby who disturbs a wasps' nest (Homer, *Iliad* 16.263–4). According to the other paradigm, the distinction is between willing and unwilling behavior. For example, a reluctant messenger delivers bad news to his king *akōn* (Sophocles, *Antigone* 274–7). When Zeus threatens Inachus with the destruction of his entire progeny unless he expels Io, Inachus complies, but *akōn* (Aeschylus, *Prometheus Bound*, 663–72).

The English terms "voluntary" and "involuntary" also straddle these two distinctions. The first paradigm underlies the notion of "involuntary manslaughter," while the second applies to the case of a person committed involuntarily to a psychiatric institution, or to a soldier who volunteers (rather than is drafted) to enlist in the army. Thus "voluntary" and "involuntary" are very apt translations of the Greek terms.

These two ways of drawing the distinction yield the two generally recognized categories of involuntary actions in Aristotle's day: those due to ignorance, and those due to compulsion (*bia* or *anagkē*). But the two paradigms fail to yield a clear set of criteria for distinguishing voluntary from involuntary actions. The first paradigm assumes a weaker criterion for voluntariness: as long as the agent knows what she is doing, her action counts as voluntary. The second paradigm requires that the agent be whole-hearted in her action, with no reluctance or resistance or feeling of constraint. Thus some of the actions that will count as voluntary according to the first paradigm will count as involuntary according to the second. For example, handing over your wallet at gunpoint counts as voluntary according to the first paradigm, and involuntary according to the second. This is why, as Aristotle tells us, there are "disputes" about whether such actions are voluntary or involuntary (*NE* III.1.1110a7–8; *EE* II.8.1225a2–9).

Settling these disputes is a philosophical task rather than a linguistic one, and it is the former sort of task that Aristotle sets out to accomplish in his discussions of voluntariness. In providing an account of voluntariness and involuntariness that gives precise and univocal criteria for classifying actions, Aristotle is inevitably revising the "ordinary" notion of voluntariness. He is engaged in philosophical theorizing, and we will see that his discussion is a textbook case of the "dialectical" method he identifies as his general philosophical method (*NE* VII.1.1145b2–7).

A dialectical inquiry, according to Aristotle, begins with the reputable views (*endoxa*) on a subject (VII.1.1145b3–5). In the case at hand, such views include the ordinary paradigms and criteria for voluntary and involuntary action, as well as uncontroversial assumptions about the topic – for example, that praise and blame are for voluntary actions, forgiveness and pity for involuntary ones (*NE* III.1.1109b31–2; *EE* II.6.1223a9–13). Aristotle also appeals to uncontroversial examples of praiseworthy and blameworthy action, and considers rival philosophical accounts of voluntariness. To proceed dialectically is to raise the puzzles or disputes that emerge from these initial assumptions, and find a way of resolving the difficulties while preserving as much as possible of the most plausible of the original views (*NE* VII.1.1145b4–6).

While the dialectical nature of Aristotle's discussion of voluntariness is not immediately evident in the *NE*, it is readily apparent in the Eudemian account, whose notorious obscurity is due to the fact that Aristotle is there working through the reasoning that yields the account, not just presenting the results of his theorizing. Let us therefore begin with the *EE*. Once we appreciate the nature of the dialectical reasoning in that work, we will be in a position to understand some of the more puzzling aspects of the account of voluntariness that Aristotle offers in the *NE*. (See Meyer 1993: ch. 3 for a detailed analysis of the Eudemian discussion.)

The Eudemian Ethics

The governing assumption in the admittedly tortuous sequence of reasoning in *EE* II.7–8, which yields the definitions of voluntariness and involuntariness in *EE* II.9, is that voluntary and involuntary are contraries (*enantia*, II.9.1225b1–2; cf. II.8.1224a13–14). Specifically, the assumption is that voluntary action is according to (*kata*) impulse, while involuntary action is contrary to (*para*) impulse (II.7.1223a24–6; cf. II.8.1224a4–5). On this assumption, the distinction between voluntary and involuntary action is analogous to that between natural motion and "forced" or "violent" (*biaion*) motion, Aristotle tells us in *EE* II.8 (1224a15–20). Something's natural motion is according to its internal impulse, while violent motion is contrary to that impulse. Thus earth's natural motion is to go down. If it is thrown up into the air (that is, contrary to its natural impulse), its motion is forced (*biaion*). According to this governing assumption, Aristotle assumes that forced motion is the paradigm for all involuntary action – hence his repeated claim that all involuntary action is forced (*biaion*; II.7.1223a29–30, II.8.1224a10–11).

In making this assumption, Aristotle is not dismissing the other ordinary paradigm of involuntariness (unwitting behavior). Indeed, we will see that he concludes the Eudemian account by making this paradigm central to his account of involuntariness (II.9.1225b6–10). Rather, Aristotle is proceeding dialectically, with the goal of incorporating the two paradigms into a unified account that preserves the salient features of both. In the case of the second paradigm (unwillingness), the salient feature is contrariety to the agent's "impulse." Actions performed unwillingly or reluctantly are contrary to what the agent desires, wants, or values. They "go against the grain" of the person who performs them. This is why Aristotle invokes pain as a sign that an action is forced (*EE* II.7.1223a30–35, 1223b20–24, II.8.1224a30–b1). Given his goal of integrating the two paradigms of involuntariness, it is reasonable for him to begin his inquiry by considering the proposal that voluntary action is according to, and involuntary action contrary to, a person's internal impulse.

EE II.7–8 tests the plausibility of this proposal by considering it in the context of the various sorts of impulse that can move a person. These are types of desire (*orexis*): appetite (*epithumia*, 1223a29–b17), spirit (*thumos* 1223b17–29), wish (*boulēsis*, 1223b29–36), and *prohairesis* (1223b37–1224a4). Aristotle's examination shows that the proposal implies a contradiction in the case of *akrasia* (weakness of will) and *enkrateia* (self–control). In such actions, a person's rational desire conflicts with his appetite or spirit (1223a37–8, 1223b12–14). Such actions are contrary to one of these impulses, but according to the other. Thus, according to the proposal, they are both voluntary and involuntary (1223b16–17), which is impossible (1223b25–6).

The problem arises, Aristotle explains in *EE* II.8, from the fact that human agents have multiple internal impulses, and as a result, an action can be contrary to one internal impulse, but according to another (1224a27–8). He solves the problem by making explicit an additional criterion for force that he takes to be implicit in the original paradigm of forced motion. In the case of simple natural bodies, motion that is contrary to internal impulse is also externally caused – as in the case of the stone thrown upwards. So too in the case of living things and non-human animals: "we see them undergoing and doing many things by force – whenever *something from the outside* moves them against their internal impulse" (II.7.1223a22–3). In these cases, the body in question has only a single internal impulse, and thus any motion contrary to that impulse must be externally caused. So it is unnecessary, in these cases, to state the requirement of external causation in addition to that of contrariety to impulse. But once we clarify the notion of force to make external causation an explicit criterion, Aristotle claims, the paradox about weak-willed and self-controlled action disappears. In being contrary to impulse, they are only "similar" to forced actions. Since they are internally caused, they are voluntary (II.8.1224b3–10).

In making external causation an explicit criterion for force, Aristotle revises the second ordinary paradigm of involuntariness (unwillingness) in order to solve the "puzzle" (*aporia*, II.8.1225a1) about continent and incontinent action. This is not, however, the only way to solve the problem. He could, for example, have followed Plato in taking only one type of desire (*boulēsis*, wish) to be the impulse relevant to voluntariness and involuntariness (cf. *Gorgias* 467s–468c). Aristotle considers this proposal in the course of the dialectical discussion in *EE* II.7. He introduces it at 1223b5–6, and finds it problematic at 1223b6–10 and 1223b30–36 (cf. II.8.1223b39–1224a3) because it implies that incontinent action is involuntary. This is an unacceptable result, he indicates, because such actions are clear cases of wrongdoing (*adikein*), and wrongdoing, he insists, is voluntary (1223b1, 1223b15, 1223b33).

Aristotle is here appealing to his reason in discussing voluntariness in the first place: the assumption that voluntary actions are praiseworthy and blameworthy (*NE* III.1.1109b31–2; *EE* II.6.1223a9–13). This assumption functions as another governing constraint in his attempt to formulate a definition of voluntariness and involuntariness. If the point in defining voluntariness is to have a set of criteria for praiseworthy and blameworthy action, and wrongdoing (*adikein*) is a clear instance of the latter, then contrariety to wish (or any other impulse) cannot be sufficient for involuntariness. Adding the explicit requirement of external causation allows Aristotle to honor this constraint.

While modern thinkers might be inclined to solve the problem by rejecting the requirement of contrariety, this is very far from Aristotle's view. His project, we have seen, is governed by the assumption that contrariety to impulse is essential to involuntariness. Thus, even if Aristotle's conception of voluntariness is intended to capture conditions of responsibility for action, involuntariness as he conceives it is not simply lack of causal responsibility. Involuntary action must, in addition, go against the grain of the agent.

In *EE* II.8, we have seen, Aristotle clarifies the conception of involuntariness to require that, in addition to being contrary to impulse, an involuntary action must also be externally caused (1224a13–30). This solves the puzzle (and dispute) about weak-willed and self-controlled action. On the clarified account of force, they both turn out to be voluntary, since it is uncontroversial that they are "according to" the agent's own impulse (1224a30–1225a2). After concluding this clarification by discussing cases where it is controversial whether the action originates in the agent or in something external – cases of compulsion or forced choice (1225a2–36), which we will discuss below – Aristotle returns, in II.9, to his project of integrating the two paradigms for voluntariness and involuntariness. That is, he seeks to combine the requirement that involuntariness involves contrariety to impulse with the view that unwitting actions are involuntary.

His remarks in *EE* II.9 are brief and careless. He concludes by proposing that the contraries constitutive of voluntariness and involuntariness are, respectively, acting with knowledge and acting in ignorance of what one is doing (1225b1–8). These are offered as glosses for "acting according to thought" and "acting contrary to thought" respectively (1225b1). This conclusion, however, invites many objections internal to Aristotle's project. First of all, thought (*dianoia*) is not, for Aristotle, an impulse (*NE* VI.2.1139a35–6). Being according to thought is not, as he here implies, an alternative to being according to desire; thought and desire together cause action (VI.2.1139a31–5). Second, and more important for our present purposes, the account of involuntariness given here fails to preserve the contrariety to impulse that Aristotle has been at pains to preserve in the preceding discussion. Indeed, it does not even allow for a category of involuntary actions that are due to force rather than to ignorance.

Thus there is a gap, in the Eudemian account of voluntariness and involuntariness, between Aristotle's goals and what he actually achieves. It is nonetheless clear, however, that his aim there is to integrate the two ordinary paradigms for involuntariness. We are now in a position to see that the Nicomachean discussion continues and advances the dialectic of the Eudemian account, and better satisfies its goal.

The Nicomachean Ethics

The *NE* account begins by correcting the fumble at the end of the Eudemian discussion. There are, Aristotle insists, two general types of involuntary action, those due to force and those due to ignorance (III.1.1109b35–1110a1). After clarifying the criteria for these two types of involuntariness, Aristotle infers a general account of voluntariness: "Since forced actions and those due to ignorance are involuntary, the voluntary would appear to be that whose origin is in the agent who knows the particular facts about the action" (III.1.1111a22–4). These opening remarks, and the definition of voluntariness that Aristotle develops from them, often leave readers underwhelmed. Is Aristotle not simply collecting and organizing ordinary criteria for voluntariness and involuntariness, rather than engaging in a distinctively philosophical investigation of his own? However, if we read these remarks in the light of the Eudemian discussion that we have just examined, we can see that this impression is mistaken. To be sure, Aristotle here in the *NE* is insisting on the two ordinary paradigms for involuntariness, but his discussion in the *EE* concluded with a definition that inadvertently rules out one of them. From this perspective, Aristotle's insistence in the *NE* on the two ordinary categories of involuntariness is a correction to the Eudemian definition.

Furthermore, the Nicomachean definition of the voluntary as "that whose origin is in the agent who knows the particular facts" (III.1.1111a23) actually succeeds in doing what the Eudemian discussion tried but failed to do. It provides a unified conception of voluntariness that incorporates insights from both of the ordinary paradigms. From the paradigm according to which contrariety to impulse is central to involuntariness comes the requirement that voluntary action has its origin (*archē*) in the agent. In the idiom of the *EE*, it is "according to his impulse." From the paradigm according to which involuntary action is unwitting comes the requirement that the voluntary agent know what he is doing.

In any case, Aristotle in the *NE* does not simply infer this definition of the voluntary from the ordinary assumption that involuntary acts are either forced or due to ignorance. His inference depends crucially on his clarification of the criteria for these two types of involuntariness. If we turn to examine his explanation, first of force (III.1.1110a1–b17) and then of involuntariness involving ignorance (III.1.1110b18–1111a21), we will be able to recognize that he is here building upon and extending the dialectical discussion of the *EE*.

Constraint and Compulsion

Aristotle devotes most of his discussion of force in the *NE* (III.1.1110a1–b17) to a clarification of the question of what it is for the origin of the action to be external to the agent. He opts there for an extremely restrictive criterion. The agent must contribute nothing to the action (1110a1–4); that is, he must not be the one moving the parts of his body (1110a15–17). It might seem odd, in the light of this restriction, that Aristotle should even recognize a category of involuntariness due to force. Voluntariness and involuntariness are properties of actions (*EE* II.6.1222b29, 1223a15–20; *NE* III.5.1113b4), but the only "actions" that can satisfy this criterion of external causation are arguably not actions at all: for example, being driven off course by the winds, or physically abducted (III.1.1110a3–4). It is not odd at all, however, if we understand Aristotle's claim in the context of his dialectical project, for there are plenty of genuine actions that would be classified as forced and involuntary according to the ordinary paradigm of involuntariness due to force.

These are cases in which a person claims to be compelled or forced to do something bad – for example, if he has been threatened with beating, imprisonment, or torture if he fails to do it (*EE* II.8.1225a4–6), or if he acts to avoid a greater evil (*NE* III.1.1110a4–7). Such cases are described in the *MM* as ones in which external things are thought to "compel" (*anagkazein*) the person to act (*MM* I.15.1188b15–20). Aristotle discusses these cases in the *EE* and *NE* when he clarifies the conditions in which the origin of the action is external to the agent. In both cases he resists the ordinary view that such actions are involuntary.

In the *EE*, he claims that as long as the person is capable of enduring the threatened sanction, the action is "up to him" to do and not to do, and hence it is voluntary (II.8.1225a8–14). Only in cases in which the alternative to his action is so painful as to be literally unbearable is his action "not up to him," and for that reason forced – for example, if the pain of torture is so severe that it is impossible to keep from divulging the secret. This is an extremely restrictive criterion, for in most of the alleged cases of compulsion, the agent acts to avoid an alternative that, however undesirable, is still endurable.

Such are the cases on which Aristotle focuses in the parallel passage in the *NE*. A man does something shameful under orders from a tyrant – who will kill the man's family if he fails to comply (*NE* III.1.1110a4–7). A captain throws his precious cargo overboard in a storm in order to save the lives of those aboard ship (1110a10–11). The agent in such cases acts voluntarily, Aristotle insists at some length (1110a11–b9) because "the origin of moving his bodily parts is in him, and if something's origin is in him, it is up to him to do or not to do it" (1110a15–18).

Those who think that such actions are involuntary are motivated in part by the view that the agents are not blameworthy for what they do (cf. III.1.1110a19–21). They depend on the assumption that they share with Aristotle that blame is for voluntary actions. Aristotle's response is to point out that denying voluntariness is too blunt an instrument to secure this result. After all, he indicates, agents in such situations can be praised for making the right judgment about which alternative to take, or for sticking to that judgment. This is because such judgment and resolution are marks of good character. It is a mark of bad or at any rate deficient character to fail on either of these two points, Aristotle points out (1110a19–b1). Such failures are blameworthy. (The limiting type of case is one in which the person makes the right judgment about what to do, but it is beyond human nature [hence not within the scope of virtue of character] to abide by that correct judgment [1110a31]. This is the type of case that Aristotle in the *EE* has already classified as involuntary; *sungnōmē* [forgiveness] is appropriate for such agents [*NE* 1110a24], and hence the verdict "involuntary" is required.)

The actions that Aristotle in these contexts classifies as voluntary are paradigm cases of *in*voluntariness on the "unwillingness" paradigm. We have seen that it is perfectly natural Greek to describe such agents as acting *akōn*. It is Aristotle's theoretical innovation that results in the verdict that virtually no real actions are due to force. His concession that such actions are involuntary "when considered without qualification" (III.1.1110a18; cf. 1110a9) or "in themselves" (1110b3) – however we are to understand what these qualifications mean (cf. *EE* II.8.1225a11–14) – is an attempt to accommodate (or at any rate acknowledge) that ordinary, pre-philosophical view in his philosophical account.

Force and Contrariety in the *NE*

Although Aristotle's discussion of force (*bia*) in the *NE* focuses on the criterion of external causation, this is not because he has forgotten about or abandoned the Eudemian constraint that involuntary action be contrary to impulse. Indeed, it is precisely because the disputed cases in *NE* III.1 satisfy this constraint that they appear to be compelling candidates for involuntariness. Adding the requirement of external causation for force was, after all, Aristotle's own theoretical clarification in the *EE*. It is thus natural that he should be emphasizing and clarifying it here in the *NE*.

In any case, Aristotle here in the *NE* clearly still assumes, as something so obvious that it goes without saying, that forced actions are contrary to impulse. He mentions in passing, when rejecting another set of cases alleged to be forced, that of course forced actions must be painful (III.1.1110b12). As the *EE* makes clear, pain is essential to involuntariness because it is a sign of contrariety to impulse (*EE* II.7.1223a30–35, 1223b20–24, II.8.1224a30–b1).

That Aristotle has not abandoned the criterion of contrariety, and that he continues in the *NE* to pursue the homogenizing project of the *EE*, is vividly clear when he discusses involuntariness due to ignorance (III.1.1110b18–1111a21). While he has not thought it worth emphasizing, in his account of force, that forced actions must be painful, he thinks it is important to insist on this in the case of acts due to ignorance. Indeed, this is the first point he makes when he embarks on the discussion of involuntariness involving ignorance: "While everything due to ignorance is not-voluntary [*ouk hekousion*], what is involuntary [*akousion*] must also be painful or regretted" (III.1.1111a19–22). He repeats this requirement at the close of his discussion of ignorance (1111a19–21; cf. 1111a32). Once again, pain (and hence contrariety to impulse) is necessary for involuntariness.

Here we see that Aristotle has accomplished the harmonizing project begun in the *EE*, whose goal is to take the two ordinary paradigms of involuntariness and incorporate them into a single set of criteria for involuntariness and voluntariness. Contrariety, which is part of one ordinary paradigm for involuntariness, is here integrated into Aristotle's account of the other. The contrariety preserved in the resulting account of involuntariness leads some scholars to translate *akousion* as "counter-voluntary" rather than "involuntary" (for example, Broadie and Rowe 2002: 38). While this is clearly an accurate reflection of Aristotle's integrated theory of the *akousion*, it is still not a better translation than "involuntary." After all, "involuntary" in English (no less than *akousion* in Greek) is used perfectly idiomatically of actions that go against a person's will (for example: "involuntary servitude"). Furthermore, Aristotle's claim that actions due to ignorance but not regretted fail to be voluntary is a theoretical revision of ordinary usage, and makes what his audience would view as an extremely surprising claim. That such actions are not "counter-voluntary" goes without saying. The best translation of a controversial claim should not make it look like a truism.

Knowledge and Ignorance

In contrast to his very brief remarks in *EE* II.9, Aristotle devotes considerable attention in *NE* III.1 to clarifying the sort of knowledge that is required for voluntariness (1110b28–1111a19). The dialectical considerations he is engaging with here are forcefully articulated in Plato's dialogues.

Plato's Socrates famously declares that all wrongdoing is involuntary because it is due to ignorance of the good. We all want the good, he claims (*Meno* 77b–78b), and whenever we do something, we do it for the sake of the good (*Gorgias* 467c–468c). Thus, all wrongdoing is due to ignorance of what is good. Wrongdoing comes in two varieties. The first is incontinence, which in the *Protagoras* (354e–357e), Socrates argues, is due to ignorance of the good. The other is ordinary wrongdoing. Here, although one does what one wants to do (what appears to be good), it is, in fact, bad. Hence, although the wrongdoer gets what she aims at in one sense (the apparent good), she is mistaken in believing this objective to be good (*Gorgias* 468d). Her rational desire (*boulēsis*), which aims at the good, is frustrated by such actions. Thus, on this view, wrongdoing is both contrary to desire and due to ignorance. This constellation of views persists through Plato's latest work. In the *Laws*, the Athenian reaffirms that "all wrongdoing is involuntary" (860c–e; cf. 731c).

Like some of Aristotle's conclusions about voluntariness, Plato's claim that all wrongdoing is involuntary constitutes an affront to, and revision of, ordinary notions. His point, unlike Aristotle's, is not to capture conditions in which praise and blame are appropriate. Quite the contrary, Plato's dominant speakers clearly think such ignorance is reprehensible and worthy of censure. Persons ignorant in this way are in need of punishment (*Gorgias* 478a–479b), sometimes even death (*Gorgias* 480d; *Laws* 854c–e, 862e–863a). The assertion that wrongdoing is involuntary is never invoked in Plato as a defense of wrongdoers, or an attempt to escape sanctions or punishment (with the possible exception of *Apology* 26a).

Plato in his revisionist theorizing is quite happy to abandon the ordinary assumption that responsibility, praise, and blame go along with voluntariness. Rather, his aim is to underscore the importance of attaining knowledge of the good. If we lack such knowledge, he preaches, we fail to achieve what we want most dearly in life. We are frustrating our deepest desires. We are like madmen in the example from the *Gorgias*: cunningly plotting to achieve ends that frustrate our deepest and dearest purposes in life (*Gorgias* 469d–470a; cf. *Laws* 731c). Plato's goal in calling wrongdoing involuntary is protreptic: to exhort us to seek and cultivate moral knowledge.

Aristotle's theoretical interest in voluntariness, we have seen, is quite different from Plato's. His motivation for seeking a theoretical definition of voluntariness is to capture the conditions of praiseworthy and blameworthy action. We have already seen how, in the *EE*, he criticizes and rejects the Platonic view that actions contrary to wish (*boulēsis*) are involuntary (*EE* II.7.1223b5–10, 1223b30–36, II.8.1223b39–1224a3). He rejects it because it conflicts with the constraint that wrongdoing is voluntary. Here in *NE* III.1, Aristotle engages more directly with the motivation for the Platonic view.

When Plato declares that wrongdoing is involuntary because it is due to ignorance, he is relying on a perfectly ordinary criterion for voluntariness, implicit in the paradigm of unwitting behavior for involuntary action. It is uncontroversial that if you do not know what you are doing, then you act involuntarily. But Plato's inference from this, that wicked actions are involuntary, is surprising and controversial because it runs up against another well-entrenched assumption about voluntariness – that blameworthy action is voluntary. Unlike Plato, Aristotle is not prepared to sacrifice this aspect of the ordinary view in his own theoretical account. But the Platonic view does present a puzzle to be solved. If wicked behavior involves ignorance of the good (a premise with which Aristotle agrees), then how can it be voluntary?

Solving this puzzle is Aristotle's main focus in the Nicomachean discussion of involuntariness due to ignorance (III.1.1110b18–21). He sets out here to clarify the sort of knowledge that is necessary for voluntariness. Unlike Plato, Aristotle has a fairly detailed account of the structure of rational motivation. He distinguishes what an agent does (the action) from the goal for the sake of which he does it (the good) – hence the distinction between the action and the *prohairesis* on which it is done. That for the sake of which one acts is part of one's *prohairesis*, not of one's action. But voluntariness is a property of actions, not motivations. Given this distinction between an action and its motivation, Aristotle is able to distinguish two sorts of knowledge. On the one hand, there is knowledge about the action itself – knowledge of what one is doing. On the other hand, there is knowledge expressed in one's reasons for acting – knowledge that what one is doing is good.

Thus an action can involve two different types of ignorance: ethical ignorance (ignorance of what is good and bad, of what is right and wrong to pursue), and non-ethical ignorance: ignorance of what one is, in fact, doing. Examples of the latter include: whether one is drinking water as opposed to poison; whether one is fighting with an enemy or a parent, with a blunted spear rather than a sharp one; whether pushing the lever will release the catapult or just display it (*NE* III.1.1111a3–15; cf. *EE* II.9.1225b3–5). Aristotle refers to the latter as ignorance of the particulars (III.1.1110b33, 1111a23–4): who, what, where, and so on – all the factors relevant to the doctrine of the mean (*NE* II.6.1106b21–4). The former he sometimes characterizes as ignorance of the universal (III.1.1110b32; cf. VII.3.1147a3) – meaning the premise in practical reasoning that has to do with what is good: for example, "it is good to help those in need; here is a needy person; so I should help him" (cf. *NE* VII.3.1147a25–31; *Mot. An.* 7.701a10–20). He also calls it ignorance "in the *prohairesis*" (III.1.1110b31). This is ignorance manifested in the goals one pursues in acting, not in one's grasp of the action one is doing.

When Plato claims that all wrongdoing is involuntary, he collapses the distinction, central to Aristotle's account of *prohairesis*, between what one does (the action) and one's reason for doing it. Thus it is not surprising that in the *Nicomachean Ethics*, immediately after rejecting the Platonic interpretation of the knowledge requirement for voluntariness, the next topic Aristotle takes up is *prohairesis* (III.2), and its constituent parts: deliberation (III.3) and wish (III.4).

The Platonic Asymmetry Thesis

After discussing *prohairesis*, deliberation, and wish in *NE* III.2–4, Aristotle returns to the topic of voluntariness and concludes his discussion of the topic in *NE* III.5. His engagement with Plato, however, is not yet over. An additional consequence of the Platonic view of voluntariness is that there is an asymmetry between good and bad actions: our good actions are voluntary, but our bad ones are not. The asymmetry thesis is a view Aristotle is clearly concerned to reject (*NE* III.1.1111a27–9; *EE* II.7.1223b14–16; cf. *MM* I.9.1187a21–3), and this is exactly what he is doing when he opens *NE* III.5. He opens the chapter by inferring, from the discussion of *prohairesis* and its components in III.2–4, that virtuous and vicious actions alike are voluntary:

> [1] Since the end is the object of wish, while the things that promote the end are objects of deliberation and *prohairesis*, actions that concern these would be according to *prohairesis* and voluntary. Now, [2] the activities of the virtues concern these. So [3] both virtue, and likewise vice, is up to us. (*NE* III.5.1113b3–7)

It might appear that the affirmation of symmetry in the argument's conclusion [3] concerns states of character – "virtue [*aretē*] and . . . vice [*kakia*]" (III.5.1113b6–7; cf. 1113b14–17) – rather than actions. But this cannot be what Aristotle means. First of all, it is perfectly natural Greek to use such expressions as "virtue," "vice," "injustice," and their cognates to refer to good and bad actions (cf. Sophocles, *Tyro* fr. 582). Plato sometimes articulates his claim that wrongdoing is involuntary using such terminology. "No one is involuntarily wicked [*kakos*]" the Athenian says at *Laws* IX.860d5, where he is clearly talking about wicked actions (860d9). Second, if Aristotle did understand [3] to concern states of character, his inference to it from [1] and [2] would be invalid, since these premises unambiguously concern virtuous and vicious actions. Similarly, in the *EE*, the arguments Aristotle offers against the asymmetry thesis establish only a symmetry between virtuous and vicious actions, even though the thesis is there articulated using terms that might equally well refer to states of character (*EE* II.11.1228a7–11; cf. II.6.1223a15–20; *MM* I.9.1187a5–19, I.11.1187b20–21, I.12.1187b31).

In the remarks that follow immediately upon these opening lines of *NE* III.5, Aristotle makes it clear that the symmetry of concern to him is between virtuous and vicious actions. He explains, in support of [3]:

> For in those cases in which it is up to us to do something, it is also up to us not to do it, and in cases in which "No" is up to us, so is "Yes." So if doing it, which is fine, is up to us, then not doing it, which is bad, is also up to us. And if not doing it, which is fine, is up to us, then doing it, which is shameful, is also up to us. And if it is up to us to do fine actions and shameful ones, and in the same way not to do them, *and this is what it is to be good and bad*, then it is up to us to be decent and base. (III.5.1131b7–14)

Indeed, he here says explicitly that he is using "being good" and "being bad" as equivalent to "doing fine actions" and "doing shameful actions" (1113b12–13). That is, he describes actions using terms that might equally well refer to states of character. Aristotle is here responding to opponents who maintain that there is an asymmetry in voluntariness between good and bad actions.

Aristotle's motivation for rejecting the asymmetry thesis is clear. Since he inquires into voluntariness in order to capture the causal conditions of praise and blame, it is a constraint on this account that both good and bad actions turn out to be voluntary. Therefore, he must reject the asymmetry thesis. He does not, however, do so without argument. In *NE* III.5 he offers a number of independent objections to the thesis. As we have seen, he points to considerations of the psychology of action (1113b3–6, quoted above), and to the "two sidedness" involved in the notion of an action being "up to us" or its origin being in us (1113b6–14, quoted above; elaborated further at 1113b17–21). In addition, he points out that the symmetry is presupposed in normal practices of reward and punishment (1113b21–30).

After a long excursus on the voluntariness of character formation – where considerations of symmetry are notably absent (III.5.1113b30–1114a31) – Aristotle proceeds to consider an argument in favor of the asymmetry thesis: "Suppose someone says that everyone pursues the apparent good, but is not in control of the appearance. Rather, the end appears to each person according to the sort of person he is" (1114a31–b1). Aristotle's response is two-pronged. First of all, he notes that his immediately preceding argument, that we are responsible for our states of character (1113b30–1114a31), undermines the objector's premise that we are not in control of the way the good appears to us (1114b1–3). But in any case, Aristotle continues, even if the objector is right that we are not in control of the way the good appears to us (1114b3–12), this applies equally to good actions and bad ones. Hence it does not show the former to be any more voluntary than the latter (1114b12–16). (In drawing this conclusion, Aristotle sometimes uses "virtue" and "vice" to articulate the asymmetry thesis [1114b13, 19–20], but it is clear in these contexts that he is talking about the voluntariness of actions, not of character: *prattousin*, 1114b16; *en tois praxesin*, 1114b21.)

After reiterating the dilemma – that the argument fails if we are responsible for our states of character, and it also fails if we are not (1114b17–21) – Aristotle reminds us that his own position is captured by the first lemma: our virtues (*aretai*) are up to us (1114b21–3), and the same thing goes for the vices (*kakiai*) (1114b23–5). (Note the use of the plural here, "virtues" and "vices," unlike the singular "virtue" and "vice" used to refer to actions.)

In offering this refutation of the argument for the asymmetry thesis, Aristotle concludes his engagement with and rejection of the Platonic account of involuntariness. We are also at the end of his discussion of voluntariness. The remaining lines of III.5 (1114b26–1115a6) are a connecting passage that concludes the general account of virtue of character, and introduces the discussions of the particular virtues of character.

Responsibility for Character

Once we recognize that *NE* III.5, the last chapter in the discussion of voluntariness, is organized around the asymmetry thesis, and that Aristotle's main project in the chapter is to reject that thesis, we are in a position to see that the chapter's main preoccupation is not, despite initial appearances, responsibility for character. The thesis that we are responsible for the states of character we develop is indeed introduced and defended in the course of the chapter in an extended discussion that we have yet to examine (III.5.1114a4–31). It is one of the conclusions that Aristotle recapitulates in the remarks that conclude the general discussion of virtue of character at the end of III.5 (1114b26–1115a3). So it is evidently an important one for Aristotle. Just what significance he attaches to the thesis, however, we have yet to determine.

As a first step toward this goal, let us consider the context in which he invokes and argues for the thesis. Aristotle is contending, against the asymmetry thesis, that ordinary practices of legal reward and sanction presuppose that our bad actions are up to us, as long as they are not done "by force or due to ignorance for which we are not responsible" (III.5.1113b24–5; cf. *EE* II.9.1225b14–16). He goes on to point out that people are also punished for being ignorant, if they are responsible for the ignorance (1113b30–1114a10). Such people were "in control of taking care" (1114a3) to acquire (or retain) the relevant knowledge. "But," an objector responds, "presumably he is the sort of person not to take care" (1114a3–40). It is to this objection that Aristotle offers his famous argument that we are responsible for becoming the sorts of people that we are.

Before considering this argument, it is important to be clear about the objection to which it responds. Modern readers often assume that both Aristotle and the objector agree on the principle that if a person acts as he is disposed to, then his action is not up to him (or does not originate in him) unless it can be shown that the disposition itself is up to him or originates in him (for example, Hardie 1980: 175). In a nutshell, the principle is that responsibility for action requires responsibility for character. This is a very common modern assumption about responsibility, and it seems to be what motivates the hypothesis we rejected at the beginning of this chapter: that establishing responsibility for character is the main goal of the account of voluntariness. But is there any evidence that Aristotle endorses such a principle?

Two passages in *NE* III.5 may give the misleading impression of articulating or implying the principle: (a) 1113b17–21 and (b) 1114b3–4. However, (a) concerns the asymmetry thesis about action, not the thesis of responsibility for character. On Burnet's (1990) reading of 1114b3 (*ei de mē outheis*), (b) does appear to articulate the principle. But the better reading is "if no one – *ei de mēdeis* – is responsible for his wrongdoing . . ." So nowhere in *NE* III.5 does Aristotle even articulate, let alone endorse, the principle. Furthermore, if he were to endorse the principle, the argument that we are responsible for our states of character would be the "linch-pin" of his account of voluntariness; yet, as noted above, the *EE* fails to argue for, or even articulate, this thesis. (Apparent instances to the contrary – *EE* II.6.1223a19–20 and II.11.1228a7–11 – address the asymmetry thesis rather than the thesis of responsibility for character; contra Broadie 1991: 162.)

The most we can infer from the fact that Aristotle responds to the objection by arguing that we are responsible for the dispositions we develop is that he takes such responsibility to be sufficient (not necessary) for responsibility for the action that issues from that disposition. That is, he is assuming the transitivity of responsibility: if you are responsible for a disposition, you are also responsible for what issues from that disposition. This principle of transitivity is much weaker than the principle that responsibility for an action requires responsibility for the disposition from which one acts. There is no evidence that the latter principle is assumed by either Aristotle or his opponent.

It is no accident that Aristotle raises the issue of responsibility for character in a context in which responsibility for ignorance is at issue. This is because the ignorance that in Plato's view makes wrongdoing involuntary is, in Aristotle's view, constitutive of character (*NE* III.1.1110b28–30). The principle of transitivity on which Aristotle relies in his response to the objection supplies one more argument in the battery of arguments he marshals against the asymmetry thesis. Even if bad character involves ignorance of the good, it is only ignorance for which one is not responsible that exempts one from praise and blame (III.5.1113b23–5). Since we are responsible for our characters, and hence for our ignorance of the good, then (via the principle of transitivity) our wrongdoing is still up to us.

Now that we have identified the role played by the thesis of responsibility for character in the only argument in which Aristotle invokes it, let us turn to consider his argument for the thesis. Of the person who is allegedly "of the sort not to take care," Aristotle says:

> People are themselves responsible for coming to be like this, by living without restraint. So too are they responsible for being unjust or intemperate – by doing bad things or by spending their time in drinking and the like. For the way they conduct themselves in these matters makes them be like that [sc. unjust and intemperate]. This is clear in the case of those who are in training for any kind of contest of action, for they continually practice the activity. So to be ignorant that it is from one's activities in these matters that one's dispositions develop is the mark of someone without perception . . . If someone does knowingly what will make him unjust, then he is unjust voluntarily. (*NE* III.5.1114a4–13)

Aristotle's argument here, which has no parallel in either the *EE* or the *MM*, is very simple. He first appeals to the general account of character formation that he outlines in *NE* II: we become just by performing just actions, temperate by performing temperate actions, and so on (III.5.1114a4–6). His second point is that we know this when we are performing the character-forming actions. We know that we are doing what will make us just (or unjust), temperate or intemperate (1114a7–10). Thus, he concludes, we voluntarily become the sorts of people we are: "If someone knowingly does the sorts of things that make him unjust, then he is unjust voluntarily" (1114a12–13).

A familiar objection to this argument from modern readers is to say: but what if someone has been raised in deprived conditions, and does not know, for example, that stealing is unjust? Surely, we are not responsible for knowing what is just and unjust, since – as Aristotle himself emphasizes – this is a product of our upbringing and social context. Thus, the objection concludes, Aristotle is wrong to deduce that people are responsible for their states of character.

The objection, however, makes the mistake of supposing that Aristotle's argument depends on the assumption that we are *responsible for knowing* what sorts of actions are unjust, intemperate, and so on, at the stage of development when we engage in the character-forming activities he refers to at III.5.1114a5–14: living without restraint, spending time in drinking and the like, performing unjust actions, and so on. Aristotle, however, starts from a much weaker assumption: that we do in fact know this. We should not be surprised that he assumes this, since all along he has made it clear that he is addressing an audience who have received a good ethical education (*NE* I.4.1095b4–6), and that he is addressing the practical question of such an audience: "what must we do to become good?" (II.2.1103b27–9). The fortunate young people in that audience are, in Aristotle's view, no more responsible for having a correct general outlook on right and wrong at this stage of their moral development than the person raised in a den of thieves is responsible for having a mistaken one.

Aristotle is keenly aware, as Plato was before him, that only someone who has been raised in optimal conditions will have correct views about what is fine and shameful (*NE* II.3.1104b11–13). That is why he insists, in the closing chapter of the *NE*, that one needs to have been raised under correct laws. Laws must dictate not only the adult activities that people are to engage in, but also the earliest stages of the upbringing they are to receive (*NE* II.1.1103b1–6, X.9.1179b31–1180a6). Someone who fails to receive such a correct *paideia* (early education) has virtually no chance of becoming good (*NE* I.4.1095b8–13). Even at the stage of habituation by adult activities, Aristotle notes, it is necessary to have good teachers (II.1.1103b10–13). One can no more learn on one's own and in unfavorable circumstances to be a navigator than to become good. Thus it is a mistake to suppose that Aristotle is attempting to argue in *NE* III.5 that, no matter what the circumstances in which a person is raised, he is still responsible for becoming virtuous or vicious.

Aristotle's intended audience in the *NE* is young people who have been blessed with a correct upbringing, good laws, and competent teachers. He is telling this audience that now it is up to them to complete the process that will make them the sort of people they aspire to be. It they fail, it will be their own fault. Here we can see that the significance Aristotle attaches to his thesis of responsibility for character relates to the ultimate practical question he addresses in the *NE*. We become good, he insists, not by taking refuge in purely intellectual studies (*NE* II.4.1105b11–18), but by engaging actively in the practical world, where it is up to us to act in accordance with the standards we have learned from our upbringing.

References

Broadie, S. 1991: *Ethics with Aristotle*. New York: Oxford University Press.
—and Rowe, C. 2002: *Aristotle: Nicomachean Ethics*. Oxford: Oxford University Press.
Burnet, J. 1900: *The Ethics of Aristotle*. London: Methuen.
Hardie, W. F. R. 1980: *Aristotle's Ethical Theory*, 2nd edn. Oxford: Clarendon Press.
Meyer, S. S. 1993: *Aristotle on Moral Responsibility: Character and Cause*. Oxford: Blackwell.

Further reading

Annas, J. 1993: *The Morality of Happiness*. Oxford: Oxford University Press.
Bondeson, W. 1974: "Aristotle on Responsibility for One's Character and the Possibility of Character Change," *Phronesis* 19: 59–65.
Brickhouse, T. C. 1991: "Roberts on Responsibility for Character in the *Nicomachean Ethics*," *Ancient Philosophy* 11: 137–48.

Burnyeat, M. F. 1980: "Aristotle on Learning to be Good." In A. O. Rorty (ed.), *Essays on Aristotle's Ethics*, pp. 69–92. Berkeley, CA: University of California Press.

Curren, R. R. 1989: "The Contribution of *Nicomachean Ethics* III.5 to Aristotle's Theory of Responsibility," *History of Philosophy Quarterly* 6: 261–77.

— 2000: *Aristotle on the Necessity of Public Education*. Lanham, MD: Rowman and Littlefield.

Everson, S. 1990: "Aristotle's Compatibilism in the *Nicomachean Ethics*," *Ancient Philosophy* 10: 81–99.

Furley, D. J. 1967: *Two Studies in the Greek Atomists: Study II, Aristotle and Epicurus on Voluntary Action*, pp. 160–22, 184–95, and 216–26. Princeton, NJ: Princeton University Press.

— 1978: "Self-movers." In G. E. R. Lloyd and G. E. L. Owen (eds), *Aristotle on Mind and the Senses*, pp. 165–79. Cambridge: Cambridge University Press. Reprinted in A. O. Rorty (ed.), *Essays on Aristotle's Ethics*, pp. 55–68. Berkeley, CA: University of California Press, 1980.

Hursthouse, R. 1984: "Acting and Feeling in Character: *Nicomachean Ethics* 3.i," *Phronesis* 29: 252–66.

Irwin, T. H. 1980: "Reason and Responsibility in Aristotle." In A. O. Rorty (ed.), *Essays on Aristotle's Ethics*, pp. 117–56. Berkeley, CA: University of California Press.

Kenny, A. 1979: *Aristotle's Theory of the Will*. New Haven, CT: Yale University Press.

— 1994: "Self-movement and External Causation." In M. L. Gill and J. G. Lennox (eds), *Self-motion: From Aristotle to Newton*, pp. 65–80. Princeton, NJ: Princeton University Press.

— 1998: "Moral Responsibility: Aristotle and After." In S. Everson (ed.), *Ethics: Companions to Ancient Thought*, vol. 4, pp. 221–40. Cambridge: Cambridge University Press.

Moline, J. N. 1989: "Aristotle on Praise and Blame," *Archiv für Geschichte der Philosophie* 71: 283–302.

Rickert, G. A. 1989: *Hekon and Akon in Early Greek Thought*. Atlanta: Scholars Press.

Roberts, J. 1989: "Aristotle on Responsibility for Action and Character," *Ancient Philosophy* 9: 23–36.

Sauvé, S. 1988: "Why Involuntary Actions are Painful," *Southern Journal of Philosophy* 27 (suppl.): 127–58.

Siegler, F. A. 1968: "Voluntary and Involuntary," *Monist* 52: 268–87.

Urmson, J. O. 1988: *Aristotle's Ethics*. Oxford: Blackwell.

7

Aristotle on Greatness of Soul

Roger Crisp

In the recent revival of interest in Aristotelian ethics, relatively little attention has been paid to the virtue of greatness of soul (*megalopsuchia*). This is partly because of the focus on the more structurally central concepts of Aristotle's theory, in particular happiness (*eudaimonia*) and virtue (*aretē*). But in fact a study of greatness of soul can reveal important insights into the overall shape of Aristotelian ethics, including the place of external goods and luck in the virtuous life, and the significance of "the noble" (*to kalon*). Further, Aristotle describes the great-souled person in more detail than any other, and calls greatness of soul a "sort of crown of the virtues" (*NE* IV.3.1124a1–2). Many have found aspects of the portrait of the great-souled person in the *Nicomachean Ethics* repellent or absurd, but that is no good reason for the student of Aristotle to shy away from it. In this chapter, I shall elucidate Aristotle's account of greatness of soul, addressing some puzzles internal to that account and bringing out its place in, and implications for, the ethics of Aristotle and of those modern writers influenced by him.

Greatness of Soul as a Virtue

To understand greatness of soul as an Aristotelian virtue requires first understanding Aristotle's conception of virtue itself. Aristotle distinguishes virtues into two classes – intellectual virtues and virtues of character – corresponding to distinct aspects of the human soul (*NE* I.13). Greatness of soul is a virtue of character, though, like all such virtues, it requires its possessor to have the intellectual virtue of practical wisdom (*phronēsis*; *NE* VI.13). A virtue, Aristotle claims, is neither a feeling nor a capacity, but a state or disposition (*hexis*) to act or to feel in particular ways in certain circumstances (*NE* II.5–6). And, of course, the same is true of vices.

The key element in Aristotle's account of virtue is his famous "doctrine of the mean" (*NE* II.6). It has several times been suggested that greatness of soul fits awkwardly into that doctrine because greatness is itself an "extreme" (Hardie 1978: 65; Curzer 1990: 527–8; Horner 1998: 421; Kristjánsson 1998: 400). There are indeed interesting questions to be asked about why Aristotle individuated greatness of soul as he did, and also some problems relating to the details of the account of it as a mean. But once the doctrine of the mean is properly understood, it should be clear that greatness of soul fits well into that account.

Let me elucidate the doctrine using the example of even temper, the mean concerned with anger (NE IV.3). What is it to say that even temper is a mean, or that the actions or feelings of the even-tempered person fall "in a mean?" It is initially tempting to think that the mean here must consist in feeling a moderate amount of anger, but this is both to ignore Aristotle's characterization of the mean in NE II.6 and to open the way to misunderstanding how the idea of greatness can feature as an element within a mean state. According to NE II.6, anger "can be experienced too much or too little, and in both ways not well. But to have [it] at the right time, about the right things, toward the right people, for the right end, and in the right way, is the mean and best" (1106b20–22). So that is the mean in the case of anger – feeling it at the right time, about the right things, and so on. But what about the two vices, those of excess and of deficiency? In one sense, there are only two ways to go wrong with anger, which can be captured by two variant placings of the negative operator. One way to go wrong would be *not* to have anger at the right time, about the right things, and so on. If you assault me for no good reason, for example, that is something I should feel angry about, and I should feel angry with you right now. If I just shrug it off and go on my way that is a kind of culpable insensibility. Another way to go wrong is to feel anger *not* at the right time, that is, at the wrong time, and so on. This is the kind of vice one often sees in car drivers who become furious at what they see, mistakenly, as insults to their honor.

In another sense, however, as Aristotle points out (NE II.6.1106b28–33), there are many ways to go wrong, and only one way to get things right. Hitting the mean involves getting one's actions and feelings right in all the various ways listed in the doctrine. But because each variable is different, to any one variable corresponds, to speak strictly, a different vice. Thus, in the case of anger, the even-tempered person will get angry with someone at the correct point, whereas the irascible or irritable person will get angry too quickly; and the person with the virtue will remain angry for the right time, whereas the sulky person will remain angry for too long. And, of course, we can imagine corresponding vices: those of the person who takes too long to get angry, and of the person who gets over their anger too quickly.

Anger is a feeling, and it might be thought that the sphere of each virtue is a distinct feeling. While stating the doctrine of the mean, Aristotle himself lists fear, confidence, appetite, anger, pity, and pleasure and pain in general (NE II.6.1106b18–20). But some virtues do not involve any special feeling: for example, the central virtue of generosity (NE IV.1), the sphere of which is the giving and taking of money. What is essential is that there is some *neutrally describable* feeling and/or action, which can be felt or performed at the right time, toward the right person, and so on. It is the fact that these feelings and actions are neutrally describable that makes the doctrine of the mean possible, since each can then feature in a description of either the virtue or a vice. As Aristotle says: "[N]ot every action or feeling admits of a mean. For some have names immediately connected with depravity, such as spite, shamelessness, envy, and among actions, adultery, theft, homicide" (*NE* II.6.1107a8–12).

What, then, is the sphere of greatness of soul, and its corresponding vices? The answer to this question will reveal why there is no difficulty in plotting this virtue onto the map provided by the doctrine of the mean: It is thinking oneself worthy of great honor. The great-souled person will think himself worthy of great honor at the right times, for the right reasons, and so on (we have to assume that Aristotle is here taking "thinking" to be a kind of action). The person with the excessive vice – vanity – will be someone who thinks himself worthy of great honor at the wrong times, for the wrong reasons, and so on; while the person with the deficient vice of smallness of soul will fail to think himself worthy of great honor when he should, and so on.

The doctrine of the mean does not rule out the possibility of a single person's possessing both of two opposed vices. Indeed, Aristotle explicitly notes this in his discussion of generosity. Someone may be both wasteful, giving away money when he should not do so, and stingy, not giving away money when he should (*NE* IV.1.1121a30–b7). So we might imagine someone who is both vain – perhaps thinking himself worthy of honor for something rather unimpressive – and small-souled – failing to recognize the significance of what he has really achieved. Perhaps Arthur Conan Doyle, who was proud of his rather earnest historical novels and thought far less of his Sherlock Holmes stories, might provide a modern example.

The above account of the doctrine of the mean makes sense of most of what Aristotle says about individual virtues and vices. And the view itself is a powerful one. Essentially, Aristotle is recognizing that there are certain central spheres of human life – emotions such as fear and anger, control over and distribution of resources, relationships with others, and so on – and that these spheres can be characterized in terms of core feelings and/or actions. The virtuous person is then the one who gets things right in these spheres, and, as we have seen, one may be vicious in either an excessive or defective direction. This picture of morality seems both more realistic and more positive in its approach than, for example, a strictly deontological list of prohibitions: do not kill, do not steal, do not lie.

According to one traditional view, however, Aristotle was revising the *Ethics* at his death, and it may well be that he had not got around to tidying up the doctrine of the mean and its implications for his accounts of individual virtues. There are certain problems which appear to arise when he fails to select a single, neutrally describable core for the sphere he is discussing. Envy involves feeling inappropriate pain at someone's doing well, and its opposite ought therefore to be failing to feel such pain when it is appropriate. But Aristotle sets it in opposition to a different "positive" vice, feeling inappropriate pleasure at someone's doing badly (*NE* II.7.1108a35–b6). Courage would most naturally be understood, perhaps, as feeling fear in the appropriate way, its excess and deficiency being, respectively, feeling fear in an inappropriate way and failure to feel it in the appropriate way. But Aristotle describes the deficient vice in positive terms: the rash man is the one who feels excessive confidence (*NE* II.7.1107a33–b4). In the case of justice, Aristotle himself realizes that the standard doctrine of the mean cannot work (*NE* V.5.1133b32–3).

So it is perhaps not so surprising that we find a problem in the case of greatness of soul. According to the account as I have elucidated it, smallness of soul must concern great honor, and will be found only in the person worthy of great honor who thinks himself unworthy of it. But Aristotle extends the sphere of this vice, so that it can be exemplified even by those who are worthy of little, but think themselves worthy of even less (*NE* IV.3.1123b9–11). This seems a mistake, since this vice should correspond to the virtue concerned with less-than-great honor, discussed in the following chapter (*NE* IV.4). One not implausible view is that Aristotle began with the assumption of a single set of virtues and vices concerned with honor, but later separated the sphere of less-than-great honor to be the sphere of an independent set. It is worth noting that in the discussion of greatness of soul in the *Eudemian Ethics*, usually considered earlier than the *Nicomachean Ethics*, we find no virtue concerned with less-than-great honor, and the small-souled person is said to be the one who is worthy of great things but fails to think himself so (*EE* III.5.1232b31–1233a1).

At this point, it may be helpful to pause and consider Aristotle's reasons for postulating a virtue of greatness of soul in the first place, and for characterizing its sphere as that of honor. Aristotle's "official" method in ethics is to begin with what is commonly believed (*ta endoxa*; *NE* VII.1.1145b2–7). So it is not unlikely that the conceptual scheme he created for his virtue ethics would have developed out of that set of virtues and vices implicit in the commonsense morality of his time. There is no doubt that greatness of soul was a widely recognized virtue by Aristotle's time, though in ordinary language the terms *megalopsuchia* and *megaloprepeia* (which Aristotle uses for the virtue of magnificence; *NE* IV.2) were equivalent (Gauthier 1951: 20). Greatness of soul was seen as closely related to generosity, and someone could be described as great-souled who helped another in need (Dover 1974: 178). Indeed, in the first book of the *Rhetoric*, usually thought to be an early work, Aristotle describes greatness of soul as the virtue that disposes us to do good to others on a large scale (I.9.1366b17). So here we already have the idea of "greatness," and it would have been quite consistent with fourth-century usage to restrict the sphere of *megalopsuchia* to that of great honor (Cooper 1989: 192–3).

But why should Aristotle have thought honor of such centrality to human life that he devoted two virtues to it, one of which is the "crown" of all others? He himself provides an answer in the text of *NE* IV.3. Having described the sphere of greatness of soul as that of thinking oneself worthy of great things, Aristotle further narrows it down to worthiness of the *greatest* thing (and, as he himself notes in the very first sentence of IV.3, he is helped here by the very name of the virtue itself). He goes on:

> Worth is spoken of with reference to external goods; and the greatest external good we should assume to be what we render to the gods, the good most aimed at by people of worth, and the prize for the noblest achievements. Such is honor, since it is indeed the greatest external good. (*NE* IV.3.1123b17–21)

"External" goods are distinguished by Aristotle from goods of the soul and goods of the body, the goods of the soul being the most significant (*NE* I.7.1098b12–15). He defines happiness as the exercise of the virtues (*NE* I.7.1098a16–17), a good of the soul, but notes that the performance of noble or virtuous actions requires external goods as "instruments," such as friends, wealth, and political power, and that happiness can be marred by lack of other external goods, such as high birth, noble children, or good looks (*NE* I.8.1099a31–b7). Given its later elevation to the position of pre-eminent external good, it is somewhat surprising that Aristotle does not mention it here. But it is clear which category it would fall into – it is not an instrument, but a good the lack of which can mar one's happiness. Also surprising is Aristotle's apparent claim that friends seem to be the greatest external good (*NE* IX.9.1169b9–10). How should we deal with this apparent contradiction? We might put weight on the "seems" in the claim about friends, but Aristotle commonly uses the word *dokei* to express a view he himself holds. Perhaps more plausibly, we might note that Aristotle uses the definite article in neither of his claims, so that either might be understood as suggesting that the item in question is "a very great" external good, that is, one of the greatest. But Greek does not require the article in this context, and it anyway leaves unanswered the question which good Aristotle would make prior to the other.

I suggest, then, that we do here have a contradiction, perhaps one Aristotle would have removed had he lived long enough fully to revise the *Nicomachean Ethics*, and that the three criteria mentioned in IV.3 for judging the value of an external good – whether it is rendered to the gods, whether it is pursued by persons of distinction, and whether it is the prize for the noblest achievements – each speak in favor of honor's being ranked above friendship, if we take the second criterion to be referring to what people of distinction *in particular* seek (since, of course, they do pursue friendship, but along with everyone else). Perhaps worth stressing in particular here is the point that friends are, in this context, merely instrumental to the goals of the virtuous person, whereas honor – with its internal conceptual connection to "the noble" (*to kalon*) is a reward or prize that follows on, and hence augments or "ornaments," virtuous activity. Also worth noting is that by honors Aristotle does not necessarily have in mind material goods, such as wealth. The honor received by the virtuous from other virtuous people is analogous to the honor paid to the gods, in the form of respect and its symbols.

What seems most likely is that Aristotle came to recognize the great significance attached to honor by those he saw as closest to his moral ideal of the completely good and virtuous person. It was then essential to his project of showing a close connection between virtue and happiness – a project the broad lines of which he took over from Socrates and Plato – to demonstrate that his conception of happiness as the exercise of virtue "makes life worthy of choice and lacking in nothing" (*NE* I.7.1097b14–15). One might even hypothesize that, had his revision been completed, the final version of *NE* I.8 would have contained the argument that the virtuous life is the most honorable.

But a further question remains. Why did Aristotle distinguish two virtues concerned with honor, one with great honor, the other – proper ambition – with less-than-great? One answer may be the hint he took from etymology – greatness of soul has, in some sense, to do with greatness. But in fact there is a clear conceptual reason for such a distinction, arising out of the doctrine of the mean. Consider two individuals, A and B. A is, and thinks himself, worthy of great honor, while B is, and thinks himself, worthy of a little honor. If there were only a single virtue, consisting in being worthy of some degree of honor or other and in thinking oneself worthy of honor to that degree, then A and B would have to be said to be equally virtuous in this respect. But in respect of the other virtues it might well be the case that A and B are not equal, since honor is the reward for exercising virtue, so that smaller honor must be the reward for a lesser exercise of the virtues. Aristotle may well have felt this to be incongruous. Further, though he may have allowed for a spectrum of character from more to less virtuous, he tends to think in terms of the paradigm exemplar of virtue, the person who possesses and exercises all of the virtues to their fullest extent. And he may have thought that the difference in degree between such a person and the person lower on the spectrum justified postulating a difference in kind at the level of the corresponding virtues.

Some have seen this difference in kind as corresponding to the distinction between mere virtue and superhuman virtue in *NE* VII.1 (Hardie 1978: 72; Curzer 1990: 524). Superhuman virtue, however, is a virtue "heroic and godlike" (1145a20), and Aristotle's illustrative reference to Priam's claim about Hector that he seemed to be a child of a god suggests we should take the reference to heroism pretty seriously. It is indeed true, as Hardie points out, that the great-souled man will be heroic, in the ordinary sense, on the battlefield (*NE* IV.3.1124b8–9), but being brave on the battlefield is not enough to make one "godlike," a quality unusual among human beings (*NE* VII.1.1145a27–8). It is anyway conceptually impossible for greatness of soul to represent superhuman virtue. A god, Aristotle points out (*NE* VII.1.1145a25–6), possesses no virtue (his state is more honorable than that), whereas the person of greatness of soul possesses every virtue to its greatest extent (*NE* IV.3.1123b29–30). Of course, it would have been possible for Aristotle to make greatness of soul equivalent to some conception of super-human virtue, but the fact that he never refers to it as such, and often refers to it as a virtue, counts strongly against reading that equivalence into the text.

The difference between the great-souled person and the person of proper ambition, then, depends on the degree of honor of which they are worthy. As far as the correctness of their judgment goes, they are equal. Such correctness, Aristotle suggests, is in itself something admirable or valuable in itself: "Correctly distinguishing great goods from small is praiseworthy" (*EE* III.5.1232a32–3). What makes getting it wrong reprehensible depends on whether one's vice is one of excess or deficiency. The person who thinks himself worthy of great honor when he is not is just plain silly, demonstrating a lack of knowledge of himself quite inconsistent with virtue (*NE* IV.3.1123b3, 1125a28), while the small-souled person, worthy of much but having a low opinion of himself, though he also lacks self-knowledge, is not so much foolish as timid, and is especially blameworthy because his timidity prevents his performing noble actions which he would otherwise have performed (1125a19–27).

Also interesting is that the capacity to distinguish great goods from small, which in the *Eudemian Ethics* Aristotle makes characteristic of greatness of soul, is found, according to Aristotle, in every virtue (*EE* III.5.1232a35–b4). So the courageous person will not judge dangers great, in the sense of worth avoiding, when they are contrary to reason; the temperate person disdains many great pleasures on the ground that they are not great goods; and the generous person takes the same attitude to wealth. So in that sense, Aristotle suggests, greatness of soul follows from the possession of any virtue. This "orthological" conception of greatness of soul cannot easily be situated within the doctrine of the mean because it is not characterized in terms of some neutral action or feeling which one can perform or feel at the wrong time, or fail to perform or feel at the right time. In that respect, it is a bivalent quality like justice – one either has it and is admirable, or one does not and is blameworthy. But there is nothing to prevent Aristotle claiming that it is part of what makes each individual virtue admirable. Indeed, as we just saw in the case of greatness of soul, its lack is common to both of the corresponding vices and helps to explain what is wrong with them. Also worth pondering is the relation of orthological greatness of soul to the intellectual virtue of practical wisdom, which also, one might have thought, would involve the capacity accurately to judge goods and evils.

Having set out the orthological conception of greatness of soul in the *Eudemian Ethics*, Aristotle proceeds to provide a narrower conception of greatness of soul as one virtue among others, and this he does, or so it seems, by noting the great-souled person's concern for great honor alone among the external goods (*EE* III.5.1232a38–b14). Since, as we have seen, external goods are required for virtuous action, this brings us into the territory of the relation of greatness of soul to the other virtues of character, the topic of the next section.

Greatness of Soul and Other Virtues

First, we must try to account for the *Eudemian* claim that the great-souled person "takes no thought for" (*outhen phrontizein*) external goods, such as life and wealth, which most people seem to take great trouble over. Do we not here have a problem, in that if, say, wealth is necessary for virtue (in particular, of course, the virtues of generosity and magnificence), will the great-souled person not be passing up opportunities to perform virtuous actions which he might have taken had he acquired sufficient wealth?

Because passing up opportunities for virtue is precisely one of the criticisms Aristotle makes of the small-souled person, and because the great-souled person has the correct view of value, it cannot be the case that the great-souled person literally sees external goods as worthless. Imagine that a great-souled person is about to perform a large-scale noble action, which will bring him great honor, yet which he knows will require a good deal of expenditure. If he catches a thief raiding his treasure chest, he will not just turn the other cheek and let the thief get on with it. I suggest that what Aristotle is speaking of in the *Eudemian* passage is not the great-souled person's evaluation of external goods so much as the way in which they occupy his thoughts. Most people make a lot of emotional and practical investment, if they can, in acquiring and retaining wealth, to the point that wealth can become to them, at the very least, a quasi-end-in-itself. The great-souled person has no concern for wealth or even life as ends in themselves, and his thoughts will not be greatly occupied by them. Indeed, if he is required to give up all his money or even his life, for the sake of honor (or rather for the sake of virtue and the noble), he will do so, without any great sense of loss (*NE* IV.3.1124b8–9).

Sometimes, however, the acquisition of wealth requires great exertion and dedication. Will the potentially great-souled person, who might otherwise become wealthy, not let slip his chance to become wealthy and so perform noble actions? The answer is "No" since this very attitude toward wealth is inconsistent with greatness of soul and therefore with virtue. Magnificent actions are not like, say, a cruise around the world, which one can work hard and save for. To be properly magnificent, and great-souled, they have to be performed with wealth which has come to one without great effort on one's own part. As Aristotle says: "The advantages of fortune ... do seem to contribute to greatness of soul" (*NE* IV.3.1124a20–21).

This raises the question whether external goods make this contribution merely by enabling the great-souled person to perform noble actions and thus become worthy of honor, or whether they are honorable in themselves. Aristotle's view here is twofold (*NE* IV.3.1124a20–b5). First, external goods without virtue are not to be honored. Indeed, they make their possessors viciously supercilious and arrogant. Only the good person is to be honored. But, second, the person who is both good and wealthy "is more widely thought worthy of honor" because "superiority in something good is in every case more honored." Several interpreters have been tempted to claim that Aristotle is here setting out an *endoxon*, a common belief, rather than stating a view of his own. But that interpretation is unnecessary. He is quite clear that external goods alone are not honorable, so he is not providing the vicious with any reason to pursue them. By incorporating into his position the generally accepted view that wealth, power, and so on are honorable in themselves, he advances his eudaimonistic aim of showing that the happiness constituted by virtue is "lacking in nothing." Finally, it is clear that wealth, power, and indeed honor, have value here only as elements within the virtuous life itself. It is the noble which really matters, though the noble will be partly manifested in the actively virtuous possession of great wealth and other external goods.

Aristotle is unconcerned, then, by the problem of "moral luck." It may well be true that this great-souled person *P* is in a position to live a life of nobility only because he has inherited a great deal of money, while this merely properly ambitious person *Q* is unworthy of the same honor, though had he had the same inheritance he would have performed no less creditably with it than *P*. The value of the moral life lies in the performance of noble actions, and the greater the nobility, the greater the honor and the happiness. The idea that there might be something unfair or objectionable about this would not appeal to Aristotle because he believes that the acquisition of both vice and virtue is voluntary and therefore a subject of praise and blame (*NE* III.5.1114a31–b25). Indeed, in the case of greatness of soul, we can see that good fortune plays a constitutive role in the conditions for the flourishing of the virtue itself. But some will be left unsatisfied. It may be acceptable to claim that a person should be praised for voluntarily doing the best he could with the opportunities available to him, but how can two people who have both done equally well with their opportunities, though their opportunities have differed greatly independently of their own efforts, be differentially honorable? I shall go deeper into this aspect of Aristotle's ethical view in my final section.

How should we situate greatness of soul *vis-à-vis* the other virtues? The relation is not as simple as that between, say, generosity and courage, both of which are independent virtues of character governing separate spheres of human life. Greatness of soul in the orthological sense is found, in a sense, implicated within every virtue, since every virtue involves correctness of opinion about goods and evils within its sphere. The particular virtue of greatness of soul is concerned with honor, and the great-souled person is worthy of the greatest honor. For that reason, Aristotle says (*NE* IV.3.1123b26–9, 1123b34–6), he must be the best or most virtuous person of all, since "the better a person is, the greater the things he is worthy of, and the best will be worthy of the greatest things." Support for the conclusion Aristotle draws here – that the great-souled person must be good – is provided also by reflection on his lack of concern for external goods (1123b29–34).

The great-souled person cares little for anything, even for honor, so no strong desire for some external good could motivate him to perform a vicious action: "It would be quite unfitting for him to run away with his arms swinging, or to commit an injustice." The portrait of the great-souled person with which *NE* IV.3 closes also provides us with additional insight into the relation between greatness of soul and other virtues, and this will be discussed in my final section below.

What does Aristotle mean by the claim that greatness of soul is "a sort of crown of the virtues" (*NE* IV.3.1124a1–3)? He offers two explanations or points in support of the claim: that greatness of soul makes the virtues greater, and that it does not occur in isolation from them. Partly because Aristotle believes that no virtue occurs in isolation from any other (a view the implications of which for greatness of soul I shall discuss shortly), but also because many things do not occur in isolation from other things without its making sense to put the first set in some kind of ornamental relation to the second, Aristotle's second point here is not easy to interpret. Indeed, it is most easily read in the light of the ornamental claim itself. What Aristotle probably has in mind is the way in which greatness of soul "supervenes" or "sits on top" of the other virtues. First, I begin to acquire the (other) virtues. Then I reach a level of modest virtue, at which I am worthy of some modest honor – and if I am aware of that then I have the virtue of proper ambition, though not of course that of greatness of soul. My moral development continues, however, and I develop virtue to a degree worthy of the greatest honor. At that point, if I am aware of my worth, then greatness of soul has emerged out of my possession of these other virtues, and adds further luster to my moral character and worthiness of honor.

But this story leaves unanswered the question about the first of Aristotle's points in support of the ornamental claim: how greatness of soul might make *the other virtues* "greater," as opposed to ornamenting my own character as a whole. One possibility is that my possession of the virtue of, say, great courage is somehow more admirable if I am aware of it. But such a view seems to involve a kind of double-counting: one's character is improved by greatness of soul, and one gains from that and the further honor consequent on it; *and* each of the other virtues one possesses is also somehow more admirable because of one's possession of greatness of soul. Rather, I suggest, the clue to Aristotle's meaning here lies in what he says about the logic of smallness of soul. If the small-souled person is to be worthy of great honor, then we must presume that "greatness in every virtue" (*NE* IV.3.1123b30) is characteristic of him as much as of the great-souled person. But he is not perfect since his diffidence leads him to refrain from noble actions which he would otherwise have performed (*NE* IV.3.1125a25–7). Thus we see how greatness of soul could make virtues already great even greater, by spurring its possessor into action in situations where the timid will stand back.

We can now see how Aristotle's account of greatness of soul sheds further light on his thesis of the so-called "reciprocity of the virtues," according to which one can possess any one virtue of character only if one possesses them all. In *NE* VI.13, Aristotle links this thesis to the intellectual virtue of practical wisdom. Properly to possess any virtue of character requires that one possess practical wisdom in something like the following way. If I am to possess a virtue of character, then my actions and feelings must be in a mean. But to see which actions and feelings are in a mean requires a quasi-perceptual capacity for judgment, which enables me to see things correctly. This is an important part of practical wisdom. The scope of this capacity, Aristotle believes, is universal, so that it will involve seeing practical reasons correctly in the sphere of every virtue. And doing this will require possessing the virtue of character within each relevant sphere.

Now at this point one might think that greatness of soul throws up an immediate problem for Aristotle's account. According to Aristotle, happiness consists in the exercise of the virtues, and happiness so understood is "widely shared" (*NE* I.8.1099b18). But greatness of soul is surely a virtue exceptional and rare, and if the thesis of the reciprocity of virtues is correct then it would seem that hardly anyone is virtuous or happy.

An obvious response here would be that what is required is not greatness of soul, but whatever honor-related virtue is appropriate to one's worth. To be virtuous, then, would require being worthy of honor to some degree or other, and being aware of one's level of worth. But in fact in his discussion of greatness of soul, Aristotle appears to moderate the thesis of the reciprocity of virtues, allowing that the small-souled person can possess virtues of character to a high degree and yet lack the virtue of greatness of soul. It may be suggested that the virtues of the small-souled are what are called in *NE* VI.13 merely "natural" (Curzer 1990: 530). But this is unlikely since the natural virtues are those we possess "by nature," independently of intellect and from birth. Rather, Aristotle's view is most plausibly taken to be that the *perfectly* virtuous person will possess every virtue, including of course that of greatness of soul. But there is a spectrum of moral character from this individual to that of the lowest, most bestial individual, and there is no reason to assume that someone who is not perfectly virtuous is not virtuous at all. As Aristotle points out, "the spheres of what is noble and what is just . . . admit of a good deal of diversity and variation" and "it is the mark of an educated person to look in each area for only that degree of accuracy that the nature of the subject permits" (*NE* I.3.1094b14–16, 1094b23–5). So we may assume that Aristotle accepted that, to be virtuous, a person's actions and feelings had to fall into some imprecisely bounded range, and that the perfectly virtuous will always perform at the top of the range, the great-souled at the very least near the top of the range, and the small-souled slightly below the top of the range.

This raises a further question concerning Aristotle's view of the "criterion of right action." It is standardly thought that, according to Aristotle, the right action is that which the virtuous person would perform, and that any other action would be wrong. Now it will be tempting to assume that the virtuous person in this formula must be the perfectly virtuous person. But it may be misleading merely to state that any other action is wrong, without pointing out the availability within the Aristotelian scheme of an evaluative ranking of actions from best to worst. The right action is perhaps the best; but of wrong actions some are significantly better than others, to the extent that they may be highly admirable and worthy of honor and praise. One should, within one's limits, always aim as high as possible, and should not assume that falling short of the best is an utter failure to achieve the noble.

The Great-souled Person: The "Portrait" and its Problems

As we have already seen, Aristotle's official ethical methodology allows issues to arise from tensions within commonsense views. We might, then, learn something about the source of his concern with greatness of soul from a passage in the *Posterior Analytics* outlining two apparently conflicting conceptions of that virtue (II.13.97b15–25). Aristotle is discussing definition, and notes that if we are seeking to define some term applied to several things, then we should investigate to see whether the things themselves have anything in common:

> I mean, e.g., if we were to seek what greatness of soul is we should inquire, in the case of some great-souled men we know, what one thing they all have as such. E.g., if Alcibiades is great-souled, and Achilles and Ajax, what one thing do they all have? Intolerance of insults; for one made war, one waxed wroth, and the other killed himself. Again in the case of others, e.g. Lysander and Socrates. Well, if here it is being indifferent to good and bad fortune, I take these two things and inquire what both indifference to fortune and not brooking dishonor have that is the same. And if there is nothing, then there will be two sorts of greatness of soul. (trans. Barnes 1975)

Aristotle's ethical discussions of greatness of soul, then, may be read as attempts to find a common account of the greatness of soul that consists in intolerance of insults and that which lies in being indifferent to good and bad fortune. On the face of it, these two conceptions seem inconsistent, since the first seems to require an extreme concern about honor in particular, the second a lack of such concern.

Here again, the attitude toward external goods taken by the great-souled person as described in the ethical treatises comes to the fore. Aristotle seeks a rapprochement between the two conceptions of greatness of soul by claiming that the great-souled person is largely indifferent to external goods, including honor, and yet concerned above all with great honor. In particular, note that by bearing misfortunes nobly, the great-souled person wins honor for himself (*NE* I.10.1100b30–33). Both conceptions of greatness of soul, then, capture an element of the truth, yet neither is unconditionally correct.

Aristotle's dialectical method, however, does not consist in his seeking any old story about some subject matter so as to resolve tensions between different positions. Rather, the story he develops will be independently plausible to him. It is now time to face up to the surprising fact that many have found the detailed "portrait" of the great-souled person in *NE* IV.3 implausible or even repellent. In the remainder of this section, I shall outline the main lines of the portrait, bringing out the various problematic aspects of it, and then reject some of the modern attempts to "rehabilitate" the great-souled person. In the final section of this chapter, I shall suggest that if we take the portrait at face value we can learn some important lessons about the nature of Aristotle's ethics overall.

The portrait describes the great-souled person's characteristics in six broadly defined areas: risk and danger; giving and receiving benefits; attitude to others; level of activity; openness; independence and self-sufficiency. Problems have been found in most of these areas, and I shall outline the main difficulties as I proceed.

(1)   *Risk and danger* (IV.3.1124b6–9):

> The great-souled person, because he does not value anything highly, does not enjoy danger. He will avoid trivial dangers, but will face great ones, and, again because of his attitude to goods, will be unsparing even of his own life.

Presumably, no virtuous person, whether great-souled or not, would enjoy danger for its own sake, since it would threaten his potential for virtuous action. And presumably no virtuous person would face trivial dangers, since the triviality must consist in there being no overriding reason to face them. So what seems to mark out the great-souled person here is, as we might expect, an especially high degree of courage – and courage is perhaps the virtue in which eminence is especially noble and honorable. We must, however, be careful to interpret Aristotle's claims about the great-souled person's motivations. He is courageous not merely because he does not care greatly about losing the various external goods that he might otherwise acquire in his life, but because he *does* care (though not greatly) about honor and (presumably greatly) about virtuous action and nobility. He has the latter positive concern in common with an "ordinarily" courageous person, but the ordinary person is pained by the loss of goods through death (*NE* III.9.1117b9–13). The ordinarily courageous person will still see the gain of nobility through death on the battlefield as worth the loss of great goods; for the great-souled person, the decision is much easier.

(2)   *Giving and receiving benefits* (IV.3.1124b9–18):

> The great-souled person is inclined to help others readily, but he is ashamed to be a beneficiary, since it is a sign of inferiority. If he is benefited, he will repay with interest, to ensure that his benefactor becomes a beneficiary. He will remember with pleasure benefits he has conferred, but will forget those he has received and feel pain on being reminded of them.

Presumably it is quite hard to benefit a great-souled person anyway, since he is concerned really only about honor, and then not very much, and the honor has to be great and conferred by good people (IV.3.1124a4–11). But there might well be cases in which a great-souled person is in need of some instrumental good to achieve the noble ends we assume are dear to him.

This beneficent side to the great-souled person's character resonates well with the account of greatness of soul in the *Rhetoric*. Here in the *Nicomachean Ethics*, however, there is no restriction to large-scale assistance. Would the great-souled person help someone in a small way? That seems unlikely given what Aristotle says below about the level of activity of the great-souled person. It is an interesting question which, if any, other particular virtue is being exercised when the great-souled person is moved to help others. Aristotle has no virtue of beneficence, benevolence, or kindness. He does, however, see friendship as a virtue, and allows that there is a natural "friendship" between human beings, which may well provide the source of motivation for beneficent action (*NE* VIII.1.1155a16–22).

The main worry about the great-souled person's attitude here is that he is ungrateful. To be sure, he is concerned to repay benefits, but apparently he does this not so as to express his gratitude but to restore his position of superiority as swiftly as possible. And once repayment is completed, the fact that he has received a favour will slip from his mind, as a painful sign of his former inferiority.

(3)   *Attitude to others* (IV.3.1124b18–23):

> The great-souled person will be proud [*megas*] in his behavior toward people of distinction, but unassuming toward others. For superiority over the former is difficult and impressive, while over the latter it is easy and vulgar.

So the great-souled person's desire for superiority is only for that which is in itself noble and honorable. One immediate question is who "people of distinction" might be. In a more literal translation they are "those held in honor and of good fortune." This should almost certainly be read conjunctively. The great-souled person will not seek to impress the vicious, however good their fortune. But there is a worrying note here, as if the great-souled person's behavior toward a successful virtuous person will change if that person's luck changes. The person will then have lost some of his own superiority, and attempting to impress him would be vulgar.

It is commonly said that the great-souled person is objectionably supercilious, though in fact this passage counts against that view. He will be self-deprecating in the company of those inferior to him. Nor is there any evidence that he is a snob, or that he will look down on anyone for any reason other than their lacking virtue. Any superciliousness presumably emerges out of his lack of concern for external goods. To someone to whom nothing much matters except virtue, the lives of those lacking virtue will seem not to matter much. He does not seem very similar to Nietzsche's *Übermensch*, though in fact a reasonable case can be made that Nietzsche was influenced by Aristotle's portrait (Kaufman 1974: 382–4).

Is the great-souled person vain? Well, he might strike us as vain, but in the Aristotelian sense he is, of course, far from vain. The vain person is mistaken about his own worth, whereas the great-souled person's view is correct. There is here an important question about the nature of modesty as a modern virtue. Does modesty require that a person is *ignorant* of their worth, or merely that they view that worth in a particular way, focusing not so much on their own hard work, say, but their good fortune in having a certain genetic endowment or education (see Driver 2001: ch. 2)? Similar issues arise concerning whether the great-souled person lacks humility. According to Aquinas (*Summa Theologiae* 2a2ae, q61, a2), humility is in fact the other side of the coin from greatness of soul. As greatness of soul spurs the person on to great things in accordance with right reason, so humility restrains them from overstepping the mark and aiming for goals beyond reason. As a result, perhaps, of the Christian emphasis on original sin, one thing that concerns us in the portrait of the great-souled man is his *confidence* in his own worth, a confidence which cannot help but strike us as somewhat complacent.

Also problematic within a Christian or post-Christian perspective is the great-souled person's direction of attention toward himself rather than toward others. He is indeed especially concerned with the noble. But his concern is that nobility be instantiated in *his* life. Further, any concern he does have for others seems to consist largely in how he appears (albeit veridically) to them. I shall return to the issue of direction of attention in the final section below.

(4) *Level of activity* (IV.3.1124b23–6):

> The great-souled person avoids things usually honored, and activities in which others excel. He is slow to act except where there is great honor at stake, and he is inclined to perform only a few actions, though great and renowned ones.

This attitude to action comes as no surprise, given the great-souled person's lack of concern for anything except great honor. The obvious problem with the account at this point, as we have seen, is that the great-souled person might be thought to be passing up opportunities for virtuous action, albeit less great virtuous action than that to which he is inclined, which a person of proper ambition would take and thereby earn the reward of honor.

One response to this by some writers has been that the actions of the great-souled person, though few, take a good deal of time, thus leaving him unable – however much he might wish that he could – to respond to calls which might be met by those with lesser degrees of virtue. But it has to be said that this is not the obvious way to read the text here, which contains no implication that the great-souled person would be quick to act if some small honor were at stake. Further, as I said, his hesitation comes as no surprise. Why should he bother himself with something that means little or nothing to him?

But this is not to say that the great-souled person is passing up opportunities for greater honor than he might otherwise achieve. His hesitation has to be seen in the context of his patterns of concern and of action in general. There is an analogy here with a consequentialist agent who passes up individual opportunities to do good as part of a strategy to maximize overall good. The great-souled person is worthy of the greatest honor, and part of what is noble about his behavior is his very lack of concern for anything other than just that.

(5) *Openness* (IV.3.1124b26–31):

> Because the great-souled person cares little for what people think, he is open in his likes and dislikes. And because he is inclined to look down on people, he speaks and acts openly, except when using irony for the masses.

Again, we see the effects of the great-souled person's lack of concern for anything other than honor issuing in certain traits of character and behavior. And, again, superciliousness seems, to the modern reader, to be one of those traits. What the great-souled person appears to lack is any sense that, insofar as another person is a person, that entitles them to a certain degree of respect or concern. He will be open with others of his ilk because truth matters to him, and, we presume, to them. But to "the masses," to whom he considers himself entirely superior, truth cannot be significant, so he is ready not to speak straightforwardly to them.

(6) *Independence and self-sufficiency* (IV.3.1124b31–1125a16):

> The great-souled person will not depend on another, unless he is a friend, because to do so would be servile. Because nothing matters to him, he is not inclined toward admiration, resentment, gossip, praise of others, or complaining. His possessions are noble rather than useful, because this is consistent with self-sufficiency. Again because nothing matters to him, he will not be rushed: His movements are slow, his voice is deep, and his speech is measured.

Just as the great-souled man is unattached to external goods, so he lacks attachment to others, except for friends. And even here, one might assume, his friendship cannot be especially profound, given his lack of concern even for his own life.

Although he need not be especially dependent on his friends, however, it might appear that the great-souled person's concern for honor does make him dependent on others. First, note again that the great-souled person cares only for great honors from good people. And, second, notice that he is not even especially concerned about these. So if he is not honored even by those who are good enough to honor him (either because it is possible for virtuous people to commit this error of omission or because there may be no virtuous people in a position to honor him) he will be at the very most mildly displeased. It has been objected that by failing to amass useful possessions, he will waste opportunities for virtuous action. That objection I dealt with above. The nobility of the great-souled person's actions overall will be the greatest possible.

Can someone with a naturally high-pitched voice be great-souled? Probably yes, if they have the same lack of concern as other great-souled people, and take things slowly and reflectively. Still, I suspect that, given the weight attached by Aristotle to the way the great-souled person *appears*, he would have thought that a high-pitched voice, like lack of external goods, could mar greatness of soul, perhaps in extreme cases making it impossible.

The Aesthetics of Virtue

In the previous section, I sketched the main lines of Aristotle's portrait of the great-souled person's character, and mentioned some of the problems which contemporary interpreters have found in it. These problems have led some to interpretations of Aristotle on greatness of soul which provide at least the chance of sidestepping some of these problems. Here are four representative examples.

(1) *Contemplation* In the mid-twentieth century, René Antoine Gauthier (1951) revived the view of the distinguished ancient commentator Aspasius that the great-souled man is, in fact, the philosopher. He noted, for example, that the great-souled man has several of the characteristics attributed to philosophers: inactivity (so as to contemplate), self-sufficiency (because philosophy requires few material resources), and self-knowledge. In particular, one may see Socratic elements in the portrait (Deman 1942; Seddon 1975): consider the great-souled person's attachment to truth, and his use of irony. Perhaps, then, he is not to be judged by those moral standards applicable to ordinary agents.

(2) *Idealization* According to the nineteenth-century commentator J. A. Stewart (1892: I, 335–7), Aristotle's portrait of the great-souled person is to be taken not as a character sketch like those of other virtuous people in the *Nicomachean Ethics*, but as an idealization. Of what? Stewart also places the emphasis on contemplation. The great-souled person "contemplates the *kosmos* or beautiful harmony of his own nature, and allows nothing external to it to dominate his thought or conduct." We should not aim to be like the great-souled person,

but to seek to instantiate the ideal he represents into a more rounded life of practical virtue.

(3) *Description*   According to another nineteenth-century commentator, John Burnet (1900: 179), quite the opposite is true. The portrait is no idealization, but a mere description of the ideal of the average Athenian of Aristotle's day: "The description itself has much quiet humour and is surely half-ironical." The portrait, then, would exemplify that stage in Aristotle's ethical methodology when he is setting out "common beliefs" (*endoxa*) before working out any puzzles or tensions that lie within them.

(4) *Aspiration*   More recently, Michael Pakaluk (2004) has revived the view that the great-souled person is Socratic, and suggested that Socrates' advocacy of a turn to virtue in one's life enables us to see greatness of soul not as complacent or supercilious (because the contempt is for goods, not persons), but as an attitude of aspiration to virtue.

What are we to make of these varying readings of Aristotle? There is perhaps strongest evidence for the contemplative interpretation. Nevertheless, we should note the following points in response to those made above on its behalf. The great-souled person refrains from action not to contemplate, but to act on a grand scale. Though he lacks useful possessions, he does acquire noble ones. And his self-knowledge is merely knowledge of his own worth. It may well be that Aristotle had Socrates partly in mind when composing the portrait, but it is as likely to have been Socrates the man as Socrates the philosopher. In general, given the lack of any explicit reference by Aristotle to a link between philosophy and greatness of soul, the case for this interpretation is not strong.

The argument from silence applies as strongly to the other three interpretations, as well as to several other similar views expressed in the literature. They rest on the assumption that Aristotle *could not* have meant what he said about greatness of soul, so we have to find some other way of understanding him. And the only way to do that is to refuse to take what he says at face value. I suggest, however, that this is exactly what we should do, and that we can learn important lessons from reflecting on Aristotle's discussion about his conception of ethics and ours.

One aspect of Aristotle's account of greatness of soul that modern readers find particularly objectionable is its failure to incorporate any principle of the equality of moral worth of persons, a principle which perhaps finds its clearest statement in Kantian ethics. This charge, however, seems a little uncharitable to Aristotle. There is nothing inconsistent with such a principle, as it is usually understood, in his account of the great-souled person. As we have seen, in his account of friendship Aristotle allows that all human beings make some sort of moral claim on one another. And though, of course, he does not believe that all humans should be treated equally (that is, treated in the same way), this is not required by any plausible principle of equal worth. Further, a principle which does seem implicit in Aristotle's account – that goods be distributed in accordance with moral desert – is not unattractive to many modern thinkers, and indeed has recently become a focus of philosophical discussion (Olsaretti 2003).

What of the notion that honor is the greatest external good? Is the idea of honor for virtue not now obsolescent (Berger 1970)? This is something of an exaggeration. Many of us do aspire to decency in action and character, and would be disappointed not to receive due recognition for that, especially if some action we have performed is over and above the call of duty. But it has to be admitted that the prioritization of honor above all else by the great-souled person does not chime with modern evaluations. To put it more generally, what we find in Aristotle's account of greatness of soul is a commitment to an aesthetics of virtue, with the moral beauty or nobility of the agent's character being his dominant aim. The virtuous person, according to Aristotle, performs virtuous actions for their own sake, where this means performing them because they are, in themselves, noble (see, for example, *NE* II.4.1105a32, III.7.1115b11–13). Further, there is nothing in the text to suggest that this focus on the noble is somehow in the background, allowing genuine concerns for others to occupy the agent's deliberations. Indeed, in *NE* IX.8 Aristotle says that the good person "assigns to himself what is noblest and best"; that he will die for his friends, "procuring for himself what is noble"; that those who die for others "choose a great and noble thing for themselves"; that the good person who gives money to his friend "gets what is noble, and therefore assigns himself the greater good"; that in all virtuous actions "the good person is seen to assign himself the larger share of what is noble."

This aestheticization of ethics can be placed within the overall context of Aristotle's eudaimonist project. Given that he is aiming to persuade us that virtue is constitutive of happiness, it will be to his advantage to find some especially valuable quality which virtue alone has. This is the moral beauty or nobility of virtuous action. Once again, it would be an exaggeration to see this value, or its being situated as a component of happiness, as quite alien to modern sensibilities. Our stories and films, for example, frequently include accounts of noble actions which we are expected to admire; and obituaries are a good source of evidence that we continue to see the "life well lived" as a life which is, at least often, good for the person concerned. What seems remarkable in Aristotle's account of virtuous motivation, and the character of the great-souled person in particular, is not so much the concern for nobility, but the lack of concern for the well-being of others. Perhaps, though the great-souled person is not the philosopher, we do see here a move toward the unworldliness of the philosopher.

Much modern virtue ethics can be seen as continuing the Aristotelian view of nobility as a value. Some virtue ethicists are welfarists, following Hume (on one reading of him) rather than Aristotle and preferring to see the virtues as mere instruments for the promotion of what is really good in itself – well-being. But those within the Aristotelian tradition will contend that virtuous action has some value in itself, and we might describe that value as "nobility." No one disputes that well-being is a value; so a central debate in modern ethics is whether nobility is a value, and if so how valuable. Those involved in that debate could not find a better source of suggestion and insight than Aristotle's account of greatness of soul.

Acknowledgment

I am most grateful to the editor for helpful comments on an earlier draft of this chapter.

References

Barnes, J. 1975: *Aristotle's Posterior Analytics.* Oxford: Clarendon Press.

Berger, P. 1970: "The Obsolescence of the Concept of Honour," *European Journal of Sociology* 9: 339–47.

Burnet, J. (ed.) 1900: *The Ethics of Aristotle.* London: Methuen.

Cooper, N. 1989: "Aristotle's Crowning Virtue," *Apeiron* 22 (3): 191–205.

Curzer, H. J. 1990: "A Great Philosopher's Not-so-great Account of Great Virtue: Aristotle's Treatment of Greatness of Soul," *Canadian Journal of Philosophy* 20 (4): 517–38.

Deman, T. 1942: *Le témoignage d'Aristote sur Socrate.* Paris: Les Belles Lettres.

Dover, K. J. 1974: Greek Popular Morality in the Time of Plato and Aristotle. Oxford: Blackwell.

Driver, J. 2001: *Uneasy Virtue.* Cambridge: Cambridge University Press.

Gauthier, R. A. 1951: "La magnanimité Aristotélicienne." In *Magnanimité,* ch. 3. Paris: Vrin.

Hardie, W. F. R. 1978: "'Magnanimity' in Aristotle's Ethics," *Phronesis* 23 (1): 63–79.

Horner, D. A. 1998: "What it Takes to be Great: Aristotle and Aquinas on Magnanimity," *Faith and Philosophy* 15 (4): 415–44.

Kaufman, W. 1974: *Nietzsche, Philosopher, Psychologist, Antichrist,* 4th edn. Princeton, NJ: Princeton University Press.

Kristjánsson, K. 1998: "Liberating Moral Traditions: Saga Morality and Aristotle's *Megalopsychia,*" *Ethical Theory and Moral Practice* 1 (4): 397–422.

Olsaretti, S. (ed.) 2003: *Desert and Justice.* Oxford: Clarendon Press.

Pakaluk, M. 2004: "The Meaning of Aristotelian Magnanimity," *Oxford Studies in Ancient Philosophy* 26: 241–75.

Seddon, F. A. 1975: "*Megalopsychia*: A Suggestion," *The Personalist* 56: 31–7.

Stewart, J. A. 1892: *Notes on the Nicomachean Ethics,* 2 vols. Oxford: Clarendon Press.

Further reading

Annas, J. 1993: *The Morality of Happiness.* New York: Oxford University Press.

Bae, E. 2003: "An Ornament of the Virtues," *Ancient Philosophy* 23 (2): 337–49.

Casey, J. 1990: *Pagan Virtue*. Oxford: Clarendon Press.

Cordner, C. 1994: "Aristotelian Virtue and its Limitations," *Philosophy* 69: 269, 291–316.

Curzer, H. J. 1991: "Aristotle's Much-maligned *Megalopsychos*," *Australasian Journal of Philosophy* 69 (2): 131–51.

Held, D. t. D. 1993: "*Megalopsuchia* in *Nicomachean Ethics* iv," *Ancient Philosophy* 13 (1): 95–110.

Jaffa, H. V. 1952: "Magnanimity and the Limits of Morality." In *Thomism and Aristotelianism*, ch. 6. Chicago: University of Chicago Press.

Putnam, D. 1995: "In Defence of Aristotelian Honor," *Philosophy* 70: 272, 286–8.

Rees, D. A. 1971: "Magnanimity in the *Eudemian* and *Nicomachean Ethics*." In P. Moraux and D. Harlfinger (eds), *Untersuchungen zur Eudemischen Ethik*, pp. 231–43. Berlin: de Gruyter.

Schmidt, E. A. 1969: "Ehre und Tugend zur Megalopsyche der aristotelischen Ethik," *Archiv für Geschichte der Philosophie* 49 (2): 149–68.

Schütrumpf, E. 1989: "Magnanimity, *megalopsychia*, and the system of Aristotle's *Nicomachean Ethics*," *Archiv für Geschichte der Philosophie* 71 (1): 10–22.

Sherman, N. 1988: "Common Sense and Uncommon Virtue." In P. A. French, T. E. Uehling, and H. K. Wettstein (eds), *Midwest Studies in Philosophy XIII: Ethical Character and Virtue*, pp. 97–114. Notre Dame, IN: University of Notre Dame Press.

Stover, J. and Polansky, R. 2003: "Moral Virtue and *Megalopsychia*," *Ancient Philosophy* 23 (2): 351–9.

8

Aristotle's Justice

Charles M. Young

Men would not have known the name of justice had these things not occurred.

Heracleitus

John Rawls (1999: 3) begins his *A Theory of Justice*, famously, by saying, "Justice is the first virtue of social institutions, as truth is of systems of thought." For Socrates, Plato, and Aristotle, each in his own way, justice is the first virtue of individual human beings. Thus Socrates in Plato's *Crito* maintains that for an unjust person life is not worth living. Plato's *Republic* argues that justice is the natural expression in the field of human relations of a properly oriented and healthy individual life. Aristotle argues in the *Nicomachean Ethics* that justice (in one use of the term) counts as the whole of virtue and that (in another use of the term) it is the virtue that expresses one's conception of oneself as a member of a community of free and equal human beings: as a citizen.

Preliminaries

Book V of the *Nicomachean Ethics* is our principal source for Aristotle's views on justice, although passages in other texts, especially *Politics* III, are relevant as well. It will be useful to have on the table a brief summary of the main topics taken up in *NE* V.

The book divides roughly into two main sections. The first section, chapters 1–5, deals with justice as a state of character:

Chapter 1 distinguishes between *universal justice*, with connections to virtue generally and to the law, and *particular justice*, the last of the individual virtues of character that Aristotle began discussing, one by one, in *NE* III.6.

Chapter 2 argues for the existence of particular justice and distinguishes its two types, distributive justice and corrective justice.

Chapters 3 and 4 aim to establish senses in which distributive and corrective justice aim at what is intermediate, just as the other virtues of character do.

Chapter 5   begins with a discussion of reciprocity and concludes with an effort at making particular justice conform to the doctrine of the mean.

The second section of Book V (chapters 6–11) takes up questions of justice and responsibility. The treatment of these topics, however, is no sooner begun than it is interrupted by a discussion of political justice that takes up most of chapter 6 and all of chapter 7. The treatment of justice and responsibility breaks down as follows:

Chapter 6   distinguishes between doing an injustice and being an unjust person (1134a17–23).
Chapter 7   explains how just actions may be seen either as universals or as particulars and distinguishes between, on the one hand, acts of justice and injustice and, on the other, just and unjust actions.
Chapter 8   takes up voluntary action and distinguishes three ways of harming people.
Chapter 9   answers several questions about justice: Can one voluntarily suffer injustice? Can one voluntarily suffer justice? Does one who suffers an unjust action suffer injustice? Who does injustice in an unjust distribution? It also tries to clear up three misconceptions about justice and injustice and to demarcate the sphere of justice.
Chapter 10   a celebrated chapter, discusses equity.
Chapter 11   answers two more questions. Can one do injustice to oneself? Is it worse to do or to suffer injustice?

The digression on political justice, finally, goes as follows:

Chapter 6   announces that the topic all along has been political justice. Aristotle explains what it is and distinguishes it from other forms of justice similar to it.
Chapter 7   discusses the two forms of political justice, natural justice and legal justice.

In discussing justice, Aristotle uses a variety of cognates of the Greek words for "justice" and "injustice." I have been uniform in translating these terms:

dikaiosunē (n.) = justice   *adikia* (n.) = injustice
dikaios (adj., m. or f.) = just (person)   *adikos* (adj., m. or f.) = unjust (person)
dikaion (adj., neut.) = just (action)   *adikon* (adj., neut.) = unjust (action)
dikaiopragein (v.) = to do justice   *adikein* (v.) = to do injustice
to dikaiopragein (n.) = doing justice   *to adikein* (n.) = doing injustice
dikaiōma (n.) = act of justice   *adikēma* (n.) = act of injustice
dikaiousthai (v.) = to suffer justice   *adikeisthai* (v.) = to suffer injustice
to dikaiousthai (n.) = suffering justice   *to adikeisthai* (n.) = suffering injustice

Later (V.7.1135a12–13) Aristotle will argue that the term "just act" (*dikaio-pragēma*, n.) is to be preferred over the term "act of justice" (*dikaiōma*, n.) because an act of justice, strictly speaking, is a correction of an act of injustice (*adikēma*).

In what follows, I take up several of many important topics that Aristotle's discussion of justice raises. There are many other topics that I am unable to take up, and those I do take up receive limited treatment. For other topics and more detailed treatments, see Kraut (2002: 98–177) and Young (forthcoming).

Universal vs Particular Justice

In *NE* V.1–2, Aristotle distinguishes between two forms of justice. *Universal* justice (sometimes called *general* justice, sometimes *broad* justice), he tells us, amounts to the whole of virtue. *Particular* (*specific, narrow*) justice, in contrast, is an individual virtue of character coordinate with courage, temperance, liberality, and so on, and is, like each of them, a part of universal justice. Aristotle warned us about this complexity in justice at the end of his brief accounts of the various virtues of character in *NE* II.7: "After this, we'll talk about justice, since it is not a simple notion, distinguishing its kinds and explaining how each is a mean state" (1108b7–9). Aristotle does explain in *NE* V.5 how particular justice is a mean state, but he does not explain how universal justice is. Presumably he takes it for granted that universal justice is a mean state in that it comprises a number of particular virtues, including particular justice, each of which is itself in some way a mean state.

Aristotle's argument for the distinction between universal and particular justice appeals in the first instance to facts of linguistic usage. He tells us that the Greek adjective *unjust* sometimes describes one who disobeys the law and sometimes one who is greedy (*pleonektēs*), i.e., *unequal* or *unfair* (*anisos*). Aristotle is right in claiming that the language of justice in Greek is ambiguous in this way. So, for example, people accused of breaking the law in Athens were accused in the indictments against them of "doing injustice" (*adikein*). Thus the charge against Socrates stated: "Socrates does injustice in corrupting the young and in believing not in the gods in which the city believes, but in other, new spiritual beings" (*Apology* 24b8–c1). And in *Republic* I, Thrasymachus, when he recommends injustice over justice, invites us to consider "the unjust man . . . who is able to be greedy on a large scale" (343e7–344a2). Thus *unjust* can be used to describe two different kinds of people, those who break the law and those who are motivated by greed. *Just* can similarly be used of those who conform to the law and of those who are not motivated by greed, and so, too, *mutatis mutandis*, with *justice* and *injustice*. Justice in the first sense – universal justice – will prove to be the same state as virtue generally. Justice in the second sense – particular justice – is a virtue coordinate with the other individual virtues of character that Aristotle takes up in *NE* III–V.

There are problems with Aristotle's equation of universal justice with lawfulness. Aristotle thinks that the laws in any political community aim at the happiness of its citizens, whether all or some of them (*NE* V.1.1129b14–19). Laws might miss this mark in at least two ways. First, those who draw up the laws might be wrong about what the happiness of its citizens consists in but successful in creating laws that promote that ill-conceived happiness. Aristotle himself thinks that happiness consists in the realization of rationality in thought and action and that the laws in a proper human community will promote this aim. Oligarchs, in contrast, think that happiness consists in the attainment of wealth or property. Let us suppose for the sake of the point that Aristotle is right and the oligarchs are wrong. Let us also suppose that a group of oligarchs enact laws that do indeed promote the attainment of wealth. What are we to say about obedience to such laws? Is it just because it conforms to the law? Or is it unjust because it does not conform to what the law should be? Second, those who draw up the laws, whether or not they are right about what happiness consists in, might do a poor job of implementing the conception of happiness they hold. Thus a second group of oligarchs might think that a certain tax code promotes the attainment of wealth, when in fact it hinders it. Compliance with the code would conform to the law, but not with the law as it should be, nor even with the law as it should be by the oligarchs' own lights.

Aristotle does not articulate these problems, much less address them, although he does at least envisage the possibility of poorly crafted laws at V.1.1129b24–5. But a proposal that captures the spirit of his ideas would be to make ascriptions of justice and injustice relative. We might score political communities both on their views of the nature of happiness and on their success in implementing those views, and assess the justice and injustice of a community's policies accordingly. Thus policies can be just or unjust according as they promote the correct or an incorrect view of happiness, and just or unjust according as they promote the view of happiness they seek to promote. This proposal gives us a principled way of dealing with the cases raised earlier. Thus, obedience to the law in the first oligarchy, which succeeds in implementing its incorrect view of happiness, will be unjust when seen from the perspective of a proper human community, but just when seen from the oligarchy's own perspective. Obedience to the law in the second oligarchy, which fails to implement its incorrect view of happiness, will be unjust both from the point of view of a proper human community and also unjust from its own perspective.

The identity of universal justice with lawfulness carries with it, for Aristotle, an identity of universal justice and virtue of character:

> But the law also prescribes certain conduct: the conduct of a brave man, for example, not to desert one's post . . . that of the temperate man, for example, not to commit adultery or outrage . . . and so on with the actions exemplifying the rest of the virtues and vices, commanding these and forbidding those – rightly, if the law has been

rightly enacted, not so well if it has been made at random. Justice in this sense is complete virtue. (V.1.1129b20–26)

For, again, the law aims to promote the happiness of citizens, and virtuous activity promotes happiness; the law requires the same forms of conduct that the virtues of character require. The identity of universal justice, lawfulness, and virtue as a whole thus brings together two major themes of Aristotle's moral and political philosophy: the moral idea that acting virtuously promotes happiness and the political idea that the political community exists to promote the happiness of its citizens.

The Scope of Particular Justice

Aristotle limits the scope of the goods with which particular justice and injustice are concerned to external goods or goods of fortune (V.1.1129b1–3). A list of external goods that Aristotle gives at *NE* I.8.1099a31–b8 includes friends, wealth, political power, good birth, satisfactory children, and personal beauty. Plainly justice and injustice will not have to do with all of these, and at *NE* V.2.1130b2, Aristotle accordingly narrows the list of external goods with which justice and injustice are concerned to honor, wealth, and safety. These all seem to be things that one might want more than one's fair share of, i.e., things that one might be greedy for.

It is easy to see how justice and injustice are possible with regard to honor and wealth, less easy to see with regard to safety. Aristotle may have in mind cases in which one person avoids risks that others are then forced to assume. At *Rhetoric* I.13.1373b20–24, he distinguishes between doing injustice to individuals and doing injustice to the community (*to koinon*), maintaining, for example, that one who commits adultery or assault does injustice to some individual, whereas one who avoids military service does injustice to the community. It would be a mistake, however, to conclude from this example that an act of injustice to the community does not involve an act of injustice to some specific person. If I unjustly avoid military service, the victim of my injustice is not only my city but also the person, whoever he may be, who must serve in my place.

Note that particular justice, in being concerned with honor, wealth, and safety, overlaps with other virtues of character: with magnanimity (*NE* IV.3) and proper pride (IV.4), which deal with honor; with liberality (IV.1) and magnificence (IV.2), which deal with wealth; and with courage (III.6–9), which deals with safety. Presumably, particular justice has a different concern with honor, wealth, and safety from that of the other virtues. Aristotle makes no effort to tell us what the difference might be, but perhaps his idea is that, for example, my cheating on my taxes shows both something about my attitude toward wealth – a concern of liberality – and something about my attitude toward those other citizens who must shoulder the burden I have shirked – a concern of justice.

Justice and the Doctrine of the Mean:
The Problem

Aristotle thinks that each virtue of character – courage, temperance, liberality, and so on – is associated, not with a single vice, the virtue's opposite (as Socrates and Plato thought), but rather with a plurality of vices. Thus he associates courage with rashness, cowardice, and arguably other vices as well; temperance with profligacy and insensibility; liberality with prodigality and a variety of strains of illiberality; and so on. Moreover, Aristotle holds – indeed, he is famous for holding – a general thesis as to how the virtue in each sphere is related to its correlative vices: the "doctrine of the mean," as the thesis is called.

In explaining the doctrine at *NE* II.6.1107a2–6, Aristotle distinguishes two sub-theses of it, which I shall call *location* and *intermediacy*. Location is the idea that each virtue is a mean state (*mesotēs*) that is in some way "between" a pair of vicious states, one of excess and one of deficiency. Intermediacy is the idea that each virtue is a mean state expressed in actions and passions that are in some way "intermediate" (*meson*) relative to the actions and passions in which its correlative vices are expressed. Thus, courage is in some sense located "between" rashness and cowardice, and courageous actions are in some sense intermediate relative to rash actions and cowardly actions. (For more, see Young 1996: 89.)

Particular justice would seem to be a counter-example to both of these sub-theses. In the first place, Aristotle associates only one vice – injustice – with justice; he does not claim that it is a mean state between a pair of vices, one of excess and one of deficiency. This problem about location produces a problem about intermediacy. If justice is indeed associated with only one vice, it is hard to see how the notion of intermediacy can have any purchase with regard to just actions. Aristotle's solution to these difficulties is, as we shall see, to find special senses in which location and intermediacy are true of particular justice. Even after he has done this, though, he will admit that location breaks down, at least partially, in the case of particular justice: "Justice is a mean state, though not in the same way as the other virtues" (V.5.1133b32–1134a1).

Distributive and Corrective Justice

NE V.2 ends by dividing particular justice into two kinds, distributive justice and corrective justice; and these are the subjects, respectively, of V.3 and V.4. Aristotle's principal aim in these discussions is to find a way to represent what is just in distribution and correction as "intermediate" between two extremes. This will enable him in V.5 to give senses in which intermediacy and location hold for particular justice.

Distributive justice is concerned with the distribution of "honor, wealth, and other items that may be divided among those who share in a political arrangement"

(V.2.1130b31–2). Earlier in V.2, Aristotle had listed safety along with honor and wealth (1130b2); presumably he means to include it among the "other things" here. On Aristotle's analysis, distributive justice involves the allocation to *persons* of *shares* of one of these goods (V.3.1131a19–20). Such a distribution will count as *just* if and only if equal persons receive equal shares (1131a20–24). Equality of shares – what counts as an equal share of wealth, honor, or safety – will typically be easy to measure. Equality of persons will often be more difficult. "Everyone agrees," Aristotle says, "that just action in distributions should accord with some sort of worth, but what they call worth is not the same thing" (1131a25–7). The distribution of political authority is a star example: democrats propose that free citizenship is the proper basis for its distribution, oligarchs propose wealth, and aristocrats virtue or excellence (a27–9). (Aristotle tries to resolve this dispute in *Politics* III.) For our purposes, though, we can set aside these problems. What matters for us is that just action in distribution distributes equal shares to equal persons. Here the kind of equality is what mathematicians call "geometric" equality or equality of ratio. A distribution involving two parties, Socrates and Plato say, will be just if and only if the worth of the share distributed to Socrates is to Socrates' worth as the worth of the share distributed to Plato is to Plato's worth, where *worth* is measured by whatever are the correct standards.

Why does Aristotle think that this counts in some way as intermediate? We can answer this question by looking at just and unjust distributions in a simple case. Suppose that Socrates and Plato invest money in some enterprise, and the time comes when the profits earned are distributed. Distributive justice requires that equal persons receive equal shares. Here the measure of equality of persons is the size of the investment each has made. Suppose that Socrates has invested 20 minae, that Plato has invested 10 minae, and that there are now 60 minae in profits to divide between them. Plainly it is just to give Socrates, who has invested twice as much as Plato has, twice as much of the profits as Plato: 40 minae for Socrates vs 20 minae for Plato. An unjust distribution would be one that violates this proportion. Suppose a distribution goes wrong by 5 minae, either by giving Socrates 45 minae and Plato 15 or by giving Socrates 35 and Plato 25. Then the amount that Socrates receives in the just distribution – 40 minae – is intermediate between what he gets in the first unjust distribution – 45 minae – and what he gets in the second unjust distribution – 35 minae. Thus a just share is intermediate between a share that is too large by some amount and a share that is too small by that same amount.

Corrective justice, the subject of V.4, is concerned not with distributions but with restoring the equality between people when one has wronged the other. In such cases, the worth of the people involved does not matter: "It makes no difference whether a good man has defrauded a bad man or a bad man a good one . . . the law looks only to the distinctive character of the injuries, and treats the parties as equals where one is in the wrong and the other is being wronged" (1132a2–6). In a case in which one person has wronged another, an inequality between the two people has been created, and corrective justice seeks to restore equality by taking away the perpetrator's "gain" (or its fungible equivalent) and restoring it to the victim. Here the kind of equality is not geometric equality but what Aristotle calls (following the mathematical terminology of his day) "arithmetic" equality or equality of difference: the difference between the victim's position after the correction and his position before the correction is equal to the difference between the perpetrator's position before the correction and her position after the correction. An illustration: if Plato has taken 10 minae that belong to Socrates, corrective justice will take 10 minae from Plato and restore it to Socrates. Socrates will then be better off after the correction by the same amount that Plato will be worse off: 10 minae. And Aristotle claims that what is equal here is also intermediate, since the restored position of equality, in which each party has again what he had before, is intermediate between the improved position of the perpetrator and the impaired position of the victim. When Plato takes 10 minae from Socrates, Plato is up 10 minae and Socrates is down 10. When equality is restored, both are back at ground zero. Each is at a position intermediate between Plato's being up 10 minae and Socrates' being down 10. Thus both distributive justice and corrective justice aim at what is intermediate. (Note that corrective justice, as Aristotle understands it, is concerned only with the restoration of the original positions between the principals. Concerns over, for example, punishment do not arise, and indeed would in most instances be posterior to the determination, in achieving corrective justice, of the nature of the wrong done. That more will be required of the offender than what he has inflicted is noted in *Magna Moralia* I.33.1194a37–b2.)

Reciprocity

Before taking up the question of how particular justice squares with the doctrine in *NE* V.2, Aristotle launches into a discussion of reciprocity, much of which appears to be a digression. In the passage in question (1132b21–1133b28), Aristotle tells us that the Pythagoreans defined justice as reciprocity, but he does not tell us anything about the substance of their view or their reasons for holding it. He also notes that reciprocity is not to be identified with either of the forms of particular justice discussed in *NE* V.3 and *NE* V.4, distributive justice and corrective justice. He gives no reasons for thinking that reciprocity is not to be identified with distributive justice; he may assume that this is obvious. He does give reasons for thinking that reciprocity is not to be identified with corrective justice. He then makes some positive remarks about the importance of reciprocity to a city, an importance celebrated by the establishment of shrines to the Graces. After these brief remarks (1132b21–1133a5), we get an extended discussion about how reciprocity in exchange is achieved and about the importance of money in achieving it.

The first, briefer, part of the discussion is arguably on point, although it may belong at the end of *NE* IV. The idea that reciprocity in the form of the *lex talionis* – the idea that an offender's punishment should correspond in kind and degree to the wrongdoing he has committed – is corrective justice is a plausible and widely held view, and Aristotle is committed, methodologically, to taking such views seriously. Thus it would be very much in order for him to tell us why that view is mistaken. It would also be in order for Aristotle to say something about the importance of reciprocity to a city, given that it is not to be identified with either form of particular justice. However, the second, longer, part of the discussion of reciprocity, on exchange and money, is harder to connect to the discussion of particular justice. Aristotle has just told us that reciprocity is not to be identified with distributive or corrective justice, and those two types are all there is to particular justice. Moreover, the discussion of justice and the doctrine of the mean that follows the discussion of reciprocity and money reads as if the latter discussion were not there. So perhaps we should treat it as an appendix of some sort, whose relevance to the main discussion Aristotle would have clarified in a later draft.

Grace

Here is the passage in which Aristotle outlines the positive importance of reciprocity to a city:

> For people seek to return both evil for evil (if they cannot, it seems to be slavery) and good for good, since otherwise exchange does not occur . . . This is why people put up shrines to the Graces in prominent places: that there shall be paying back. For what is special about grace is that it's gracious for one who has been shown favor to do a kindness in return, and for him to go first in showing favor next time out. (V.5.1132b33–1134a5)

Aristotelian grace thus takes the good that we do for one another and returns, magnifies, and ramifies it. As a response to goodness, Aristotelian grace should be distinguished both from the grace of God and from grace under pressure (what Hemingway called "guts"), each of which responds to evil. The grace of God is God's response, if we are fortunate, to the evil that we do to one another. Grace under pressure is our response, if we are fortunate, to the evil that God – the world and other people, if you prefer – does to us.

Aristotle makes two main points about the operation of grace in the passage quoted above. First, grace enjoins us to return kindnesses that we have received: If you invite me to dinner, it is gracious for me to reciprocate. It is worth noting that the kindness done in return need not, and sometimes cannot, be done to the person who performed the original kindness. So it is, for example, with what we owe to those responsible for our training in philosophy. "For such gifts the only proper return is the endeavor to make worthy use of what one has learned," as Myles Burnyeat (1982: 40 n40) says in connection with Bernard Williams. Indeed, a kindness done in return need not be done to the specific individuals who benefited from the original kindness: "Lafayette, we are here."

Aristotle's second point is that grace enjoins one who has received a kindness "to go first . . . next time out." If you have invited me to dinner, you have done me the kindness of the invitation. You have also done me the kindness of extending an invitation that is not a response to a previous invitation. It is gracious for me to return both kindnesses. Thus it is gracious for me to reciprocate the kindness of your original invitation by inviting you to dinner. It is also gracious for me to reciprocate the kindness of your extending an invitation that is not a response to a previous invitation by extending a similar invitation to you.

There would seem to be an appealing regress here: a gracious regress, if I may. You invite me to dinner (Y). According to Aristotle's first point, it is gracious for me to reciprocate (M). That is a cycle, YM. According to his second point, it is gracious for me to initiate the next cycle, MY. But now we have a larger cycle, $YMMY$, which you initiated. So it is gracious for me to initiate a second larger cycle, $MYYM$. And so on, and on. It is thus a theorem of Aristotelian grace that if you do me a kindness, I will be forever in your debt. Aristotle may think that in "going first . . . next time out" I square things with my benefactor. If so, our gracious regress is vicious against this thought. Kant goes straight to the heart of the matter: "For even if I repay my benefactor tenfold, I am still not even with him, because he has done me a kindness that he did not owe. He was the first in the field . . . and I can never be beforehand with him" (Kant 1930: 222).

Political Justice

Having wrapped up his discussion of justice and injustice as states of character at the end of V.5, Aristotle takes up a new topic in V.6, only to drop it forthwith and return to the subject of justice and injustice:

> We must not forget that what we are seeking is also unqualifiedly just action and politically just action. This is found among people who share in a life aimed at self-sufficiency, people who are free and either proportionately or arithmetically equal, so that for those who do not have these features there is no politically just action, but only a certain just action, just in virtue of a similarity. For there is just action among those in relation to whom there is also law . . . (1134a24–30)

A problem in understanding this important remark is whether, in describing "what we are seeking" as "unqualifiedly just action and politically just action," Aristotle is referring to two separate actions (as in "I'll start my car and drive to town") or to one thing twice, the second time in a way that explains or explicates the first (as in "I'll obey the law and pay my taxes in full"). Are "unqualifiedly just action" and "politically just action" two names for two things or two names for one thing?

The text of *NE* V.6, though not conclusive, leans toward the second option. In the first place, 1134a24–30 goes on to say that politically just action is found among people "who share in a life aimed at self-sufficiency," who are "free," and who are "either proportionately or arithmetically equal," but it nowhere tells us what unqualifiedly just action is. This makes sense if "politically just action" explicates "unqualifiedly just action," since the statement of what politically just action consists in will also be a statement of what unqualifiedly just action consists in. If unqualifiedly just action and politically just action are two different things, the lack of an explanation of what unqualifiedly just action is would be mysterious.

Second, 1134a24 goes on to say that there is no politically just action among people who are not free and equal, only "something just in virtue of a similarity [*ti dikaion kai kath' homoiotēta*] (1134a29–30). Presently (1134b8–18), he will tell us that no unqualifiedly just action or politically just action obtains between master and slave, between father and child, or between husband and wife, only something "similar" (*homoion*). Thus, the first passage contrasts politically just action with action that is just "in virtue of a similarity," while the second contrasts unqualifiedly just action and politically just action with something "similar." Presumably, we have the same contrast both times. If so, again unqualifiedly just action and politically just action are the same thing.

Politics III.6–7 confirms the point. There, Aristotle classifies political arrangements or constitutions into types according to whether (a) *one* person, a *few* people (typically the rich), or *many* people (typically the poor) rule, and (b) the arrangement is *correct* in promoting the common interest or *incorrect* in promoting the rulers' interest. Thus we have six possible political arrangements:

	Correct	Incorrect
One	Monarchy	Tyranny
Few (rich)	Aristocracy	Oligarchy
Many (poor)	Polity	Democracy

Near the end of *Politics* III.6, Aristotle makes it plain that unconditional justice is restricted to cities with good rulers: "It is clear that those political arrangements that aim at the common interest are correct in conforming to what is unqualifiedly just, while those that aim at the interest of their rulers alone are all mistaken and are perversions of the correct political arrangements" (1279a17–20). Thus Aristotle affirms that political justice, as it is found in communities with correct constitutions, conforms to what is unqualifiedly just. It will be clear that unqualified justice and political justice coincide if he also holds that *only* such communities enjoy political justice. And indeed he does. *NE* V.6.1134a27 asserts that politically just action is possible only among people who are free and equal. And according to *Politics* III.6.1279a21, communities with incorrect political arrangements do not meet the condition of freedom: "These political arrangements [viz., the incorrect ones] are despotic, and a city is an association of free men." Indeed, it is precisely because they are despotic that these arrangements are mistaken and perverted (a19–21). It is safe to conclude, therefore, that unqualifiedly just action and politically just action in *NE* V.6 are one and the same thing, differently described.

Pleonexia

Aristotle begins his development of the distinction between universal and particular justice with the observation "Both one who breaks the law and one who is greedy seem to be unjust" (V.1.1129a31–2), and his first argument for the existence of particular justice appeals crucially to the notion of greed (V.2.1130a16–24). Thus greed is central to Aristotle's conception of particular justice. Here "greed" translates *pleonexia*; literally, "having more." Other translations include "overreaching," "getting more than one's fair share," "aggrandizement," and "graspingness." So what, exactly, is *pleonexia*, that is, Aristotelian greed?

Nobody knows. Aristotle says at one point, though, that the motive for particular injustice is the pleasure that comes from gain (V.2.1130b19–22). This remark requires some qualification, since plainly it is common for people to act on the desire for gain without being unjust: consider, for example, business owners or investors. But the notion of excess is built into the word *pleonexia*, so perhaps Aristotle's idea is that a desire for excessive gain is at the heart of greed: in particular, a desire for gain that goes beyond one's fair share (see Hardie 1968: 187). A case will help to illustrate the idea. Suppose that I owe you some money. I might want to keep the money I owe you so that I will have more money rather than less. If I act on that desire, on the current suggestion I will act unjustly.

One difficulty with this suggestion is that Aristotle associates the desire for excessive gain with the vice of illiberality (see, for example, *NE* IV.1.1122a2–3, and *EE* III.4.1232a11–12). If he was right in saying that, then he is wrong in saying, at V.2.1130b19–20, that actions done from greed are not expressions of any of the vices discussed in *NE* III–IV. A second difficulty is that if there is such a thing as desire for excessive gain, and that desire were distinctive of injustice, then presumably there is also such a thing as a desire for deficient gain, i.e., for less than one is entitled to, and such a thing as a vice of deficiency, which is also associated with justice – injustice to oneself, say. But Aristotle makes no provision for any such vice (see V.5.1133b32–1134a1); indeed, he vigorously denies that one can be unjust to oneself (see V.11.1138a4–28). Furthermore, far from thinking that desiring less than one's fair share is vicious, Aristotle counts the willingness to accept less than one is entitled to as a mark of equity (V.10.1138a1–2), something better than justice.

A second suggestion regarding Aristotelian greed as the desire for more than one's fair share is that greedy people desire not simply to have more rather than less, but also to have more than their fair share (on one form the suggestion might take, see Engberg-Pedersen 1988: 59; Curzer 1995: 215–17) or to cause others to have less than their fair share (on another form of the suggestion, see Kraut 2002: 138–41). Thus, in the example in which I want to keep the money I owe you, I desire to have more rather than less. But I also desire to have more than my fair share (on the first version of the suggestion) or in causing you to have less than your fair share (on the second): the unfairness is part of what appeals to me.

There is no doubt, I think, that the states of mind under discussion are possible states and that they are bad states. The question is whether they are the states of mind that Aristotle thinks are constitutive of greed. Consider the first case he gives in arguing for the existence of particular injustice at the beginning of V.2. One man commits adultery for pleasure, another for profit. The former action is profligate, the latter unjust. The most straightforward way to construe the profit example is to say, for example, that the second man seduces the woman because someone paid him to do it, or because he wished to gain entry into her house in order to steal something. Perhaps we could construe profit broadly, so that getting more physical pleasure than he deserves, or disgracing the woman, or her husband, or her family, counts as profit (though it is unclear how this counts as securing excessive money, honor, or safety – the goods with which justice and injustice are concerned). But there is no good reason to read the example in this way, except to save the interpretation. So, too, with the other cases of unjust action in the *NE*.

Further, it is not clear that the states of mind under discussion are plausibly to be seen as unjust at all. As Rawls (1999: 385–6) notes, unjust people and evil people are both prepared to do wrong or unjust things. They differ in that unjust people want more than their fair share of goods, the appropriate pursuit of which is legitimate, whereas evil people want this and more. Evil people want, in addition, to display their superiority over others and to humiliate them. They love injustice itself, and not merely the external goods that injustice can bring. The states of mind under discussion are, I take it, much closer to that of Rawls's evil man than that of his unjust man.

Rawls says that unjust people want more than their fair share of goods, the appropriate pursuit of which is legitimate. This remark suggests a way of understanding Aristotelian greed different from those we have considered so far. For if this is what unjust people are like, then the difference between just people and unjust people will be that just people desire external goods only when their appropriate pursuit is legitimate, while unjust people continue to desire such goods even when their pursuit is illegitimate. In our example, if I owe you money and I am just, I will not want to keep your money. If I am unjust, I will. So understood, Aristotelian greed is not to be identified simply with some form, simple or complex, of the desire for excessive gain. It consists, rather, in the absence of a certain restraint on the desire for gain. A just person does not want gain when it involves taking what belongs to another. An unjust person is not similarly restrained.

If this is indeed what Aristotle means by greed, he is right to say, as he does at V.2.1130b19–20, that actions performed from greed are not expressions of any of the vices discussed in *NE* III–IV, illiberality in particular. For the mark of illiberality is the desire for excessive gain, and the mark of injustice is the absence of a particular inhibition on the desire for gain. Evidently Aristotle is also right not to seek a second vice to associate with justice. For if justice consists in the appropriate curbing of the desire for gain, and injustice in the failure to curb that desire appropriately, it is hard to see what is left for a second vice to consist in.

Justice and the Doctrine of the Mean: Aristotle's Solution

Aristotle attempts at the end of V.5 to square his account of justice with the doctrine of the mean. Recall that the doctrine has two parts: location, according to which each virtue is in some sense "between" two vices, one of excess and one of deficiency, and intermediacy, the idea that virtuous action is in some sense "intermediate" between the actions expressive of those vices. Here is what Aristotle says about justice and intermediacy: "We have now defined the unjust and the just. These having been marked off from each other, it is plain that just action is intermediate between acting unjustly and being unjustly treated; for the one is to have too much and the other to have too little" (V.5.1133b29–1134a1). This should come as a surprise. In the first place, intermediacy should place just action between two sets of actions that are not just. Here, though, Aristotle places just action between acting unjustly and being unjustly treated. Furthermore, as we saw earlier, Aristotle argued in V.3 that what is just in distribution is intermediate between a share that is too great and a share that is too small. He argued in V.4 that what is just in correction is intermediate between profit (viz., the profit that an unjust agent secures) and loss (viz., the loss that the agent's victim suffers). Here he tells us, with no preparation, that doing justice – doing what is just – is intermediate between acting unjustly and being unjustly treated. It is hard to see how the remarks on intermediacy here fit with the remarks on intermediacy in V.3–4.

One possibility is this: Aristotle means that (a) my treating you justly is intermediate between (b) my treating you unjustly, in which case I get more than my fair share, and (c) my treating myself unjustly, in which case I get less than my fair share. Some scholars (for example, Curzer 1995: 218–22) think this is what Aristotle should have said in any event, since it represents justice as "between" a pair of vices, injustice and self-abnegation, as we might call (c) injustice to oneself.

One problem with this interpretation is that it takes no account of the explanations of intermediacy in V.3–4. A second problem is that, even if Aristotle would have a better view if he took this line – and this is not obvious – the fact remains that he does not. He never attempts to associate justice with a pair of vices. Moreover, he has what he regards as good and sufficient reason not to take this line – for he will argue at V.11.1138a4–28 that one cannot do injustice to oneself. Indeed, it is not far-fetched to suggest that part of the point of Aristotle's including the discussion of justice and responsibility that occupies most of the rest of *NE* V is precisely to explain why he does *not* take the line under discussion.

A second possibility is this: Aristotle means that (a) my treating you justly is intermediate between (b) my treating you unjustly, in which case I get more than my fair share, and (c) your treating me unjustly, in which case I get less than my fair share. This interpretation has two disadvantages. First, it is awkward that in (a) and (b) I am the agent and you are the patient, while in (c) you are the agent and I am the patient. And, second, apparently, the interpretation, like the preceding one, takes no account of the explanations of intermediacy in V.3–4.

We can, I suppose, swallow the first difficulty. And perhaps we can answer the second. Suppose I refuse to repay the money I owe you. Corrective justice will then require that my unjust gain – the money of yours that I have kept – be taken from me and restored to you. Thus corrective justice will bring about the very same outcome that would have been brought about if I had acted justly toward you in the first place. And since corrective justice aims at what is intermediate between gain and loss – between what I get if I act unjustly and what you lose if you are unjustly treated – we can say that just conduct aims at that intermediate situation as well. Similar remarks can be made about cases involving distribution.

An advantage of this interpretation is that it may go some way toward explaining why Aristotle thinks the discussion of distributive and corrective justice in V.3–4 is relevant to the analysis of justice seen as the contrary of Aristotelian greed, the subject of V.1–2. Unjust conduct as described in V.1–2 is conduct that corrective justice as described in V.3 exists to make good on: theft, adultery, murder, assault, robbery, breach of contract, and so on (see the end of V.2 for the complete list). So why does Aristotle think that the discussion of distributive and corrective justice is even relevant to the understanding of justice as the contrary of Aristotelian greed? Perhaps because he thinks the perspective of a distributor or corrector is a perspective my assumption of which will allow me to bracket my personal interest in the outcomes of the various choices I might make, and thus allow me to see, in a disinterested way, what justice requires of me.

In Young (1989: 246) I give an example that illustrates what Aristotle may have in mind. I back my car out of my driveway, destroying your bicycle, which you have left there. A predictable dispute arises. We agree that I owe you compensation to the degree that I was negligent in not looking before backing my car out and to the degree that you were negligent in leaving your bicycle in my driveway. But we disagree about which of us was the more negligent. You stress my error in not looking before backing out my car. If you are rude, you note that it might have been a child, not just a bicycle, that I ran over. I stress your error in leaving your bicycle where you did. If I am rude, I express the hope that you take better care of your child than you do of your bicycle.

To settle our dispute we might take it to a third party for adjudication. Each of us would expect the arbiter to decide the case from a disinterested perspective. The arbiter will treat each of us, and our respective claims, equally. She will look only at the fact that a bicycle left in a driveway by one person was destroyed by a second person who backed over it, and not care which of us owned the bicycle and which the car. And she will fix responsibility as the facts and the relevant principles demand.

The arbiter's decision helps us to see what justice requires of each of us in the original case. The arbiter assumes a disinterested perspective on the matter, seeing us only as two members of a community of free and equal persons, each with our own needs and interests. She is made aware of the facts of the case, and she is asked to fix responsibility as the facts and principles require. But this is a perspective that is open to each of us, independently of our actually submitting our case to a third party. Each of us can look at the situation from the arbiter's point of view without actually submitting the case to an arbiter. I can base my claims on a view of the appropriate degree of responsibility attaching to someone who, in such circumstances, ran over some else's bicycle that brackets the fact that the responsibility is mine. You can do the same, *mutatis mutandis*. To the extent that we have achieved Aristotelian justice, I am suggesting, this is what we will be disposed to do.

Aristotle's attempt to square his account of particular justice with location, according to which each virtue is in some sense "between" two vices, one of excess and one of deficiency, is this: "Justice is a mean state of a sort, but not in the same way as the other excellences, but because it is related to an intermediate, while injustice is related to the extremes" (V.5.1132b32–1134a1). Here Aristotle makes no effort to locate justice between a pair of vices. This is understandable since there is no vice other than injustice with which it is associated. But he apparently thinks that justice nonetheless counts as a mean state since it is "related to an intermediate, while injustice is related to the extremes." Evidently, this is an attempt to exploit the analyses of distributive and corrective justice in V.3 and V.4, where what is just is identified with what is intermediate, and what is unjust is shown to involve both excess and deficiency. But it is far from clear that it gives us an interesting sense in which justice is a mean state. Aristotle does have a verbal point: as kindness aims at what is kind, so a mean state (*mesotēs*) aims at what is intermediate (*meson*). But one could argue that the practical crafts (such as, for example, medicine) aim at what is intermediate – indeed, Aristotle argues exactly this himself in *NE* II.6.1106b8–14. But would one draw the conclusion that the practical crafts are mean states? Aristotle himself does not.

Responsibility

Although the two discussions of responsibility at *NE* III.1–5 and *EE* II.7–10 differ in many important ways, they share the idea that voluntary action is action that has its source in an agent who in certain ways knows what he is doing. They also share the idea that responsibility is an all-or-nothing matter. The remarks on responsibility in *NE* V.8 supplement these discussions by allowing for *degrees* of responsibility.

The theory developed in V.8 distinguishes three ways of harming people: by performing an unjust action *in ignorance, knowingly*, or *from choice*. If I perform an unjust action in ignorance, I commit an *error*, but I do not do an injustice, and I do not show myself to be an unjust person. If I have reason to have anticipated my error (for example, if I release my guard dog into my unfenced front yard, and he bites the letter carrier), I have committed an *error proper*. If I have no reason to have anticipated my error (for example, if I release my dog into my fenced back yard and he bites the letter carrier, who has jumped the fence to retrieve mail that has been blown there), I have caused a *misfortune*.

If I perform an unjust action knowingly but not from choice (if, for example, I release my dog into my front yard because I am enraged to see the letter carrier walking through my flower bed), then I *do injustice* and I *do an act of injustice*, but I do not show myself to be an unjust person. Finally, if I do an unjust action from choice (if, for example, I release my dog into the front yard because I want him to bite the letter carrier), then I not only do injustice and do an act of injustice, but I also *show myself to be an unjust person*.

Evidently Aristotle's distinctions between causing misfortune, committing errors, doing an injustice, and doing an injustice that shows one to be an unjust person classify acts of increasing culpability. His distinctions correspond more or less roughly to distinctions that we draw between acting in non-culpable ignorance, acting in culpable ignorance, acting in the heat of passion, and acting with premeditation and malice aforethought, though we draw other distinctions than just these. Plato, at *Laws* IX.866d–867c, distinguishes those who kill out of immediate impulse and subsequently regret what they did from those who kill with premeditation and feel no regret, and he argues that the latter deserve the greater punishment. Since Aristotle thinks that choice by definition involves deliberation (see, for example, *NE* III.3.1113a9–12), it is reasonable to speculate that he is attempting in V.8 to express Plato's distinction in terms of his own moral psychology. For in telling us at 1135b25 that acts that express an unjust character do involve choice, he clearly implies that these acts involve deliberation. So Aristotle's chosen actions seem to be Plato's premeditated actions. Similarly, in saying at 1135b26 that actions performed from passion do not involve forethought, he suggests that his voluntary but not chosen actions are Plato's impulsive actions.

If this is indeed part of what Aristotle is up to in V.8, however, it is not clear that he succeeds. For he himself allows for premeditated actions that are not chosen. Incontinent people, he thinks, do something other than what they choose to do (see, for example, VII.3.1146b22–4). But he also allows that incontinent people sometimes exercise forethought (see, for example, VI.9.1142b18–20). So, by Aristotle's own lights, the class of premeditated actions does not coincide with the class of chosen actions.

Conclusion

In coming to a final view of Aristotelian justice, we must appreciate how thoroughly *political* it is. Justice does have a political dimension for Socrates and Plato, but each sharply limits that dimension. Socrates, in Plato's *Crito*, believes that it is unjust to disobey the city's laws, except under very special circumstances. But the injustice of disobeying the law is secondary; it derives from the injustice of harming those responsible for our existence or those who have benefited us and the injustice of reneging on our promises (if we believe that the laws speak for Socrates) or from the injustice of harming others *simpliciter* (if we do not). Plato's *Republic* notoriously defends a strong analogy between justice in a city and justice in an individual. But justice in the city is principally a heuristic facilitating the discovery of justice in the individual, and what matters in individual justice is not its connection with the city but its role in helping us to achieve and sustain what really matters: an apprehension and appreciation of formal reality.

Aristotle goes further than Socrates or Plato in making justice political. One way in which he does this is, of course, by equating universal justice with lawfulness. But with his analysis of particular justice he cuts more deeply even than this. For on the account offered earlier, Aristotelian particular justice invites us, in conducting our relations with others, to assume a perspective from which we view ourselves and those others as members of a community of free and equal human beings, and to decide what to do from that perspective. If we are able to achieve that perspective, and to embody it in our thoughts, feelings, desires, and choices, we will have achieved Aristotelian particular justice. When we act from that perspective, we will express a conception of ourselves as free and equal members of a political community: as citizens.

References

Burnyeat, M. F. 1982: "Idealism and Greek Philosophy: What Descartes Saw and Berkeley Missed," *The Philosophical Review* 91: 3–40.

Curzer, H. J. 1995: "Aristotle's Account of the Virtue of Justice," *Apeiron* 28: 207–38.

Engberg-Pedersen, T. 1988: *Aristotle's Theory of Moral Insight*. Oxford: Oxford University Press.

Hardie, W. F. R. 1968: *Aristotle's Ethical Theory*. Oxford: Clarendon Press.

Kant, I. 1930: *Lectures on Ethics*, trans. I. Infield. London: Methuen.

Kraut, R. 2002: *Aristotle: Political Philosophy*. Oxford: Oxford University Press.

Rawls, J. 1999: *A Theory of Justice*, rev. edn. Cambridge, MA: Harvard University Press.

Young, C. M. 1989: "Aristotle on Justice," *The Southern Journal of Philosophy* 27 (suppl.): 233–49.

—1996: "The Doctrine of the Mean," *Topoi* 15: 89–99.

—forthcoming: *Aristotle*: Nicomachean Ethics V. Project Archelogos.

Further reading

Balot, R. K. 2001: *Greed and Injustice in Classical Athens*. Princeton, NJ: Princeton University Press.

Jackson, H. 1879: *The Fifth Book of the Nicomachean Ethics of Aristotle*. Cambridge: Cambridge University Press.

Keyt, D. 1991: "Aristotle on Distributive Justice." In D. Keyt and F. D. Miller (eds), *A Companion to Aristotle's Politics*, pp. 238–78. Oxford: Blackwell.

MacDowell, D. M. 1978: *The Law in Classical Athens*. Ithaca, NY: Cornell University Press.

Ritchie, D. G. 1894: "Aristotle's Subdivisions of Particular Justice," *Classical Review* 8: 185–92.

Santas, G. 2001: *Goodness and Justice: Plato, Aristotle, and the Moderns*. Oxford: Blackwell.

Williams, B. 1980: "Justice as a Virtue." In A. O. Rorty (ed.), *Essays on Aristotle's Ethics*, pp. 189–200. Berkeley, CA: University of California Press.

9

Aristotle on the Virtues
of Thought

C. D. C. Reeve

A ristotle thinks that there are two kinds of beings: those whose first principles (*archai*) "admit of being otherwise"; and those whose first principles
do not (*NE* VI.1.1139a6–8). He thinks that there are such things as first
principles because he thinks that (true) sciences mirror the structure of the world,
and that such sciences themselves have a particular structure: they consist of syllogistic deductions (*sullogismoi*) from first principles, which are necessarily true
definitions of the essences of the beings with which the sciences deal (VI.11.1143
a36–b2). Finally, he thinks that this divide among the beings and sciences must
itself be mirrored in the structure of our souls. Let us accept his own terse explanatory formula without much probing the largely arcane account it summarizes: "it
is through a certain similarity and kinship" with their objects that parts of the soul
have knowledge of them (VI.1.1139a10–11). The part of the soul that cognizes
beings with necessary first principles is the scientific part (*epistēmonikon*); the part
that cognizes beings with contingent ones, the calculating part (*logistikon*). Each
is a sub-part of the part that has reason (*logos*) (1139a3–15).

The function or work (*ergon*) of these parts is reliably to cognize truth (*NE*
VI.2.1139a29). In the case of the scientific part (or of the contemplative thought
it enables), the truth in question is (plain) truth. In the case of the calculating
part (or practical thought), it is *practical* or *action-related* truth, which is "truth
agreeing with correct desire" effective in producing appropriate action (*NE*
VI.2.1139a29–31). When we see why this is so, we will be well on our way to
understanding the virtues of thought – theoretical wisdom (*sophia*) and practical
wisdom (*phronēsis*). For, since "virtue relates to proper function," these are – pretty
much by definition – simply the states that enable the rational parts to discharge
their functions in the best possible way (1.1139a14–15).

1 The Scientific Part of the Soul

"If we must speak exactly and not be guided by [mere] similarities," we will not class anything as a genuine science unless it gives us knowledge of what "does not admit of being otherwise" (*NE* VI.3.1139b18–24). At the same time, "scientific knowledge is of what holds . . . for the most part [*hōs epi to polu*]" (*Meta.* VI.2.1027a20–21) and what holds for the most part does admit of being otherwise: "nothing can happen contrary to nature considered as eternal and necessary, but only where things for the most part happen in a certain way, but may also happen in another way" (*Gen. An.* IV.4.770b9–13). "What admits of being otherwise" covers two quite different spheres, however: "what holds for the most part but falls short of [unqualified] necessity" and "what happens by luck, since it is no more natural for this to happen in one way than in the opposite" (*An. Pr.* I.13.32b4–13). In the former case, scientific knowledge is possible within the sphere; in the latter, it is not: "There is no scientific knowledge through demonstration of what holds by luck; for what holds by luck is neither necessary nor does it hold for the most part but comes about separately from these; and demonstration is of either of the former" (*An. Post.* I.30.87b19–22). Since "demonstration is a necessary thing," it follows that what holds for the most part must also hold by some sort of necessity, even if not by the unqualified sort applying to things that do not "owe their necessity to something other than themselves" (*Meta.* V.5.1015b6–11) and neither come-to-be nor pass-away (*NE* VI.3.1139b23–4).

The realm of necessity, qualified or unqualified, is the realm of scientific knowledge in the broad, or non-strict sense. The division within it is mirrored within science itself (*Meta.* VI.1). *Theoretical* sciences – theology, astronomy, mathematics – deal with what is unqualifiedly necessary; *natural* sciences – physics and biology – with what is qualifiedly so. The underlying explanation for the division is, again, arcane. No natural science has a perfect model (just as no physical theory in our way of thinking has a perfect physical model) because sublunary matter – air, water, fire, and air in some combination – is "irregular," "not everywhere the same," and "capable of being otherwise than it for the most part is" (*Gen. et Corr.* II.10.336b21–2; *Meta.* VI.2.1027a13–14). Theoretical sciences, by contrast, do have perfect physical models. For they deal either with abstract, immaterial objects (mathematics), or with superlunary material ones (astronomy, theology), whose matter – ether or primary body – is as uniform and invariant as Euclidean space (*Cael.* I.2.268b26–3.270b31).

If we want to know why or whether bird meats are healthy, then the relevant Aristotelian science might answer as follows:

1 All light meats are healthy.
2 All bird meats are light.
3 Therefore, all bird meats are healthy.

This answer will be correct if – among other things – (1), the major premise, and (2), the minor, are both necessarily true, and (3), the conclusion, follows validly from them.

Though we cannot grasp first principles by demonstrating them in this way from something yet more primitive, they must, if we are to have any scientific knowledge at all, be better known than anything we demonstrate from them (*An. Post.* I.3.72b18–23). Such knowledge is provided by understanding (*nous*) (*NE* VI.6.1141a7–8). Induction (*epagōgē*) is the process by which universals come within its purview (VI.3.1139b29–31; *An. Post.* II.19).

Induction begins with (1) the perception of particulars. In some animals, such perception gives rise to (2) retention of perceptual contents or memory. When many perceptual contents have been retained, animals with understanding (3) "come to have an account from the memory of such things" (*An. Post.* II.19.100a1–3). This account, or the unified set of memories from which it arises, is experience (100a3–6). Then, "for the first time there is a universal in the soul" (100a16). Finally, (4) it is through experience that craft knowledge and scientific knowledge arise "when from many notions gained by experience one universal supposition about similar objects is produced" (*Meta.* I.1.981a1–8).

The universal appearing at stage (3) is characterized as "indeterminate" and "better known in perception" (*Phys.* I.1.184a24–5). It is the sort that experience enables us to grasp. The universal at stage (4) is reached when an indeterminate universal, which is better known or more familiar to us, is analyzed into its "elements and first principles" (184a16–23), so that it becomes intrinsically clear and unqualifiedly better known (*NE* I.4.1095b1–4). These analyzed universals are the first principles of the (rationally) teachable sciences and crafts (VI.3.1139b25–7; *Meta.* I.1.981a28–30, b7–10).

Induction thus includes two rather different sorts of transitions from particulars to universals: the broadly perceptual and non-inferential process by which we reach (3) unanalyzed universals from the perception of particulars, and the other, obviously more intellectual and discursive one, by which we proceed from unanalyzed universals to (4) analyzed ones and their accounts. The latter are the first principles from which deduction then proceeds.

When a science has identified first principles from which all its theorems can be demonstrated, it falls to dialectic to defend them against various sorts of attack. This defense consists in a discussion of them "through the *endoxa* about them" (*Topics* I.2.101a36–b4) – *endoxa* being opinions accepted by "everyone or by the majority or by the wise, either by all of them or by most or by the most notable and reputable" (I.1.100b21–3, I.11.104b32–4).

Discussing first principles on the basis of *endoxa* is a matter of going through the problems (*aporiai*) "on both sides of a subject" until they are solved (*Topics* I.2.101a35), since "if the problems are solved and the *endoxa* are left it will be an adequate proof" (*NE* VII.1.1145b6–7). Thus, the hypothesis for dialectical investigation might be: is happiness pleasure or not? A competent dialectician will be able to follow out the consequences of each alternative to see what problems they face, and to go through these and determine which can be solved and which cannot (*Topics* VIII.14.163b9–12). In the end he will have concluded, if Aristotle is right, that happiness is not pleasure, though pleasure is intrinsic to it (*NE* I.8.1099a7–21). Along the way, many of the *endoxa* on both sides will have been modified or clarified, partly accepted and partly rejected (*Topics* VIII.14.164b6–7), whereas others will have been decisively rejected. These he will need to explain away (*NE* VII.14.1154a22–5). If most of the most compelling *endoxa* remain standing at the end of this process, that will be an adequate proof of the philosopher's conclusion, since there will be every reason to accept it and none not to.[1]

By defending a first principle against all dialectical objections, then, we show how it, and so the theorems that follow from it, can be knit into the larger fabric of our unproblematic beliefs. This gives it a kind of intelligibility, credibility, and security it would otherwise lack (*NE* I.8.1098b9–12, X.1.1172a34–b1, 8.1179a20–22). What dialectic offers us in regard to the first principles of the sciences is no problematic knots – no impediments to knowledge and understanding (*NE* I.7.1097b22–4, VII.2.1146a24–7).

2 Theoretical Wisdom

Given this picture of science, we can readily understand why theoretical wisdom, as the virtue or excellence of the scientific part of the soul, must deal with universal and unqualifiedly necessary truths: other sorts are less sure and less general. We can see, too, why it must comprise not just knowledge of what follows from a science's first principles, but a grasp by understanding of those first principles themselves: "theoretical wisdom is understanding combined with scientific knowledge; scientific knowledge – having a crown, so to speak" (*NE* VI.7.1141a18–19). Failure to know first principles, after all, is an obvious epistemic liability (Plato, *Republic* VI.510c–511d). At the same time, however, we are bound to feel that theoretical wisdom is very limited in scope, restricted as it is to such sciences as theology, astronomy, and mathematics.

The feeling is unlikely to be much diminished by Aristotle's own reason for thinking it misplaced. In his view, the god, as sole unmoved mover, is the final or teleological cause of everything else in the universe (*Meta.* I.2.983a8–9, XII.7.1072a25–7), and so enters as an explanatory factor in all the other sciences (for example, *De An.* II.4.415a26–b7). Since a science, S, is more exact than another science, S*, if (among other things) S offers demonstrations of the first principles of S*, it follows that theology is the most exact science (*An. Post.* I.27.87a31–5; *Meta.* VI.1.1025b1–18). That, in essence, is why it gets identified with primary (or first) philosophy, the most universal science of being *qua* being (*Meta.* VI.1.1026a13–32). But as most universal, its scope is, of course, greater than that of any other science. Since the god is also the best or most estimable thing, theology, which deals with him, is both the best or most estimable science (*Meta.* XII.9.1074b34, 10.1075a11–12).

When Aristotle, not unreasonably, requires theoretical wisdom to be "the most exact of the sciences," then, he is requiring its unqualified universality; when he tells us – almost as an afterthought – that it must deal with "the most estimable things," he is identifying it with theology, which he already believes to have alone the former trait (*NE* VI.7.1141a16–17, 1141a19–20).

3 The Calculating Part of the Soul

Outside the sphere of the necessary and scientifically explicable lies the sphere of what admits of being otherwise in the second sense of happening by luck. This is the sphere within which production (*poiēsis*) and action (*praxis*) operate (*Phys.* II.6.197a36–b3; *NE* VI.4.1140a17–20). For what happens by luck is the sort of thing that might be "an outcome of thought," but is not (*Phys.* II.5.196b21–2). So, for example, there is no explanation in any Aristotelian theoretical or natural science for the fact that (as it happens) this tree is at such-and-such a place. Since the tree is just where I would have put it in planning my garden, however, it is lucky that it is there. If, on the other hand, I had actually planted it there, it would be where it is because of my voluntary actions and the beliefs and desires that gave rise to them. So *I* would be the first principle of its being there (*NE* VI.2.1139a31–b5). Still, from the point of view of Aristotelian science, it remains in the sphere of luck in either case.

Because what is in that sphere is outside the sphere of necessity, and so cannot be an object of strict scientific knowledge (*epistēmē*), cognition of it is always simply just belief (*doxa*): "belief is about what is true or false but admits of being otherwise" (*An. Post.* I.33.89a2–3). Hence the calculating part is also referred to as "the part that forms beliefs [*doxastikon*]" (*NE* VI.5.1140b25–8, 13.1144b14–15).

When we believe that something in the sphere of luck is thus-and-so, we either like that it is (luckily, the tree is just where I want it), or we do not (unluckily, it is not). Our desires and feelings are positively or negatively engaged. That is why the realm is precisely one of luck: how we *see* it is determined, in part, by how we feel about it. Which raises the question of how (normatively) we *should* see it. And that is a two-part question: how should our desires and feelings be, so that we will see it correctly? And – since it is alterable through our actions – how should it be?

What makes an item in the realm of luck a piece of good, rather than bad, luck is its relationship to happiness: "when it [good luck] is excessive, it actually impedes happiness; and then it is presumably no longer called 'good' luck, in that the limit [up to which it is good] is defined in relation to happiness" (*NE* VII.13.1153b21–5). Since happiness "is what we all aim at in all our other actions"

(I.12.1102a1–3), our desires and feelings will be as they should – they will be "correct" – when they are for, and so represent as good luck, what will in fact promote our happiness. Since the virtues of character alone ensure that we feel the right things "at the right times, about the right things, toward the right people, for the right end, and in the right way" (II.6.1106b21–3), we will see correctly in the realm of luck only if we possess these virtues. That, in a nutshell, is why "virtue makes the target correct" (VI.12.1144a8) – it makes us see as happiness-promoting what is in fact *happiness*-promoting.

The desiring part of the soul (*orektikon*), whose virtues the virtues of character are, is not fully rational, because it cannot give reasons or construct explanatory arguments as the rational part can. Nonetheless, because it can "listen to reason and obey it" as a child can its father, it "shares in reason in a way" (*NE* I.13.1102b13–1103a3). What enables it so to listen is rational wish (*boulēsis*) – a desire specifically for the human good or happiness, and hence responsive to the rational part's prescriptions regarding it (III.4.1113a22–33; *De An.* III.10.433a9–26). Since the division between the scientific and calculating part is made "in the same way" (VI.1.1139a5–6) as that between the rational part and the desiring one, we should expect the calculating part, too, to listen to the scientific one on matters to which it has no autonomous access. These are universal necessary truths, which are objects of scientific knowledge but not of belief – truths that are "co-incidentally useful to us for many of the things we need" (*EE* I.5.1216b15–16). If we want to know whether this particular bit of bird meat is healthy, for example, the scientific explanation we looked at in section 1 will help us to decide.

Armed with the knowledge, provided by the scientific part, that all bird meats are healthy, and the (as we may suppose) true belief that this is bird meat, the calculating part does some reasoning of its own:

1   All bird meats are healthy.
2   This is a piece of bird meat.
3   Therefore, this meat is healthy.

But this reasoning has, as yet, no prescriptive force: "thought by itself moves nothing" (*NE* VI.2.1139a35–6; also *De An.* III.9.432b26–10.433a30). It is to drive this very point home, indeed, that Aristotle distinguishes practical wisdom, which is "a prescriptive capacity [*epitaktikē*]," to which the desiring part should listen, from sound judgment (*eusunesia*), which is critical but not prescriptive (*NE* VI.10). For a sound judge might argue in this way in order simply to evaluate critically someone else's reasoning or course of action. When such reasoning occurs in a hungry person, however, who is trying to decide whether to eat the piece of meat in question, the conclusion gains prescriptive force, not from his hunger, but from his rational wish for happiness: "deliberate choice will be a deliberate desire to do an action that is up to us; for when we have judged, as a result of deliberation [that it is what we should do], our desire to do it is in accordance with our rational wish [*boulēsin*]" (III.4.1113a10–12). So (3) takes on prescriptive, wish-backed force for a hungry person because he believes (as we may imagine) that healthy food is happiness-promoting food, and so is led to conclude:

4   I *should* eat this.

But suppose he lacks the virtue of temperance, so that his appetites for such things as food, drink, or sex, are not in a mean. Then his hunger for the fat-saturated, unhealthy Big Mac may be stronger than his wish for the lean and healthy bird meat. If so, he will succumb to *akrasia* and not act as he should. For him, there-fore, (4) is not a practical truth, since though his thought (the calculating part) asserts it, his desiring part does not act on it. But just as what one believes is what one asserts in the calculating part of one's soul, what one believes *in a practical or action-related way* is what one both asserts there, effectively desires in one's desiring part, and so pursues (*NE* VI.2.1139a21–7).

   We can now see why the function of the calculating part is to cognize specifi-cally practical truth, rather than contingent truth in general, and why, because the sphere within which it operates is the sphere of luck, it must involve correct desire, and so the virtues of character (*NE* VI.13.1144b30–32). What is bound to surprise – and somewhat disappoint – is that Aristotle has so little to say about deliberative reasoning *per se*. But that, as we are about to discover, is very largely because of the extremely narrow sphere he assigns to it.

4   Deliberation and Ends

Happiness (*eudaimonia*) or doing well in action (*eupraxia*), which is the best human good, is the (teleological) first principle of practical wisdom, the goal, end, or target at which unqualifiedly good deliberation aims (*NE* I.4.1095a14–20, 13.1102a2–3, VI.9.1142b16–22, 12.1144a31–3). Since happiness is a universal of a sort – something with many instances – we reach it, as we do all universals, by induction from the understanding-involving perception of particulars. These particulars, therefore, are the "first principles of the end in view" (VI.11.1143b4–5), the starting-points of our induction.

   But what particulars are they? People generally agree that happiness is the highest practical good, and so accept a formal but somewhat empty characteriza-tion of it as what "all by itself makes life choiceworthy and lacking in nothing" (*NE* I.4.1095a18–20, 7.1097b14–16). They acquire their different concrete conceptions of what happiness actually consists in, however, "from their lives" (I.5.1095b14–16) – that is to say, from what, as a result of their acquired habits, they have come to be pleased or pained by. If they have been brought up with good eating habits, for example, they will take pleasure in, and so judge as pro-moting happiness (formally conceived), things like bird meats. If they have been brought up with bad eating habits, they will find bird meats unpleasant, preferring instead the non-happiness-promoting Big Macs.

At the same time, more general scientific theorizing about themselves and the universe of which they are a part may have led them to conclude that their happiness must consist in rational activity that is in accordance with "the best and most complete virtue" (*NE* I.7.1098a16–18). But this conclusion cannot simply trump their inductive experience: "Arguments about actions and feelings are less credible than the facts; hence any conflict between arguments and perceptible facts arouses contempt for the arguments and undermines the truth as well as the arguments" (X.1.1172a34–b1). We must always evaluate a theory of happiness "by applying it to what we do and how we live; and if it harmonizes with what we do, we should accept it, but if it conflicts, we should count it mere words" (X.8.1179a20–22; also I.8.1098b9–12). The experience gained from reflective living, therefore, is by and large the evidentiary bottom line in Aristotelian ethics. Theory can illuminate and deepen experience but cannot go too much against its grain without undermining itself. In this respect, Aristotelian ethics is no different from Aristotelian natural or theoretical science.

It is the conception of happiness emerging from this two-pronged process that practical wisdom takes as a first principle – as something given. For practical wisdom is primarily a deliberative capacity (*NE* VI.5.1140a25–8, 1140a30–31), and "we deliberate not about ends, but about what promotes ends [*tōn pros ta telē*]" (III.3.1112b11–12). That is why someone can be a good deliberator with regard to any end whatever. But if he is to be an unqualifiedly good one, his end must be the unqualifiedly good end – happiness (VI.2.1139b1–4).

While deliberation is restricted to what promotes ends, it is not restricted to what promotes them in the way *external* means do – intrinsic constituents or components can be deliberated about, too (*Meta.* VII.7.1032b18–29). We can also, of course, deliberate about relative ends – ends that are means to other ones. What we cannot deliberate about is just our unqualified end. For "what we deliberately choose would seem to be what is up to us" (*NE* III.2.1111b29–30). But that happiness is our end is not up to us, since, as something determined by our function or essence (I.7.1097b22–1098a20), it does not admit of being otherwise.

Deliberation about some more restricted ends is excluded for a parallel reason. A doctor, for example, "does not deliberate about whether he will cure, or an orator about whether he will persuade, or a politician about whether he will produce good order, or any other about the end" (*NE* III.3.1112b12–15). For medicine is a craft partly defined by its end or goal – health. Insofar as that craft dictates our actions, therefore, we necessarily pursue health. (In the same way, oratory is defined by persuasion, politics by good order, and other such things by their defining ends.) The point, then, is not that *no one* can deliberate about whether to cure or to persuade or to produce good order, but rather that just as human beings cannot deliberate about their unqualified end, so too the doctor *qua* doctor, the orator *qua* orator, and the politician *qua* politician cannot deliberate about theirs.

When deliberation is said not to be about ends, therefore, all that is being absolutely excluded as a topic of deliberation is happiness. And even in its case, it remains possible, first, to deliberate about constitutive means, and, second, to engage in dialectical clarification of what happiness actually is (section 1). Much of the *NE*, indeed, though practical in intent, consists in precisely the latter (*NE* I.2.1094a22–6). Aristotle does not consider such clarification to be deliberative, but this is perhaps more a matter of terminology than of substance.

5 Deliberation, Practical Sciences, and Perception

The sphere of luck is delimited by the sphere of necessity, although, as we saw, the sciences dealing with the latter are coincidentally useful within it. Also useful are some other bodies of knowledge that Aristotle classes as sciences. These include practical sciences, such as household management, legislative science, and political science, which deal with action (*praxis*), as well as crafts (*technai*), such as medicine and building, which deal with production (*poiēsis*) (*NE* VI.7–8). Aristotle talks about first principles in the case of these sciences, too, and refers to deductions and demonstrations within them, but it is not clear just how closely they conform to the paradigm established by the theoretical sciences.

What *is* clear is that, like the natural and theoretical ones, these sciences further delimit the sphere of deliberation:

> Where the exact and self-sufficient sciences are concerned, there is no deliberation, for example, that of forming the letters of the alphabet, since we are not in two minds about how to write them. But those things that come about through us, although not in the same way on every occasion, about *them* we do deliberate, for example, about those in the sphere of medicine or wealth-acquisition, and more so where navigation is concerned than where physical-training is, to the extent that the former is less exactly worked out, and similarly where the remaining ones are concerned, but more so where the crafts are concerned than where the sciences are, since we are more in two minds about them. Deliberation occurs, then, where things for the most part happen in a certain way, but where the outcome is unclear and the correct way to act is undefined. (*NE* III.3.1112a34–b9)

Hence, even within the sphere of luck, the practical sciences or crafts often tell us exactly what to do – how to make a letter alpha, or miter a joint, or trim a topsail, or cauterize a wound. It is when they do not that deliberation comes into play: we "speak of people as practically wise in some [area], when they calculate well about what promotes some good end, *concerning which no craft exists*" (VI.5.1140a29–30).

In between the cases where a science or craft tells us exactly what to do and those where no craft or science exists lie two other sorts of cases: first, where the relevant universal laws, like all those in natural sciences, hold only for the most part, and so with less than unqualified necessity; second, where the laws are incomplete or inexact "owing to the endless possible cases presented, such as the kinds and sizes of weapons that may be used to inflict wounds – a lifetime would be too short to make out a complete list of these" (*Rhet.* I.13.1374a26–b1). For example, it is a natural law that all adult males have hair on their chins, but it holds only for the most part (*An. Post.* II.12.96a9–11). Hence, if having a beard is used as a legal test for adulthood, we will face disputable cases, where deliberation is needed. Similarly, it may be unclear whether a ring, or a professional boxer's fist, is or is not a deadly weapon, given the incomplete specification contained in the law. When an assault involves such things, deliberation will again be required in order to determine how the law applies to them. The sphere of deliberation is delimited at the other end, too; this time by perception: we do not deliberate "about particulars – for example, about whether this is a loaf or is cooked as it should; for these are questions for perception, and if we keep on deliberating at each stage, we shall go on indefinitely" (*NE* III.3.1112b34–1113a2).

The overall picture, then, is something like this: perception provides us with such information as that this meat is bird meat; natural science tells us that bird meat is healthy; the craft of culinary science (aided perhaps by that of medicine or dietetics) tells us that bird meat is cooked as it should when the juices run clear; perception tells us that these juices are clear. In this case, there may be no need for deliberation at all, so that the bird meat is simply eaten straight off. But when there is a gap between what science and craft tell us about universals, on the one hand, and what perception tells us about particulars, on the other, deliberation is required.

We see the effects of this way of conceiving the sphere of deliberation most clearly, I think, in Aristotle's discussion of the ways in which deliberation may be incorrect. He appears to recognize just two of these: first, we may deliberate well about how to achieve an incorrect end, something that does not promote happiness; second, we may reach the correct end "by a false deduction, that is, reach the thing that should be done, but not why, *the middle term being false*" (*NE* VI.9.1142b22–4). So suppose the deduction in question is:

1 All bird meats are healthy (happiness-promoting).
2 This is bird meat.
3 This is healthy (happiness-promoting).

The first error lies in one's conception of happiness, and so in what promotes it: this error, the virtues of character correct. The second error lies in believing falsely that the middle term, "bird meat," applies to this particular bit of meat. This is an error in (a sort of) perception. But what about the other errors Aristotle omits:

namely, the possible falsity of (1) and the possible invalidity of the inference? The most plausible answer is that these are omitted because neither is narrowly deliberative. The first is a scientific error; the second a logical one.

The following somewhat difficult text suggests that this is precisely what Aristotle has in mind:

> [A] The error may be about the universal in deliberation or about the particular; either [in supposing] that all heavy types of water are bad, or that this particular one is heavy. [B] But that practical wisdom is not scientific knowledge is evident. [C] For . . . practical wisdom concerns the last thing, of which there isn't scientific knowledge, but rather perception – [D] not the [perception] of special objects, but the sort by which we perceive that the last thing among mathematical objects is a triangle, since there too will come a stopping-point. And it is more this perception that is practical wisdom [*phronēsis*], but it is a different kind from the other. (*NE* VI.8.1142a20–30)

(A) acknowledges that a deliberator may be in error about the universal premise, (1). But (B) quickly excludes this as being an error in practical wisdom (which is quintessentially a deliberating capacity, as we saw), attributing jurisdiction over (1), and the like, to scientific knowledge. (C) restricts the sphere of practical wisdom to particular premises, such as (2), which are matters of perception. (D) then gives a laconic characterization of the sort of perception involved, saying that practical wisdom consists more in it than in knowledge of such things as (1). For though practical wisdom must be concerned with universal premises (VI.7.1141b14–15), it gains its knowledge of them at second hand from the scientific part. Practical perception of such things as (2), by contrast, is its own unique contribution.

With practical perception, then, we come to the very heart of deliberation. But what exactly is it? (D) analogizes it to a sort of perception involved in a mathematical construction – an analogy filled out slightly in an earlier passage: "a deliberator would seem to inquire and analyze in the way stated as though [analyzing] a diagram (for apparently all deliberation is inquiry, but not all inquiry – for example, mathematical – is deliberation), and the last thing in the analysis is the first that comes to be" (*NE* III.3.1112b20–24). The mathematician, apparently, is trying to figure out how to construct a complex figure, using, for example, a pencil and set square. He analyzes this figure until he reaches simpler ones (triangles, in Aristotle's example) that he can readily draw with such implements. These figures are the last things reached in the analysis, but the first ones that come to be in the subsequent construction.

Similarly, in practical matters, a plan of action couched in universal terms – "Confiscate all lethal weapons. Imprison all adult males" – has to be broken down into terms we can act on directly because we can apply them on the basis of perception: "Confiscate all sharp, pointy metal objects. Imprison all those with hairs on their chins." However, the relevant sort of perception is not perception of colors, shapes, or sounds (special objects). That is not, as we would say, theory-laden enough. Instead, it is the desire-infused perception, appropriate to the sphere of luck, which the virtues of character make correct.

A timorous person does not just overreact to danger, he misperceives minor dangers as major ones that fully justify his reaction, "so that even from a very slight resemblance he thinks that he sees his enemy . . . and the more emotional he is, the smaller is the similarity required to produce this effect" (*De Insomniis* 2.460b3–11). Think of what would happen if we sent him out to collect weapons! The perception of the practically wise man, by contrast, since his fears are in a mean, neither over-estimates nor under-estimates the dangers he faces. In the last analysis, in fact, his perceptions set the very standard of correctness: "the good man judges each thing correctly and the truth in each matter appears [so] to him . . . since he is a sort of standard and measure of these things" (*NE* III.4.1113a29–33; also X.5.1176a15–19).

6 Deliberation and Time

Virtuous actions must be deliberately chosen (*NE* II.4.1105a28–33). Actions done "on the spur of the moment are . . . voluntary, but not [done] by deliberate choice" (III.2.1111b9–10). "What is without prior deliberate choice is what is without prior deliberation" (V.8.1135b10–11). "One deliberates for a long time" (VI.9.1142b3–4). Apparently, then, all virtuous actions must be the result of lengthy, explicit, prior deliberation.

Just how implausible this view would be, is revealed by Aristotle himself. Suppose the hungry agent in section 4 knows that in order to be beneficial to him the bird meat must be eaten within ten minutes. Then his deliberation will be defective if it takes longer than that. So taking a long time to reach a decision may make one a bad deliberator, not a good one (*NE* VI.9.1142b26–8). Sometimes, indeed, the need for instantaneous action precludes prior deliberation altogether: "someone who is unafraid and unperturbed in a sudden alarm seems more courageous than someone who stands firm in dangers that are obvious in advance . . . For if an action is foreseen, we might deliberately choose to do it also by reason and rational calculation, but action done on the spur of the moment expresses our state of character" (III.8.1117a18–22). Moreover, when something is just plain obvious, we do not deliberate about it either: "if walking is good for a man, reasoning does not waste time on the fact that he is a man. That is why whatever we do without calculation, we do quickly" (*Mot. An.* 7.701a26–9). Presumably, then, in cases where everything is obvious, no deliberation is required.

All this seems right, yet it is in some degree of tension with the picture of virtuous action as requiring explicit prior deliberation that Aristotle often seems eager to convey. There are, however, some resources available to him by which that tension might be reduced. If, like the courageous person in a sudden alarm, we see right off what to do, it would just be silly for us to deliberate. But it would be wrong to conclude that we do not then act without prior deliberation. A weak-willed person, for example, has a state of character of the sort required for deliberate choice (*NE* VI.2.1139a33–5, 9.1142b18–20). It is not a virtuous state, of course, since his appetites and feelings, not being in a mean, oppose his rational wish. But since it may not be unchangeable or incurable (VII.8.1150b29–35), he can deliberately choose to try to change his appetites. If he succeeds and becomes virtuous, he will have his virtuous state in part because he has deliberately chosen it. Actions done on the spur of the moment from that state will then be – indirectly – the result of prior deliberation and deliberate choice.

What is true of the weak-willed person, however, is also true of all fairly decent but non-saintly people, whose habituation has not succeeded in completely harmonizing their rational wish with their appetites and feelings (*NE* X.9.1179b16–20). For they, too, can plan and deliberately choose to become more internally harmonized, less weak willed. If they succeed, they will have their states of character in part because they have deliberately chosen them. When they act on the spur of the moment out of such states, therefore, their actions will be – indirectly – the result of deliberate choice.

It is difficult to be sure that this is how Aristotle would reconcile his picture of virtuous actions as deliberately chosen with the facts of human experience. But it has, at least, the virtue of honoring the underlying motivation of that picture, namely, to ensure that the virtuous agent performs virtuous actions willingly, in full knowledge of what he is doing, and because he values such actions for themselves (*NE* VI.12.1144a11–20).

7 Practical Wisdom as Political Science

Practical wisdom is the same state of the soul as political science (*politikē*), so that what the former accomplishes in relation to the individual, the latter accomplishes in relation to the city (*polis*): ethics is politics for the individual; political science, ethics for the city or state (*NE* I.2, VI.8). The individual citizen's exercise of practical wisdom, as a result, typically takes place under the legislative authority and architectonic guidance of that of his community's rulers: "political science . . . prescribes which of the sciences ought to be studied in cities, and which ones each class in the city should study and to what extent they should study it . . . Furthermore, it uses the other practical sciences, and legislates what must be done and what avoided in action" (*NE* I.2.1094b4–6; also VI.8.1141b22–3).

The extent of such authority and guidance is, moreover, extremely large. For the aim of political science is to make citizens virtuous, and so happy, by enacting and enforcing the appropriate *universal laws* (*NE* V.10.1137b13–15; *Pol.* VII.1–3). And though "to legislate about matters that call for deliberation is impossible"

(*Pol.* III.16.1287b22–3), nonetheless, these laws must be sufficiently complete and detailed as to leave as little as possible to "so unreliable a standard as human wish" (II.10.1272b5–7). Ideally, in other words, the scope of deliberation should be minimal; that of universal law maximal.

Deliberation may be the avatar *par excellence* of Aristotelian so-called *particularism* – the place at which guidance by universal laws gives out and the individual agent must come to his own virtue-aided conclusions. If so, political science is surely the avatar of Aristotelian *universalism*. To see practical wisdom correctly, we must keep both its aspects in mind – something we will be more likely to do if, as Aristotle intends, we read the *Nicomachean Ethics* as a prelude to the *Politics*.

8 Practical Wisdom as Theoretical Wisdom's Steward

The exercise of theoretical wisdom in contemplation is "complete happiness" (*NE* X.7.1177a17–18, 8.1178b7–32, 1179a22–32); that of practical wisdom itself, happiness of a secondary sort (X.7–8.1178a4–10). Hence, among the universal laws practical wisdom (political science) enacts, are those pertaining to the education of (future) citizens in the virtues of character and thought (*Pol.* III.9.1280b1–8, VII.14.1333b8–10, VIII.4.1338b4–8), and to the external goods and leisure needed for virtuous activities (VII.8.1328b2–23, 15.1334a18–19; *NE* I.8.1099a32–b8).

Some virtues, such as courage and endurance, (1) "fulfill their function" exclusively in un-leisurely activities or work, such as war or politics; some, such as theoretical wisdom, (2) do so exclusively in leisurely activities, such as contemplation; and some, such as justice and temperance, (3) do so in both work and leisure activities, though primarily in the latter (*Pol.* VII.15.1334a11–40). Since leisure is the end aimed at in work, as peace in war (*NE* X.7.1177b4–6), the virtues in (2) take teleological precedence over those in (1) and (3): "reason and understanding constitute our natural end. Hence they are the ends relative to which procreation and the training of our habits should be organized . . . But supervision of desire should be for the sake of the understanding, and that of the body for the sake of the soul" (*Pol.* VII.15.1334b15–28). Practical wisdom, therefore, which has as concomitants the virtues in (1) and (3), is "a sort of steward of theoretical wisdom, procuring leisure for it and its function by restraining and moderating the feelings" (*MM* I.35.1198b17–19).

The goal at which practical wisdom aims in designing a constitution (at any rate, in ideal circumstances) is leisure, then, and the leisured activities, such as contemplating in accordance with the virtue of theoretical wisdom, that are impossible without it (*NE* X.7.1177b1–18; *EE* VIII.3.1249b9–25; *Pol.* I.7.1255b37, II.7.1267a12). This explains why practical wisdom's relationship to theoretical wisdom is analogized to that between medicine and health: practical wisdom "doesn't have authority over theoretical wisdom or the better part (just as the craft of medicine doesn't over health); for it doesn't use it, but sees to its coming-into-being: it prescribes for its sake, therefore, but not to it" (*NE* VI.13.1145a6–9). Medicine prescribes for the sake of health, as practical wisdom for the sake of leisure and leisured activities. But it does not prescribe about how such-and-such a healthy activity is to be performed. Similarly, practical wisdom does not prescribe to theoretical wisdom about how to carry out the leisured activity of contemplation.

Given practical wisdom's stewardship role, and the un-leisured nature of its exercise, to aim at maximizing that exercise would be like aiming to maximize the amount of fighting or working we do. We should maximize the *cultivation* of our characters, because "a happy life for human beings is possessed more often by those who have cultivated their character and mind [*dianoia*] to an excessive degree" (*Pol.* VII.1.1323b1–3). But, when it comes to activities, it is on the leisured ones that we should aim to spend the greatest possible amount of time: "the more excessively someone engages in contemplation, the more happy he is" (*NE* X.8.1178b29–30). Just how that aim is best achieved is another matter.

Unlike a god, a human being needs friends and other external goods if he is to have a happy life; he cannot survive on a diet of contemplation alone (*NE* X.8.1178b33–5). If he is to contemplate successfully, moreover, his appetites and feelings must be in a mean, since otherwise they will distract and importune. A strategy of starving them, therefore, is bound to be wrecked by its own success, though "it is the best limit for the soul to be as aware as little as possible of the part of the soul that lacks reason as such" (*EE* VIII.3.1249b21–3). Hence, at the level of character design, a habituated readiness to sacrifice external goods for contemplation would not promote a happy life nearly as well, if Aristotle is right, as having the virtues of character. Once one is virtuous, however, one will not be tempted to try to maximize one's leisure time for contemplation come hell or high water, since one will have practical knowledge that this is not the optimal strategy in the long term: "Insofar as someone is human, and so lives together with a number of other human beings, he deliberately chooses to do the actions that are in accordance with virtue" (*NE* X.8.1178b5–7).

It is a mistake, nonetheless, to treat the demand that one develop and act on *the virtues of character* as simply overriding. For in Aristotle's view, practical wisdom (political science) should develop in people those states of character that suit them to be good citizens under the constitution of their own political system (*Pol.* I.13.1260b8–20, VIII.1.1337a11–21). And these will be the full-blown virtues of character in only a very few cases (*Pol.* III.18.1288a37–9, IV.7.1293b5–6). In an oligarchy, for example, what one develops as justice will not be the unqualified justice that promotes true happiness, but an analogous state of character that promotes the wealth-acquisition oligarchs conceive of as happiness (*Pol.* III.9.1280a25–32, V.9.1309a36–9, VII.9.1328a41–b2). What is absolute from the point of view of practical wisdom is not *virtue* of character, in other words, but whatever state of character will, in one's actual political circumstances, make one's life go best. This may involve compromises not just on what promotes one's end, then, but on what one takes that end itself to be. Virtue ethics, as one might put it, is *the preferred system* of states of character and thought in the abstract, as contemplation is the preferred end, but neither is the system or end that practical wisdom must, in all circumstances, promote if it is to do its job.

The practically wise man possesses a complex array of well-entrenched and stable capacities to be richly aware and effectively responsive to all the good and bad things salient in any situation, and all the considerations bearing on them. But there is no requirement on him, as there is on a so-called direct-aim maximizer, such as a hedonistic act-utilitarian, to see all goods as commensurable. At stake in the situation may be the values of friendship, family, honor, and personal pleasure, and there may be no uncontroversial way to weigh these against one another. Rather, sensitive to all of them, and aware that no deliberation can result in their value being simply canceled or trumped by another, he tries to figure out how to be true to them. This task cannot be made routine. Universal laws come significantly into play, certainly, but as other factors to which he must be true in his deliberation, not as saving solutions.

Unlike the direct-aim maximizer, moreover, the practically wise man aims "not at some benefit close at hand, but at benefit for the whole of life" (*NE* VIII.9.1160a21–3). His primary aim, in other words, is to choose from among life plans the one that, when psychologically realized, will result in his living the happiest life possible in the political community of which he is a citizen. Happiness is not just to be maximized, then, but appropriately distributed throughout a life that is itself sufficiently long (I.7.1098a18–20, X.7.1177b24–6): "no one would count happy" someone, such as Priam, whose life was initially happy but came to "a miserable end" (I.9.1100a5–9), or someone whose happy life is cut prematurely short. But distribution of happiness, like just how long a life needs to be to count as happy, seems to be fixed by nothing more precise than the requirement that the overall life should be choiceworthy and lacking in nothing.

Also included among the laws practical wisdom (political science) enacts for a city are laws about the distribution of priesthoods, the location of temples, and other things pertaining to the public service of the gods (*Pol.* VII.9.1329a27–34, 10.1330a11–13, 12.1331a24–30). These are for the sake of the gods, ensuring their proper honor and worship. But we do not, for this reason, think that the gods are subject to these laws, or to political science (*NE* VI.13.1145a10–11). So we should not think that theoretical wisdom is subject to them either. The part of the soul in which such wisdom is located – *nous* (understanding) – is "something divine" (X.7.1177b28), after all, and practical wisdom legislates to provide leisure precisely for it:

The god . . . is that for the sake of which practical wisdom prescribes . . . So if some choice and possession of natural goods – either goods of the body or money or of friends or the other goods – will most of all produce the contemplation of the god, that is the best, and that is the finest limit. But whatever, through deficiency or excess, hinders the service and contemplation of the god is bad.[2] (*EE* VIII.3.1249b14–21)

9 Aristotelian Practical Reason

On what we may call the *Simple Humean Model*, practical reasoning consists exclusively in instrumental means–ends inferences and (ultimate) ends are determined by desire (broadly construed) alone. So practical inferences have the following (simplified) form:

(A) X has a desire for e
 X believes that f -ing will bring about e (or will better bring it about than anything else he can do in the circumstances)
Therefore, X f s.

On this model, nothing can be a practical reason for X to f unless either X desires to f or f -ing is a means to some end X desires.

On the *Iterated Humean Model*, X , motivated by his desire for ends $e_1, \ldots, e_n$, has done $f_1, \ldots, f_n$ on a number of occasions and found that while doing them promotes these ends doing $f_{m+1}, \ldots, f_n$ does not. By repeated "experiments in living" of this sort, he discovers what the reliable means to his various ends are. (This is the sort of information that X might bring to bear in forming the belief that figures in the second premise of A.)

Inter alia, however, X also discovers that achieving $e_1, \ldots, e_m$ makes his life pleasant or satisfying, makes it go better, more worth living, whereas achieving $e_{m+1}, \ldots, e_n$ does not. On the natural assumption that pleasure engenders desire, X will come to have a desire that supports his desires for the former ends, not the latter. This new desire is rational in the following sense: it is based on inductive evidence bearing on pleasure or satisfaction and on inferences from it. There is no guarantee, of course, that it will always be effective in causing action. By the time X makes his discoveries, his desires for $e_{m+1}, \ldots, e_n$ may have become too deeply ingrained in his character or motivational set for that.

We can now say that X has a reason to f not simply if he desires to f (or something to which f -ing is a means), but if, in addition, that desire is supported by a rational desire. It seems natural to think at this point that reason has acquired a locus in (A) beyond its second premise. For X can now claim to have inductive reasons for thinking that e is (or is not) desir*able* to him, or rational for him to desire. And this will still be true even if his rational desire is ineffective in producing actions. To be weak willed, after all, is just knowingly to have better reasons to do something other than what one actually does.

On the *Transgenerational Humean Model, X* draws on what he has learned from experiments in living to shape his children's desires by rewards and punishments, so that their effective desires will be for ends that he has found – and so they, as relevantly similar to him, are likely to find – more pleasant or satisfying to pursue. On the assumption that *X* is a social being, he can, of course, also draw on the experiences of other similar beings, trusting those that seem to have lived satisfying lives, and such practical advice as has withstood the test of time. The ends that are sanctioned by this inductive process, we may call the (putatively) *objective* ends – the ones that are not merely desired by someone, or desirable to someone, but unqualifiedly desirable, and so unqualifiedly valuable. The habits that promote their achievement, we may call the (putative) virtues.

Imagine this process continuing until such time as it can be somewhat systematized into a body of laws suitable for ensuring a stable, well-ordered form of social life for beings with these objective ends and these virtues, and will result in future generations of similar people (*NE* X.8.1178a33–9.1181b22).

Within a community of such people, we can distinguish four groups: first, those whose desires are always in accord with their rational desires – these are the virtuous; second, those whose effective or action-producing desires are always in accord with their rational desires, while some of their ineffective desires are sometimes not in such accord – these are the self-controlled; third, those whose effective desires are sometimes not in accord with their rational desires – these are the weak willed; fourth, those whose rational desires are not for objective ends – these are the vicious.

Relative to these four groups we may license a number of different locutions bearing on practical reasons. First, we can say that all virtuous, self-controlled, or weak-willed members of the community have a (not necessarily effective) reason to do what promotes objective ends. Second, we can say that all members of the community that are virtuous or self-controlled have an effective reason to do what promotes objective ends. Third, we can say that the vicious have no reason to do what promotes objective ends, except insofar as doing so promotes some (subjective) end of theirs.

In this model, then, we have licensed a rich array of locutions dealing with practical reasons, and a broader base for such reasons in the world. We have not, however, exceeded the resources of the Humean model of practical reasoning, merely enriched it in ways the basic version clearly permits.

Let us imagine now, not implausibly, that one of the ends sanctioned as objective in the transgenerational model is that of acquiring knowledge about the world, including knowledge about rational agents and their goals. Such knowledge would, of course, have to be a part of the best overall theory of the world as a whole. In Hume's view this theory will not be teleological or essentialist. In Aristotle's, it will be both. Suppose that Aristotle is right. Then the best overall theory may underwrite, or partially underwrite, the conclusions about ends reached in the

Transgenerational Model. It might tell us, for example, that given what our nature, essence, or function is, one among these ends has a claim to be our unqualifiedly absolute end, happiness – the one for whose sake, at least in part, all other ends should be pursued. Theoretical knowledge of this fact, together with a more detailed knowledge of the nature of that end itself, will then be available to enrich practical reason, so that armed with a better understanding of our end, it will be in a better position to achieve it.

We can now license a stronger locution about practical reason than before. We can say that *everyone* has a reason to do what promotes his natural end, since this alone will promote his genuine happiness and satisfaction. We can then recognize the vicious person, who has no general motivation to act on such reasons, as a pathological case – as someone whose failure to be moved by them has no tendency to undermine their objectivity.

In essence, this is the picture of practical wisdom Aristotle has given us in *Nicomachean Ethics* VI. It might with some justification be characterized as broadly Humean, since its non-Humean elements stem not from views about practical reason in particular, but from those about the nature of reality (including human reality) and of the sorts of theories that best capture it.

Notes

1 For a fuller and more nuanced account, see Reeve (1998).
2 The phrases *tēn tou theou theōrian* ("the contemplation of the god") and *ton theon therapeuein kai theōrein* ("the service and contemplation of the god") could refer to (1) human understanding (as a divine thing) and its contemplation of any appropriate object, or (2) contemplation specifically of the god. If the contemplation is of the best kind, however, the kind in accordance with theoretical wisdom, it must be the most exact form of scientific knowledge, and so must be the kind the god has of himself.

Reference

Reeve, C. D. C. 1998: "Dialectic and Philosophy in Aristotle." In Jyl Gentzler (ed.), *Method in Ancient Philosophy*, pp. 227–52. Oxford: Clarendon Press.

Further reading

Allan, D. J. 1953: "Aristotle's Account of the Origin of Moral Principles," *Actes du Xième Congrès International de Philosophie* 12: 120–7.
Anscombe, G. E. M. 1957: *Intention*. Oxford: Blackwell.
Bostock, David 2000: *Aristotle's Ethics*. Oxford: Oxford University Press.
Charles, David 1984: *Aristotle's Philosophy of Action*. London: Duckworth.

Dahl, N. O. 1984: *Practical Reason, Aristotle, and Weakness of Will*. Minneapolis, MN: University of Minnesota Press.

Fortenbaugh, W. W. 1991: "Aristotle's Distinction between Moral Virtue and Practical Wisdom." In J. P. Anton and A. Preus (eds), *Essays in Ancient Greek Philosophy, IV: Aristotle's Ethics*, pp. 97–106. Albany, NY: State University of New York Press.

Kenny, Anthony 1979: *Aristotle's Theory of the Will*. New Haven, CT: Yale University Press.

Reeve, C. D. C. 1992: *Practices of Reason*. Oxford: Clarendon Press.

Smith, A. D. 1996: "Character and Intellect in Aristotle's Ethics," *Phronesis* 41: 56–74.

Sorabji, R. 1973–4: "Aristotle on the Role of Intellect in Virtue," *Proceedings of the Aristotelian Society* 74: 107–29.

Woods, M. 1986: "Intuition and Perception in Aristotle's Ethics," *Oxford Studies in Ancient Philosophy* 4: 145–66.

10

The Practical Syllogism

Paula Gottlieb

Aristotle makes the controversial claim that it is impossible to have all the ethical virtues – bravery, temperance, generosity, magnificence, magnanimity, the virtue concerned with honor on a small scale, mildness, truthfulness, wit, friendliness, and justice – fully without having practical wisdom (*phronēsis*), and that it is impossible to have practical wisdom without having all of the Aristotelian ethical virtues fully (*NE* VI.13.1144b30–1145a1). This raises a puzzle about what sort of reason is involved in practical wisdom that would make this the case.

In the sphere of formal logic Aristotle is famous for discovering the syllogism (a piece of reasoning consisting in two premises and a conclusion), and for categorizing all the valid forms of syllogisms with premises containing subject and predicate terms. One of these valid forms, according to Aristotle, and as I explain below, is the basis for the appropriate form for setting out reasoning in the theoretical sciences, but it is controversial whether there is any such analogous form for practical reasoning.[1] I shall argue that there is indeed such a thing as a syllogism that is practical and of specific ethical import, that it is analogous to the correct theoretical syllogism in an important way, and that the explanation for its practical and ethical nature is to be found in the much-neglected part of the minor premise that reveals the agent to have the virtue salient to the situation at hand.

Formulating a correct ethical practical syllogism presents various difficulties. First, Aristotelian "practical" wisdom is not broadly practical. Aristotle draws a sharp distinction between practical wisdom and productive reasoning or skill (*technē*), and yet almost all of the examples in the *Nicomachean Ethics* and elsewhere relate to skills, for example medicine, which, while analogous to practical wisdom, according to Aristotle, is not the same. In his *Nicomachean Ethics*, instead of presenting a complete and detailed example of a valid ethical practical syllogism, Aristotle supplies snippets of medical reasoning, albeit applied to the agent and not to a separate patient, and parts of reasoning that have gone awry in the sphere of temperance. Secondly, it is not immediately clear whether the practical syllogism is supposed to represent the actual reasoning processes of the good person or an *ex post facto* explanation of action or the person's motivation or the justification for their action or some combination of the above.

Therefore, in order to formulate a correct ethical practical syllogism, I shall begin by considering the parallels between it and the theoretical syllogism and examining some more complete pieces of reasoning in *De Anima* and *De Motu Animalium*. With regard to the role of the practical syllogism, I shall argue below for the narrow claim that it is its role in explanation (explaining why the good person acts as he does and why he is licensed in drawing the conclusion he does) that makes it analogous to the theoretical case. The other functions of the practical syllogism are beyond the scope of this chapter.

I shall then discuss the minor premise of the ethical practical syllogism in more detail, and consider the way in which the ethical practical syllogism will only be used by the good human being. I shall preface my remarks with a brief discussion of Aristotelian deliberation with the aim of giving an intuitive picture of why Aristotle should introduce a practical syllogism in the first place, and what aspects of reasoning it is supposed to represent.

The Practical Side of Deliberation

Aristotle says that:

> in order to grasp what practical wisdom is, we should first consider who are the people we call practically wise. Indeed, it seems to be the mark of the person who has practical wisdom to be able to deliberate finely about what is good and beneficial for himself, not in some particular respect, for example, about what sorts of things are conducive to health or strength, but about living well in general. (*NE* VI.5.1140a25–8)

Despite this fine pronouncement, Aristotle fails to present a complete and detailed piece of deliberation about living well in general, so commentators often turn to Aristotle's discussion of deliberation in Book III, chapter 3 for elucidation. However, as we shall see, this discussion relates not to deliberation in general, but to deliberation in some particular respect, for example, health.

Aristotle begins by explaining that there is no deliberation concerning eternal truths of metaphysics or nature, nor of chance occurrences, nor of practical matters that do not concern ourselves; for example, how a remote nation of people might best govern themselves. Deliberation, then, is not the same as inquiry, which may deal with such matters and, in the case of metaphysics and science, have such truths as axioms and conclusions. While it may seem unclear whether deliberation can make use of such truths at all, what is clear is that the goal of deliberation must be practical. It is not the role of deliberation to reason through to the conclusions of other disciplines, though it may use the conclusions to come to a practical conclusion.

The more variable the subject matter, the more need there is for deliberation, according to Aristotle. Therefore, he claims, spelling calls for no deliberation and gymnastics calls for less deliberation than navigation does. (Aristotle had clearly not encountered the English language!) Be that as it may, disciplines like medicine and making money, according to Aristotle, are about things that are "for the most part" where it is not always clear how things will turn out (*NE* III.3.1112b8). Deliberation, then, occurs when everything is not already set in advance, and yet it is not completely arbitrary what to do.

Having explained the difference between deliberation and inquiry, Aristotle then discusses the similarity, explaining that the deliberator works out what to do in the same manner as a mathematician analyzing a diagram. The last step in the analysis is the first step in the construction. Although not all inquiry, for example mathematics, is deliberative, he comments, all deliberation is inquiry.

To see what the difference is between deliberation and other types of inquiry, we have to look at its goal. Famously, Aristotle says that we do not deliberate about goals, but only about what relates to the goal. The doctor does not deliberate about whether to cure, the orator whether to persuade, or the politician whether to create law and order (*NE* III.3.1112b12–14). The goal is wished for, and the things that are related to the goal are deliberated and chosen (*NE* III.5.1113b3–4). The claim echoes Hume's view that goals are set, not by reason, but by desire. Against such a view, commentators have argued that, on Aristotle's view, unlike Hume's, we can deliberate about goals because deliberating about what relates to the goal includes deliberating about what the goal consists in, or how to make it more specific so that it can be followed. It also seems obvious that someone can deliberate about whether to become a doctor.

There has been much discussion about whether the doctor can deliberate about his career, or whether, more generally, one can deliberate about what one's goals consist in, including happiness, or how to make them more specific so that they can be effectively pursued.[2] Fortunately, the particular reason why the doctor does not deliberate about whether to cure emerges from the preceding text. The reason is a practical one, and has nothing to do with rational justification. It is not that the doctor could not, if he so wished, consider whether he should continue with his career, but that insofar as he is a doctor he already has a practical interest in curing the sick, or, at least, in making his patients as well as he can. He does not need to deliberate about whether he should have that interest or not. Nor, insofar as he is a doctor, does he deliberate about whether he should treat this particular patient or, for example, continue watching the play. The reason we do not deliberate about ends is that they are practical, and to have a particular end requires being a particular sort of person, the sort of person who is disposed to act on the end in question when appropriate, and without further deliberation about the appropriateness of the end itself. If the doctor did not see the point in treating his patients, he would not be a doctor.

To start deliberating, the doctor not only has to see that it is the right time to cure, but also that it is the right time *for him* to cure. Once he sees that it is appropriate, deliberation about *whether* it is appropriate would be superfluous. How does the doctor carry out the deliberation? The aim of the doctor is the health of this patient, or as near as he can get to that objective (*NE* I.6.1097a11–13; *Rhet.* I.1.1355b11–14). To achieve that aim, the doctor needs to find out exactly what is ailing the patient, and consider the appropriate way to return the patient to health. The first requires perception and experience. The second, at the least, requires knowing what has cured, or at any rate helped, patients with similar conditions. (Even if the doctor went by trial and error, his experience with previous patients would still give him some general thoughts about what remedies to try.) This sort of general knowledge will not be simply book knowledge. Reading a Hippocratic treatise on the topics would not be sufficient for practical understanding; the doctor's grasp must involve experience. Furthermore, the general knowledge in question will only be what Aristotle calls "for the most part" because it will not necessarily be applicable to every single patient (for example, *NE* X.9.1180b7–12).

Therefore, while one might represent the doctor's deliberation as mechanically starting from a certain goal – the health of this patient – and then proceeding by steps to an action he can do now – say, massage the part of the body that is in pain (for example, *Meta.* VII.7.1032a32–1033a5) – this hardly captures all of what is required for successful medical reasoning. Correct deliberation here requires being a doctor, using some general knowledge, knowing which knowledge is relevant and why, and being able to perceive what needs to be done here and now with regard to this particular patient. As we shall see, these aspects of reasoning are not emphasized by Aristotle until the more general discussion of practical wisdom in Book VI, where, I argue, they are applied to the agent himself and come to the fore in the Aristotelian practical syllogism.

The Analogy between the Theoretical and Practical Syllogism and the Importance of the Middle Term

At *De Motu Animalium* 7, Aristotle raises the following question: "But how is it that thought sometimes results in action and sometimes does not, sometimes in movement, sometimes not?" He answers by pointing out a parallel between theoretical and practical reasoning: "What happens seems parallel to the case of thinking and inferring [*dianooumenois kai sullogizomenois*] about immovable objects. There the end is speculation (for, when one thinks the two premises, one thinks and puts together the conclusion), but here the conclusion drawn from the two premises becomes the action."[3] In drawing an analogy between theoretical and practical reasoning, Aristotle uses the terminology of a syllogism, mentioning premises and conclusion. The analogy is confirmed in the *Nicomachean Ethics* where Aristotle says that in ordinary reasoning the soul affirms the conclusion, but in the productive case it immediately acts (*NE* VII.3.1147a26–8). To examine the analogy in more detail, my discussion begins with the theoretical syllogism and its application to Aristotelian science.

Aristotle's main discussion of the theoretical (sometimes referred to as "demonstrative") syllogism appears in the *Posterior Analytics*. The details of the theoretical syllogism are the subject of nearly as much controversy as Aristotle's practical syllogism. In addition, Aristotle's own examples of syllogisms often do not live up to his own stringent requirements.[4] The medievals helpfully formulated the following example to fit Aristotle's specifications. It consists of a major premise, a minor premise, and conclusion thus:

Major premise: Rational animals are grammatical.
Minor premise: Human beings are rational animals.
Therefore,
Conclusion: Human beings are grammatical.

Here is the Aristotelian schema:

       C   B
(1) Being grammatical belongs necessarily to rationality.

       B   A
(2) Rationality belongs (essentially and necessarily) to human beings.

       C   A
So (3) being grammatical belongs necessarily to human beings.

B is the middle term. It is the cause or explanation why the conclusion holds true. Human beings are grammatical, i.e., capable of learning a language, *because* they are rational. Their rationality explains why they are capable of learning a language. According to Aristotle, the premises are true, necessary, primary, immediate (they themselves do not have any further middle terms) and both prior to and explanatory of the conclusion.

This type of syllogism is not intended to mirror the research or inquiry of the working scientist. The scientist does not start with definitions and work out the science a priori. Nor does putting terms in the order of a syllogism alone guarantee success. The scientist must make sure that the middle term really is explanatory. In other words, she must make sure that what appear in the premises are not mere correlations, but are etiologically grounded (*An. Post.* I.2–6, II.8–10; *An. Pr.* II.23).[5] Furthermore, Aristotle gives examples to show that the middle term must not be too remote (*An. Post.* I.13.78b22–8). Aristotle compares his examples to Anarchasis' riddle, "Why are there no female flute-players in

Scythia?" and its answer "because there are no vines there" (78b28–31). Presumably, the answer is short for the following train of reasoning: "Where there is no drunkenness there are no female flute-players. Where there is no wine there is no drunkenness. Where there are no vines there is no wine. In Scythia there are no vines. Therefore, in Scythia there are no female flute-players." As Ross points out, the problem is that there might be drunkenness and yet no female flute-players, wine and yet no drunkenness, or vines and yet no wine. The point is that if the middle term gives an explanation that is too remote, it may also turn out not to be the correct explanation for the conclusion of the syllogism at all (Ross 1949: 553–4).

Jonathan Barnes notes that Aristotle thought that the final results of a science would be written up in syllogistic format and he accordingly considered Aristotle's biological works unfinished since they contain no complete syllogisms (Barnes 1975; cf. Barnes 1994: esp. p. xii). However, he also thinks that Aristotle's works would point the way to a more complete science. The pioneering work of Gotthelf and Lennox supports this idea. For example, Gotthelf has shown that proto-syllogistic reasoning does in fact abound; many explanations of facts about animals are given in terms of features of the animal which are explained by the nature of the animal or its parts (Gotthelf 1987: esp. pp. 168–7; Lennox 1987).

According to the *Posterior Analytics*, any of Aristotle's four causes can play the role of middle term, but in the biological works, not surprisingly, it is the final cause, the explanation in terms of point or function, which usually takes pride of place. Gotthelf and Lennox's conclusions are controversial because of the laxer type of reasoning involved in the biological works.[6] However, if it be allowed that what appears in the biological works is in an important sense syllogistic (and more recent inquiry supports this view), then it becomes less of a leap to suppose that the practical syllogism counts as a syllogism too, even if it contains particular terms. That is not to say that the practical syllogism is a type of theoretical syllogism; rather, it is analogous to one. Aristotle carefully distinguishes practical and theoretical reasoning in *Nicomachean Ethics* VI.

Formulating the Practical Syllogism and the Analogous Middle Term

The clearest example of the premises of a practical syllogism appears in Aristotle's *De Anima*. Aristotle says:

> Since the one supposition and proposition [*hupolēpsis kai logos*] is universal and the other is particular (the one saying that such and such a human being ought to do such and such a thing, while the other says that this then is such and such a thing, and I am such and such a human being), then either it is the latter opinion [*doxa*],

not the universal one, which produces movement, or it is both, but the first is more static while the other is not. (*De An.* III.11.434a16–22, trans. Hamlyn 1993)

In the *De Motu Animalium*, Aristotle says that the conclusion drawn from the two premises *becomes* the action (*Mot. An.* 7). This comment is cryptic. Aristotle seems to imagine that the agent will act immediately. He says, "For example, when one thinks that every human ought to walk, and that one is a human being oneself, immediately one walks," but he elsewhere points out that the agent will act if not physically prevented (*NE* VII.3.1147a31–2). Presumably, then, the conclusion of the syllogism is the action itself. The default conclusion is a specification of the action to be performed.

In *De Motu Animalium* 7, Aristotle considers the productive reasoning resulting in making a coat. Aristotle renders the conclusion as "a coat must be made," or, in more idiomatic English, and applying the major premise to oneself, "I should make a coat." (Negative conclusions, such as that I should avoid doing something now, are also possible as we shall see below.) In the following, I shall give the idiomatic rendering of the (default) conclusion, with the caveat that, in Aristotle's view, it is not possible to reach that very conclusion except by way of the major and minor premises.

Putting these two passages together provides the following schema:

Universal premise: Such and such a human being ought to do such and such a thing.
Particular premise: I am such and such a human being. This is such and such a thing.[7]
Conclusion: I should do this (now etc.).

In the passage in *De Motu Animalium*, Aristotle uses the phrase "I am a human being" as opposed to "I am such and such a human being." The reason for this, I suggest, is that here Aristotle is contrasting human behavior with that of other animals, so "human" is the salient term. The appropriate kind of behavior is related to the kind of creature one is. However, a more plausible reconstruction of the syllogism in question might refer to the health of the agent as follows:

Universal premise: Healthy human beings ought to take constitutionals (at the right times etc.).
Particular premise: I am a healthy human being. (This is the right time for a walk etc.)
Conclusion: I should go for a walk (now).[8]

A few paragraphs further on, Aristotle mentions that walking is good for human beings. Presumably, it is good for their health. He also notes, plausibly, that, when acting, people do not dwell on the premise "I am a human being." I shall return to this point later.[9]

I now turn to the snippets of syllogizing in the *Nicomachean Ethics*. In explaining why the person with practical wisdom must be concerned with particulars as well as universals, Aristotle says: "For someone who knows that light meats are digestible and healthy, but not which sorts of meats are light, will not produce health; the one who knows that bird meats are healthy will be better at producing health" (*NE* VI.7.1141b18–21, trans. Irwin). He also comments: "Moreover . . . deliberation may be in error about either the universal or the particular. For [we may wrongly suppose] either that all sorts of heavy water are bad or that this water is heavy" (*NE* VI.8.1142a20–22, trans. Irwin).[10]

The above examples suggest that the more specific information one has, the better able one is to act. However, Aristotle seems to define the particulars in relation to the universal. If "light meats are digestible and healthy" is a universal claim, "bird meats are light" counts as a particular claim. None of this detracts from the view of *De Anima* that the very final minor premise contains indexicals: "I am . . . and this is . . ." The doctor in the first example who knows that bird meats are healthy would still have to know that *this* is bird meat.

This point emerges more clearly in *NE* VII.3.1147a1–10. Here Aristotle notes that there are two types of premise, the universal and the particular,[11] and he presents a syllogism which has two particular premises. He says: "Perhaps, e.g., someone knows that dry things benefit every human being, and that he himself is a human being, or that this sort of thing is dry; but he either does not have or does not activate the knowledge that this particular thing is of this sort." In other words, it is no good knowing that dry foods benefit you, and that, say, bread is dry, if you do not know that this is bread.[12]

The correct syllogism, then, would run as follows:

Major premise: Dry things benefit human beings.
Minor premise: I am a human being. Bread is dry.
Final minor premise: I am a human being. This is bread.
Conclusion: I should eat this now.

Although the final minor premise is not arbitrary, how many premises there are between major and final minor premise seems to me to be arbitrary. If one thinks of the syllogism on analogy with an accordion, one can insert as many premises as one likes between major premise and final minor premise.

In the same passage in Book VII, Aristotle also distinguishes two types of universal, one relating to the agent, the other to the thing (*to men eph'heautou to d'epi tou pragmatos estin*; 1147a4–5). The distinction is puzzling if one takes Aristotle to be referring to two universal premises because the distinction between what refers to the agent and what refers to the thing seems only to appear in the minor premise. Irwin's translation refers to two universal terms. But this is equally puzzling, for how is the part of the premise that refers to the agent a universal term?

The solution is to consider the agent in the light of some universal attribute which she possesses, just as, in the passage in *De Anima*, the agent in the first part of the minor premise appears as "such-and-such a human being" (cf. Kenny 1973: 28–50). Putting all the information together, we get the following good medical syllogisms:

(1) *Universal premise*: Healthy human beings ought to eat light foods.
   Minor premise: I am a healthy human being. This is chicken.
   Conclusion: I should eat this now.
(2) *Universal premise*: Healthy human beings ought to eat dry food.
   Minor premise: I am a healthy human being. This is wet.
   Conclusion: I should not eat this now.
(3) *Universal premise*: Healthy human beings ought not to drink polluted water.
   Minor premise: I am a healthy human being. This is polluted.
   Conclusion: I should avoid this now.

According to Aristotle, the universal premise represents the result of deliberation. The content of the minor premise is given by perception. Presumably, what licenses the conclusion is the fact that the agent is the sort of person she is. If she is not that sort of person, then the universal and second part of the minor premise will have no effect on her whatsoever. This is different from the scientific syllogism, where the inference from premises to conclusion holds whatever kind of character one has. However, there is one extremely important point of similarity. The explanatory role of the middle term in the practical syllogism is played by the part of the minor premise which refers to the agent. Indeed, its explanatory nature may explain why Aristotle calls it a "universal term."[13] The part of the minor premise which refers to the agent not only licenses the move from premises to conclusion, but it also explains why the agent acts the way she does.

What Aristotle says about the akratic dieter is consistent with the above schema. There are two beliefs, one universal and the other about particulars (*NE* VII.3.1147a25–7). The universal belief hinders the akratic from tasting (1147a33) and he also has the belief that this is sweet. On my account, the full *correct* ethical practical syllogism would be as follows:

Universal premise: Temperate human beings should avoid (too many) sweets.
Final minor premise: I am a temperate human being and this is a sweet (too many).
Conclusion: I should not eat this now.

Here again, the first term in the final minor premise plays an important explanatory role. It is the agent's temperance that licenses the inference from premises to conclusion and it is because the agent is temperate that she avoids the sweet.

The Middle Term and the Ethical Agent

It might be objected that in the *Nicomachean Ethics*, despite drawing the distinction between what refers to the agent and what refers to the thing, Aristotle routinely omits the part of the syllogism which refers to the agent, and when he mentions it, he often does so in the form "I am a human being" as opposed to "I am such and such a human being."

My explanation for the omission goes back to the discussion in *De Motu Animalium* where Aristotle says that the agent does not dwell on the part of the premise which says "I am a human being." This makes perfect sense as long as one thinks of the parts of the syllogism simply from a first-person point of view, for it is most implausible that the agent thinks to herself "I am a human being." All the good person will have in mind when he or she acts will be the other parts of the minor premise. None of this shows that the first part of the minor premise of the syllogism does not play an important explanatory role from a third-person point of view. To explain why the person acted as she did, one needs to invoke her character.

If the part of the minor premise which refers to the agent himself is truly explanatory, why does Aristotle sometimes represent this as "I am a human being" rather than "I am such and such a human being?" I wish to suggest that here too he is referring to what a human being ought to be, namely, a good human being. As we saw in the theoretical syllogism of the *Posterior Analytics*, the explanatory term must not be too remote. "I am a human being," taken *tout court*, is too remote to play a suitable role in the syllogism. Just because I am a human being does not explain why, for example, I do the generous action (many human beings do not), unless I am a *generous* human being. But if that is the case, then "human being" in the minor premise must be short for "such and such a human being" after all.

The Middle Term and Ethical Virtue: Deliberation Re-visited

So far, I have argued that the first part of the minor premise of the practical syllogism plays the same explanatory role as does the middle term of the scientific syllogism. I have not argued, and I do not mean to argue, that the first part of the minor premise *is* the middle term of the practical syllogism, but it may be worth considering a passage about deliberation in *Nicomachean Ethics* VI.9, where Aristotle does explicitly refer to a "middle term." I wish to argue that one way of understanding this passage is clearly at odds with my reconstruction, but another and preferable way of understanding the passage is congenial to my project.

In this passage, Aristotle is trying to explain what good deliberation is by contrasting it with other types of thought. In the midst of his discussion, he makes the following comment:

> However we can reach a good by a false inference [*pseudei sullogismōi*], as well [as by correct deliberation], so that we reach what we should do, but by the wrong steps, when the middle term is false. Hence this type of deliberation, leading us by the wrong steps to what we should do, is not enough for good deliberation either. (*NE* VI.9.1142b22–6)

The implication is that in good deliberation, the middle term is true. But what is the middle term?

Aquinas, in his lectures commenting on Aristotle's *Ethics*, suggests that what has gone wrong in the false syllogism is that the agent has arrived at what he ought to do but by the wrong means. The correct middle term would then be the correct means. Along similar lines, Sarah Broadie too suggests that the parallel to the "why" in the scientific syllogism is the "how" of the practical syllogism (Broadie 1991: 225–32). Aquinas's example is of someone who rightly concludes that he ought to help the poor, but by the wrong means, stealing (VI.L.VIII: C 1230).

The example is puzzling. According to Aquinas, the line of reasoning must be as follows:

1 My aim is to help the poor.
2 Stealing is the correct way to help the poor.
3 I should steal this. (Or I should help the poor by stealing this.)

According to Aristotle, the correct action would be to help the poor at the right time in the right way from the right sources and so on, and so the false syllogism would *not* have the right conclusion, since it is never the right time to help the poor from the wrong sources. We need to find an alternative interpretation where the middle term is incorrect but the conclusion is still true.

Interestingly, Aquinas's own comments suggest an alternative. He says, "Although the end in the order of intention is like the principle and the middle term, nevertheless . . ." if the aim is to be generous and to help the poor, what the agent gets wrong is what that consists in.[14] According to Aristotle, it does not consist in helping people at the wrong times from the wrong sources and so on. Being a generous person enables one to discern what the appropriate circumstances for generosity are. Hence the middle term, correctly understood, is the universal attribute under which the good person falls – being generous. Such an account is well within the spirit of my proposed general interpretation. In the following syllogism, what the reasoner gets wrong are the italicized passages. However, the conclusion is still true:

1 Generous people ought to help the poor (at the right times, from the right sources etc.).

2 *I am a generous person.* This is a poor person in need of help. *This is the right source* etc.
3 I should help this person (now etc.).

The reasoner is right that the poor person needs help, but he is not a generous person and so lacks the appreciation to see what the correct source for the help should be. He thinks that there is nothing wrong with stealing. In short, he is wrong about what generosity consists in and that is because he is not a generous person.[15]

A Note on the Enkratic, the Akratic, and the Learner

It has been objected that if, on my interpretation of Aristotle, a good character explains good action, it will be impossible to explain the good action of the Aristotelian enkratic agent. While the akratic person, according to Aristotle, has the correct view of what she should do, but fails to do it because of a recalcitrant desire,[16] the enkratic person apparently manages to "do the right thing" despite her recalcitrant desire to do something else. How can the enkratic person do this if she is not a good person? The answer again turns on what it is to do the right thing. On Aristotle's account, having the right motivation is part and parcel of doing the right thing. "Doing the right thing although I would rather be doing something else" means that one is not doing the right thing *tout court*, but one is doing something that only looks as if it is the right thing. In the case of justice, Aristotle draws a distinction between those acts that are unjust – done from unjust motivation – and those that result in injustice even though they may not have been unjustly motivated (*NE* V.8. esp. 1135b20–25). He draws no such distinction explicitly elsewhere,[17] but I think that he would not consider the actions of an enkratic person to have the same status as those of the good person. What explains the actions of the enkratic person is her *enkrateia*, not her virtue, and it is her *enkrateia* that leads to enkratic, rather than virtuous, action. At the very least she lacks the first part of the minor premise of the correct syllogism.

A similar objection can be made regarding the people who are learning to be good or who aspire to improve their character. Again, the explanation for any of their behavior cannot be their ethical virtue as they do not already have it. They may aspire to be virtuous and to use the practical syllogism, but will not actually be using it until they have improved their characters.[18]

Conclusion

There are several advantages in taking the first part of the minor premise seriously. First, Aristotle is often mentioned as the forefather of modern virtue ethics, a type of ethical theory that is supposed to be an alternative to Utilitarianism and Kantian theory. If, as I have argued, the agent's virtue plays an important explanatory role in practical reasoning, Aristotle's account can act as a good starting-point for developing an account of virtue ethical reasoning that is not easily subsumed under Utilitarian or Kantian reasoning.

Second, the fact that the agent must be a certain kind of person and apply the general knowledge that comes with being such a person to himself, shows how the practical syllogism can be practical. In order to act, the agent must be a certain kind of person and apply his know-how to himself, here and now. A practical syllogism with all general terms could not be practical, and it is no small achievement on Aristotle's part to grasp this point.[19]

Finally, the minor premise of Aristotle's practical syllogism shows how and why one cannot have practical wisdom without ethical virtue and vice versa (*NE* X.8.1178a16–17; cf. VI.13.1144b30–1145a1). The noted Aristotelian scholar G. E. M. Anscombe was therefore wrong to say that "the practical syllogism as such is not an ethical topic," but right to claim that "'[p]ractical reasoning' or 'practical syllogism', which means the same thing, was one of Aristotle's best discoveries" (Anscombe 1957: 78, 57–8).

Acknowledgments

I should like to thank the following for detailed comments on earlier versions of this chapter: Norman Dahl, R. J. Hankinson, R. Kamtekar, J. Longeway, H. Newell, T. M. I. Penner, R. Saunders, E. Sober, and L. Weitzman. Especial thanks go to R. Kraut for a host of helpful comments on the penultimate draft.

Notes

1 See, for example, Annas's doubts (1993: 92). Broadie (1991: esp. p. 229) and Reeve (1992) think there is an analogy, but Broadie draws a different parallel from mine, which I discuss below, and Reeve concentrates on the status of the major ("universal") premise.

2 For the two sides to the debate, see, for example, Wiggins (1975–6: 226–7) and Tuozzo (1991: esp. pp. 197, 202).

3 I explain this comment in the following section.

4 See Lloyd (1996: 13), who goes on to argue that there are more stringent and laxer versions of demonstration.

5 I do not mean to suggest that Aristotle does not also discuss inductive reasoning and "demonstrations of the fact," but I take these to be earlier stages in an Aristotelian science.

6 See Lloyd (1996: 7–37), addressed by Lennox in his introduction to Lennox (2001). On the complexities of Aristotelian demonstration, definition, and explanation, see also Charles (2000: pt II).

7 It has been suggested that my particular premise is in fact two premises and that there are two syllogisms involved, not just one. Briefly, against this suggestion, I would argue that Aristotle himself claims to be describing only two premises and one conclusion, that my account makes more perspicuous the connection between being a good person and having a correct appreciation of the circumstances, and that Aristotle's account of *akrasia* (lack of self-control) can also be formulated with only one syllogism.

8 A separate account is required for the actions of the person who is sick and merely wishes to do what is healthy. Compare section 6 of this chapter.

9 The passage in the *De Motu Animalium* also introduces two types of premises in productive reasoning; some describe what is good for human beings, others describe what is possible for them. For example, if a tailor needs a coat (something that would be good), she will work out what she needs to do first in order to make it, i.e., what is possible. Controversy surrounds whether these are two types of major premise or whether the good premises are major, while the possible are minor (Allan vs Wiggins in Wiggins 1975–6). My solution is that the two types of premise alternate as follows:

Major premise: Healthy human beings should wear coats when they go out.
Minor premise: I am a healthy human being. I need a coat.
Possible premise: To make a coat, I need material etc.
So (*new major premise*): Healthy human beings should find the right material.
Minor premise: I am a healthy human being. This is the right material etc.

10 Although this may look like decisive evidence against Cooper's view that deliberation ceases at the major premise (Cooper 1975: 46), there is a problem involving scope in this sentence.

11 The particular here is *to kata meros* (cf. *An. Post.* I.24).

12 *Contra* Cooper (1975: e.g. 184) and with Dahl (1984: esp. 29 and n 12).

13 See *An. Post.* I.24 for the connection between the universal and the explanatory.

14 See, too, *An. Post.* II.11 where Aristotle seems to be envisaging the final cause as a middle term, although the passage is obscure.

15 An alternative suggestion is that the reasoner is wrong about a matter of fact, but this has the awkward consequence that the resulting action will not then be voluntary.

16 She also lacks part of the correct syllogism, but a full account of how this works is beyond the scope of this chapter.

17 Aristotle's distinction between bravery and ersatz states that resemble bravery presupposes a distinction between virtuous action and merely virtuous-looking behavior (*NE* III.6–9).

18 For a fuller discussion of the difference between the learner and the person who is good, see the analysis of *NE* II.4 in Gottlieb (2001).

19 In the twentieth century, much work has been done on the related, though slightly different, problem of the indexical "I" in action. See, for example, Perry (1979).

References

Annas, J. 1993: *The Morality of Happiness*. Oxford: Oxford University Press.

Anscombe, G. E. M. 1957: *Intention*. Oxford: Blackwell.

Barnes, J. 1975: "Aristotle's Theory of Demonstration." In J. Barnes, M. Schofield, and R. Sorabji (eds), *Articles on Aristotle*, vol. 1: *Science*, pp. 65–87. London: Duckworth.

—1994: *Aristotle: Posterior Analytics*. Oxford: Clarendon Press.

Broadie, S. 1991: *Ethics with Aristotle*. New York: Oxford University Press.

Charles, D. O. M. 2000: *Aristotle on Meaning and Essence*. Oxford: Oxford University Press.

Cooper, J. M. 1975: *Reason and Human Good in Aristotle*. Cambridge, MA: Harvard University Press.

Dahl, N. O. 1984: *Practical Reason, Aristotle, and Weakness of the Will*. Minneapolis, MN: University of Minnesota Press.

Gotthelf, A. 1987: "First Principles in Aristotle's *Parts of Animals*." In A. Gotthelf and J. G. Lennox (eds), *Philosophical Issues in Aristotle's Biology*, pp. 167–98. Cambridge: Cambridge University Press.

Gottlieb, P. L. 2001: "An Analysis of Aristotle's *Nicomachean Ethics* Books 1 and 2 for *Project Archelogos*" (http://www.archelogos.com).

Hamlyn, D. W. 1993: *Aristotle's De Anima Books II, III*. Oxford: Clarendon Press.

Hume, David 1967: *A Treatise of Human Nature*, ed. L. A. Selby-Bigge [1888]. Oxford: Clarendon Press.

Irwin, T. H. (trans.) 1985: *Aristotle's Nicomachean Ethics*. Indianapolis, IN: Hackett.

—(trans.) 1999: *Aristotle's Nicomachean Ethics*. Indianapolis, IN: Hackett.

Kenny, A. 1973: "The Practical Syllogism and Incontinence." In A. Kenny, *The Anatomy of the Soul: Historical Essays in the Philosophy of Mind*, pp. 28–50. Oxford: Blackwell.

Lennox, James G. 1987: "Divide and Explain: The *Posterior Analytics* in Practice." In J. G. Lennox, *Aristotle's Philosophy of Biology: Studies in the Origins of Life Science*, pp. 7–38. Cambridge: Cambridge University Press, 2001; reprinted from A. Gotthelf and J. G. Lennox (eds), *Philosophical Issues in Aristotle's Biology*. Cambridge: Cambridge University Press, 1987.

—2001: *Aristotle's Philosophy of Biology: Studies in the Origins of Life Science*. Cambridge: Cambridge University Press.

Lloyd, G. E. R. 1996: *Aristotelian Explorations*. Cambridge: Cambridge University Press.

Perry, J. 1979: "The Problem of the Essential Indexical," *Nous* 13: 3–21.

Reeve, C. D. C. 1992: *Practices of Reason*. Oxford: Oxford University Press.

Ross, W. D. 1949: *Commentary on Aristotle's Prior and Posterior Analytics*. Oxford: Clarendon Press.

Tuozzo, T. M. 1991: "Aristotelian Deliberation is Not of Ends." In J. P. Anton and A. Preus (eds), *Essays in Ancient Greek Philosophy*, vol. 4: *Aristotle's Ethics*, pp. 193–212. Albany, NY: State University of New York Press.

Wiggins, D. 1975–6: "Deliberation and Practical Reasoning." In A. O. Rorty (ed.), *Essays on Aristotle's Ethics*, pp. 221–40. Berkeley, CA: University of California Press.

Further reading

Ackrill, J. L. 1973: *Aristotle's Ethics*. New York: Humanities Press.

Bostock, D. 2000: *Aristotle's Ethics*, pp. 140–42. Oxford: Oxford University Press.

Burnyeat, M. F. 1980: "Aristotle on Learning to be Good." In A. O. Rorty (ed.), *Essays on Aristotle's Ethics*, pp. 69–92. Berkeley, CA: University of California Press.

Engberg-Pedersen, T. 1983: *Aristotle's Theory of Moral Insight*. Oxford: Clarendon Press.

Hardie, W. F. R. 1980: *Aristotle's Ethical Theory*, pp. 212–58. Oxford: Clarendon Press.

Hursthouse, R. 1999: *On Virtue Ethics*, esp. pp. 121–40. Oxford: Oxford University Press.

Irwin, T. H. 1975: "Aristotle on Reason, Desire, and Virtue," *Journal of Philosophy* 72: 567–78.

Kraut, R. 1989: *Aristotle on the Human Good*, pp. 197–266. Princeton, NJ: Princeton University Press.

McDowell, J. 1979: "Virtue and Reason," *Monist* 62: 331–50.

—1996: "Deliberation and Moral Development in Aristotle's Ethics." In S. Engstrom and J. Whiting (eds), *Aristotle, Kant and the Stoics: Rethinking Happiness and Duty*, pp. 19–35. Cambridge: Cambridge University Press.

Nussbaum, M. C. 1978: *Aristotle's De Motu Animalium*. Princeton, NJ: Princeton University Press.

Richardson, H. S. 1994: *Practical Reasoning about Final Ends*. Cambridge: Cambridge University Press.

Sherman, N. 1997: *Making a Necessity of Virtue: Aristotle and Kant on Virtue*, esp. pp. 239–331. Cambridge: Cambridge University Press.

11

Acrasia and Self-control

A. W. Price

1 Prelude

I start with an ostensibly Aristotelian account of acrasia[1] that is *not* Aristotle's. It will pose two questions to occupy us thereafter: *how* different is Aristotle's own account, and *why* is it as different as it is?

When a person acts voluntarily, he acts as he wants because he wants to act so. His desire to act so is then *effective*. What is the origin of effective desire in a human agent? Socrates offered a simple answer: it is practical judgment. An effective desire to act in a certain way is a corollary of a judgment that it is best to do so (*Protagoras*, 358b6–c1, c6–d2). Consequently, in Aristotle's words (*NE* VII.2.1145b26–7), "No one acts against what he believes best – people act so only because of ignorance." Yet "this view plainly contradicts what appears to be the case" (literally "the phenomena," *tois phainomenois*, b27–8), whether this phrase means the things we see (or seem to see), or the things we say. Men are rational animals, that is, rational as animals go. Our agency displays our composite nature, above all in the disunity of our desires (*orexeis*).[2] Wishes (*bouléseis*) and choices (*prohaireseis*) respect the Socratic paradigm: wish is for a goal (III.2.1111b26, III.4.1113a15) that one thinks *good* (V.9.1136b7–8), whereas choice is of something in one's power (III.2.1111b30) that one discriminates as *best* (III.3.1112b17, 1113a4–5). Ultimately, both derive from conceptions of *eudaimonia* or of what it is to live well, which is the end of ends of action (I.2.1094a18–22, I.12.1102a2–4).

Yet there are also irrational desires, many of which are ascribable, after Plato, to appetite (*epithumia*) or spirit (*thumos*). Appetites aim at the pleasure of the moment (VIII.3.1156a32–3), and so are dangerous even for a rational hedonist who aims to maximize pleasure over a lifetime. Within spirit, Aristotle most often mentions anger (as at III.1.1111a30–31). Human appetite and spirit are not impermeable to reason. They can share in reason to the extent of being, ideally, persuadable by it (I.13.1102b25–1103a3). This entails that they take on some of reason's vocabulary. Appetite inclines us to think its objects absolutely pleasant *and good* (*De An.* III.10.433b8–9); spirit inclines us to think that its objects *must* be combated (*NE* VII.6.1149a33–4). They thus become distinctively human, like reason itself (*EE* II.1.1219b37–8). Ethical education aims to refashion them into aids, and not obstacles, to the ends that virtue inculcates (VI.12.1144a8, VI.13.1145a5; see McDowell 1998b: §§ 6, 11). However, a reliable coincidence between feeling and reason remains a contingency and an achievement. Virtue proper may demand a generous endowment of natural virtues (VII.13); and what one is taught "has to become second nature, which takes time" (VII.3.1147a22). In most men, success is at best imperfect and precarious.

When an agent finds the demands and solicitations of a situation coming into conflict, various failures are possible. His judgment may be temporally perverted or obscured by sentiment or temptation, so that he acts in a manner of which he would normally disapprove; he shows *weakness in judgment*. Or his judgment may be neither dimmed nor distorted, and yet he shows *weakness in execution* by acting otherwise. We may label the first "soft," the second "hard," acrasia. In either case, what looks like being decisive is what the agent *wants most*. Given the link between forming desires and conceiving ends, he cannot regularly desire most to act in one way while thinking it best to act in another. Yet, on occasion, a lively experience of mental conflict may confirm the sincerity of contrary states of mind. Aristotle is here a rich source (see Price 1995: 104–5). Within divided minds, reasoning and desire, being separate, knock out one another (*EE* II.8.1224b23–4), with victory going to the reasoning of the self-controlled, but to the desire of the uncontrolled or acratic. And this is not really puzzling. Rather, it is a consequence of the heterogeneities integral to the nature of man as a rational animal that a spontaneous desire may prevail in action over a reasoned decision without dissolving the judgment upon which the decision rests.

Such is a story that is Aristotelian, up to a point, and yet not Aristotle's. My main task is to try to establish this fact through an analysis of part of his text, and a discussion of certain difficulties and alternatives. An ancillary hope is to explain the fact through reflections on his behalf. These two aims are not really independent: to apply a distinction of his (*NE* I.4.1095b6–7), the *that* properly comes before the *because*; and yet confidence about the fact can hardly survive despair about the explanation.

2 Aristotle's Account

Aristotle's reaction to Socrates orients his own approach:

(a) It would be strange – so Socrates thought – if, when knowledge is in a person, something else masters it and drags it about as if it were a slave. Socrates for his part fought against that view root and branch, holding that (b) acrasia does not exist. For (c) no one, he said, acts against what is best, judging it to be best; rather, he acts so because of ignorance. Now this view plainly takes issue with what appears to be the case, and we must inquire about the change that such a person undergoes: if he acts so because of ignorance, what is the manner in which the ignorance arises? (VII.2.1145b23–9)

How much of the Socratic view "plainly takes issue with what appears to be the case?" Aristotle will not, eventually, contest (a) (cf. VII.3.1147b13–17). While he certainly rejects the gratuitously paradoxical (b), the disagreement might be verbal. (c) is the most pertinent, since it denies one of the "phenomena" given in the previous chapter (VII.1.1145b12–14): "The acratic person, knowing that what he does is bad, does it because of sentiment [*pathos*]" (cf. VII.9.1151b25–6).[3] Yet Aristotle's response is surprisingly concessive (VII.2.1145b28–9): we must inquire, if what happens is "because of ignorance," what is the origin of the ignorance. A parallel narrowing of focus upon a mode of cognition introduced the present chapter ("We may ask in what manner the man who acts acratically judges correctly," b21–2), and will introduce the next (VII.3.1146b8–9): "One might raise the problem whether acratic people act knowingly or not, and in what manner knowingly." It becomes clear that, in apparent independence from the "phenomena" that he has stated, Aristotle will qualify the attribution of knowledge to the acratic agent through ascribing to him also a qualified ignorance.

In pursuit of this, Aristotle introduces a sequence of distinctions, which I quote:

(a) (VII.3.1146b31–5): Since we use the word "know" in two senses (for both the person who has knowledge but is not using it and he who is using it are said to know), having but not considering what one shouldn't do will differ from having and considering it; for the latter seems strange, but not if he acts without considering.[4]

(b) (VII.3.1146b35–1147a4): Further, since there are two [a1] kinds of premises, there is nothing to prevent a person's having both premises and acting against his knowledge, provided that he is using only the universal one and not the particular one; for it is particular acts that are done.

(c) (VII.3.1147a4–10): And the universal admits a distinction: one term applies to the agent, [a5] the other to the object. E.g., "dry food benefits every man," and "I am a man," or "such-and-such food is dry"; but whether this food is such and such, he either does not have or does not activate. There will, then, be an enormous difference between these ways of knowing, so that to know in one way does not seem anything peculiar, but in the other way extraordinary.

(d) (VII.3.1147a10–24): Further, that they have knowledge in another way than those just mentioned is true of men. For within having but not using we see a distinction of state, so as both to have in a way and not to have; e.g., a person asleep, raving, or drunk. But now this is just the condition of men under the influence of [a15] the sentiments; for outbursts of anger and sexual appetites and some other such sentiments, it is evident, actually alter the body, and in some men even produce fits of madness. It is clear, then, that acratic people must be said to be in a similar condition to these. That they *say* the sentences that come from knowledge indicates nothing; for men under the influence of [a20] these sentiments say scientific proofs and verses of Empedocles, and those who have just begun to learn string together the sentences, but do not yet have knowledge; for it has to become second nature, which needs time. Therefore we must also suppose people in an acratic state to say things in the manner of those who are reciting.

He then applies these distinctions in order to give a focused account of acrasia:

(VII.3.1147a24–b19): Further, one might look at the cause scientifically [a25] as follows. The one opinion is universal, while the other concerns particulars, of which perception is determinant. Whenever a single opinion results from them, the conclusion must in the one case be asserted by the soul, and in the case of practical reasoning immediately be done; e.g., if everything sweet should be tasted, and this is sweet [a30] (which is *one* of the particular premises), the agent who is able and not held back must simultaneously actually *do* this.[5] So whenever the universal opinion is in an agent holding him back from tasting, and the other opinion is that everything sweet is pleasant and this is sweet (and this opinion is activated), and appetite happens to be in him, the one says to avoid this, but appetite leads the way; [a35] for each of the parts can cause motion. So it comes to pass [b1] that he behaves acratically under the influence in a way of some reasoning and an opinion, but of an opinion that is opposed not in itself but only incidentally – for it is the appetite and not the opinion that is opposed – to the correct reasoning. Thus it is because of this that non-human animals are not acratic, because they do not have any universal judgment, [b5] but only imagination and memory of particulars.

Of how the ignorance dissolves, and the acratic man regains his knowledge, the account is the same as about the man drunk or asleep and is not peculiar to this state; we must hear it from scientists. Since the final premise is a perceptual [b10] opinion and determinant of actions, the agent in this state either lacks it, or so possesses it that the possessing is not knowing but saying things, like the drunkard saying the verses of Empedocles. And because the last premise is taken not to be universal, nor expertly cognitive as the universal premise is, what Socrates was looking for actually [b15] seems to result: for it is not so-called knowledge proper that the sentiment overcomes (nor is it this that is dragged about as a result of the sentiment), but perceptual knowledge.[6]

About knowing and not knowing, and with what mode of knowing it is possible to act acratically, let so much be said.

I shall present a fairly traditional reading of this passage, according to which the acratic agent is cognitively deficient at the moment of action, and does not then really comprehend that he ought to act otherwise.

Traditionally, (a) is read as making a distinction recurrent in Aristotle between two degrees of "actualization" of a capacity.[7] A capacity for knowledge has two actualizations: the first is achieved when one has acquired the knowledge; the second when one is actually rehearsing it. (b) then distinguishes, within the premises of a syllogism, the universal and the particular. (c) adds a third distinction, within the universal premise, between the subject and the predicate terms. Aristotle then supplies an illustrative syllogism, which may be structured as follows:

Universal premise: Dry food is good for every man.
Particular premise: I am a man, and such-and-such food is dry and this food is such and such.[8]

An agent who fails to supply the final premise ("this food is such and such") will be in no position to draw a conclusion; hence he cannot be expected to eat this. (d) then adds a fourth distinction, primarily and explicitly between degrees of *having* a proposition, secondarily and implicitly between degrees of *using* it. This distinction was later labeled by the Scholastics "*habitus solutus*" and "*habitus ligatus*": I fully possess my knowledge if I can activate it at will (it is *solutus* or free); I possess it only in a sense if I cannot activate it at will (it is *ligatus* or bound; Kenny 1973: 40).

Aristotle illustrates this by adducing various parallels. The first is of (A) "a person asleep, raving, or drunk" (1147a13–14): he is temporarily in no condition to activate what yet remains *his own* knowledge. His usual state is one of fully possessing the knowledge; it is only transiently that he cannot retrieve it. The second case is of (B) students who do not yet possess the knowledge for themselves – they have not yet, as we say, *internalized* it. All they have as yet learnt is to be able to "string together" some of the sentences. This is a capacity that they share with (A): inebriates and students can equally quote verses from Empedocles. Aristotle first remarks (a17–18) that acratic agents resemble (A); so when he *concludes* (note *hōste*, a22) from mention of (B) that the acratic too are like "those who recite" (*tous hupokrinomenois*, a23), he must intend a comparison that also applies both to (A) and to (B).

Translators commonly take "those who recite" to be *actors*. This is possible, so long as Aristotle thinks he has just shown that the members of his three classes (inebriates, students, and acratic agents) do resemble actors. However, we do not really want a fourth category (actors) to be introduced within what purports to be a conclusion; and the verb *hupokrinesthai* can be understood more widely to mean "recite." Aristotle's distinction becomes one between modes of activating a piece of knowledge (one's own or someone else's): when I say "Water is H_2O," I may be expressing an acceptance of the proposition that water is H_2O, or I may be rehearsing the sentence "Water is H_2O" as an echo or pre-echo of that. The difference may not be readily introspectible: both the young, who are naturally intoxicated (VII.14.1154b9–10; *Rhet.* II.11.1389a18–19), and the actually intoxicated tend to speak with what they mistake for conviction. Yet if the speaker cannot explain what he says when asked, he may be taken to mean little. Aristotle is illustrating by example that *saying* can fall far short of *meaning* (in a fairly rich sense). The Greek *legein*, like our "say," can take for its object either a sentence (as in direct speech), or a proposition (as in indirect speech). Yet in this context we are warned to read *all* occurrences of *legein* pretty minimally, as connoting more than parrot talk but less than real commitment. When Aristotle has in mind a saying that is a serious asserting for which the speaker is answerable, he uses a different word (such as *phanai* at 1147a27–8). *We* might wish to make distinctions between and beyond Aristotle's examples; yet they serve to make his point.[9]

Having introduced a series of distinctions that apply very widely, Aristotle proceeds to put them at the service of an explanation of acrasia.[10] To start identifying his topic, he makes a distinction between what happens "in the one case" (*entha*, 1147a27) and "in the case of practical reasoning" (*en tais poiētikais*, a28). This half inexplicit contrast has been interpreted variably.[11] But evidence elsewhere makes it certain that the comparison is between theoretical thinking (in a broad sense that goes beyond the proper spheres of science) and practical thinking. First, the term *poiētikos* is standardly used in the *Eudemian Ethics* (to which *NE* VII may well properly belong) indistinguishably from *praktikos* ("practical"), and in explicit contrast to *theōrētikos*.[12] Secondly, we should not neglect a close parallel between 1147a26–31 and some lines in the *De Motu Animalium* (7.701a10–16):

> There [*ekei*, i.e. "in thinking and inferring about immovable things," a9] the end is a piece of theoretical knowledge [*theōrēma*] (for, whenever one thinks the two premises, one thinks and puts together the conclusion), but here [*entautha*] the two propositions result in a conclusion which is the action.[13] E.g., whenever one thinks that every man has to walk and one is a man, immediately one walks; or if one thinks that, in this case, no man should walk and one is a man, immediately one remains at rest. And one so acts in the two cases, if nothing holds one back or compels one.

The two passages agree that to draw a conclusion is to make an assertion when the thinking is theoretical, but to perform an act when the thinking is practical.[14] Not that acting is ceasing to think, for taking action may *include* giving thought to its execution (as at *Mot. An.* 7.701a17–23). As Nussbaum illustrates (1978: 344), "At once he makes a house" (a17) need not imply that "the man breaks the ground immediately, without going out to look for helpers, supplies, etc." Equally, writing a letter can involve thinking how to open it, and conducting a conversation need not be wholly spontaneous. Action, in a full sense, has an outer face and an inner one. So Aristotle can also allow a practical pair of premises to entail an opinion (1147a26–7), and thought leading to action to involve a choice (VI.2.1139a21–33). To interpret him as consistent, we must place these, together with physical motion, as inseparable aspects of *a man in action*.

A more distant relation of thought to action is implicit when he spells out a distinction between two species of acrasia, weakness (*astheneia*) and impetuosity (*propeteia*) (VII.7.1150b19–22): "Some men after deliberating fail, owing to their sentiment, to stand by the results of their deliberations, others because they have not deliberated are led by their sentiment." Among the initial "phenomena" to be accommodated was a distinction between the self-controlled agent who abides by (*emmenetikos*) his reasoning (*logismos*), and the acratic agent who departs from it (*ekstatikos*, VII.1.1145b10–12; cf. VII.2.1146a16–21, VII.8.1151a26–7). This envisages a mode of deliberation concluding in a decision taken in advance of action – whether this be *well* before, or *just* before; and this is easily accommodated within the account of deliberation and decision in *NE* III.3.[15]

Yet Aristotle finds it explanatory of rational action to suppose that, given certain conditions, the practical premises that necessitate a conclusion thereby necessitate accordant action, so that, in respect of the conclusion, *assenting* is *acting*.[16] Obvious conditions include these: the time for acting must be *now*; the agent is not paralyzed (cf. I.12.1102b18–20); he knows what he is doing (cf. III.1.1110b33–1111a19). Aristotle may have in mind interference between conclusion and action when he adds the qualification that action follows on the premises when the agent is "able and not held back" (VII.3.1147a30–31, cf. *Mot. An.* 7.701a16).[17] He may also, or alternatively, have in mind obstacles that apply equally to acting and to concluding. These could include not only constraining circumstances, but also inhibiting considerations: concluding the syllogism by acting may be impeded by a realization either that one lacks the ability or opportunity, or that there is sufficient reason against.[18]

How does Aristotle intend to illustrate the syllogism whose conclusion is an action? What we read is spare (1147a29–30): "Everything sweet should be tasted, and this is sweet (which is *one* of the particular premises)." The words between brackets could equally mean no more than "which is some particular item." I prefer to read them as a reminder, in the light of the general statement at a4–5, that we also need to identify an appropriate agent. But who is he? If, as at a6, he is just *a man*, the universal premise becomes (1) "Every man should taste everything sweet." We might interpret this, more sanely, as "Every man should taste *anything* sweet," meaning that he should taste something sweet, and anything sweet will do.[19] (It then fails to entail "I should taste this," but Aristotle might overlook that.) This would make a kind of sense as a principle of intemperance. Alternatively, as Anthony Kenny has proposed (1979: 158), we could understand the agent-term more specifically, say as within (2) "Every pastry cook should taste everything sweet." Whether we suppose (1) or (2), we hardly have a principle that is absolute, applying without exception. Hence one possible impediment is some consideration that creates a special case, such as "I am a diabetic" or "I have an undercook," which would invite qualification to (1) or (2), respectively.

At last we come to the special case of the acratic agent (1147a31–5): "So whenever the universal opinion is in a man holding him back from tasting, and the other opinion is that everything sweet is pleasant and this is sweet (and this opinion is active), and appetite happens to be in him, the one says to him to avoid this, but appetite leads him on; for each of the parts can cause motion."[20] This is over-concise, and has been interpreted and supplemented very variably. The first question is whether we have one syllogism, or two as most interpreters suppose. I am persuaded by Kenny that we have a single syllogism. This both matches and motivates the complications of the example set out at a5–7, with its composite minor premise incorporating a universal statement.[21] We are no more told here *why* tasting is advised against than we were told at a30–31 what might inhibit tasting. The consideration that holds the agent back (or would aptly do so) may fall under the subject term or the predicate term. An instance of the former would be that potential gluttons should not taste pleasant things (they should keep to dry food instead).[22] Then Aristotle's example turns out like this:

A potential glutton should not taste pleasant things.
I am a potential glutton, and everything sweet is pleasant to taste and this is sweet.
Conclusion/action: I don't taste this.

Alternatively, an inhibitor is contained within the predicate. The thought might be that no man should taste pleasant things in a way that is unhealthy. We would then have this:

No man should taste pleasant things unhealthily.
I am a man, and everything sweet is pleasant to taste and this is sweet, but tasting this would be unhealthy.
Conclusion/action: I don't taste this.

What goes wrong so that the agent *does* taste?

We are told that the major premise is present as an inhibitor (1147a31–2), and indeed "says to avoid this" (a34). This last remark has to be approximate, and is interpretable in two ways. If it really means that a *universal* premise tells the agent to avoid *this*, it sounds self-contradictory – but one may compare saying loosely: "The Ten Commandments tell you, James, to respect your father, John." Alternatively, but only in the case of weakness, we may take the meaning to be that, in context, the major premise yields the sentence "I shouldn't taste this." This will play two successive roles: first, in advance of action, it expresses a piece of particular knowledge (which is then lost, and finally regained, b6); then, at the moment of action, it becomes the mouthing of a sentence that is the vestige of a judgment – as Aristotle may be indicating by his choice of the word "says" (*legei*, cf. a10–24, b12) rather than "asserts" (*phanai*, cf. a27–8). What is *then* fully active is the seductive part of the composite minor premise, viz. "Everything sweet is pleasant and this is sweet" (a32–3). What arises is a special kind of irrationality whose driving force is desire ("appetite leads the way," a34) and not judgment (a35–b3): "It comes to pass that he behaves acratically under the influence in a way of some reasoning and a judgment, but of a judgment that is opposed not in itself but only incidentally – for it is the appetite and not the opinion that is opposed – to the correct reasoning." This is easy to explain if there was only a single syllogism, and that a logically consistent one. Neither the judgment that everything sweet is pleasant and this is sweet, nor the implicit reasoning to a conclusion that this is pleasant, can itself be in any logical conflict with the syllogism as a whole; yet they become a necessary part of a sufficient causal condition for the syllogism's failure to be completed in action. Appetite is the instigator, who recruits part of the truth as its accomplice.[23]

The acratic agent is not as irrational as a brute, for he acts *against* (as also, in this case, *with*) a universal generalization. Yet he is in a state of "ignorance," like that of a man asleep or drunk, whose origin, and later lifting, are to be explained not by the rational interpreter but the natural scientist (1147b6–9). What, despite appearances, is he "ignorant" of? We are told that what the acratic agent "either lacks, or so possesses that the possessing is not knowing but saying things, like the drunkard saying the verses of Empedocles" (b10–12) is the "final premise" (*teleutaia protasis*, b9) or "last premise" (*eschaton horon*, b14). Some interpreters take *protasis* and *horos* here to signify not specifically "premise" but generally "proposition"; the "final" or "last" proposition may then be the conclusion.[24] This would go happily with the reading of "one says to avoid this" (a34) that takes it to express a quasi-conclusion which is only the shadow of an action and expresses no conviction. Now a *protasis* can be a proposition (with the connotation of something *proposed*) and a *horos* a definition; yet both remain apt to be premised rather than inferred, and there is no parallel for applying either term, even with a qualification ("final" or "last"), specifically to a conclusion.[25] We may rather adduce 1147a5–7, where it was the last clause of the minor premise ("This food is such and such") that was either not possessed or not activated. Within my reconstructions, what is not present in any real sense is either "I am a potential glutton" or "Tasting this would be unhealthy," which may both be ascribed to perception if this includes memory of past perceptions. It will then be a corollary that no conclusion can be fully present either.

Why does Aristotle suppose that it is not only the conclusion, but also the "final premise" that is either simply lacking, or present only vestigially (1147b10–12)?[26] To answer this, we have to appreciate his conception of the force of "syllogisms of things to be done" (*sullogismoi tōn praktōn*, VI.12.1144a31–2). The phrase invites the application of a general principle stated in the *Prior Analytics* (I.1.24b18–22, abbreviated): "A syllogism is a *logos* in which, certain things being laid down, something follows of necessity from them; that is, because of them, without any further term being needed to produce the necessity." When we read in the *Nicomachean Ethics* of a single opinion resulting from a pair of premises (VII.3.1147a26–7), the meaning is not that a conclusion is freely drawn, but that it is rationally compelled. The same, *mutato mutando*, must hold when the syllogism is practical, and the conclusion an action. Apparently Aristotle does not envisage that a sentiment such as appetite might break this link. Why not? We cannot simply appeal to the power of logic, since the *relata* are not the truth-values of propositions, but the states and actions of agents, and it is not a logical truth (nor a truth at all) that these are always logical. I suspect here the influence of Aristotle's stratification of the capacities that constitute the human soul.

While disclaiming the precision of a scientific psychology (I.13.1102a23–6), the *Nicomachean Ethics* operates with a division between a rational and an irrational part of the mind.[27] (This structures the demarcation between ethical and intellectual virtues, and arguably makes for trouble when it comes to relating practical wisdom to virtue of character.) Even that level of the irrational part which is distinctively human and influenced by reason (b13–14) contains a variety of functions, including sentiment, perception, memory, and locomotion. The proximity of these functions makes sentiments particularly sensitive to appearances (see Price 1995: 115–17), which has its dangers: fear makes the coward think he sees the enemy approaching (*On Dreams* 2.460b3–11). There is no equally close connection between sentiment and the exercise of our logical capacities. Hence, perhaps, Aristotle supposes that, from the point of view of sentiment, the weak link in the practical syllogism is not the linking of premises, or the transition from premises to conclusion, but the particular elements of the minor premise, "of which it is perception that is determinant" (*NE* VII.3.1147a26). Hence, like a calculating saboteur (cf., but specifically of appetite, VII.6.1149b13–17), sentiment that cannot stomach a practical conclusion loosens the agent's grasp upon one of the particular premises.[28] This will preclude genuinely drawing the conclusion, and leave (at most) an enunciating in place of an enacting.[29]

The upshot is, we may think, all too concessive to Socrates:

> Because the last premise is taken not to be universal, nor expertly cognitive as the universal premise is, what Socrates was looking for actually seems to result: for it is not so-called knowledge proper that the sentiment overcomes (nor is it this that is dragged about as a result of the sentiment), but perceptual knowledge. (1147b13–17)

In Aristotle's account, knowledge of the major premise escapes both maltreatment (*it* is not obscured) and disrespect (it is not bluntly disobeyed). Yet an element of ignorance is confirmed later (VII.10.1152a9–15): unlike the practically wise man, "The acratic agent is not active . . . nor is he like the person who knows and considers, but like the man asleep or drunk." These statements most easily fit a traditional reading. What is accounted for is a form of soft, not hard, acrasia. Even in cases of what is distinguished from impetuosity as weakness, the agent does not really know as he acts that he is acting wrongly.

3 Difficulties and Alternatives

If this is, indeed, Aristotle's meaning, it is, we may think, disappointingly distant from the quasi-Aristotelian account that I offered in anticipatory contrast. However, before I go in search of his motivation, I shall raise two difficulties, and discuss one very different line of interpretation.

In two ways, Aristotle wishes to remain closer to common sense than to Socrates. First, he wants to hold the acratic responsible for acting as he does. Yet it is part of his account of responsibility that, while men are blamed for ignorance of the universal, "ignorance of the particular circumstances of the action and the objects with which it is concerned" makes an act involuntary (*akousios*, III.1.1110b32–1111a2), so long as it is later rued (1110b18–24). So the acratic's loss of "the last premise," which *is* rued (VII.8.1150b30–31), should preclude voluntary action. Yet Aristotle is explicit that he is a voluntary agent (*hekōn*, VII.2.1146a5–7), remarking that "he acts voluntarily (for in a way he knows both what he does and its result)" (VII.10.1152a15–16). Now this could equally apply to cases of exculpating ignorance: as Aristotle earlier noted (III.1.1111a6–7), only a raving lunatic can know *nothing* about what he is doing. However, Aristotle has a better point in his repertory (1110b24–7): "Acting *because of* ignorance seems also to be different from acting *in* ignorance; for the man who is drunk or in a rage is thought to act as a result not of ignorance but of one of the causes mentioned, yet not knowingly but in ignorance." He accordingly approves of legislators who do not accept as an excuse *any* ignorance for which the agent is himself responsible (III.5.1113b24–5, 1114a1–3). Though acratic action manifests a degree of ignorance without which it would not occur, the cause of the ignorance is identical to the cause of the action, viz. a disorderly sentiment; and "presumably acts done because of spirit or appetite are not rightly called involuntary" (1111a24–5).[30]

Secondly, as I noted in section 1, when presenting a quasi-Aristotelian account, Aristotle is alive to the experience of mental conflict within acrasia and self-control. Thus he writes that sometimes rational desire "defeats and moves" other desire, and at other times is defeated and moved by it, like one ball hitting another, when acrasia occurs (*De An.* III.11.434a12–14). If this is to be a struggle of which the agent is conscious, does it not require a clear-eyed co-awareness of a strong desire that favors one option, and a judgment that approves another? If the acratic agent does not fully recognize, at the time of action, that decisive considerations exclude *the very act* that he is performing, how can he feel conflicted?[31] Now it may well be that, on occasion, Aristotle lapses into saying things that are commonsensical but inconsistent with his own account.[32] Yet it is not true that this account cannot accommodate any experience of conflict. Take the case of a sentry who is trying hard not to fall asleep: this can be a real struggle, which may only end when it is lost. Similarly, a sweet-toothed but not yet self-indulgent agent who is presented with an exquisite praline may strive to remember "I am a potential glutton," but find it hard to focus his mind upon the fact even as he repeats the words.[33] Very likely, acrasia gives rise to other struggles to which Aristotle, as traditionally interpreted, is blind; but not all conscious conflict is excluded.

And yet it might be welcome if we could reconcile the texts with the quasi-Aristotelian account with which I began, and so accommodate hard as well as soft acrasia. Such an interpretation may still seem to us more credible, and more credibly Aristotelian, than the one that I have offered of *NE* VII.3. What has recently become an alternative tradition aims to achieve this.[34] It is to be noted that Aristotle uses not one but a variety of terms to signify what it is fully to think a proposition: "use" (*chrēsthai*, 1146b32, 1147a2, a10), "consider" (traditionally "contemplate," *theōrein*, 1146b33–5), "activate" or "be active" (*energein*, 1147a6, a33). All are used in theoretical contexts to signify the actualization of a potentiality or disposition, with a contrast between having a potentiality, whether "first" (for example, sight) or "second" (for example, knowledge of grammar), and exercising it (for example, in seeing a thing, or speaking Greek; cf. *De An.* II.1.412a10–11, II.5.417a21–b2; *Meta.* V.7.1017a35–b6). Yet it may be that the terms can take on distinctive connotations in practical contexts, so that a piece of knowledge that is (as we would say) fully understood and accepted may still count as unactivated, in that the agent fails to put it to use appropriately.[35] Kenny (1979: 161) has a unified but flexible proposal:

> What is the difference between a piece of knowledge being merely present, and being actually operative? In the case of practical knowledge, an item is operative if it thrusts towards action. What this metaphorical expression means will differ from case to case, according to the nature of the individual items in question. A practical generalisation, a universal premise, will be operative when consequences are drawn from it that are more particular and therefore closer to practical implementation . . . A particular premise will be operative when it leads to a practical conclusion being drawn . . . A practical conclusion, in its turn, is operative when it is actually acted upon.

This is elegant, and – for the Aristotelian advocate of hard acrasia – well motivated.[36] More problematic is where to find the evidence.

A passage is often cited from the *Prior Analytics* which speaks of *considering* premises *together* (*suntheōrein*):

> There is nothing to prevent a man's knowing that A belongs to all B *and* B to all C, and yet thinking that A does not belong to C (e.g., knowing that every mule is barren and that this is a mule, and thinking that this animal is pregnant); for he does not know that A belongs to C unless he considers the two premises together. (II.21.67a33–7; adapted from the paraphrase *ad loc.* in Ross 1949)

This would be highly pertinent if it said what it does not say, viz. that I do not fully consider "A belongs to all B" unless I put it to further use, say in inferring "A belongs to all C" from "B belongs to all C." As it is, it says nothing to deter us from the simple and satisfactory thought that, just as to consider the premises together is to consider that A belongs to all B *and* B belongs to all C, so to consider the premise "A belongs to all B" is to consider that A belongs to all B. What follows also falls within the target area but misses the desired target (a37–b3):

> A person may err if he knows the major premiss and *not* the minor, which is the position when our knowledge is merely general. We know no sensible thing when it has passed out of our perception, except in the sense that we have universal knowledge, and *possess* the knowledge appropriate to the particular without *exercising* it. (Ross's paraphrase)

On Kenny's proposal, the person ought to count as having universal knowledge without exercising it, since it gets him no further forward. Instead, Aristotle ascribes his failure to having but not exercising particular knowledge. By "knowledge appropriate to the particular" he has in mind knowledge specifically about *it* that is already possessed inasmuch as it is readily acquirable by perception; for he counts perceiving (*De An.* II.5) as the actualization of a potentiality, and not as an alteration from one state to another.

What does invite reflection of the traditionalist interpreter is this question: what establishes that a subject accepts a proposition? Does the acratic agent in Aristotle's example (*NE* VII.3.1147a31–4) really embrace the thought that he should not taste? Kenny (1979: 166) writes pertinently: "Here we have the clash between the verbal criterion for what the person believes (he says he is not to do it) and the behavioural criterion (he goes on to do it) which was precisely what Aristotle's distinction between having and half-having was introduced to take account of." Thus rehearsing a thought may not be a sufficient condition of making it one's own. In another case, it is not even a necessary condition (*Mot. An.* 7.701a25–8): "Thought does not stop and consider the other premise if it is obvious; e.g., if walking is good for a man, it does not spend time upon the premise 'I am a man.'" Here, it is actually walking that is the criterion of the agent's taking into account that he is a man, given that he is considering the major premise. When the premises of a practical syllogism have immediate application, action becomes the *criterion* of choice and judgment, in this sense: the test of whether an agent really chooses to φ, judging that he should φ, is whether he actually φs – rather as, within a valid inference, the truth of a conclusion is a test of the truth of the premises (in that, if it is false, they cannot both be true).

David Charles (1984: 167) makes explicit an assumption that is fundamental to the alternative line of interpretation when he defends the possibility of hard acrasia by *adding* or *appending* a motivational condition to an apprehension condition: "The *acratēs'* failure 'fully to understand' the good conclusion (through the presence of an opposed, recalcitrant desire) is compatible with his knowing (intellectually) full well that *x* is the better course, and his realizing that he has strong reasons against *y*." Would such a conjunctive account of practical knowledge (as *both* comprehending which option is best, *and* being sufficiently inclined to pursue it) have been acceptable to Aristotle? This, in effect, is the question that we have to consider if we are to understand what motivates his account of acrasia (as of much else in his ethics) without either, as I see it, translating it into a different account, or writing it off in disappointment.

4 Aristotle's Motivation

The traditionalist will ask not "what mode of accepting premises is practical?" but "how can premises have a content that is practical?" He will appeal not to cognition *plus* motivation, but to motivation *through* cognition. How may he do this?

Two writers who are illuminating here are David Wiggins and John McDowell.[37] They start from Aristotle's conception of *eudaimonia*, of which Wiggins (2002: 254) writes: "For the agent to embrace a specific conception of *eudaimonia* just is for him to become susceptible to certain distinctive and *distinctively compelling* reasons for acting in certain sorts of ways." Aristotle can describe him as free of regret (IX.4.1166a27–9): "He grieves and rejoices, more than any other, with himself; for the same thing is always pleasant, and not one at one time and another at another; he has just about nothing to regret." We must then be cautious about a notoriously hard claim (I.7.1097b14–17): "The self-sufficient we now define as that which when isolated makes desirable and lacking in nothing; and such we think *eudaimonia* to be; and further we think it most desirable of all things, without being counted as one good thing among others." This is taken to mean that *eudaimonia* is the enjoyment not, *per impossibile*, of every possible good, but of distinctively valuable goods that leave a man free of regret inasmuch as he *needs* nothing more (see McDowell 1998b: § 12).

McDowell explains this further through his idea that, if an agent fully comprehends that the requirements of *eudaimonia* demand, in a certain context, that, of two goods *A* and *B* both at hand, he pursue *A* and set *B* aside, he will appreciate that he has *no reason* to pursue *B* instead. Any general reason to pursue *B* is *silenced* in the context (1998b: §§ 9–10). While the concept of silencing is not clearly evidenced in Aristotle (and McDowell suggests no way of expressing it in his Greek), it supplies one way of explaining remarks such as this (III.11.1118b32–3): "The temperate man is so called because he is not pained at the absence of what is pleasant and at his abstinence from it." For this may now be paraphrased as follows: he is not pained by missing pleasures which he has no reason to pursue that is not silenced in the context. Such a man will feel no regret for the opportunities that he rightly passes by.

What then of acrasia? Wiggins writes (2002: 254, abbreviated):

> The incontinent man is *party* to the Aristotelian conception of activity in accordance with human excellence, and he understands the claims it makes. How then, understanding *so* much, can he prefer weaker and different claims, or allow himself to pursue a different goal whose pursuit is actually incompatible with what he recognizes as the supremely important goal?

It may thus appear inexplicable that an agent could fully appreciate, within a given context, that a course of action is supported by compelling considerations and

opposed by no considerations that amount to anything, and yet freely opt otherwise. McDowell's solution (1998b: § 14) is to suppose that the acratic agent falls
short of a perfect understanding: his thoughts and perceptions only approximate
to those of the virtuous man, and so admit certain reasons that are really no reasons
there and then. It is indeed nothing less than *virtue* of character that is needed
for correct goals and choices (VI.12.1144a8, a20).[38]

Such an explanation places the acratic agent in relation to the practically wise
man: the problem is how he can act contrary to his *knowledge* of how best to live.
Aristotle may share that focus, and yet his concerns extend more widely; for he
asserts that it makes no difference whether the agent has knowledge or true
opinion, so long as his opinion is confident (VII.3.1146b24–31). He cannot go
further and say that it does not even make any difference whether the opinions
are *true*; for he has defined acrasia as blameworthy (VII.1.1145b9–10), and so is
embarrassed by cases of what we might count as *good* acrasia, such as Philoctetes'
failure to stick by his promise to Odysseus through his reluctance to tell a lie
(VII.2.1146a18–21, VII.9.1151b19–21). Yet he admits this kind of case, together
with most varieties of acrasia (including that of spirit, cf. VII.4.1148a10–11), as
acrasia *with a qualification* (VII.9.1151a29–b4). He gives no indication whether
it operates differently from other varieties; presumably not greatly – not more, say,
than acratic anger differs in its workings from acratic appetite. McDowell reads
Aristotle as concerned "to characterize a person whose practical thought comes
as close as possible, consistently with a failure of action, to matching the practical
thought . . . specifically of a person who has 'practical wisdom'" (1996: 101). This
restriction of focus does not entail that he has explained nothing; it does mean
that there is more explaining to be done.

What we need, as a supplement if not a replacement, is a more general story
that applies equally to correct and faulty conceptions of *eudaimonia*. Suppose that
an agent's conception of *eudaimonia* commits him to weighing up not just certain
"distinctively compelling" reasons (Wiggins), but *all* the goods by which he is
attracted.[39] Such a conception takes on determinacy through a reflective mingling
of all the motivations that derive from a man's composite make-up and social
acculturation. Forming a conception of one's end is not mechanical, and demands
the intelligent application of experience in sifting and reconceiving one's goals
(VI.11.1143a35–b5). Yet every surviving or resulting desire becomes not just a
datum but an input. Inasmuch as we are creatures of desire, our goal is a way of
life "such that one who obtains it will have his desire fulfilled" (*EE* I.5.1215b17–
18). An all-in practical judgment comes of applying one's total goal to the context
of action. So long as the judgment is sincerely meant, then, since it is practical,
the desires that influence it must exert an equal influence upon action; to the
extent that it is all-in, in the sense of taking *all* desires into account, what is decisive
for judgment must be decisive for action. Provided that the all-in view connects
fully with the context of action (which excludes oversight and other obstacles),
the reasoning must result in action.[40]

We might now offer Aristotle a disjunctive rationale. Agents who fully appreciate the ethical value of *eudaimonia*, correctly conceived, are alone well placed to refuse to allow some of their desires, general or particular, to count at all in defining its content; those who lack that appreciation, at least as yet, have to take account of all their desires within their conception of *eudaimonia*. Acrasia is made problematic by either of two considerations: the objective sufficiency of *eudaimonia* correctly conceived (as dominant), and the subjective sufficiency of *eudaimonia* to the agent (if he conceives it inclusively). On the subjective conception, *eudaimonia* takes in as much as is practicable of what he wants; on the objective conception, it offers him and every man enough to satisfy his heart's desire. In either case, how could an agent ever clear-headedly resist the pull of *eudaimonia* by drawing back from what he knows, or thinks, to be best? Aristotle may be driven to the ingenuities of his own account of a soft acrasia that mimics hard acrasia because he sees no answer to the question.

Acknowledgments

This chapter has benefited from the comments of Robert Heinaman, Michael Pakaluk, and David Wiggins.

Notes

1   I find the term *akrasia* untranslatable, and shall keep to the quasi-English "acrasia." Attempts have been "incontinence" (which suggests bowel movements) and "weakness of will" (which suggests the will); "lack of self-control" is better, but long-winded. However, I shall render its opposite, *enkrateia*, by "self-control."

2   Here I draw on Price (1995: esp. 106–8).

3   A human *pathos* is an intentional mental state (having or involving a propositional content) which is intimately tied to the body and not automatically responsive to reason (see Price 1995: 114–25).

4   Here I follow D. J. Allan (in the margin of his copy of Bywater 1890) in deleting *kai to theōrounta* instead of *tou echonta kai theōrounta* (1146b34).

5   "Immediately" (*euthus*) may not mark a temporal distinction from "simultaneously" (*hama*). For, in this and related contexts (cf. *Mot. An.* 7.701a15, 17, 22), it may signify not temporal but explanatory immediacy; see Bonitz (1870: 296a16–21). Clear examples in the *NE* are VI.5.1140b17–18 and VI.12.1144b5–6.

6   On the text, see Price (1995: 196 n30).

7   Bostock (2000: 126 n9) cites, among other passages, *De An.* II.5.417a21–b2.

8   This is only slightly more complex than the structure proposed at *De An.* III.11.434a16–19, which also involves a conjunctive particular premise. Here one of the conjuncts is a universal proposition ("such-and-such food is dry"). Aristotle is happy to count as "particular" a minor premise that is universal in form, but of narrower extension than the major premise (see Kenny 1973: 36–7; Bostock 2000: 126 n12).

9 This paragraph is indebted to Lawrence (1988).

10 The distinction is not between the logical and the physiological (in which (d) was already rich), but between the problem that we have to explain and general points that may contribute to its explanation; so Charles (1984: 128 n27).

11 Compare Kenny (1973: 43; 1979: 157 n2), Charles (1984: 128–9 n28), and McDowell (1996: 98–9).

12 This is pointed out by Wiggins (1996: 259), who cites Woods (1992: 57). The passages are *EE* I.5.1216b16–18, II.3.1221b5–6, and II.11.1227b28–30; cf. also *Mot. An.* 7.701a23–5. It is true that in *NE* VI, which is also *EE* V, Aristotle distinguishes "acting" (*prattein*) from "producing" (*poiein*), and "practical" (*praktikos*) from "productive" (*poiētikos*): see *NE* VI.2.1139a27–8, 1139b1–3, VI.4.1140a1–3, VI.5.1140b6–7. Yet in the undisputed *NE poiētikos* can contrast very generally with *pathētikos* as "active" with "passive" (X.4.1175a2–3). McDowell (1996: 99) fails to make it plausible that the distinction between acting and producing is at work in *NE* VII.3.

13 For a defence of this translation, see Nussbaum (1978: 342–3).

14 Cf. also *De An.* III.11.434a16–21, which offers a schema for a pair of practical premises, and discusses, without mention of a conclusion, which premise is more the cause of movement.

15 Thus choice in advance of action is to be ascribed to the weakly acratic agent. However, if a remark that the acratic differ from the vicious in acting contrary to *prohairesis* (VII.8.1151a6–7, cf. VII.10.1152a17) is to apply to impetuosity as well as to weakness (a distinction recalled at 1151a1–3), *prohairesis* must there signify aiming at an *end* (as at VI.12.1144a20, and VII.10.1152a14), and so to be equivalent to *hē tou telous ephesis* (III.5.1114b5–6).

16 We might say, in an Aristotelian form of words (e.g., *De An.* III.2.426a15–17), that these are the same, though their *being* is not the same. This already holds of practical judgment and choice, which always coincide, but differ in their logical grammar (*NE* III.2.1112a3–5).

17 This is uncertain. The phrase *hama touto kai prattein* (VII.3.1147a31), which I have translated by "simultaneously actually *do* this," may convey that the practical conclusion is both asserted, and also – *if* certain further conditions are met – simultaneously enacted. Yet Charles (1984: 91) is wrong to infer this simply from the *kai*; for that can mean "actually" (as evidently at a16, a19, b3, and b14) rather than "also" (though it probably means "also" at a23). What may support his inference, however we translate the *kai*, is the term "simultaneously" (*hama*, which he quite overlooks) – so long as the simultaneity holds between asserting the conclusion and enacting it. However, it may hold instead between grasping the premise-pair and enacting a conclusion (cf. *Mot. An.* 7.701a10–11, where the untranslatable aorists convey how, within theoretical reasoning, a conclusion is drawn *instantaneously* once a premise-pair is entertained; also *An. Post.* I.1.71a17–21). The same ambiguity affects *Mot. An.* 8.702a15–17: "So it is pretty well simultaneously that a man thinks that going is called for [*poreuteon*] and goes, unless something else impedes him." This suits Charles, if his thinking is concluding "I should go"; however, Nussbaum (1978: 358) identifies it instead with thinking "Every man should go" in a context where this serves as a major premise.

18 See Charles (1984: 129) and Broadie (1991: 311 n32). By contrast, it seems that, when Aristotle only has in mind external impediments to successful execution, he

makes this explicit (cf. *De An.* II.5.417a28; *Meta.* IX.5.1048a16–17). It reduces the unreality of his examples of practical major premises (e.g., "Every man has to walk," "I have to produce a good," *Mot. An.* 7.701a13, 16–17) if they are to be understood as *prima facie* principles, subject to an implicit "for the most part" (*hōs epi to polu*), which may be qualified or overridden.

19   Dick Hare suggested this to me, citing the *pamphagos* or omnivore, who is willing to eat *anything*, but can hardly eat *everything*.

20   The last clause could mean not "each of the parts [sc. of the soul] can cause motion," but "it [sc. appetite] can move each of the parts [sc. of the body]"; yet the former is surely the more pertinent.

21   Cf. Kenny (1973: 44–6). It also fits the wording of the present passage ("the universal judgement . . . the other one . . . ," a31–2), and its echo of a sentence shortly before ("The one judgment is universal, while the other . . . ," a25). If this is right, Aristotle evidently finds it piquant to imagine acratic appetite and spirit both as responding inappropriately to some element in the inhibiting syllogism, appetite to "Everything sweet is pleasant and this is sweet" (a32–3), spirit to "I have been outraged" or "insulted" (VII.6.1149a32–3). However, this cannot always be the case: reason and feeling may ascribe salience to altogether different aspects of a situation. It differentiates spirit and appetite that appetite acts upon a *contingently* motivating thought or perception "This would be pleasant"; spirit indulges in a display of anger that presents itself as the active conclusion ("therefore immediately it flares up") drawn from a prescriptive premise "One must combat such and such a thing" (a33–5). In Aristotle's view, this makes spirit the more rational of the two (b1–3). Yet it is only "as it were" (*hōsper*, a33) and "in a way" (*pōs*, b1) that it follows an inference, perhaps because the words "One must combat such and such a thing" *express* anger instead of *prompting* it. Spontaneous anger equally causes what the agent *says*, and what he *does*; hence he invokes a principle without really making a choice (cf. III.2.1111b18–20). If spirit or appetite *really* reasoned practically, there would be the absurd implication (which Bostock actually draws, 2000: 133–4) that acrasia and self-control are on a par, since each has to sabotage a practical syllogism by suppressing a perceptual premise (as at 1147b9–17).

22   This may seem a little severe: are potential gluttons *never* to indulge a sweet tooth? However, one may recall the advice of II.9.1109b1–12, which was to drag oneself away from whatever tends to carry one away, with a special warning against pleasure.

23   For a succinct commentary which partly coincides with mine, I recommend Irwin (1999: 260).

24   See Kenny (1973: 49) and Charles (1984: 120–21). Slightly different is Kenny (1979: 164).

25   Bostock (2000: 132) is unanswerable, I think. Thus *An. Pr.* I.24.42b2–5 segregates *protaseis* from "conclusions" (*sumperasmata*) when they say that syllogisms contain an even number of *protaseis*, an odd number of *horoi* (in the sense of "term"), and twice as many *protaseis* as *sumperasmata*.

26   It is tempting to apply the first disjunct (absence) to cases of impetuosity, and the second (vestigial presence) to cases of weakness.

27   However, there is no unequivocal terminology: *to logon echon* can be applied widely within the soul (I.13.1103a2–3), while *to logistikon* is used narrowly (VI.1.1139a11–

15). A suggestive phrase in the *Politics* for the irrational part is *to pathētikon morion* (I.5.1254b8).

28 See, more fully, Price (1995: 197–9 n33). I also discuss there, and on pp. 137–8, why Aristotle does not envisage something that we might find more plausible, viz. a temporary clouding of the *major* premise.

29 This confirms the fine line traced by Aristotle's distinction between saying and meaning: a premise that is not fully meant can still yield a quasi-conclusion, so long as this too is not fully meant. We might compare the quasi-inferences of dreamers.

30 Cf. Kenny (1979: 162–3). However, Robert Heinaman alerts me to a series of obstacles that I need to surmount: (a) *NE* III.1 often asserts (finally at 1111a22–4, *after* making the "in"/"because of" distinction), and never explicitly denies, that voluntary action involves knowledge of the particulars; (b) V.8 counts as "mistakes," and involuntary, actions that come, without vice (*kakia*), of a particular ignorance for which the agent is responsible (1135b17–19); (c) V.8 ends by classifying certain acts done in ignorance and because of a *pathos* as *in*voluntary, though not pardonable (1136a5–9). On (a), I would remark that 1111a21–4 leave acts that are done in, but not because of, particular ignorance in a limbo, and so cannot be definitive; on (b), that acrasia is a *kind* of vice (VII.4.1148a2–4, 8.1151a5–6) which, involving a *kind* of particular knowledge (VII.10.1152a15–16), causes actions that come close to "acts of injustice" (which involve such knowledge, are caused by "anger and other sentiments that are necessary or natural to men," and count as voluntary) (1135b19–24); on (c), that the *pathos* that makes the actions it causes involuntary is specified as "neither natural nor human" (1136a8–9), and may be ascribable to causes that, *never* having been within the agent's control, make his present action (unlike ordinary acratic action) involuntary, even though it remains, as we might say, beyond the pale (cf. VII.5 on the aetiology of *pathē* that are not "human," but "bestial" or "morbid").

31 Wiggins (2002: 250) takes this to create real trouble for Aristotle, whereas Dahl (1984: 190–94) takes it to embarrass his traditional interpreters.

32 Consider *EE* II.8.1224b19–21 and VII.6.1240b21–3.

33 Compare the mental struggle that the would-be repentant Claudius reports when he says (*Hamlet* III.iii.97), "My words fly up, my thoughts remain below."

34 Forms of it are to be found in Kenny (1973: 34–6; 1979: 161), Charles (1984: 164–90), Dahl (1984: 208–10), Irwin (1989: 55–6; 1999: 261–2), Gosling (1990: 29–30, 32–7), Broadie (1991: 280–97), and Broadie and Rowe (2002: 385–7). Bostock (2000) is dismissive.

35 Thus Broadie (Broadie and Rowe 2002: 389) cites a passage in the *De Anima* that distinguishes activation (*energein* or *entelecheia*) from alteration (*alloiōsis*), noting that there, while to activate knowledge (*epistēmē*) is *theōrein*, to activate the art of building is to *build* and not to think about building (II.5.417b5–9). This is a nice point. Yet that contrast does not encourage reinterpretation of *epistēmē* and *theōrein* within *NE* VII.3, which anyway counts a man who fails to act as still "using" the universal premise (1146b35–1147a7).

36 Kenny may come to grief over the identity of the *teleutaia protasis* of 1147b9 (see the text to note 25 above), though not if one thinks, as he does not, that the conclusion is an action. If it is, we can cut my quotation short, since failure to act will count as failure to use the final *premise*.

37 They have their differences, and have often rehearsed them. The line of thought that I wish to take over in *explaining* Aristotle is, where they differ, taken rather from McDowell than from Wiggins. Were I *assessing* Aristotle, I would draw rather from Wiggins than from McDowell (see note 38 below).

38 According to Wiggins (1996: 259–60), however, the acratic agent lacks the virtues, in part executive, that are needed to sustain *in action* a perspective within which acting well shows up as sacrificing nothing that matters. His achievement of virtue is thus incomplete in a special way: he is not brave enough, or not single-minded enough, or not persistent enough. This finds room for executive virtues that are necessary for reliable action, but not for perfect understanding.

39 Such an interpretation, "inclusive" instead of "dominant," has no trouble with the continuation of a sentence already quoted (I.7.1097b17–18): "If it [*eudaimonia*] were so counted [as one good thing among others], it would clearly be made more desirable by the addition of even the least of goods." But the passage is much debated.

40 Compare, more fully, Price (1995: 129–32). The idea itself, without its application to Aristotle, had already occurred to Wiggins (cf. McDowell 1998a: 92–3).

References

Bonitz, Hermann 1870: *Index Aristotelicus*. Berlin: Reimer.

Bostock, David 2000: *Aristotle's Ethics*. Oxford: Oxford University Press.

Broadie, S. 1991: *Ethics with Aristotle*. New York: Oxford University Press.

—and Rowe, C. 2002: *Aristotle: Nicomachean Ethics*. Oxford: Oxford University Press.

Bywater, I. 1890: *Aristotelis Ethica Nicomachea*. Oxford: Clarendon Press.

Charles, David 1984: *Aristotle's Philosophy of Action*. London: Duckworth.

Dahl, Norman O. 1984: *Practical Reason, Aristotle, and Weakness of Will*. Minneapolis, MN: University of Minnesota Press.

Gosling, Justin 1990: *Weakness of Will*. London: Routledge.

Irwin, T. H. 1989: "Some Rational Aspects of Incontinence," *Southern Journal of Philosophy* 27 (suppl): 49–88.

—1999: *Aristotle: Nicomachean Ethics*, 2nd edn. Indianapolis, IN: Hackett.

Kenny, Anthony 1973: "The Practical Syllogism and Incontinence" [1966]. In *The Anatomy of the Soul*, pp. 28–50. Oxford: Blackwell.

—1979: *Aristotle's Theory of the Will*. London: Duckworth.

Lawrence, Gavin 1988: "Akrasia and Clear-eyed Akrasia in *Nicomachean Ethics 7*," *Revue de Philosophie Ancienne* 6: 77–106.

McDowell, John 1996: "Incontinence and Practical Wisdom in Aristotle." In S. Lovibond and S. G. Williams (eds), *Identity, Truth and Value: Essays for David Wiggins*, pp. 95–112. Aristotelian Society Monographs. Oxford: Blackwell.

—1998a: "Are Moral Requirements Hypothetical Imperatives?" In *Mind, Value, and Reality*, pp. 77–94. Cambridge, MA: Harvard University Press.

—1998b: "Some Issues in Aristotle's Moral Psychology." In *Mind, Value, and Reality*, pp. 23–49. Cambridge, MA: Harvard University Press.

Nussbaum, Martha Craven 1978: *Aristotle's De Motu Animalium*. Princeton, NJ: Princeton University Press.

Price, A. W. 1995: *Mental Conflict*. London: Routledge.

Ross, W. D. 1925: *Ethica Nicomachea*. Oxford: Clarendon Press.

—1949: *Aristotle's Prior and Posterior Analytics*. Oxford: Clarendon Press.

Wiggins, David 1996: "Replies." In S. Lovibond and S. G. Williams (eds), *Identity, Truth and Value: Essays for David Wiggins*, pp. 219–84. Aristotelian Society Monographs. Oxford: Blackwell.

—2002: "Weakness of Will, Commensurability and the Objects of Deliberation and Desire" [1978/9]. In *Needs, Values, Truth*, 3rd edn, pp. 239–67. Oxford: Clarendon Press.

Woods, Michael 1992: *Aristotle: Eudemian Ethics Books I, II, and VIII*, 2nd edn. Oxford: Clarendon Press.

12

Pleasure and Pain in Aristotle's Ethics

Dorothea Frede

Pleasure as a Good

Some ideas are at once so good and so convincing that it seems a pity that there is no such thing as a Nobel Prize for philosophy. Not only that, it seems strange that they had to be invented at all and have not been with humankind from the dawn of creation on.

One of those bright ideas that we should be grateful to have to this very day is Aristotle's ingenious device of integrating pleasure and pain in ethical thought.[1] Before Aristotle, this point presented a real problem to Greek philosophers. There were two parties, or rather three, because there is always a middle party: (1) There were those who did not want to have anything to do with pleasure at all because they saw it as an impediment to the good. (2) The other side simply identified pleasure and the good. (3) Then there were those who advocated a mixed position. No doxography of the different positions that existed before Aristotle can be attempted here. It would exceed the limits of this chapter, especially since a clarification would be needed of what nature each of these parties attributed to pleasure and pain in the first place.[2] Instead, a brief sketch of the difficulties Plato encountered in his various attempts to come to terms with pleasure in his moral thought will be given as a foil for our assessment of Aristotle's innovations. For in Plato examples of all of the positions can be found: pro-hedonist, anti-hedonist, as well as a mixed account.[3]

In the *Gorgias*, for instance, Plato lets Socrates reject pleasure *tout court*. Pleasure is nothing but the filling of a painful lack (*Gorgias* 491e–500e). The hedonist is therefore condemned to Sisyphean labors: trying to satisfy ever-new desires is like filling a leaky jar with a sieve. Everyone in his right mind, so Socrates suggests, would prefer a life of undisturbed peace. That a life of pleasure is a laborious and unsatisfactory task is, of course, not the only argument ventured against Callicles. But we shall not pursue that matter any further here. The *Phaedo*, notoriously, shares the *Gorgias'* negative attitude toward pleasure. Pleasure is the "wrong coinage" in measuring the good, so Socrates claims there. It is a disturbance of the mind and the cause of all the evils that plague humankind: it leads to greed, injustice, upheaval, and war (*Phaedo* 64d–69d).

Much to one's surprise the dialogue *Protagoras* seems to presuppose a quite different conception of pleasure. Socrates wins his last argument against the famous sophist via the definition of virtue as the "art of measuring pleasure" (*Protagoras* 351b–358e). He thereby proves the supremacy of knowledge over all else, for only reason is capable of measuring. Whether he is serious about using pleasure and the avoidance of pain as the ultimate unit or "coinage" in that calculus remains an open question of scholarly debate. At any rate, Socrates does use it to refute the argument that people act against knowledge because they are overcome by a desire for pleasure. Not so, says Socrates. It is reason that is mistaken in its calculus of pleasure over pain. The nearness of an imminent pleasure gives a distorted view of the amount of pain that will result from it later. Far from being "overcome by pleasure," reason simply "mismeasures" pleasures against pains or pleasures against other pleasures.

The *Republic* once again presents a different picture (*Republic* IX. 580d–588a). There is neither stark anti-hedonism nor unmitigated hedonism; instead, we find a mixed position. Plato now distinguishes between different kinds of pleasure. The vulgar pleasures are those criticized in the *Gorgias*: they are mere fillings of a lack and are therefore mixed with pain. Only the philosophers' pleasures are true and unadulterated. They are far above the common "bastard-pleasures." The life of a philosopher is therefore supposedly 729 times as pleasant as the life of a tyrant.

This list still does not exhaust the Platonic positions. In the *Philebus* he once again raises the question of the role of pleasure in the good life and comes to a more sophisticated result. A brief summary of its upshot must suffice: pleasure as a whole turns out to be at best a second-rate good because it consists in the filling of a lack or in the restoration of some imbalance (*Philebus* 53c–55a). If some pleasures are treated as an integral part of the good life, it is not just on account of ineradicable human deficiencies, but because certain pleasures have a positive function: they are incentives toward self-improvement and self-completion (*Philebus* 51a–52e, 63a–64a).

In the *Laws*, finally, pleasure and pain play an important role as a means of education and as a test of its success (especially II.663a–b). The good citizen of Plato's "nomocracy" is pleased and displeased by the kinds of things that one ought to enjoy or avoid. Education is supposed to make the citizens enjoy and dislike the right things in the right measure. Once they have acquired this condition, they will invariably act in the appropriate way. But in spite of this positive function, pleasure remains a mere by-product (*parepomenon*, 667d) of the actions that the laws prescribe.

As this review shows, Plato saw the need to somehow *integrate* pleasure in human life, once he realized that it was better neither to suppress nor to deny it, but to use it for the good cause. But somehow his attempts do not seem quite satisfactory. This is true even in the case of the pleasures that Plato approves of in his catalogue of goods in the *Philebus*, namely the pleasure of pure sense perceptions, the pleasure of learning, and the pursuit of virtue. The underlying assumption that those pleasures are based on an unfelt and therefore harmless *lack* seems plausible in some cases, but it clearly begs the question in others (*Philebus* 51b). It seems highly implausible to assume an "unfelt lack" that needs compensation in the case of those activities we are best at and take most pleasure in. Our most cherished pleasures should obtain a higher rank, among the goods of life, than as a remedy for some deficiency. This seems to be the very point where the pro-hedonist position gets the better over the austere "remedial-model" of pleasure.

Now hedonism cannot be quite "it" either. We are all aware of the shortcomings of hedonist ethics of all kinds, from Epicurus down to the Utilitarians. For whose pleasure or satisfaction is at stake? What should be the proper object of pleasure, and how long should it last? These questions do not present the only difficulties with hedonism. What seems wrong, quite generally, is that pleasure should constitute the ultimate motive of all of our actions. The reason for our discomfort with that idea comes to the fore if we look at a version of the Protagorean argument that most of us must have encountered in everyday life at some point or other. It is the argument that all our actions are ultimately motivated by pleasure since we *like* doing them. Even the most sublime kind of aim is, after all, my aim, and its attainment is therefore a sublime form of pleasure. Hence even the most unselfish acts ultimately seem motivated by one's own satisfaction.

Our justified discomfort with such arguments shows that we need to find a better place for pleasure in our moral discourse. It also shows, however, why that is no easy task. It comes as no surprise, then, to learn from Aristotle that Plato was not the only one who tried to find a suitable role for pleasure in human life. As the two sections on pleasure in the *Nicomachean Ethics* indicate, an extended debate on that issue must have taken place among the members of the Academy. We shall return a little later to these two texts and their relationship. Right now it suffices to see that the Aristotelian conception of pleasure reflects a long-standing controversy and that Plato was not the only contributor to that discussion.

Aristotle on Pleasure

This takes us to the promised advantage of Aristotle's conception of pleasure and pain. He manages to integrate pleasure in his moral philosophy and to assign an intrinsic value to it without treating it as the ultimate motive of our actions. Thus his position is immune to the attack of the cunning hedonist of Plato's *Protagoras*. But before we take a closer look at Aristotle's solution, a general clarification of the concept of pleasure and pain is necessary. Just as in English, the Greek terms *hedonē* and *lupē* are not names for simple phenomena. They encompass a wide field of psychological states. Pleasure and pain designate any kind of positive or negative type of sensation, perception, feeling, mood, or attitude. This enumeration indicates how wide a spectrum is covered by those two terms. It comprises simple pleasures like munching a juicy apple, but also complex ones such as the enjoyment of a great work of art or the admiration of a morally outstanding action. The field covered by its counterpart, pain, is just as wide. It reaches from the simple sensation of the pain of a mosquito-bite to the feeling of disgust at some cruelty, or the *ennui* of having to listen to a boring lecture. In each case "pleasure" and "pain" may, of course, be replaced by more specific expressions. But for economy's sake we shall here stick to the accustomed generic names.

That pleasure and pain are not simple phenomena but cover a wide variety of experiences was already noticed by Plato. As he frequently indicates, pleasure does not simply consist in wine, woman/man, and song – it also includes moral attitudes as well as intellectual activities. Thus it was Plato who discovered that certain pleasures have an intentional content. That is why he not only claims that the philosopher's pleasures are the greatest, but also that they are concerned with pure and true being, and assigns to some of them what we would nowadays call "propositional content." This is the upshot of his discussion of true and false pleasures (cf. Frede 1996, 1997: 242–95.).

Aristotle in his moral philosophy also pays attention to the complexity of pleasure and pain. For moral virtues are concerned with the appropriateness of pleasant and unpleasant actions, and that clearly depends on their content. We enjoy or are displeased by a morally right or wrong action. Since it is the intentional content of the feeling or attitude that determines its nature, a pleasure can be judged as good or vicious, as appropriate or inappropriate, as exaggerated or insufficient. That Aristotle is concerned with propositional attitudes is confirmed by the fact that the "right measure" he demands for pleasure and pain does not just depend on the sheer quantity, i.e. whether there is too much or too little. It also concerns the motive, the opportunity, and all other qualifications of an action that he carefully specifies: the persons involved, the object, the occasion, and the means employed to achieve a certain end. That Aristotle's conception of the "right mean" as a criterion of moral judgment was inspired by Plato's *Laws* and its demand for an appropriate emotional education, is well known. That background probably explains why he spends comparatively little time in the *Nicomachean Ethics* on an explanation of the moral functions of pleasure and pain, but presupposes his readers' familiarity with that idea.

The two sections in the *NE* that explicitly discuss the nature of pleasure come rather late in the day, in Books VII and X, long after pleasure has been assigned its proper place in the good life. This already happens in Book I, and it happens in a quite unobtrusive way. After the definition of happiness as the "actualization of the soul's best abilities" (chs 6–8), Aristotle adds that the best life is also the most pleasant one (*hēdus*, 8.1099a7). Since everyone takes pleasure in the activities that come naturally to them, virtuous persons – the *philokaloi* – enjoy virtuous actions and hence their lives will quite automatically contain pleasure as an integral part:

> just acts are pleasant to the lover of justice and in general virtuous acts to the lover of virtue . . . Their life, therefore, has no further need of pleasure as a sort of adventitious charm [*periaptou tinos*], but has its pleasure in itself. For besides what we have said, the person who does not rejoice in noble actions is not even good: since no one would call a man just who did not enjoy acting justly, nor any man liberal who did not enjoy liberal actions; and similarly in all other cases . . . If this is so, virtuous actions must be in themselves pleasant. But they are also good and noble and have each of these attributes in the highest degree, since the good man judges well about these attributes. (*NE* I.8.1099a10–11, 15–23).[4]

There it is! Aristotle has come up with a kind of pleasure that is well integrated into moral action and that is immune to the complaint just ventured against hedonism. Pleasure in this case is not the ultimate motive of an action, but a characteristic of its performance. For everything one is naturally inclined to do – and has a natural talent for – is at the same time pleasant. That does not just apply to morally virtuous actions, it applies to all activities whatsoever. If Aristotle does not emphasize this fact, it is due to the focus on moral actions in the *Nicomachean Ethics*.

It is easy to see the importance of this innovation. Pleasure is no longer an aim beyond the action itself; it does not constitute an end of its own. (For brevity's sake, the problem will be ignored that in X.4.1174a31–3 Aristotle, somewhat misleadingly, depicts pleasure as if it were an additional end of a perfect natural activity. With others, I assume that he wants to say no more than that the pleasure is part and symptom of such an activity.)[5] It is not the motive of the action, but it arises as a natural concomitant due to the agent's personality. Pleasure can therefore serve as a kind of litmus test. Someone who gladly supports worthy causes is magnanimous; someone who treats others graciously is of a friendly disposition; someone who enjoys hard thought is a true philosopher. Similarly, certain pleasures and pains are indicators of character flaws. A reluctant contributor is usually a stingy person, while someone who enjoys giving pain to animals or humans is a sadist.

According to Aristotle, all morally right and wrong attitudes are the products of the corresponding kind of habituation from early on. Though he admits that there are natural predispositions, he holds that everyone – up to a certain age – is corrigible by the right kind of moral training, just as everyone is corruptible by the wrong kind. That is why he puts so much emphasis on the habitual acquisition of the right mean between too much and too little in his definition of virtue (II.2 *et passim*). The "right mean" at the same time determines the amount of pleasure and pain contained in the corresponding action. As in the case of other properties and abilities that are not inborn, human beings must acquire their character by the right kind of exercise. We become good piano-players – or kithara-players, as Aristotle has it – by practicing well and bad ones by practicing badly (II.1.1103a34).

The basis and justification of Aristotle's own standards of "doing well morally" and of the "right mean" shall not be our concern here. This brief summary of the inner connection between actions and pleasures serves merely as a reminder of Aristotle's principle that what is good *in* a person is also what is good *for* that person and that it should be felt to be so *by* that person. That this should be so is at least not self-evident. There is the possibility that others may take much more pleasure in the activity than the originator himself, if the benefits are all on the recipient's side. Nevertheless, if it is the right thing for that person to do, the action is part of his overall good, too. And there is also the possibility that we do not take pleasure in the kinds of things that we are good at, even if we might benefit from them. Aristotle does not seem to have recognized the phenomenon of the gifted but lazy or of the moody person. This may, of course, be due to the fact that for him *euphuia* ("a good nature") is not just a natural potential but also entails a natural inclination. If we grant him that point, we may also be ready to admit that we normally do take pleasure in performing those actions we are good at and have a natural inclination for. This does not just apply to moral dispositions, of course, but also to intellectual and artistic talents of all sorts. Someone who is good at the piano but does not enjoy playing at all, may be considered a technically good player but not a real musician.

As this sketch shows, Aristotle is not a hedonist. For not pleasures as such are good, but only good pleasures. This seems like circular reasoning, but there is actually no vicious circle in this qualification. For though Aristotle considers good pleasure as an integral part of the good life, the goodness of pleasure is not contained in the definition of the human good as such. More importantly, because morally good pleasure is part of the corresponding action, pleasure and the activity of the soul are no longer rival candidates for the *summum bonum*; they are, in a way, mutual complements. Furthermore, Aristotle's conception also explains why the morally good person does not automatically lead a life of sheer pleasure: pain and displeasure are also integral parts of his or her life. For even in the best life there are occasions for moral indignation, for disappointment, and for anger – in the right way, at the right occasion, and so on.

Now this integration of pleasure and pain in his moral theory may be a brilliant move on Aristotle's side because it settles many of the difficulties that have riddled the accounts of both friends and foes of pleasure among his predecessors. But what is so great about this idea that makes it worthy of the Nobel Prize? One major point of advantage of the Aristotelian theory has already been mentioned: it liberates morally good actions from the suspicion of hidden hedonistic egoism. If I help someone, according to the Aristotelian account, I do not do so in order to obtain for myself the pleasure of helping, but I do it because it is the right action in the situation. And that is why it pleases me.

But this clean-up of the muddle of cause and effect in human motivation is not the only advantage of the Aristotelian conception. It also disposes of another problem that those among us should be most familiar with who have been raised with an exaggerated Lutheran morality or with a perversion of Kantian principles. I am referring here to the misconception that actions have a particular moral value if they are done against one's own inclinations. This idea may have lost some of its attractiveness in recent decades. But even today public discourse sometimes treats it as a symptom of the hedonism of the present age that people show little readiness to act against their own inclinations. There still seems to be the belief that "self-overcoming" and "self-sacrifice" are the hallmarks of a moral action, rather than its enjoyment. This attitude also seems to agree with the Kantian principle that an action has proper moral worth only insofar as it is done on account of duty (*aus Pflicht*) and not from inclination (*aus Neigung*). Aristotle, by contrast, does away with the separation of duty and inclination in the determination of moral worth. In his account a morally right action should be done *with* inclination but not *because of* the inclination.

At first sight this may seem like an overly smooth solution since it suggests that the morally educated person carries out his/her actions automatically. But a closer look will show that there is no such automatism. Aristotle treats the respective inclination as a criterion for determining whether a particular action is a truly virtuous action rather than an action that merely happens to concur with the appropriate standards. But the inclination is not a sufficient determinant of the action itself. For the decision, the *proairesis*, presupposes a rational judgment about whether a particular action agrees with the appropriate rules and standards. Though deliberation does not make use of Kant's categorical imperative, it is also not just decided by personal inclinations. Though feelings, likes, and dislikes play an important role in fixing the ultimate aim of an action, they do not determine the rational deliberation of the appropriateness of an action. It is true that Aristotle is less suspicious of human inclinations than Kant. Instead, he presupposes that they must be molded and trained in the right way – a thought that Kant treats with skepticism. For he sees human beings as made "from such crooked timber that you can't easily get anything straight out of it" (Kant 1991: 46). Though Aristotle also acknowledges the possibility of twists, even natural twists, in the character of a person, and also uses the metaphor of "crooked timber," he assumes that the right kind of training will straighten it out and thereby produce well-tempered characters (II.9.1109b1–7). There is, then, no need to separate duty and inclination once they have become perfectly adjusted to each other: good persons take pleasure in the kinds of things that ought to be enjoyed, and they despise what is despicable.

As has been said before, this does not mean that for Aristotle the good person automatically acts in the right way. That may be so in unproblematic cases. But as the reference to decision-making shows, a lot of deliberation may be necessary. The truly liberal person is not the one who automatically reaches for his or her purse and gladly supports every cause. Instead, it is the person who gives at the right moment to the right person for the right purpose in the right measure – and who does so gladly. If Aristotle emphasizes the right mean and practical reason as the decisive conditions, he does do so for a reason. In critical cases, all factors have to be carefully weighed and measured in order to ensure that the right choice is made. The morally appropriate pleasure is not based on something like perfect pitch in music; it is rather like good taste in the judgment of works of art. It presupposes not only a natural aptitude, but also training, experience, deliberation, and hard thought.

That Aristotle was conscious that his conception of "integrated pleasure and pain" presents decisive progress in the controversy over hedonism is emphasized in the two sections on pleasure in Books VII.12–15 and X.1–5 of the *Nicomachean Ethics*. The problems concerning these two pieces – why there are two of them, why they do not refer to each other, and what conclusions we should draw from the discrepancies between them – cannot be addressed here. The answer to the first question depends on the relation between the "middle" books of the *NE* (V–VII) that it shares with the *Eudemian Ethics* (IV–VI). Whoever put together the *NE* in its present form ignored, accidentally or deliberately, that it contains two versions of the discussion of pleasure. The compatibility of the two views is a much-disputed question. Owen (1971–2) went even further by claiming that the two views are too divergent to be incompatible: they answer different questions. Version *A* he takes to be about the objects of pleasure, while version *B* is an analysis of the acts of enjoyment or enjoying. But his attempt at severing the Gordian knot has been critically reviewed, among others, in Gosling and Taylor (1982: esp. 193–344).

One significant distinction between the two sections that is relevant for our topic is that version *A* (Book VII) aims in the main at a systematic discussion of other philosophers' conceptions of pleasure, especially those of the anti-hedonists. This seems to be the reason why Aristotle gives only a very brief sketch of his own conception of pleasure at that point. In version *B* (Book X), by contrast, Aristotle keeps the polemics much shorter (cf. his critique of Eudoxus' hedonist position, 2.1172b9–25), while expanding on his own conception. As far as his own concept of pleasure is concerned, in version *A* Aristotle defines pleasure as an "unimpeded activity [*energeia*] of a natural state/disposition" (VII.12.1153a14–15). He thereby justifies his rejection of the rival view supported by Plato in the *Philebus* (especially 51a–55a) and, as Aristotle's discussion indicates, in a somewhat modified form by others as well, that pleasure is a *becoming* or a "perceptible process of restoration." The existence of bad pleasures, which seem to support the anti-hedonists' stance, he explains by the circumstances: pleasures may be bad if they result from activities in a diseased state, or if they lead to such a state.

In version *B* Aristotle once again rejects the Platonist attempt to treat pleasure as a kind of process or becoming. But his main point of criticism does not here concern an inherent inconsistency in his opponents' theory itself. He rather objects to the fact that it does not meet his own preconceptions of pleasure: if pleasure were a process it could not be perfect at every moment. He thereby confirms the close connection between pleasure and action: an activity in the full sense must contain its end in itself. The condition of perfection or completeness represents a crucial factor in Aristotle's own, fuller, account of pleasure. It is not sufficient that the activity should be natural and unimpeded; it must, in addition, be perfect at every moment. The importance of this additional consideration comes to the fore especially in the summary that is quoted so often because of its poetic flair: "Pleasure completes the activity not as the corresponding permanent state does, by its immanence, but as if it were an end which supervenes as flourishing does on those in the flower of their age" (X.4.1174b31–2).[6]

About the corresponding concept of pain or displeasure, Aristotle has little to say (X.5.1175b17–24). He seems to regard it as the mirror image of pleasure. He merely indicates that negative experiences are actions that are alien to the agent. Such actions, he claims, are accompanied by an "alien pleasure" that impedes the proper activity, and he draws the conclusion that such alien pleasures are really no better than pains. In such circumstances the activity is either carried out badly or not at all. Aristotle does not add any further specifications on that issue. He does not, for instance, distinguish between the frustration of a person who is hampered in his activities, like a pianist forced to play on a bad instrument, and the displeasure of a person forced to act against his/her natural inclination, like an unmusical and unwilling child forced to practice the piano. This neglect of pain as the counterpart of pleasure is in part due to the topic: Aristotle is not concerned with the bad, but rather with the good life. Though at times he recognizes not only the inevitability of pain (for example, II.7.1107b4) but even admits that the good life contains some – justified – pains (for example, III.9 on the pain involved in courageous actions), this is not a point he ever really focuses on in his account of pleasure.

As has been mentioned before, the definition of pleasure as the "perfection of complete activities" is not confined to moral actions, but applies to all activities that contain their end in themselves. Naturally, in his ethics Aristotle concentrates on the moral aspect of the question. The good and righteous person is for him the ultimate criterion for the assessment of pleasure: an action that appears pleasant to him *is* a true pleasure (X.5.1176a15–19). Aristotle does not give any further justification for this claim; he seems to presuppose that his conception of the good life as a whole provides a sufficient explanation, since it is the life that fully actualizes our best abilities.

Limitations and Drawbacks

The task of this chapter is not to deliver a eulogy of the Nobel Prize-worthy Aristotle by summing up what is obvious to any careful reader of the *Nicomachean Ethics* anyway. Even prize-worthy ideas have their limitations and drawbacks. That there are various problems in Aristotle's conception of pleasure is, of course, well known.[7] To keep the discussion within reasonable limits, it will be confined to four points. Not all of them represent serious objections to the Aristotelian theory, not all are new, nor do they exhaust what is problematic. They are supposed to open up the field for further discussion, not to close it. Their main purpose is to show that the identification of pleasure with the perfection of an activity comes at a price. For Aristotle's conception of pleasure does not offer a full or satisfactory account of all the kinds that he does or should recognize. (1) The first point concerns the ordinary pleasures of *hoi polloi* that Aristotle refers to in his discussion of the human good. (2) The second point deals with the exclusiveness of the definition of pleasure as the perfection of an activity. (3) The third point focuses on the neglect of the "passive" side of moral activities and the problem of "bad pleasures." (4) The final point concerns the connection between pleasure as the object and pleasure as the integral part of moral actions.

(1)   That for Aristotle not all pleasures are integral parts of morally or intellectually good actions is obvious already in Book I of the *NE*. In the discussion of the candidates for the greatest good that makes life happy, "pleasure" is presented as the champion of *hoi polloi* (I.5). Though Aristotle does not there comment on the nature of vulgar pleasures, it seems clear that he does not regard them as perfect activities, for they are treated as rivals to the life of virtue. But he does not specify whether he takes "the many" to be either metaphysically confused by mistaking pleasures to be *ends* rather than integral parts of activities, or to be morally deluded in picking the wrong activities.[8] The fact that he reproaches the many for sharing the pastime of beasts (I.5.1095b19–22) seems to confirm the latter assumption. So does his claim that most people take delight in what is not "by nature" pleasant and hence their pleasures conflict with each other (I.8.1099a11–13; on the difference between good and bad pleasures, cf. especially *NE* VII.4.1148a23, VII.9.1151b19). Perhaps Aristotle would attribute both faults, metaphysical as well as moral, to the many: they neither have the right view of what pleasure is, nor do they pick the right activities as life's aim, if all they care about is food, drink, and sexual pleasures. Though there is nothing intrinsically wrong with those pleasures, they are – because they are the manifestations of life in all animals (X.5.1175a21–1176a29) – not to be taken as the overall aim of human life, and they ought to be enjoyed in moderation, as Aristotle points out in Books II and III, where pleasures are discussed as the objects of *sōphrosunē* and *akolasia*, the right and wrong attitude toward eating, drinking, and the *aphrodisia* (II.7.1107b4–8, III.10.1117b23–12.1119b18). As has been observed, in his evaluation of the pleasures of the flesh Aristotle seems to waver (cf. Annas 1980), which may be intended to mitigate his warnings against the lures of "pleasure" *tout court* (II.9.1109b7–12).

But even if we grant Aristotle that the many have a rather primitive view of the ultimate aims of life, the question is whether he is right *if* he regards these pleasures as parts of the performance of activities. As a closer look shows, it would be quite odd to treat the common pleasures of seeing, hearing, touch, or taste as integral parts of such a performance. Though eating, drinking, and sexual delights are sensual activities and therefore involve the soul, the pleasures they provide are not aspects of a perfect and unimpeded performance. In fact, the claim that someone enjoys the perfect performance of eating, drinking, and so on sounds rather artificial. It would take quite some training and aesthetic connoisseurship to achieve such a state of mind. To most human beings, it would sound snobbish to claim that one does not enjoy the taste, but "the act of tasting," or whatever other pleasure one may describe in that way. Nor is the enjoyment of such an act the same as the pleasant taste. Perhaps one could even enjoy "tasting" something that does not actually taste all that good. Be that as it may, it seems that the life of ordinary pleasure is concerned with what we would normally take it to be: namely just *sensuous feelings*, "the kick," or whatever one may prefer to call it. Thus with respect to feelings and sensations, the Aristotelian conception of pleasure as an integral part of activities seems to be openly deficient, as has been pointed out succinctly by Urmson (1967, 1988: 105–8).

That the *adverbial* or *performative* aspect cannot be decisive in the case of the pleasures of the body, anyway, is confirmed by the fact that not all natural unimpeded activities are pleasures; in fact, most of them are neutral. We hear, see, touch, or taste many things in the most natural and therefore "perfect" way without either pleasure or pain, as the examples of everyday activities of eating and drinking and so on show; they are generally unimpeded, but often neither pleasant nor unpleasant. It would be quite a bad ad hoc explanation that neutral sense-experiences lack pleasure because of some unknown impediment in their performance. If there is pleasure, it seems to be concerned with the *object* of that particular experience: seeing, hearing, touching something particularly beautiful or attractive that pleases us. The claim that the pleasure depends on *how* the eating of an apple, the sniffing of perfume, the touching or being touched is carried out seems quite unconvincing. The explanation would fare no better if it said that some of our sense-experiences are more natural than others, so that we enjoy certain sounds, colors, tastes, and whatnots while others leave us cold, or that certain persons are in a more natural state than others. In short: the "performative explanation" of pleasure seems quite unsatisfactory, in the case of these types of pleasure. That it is a mistaken approach comes to the fore even more when we reflect on the corresponding pains. When eating, drinking, or touching something that gives us pain or nausea, it is not the *act* that is either unnatural or impeded, but it is the immediate "feel" or sensation that is at stake. Had Aristotle taken a closer look at the corresponding pains or negative feelings, this fact could hardly have escaped his notice.

Now, Aristotle was clearly not much concerned with an analysis of ordinary pleasures and pains. The life of pleasure of *hoi polloi* as such is largely ignored after the first book of the *Nicomachean Ethics*. Although the ordinary pleasures continue to play an important role in the discussion of the right and wrong moral attitudes, Aristotle does not concern himself with the refutation of "the life of pleasure" any further. But precisely because handling the ordinary pleasures and pains does play a significant role in the determination of some of the moral virtues, it is important to see that there is an ambiguity that Aristotle does not solve. Admittedly, he nowhere states that the "common pleasures" are involved in unimpeded activities. But he also nowhere says that they are not. Nor does he say what he takes their nature to be.

(2) The second problem lies in the confinement of pleasure proper to *complete activities*, i.e. to activities that contain their own ends, to the exclusion of pleasures taken in what Aristotle regards as processes (X.4.1174a13–1175a3).[9] As a survey would show, many of our pleasant and cherished activities are neither perfect nor complete at every moment in the sense intended by Aristotle (cf. Bostock 2000: ch. 7). We often enjoy doing things that have an external end, an end we may or may not attain. Though Aristotle was aware of that fact, he seems to have held that in their case it is not the process as a whole that is pleasant, but only the particular part or aspect that *is* a perfect actualization of a particular potential. An example will show what is problematic about this position. Take the case of playing a Beethoven sonata. For Aristotle it must be a process, for it goes through several different movements and it is not complete while the performance goes on, just as in the case of the process of building a house, which reaches its end only with the completion of the house. Since the performance of the whole piece attains its end only with the final chord, there is either no pleasure in playing the sonata as a process, or the pleasure consists in playing individual chords as we go along. Since Aristotle does not discuss the performance of music or any kind of complex activity, it must remain an open question how he would treat this problem, but it can hardly be denied that there *is* a problem in such cases.

That this is not just an odd construction of a modern interpreter becomes apparent if we reflect on the fact that, in his account of intellectual pleasures, Aristotle seems to pass over the pleasures of the scientists' actual research, the work on a philosophical problem, in favor of "contemplating the truth" (cf. IX.9.1169b30–1170a4, X.7.1177a12–1178a8). Occasionally he does include the "pleasure of learning" with that of thinking in his account, without mentioning, however, that he regards it as a process (VII.12.1153a22–3). Because he includes activities such as "doing geometry" (X.5.1175a33), we may in any case have to take the static picture of *theōria* with more than a pinch of salt, despite the fact that he seems to impose rigid limitations on what counts as a perfect *energeia* when he makes it a condition that the activity must not take time but be complete at every moment (X.4), a condition that in *Metaphysics* IX receives its canonic form: it must be possible to say at the same time that we are doing *p* and that we have done *p* (6.1048b18–36).

It is possible to construct rejoinders to some of these queries. Aristotle might insist, for instance, that what is pleasant in such activities is the employment of our faculties *with* the anticipation of their end. So the end is virtually, if not actually, contained in the activity; you have the whole Beethoven sonata in mind while you play along, just as a statue's form already exists in the artist's mind while he creates it. Alternatively he might claim that it is working on the Beethoven sonata that can be enjoyed to perfection at every moment, even if I have to stop and the playing remains an unfinished task. But the virtual enjoyment of the entire piece or the joy of playing is not the same as the enjoyment of playing the Beethoven sonata. The same applies to physical activities like that of a mountaineer who enjoys working his way up the northern route of the Matterhorn. The explanation would sound quite artificial that the hiker enjoys "working on the climb up the Matterhorn," i.e. every grip of the fingers, every perfect hoist of his body. Of course, this may be true; he may enjoy every move of his body as part of the hike, and enjoy it because he is on his way up the Matterhorn; and the musician may enjoy every chord because it is part of that particular sonata by Beethoven. Nevertheless, it seems natural to claim for both cases that they are processes toward an end and not perfect activities at every moment. An Aristotelian, by contrast, who wants to make sure that he/she is really enjoying the activity itself must always be very careful to spell out that he/she is not concerned with attaining a particular end, but with what he/she is doing right now. This position seems needlessly complicated and contrived. Not all processes that are done for an end are processes of replenishment, let alone of self-replenishment. If Aristotle thought so, then this seems like an over-reaction to the Platonic conception of pleasure.

Given that there are good arguments for the assignment of intrinsic pleasures to activities that do not contain their own ends in themselves it should come as no surprise that Epicurus later distinguished two cases of pleasure, namely *kinetic* or process pleasures and *katastēmatic* or static pleasures. Though he treats the *kinetic* pleasures as inferior in kind, he clearly saw the need to recognize both types as real *pleasures*, while Aristotle in the *Nicomachean Ethics*, at least in his official definition of pleasure, acknowledges only the latter kind because of its instantaneousness (cf. X.4.1174a17–23). This peculiarity, as it must strike us, seems to have one major cause: it is due to the fact that Aristotle takes processes to be "Platonist" processes of repletion or regeneration. As some of the counter-examples are meant to show, the condition that the activity, and therefore also the pleasure, be complete leaves an uncomfortable gap in Aristotle's theory, for it gives no proper account of the enjoyment taken in processes of generation and creation.

(3)   The third point of critique turns on the fact that Aristotle treats pleasure almost exclusively from the perspective of the actively engaged person and equates completeness of the activity with its perfection from a moral point of view. This conception certainly does not even cover all cases of morally relevant positive or

negative experiences. That there may be problems comes to the fore already if we look at the passive counterpart in such an activity. What, precisely, is the nature of the pleasure of the person who is the *recipient* of someone's virtuous act, like an act of generosity? Does this person experience pleasure because he/she fully and unimpededly activates his/her potential to receive a generous gift gratefully? There may be something to that claim. For the naturally ungrateful person will not be pleased, but will receive the gift with bad grace since he/she does not have the appropriate disposition. The reception of gifts is in fact the only example of "being acted on" that Aristotle discusses in the *NE* (II.7.1107b9–14, the *lēpsis chrēmatōn*): the profligate is excessive in handing out money and deficient in taking it; the avaricious person is excessive in taking and deficient in handing it out. Aristotle in that connection does not comment on the respective pleasures and pains. He may not have given much thought to the question whether in the recipient's case the pleasure consists in his own unimpeded activity of receiving, rather than in his admiration of the other's generous action. The problem also applies to observers of virtuous acts. No doubt, if a person has the right moral attitude he/she will be pleased to observe acts of generosity, but the pleasure does not consist in the activity of observing. Once again, what constitutes the moral pleasure is not the "performative" or *adverbial* aspect of the observation; it is the object of the experience, the generous deed itself that is enjoyed. This criticism of the Aristotelian point of view is analogous, then, to the one ventured against the "performative" explanation of the pleasures of the body: there are pleasures that are directly related to their intended objects, not to the performance of an activity. Why this point – which seems obvious once one tries out different cases – escaped Aristotle's notice is a question that needs explanation.

That Aristotle is on thin ice as soon as the moral agent's point of view is not the focus should be clear by now. It should be equally clear that the ice is also thin when we look at the question of the bad person's pleasures. How, in general, does Aristotle account for "bad pleasures" in opposition to good pleasures? Given the symmetry in his conception of moral virtues and vices, it seems there must be pleasures taken in vices as well as in virtues (cf. Gottlieb 1993). For if virtue consists in taking pleasure in the right act in the right measure between too much and too little, vice must consist in taking pleasure in doing either too much or too little. Everyday observations would speak for the soundness of such a view. Don't stingy people take pleasure in successfully pinching a penny, and don't resentful characters take a full dose of *schadenfreude* when they see their neighbors come to grief? Unfortunately, in the books that discuss the moral virtues and vices in detail (II, III.6–V) Aristotle is not very specific about the quality of the respective pleasures or pains. He contents himself largely with the assertion that there is in each case a right mean and a way of missing it by overdoing or by "underdoing" it.

Are there, then, for Aristotle, perfectly bad acts with the corresponding perfect pleasures, i.e. unimpeded actualizations of one's potential for the bad, once the person has acquired a thoroughly bad character? One would expect it, on account of the alleged symmetry between virtue and vice, but this expectation is not fulfilled. Aristotle's conception of what it is to be a human being, in fact, rules out that there can be perfect morally bad pleasures or perfectly performed bad activities. Bad actions can be extreme, but they are never "complete" nor can they be "unimpeded" activities because they are not natural to human beings. In *Metaphysics* IX.9.1051a16–21, Aristotle denies, quite generally, that there is a proper actuality of the bad: it is posterior to potentiality because the potential can at least be both good and bad. As Aristotle sees it, the bad man does not fulfill his human potential, and therefore cannot consistently lead a happy life. For precisely the same reason, Aristotle denies that there can be real and lasting friendships among bad people (*NE* VIII.8.1159b7–10). In the end, he concludes that the bad person cannot even be his own friend, since there is nothing lovable in him (IX.4.1166b5–29). As in Plato, so in Aristotle, the "happy scoundrel" seems to be a *contradictio in adiecto*.

Though Aristotle says little about the bad man's pleasures, we may try to extrapolate from his general remarks on the types of pleasure experienced by a person in a bad condition. In Book VII he explains such pleasures as the activity of part of the person's soul that remains in good condition (VII.12.1152b33–1153a7). As far as physical impairments are concerned, the explanation seems plausible that if there is pleasure, it must be due to a healthy residue, a function that is left intact (cf. Owen 1971–2: 142–5). But what about moral impairments? Does an analogous explanation strike us as convincing? Take the case of a wicked person enjoying a certain wicked act. Aristotle may presuppose that in such a case only a part of the perpetrator's soul is properly and pleasantly active, his "cleverness." In that case, the scoundrel takes pleasure in activating his cleverness, not in the performance of the crime itself. But such explanations would be desperate remedies. It comes as no surprise then, that Aristotle, with the exception of such less than satisfying side-remarks, leaves the bad man's pleasures aside in the *Nicomachean Ethics*.

That so little is said about negative moral attitudes in the *NE*, quite generally, must seem strange, given the fact that moral actions involve both pleasures and pains, as Aristotle states in his introduction to the moral virtues. Moral virtue, so he claims in Book II (3.1104b12), presupposes the right upbringing:

> so as to delight in or be distressed by the things we should. This is what the correct education is. Again, if the excellences have to do with actions and affections, and every affection and every action is accompanied by pleasure and pain, this will be another reason for thinking that excellence has to do with pleasures and pains.

As has been pointed out, Aristotle concentrates on actions and pleasure but neglects both pains and affections. This one-sidedness seems to account for the blind-spots in his theory.

(4)　The final point takes up a peculiarity that has emerged in the discussion of the "vulgar pleasures" but not been pursued any further, namely that in certain moral actions pleasures and pains play a significant role at *two* different levels. For pleasure and pain figure not only as *integral parts* of moral attitudes, but also both as their *objects*. Aristotle must have been aware of this distinction. For in his discussion of some of the moral virtues, he treats pleasures and pains (a) as the subject matter of acts of pursuit and avoidance alongside the noble (*kalon*) and beneficial (*sumpheron*) (II.3.1104b30–32), and (b) as the characteristics of the activities themselves (1105a6–7). As a consequence, the morally educated person both has to seek the right kinds of pains and pleasures and to act in the right – enjoyable – way. This applies, for instance, to courage. It is a disposition to (a) face the pain of injury and death – and (b) do so gladly. The same applies, *mutatis mutandis*, in the case of moderation, which is concerned (a) with the pleasures of the body and (b) with the appropriate actions. Aristotle addresses the twofold role of pleasure and pain in his comments on moderation: "For the man who abstains from bodily pleasures and delights in this very fact is temperate, while the man who is annoyed at it is self-indulgent" (II.3.1104b5–7). It is the abstention from bodily pleasure, then, that he takes moral delight in: "It makes no small difference with regard to action whether someone feels pleasure and pain in a good way or a bad way" (1105a6). Not to indulge in a physical pleasure is then the moderate person's moral enjoyment.

Because Aristotle does not emphasize that in moral activities pleasure and pain show up at two different levels, the novice will at first find his discussion of certain moral virtues, such as moderation or courage, confusing (the same applies to the social virtues concerning everyday life and amusement in IV.6 and 8). But once the difference has been recognized, it is clear that the moral attitude needs to be kept separate from the first-order pleasure or pain. Thus, in the case of courage, Aristotle asserts that the courageous person faces the fearful (and therefore painful) situation either "with pleasure or at least not with displeasure" (II.3.1104b7–8); later on, he is less confident about the sweetness of dying for the fatherland, but insists that the courageous person derives a certain satisfaction from facing death in the morally right way (III.6.1115a30–34, 9.1117a34–b22).

Because the need to separate two different kinds of pleasure and pain is confined to those kinds of virtue where pleasure and pain are the objects of the actions, Aristotle can disregard it where "higher goods" like honor or knowledge are the objects. He also does not address it in that part of his discussion of the nature of pleasure, in Books VII and X, that focuses on the perfect activities irrespective of their content. No such insouciance is justified, however, where the acquisition of the moral virtues is concerned because it involves – at least in principle – the practice of the right attitude toward all the emotions (*pathē*) on Aristotle's list: "By affections I mean appetite, anger, fear, boldness, envy, joy, friendliness,

hatred, longing, envy, pity – generally, feelings connected with pleasure and pain"
(II.5.1105b21–23).

Because Aristotle does not discuss those types of pleasure and pain that are
involved in the *pathē*, it is necessary to turn to his *Rhetoric* for further enlightenment on his theory of the emotions. There he provides a detailed analysis of each
of the most important pleasant or unpleasant affections: the respective state of
mind, the reasons that cause the *pathē*, and the kinds of people who cause or suffer
them (cf. *Rhet.* II.1.1387a25). What is significant for our topic is that Aristotle
in the *Rhetoric* uses precisely the Platonic account of pleasure as a *process* that he
rejects unqualifiedly in Books VII and X of the *Nicomachean Ethics*: "We may lay
down that pleasure is a kind of change [*kinēsis*], an intensive and perceptible
restoration [*katastasis*] of the natural state and that pain is the opposite" (*Rhet.*
I.11.1369b33–5). It is, in fact, not hard to see why Aristotle resorts to the definition of pains and pleasures as "processes of disruption and restoration": emotions
are based on needs, wants, and desires or the corresponding aversions. All these
phenomena therefore presuppose some kind of lack of something, a need that has
to be filled. Orators are concerned with human needs in different ways. In the law
courts, accusers as well as defendants have to deal with the motives involved in
breaking the law, i.e. the alleged perpetrator's *desires* or *dislikes*. In political speech,
the speakers have to address their audience's own needs, desires, or aversions in
order to get their consent to some proposal. In both cases the relevant pleasant
and painful feelings are connected with people's needs and wants. Hence the
rhetorician must know how to work on those feelings, both positive and negative.
It is therefore quite implausible (*pace* van Riel 2000: 51 n53 and others) that
Aristotle should resort here to the "scholastic definition circulated in the Academy"
that he does not accept.

Though this is not the place for a lengthy discussion of the emotions in Aristotle's
Rhetoric, it is clear that it contains the kind of analysis that Aristotle must presuppose for the *pathē* in the *Nicomachean Ethics* as well (cf. Frede 1996, 1997: 418–27;
Rapp 2002: II.543–83). Hence there is no need to assign the different treatments
of pleasure and pain to different stages in Aristotle's life: an early "Platonist" phase
reflected in his definition of pleasure and pain in the *Rhetoric* and a late "Aristotelian"
stage with a full-fledged account of pleasure as the perfection of activities in Books
VII and X of the *Nicomachean Ethics*. That the two concepts of pleasure must have
existed side by side in Aristotle's mind from early on is shown by his rejection of
the "Platonic" account of pleasure in *Topics* IV.1.121a35–6 – a relatively early text.
Though parts of the *Rhetoric* seem of an early origin, Aristotle kept using it as a
textbook, as the traces of later revisions show, and clearly saw no need to change
the explanation of pleasure and pain in his account of the emotions. He may, in fact,
have counted on his reader's familiarity with that discussion when he refrained from
an extensive discussion of the *pathē* in the *Nicomachean Ethics*. It seems, then, that
Aristotle recognized different types of pleasure and pain in his ethics without
drawing his audience's attention to that fact.

The Coherence of Aristotle's Treatment of Pleasure and Pain

It seems prima facie hard to explain this tension in Aristotle's treatment of pleasure because "duplicity" seems as untypical for him as is a lapse of memory so extensive that in his elucidation of the nature of pleasure in Books VII and X of the *Nicomachean Ethics* he was no longer aware of the different kinds of pleasure presupposed in its earlier books. Two considerations may help explain the discrepancy: First, Aristotle's aim was not a comprehensive treatment of the concept of pleasure in those two essays, but to establish, in opposition to rival theories, his own conception of pleasure as an ingredient of actions. The exclusivity of this focus and the "oblivion" of what went on before are intelligible if the treatise on pleasure originated from a different context and was incorporated into the *Nicomachean Ethics* (as well as into the *Eudemian Ethics*, if Book VII, as seems most likely, belongs to the earlier version) only at a fairly late stage by Aristotle. A separate origin and a late interpolation would explain certain peculiarities in both treatises that are notably absent in the rest of the *Nicomachean Ethics*, namely the unusual amount of doxographical information and the intensity of Aristotle's polemics against rival theories. These two factors suggest that the two essays were the results of intensive debates with members of the Academy and explain why Aristotle regards it as his main task to defeat the different varieties of the Platonist position that pleasure is at best a "remedial good." He therefore argues for the counter-position and confines pleasure to complete activities. Once this polarization between the two positions is in place, there is no room for compromise, and Aristotle clearly does not want to weaken his own position by making concessions to the other side.

Second, in the treatises on pleasure the main bone of contention is whether and in what sense pleasure is *a* good or *the* good in life. Aristotle therefore focuses only on the best kind of pleasure: the pleasure that is contained in the full actualization of our highest potential as the best state imaginable. That such is Aristotle's preoccupation is noticeable in his treatment of the rival theories of pleasure. He does not even question whether these theories are concerned with the same *phenomenon* as he is. If he concurs with some of them, he does so only to the extent that they agree with his notion of pleasure as an integral part of a perfect activity of the soul. According to Aristotle, the self-sufficient life has to be lived by the *agents* themselves and it has to be lived in an active fashion. This explains why at this point he passes by those pleasures that are not at stake in the best life: the sensuous pleasures of *hoi polloi*, the pleasures of the recipient or witness of a virtuous act, the pleasure of the wicked, and the emotive pleasures.

The assumption that Aristotle never intended to give an all-encompassing treatment of pleasure in the two short essays on this topic does, however, not settle the philosophically most pertinent question: Did he realize that neither "pleasure" nor "pain" constitutes a unitary genus and that therefore any attempt to give a unified definition of its nature must fail? Aristotle is not usually shy to admit a plurality of meanings for key terms. So why did he not come up with the solution he resorts to in other connections, namely that "pleasure is used in many ways," with his favorite type of pleasure as the "focal meaning" of the other, secondary kinds (cf. *Meta.* IV.2.1003a32–b10)? In the case of pleasure, such a solution would be highly problematic: it would presuppose that all pleasures relate to the central type in the way that all healthy things depend on health as their focus (preserving health, indicating health, causing a state of health and so on). No such relation seems to exist between pleasure as an integral part of a perfect activity and the other kinds that consist in the fulfillment of a desire, in the restoration of a mental (or physical) equilibrium, or in the sheer "feel" of sensuous pleasures. Although the different types of pleasure may coexist, they are not related to each other in the way that Aristotle presupposes for focal meaning.

We cannot be sure whether Aristotle was fully aware that in the case of pleasure and pain the use of their "generic" names is a dangerous thing because it suggests a unity that simply is not there. If he did not realize it, then he is not alone in that predicament. Philosophers after Aristotle have struggled for centuries in their attempts to account for "pleasure" and "pain" and their role in human life. Though many of them saw the need for differentiations, the general assumption seems to prevail to this very day that pleasant and unpleasant sensations, feelings, emotions, moods, and activities must have something in common, since they are all positive or negatives states of the soul.

Conclusions

In view of these drawbacks and deficiencies in Aristotle's discussion of pleasure and pain, readers of this chapter may wonder why it started with a plea to award him a Nobel Prize in ethics. The long list of critical points should not obliterate the importance and ingenuity of Aristotle's treatment of pleasure. It is advisable, however, to adopt the practice of the Nobel committees in Stockholm and Oslo, and specify quite clearly the particular achievement for which the prize is awarded. What the specifications are, in the case of Aristotle's treatment of pleasure, should be clear by now. The Nobel Prize in moral philosophy should be awarded for his contention that *certain* pleasures are an integral part of the human life that finds its fulfillment in morally and intellectually worthy activities, and this is, after all, the central type of pleasure he is concerned with.

One may well raise the question to what positive use *we* can put this noble idea nowadays. For if we speak of Nobel Prize-worthiness the achievement should have a lasting importance and relevance for our own time. Is there any actual use for the Aristotelian conception of pleasure – except as an *antidote* to undue Lutheran or Kantian austerity? There are, in fact, two aspects of the Aristotelian notion of pleasure that address contemporary concerns. First, his theory explains the need for a proper *emotional* moral education: education should aim at personalities that take pleasure in the right activities and in the right attitudes. That would make for a more peaceful private and public life. What general standards there should be for what is right and wrong must remain an open question here. It is a highly complex problem that every society will have to work out for itself. The second point concerns the much debated *quality of life*. And there a lot can be learned from Aristotle. It ought to be an important consideration in education at all levels that students discover and develop their natural abilities and talents so that they can lead satisfactory active lives. It must remain a moot point why education nowadays concentrates almost exclusively on technocratic skills and pays so little attention to the central point in the Aristotelian theory of the good, worthwhile life – that it must be a life of satisfactory activities. Proper incentives in that respect would greatly reduce the problems in affluent societies that are marked by discontent and idleness.

Apart from pedagogy, there is also a philosophical point that is worth keeping in mind: The declaration of Aristotle's prize-worthiness does not mean that his is *the* ultimate theory of pleasure that accounts for all its varieties and kinds. But this does not detract from the importance of his discovery that morality is not only quite compatible with personal inclinations, but actually presupposes them. That our actions should be done *with* inclination rather than *because* of inclination is an insight that should never have dropped out of moral discourse. It would have saved philosophers a lot of unnecessary detours and debates.

Notes

1 Aristotle is actually doing quite well for Nobel Prizes. The Nobel-laureate physicist and physiologist Max Delbrück (1971) awarded him the Nobel Prize for his anticipation of DNA by making the form contain the plan and program for the development of embryos.

2 An overview is provided by Gosling and Taylor (1982).

3 For a review of Plato's positions see Frede (1985: 151–80, esp. 151–60).

4 The translation follows that by Ross, revised by J. Urmson in Barnes (1984).

5 For a summary on this issue cf. van Riel (2000: 52–8).

6 Following Gauthier and Jolif's (1958–9: II.2.842) contention that *akmē* is not confined to youth only; see also van Riel (2000: 57).

7 Cf. Owen (1971–2) for criticism launched by analytic philosophers.

8 On this confusion, cf. Rorty (1980: 272).

9 On the distinction between activity and process, cf. Ackrill (1965).

References

Ackrill, J. L. 1965: "Aristotle's Distinction between Energeia and Kinesis." In R. Bambrough (ed.), *New Essays on Plato and Aristotle*, pp. 121–41. London: Routledge and Kegan Paul.

Annas, J. 1980: "Aristotle on Pleasure and Goodness." In A. O. Rorty (ed.), *Essays on Aristotle's Ethics*, pp. 285–99. Berkeley, CA: University of California Press.

Barnes, J. (ed.) 1984: *The Complete Works of Aristotle*. Princeton, NJ: Princeton University Press.

Bostock, D. 2000: "Pleasure." In *Aristotle's Ethics*, pp. 143–66. Oxford: Oxford University Press.

Delbrück, M. 1971: "Aristotle-totle-totle." In J. Monod and E. Borek (eds), *Of Microbes and Life*, pp. 50–55. New York: Columbia University Press.

Frede, D. 1985: "Rumpelstiltskin's Pleasures: True and False Pleasures in Plato's *Philebus*," *Phronesis* 30: 151–80; reprinted in G. Fine (ed.), *Plato 2*, pp. 345–72. Oxford: Oxford University Press, 1999.

— 1996: "Mixed Feelings in Aristotle's *Rhetoric*." In A. O. Rorty (ed.), *Essays on Aristotle's Rhetoric*, pp. 258–85. Berkeley, CA: University of California Press.

— 1997: *Platon Philebos*. Göttingen: Vandenhoeck and Ruprecht.

Gauthier, R. A. and Jolif, J. Y. 1958–9: *L'Éthique à Nicomaque, introduction, traduction et commentaire*. Louvain: Nauwelaerts (reprinted 2002).

Gosling, J. C. B. and Taylor, C. C. W. 1982: *The Greeks on Pleasure*. Oxford: Oxford University Press.

Gottlieb, P. 1993: "Aristotle's Measure Doctrine and Pleasure," *Archiv für Geschichte der Philosophie* 75: 31–46.

Kant, I. 1991: "Idea for a Universal History with a Cosmopolitan Purpose." In H. Reiss (ed.), *Kant: Political Writings*, trans. H. B. Nisbet, 2nd edn. Cambridge: Cambridge University Press.

Owen, G. E. L. 1971–2: "Aristotelian Pleasures," *Proceedings of the Aristotelian Society* 72: 135–52.

Rapp, C. 2002: *Aristoteles Rhetorik*, 2 vols. Berlin: Akademie Verlag.

Riel, G. van 2000: *Pleasure and the Good Life: Plato, Aristotle, and the Neoplatonists*. Leiden: Brill.

Rorty, A. O. 1980: "Acrasia and Pleasure: *Nicomachean Ethics* Book 7." In A. O. Rorty (ed.), *Essays on Aristotle's Ethics*, pp. 267–84. Berkeley, CA: University of California Press.

Urmson, J. 1967: "Aristotle on Pleasure." In J. M. Moravcsik (ed.), *Aristotle: A Collection of Critical Essays*, pp. 323–33. Garden City, NY: Anchor Books.

— 1988: *Aristotle's Ethics*. Oxford: Blackwell.

13

The Nicomachean Account
of *Philia*

Jennifer Whiting

1 Preliminary Note

Those translating Aristotle into English so readily agree in rendering *philia* as "friendship" and *philos* as "friend" that it is easy to overlook two related difficulties with this. The first is that of preserving the etymological connections present in the original; the second that of finding terms having roughly the same extensions and connotations as the Greek for which they do duty.

Philia is an abstract noun derived from the verb *to philein*, which means "to love" or "hold dear" in a general sense: one can love or hold dear all sorts of things, from a bottle of wine or a dog through one's family and friends. So we *could* preserve the etymological connection by rendering *philia* and its cognates with "love" and its cognates. But this suggests "lover" for *ho philōn* (from the active participle) and "beloved" for *ho philoumenos* (from the passive participle). And this involves changes in both connotation and extension. For "lover" and "beloved" have erotic connotations, and tend to refer narrowly to the subjects and objects of specifically erotic love.

We might seek to rectify the problem by reserving "to love" and its cognates for *to eran* and its cognates. But we bump immediately into the problem of how to render *to philein*. "To befriend" is awkward. More importantly, it is too weak to capture paradigmatic forms of *philōn*, such as that of parents for their children. We need a verb covering both weak and strong forms of attachment. So I propose to continue using the generic "to love" for *to philein*.[1] We can then use the less erotically charged "one who loves" and "one loved" for *ho philōn* and *ho philoumenos*, while keeping the more erotically charged "lover" and "beloved" for the relevant forms of *to eran*, which we can render "to love erotically." This seems appropriate insofar as Aristotle treats *erōs* as a kind of *philia*.

This would allow us to render *philia* simply as "love," thus preserving the etymological connections between *to philein* and the abstract noun. But *should* we work so hard to preserve this connection? For two reasons, I think we should not. First, we must eventually sacrifice the connection in order to render the adjective *philos* and the substantive noun derived from it: the adjective is best rendered "dear," while the noun (which is non-directional and refers indifferently to those who love and to those who are loved) is best rendered "friend." Second, "friendship" is so well entrenched in translations and the secondary literature that it would be disruptive to depart from it. So I shall retain "friendship" for *philia* and "friend" for (the noun) *philos*, but abandon the etymological connection by using "to love" (rather than "to befriend") for *to philein*.

2 Eudaimonism and Rational Egoism

The *Nicomachean Ethics* opens with – and is organized around – what Vlastos (1991) calls "the eudaimonist axiom": *eudaimonia* is the ultimate end of human action in the sense that (a) it is never chosen for the sake of any further end, and (b) it is that for the sake of which all actions should be (and in some sense are) performed.[2] Many commentators read this as a form of rational egoism according to which each agent should aim primarily at her *own eudaimonia*, construed more or less broadly so as to include the *eudaimonia* of at least some "significant others." Such commentators sometimes read Aristotle's conception of the friend as an "other self" as explaining how the agent's *eudaimonia* comes to *include* that of others: because the agent's friend is her other *self*, her friend's *eudaimonia* is *part* of her *own* and promoting her friend's *eudaimonia* is a *way* of promoting her *own*. Some even read Aristotle as making the friend a literal extension of oneself. Irwin (1988), for example, reads Aristotle as treating the character and activities of one's friend as an "extension of [one's] own activity": friendship is thus conceived as a mode of "*self*-realization."[3]

But there is some question whether such readings honor Aristotle's repeated insistence that a true friend loves and seeks to benefit her friend for her *friend's* sake. For rational egoism gives normative – and not just explanatory – primacy to the *agent's eudaimonia*: loving and seeking to benefit one's friend for her sake is acceptable *because*, and *only insofar as*, it is a way of loving and seeking to benefit *oneself*. Moreover, the *NE* does not actually specify the agent's own *eudaimonia* as the ultimate end of all of her actions: it is compatible with what Aristotle says that an agent at least sometimes, perhaps often, takes the *eudaimonia* of others as the ultimate end for the sake of which she acts in the sense that she aims at their *eudaimonia simply as such* (and *not* as parts of her own).[4]

Aristotle's account of *philia* must, of course, be interpreted within his eudaimonist framework. But we should not assume straightaway that his eudaimonism is a form of rational egoism. For his account of *philia*, if read without this assumption, may tell *against* rational egoist readings of that framework. There is, of course, no escaping the hermeneutic circle. But I propose to reverse the usual order by starting with Aristotle's account of *philia* and then asking what (if anything) it suggests about the nature of his eudaimonism.

3 *NE* VIII.1: Nicomachean Context and Platonic Background

NE I characterizes *eudaimonia* as "an activity of soul in accordance with virtue, and if there are several virtues, in accordance with the best and *teleiotatēn*" (I.7.1098a16–18). Commentators are famously divided over how to take this. Some take *teleiotatēn* to mean "highest" and read this as pointing either to the purely contemplative activity of theoretical intellect apparently championed in *NE* X.7 or to the distinctively human activity of practical intellect and the virtues associated with it (1177b24–1178a22). Others take *teleiotatēn* to mean "complete" and read this as referring to a compound activity in accordance with the panoply of practical and theoretical virtues covered in the *NE*. We cannot resolve this controversy here. The point is that *whichever* way Book X goes, Aristotle seems to model human on divine *eudaimonia*: he seems to think that human subjects – even those living primarily political lives – are more *eudaimōn* the more their activities and lives resemble those of the gods. And he takes self-sufficiency to be a prominent feature of divine activities and lives.

This is the context in which the Nicomachean books on *philia* appear. They precede Book X's problematic return to the topic of *eudaimonia* and open with a reference back to Book I's account of *eudaimonia* as something self-sufficient in the sense that it "taken by itself makes life choiceworthy and lacking in nothing" (I.8.1098b14–15):

> After these things comes the discussion of *philia*. For it is a kind of virtue or something involving virtue. Further, it is most necessary for life; for without friends, no one would choose to live, even if he had all other goods. (VIII.1.1155a3–6)

NE VIII.1 cites various *endoxa* – or common beliefs – in support of this. But the claim itself seems to be in Aristotle's own voice: he seems to think that a life without friends is not simply lacking but not even choiceworthy.

But this generates a puzzle. For the need for friends seems to undermine the self-sufficiency of the would-be *eudaimōn*. The more she needs friends, the less (it seems) her life can approximate that of the gods. And the more her relationships with her so-called friends are grounded in *her* needs, the less (it seems) her relationships with them qualify as true friendship, which must be based on appreciation of one's friend and not on one's own needs. So the more self-sufficient an agent is, the more capable she will be of true friendship. But the more self-sufficient she is, the harder it is to explain why she will (or should) have friends in the first place.

In seeking to resolve such puzzles, Aristotle follows his standard "endoxic" method: he seeks an account that resolves the puzzles to which common beliefs give rise, while preserving as many of these beliefs as possible. His strategy is to argue that apparently opposed beliefs can be reconciled insofar as each is true in one sense (or one set of cases) but not in another (*EE* VII.2.1235b13–18). *NE* IX.8 provides a classic example: by distinguishing two kinds of self-love, he preserves the claims both of those who commend self-love and of those who condemn it.

NE VIII.1 dismisses the puzzles raised by natural philosophers – such as whether like is friend to like or whether friendship arises only between contraries – as "not appropriate" to Aristotle's inquiry: they are, as he explains at *EE* VII.1.1235a30, "too universal." But VIII.1 admits specifically human variants, involving human characters and emotions: most notably, whether (as some think) only *good* people can be friends (since friendship requires us to trust our friends in ways we cannot trust those who are bad); or whether (as many think) *any* sort of person can be friends with *any* sort (1155b9–13). These puzzles can be traced to Plato's *Lysis*, which provides immediate and indispensable background for Aristotle's discussion. At 215a–b, Socrates gets Lysis to agree that the good agent is sufficient, and that one who is sufficient will *need nothing* and so will neither cherish (*agapein*) nor love (*philein*) anything. How then, they wonder, can good agents value one another?

Aristotle's conception of the true friend as an "other self" is largely a response to this question – a response at which Socrates himself hints at the end of the *Lysis*, where he distinguishes what is *oikeion* (roughly "appropriate") to a person from what is merely *like* her, and then suggests that the good may be *oikeion* to *everyone* (222b–c). Socrates gestures here toward a kind of loving that is neither need-based nor a function of what its *subject* is like – a kind of loving motivated not by some deficiency or mere taste in its subject but rather by some positive quality in its *object*. And he has hinted (at 216c) at the relevant quality: *to kalon* (there rendered "beauty"). Aristotle uses the same term to characterize the end for the sake of which virtuous agents act (in which contexts *to kalon* tends to be rendered "nobility" or "the fine").

4 *NE* VIII.2: Aristotle's Preliminary Account

Aristotle begins, following Socrates' lead, with a discussion of the *object* or "what is lovable" (*to philēton*). This has normative connotations: it refers to what people are *apt* to love because they deem it *worthy* of love. Aristotle recognizes three such objects: what is good (*agathon*), what is pleasant, and what is useful (VIII.2.1155b18–19). These almost certainly correspond to the three objects of choice listed at II.3.1104b30–31: the fine (*to kalon*), the pleasant, and the advantageous. For it is likely, as Broadie suggests, that Aristotle avoids using *to kalon* here lest he be misunderstood as referring simply to physical beauty (Broadie and Rowe 2002:

408). Associating the good mentioned here with *to kalon* is especially reasonable given the three corresponding forms of friendship that Aristotle goes on to discuss: those based on virtue (where *to kalon* is key), those based on pleasure, and those based on utility.

Aristotle adds immediately that things are useful because some good or some pleasure comes to be through them, so that it is ultimately only the good and the pleasant that are lovable "as ends" (VIII.2.1155b19–21). It is worth noting that Aristotle here associates what is pleasant with what is good and opposes *both* to what is useful. For commentators tend to speak as if he associates pleasure-friendship primarily with utility-friendship and takes the two together to be uniformly opposed to character-friendship. But there is evidence here (and elsewhere) that Aristotle associates pleasure-friendships more closely with character-friendships than with those based on utility.[5]

Aristotle next asks whether people love what is good (simply) or what is good *for themselves*, and whether people love what is pleasant (simply) or what is pleasant *to themselves*. For these do not always agree (1155b21–3). As explained in the *EE*, they agree in the case of properly constituted subjects: what is good simply (*haplōs*) is what is good *for* a healthy body or a well-ordered soul, but some things (such as drugs and surgery) are good *for* a subject only because of peculiarities of her condition. Aristotle draws a similar distinction between what is pleasant *haplōs*, and so pleasant *to* a mature and non-defective body or soul, and what is pleasant *only* to an immature or otherwise defective body or soul (*EE* VII.2.1235b30–1236a7).

The *Eudemian* account does not separate the distinction between what is good *haplōs* and what is good *for* someone as clearly as it might from that between what is *really* good and what is *apparently* good. But the Nicomachean account makes it clear that there are two distinctions here. For it explicitly contrasts what is *really* good for oneself with what is *apparently* good for oneself (VIII.2.1155b25–6). Note that the contrast here is not between what is *really* good for oneself and what is *only apparently* good for oneself. For what is *really* good for oneself may also (and should ideally) *appear* to oneself as such.

Aristotle recognizes that a subject can pursue what *is* good only by pursuing what *appears* to her good, and that this applies equally to what is good *haplōs* and to what is good *for* her. And he thinks (following *Gorgias* 466b–468e) that those who pursue what appears good *because* it appears good are ultimately pursuing what is really good, even if (thanks to defective appearances) they are mistaken about what is really good. His view is not just that people *do* tend to pursue what is (really) good for themselves, but also that they *should* do so: he says at V.1.1129b5–6 that people should *choose* things that *are* good for themselves, given their actual circumstances, while *praying* that the things that are *haplōs* good *be* good for them. This ideal plays an important role in Aristotle's account of *philia*: true friends are good both *haplōs* and *for one another* (VIII.3.1156b12–13).

With these distinctions in place, Aristotle produces the following preliminary account: *philia* requires (a) reciprocal loving or affection (*antiphilēsis*); (b) each party wishing good to the other for the *other's* sake; and (c) mutual awareness of this reciprocal well-wishing (VIII.2.1155b27–1156a3). (a) and (b) rule out friendship with inanimate objects. Even if a bottle of wine is *philon* (i.e., dear) to me because I have affection for it, it does not return my affection. And even if I wish for its good, I do not wish that for *its* sake; I wish for it to be preserved so that I might enjoy (or perhaps sell) it. But even reciprocal well-wishing for the other's sake is *not sufficient* for *philia*: each party must be *aware* of the other's well-wishing (1155b34–1156a5). The importance of such awareness should become clear in section 11 below.

It is worth noting that when Aristotle explains condition (b), he seems to be reporting how the term *eunoia* is *commonly used*: he says that those who wish goods to another for the other's sake are *said* to have goodwill (*eunoia*) toward the other whenever such wishing is not reciprocated by the other; and that *philia* is *said* to be reciprocal *eunoia* (1155b31–4). Aristotle's own account of *eunoia*, in IX.5, is more restricted: he claims that *eunoia* "generally comes about on account of virtue or a certain decency" (1167a18–20) and he seems to restrict *eunoia* to friendships based on virtue (1167a14–17). And some commentators (such as Irwin) take this later restriction to suggest that there is no genuine wishing-goods-to-the-other-for-the-*other's*-sake in friendships based on pleasure or utility.[6]

But this does not follow if, as I suggest, Aristotle starts in the endoxic phase of his discussion with the common use (according to which *eunoia* is simply wishing-goods-to-the-other-for-the-other's-sake *however such wishing comes about*) and then moves in his own positive account to what he regards as the proper use (according to which *eunoia* is such wishing *when it comes to be on account of the parties recognizing some decency or virtue in one another*). For in that case it may be only *eunoia* proper, and not wishing-goods-to-the-other-for-the-other's-sake, that Aristotle takes to be missing in friendships based on pleasure and utility. And if (as I argue in section 6 below) it is only wishing-goods-to-the-other-for-the-other's-sake, and not *eunoia* proper, that is necessary for *philia*, then friendships based on pleasure and utility may still (as Cooper insists) make the grade.

5 *NE* VIII.3–4: Three Forms of *Philia*?

The next two chapters suggest that Aristotle counts at least some relationships based on pleasure and utility as genuine friendships. For VIII.3 describes the three forms of *philia*, and VIII.4 defends the practice of calling the lower two forms of *philia*. But VIII.4 tends to be misunderstood: because commentators miss a key distinction, they read Aristotle's defense of this practice as more concessive than I think he means it to be.

Note first how vehemently the *EE* rejects the restriction of *philia* to character-friendship. After arguing that the various forms of *philia* are so-called in relation to some primary form, Aristotle objects to those who would restrict *philia* to its primary form:

> Because they take the universal to be first, they take the first also to be universal. But this is false. So they are not able to admit all the phenomena. Because one account does not fit [all the forms] they deny that the others are friendships. But they are, only not similarly [in each case]. But these people, whenever the first does not fit [a case] say that the others are not friendships, because they think an account would be universal if it were first.[7] But there are many forms [*eidē*] of friendship . . . in fact, we have already distinguished three, one *dia* virtue, one *dia* the useful, and one *dia* pleasure. (VII.2.1236a23–32)[8]

The *NE* is at least superficially similar to the *EE* on this point: it speaks of the lesser forms of *philia* as so-called on account of their similarity to the primary form. So we need compelling evidence for seeing the alleged restriction in the *NE*.

We can best appreciate the Nicomachean defense by starting at VIII.3.1156b17–21:

> It is reasonable that such *philia* [character-friendship] should be enduring. For it contains in itself all the things that should belong [*dei huparchein*] to friends.[9] For all *philia* exists *dia* [what is] good or *dia* pleasure, either *haplōs* or for the one who loves, and is [*philia*] in virtue of some similarity [to character-friendship].

The defense culminates at VIII.4.1157a20–33:

> [A] And only the *philia* of good people is immune to slander. For it is not easy to trust someone who has not been tested by oneself for a long time. But trusting belongs among these [i.e., good people], and so does never doing injustice to one another, and whatever else people think worthy of true friendship. [B] And nothing prevents *such things* coming to be in the other [forms]. For since people apply the term "friends" both to those who [are friends] *dia* what is useful . . . and to those who are fond of one another *dia* pleasure . . . we should presumably say that such people are friends and that there are several forms of friendship, first and in the controlling sense, the friendship of good people insofar as they are good, and the remaining [forms] according to their similarity [to this].

Most English translations take the italicized "such things" as referring to the sort of "distrust" (Irwin), "slander" (Rowe), or "evils" (Ross) that Aristotle has just said arise in the other forms of *philia*. So they read the "nothing prevents . . ." sentence as summing up the reasons *against* counting the others as genuine forms of *philia*. They then read the rest of (B) as saying that we should *nevertheless* continue to call the others forms of *philia*.

But it should be clear from (A) that this *cannot* be the correct reading. For "such things" obviously refers back to "trusting . . . and . . . never doing injustice . . . and *whatever else people think worthy of true friendship.*" Aristotle's point is that even though such things do not always *in fact* belong to friendships based on pleasure or utility, nothing prevents such things *sometimes* belonging (even if only accidentally) to such friendships. And his "nothing prevents . . ." sentence is surely better read as supplying an argument for his ostensible conclusion (i.e., that there are several forms of friendship) than as posing an obstacle to it.

Moreover, "whatever else people think worthy [*axioutai*] of true friendship" seems to refer back to two previous occurrences of "the things that should belong to friends" – one (quoted above) and one in the opening sentence of VIII.4. This suggests that "the things that should belong to friends" refers not to constitutive conditions of *philia* (such as wishing-goods-to-the-other-for-the-other's-sake) but to features that are thought to flow from the constitutive conditions (features like durability, trusting, and not doing injustice to one another). Irwin's (1999) translation obscures this by rendering the *dei* (in *dei huparchein*) as "must" rather than "should," thus making it seem as if Aristotle means to refer to necessary conditions of *philia* and not – as his argument actually *requires* – to features that should ideally belong to friends but do not always in fact do so. And this makes it seem as if Aristotle's argument is more concessive than I take it to be.

Aristotle is *not* saying (what seems only marginally coherent) that, in spite of the distrust et cetera endemic to the relationships based on pleasure and utility, and in spite of their failure to exhibit the features that *must* belong to friends, we should *nevertheless* go on calling such relationships forms of *philia* because that is how people in fact speak. He is rather *defending* the practice of speaking that way by arguing not just that some such relationships exhibit the defining features of *philia* (such as mutually acknowledged and reciprocal well-wishing for the other's sake) but also that nothing prevents those that do exhibit the defining features from sometimes exhibiting (at least to some extent) other features (such as durability) that should ideally belong to friendships but do not always do so. His claim is that these other features belong to character-friends *in themselves*, while they belong *only accidentally* (if at all) in relationships based on pleasure or utility.

6 *NE* IX.4–6: *Ta Philika* versus the Defining Features of *Philia*

There is evidence in *NE* IX.4–6 that Aristotle distinguishes the defining features of *philia* from other features of it in precisely the way required by my account. *NE* IX.4 begins as follows: "*Ta philika* in relation to one's neighbors *and* the features by which friendships [*philiai*] are defined would seem to be derived from the features of one's relation to oneself" (1166a1–2).[10] Aristotle then presents a list of various features by which *philia* is said to be defined:

1 Wishing and doing goods or apparent goods for the sake of the other.
2 Wishing the other to exist and to live for his sake (which is what mothers, and friends who have quarreled, experience).
3 Spending time together and choosing the same things.
4 Experiencing pain and pleasure together with one's friend (which happens most of all in the case of mothers).

There is no explicit mention of *eunoia* here, nor anywhere in the remainder of IX.4's comparison of friendship to (proper) self-love. *Eunoia* reappears as such at the start of IX.5, which is devoted to *eunoia* and begins: "*eunoia* seems like [something] *philikon*." And IX.6, which is devoted to like-mindedness (*homonoia*), begins in much the same way: "*homonoia* seems to be *philikon*." So IX.5 and 6 seem to be moving on, after IX.4's discussion of the defining features, to *ta philika*.

NE VIII.6 contains a hint (borne out here) about how Aristotle may distinguish *ta philika* from the defining features. He is speaking there about things like good-temper and enjoying one another's company, which he says are "most *philika* and productive [*poētika*] of *philia*" (1158a2–4). So *ta philika* may sometimes refer to things insofar as they are *productive* of *philia*. This does not exclude its sometimes referring to things characteristic of *philia* or even constitutive of it. But it seems that the emphasis, in calling things *philika*, is on their being productive of *philia*. This is borne out at IX.5.1167a2–3, where Aristotle says that *eunoia* is a source (*archē*) of *philia*, just as the pleasure occasioned by sight is a source of *erōs*.

If Aristotle regards *eunoia* proper as one of *ta philika* and not as one of the defining features, then it would not follow from any restriction of *eunoia* proper to character-friendship that the lower forms fail to exhibit one of the defining features: they can still count as forms of *philia* if they involve reciprocal wishing-of-goods-to-the-other-for-the-other's-sake (along with whatever other features are required for something to count as *philia*). So we need to ask: what exactly are the defining features? And to what extent (if at all) are they present in the lower forms?

We will see below that (3) and (4) play important roles in Aristotle's account of the character-friend as an "other self." But which of (2) – (4) he counts as a defining feature must take a back seat to the question to what extent he takes (1) to be satisfied in friendships based on pleasure and utility. For he clearly takes (1) to be a defining feature.

7 Digression on *Dia*: Efficient Causal, Final Causal, or Both?

Much of the dispute about whether friendships based on utility and pleasure satisfy (1) has focused on the question of how to understand the preposition *dia* in

Aristotle's talk of friendships *dia* virtue, pleasure, and utility. This could refer simply to what causes the parties to have the relevant attitudes toward one another in an *efficient* causal sense; or it could refer to the *final* cause, i.e., to the end or purpose for the sake of which their relationship exists; or it could refer to *both*. Irwin (1999: 274) argues that the *dia* expresses both efficient causal and final causal relations. On his account, those who love *dia* pleasure (or *dia* utility) love each other not simply as a result of the pleasure (or utility) each *has received* from the other, but also for the sake of such pleasure (or utility) as each *expects to receive* from the other.

Cooper (1999) argues, against this, that *dia* is primarily (efficient) causal and "at least as much retrospective as prospective." He reads Aristotle as

> making, in effect, the psychological claim that those who have enjoyed one another's company or have been mutually benefited through their common association, will, as a result of the benefits or the pleasures they receive, tend to wish for and be willing to act in the interest of the other person's good, independently of consideration of their *own* welfare or pleasure. (Cooper 1999: 323)

Cooper says it is "compatible" with this that each party should *expect* the friendship to yield pleasure (or utility) for himself. But pleasure (or utility) is nevertheless the "cause, not the goal, of the well-wishing" (1999: 324).

As we shall see below, Aristotle himself takes his account of *philia* to rely on the sort of psychological tendencies on which Cooper's reading of it relies. So it is plausible to read Aristotle as claiming that people tend, as a matter of psychological fact, to become fond of those they find pleasant or those who have been useful to them; and that people tend, as a matter of psychological fact, to wish goods to those of whom they are fond and to do so for the latter's sake (as distinct from their own). But we cannot read Aristotle this way if we are required to read his talk of friendship *dia* pleasure (or *dia* utility) as expressing final (as well as efficient) causal relations.

Irwin (1999: 274) cites two passages that he takes to "associate '*dia*' clearly with the final cause." His translation of the second (X.2.1172b21) associates them clearly: "What is most choiceworthy is what we choose not because of, or for the sake of, something else." But in suggesting that "for the sake of" explicates "because of" Irwin ignores the clear "neither/nor" structure of Aristotle's sentence, which (non-tendentiously translated) reads as follows: "what is most choiceworthy is what we choose *neither* on account of something else *nor* for the sake of something else [*mē di' heteron mēd' heterou charin*]." Properly translated, this sentence tells more against than for the association of *dia* with the final cause.

And this is just what we should expect, given the prominence of the *Lysis* in the background. For Socrates clearly distinguishes that *dia*-which (or on account of which) *A* is friend to *B* from that *heneka*-which (or for the sake of which) *A* is friend to *B*: it is *dia* something bad (namely, disease), but *heneka* something good (namely, health), that the sick person loves or is friend to the doctor (217–19).

And Socrates explicitly *rejects* the idea that we should equate loving *B heneka* some good with loving *B dia* some bad: he argues that even if all the bad things *dia* which *A* is friend to *B* were abolished, *A* might still be friend to *B heneka* some good (220c–d). Aristotle might, of course, reject the Socratic distinction. But in that case, we would expect him to call attention (as he does elsewhere) to his disagreement with Socrates.

So Irwin's case rests primarily on VIII.3.1156a31. But this, when read in context, provides, at most, weak support:

> The *philia* of young people seems to be *di' hēdonēn*. For they live in accordance with their passion, and pursue above all what is pleasant for themselves and what is present [*to paron*]. Since they are of a volatile age, their pleasures are different [at different times]. Hence they become friends quickly and stop [quickly]. (1156a31–5)

This is compatible with Cooper's view: because young folk tend to pursue what is pleasant, they may (as a matter of psychological fact) tend to wish and do goods to those they find pleasant, and they may do so at least as much for the sake of those they find pleasant as for their own sakes (though they may do so only as long as they continue to find one another pleasant). Aristotle may simply be citing the common tendency of young folk to do all sorts of crazy things for their friends, without much regard for their *own* interests. This seems, in fact, to be the point of his reference to "what is present": young folk act according to their present passions without regard to their own future interests (including their own future passions). This is why, as Aristotle explains in *Rhetoric* II.12–13, it is so much easier to take advantage of young than of old folk, who tend to be so jealous of their own interests that they do not even enjoy one another's company. These chapters explicitly oppose the sort of calculating attention to one's own advantage that Aristotle takes to be characteristic of old age to the sort of non-calculating attitude he takes to be characteristic of youth; and they explicitly associate the latter with preferring what is *kalon* to what is advantageous.

Note that even if we accept Irwin's association of *dia* with the final cause, *Politics* I.2 shows that we cannot move immediately from the claim that a relationship *comes to be* for the sake of some end to the conclusion that the relationship *continues to exist* for the sake of that end. After explaining that man and woman couple to produce offspring, and that the resulting families (*oikoi*, which exist in order to serve daily needs) form villages for the sake of satisfying other (not merely daily) needs, and that villages come together to form the *polis*, Aristotle says that the *polis* is the first community that is virtually self-sufficient and that it "*comes to be* for the sake of living, but *exists* for the sake of living well" (I.2.1252b29–30). Moreover, Aristotle explicitly allows some such phenomenon in the case of *philia*: some friendships that come to be for the sake of pleasure later exist in the absence of the relevant sort of pleasure if, from the friends' association with one another, they have become fond of one another's characters (*NE* VIII.4.1157a10–12).

Still, Aristotle's claim that friendships based on pleasure and utility tend to dissolve when the parties cease to find one another pleasant or useful seems to support Irwin's general view. For even if, as a result of the pleasure or utility I have received from my friend, I wish well to her, and seek occasion by occasion to benefit her *without* an eye to my own pleasure or utility, the fact that I would *not* continue to do so if I ceased to expect pleasure or utility from the relationship seems good reason to say that my primary goal is *my* pleasure or *my* utility. And Aristotle himself seems to agree when he says that those who love on account of what is useful or pleasant love one another not "in themselves" (*kath' hautous*) – nor "for being persons of a certain sort" (*tō[i] poious tinas einai*) or "insofar as each is who he is" (*hē[i] estin hosper estin*) – but rather insofar as the other is pleasant or useful to themselves (VIII.3.1156a10–16).

But *why* does Aristotle introduce the technical language he typically uses to characterize the distinction between a thing's essence and its accidents? Why does he not say simply that those who love on account of utility (or pleasure) love only themselves and not the other – full stop? One (I think good) way to explain this is to read him as allowing that those who are friends on account of pleasure or utility really *do* wish one another well for the *other's* sake, and so satisfy the most important condition for being friends, with the result that he needs to explain what is *special* about the sort of wishing-well-for-the-other's-sake we find in character-friendship. So he appeals to the idea that *this* wishing is based on something essential to who the *other* is, and not simply on accidental features of her that might change with time, including the relationships in which she stands to the agent's own contingent tastes and/or needs. By focusing on essential features of the object, he minimizes the role played by the merely accidental tastes and needs of the agent as things *dia* which she might come to be fond of the other and so to wish him well for *his* sake. But in cases where accidental features of the parties do result in each being fond of the other and wishing the other well for her sake, Aristotle seems to allow that (1) *is* satisfied, even if only accidentally and only temporarily: that is why these cases do not exhibit all the features (such as durability) that should ideally belong to friends.

8 *NE* IX.7 (VIII.8 and 12): Benefactors, Poets, and Parents

We now begin to see the role played in Aristotle's account by facts about what people tend, as a matter of psychological fact, to love and cherish. Aristotle makes prominent use of such facts in IX.7, where he seeks to explain why benefactors seem to love their beneficiaries more than their beneficiaries love them. People find this puzzling because they expect beneficiaries to love their benefactors, on account of the benefits received from them, *more* than their benefactors love them. Aristotle rejects the common attempt to explain this by comparing benefactors to creditors and beneficiaries to debtors, and then claiming that debtors wish their creditors did not exist while creditors actually wish for the preservation of their debtors. For he denies that benefactors resemble creditors, who wish their debtors to be preserved for the sake of (*heneka*) recovering what they themselves are owed and so fail to satisfy (2): benefactors often love and cherish (*philousi kai agapōsi*) those whom they have benefited even if the latter are in no way useful to them and unlikely to become so later (IX.7.1167b28–33). The true explanation, he says, seems to be "more natural":

> It is just what happens in the case of artists. For every [artist] loves and cherishes his own work [*to oikeion ergon*] more than he would be cherished by the work if it came to be ensouled. This happens especially perhaps in the case of poets; for they over-cherish their own poems [*ta oikeia poiēmata*], being fond of them as if they were [their own] children. And the case of benefactors seems to be like this. For the one benefited is their work, and they cherish this more than the work cherishes the one having produced it. The explanation of this is that being is choiceworthy and lovable for all; and we exist in [our] activity, for to live is to act; and in activity, the producer is in a way the work [itself]; indeed he is fond of the work because [he is fond] also of [his own] being. And this is natural. (IX.7.1167b33–1168a8)

This explanation appeals to human nature: to facts about what people, as a matter of psychological fact, tend to love and cherish and not (as the explanation Aristotle seeks to supplant) to the specific motives of particular sorts of agents.

Aristotle cites several other such facts: for the benefactor, the beneficent activities are *kalon*, but for the beneficiary, they are merely advantageous, which is less pleasant and lovable than what is *kalon* (IX.7.1168a9–12); everyone is fonder of the things that come about as a result of their own labor, which is why those who have earned their money are fonder of it than those who have inherited it (a21–3). The points have little to do with the ends for the sake of which particular individuals act: people *just do* tend to find what is *kalon* more pleasant and more lovable than what is merely advantageous; and they *just do* tend to be fonder of things that have come about as a result of their own labor than of things that have not. Moreover, Aristotle's appeal to what is *kalon* may signal the *lack* of any ulterior motive: for he routinely associates the virtuous agent's choice of virtuous actions *for themselves* with acting for the sake of *to kalon*.

The chapter concludes: "And it seems that receiving benefit is effortless, while doing benefit involves work. On account of these things, mothers are more child-loving [*philoteknoterai*] [than fathers are]. For the genesis involves more labor on their part, and they know better [than fathers do] that the children come from themselves" (1168a23–7). This should be compared with two other passages where motherly love is cited as paradigmatic. The first is in VIII.8, where – after arguing that being loved is better than being honored because being loved is enjoyed for itself in a way that being honored is not – Aristotle claims that *philia* consists even more in loving than in being loved. He cites as evidence the fact that some mothers give up their own children to be raised by others and then love their children without seeking to be loved in return (if they cannot have both), it being sufficient for them to see the children doing well (1159a16–34).

The second appears in VIII.12:

Parents are fond of their children as being something of themselves [*hōs heautōn ti onta*], and children [are fond of] their parents as [themselves] being something from them [i.e., the parents]. But parents know the things coming from themselves more than their offspring know that they are from them [i.e., the parents]; and the one from which is more familiar with [*sunōkeiōtai*] the one generated than the one coming to be is with its producer. For what comes from oneself is *oikeion* to the one from which it comes . . . but the one from which [the latter comes] is in no way [*oikeion*] to it, or less so. And [these phenomena vary] with the length of time [involved]. For [parents] are fond of [their children] immediately upon their coming to be, while children [are fond of] their parents only after some time, when they have acquired comprehension [*sunesis*][11] or perception. From these things it is clear why *mothers love* [*their children*] *more* [*than their children love them*].[12] Parents, then, love their children as themselves [*hōs heautous*] (for the ones coming to be from them are like other selves [*hoion heteroi autoi*], by being separated [from them]).
(1161b18–29)

Note the role played here not just by what is *oikeion* to a subject, but also by the subject's *recognition* of it as such: this is supposed to help explain the kind of affection people tend as a matter of fact to have. Note especially my rendering of *sunōkeiōtai* as "familiar with." Ross (1980) has "attached to," which is good insofar as it suggests some sort of emotional bond; Irwin (1999) has "regards . . . as more his own," which is less good insofar as it suggests something primarily cognitive. I prefer "familiar with" both because it preserves the etymological connections with *sun-* (meaning "with") and *oikos* (whose focal referent is the family), and because it has both cognitive and affective aspects: it suggests not only recognizing *that* something is *oikeion* to one, but also the sort of emotional affiliation people tend to have with those with whom they have lived. It suggests a bond requiring a certain kind of perception or understanding, which is why it takes time for children to achieve it.

Aristotle is preparing here for his account of character-friendship, which is also a developmental achievement: it takes time and intimacy for the parties to become familiar with one another in ways such that they are "other selves" to each other, each appreciating and enjoying the other's activities in something like the way she appreciates and enjoys her own. But the apparent assimilation of character-friendship to the attitude of parents toward their children may give us pause. For this makes it seem as if Aristotle's account of character-friendship is grounded in the sort of egocentric bias on which ethnocentric and other objectionable forms of bias are based. So we must pause to see that this is not the case.

The first step is to see that even in the case of relations among kin Aristotle treats character-friendship as the ideal. He compares *philia* between brothers to that between companions, especially to that between companions who are decent (presumably character-friends or those on the way to becoming so) but more generally to that between companions who are similar to one another (presumably pleasure-friends, who tend to enjoy the same things, rather than utility-friends, who tend to differ in ways that allow each to provide the other with things he cannot provide for himself) (VIII.12.1162a9–15). I think it significant that Aristotle runs the comparison this way, rather than the other way round: pleasure-friendships are his most common paradigm, and character-friendships his most esteemed paradigm, so he points to ways in which *philia* between brothers is similar to these, not to the ways in which these are similar to it. And as he goes on to say, relations among family members – particularly between husband and wife – typically involve a mix of pleasure and utility, but they *can* also be "*dia* virtue *if* the parties are decent, for there is a virtue [characteristic] of each, and [each] will delight in such [virtue as the other has]" (VIII.12.1162a25–7).

Aristotle clearly represents character-friendship as the ideal toward which even blood-relations should aspire. This suggests that his appeal to psychological facts about whom and how we *do* love is not a crude attempt to justify conclusions about whom and how we *ought* to love, but rather a strategy for establishing the *possibility* of attitudes he seeks eventually to *recommend*. Given the prevalence of skepticism about the very *possibility* of these attitudes – the sort of skepticism betrayed, for example, in the common attempt to assimilate benefactors to creditors – Aristotle seeks to show how the attitudes he would recommend are made *possible* by natural human tendencies (such as parents' affection for their children and artists' affection for their work).

9 Ethnocentrism and Aristotle's Ethocentric Ideal

We may better appreciate Aristotle's strategy once we note a common error in recent translations of VIII.1. After saying that *philia* seems to belong by nature to parents in relation to their offspring, and to offspring in relation to their parents, Aristotle says that such *philia* (perhaps including natural *philia* more generally) occurs

> not only among human beings, but also among birds and most animals, and [among] those belonging to the same clan [*tois homoethnesi*], especially human beings; whence we praise those who are lovers of humankind [*philanthrōpous*]; for one might see in traveling widely that every human is *oikeion* to every other and [likewise] dear [*philon*]. (VIII.1.1155a14–22)

Ross (1980) renders *tois homoethnesi* "members of the same *race*." Irwin and Rowe each replace this with talk of belonging to the same *species*. Irwin defends "species" by saying that "the rest of the paragraph shows that Aristotle has species in mind (i.e., friendship among dogs or human beings, rather than friendship among greyhounds or Greeks)" (1999: 273). But this misses Aristotle's point, which is that human beings stand out among animals as especially *clannish*. We are the most *ethnocentric* – or, as Aristotle puts it, the most *homoethnic* – of animals. That is why we *praise* those who are (simply) *philanthrōpoi*: they have managed to overcome this common but regrettable tendency.

Those who take Aristotle's conception of the friend as an "other self" as endorsing bias toward those similar to oneself may be tempted to dismiss the point about praising those who are simply *philanthrōpoi* as mere endoxic chatter. But that would be rash. For taking Aristotle to *endorse* such bias rests on the mistaken view that he takes similarity as such not simply to *explain* but also to *justify* partiality toward those similar to oneself. But part of his point in recommending the character-friendship ideal is to reject such egocentric views.[13]

Instead of taking the legitimacy of brute self-love for granted and seeking – as on rational egoist readings – to extend it to others, Aristotle argues in IX.8 that brute self-love is *not* justified.[14] As the *Magna Moralia* puts it, "[the good man] is a lover-of-good [*philagathos*], not a lover-of-self [*philautos*]; for he loves himself only, if at all, because he is good" (II.14.1212b18–20). So if, as IX.4 suggests, the virtuous agent's attitudes toward his friends derives from his attitudes toward himself, he will not love his friends because they are his "other selves" in the sense that they are simply *like* him: he will love them, as he loves himself, because they are *good*. Any likeness they bear to him is a mere sign of what really matters – namely, their respective goodness.

Note, in support of this, that in listing what seem to be the constitutive conditions of *philia*, the closest Aristotle comes to mentioning sameness or even similarity of character is in (3), when he speaks of friends "choosing the same things." But this does not require friends to be the same or even similar in character. People who are radically different may choose the same objects – perhaps because they agree (in spite of their differences) on the goodness of those objects, or perhaps because (as we tend to think characteristic of friendship) each chooses some objects for the sake of the other in the sense that she chooses these objects primarily because they are what the *other* wants.

Nor does Aristotle mention *homonoia* among the candidates for constitutive conditions. He no doubt thinks that character-friends are both similar in character and like-minded. But he may think that such similarity and like-mindedness are more productive of *philia* than constitutive of it. Such similarity and agreement may also result from or be reinforced by the relationship. There is clearly a complicated nexus here. But let us recall the *Lysis*, where Socrates and his interlocutors failed to account for *philia* either in terms of similarities between the parties or in terms of dissimilarities: Socrates then suggests that they appeal instead to the idea of what is *oikeion* to the parties, but insists that they refuse to *reduce* talk of what is *oikeion* to talk of what is *similar*.

Let us turn, keeping this in mind, to Aristotle's initial description of character-friendship:

> Each [friend] is good both *haplōs* and *for his friend*. For good people are both good *haplōs* and beneficial to one another. And they are similarly pleasant. For good people are pleasant both *haplōs* and *to one another*. For each finds his own actions [*hai oikeiai praxeis*] and such [actions in general] [*hai toiautai*] pleasant, and [the actions] of good people are the same or similar [in kind] [*hai autai ē homoiai*]. (VIII.3.1156b12–17)

We are now in a position to see that "his own" may not quite capture what Aristotle intends: *oikeiai* might mean not (or not simply) that the actions are strictly speaking the agent's *own*, but rather (or also) that they are somehow *familiar* or even *appropriate* to him.

It is clear from Aristotle's reference to the proverbial potters that he does not think that everyone finds actions *like* her own pleasant (*EE* VII.1.1235a18–19). Those who compete in some arena are often *pained* when they see *others* performing the sort of actions they *enjoy* seeing *themselves* perform. Whether one is pained or pleased depends on whether one values the actions in question *for themselves*, in which case one is likely to take pleasure in such actions simply as such; or whether one values the actions *as means to some further end* (such as wealth or honor) for the sake of which one competes with others. The point about good agents is that they value virtuous action *for itself* and *not* (either not simply or not primarily) *insofar as it is their own*. So virtuous agents tend, as a matter of psychological fact, to be similarly pleased by their own and others' virtuous actions.

This is part of the point of IX.4's talk of the way in which the virtuous person's attitudes toward others are derived from her attitudes toward herself. Some would take Aristotle's derivation in a more linguistic way, as saying that we *call* a relationship *philia* whenever two parties exhibit toward one another the sort of attitudes that each of us, given our natural tendency to *self*-love, takes toward him- or herself. But we can make better sense of the overall argument if we read IX.4 as making instead (or perhaps in addition) a somewhat different and primarily psychological point: namely, that the attitudes constitutive of *philia* are derived, as a matter of psychological fact, from the attitudes constitutive of the virtuous person's love for herself. For much of the surrounding argument appeals to such psychological facts. And Aristotle's point seems to be (at least partly) that insofar as a genuinely virtuous person loves and values virtue simply as such, and so loves and values herself (at least partly) insofar as she is virtuous, the virtuous person will (as a matter of psychological fact) be disposed to love other virtuous persons on account of *their* virtues. This contributes to a puzzle Aristotle goes on to discuss in IX.8 – namely, whether one should (*dei*) love oneself, or someone else, most of all.[15]

Aristotle resolves this puzzle by rejecting the dichotomous assumption on which it turns: that one must *either* love oneself most of all *or* love someone else most of all. Once we accept his distinction between self-love properly construed and self-love as it is usually (but mistakenly) understood, we are supposed to see an important sense in which self-love properly construed is *impartial*: insofar as self-love properly construed involves the virtuous person's love for herself *qua virtuous*, and insofar as a genuinely virtuous agent will value virtue as such, the virtuous agent should love other virtuous agents in much the same way that she loves herself (i.e., *qua virtuous*). By the end of IX.8 the "most of all" has dropped out: Aristotle concludes by saying simply that one *should* love oneself in the proper sense but *not* in the vulgar sense. It is compatible with this that one should also love others in the proper sense, and even that one should love at least some others *equally* with oneself: perhaps this is how one should love one's "other selves."

This might be taken to suggest that the pleasure virtuous agents take in the virtuous actions of their friends (and perhaps even in the virtuous actions of strangers) is at least potentially equal to the pleasure they take in their own virtuous actions. But this does not follow. The point is that virtuous agents can sometimes take the same *kind* of pleasure in their own and others' virtuous actions. Other factors, especially epistemological ones, may limit the *extent* to which virtuous agents can appreciate (and so enjoy) the actions of others in the same way that they can appreciate (and so enjoy) their own. That Aristotle is aware of such factors is clear from his emphasis on the need for time and intimacy (*sunētheia*).

Aristotle has two related reasons for requiring intimacy – one epistemological and one hedonic. Their relation is clear from *Poetics* 4, where Aristotle calls humans the "most mimetic of animals" and says that all enjoy imitations: even in cases where seeing the objects themselves is painful – for example, with disgusting creatures or corpses – we enjoy viewing images of them because understanding is most pleasant, and in contemplating (*theōrountas*) such images we understand or work out what each is (1448b5–17). Aristotle speaks here of the sheer joy of recognition, which increases when the object is *kalon* – as, for example, when we witness virtuous actions and recognize them as such.

But matters are more complicated when it comes to observing *actions*. For superficially similar behaviors can result from radically different motives and can thus constitute radically different sorts of action. So we must know something about the *reasons* for which another acts, which involves having some knowledge of her *character*, before we are in a position to understand (and so enjoy) her actions in ways like those in which we typically understand (and so enjoy) our own. There are thus *epistemological* constraints on the extent to which a virtuous agent can *enjoy* the virtuous actions of others. But we should not forget that these are constraints on a kind of *enjoyment*. For this gets lost in Cooper's interpretation of IX.9, which emphasizes epistemological aspects of the character-friends' contemplation of one another's actions at the expense of hedonic ones.

10 *NE* IX.9: The *Lysis* Puzzle Revisited

NE IX.9 begins with a puzzle:

> [On the one hand] people say that those who are blessed and self-sufficient have no need of friends. For the good things [in life] belong to them, and being self-sufficient they will need nothing in addition. But the friend, being another self, [is one who] provides the things one is unable to get on one's own . . .
>
> [On the other hand] it seems strange, when assigning all good things to one who is *eudaimōn*, not to grant him friends, which seem to be the greatest of external goods . . . And it is strange to make the blessed person solitary. For no one would choose to have all good things by himself [*kath' hauton*]. For man is political and by nature such as to live with others. So this [i.e., living together with others] will belong to one who is *eudaimōn*. For he has all the things that are good by nature.

Aristotle proceeds to diagnose the error behind the first view while preserving the element of truth contained in it. Its proponents are right, he thinks, that the friend is an "other self." But they have the wrong conception of this: they think it means someone who provides one with goods one *cannot* provide for oneself. This is largely because they think of friends as *useful*. So they move illegitimately from the claim that the blessed person has no need of *such* friends (i.e., *utility* friends) to the conclusion that she has no need of *any* friends (1169b23–8).[16]

The rest of IX.9 aims to clarify the "other self" doctrine with a view to elucidating the sense in which (as the final sentence says) one who is going to be *eudaimōn* will need (*deēsei*) to have excellent friends. Many commentators have found Aristotle's arguments for this disappointing. But that may stem more from their failure to understand his intended conclusion than from his failure to provide adequate arguments for it.

Consider, for example, Cooper. Like others, he takes Aristotle to be asking a *justificatory* question analogous to the familiar "why be moral?" question. In his view, Aristotle seeks to provide reasons why someone who aims to flourish *should* arrange things "so that he becomes attached to certain people in the ways characteristic of friendship" (1999: 337). Cooper is thus troubled by the fact that the arguments Aristotle actually gives seem to answer a different and less interesting question: namely, why will someone who already has friends "need or want to do things for them or with them?" Cooper thinks the answer, which is primarily *explanatory* of the actual attitudes and tendencies of friends, is less interesting in two ways. First, it is too easy: for it simply follows from what it *means* to be a friend that one who has a friend will, as a matter of psychological fact, want to do things with and for her friend. Second, and more importantly, the answer begs the question why one who aims to flourish should have friends in the *first* place. So Cooper seeks to tease out of Aristotle's explicit arguments two implicit arguments that *justify* having friends in the first place.

Cooper turns for help to the *Magna Moralia*. For he takes *MM* II.15.1213a7–26 to argue that self-knowledge is *necessary* for *eudaimonia* and that character-friendship is the only (or at least the best) way to achieve self-knowledge. The idea there is that bias toward oneself prevents one from seeing clearly what one is really like; and that just as one needs to look into a mirror to see one's own face, so one needs to look upon someone similar in character to oneself in order to study one's own character. Cooper thinks the argument at *NE* IX.9.1169b18–1170a4 similar insofar as it claims first "that the good and flourishing man wants to study (*theōrein*, *NE* IX.9.1169b33, 1170a2; *theasasthai*, *MM* II.15.1213a16) good actions"; and second "that one cannot, or cannot so easily, study one's own actions as those of another."

But it may be significant that Aristotle describes the object of the virtuous agent's choice as, simply, to contemplate decent and appropriate *actions* (IX.9.1170a1–3): he does not suggest that the agent seeks primarily to contemplate her *own* actions. When he says that the virtuous agent will need virtuous friends if she chooses to study such actions (i.e., decent and appropriate ones), his point may be simply that she cannot (or cannot easily) contemplate her own actions, and so will have to get her contemplative pleasures (as distinct from her engaged pleasures) from observing the actions of others whose actions she is in a position to appreciate. His point need not have anything to do with her pursuit of self-knowledge.

The main obstacle to finding the *MM* argument in the *NE* is that where the *MM* talks about coming to know (*gnōnai*) oneself, the *NE* speaks of perception or awareness (*aisthēsis* or *sunaisthēsis*) of oneself. And one might be aware of oneself and one's own activities without knowing what they are really like. Cooper attempts to bridge the gap partly by rendering *theōrein* as "to study" rather than (as often appropriate) "to contemplate" or "to observe" (1999: 344 n13). He is effectively providing the contemplation of virtuous actions with an *end*: namely, the subject's acquisition of the kind of self-knowledge he takes Aristotle to view as a "prerequisite of flourishing" (1999: 345). But this makes the reason Aristotle gives for having friends more instrumental than I think Aristotle wants to allow. For it assimilates the value of having friends to the value of being honored.

On Cooper's account, we value decent friends insofar as they serve, like honor from decent people, to confirm our sense of our own worth. But Aristotle regards the value even of such honor as "more superficial" than the value he seeks in would-be components of *eudaimonia* (*NE* I.5.1095b22–6). And he explicitly contrasts the instrumental value of honor with the intrinsic value of both loving and being loved when he says that being loved is valued for itself in a way that being honored is not, and then cites the joy mothers take in loving, even when their love is not returned, as evidence that loving is even *more* valuable than being loved. So it seems unlikely that Aristotle would assimilate the value of having friends to the value of honor.

The second argument that Cooper teases out of IX.9 (from 1170a4–11) is similar to the first: he takes Aristotle's claim that it is easier to be continuously active in the company of friends than by oneself as resting partly on claims about the ways in which activities engaged in with those we respect provide "concrete and immediate" "confirmation of the worth" of our own pursuits (Cooper 1999: 346–8). But IX.9 seems to point in the opposite direction: its point is that contemplating the virtuous activity of one's character-friend is something good and pleasant *in itself*. And Aristotle may well have used *theōrein* precisely to capture the *intrinsic* value of the activity in question, as distinct from any instrumental value it might have. For *theōria* is his paradigm of an activity engaged in for itself.

Cooper mentions other ways in which Aristotle may think that sharing in activities with others serves to augment one's own activity. For example, the agent "can be said to be active – indirectly – whenever and wherever any of the group is at work." But this approximates Irwin's suggestion that Aristotle regards the activity of one's friend as an "extension" of one's own: where Irwin speaks of the ways in which having friends allows an agent "to realize *himself* more fully than [he would] if he had no friend" (1988: 393),[17] Cooper speaks of shared activities as "expand[ing] the scope of one's activity by enabling one to participate, through membership in a group of jointly active persons, in the actions of others" (1999: 349). So Cooper and Irwin seem in the end to share the same fundamental outlook. Each takes Aristotle to be concerned primarily with the *justificatory* question: why have friends in the *first* place?

Aristotle no doubt believes that someone who has good friends will realize herself more fully than she would if she had no friends. But if he allows this to serve as the agent's reason for having friends in the first place, he threatens to undermine the primacy of wishing and doing well to another for the *other's* sake. For even if having friends involves some sort of wishing them well for *their* sakes, it is problematic for the agent to take as her reason for having friends the fact that doing so is the only (or the best) way to achieve the sort of self-knowledge or self-realization in which *her eudaimonia* consists. But we *need not* read Aristotle as arguing in this way.

We could resolve Cooper's original problem by reading Aristotle *either* as less concerned with the justificatory project than Cooper takes him to be *or* as concerned with a somewhat weaker justificatory project than the one Cooper has in mind. For the explanatory arguments Aristotle gives may be more interesting than Cooper allows. Consider a context in which it is assumed that friendship involves conditions like wishing good to another for the other's sake but there are people who doubt that such conditions are ever – or can ever – be satisfied. In such contexts, there might be some point to *explaining* how it is *possible* for someone to take the same sort of intrinsic interest in another's good (or to derive the same sort of intrinsic enjoyment from another's activity) as she takes in her own good (or derives from her own activity). There might even be some point in arguing that virtuous agents are, as a matter of psychological fact, disposed to take this sort of interest in the good of other virtuous agents with whom they are acquainted and to derive this sort of enjoyment from the virtuous activities of those with whom they are intimate. For one could then argue that, given this tendency, a virtuous person who aims to flourish not only will but *should* have virtuous friends in the sense that there is *good reason* for her to do so: such friends are pleasant (and in that sense goods) to her. This provides a kind of justification for having friends that does not threaten the self-sufficiency of the would-be *eudaimōn*.

Note that the conclusion of IX.9 is open to stronger and weaker interpretations. For *deēsei* can be taken either (as Cooper and Irwin take it) as expressing a hard "must" or (as I suggest) as expressing a somewhat softer "should" (as forms of *dei* are often taken in surrounding contexts).[18] If Aristotle is following Socrates' lead, and seeking to establish the *possibility* of a kind of love that is based not in the subject's needs but rather in her appreciation of the object's positive qualities, then "should" may better capture his thought than does "must" or "needs."

11 Contemplative (versus Engaged) Pleasures

The *eudaimōn* agent *should* have excellent friends, but *not* because she *needs* to. She *should* have them in the same sense in which she *should* contemplate or engage in virtuous action. Each of these activities is an *appropriate* response to ways the world is: contemplation is an appropriate response to the wonders of nature or the beauty of mathematical truth; and virtuous action is an appropriate response to (for example) the needs of others. Similarly, wishing another's good for her sake is an *appropriate* response to the recognized virtues of another, a response that is (as a matter of psychological fact) characteristic of virtuous agents and that tends (as a matter of psychological fact) to lead – with time, intimacy and mutual recognition – to character-friendship.

In saying that such activities – i.e., friendship, contemplation, and virtuous action – are *appropriate* responses to ways the world is, I aim to challenge the tendency of some commentators to represent the would-be *eudaimōn* as engaging in these activities primarily *qua* forms of *self*-realization. For even if the agent's self-realization (or *eudaimonia*) consists in engaging in such activities, the nature of these activities may be such that an agent can engage in them and so realize herself (or achieve *eudaimonia*) *only if* she engages in them *for themselves* and *not qua* forms of self-realization.[19] The idea that I should wish-well-to-another-for-*her*-sake *qua* form of my *own* self-realization – or *because* doing so is a component of *my eudaimonia* – is not only morally but also conceptually problematic. For to the extent that I do what I do *qua* form of self-realization, it seems that I fail to do it *for itself*. And I take Aristotle's requirement that we choose virtuous actions *for themselves*, along with his requirement that we wish our friends well for *their* sakes, to be incompatible with the view that our primary reason for engaging in such activities is that doing so is a form of self-realization.

But some commentators seem to read the following lines as saying that the activities in which my friend's being consists are choiceworthy *for me* in the same way that the activities in which my *own* being consists are choiceworthy *for me* – i.e., as forms of my own self-realization: "As the excellent person stands to himself, so he stands to his friend, for his friend is another himself.[20] So just as his own being is choiceworthy for each, so also (or nearly so) is the being of his friend [choiceworthy for him]" (IX.9.1170b5–8). So we need to examine these lines in context.

These lines state the conclusion of an argument that runs from 1170a25 to 1170b8. But we should begin back at 1170a13, where Aristotle makes it clear that he is once again arguing *phusikōteron* – i.e., by appeal to natural psychological facts. Aristotle then identifies the activities in which human *life*, and so human *being*, consists – i.e. perceiving and thinking – and explains that he is talking about the life of someone who is good, since such a life is determinate (*hōrismenon*), and not about the life of the vicious or corrupted person, or a life full of pain, since such lives are indeterminate (*ahoristos*). We shall return shortly to these puzzling remarks. We must first survey the argument they introduce.

> *If* [a] [such] living[21] is itself good and pleasant . . . and [b] the one seeing perceives [*aisthanetai*] that he sees, and the one hearing [perceives] that he hears, and the one walking [perceives] that he walks, and similarly in the case of other activities there is something perceiving that we are acting, so that if we perceive, we perceive that we perceive, and if we think, [we perceive] that we think; and [c] [perceiving] that we perceive or think is perceiving that we exist . . . and [d] to perceive that one lives is one of the things pleasant in itself (for living is by nature good, and to perceive what is good belonging in oneself is pleasant); and [e] living is choiceworthy above all to good people, because being is good for them and pleasant [as well] (for they are pleased when they are aware of [*sunaisthanomenoi*] what is good in itself); and [f] as the excellent person stands to himself, so he stands to his friend (for his friend is another self), *then* [g] just as his own being is choiceworthy for each, so also (or nearly so) is the being of his friend [choiceworthy for him]. (1170a25–b8)

Hardie – presumably relying on Cartesian assumptions about the privacy of our own thoughts – objects that "the weak link in the argument [of IX.9] lies in the claim that a friend is an *alter ego* in the sense that we can be aware of his thoughts as we can be aware of our own" (1980: 332). But even were it obligatory for Aristotle to grant the Cartesian assumptions, there is no reason to suppose that he must be flouting them. For he says at 1170b10 that awareness (*sunaisthēsis*) of the life-constituting activities of one's friend requires living together and *sharing in conversation and thought*, and he may well require this precisely *because* he recognizes that we do not have the sort of privileged access to the thoughts of another that we have to our own. But Aristotle is not a Cartesian, so he may even think that a person can come to know what she *herself* thinks only through sharing in conversation and thought with others. If so, he may well assimilate a person's awareness of what her friend thinks to her awareness of what she herself thinks, which would yield something like the *MM* argument for the role of friends in achieving self-knowledge.

But Aristotle's point in IX.9 is different. Here, he emphasizes the *pleasure* taken both in our awareness of our own activities and in our awareness of our friend's activities. The key to understanding this lies in seeing that his puzzling remarks about determinacy and indeterminacy point (as X.3's discussion of pleasure points) to views expressed in Plato's *Philebus*. The relevance of the *Philebus* should be clear. For the *Philebus* is structured around questions about the sufficiency of various candidates for *eudaimonia* or "the good." Socrates' argument is, roughly, that neither pleasure by itself nor intelligence by itself can be *the good*, since the conjunction of pleasure and intelligence is better than either of these taken alone, whereas *the good* is *teleion* and sufficient in the sense that it cannot be improved – as either pleasure or intelligence can be improved – by the addition of other goods. Aristotle is running a similar argument about having friends: if an otherwise happy life can be improved by the addition of friends, then a life without friends cannot be *the good*.

But the relevance of the *Philebus* extends far beyond this. "Intelligence" stands there for a range of cognitive capacities or states, including memory, knowledge, and opinion. And Socrates argues there that a life of pleasure without any of these cognitive states is less good than a life of pleasure that involves these states:

> without memory, it would be impossible for you to remember that you had ever enjoyed yourself or for any pleasure to survive from one moment to the next . . . and without true opinion, you would not realize that you were enjoying yourself even when you were; and being deprived of reasoning, you would not be able to reason about how you might enjoy the future; [you would be] living a life not of a human being but of a jellyfish or some one of the encrusted creatures living in the sea. (21c).

Socrates' point is not simply that (as with rudimentary somatic pleasures) pleasure *plus* awareness of it is better than pleasure taken alone. There are (at least) two further points.[22]

First, in the case of more sophisticated pleasures – such as those involved in writing a poem, doing a mathematical proof, or helping a friend – the first-order activities in which the pleasure is taken themselves involve cognition, typically of things apart from the agent's activity and the pleasure taken in it, things such as the meanings, sounds, and rhythms of words, the nature of mathematical truth, or the needs of others. It follows from this, in a way important to Aristotle's argument, that these activities require the agent's attention to be directed *outwards*, toward such things.

Second, a subject's higher-order awareness of these activities and their value is *itself* pleasant in ways that depend on the subject's cognitively loaded appreciation of them: she must *recognize* what is being done and *appreciate* the value of doing *that*. Suppose, for example, that I talk in my sleep, always in verse, and my partner records and publishes my poems under a pseudonym. Suppose further that I do not recognize the products as my own or have any independent appreciation of them. (Perhaps I was punished for versifying as a child and have, consciously at least, forsworn all such activity. And now, having been to college, I regard such verse as an objectionably anachronistic genre, so I write reviews attacking these poems.) Suppose further that these poems are great works, so widely appreciated that the Nobel Prize committee would like to be able to identify their author. Now compare the value *to me* of the mere activity of producing these poems to the value *to me* of the activity of producing the same poems in full awareness of what I am doing and with appreciation of the value of doing that: however good these poems are, and however good *haplōs* their production is, the activity of producing them will not be a good *to me* if I am neither aware of what I am doing nor appreciative of its value.

Or suppose I am depressed and operating on "automatic pilot." Because I have promised to teach a disadvantaged child to read, I go through the motions, showing up weekly and contributing (as a matter of fact) greatly to her progress, all the while thinking how pointless the whole business is and wishing I had not made the promise in the first place. Here again, what I am doing may be good for *her*, and even good *haplōs*; but it will not have the sort of value *to me* that it would have if I were both aware of what I was doing – namely, opening up new worlds for her – and appreciative of the value of doing that. We can, of course, distinguish *awareness* of what I am doing from *appreciation* of it: I may be aware that I am writing rock music, but (having read Allan Bloom) be ashamed of what I am doing. The point here is that awareness *without* appreciation is less good *to me* than awareness *with* appreciation (justified, of course, by the value of my activity).

These two points apply as much, via memory and anticipation, to past and future activities as to present ones; and, as I take Aristotle to be arguing in IX.9, as much, via intimacy, to the appreciation of my friend's activities as to my own. For the argument quoted above is roughly that my appreciative awareness of my *friend's* activity serves (if my friend's activity is good) to *make* my friend's activity a good *to me* in much the same way that my appreciative awareness of my own activity serves (if my activity is good) to *make* my own activity a good *to me*. The two are not exactly alike, since my own activities would not in general *be* the kinds of activities they are, nor have the kinds of value they have, independently of *my* appreciation of them as such, whereas my friend's activities may *be* the kinds of activities they are, and have the kinds of value they have, independently of *my* appreciation of them as such (though *not* independently of *her* appreciation of them as such). But the point remains that there is a distinction between the value *haplōs* of an activity, and the value of that activity *to* (or *for*) any given subject, including its agent but not necessarily limited to its agent. To the extent that intimacy allows me to appreciate another's activity in something like the way I appreciate my own, her activity can come to have *to* (or *for*) me some of the kind of value my own activity typically has *to* (or *for*) me in virtue of my (admittedly constitutive) appreciation of it.[23]

The pleasures associated with such appreciation depend on their subject's beliefs about the value of their objects and are a sign of what their subject values. And while we can (and often do) take pleasure in the sight of things we take to be instrumental means to things we value for themselves, Aristotle's point in IX.9 seems to be about the sort of intrinsic pleasure we take in the sight of things we value for themselves. This is the sort of pleasure the genuinely virtuous agent experiences both when she performs virtuous actions and when she sees others performing virtuous actions and recognizes them as such.

But Aristotle seems to think that there are special difficulties involved in contemplating one's *own* activities. His point may be partly that one can no more readily observe oneself engaging in virtuous action than one could before the rise of video-cameras observe oneself wrestling. So his point may be partly that one can get the sort of pleasure involved in *observing* virtuous actions only where the virtuous actions of *others* are in play. But he may also be thinking of a deeper problem here, one not amenable to technological resolution.

He may be thinking about the ways in which contemplating one's own virtuous activity as such can *impede* that activity. Contemplating one's own activity in progress may prevent one from focusing outwards in ways required by such activity, and so prevent one from seeing and doing what one ought to do. And even contemplation after the fact – if, for example, one were to watch videos of oneself performing virtuous actions – might reflect a kind of self-indulgence incompatible with genuine virtue. But there is no such problem in contemplating, even with great admiration, the virtuous actions of *others*. For my admiration of another's activity need not interfere with her activity nor undermine *its* status as virtuous.

I say "need not" because the other's desire for admiration *might* tempt her to do the sorts of things virtuous persons do, but not *as* the virtuous person does them – i.e., not for themselves and with her attention focused, as it should be, on the needs of others or on what justice requires et cetera. That is why I must *really* know her, in order to know *what* she is doing, if I am to appreciate (and so enjoy) her actions in anything like the way I can (absent self-deception) appreciate (and so enjoy) my own. But if I *do* know her, it may be far easier to achieve contemplative enjoyment of her actions than to achieve contemplative enjoyment of my own. So Aristotle's point may have less to do with the difficulty of self-knowledge than with the difficulty of finding *contemplative* enjoyment in one's own actions, which typically require one's attention to be focused elsewhere.

Reading Aristotle this way allows us to explain his emphasis on pleasure in ways that Cooper's interpretation does not. It also helps to explain why Aristotle associates pleasure-friendship so closely with character-friendship. For even in relationships where virtuous activity is not the principal source of the pleasure the parties find in one another's company, each party may be disposed to take some of the same sort of pleasure in the other's activities as she takes in her own. Each may be disposed, for example, to enjoy the other's athletic victories, or the other's musical accomplishments, *for themselves*. And this may lead each to promote the *other's* activities *not* as extensions of her own, or as forms of (her own) self-realization, but rather *for themselves*.

12 Conclusion: Eudaimonism Revisited

Insofar as my friend's activities are constitutive of her *eudaimonia*, I am, of course – *in* promoting her activities *for themselves* – promoting her *eudaimonia* for *itself*. And while it may also be true that I am, in doing so, *realizing* my own *eudaimonia*, this is *not* the reason *why* I promote her activities, at least not if I am a genuine friend: I do so simply because I value her activities *for themselves*. So the fact that I am *realizing* my own *eudaimonia* does *not* require us to say that I am acting for the *sake* of my *eudaimonia*.

In sum, we need not read the "eudaimonist axiom" as requiring that all actions be performed ultimately for the sake of the agent's *own eudaimonia*: for Aristotle's account of *philia* shows how, given human nature, it is *possible* to act directly for the sake of *another's eudaimonia*. His account of *philia* thus serves to rescue the ethical credentials of his eudaimonism: there is no need to read it as a form of rational egoism. As Aristotle himself says of those who would assimilate the motivations of benefactors to those of creditors, "Epicharmus would perhaps say" that those who read Aristotle as a rational egoist may do so because they read him "from a base point of view" (IX.7.1167b25–7).

Notes

1　*Pace* Cooper (1977a: n5); reprinted, with Cooper's (1977b), in his *Reason and Emotion* (1999), to which I henceforth refer. I am much indebted to these two canonical papers, which are efficiently combined (for less specialist readers) in Cooper (1980). For more on linguistic (and other) issues, see Konstan (1997).

2　Vlastos defends the traditional rendering of *eudaimonia* as "happiness" (1991: 200–203). This is potentially misleading because modern conceptions of happiness tend to be more subjectivist than Aristotle's conception of *eudaimonia*. So "flourishing" (used by Cooper) or "well-being" is sometimes preferred. I prefer simply to use the Greek.

3　Irwin (1988: 614 n6, 391–7). For criticism of this "colonizing ego" view, see Whiting (1991).

4　The issue of egoism in Aristotle is well discussed in Kraut (1989).

5　This is distinct from the familiar point that pleasure-friendships are closer to character-friendships than utility-friendships are. I take the label "character-friendship" from Cooper (1999).

6　See especially the notes to VIII.2 and IX.5 in Irwin (1999).

7　Aristotle does not specify his opponents here, but the mistake sounds Academic. Perhaps Plato himself proposed this restriction.

8   On *dia* (best rendered "on account of") see section 7.

9   Or perhaps "*must* belong" (discussed below).

10 Irwin's (1999) translation elides the alleged distinction: "The defining features of *friendship* that are found in friendships toward one's neighbors would seem to be derived from features of friendship toward oneself." Irwin also removes the potentially significant plural in Aristotle's talk of the features "by which *friendships* are defined." But the plural may indicate that Aristotle takes himself to be talking about more than one kind of *philia*.

11 *Sunesis* is what *Republic* 376 says dogs have when they recognize people as *oikeion* (familiar) or *allotrion* (alien): it is a kind of *comprehending perception*, which is what is needed to engender a child's fondness for its parents.

12 The point here is *not* (as Ross and Irwin render it) that mothers tend to love their children *more than fathers do*: the thrust of this argument (as distinct from that in IX.7) is that parents (at least initially) tend to love their children *more than their children love them*. If mothers are suddenly singled out here, that may be because Aristotle thinks (for reasons cited in IX.7) that mothers tend to love their children more than fathers do.

13 I do *not* take the fact that Aristotle sometimes *expresses* ethnocentric (and other) biases to show that he *endorses* such bias. He may simply fail (like most of us) to recognize his own biases for what they are. For more on the ethocentric – or character-centered – ideal, see Whiting (1991).

14 For detailed analysis of IX.8, which I cannot provide here, see Whiting (1996).

15 Note (for future reference) that *dei* is here rendered "should" by Ross and Rowe, and "ought to" by Irwin.

16 I take "such friends" (*tōn toioutōn philōn*) in b27 to refer back to *tōn toioutōn* in b24, and read the intervening remarks about pleasure-friendship as parenthetical.

17 See, more generally, sections 197–215 of Irwin (1988).

18 See above, note 15.

19 For more detailed argument, see Whiting (2002).

20 "Another himself" is Irwin's rendering of "*heteros . . . autos*"; Ross and Rowe each say "another self."

21 That is, the sort he has just specified, not that of someone who is corrupted or whose life is full of pain.

22 I am much indebted, throughout this section, to the second chapter of Bobonich (2002).

23 The depression example shows that there may be cases where my intimate can have the relevant sort of awareness even when I do not. But that is not a problem for Aristotle, who surely takes himself to rely on premises that hold only "for the most part."

References

Bobonich, Christopher 2002: *Plato's Utopia Recast: His Later Ethics and Politics*. Oxford: Oxford University Press.

Broadie, S. and Rowe, C. 2002: *Aristotle: Nicomachean Ethics*. Oxford: Oxford University Press (introduction and commentary by S. Broadie and translation by C. Rowe).

Cooper, John 1977a: "Aristotle on the Forms of Friendship," *Review of Metaphysics* 30: 619–48; reprinted in John Cooper, *Reason and Emotion: Essays on Ancient Moral*

Psychology and Ethical Theory, pp. 312–35. Princeton, NJ: Princeton University Press, 1999. All citations follow pagination of reprint.

— 1977b: "Friendship and the Good in Aristotle," *Philosophical Review* 86: 290–315; reprinted in John Cooper, *Reason and Emotion: Essays on Ancient Moral Psychology and Ethical Theory*, pp. 336–55. Princeton, NJ: Princeton University Press, 1999. All citations follow pagination of reprint.

— 1980: "Aristotle on Friendship." In A. O. Rorty (ed.), *Essays on Aristotle's Ethics*, pp. 301–40. Berkeley, CA: University of California Press.

— 1999: *Reason and Emotion: Essays on Ancient Moral Psychology and Ethical Theory*. Princeton, NJ: Princeton University Press.

Hardie, W. F. R. 1980: *Aristotle's Ethical Theory*, 2nd edn. Oxford: Clarendon Press.

Irwin, Terence 1988: *Aristotle's First Principles*. Oxford: Oxford University Press.

— 1999: *Aristotle: Nicomachean Ethics*, 2nd edn. Indianapolis, IN: Hackett.

Konstan, David 1997: *Friendship in the Classical World*. Cambridge: Cambridge University Press.

Kraut, Richard 1989: *Aristotle on the Human Good*. Princeton, NJ: Princeton University Press.

Ross, W. D. 1980: *The Nicomachean Ethics*. Oxford: Oxford University Press. This is a revised version of Ross's translation, originally published by Oxford in 1925. The revised version is also available in vol. 2 of Jonathan Barnes (ed.), *The Complete Works of Aristotle*. Princeton, NJ: Princeton University Press, 1984.

Vlastos, Gregory 1991: *Socrates: Ironist and Moral Philosopher*. Ithaca, NY: Cornell University Press.

Whiting, Jennifer 1991: "Impersonal Friends," *The Monist* 74: 3–29.

— 1996: "Self-love and Authoritative Virtue: A Prolegomenon to a Kantian Reading of *Eudemian Ethics* viii 3." In S. Engstrom and J. Whiting (eds), *Aristotle, Kant, and the Stoics: Rethinking Happiness and Duty*, pp. 162–99. Cambridge: Cambridge University Press.

— 2002: "*Eudaimonia*, External Results, and Choosing Virtuous Actions for Themselves," *Philosophy and Phenomenological Research* 65: 270–90.

Further reading

Cooper, John 1990: "Political Animals and Civic Friendship." In G. Patzig (ed.), *Aristoteles "Politik,"* pp. 221–41. Göttingen: Vandenhoeck and Ruprecht; reprinted in John Cooper, *Reason and Emotion: Essays on Ancient Moral Psychology and Ethical Theory*, pp. 356–77. Princeton, NJ: Princeton University Press, 1999.

Pakaluk, Michael 1998: *Aristotle: Nicomachean Ethics Books VIII and IX*. Oxford: Clarendon Press.

Price, A.W. 1989: *Love and Friendship in Plato and Aristotle*. Oxford: Clarendon Press.

Stern-Gillet, Suzanne 1995: *Aristotle's Philosophy of Friendship*. Albany, NY: State University of New York Press.

14

Aristotle's Political Ethics

Malcolm Schofield

1 Ethical Politics

The *Nicomachean Ethics* is framed by a beginning (*NE* I.1–3) and an ending (*NE* X.9) which, in rather different ways, communicate a single message: *politics* is the activity and branch of study that deals with the subject matter of the work. For us, ethics and politics signify two distinct, if overlapping, spheres. For Aristotle, there is just one sphere – politics – conceived in ethical terms. This startling truth is generally downplayed (if not totally ignored) in many presentations of the *Nicomachean Ethics*. Seeing that, and in what sense, it is true, and why its truth is important for understanding not only Aristotle's project as a whole but also many of its key theses, is the challenge taken on in this chapter.

A good place to start is Aristotle's summary later in Book I of the upshot of the opening section: "We stated that the chief good is the goal of politics; and it devotes most of its concern and effort to making the citizens be of a certain kind, viz. good and capable of fine deeds" (*NE* I.9.1099b29–32). When he turns a little later to the topic of virtue he amplifies the thesis:

> The true politician [i.e. the person possessed of real political understanding] is thought to have put most of his effort into studying virtue. For he wants to make the citizens good and obedient to the laws. As an example of this we have the lawgivers of the Cretans and the Spartans, and any others there may have been with the same concerns. (*NE* I.13.1102 a7–12)

Three comments: (1) If making people good is the principal job politics needs to undertake, then it is obvious that (as Aristotle says) the study of virtue, i.e. getting clear about what goodness consists in, has to be at least a main ingredient in the intellectual effort a politician makes in preparing himself for his task – at any rate if he wants to act on the basis of understanding, not just his prejudices. The *NE* is a work well designed to supply that need for understanding. It is devoted mostly to a treatment of virtue and the virtues. Its very title expresses this focus on virtue, as good *state of character* (*ēthos*). The last chapter of Book I – where Aristotle makes the second of the two remarks just quoted – in fact performs the transition from the opening discussions of happiness as the chief good to the rest of the treatise, and most immediately to the general account of virtue in Book II. Aristotle's comment about the politician is offered as one reason why virtue has to be his chief topic, and also explains why in the *Rhetoric* he speaks of ethics as "the enquiry regarding matters of character which is rightly designated politics" (*Rhet.* I.2.1356a26–7).

(2) If we ask *how* politicians are to make the citizens good, we get a hint of Aristotle's answer in the phrase "obedient to the laws." He begins the final chapter of the whole work by observing that with goodness (as with other practical matters) "it is not sufficient to *know* about it – people must make the attempt to possess and employ it." The goal in this sphere is *doing* things (*NE* X.9.1179b2–3). This thought leads him into reflections on the stock topic of the role of nature, teaching, and habituation in the acquisition of virtue. The importance of laws for the business of habituation quickly becomes apparent. For example:

> Before someone can acquire goodness there is a sense in which they must already have a character akin to it – one that is attracted by what is fine and repulsed by what is shameful. But it is hard for people to get the right upbringing directed towards goodness, from childhood on, if they have not been brought up under *laws* that promote it (for the average person a life of restraint and endurance is not pleasant, especially in childhood). So it is by *laws* that their upbringing and patterns of behavior must be ordered, since that sort of life won't be irksome to them if they have got used to it. (*NE* X.9.1179b29–1180a1)

This chimes with earlier remarks Aristotle has made about the particular interest politics must take in the way in which someone with a good character copes with pleasure and pain (*NE* II.3.1105a10–12, VII.11.1152b1–3). But habituation to practice of the right kind of behavior is not just something for children. Aristotle argues that adults are in similar need. So we shall need appropriate laws to promote virtuous behavior in adults, too – in fact, laws covering "the whole of life." Aristotle takes the view that "only in Sparta, or a few other places" has the lawgiver "given sufficiently careful attention to upbringing and patterns of behavior" (*NE* X.9.1180a24–6). But he supposes that *everywhere* laws are concerned with restraining people from morally undesirable behavior, "ordering us to do some things and forbidding others" more or less appropriately according as they are correctly or less well framed (*NE* V.1.1129b19–25). Of course, for many people it is the fear of the punishments prescribed by law that makes them behave decently rather than voluntary internalization of its norms (cf. *NE* X.9.1179b10–16, 1180a4–5), but even in that case the compulsion of law is less resented than would be the dictates of an individual, since it is "reason proceeding from a kind of wisdom and understanding" (*NE* X.9.1180a18–24).

(3) As examples of the "true politician," Aristotle instances "the lawgivers of the Cretans and the Spartans." And as (2) already leads us to expect, it will be by making legislation the prime business of politics that he will be able to indicate the way "it devotes most of its concern and effort to making the citizens good." Needless to say, this was not how everyone in Aristotle's time thought of politics. In a passage we shall be discussing in section 2.3, he comments on the issue in *NE* Book VI:

> Political understanding and practical wisdom are the same state of mind, but their essence is not the same. Of the practical wisdom concerned with the city, the architectonic form is legislative understanding, while the form comparable to particular instances of a universal is what is known by the name common to them both, "political": this has to do with action and deliberation, for a resolution [i.e. of a council or an assembly], as the outcome of deliberation, is something requiring action. That is why people say that they [i.e. those politicians involved in deliberation and consequent action] are the only ones engaged in politics, because they are the only ones who "do things" – in the same way that artisans "do things" [i.e. as opposed to master builders]. (*NE* VI.8.1141b23–9)

The identification of the lawgiver as the sort of politician who commands a strategic and directive understanding comparable to that of the *architectōn* or master builder takes us right back to the beginning of Book I:

> The chief good would seem to be the object of the most authoritative form of knowledge, and the one that is most architectonic. And that seems to be the knowledge characteristic of politics. For it is this which ordains what other forms of knowledge should be studied in cities, and which each class of citizens should learn and up to what point. And we see even the most highly esteemed of capacities subordinated to it – e.g. generalship, household administration, oratory [cf. *Rhet.* I.2.1356a26–8, I.3.1359b10]. So since politics [i.e. in this strategic sense] uses the other forms of knowledge, and since again it legislates as to what we are to do and what we are to keep away from, the goal aimed at by this form of knowledge will include that of the others. Hence it is politics which has as its goal the human good. (*NE* I.2.1094a26–b7)

At this point we might want to ask: *why* does "the most authoritative form" of practical wisdom have to be politics, i.e. "legislative understanding?" If an ordinary person has a practical understanding not focused on legislation, why should that not be authoritative for that individual because architectonic or strategic so far as his or her own pattern of activities is concerned? Aristotle has already anticipated this line of objection:

> The human good is in fact the same for an individual and a city. But it is apparent that achieving and preserving the good of the city is something greater and more

complete. While to secure the good is satisfactory enough for one person on their own, for a nation or for cities it is finer and more divine. (*NE* I.2.1094b7–10)

Or to put it a bit differently, the human good both is and is not the same for an individual and a city. In each case, it is happiness or human fulfillment – for one person or for the members of the population at large. But given the choice of achieving and preserving the happiness of the population at large rather than just one's own, it is plain that the first option represents a greater good, something we would prefer to pursue as our goal. It is finer, more admirable; more the sort of thing a providential god would have arranged.

If the principal proper subject of politics is ethics, why does Aristotle write an entire separate treatise entitled *Politics* – a work which appears to operate with a rather different understanding of what politics is? The *Politics* certainly envisages making citizens "good and capable of fine deeds" as a fundamental purpose of a good city (for example, *Pol.* III.9.1280b5–12, 1281a2–4, VII.13.1332a7–38), although its overall emphasis is on their attainment of happiness and the good life (for example, *Pol.* III.9.1280b39–1281a2, VII.13.1331b24–1332a7). But it is a political work primarily in the straightforward sense that it studies the *polis* – the city – as the most complete and important kind of human community, and in particular *politeia* – social and political systems, or more narrowly constitutions. For what *politeia* a city has – democracy, oligarchy, or some other – makes all the difference as to whether it is capable of achieving the good life.

In the concluding section of *NE* Book X, Aristotle says some things which explain the relationship between politics conceived as that kind of enterprise and politics as legislation. Given his specification of legislation as the means whereby the politician will try to make the citizens good, it comes as no surprise to find him approaching the need for a work on "constitutions" – the principal subject of the *Politics* – *via* a proposal for a general study of legislation. He indicates a reason for undertaking such a project (*NE* X.9.1180b28–1181b15). Successful lawgiving and the ability to assess the merits of particular legislation are largely a matter of experience, just as people learn to be skilled in medicine not by reading the textbooks, but by practicing as doctors. Nonetheless, collections of remedies and suggestions about how different sorts of patients should be treated are thought to be useful for those with the relevant experience. Similarly, collections of laws and constitutions could be useful to those who have the ability to study and judge what is good or bad in them, and what provisions suit what sorts of city. Even those who lack it might perhaps come to comprehend these things better. Aristotle ends by complaining that his predecessors have left the field of legislation uninvestigated. It is time for a proper examination. Without it, philosophical inquiry into things human will be incomplete.

Anybody who has waded through Plato's *Laws* may be forgiven for feeling some surprise at this claim about previous work on the subject. I suspect, however, that what Aristotle missed in the *Laws* – and what provokes his criticism – is its failure to adopt an empirical approach to the subject, or to provide precisely the kind of survey of existing laws and constitutions he has just been mentioning. Certainly, he makes it clear that his own work in this field is to be based on "the collected constitutions." We know what he had in mind. The ancient catalogues of Aristotle's writings list such a collection, consisting (according to the more reliable versions) of accounts of the constitutions of 158 cities. These are generally presumed to have been the work of his school, even if he himself had a hand in preparing some of them. Only one of the 158 survives, the *Constitution of the Athenians*, preserved more or less intact on papyrus rolls acquired for the British Museum from an Egyptian source in 1888–9. It contains a history of the changes to which the Athenian constitution had been subject from the earliest times to the restoration of democracy in 403 BC, followed by an analysis of the constitution in the author's own day. The assumption underlying the massive research project required to compile the collection was apparently that only by this means would it be possible to acquire the evidence needed for solid explanations of what makes a constitution and its legislative provisions successful or not. For Aristotle says that he will try to use the collection "to study what sorts of things preserve and destroy cities, and likewise the particular kinds of constitutions, and what causes some cities to conduct their political life well, others badly" (*NE* X.9.1181b17–20). And if we now turn to the *Politics*, we find that it does in fact contain material corresponding precisely to what this passage promises. Book V is a treatment of what causes the preservation and destruction of constitutions; and it makes frequent reference to practices and incidents in a wide range of Greek cities (and among non-Greek peoples too).

NE Book X ends with a statement of the ultimate destination to which such a causal account will lead: "When we have studied these matters we will perhaps get a better overview of the question of what sort of constitution is best, and how each should be organized and what laws and customs it must use if it is to be at its best. So let us make a beginning on the discussion" (*NE* X.9.1181b20–23). The intention is thus to return in the end from study of constitutions to the architectonic project of legislation which is the prime function of the true politician. The later books of the *Politics* do in a sense work out the prospectus Aristotle offers in the statement just quoted. This may indeed explain why they are placed as they are at the end of the treatise, after the treatment of what preserves and destroys constitutions in Book V. Book VI discusses how democracy and oligarchy can be constructed for greater stability, and Books VII and VIII what conditions and provisions would be needed to achieve the ideal city and to produce for it an ideal aristocracy. Finally – something of vital importance in the light of the *Nicomachean Ethics'* identification of legislation as the main task of true politics – the later chapters of Book VII (13–17) and all of the incomplete Book VIII are specifically concerned with the laws and customs necessary for educating citizens for virtue. In beginning the discussion, the last section of *Politics* VII.13 introduces a trichotomy of nature, reason, and habituation – as the things that make people become good – which more or less mirrors the trichotomy of *NE* X.9 (*Pol.* VII.13.1332a38–b11; *NE* X.9.1179b20–1180b28). What follows is paradoxically highly reminiscent of the *Laws*, both in its assumption of the need for a high degree of social regulation by the city and in its specific legislative provisions.

Not that there should be any real surprise about this. The ideal city and constitution of Book VII, for which the laws and customs Aristotle now prescribes are devised, is itself a close cousin of Plato's Cretan polity in the *Laws*. The very idea that the true politician seeks above all to "make the citizens good" is fundamental to the political philosophy of the *Laws* (for example, *Laws* I.630C–631A, IV.705D–706A, VI.770C–E, XII.963A); and when Aristotle infers that this calls for the study of human virtue by the politician, and consequently for knowledge at an appropriate level of "things to do with the soul" (*NE* I.13.1102a13–26), here too he is simply following Books I and XII of the *Laws* (Book I concludes with a statement of the huge importance of "knowing the natures and conditions of souls" as a task for political understanding [*Laws* I.650B]). The legislation at the end of the *Politics* bears the same pedigree. Like Plato at the start of the *Laws*, Aristotle begins by arguing that educating people for peace and leisure, not war (as at Sparta), must be the prime objective (*Pol.* VII.14–15). Like Plato, he gives prominence to rules governing marriage and the rearing of young children (*Pol.* VII.16–17). As in the *Laws*, communal arrangements for physical training and for musical performance, conceived as key ingredients in the moral education of children and adolescents, are a predominating theme (*Pol.* VIII).

These chapters therefore round off the project of ethical politics launched in the very first pages of the *Nicomachean Ethics*, as further elaborated in the account of the lawgiver's educational role in chapter 9 of Book X. Scholars have sometimes suggested that the last paragraph of the *NE* simply does not supply a "recognizable synopsis" of the *Politics*. Some have concluded from this that Aristotle there looks forward to a new version of the *Politics*, in the event never realized, or to a different kind of treatise altogether. It seems better to suppose that the remarks he makes at the end of the *NE* are intended not as a synopsis, but as a characterization of the *Politics* we actually have from a particular point of view – one which explains the focus on the later rather than the earlier books. It is presented as analogous to a medical textbook: offering general but practical guidance, based on case studies, to the practitioner, and concluding with an account of "what laws and customs a constitution must use" (*NE* X.9.1181b22). The *NE* and *Politics* alike are best interpreted as writings that are addressed not to individuals in their private capacities, but to someone who is or aspires to be a politician – that is to say, a lawgiver.

2 Political Dimensions of Virtue

Does the goodness that the true politician is to cause citizens to acquire have political dimensions itself? Or are goodness and the happiness of a life lived virtuously conceived in terms which, while not in any crude sense egoistic, make no indispensable appeal to the city or the sphere of the political? In this section, I shall bring together a range of evidence – mostly from the *NE*, but some from the *Politics* – confirming that for Aristotle the humanness of the good and the happiness and the virtue with which the *NE* is preoccupied are things essentially social and political. I shall be concentrating on the way in which he works this out in his treatment of just three topics: self-sufficiency, the general virtue of justice, and practical wisdom. But there are, in fact, a huge number of passages where it comes home to the reader that Aristotle takes it for granted that the city is the major forum in which life, and therefore the good life, is lived. The assumption permeates the books on justice and friendship in particular, but is also operative – as we shall glimpse in section 2.2 below – in the treatment of other virtues. As Ross's (1925) translation puts it with customary Aristotelian pithiness: "man is born for citizenship" (*NE* I.7.1097b11).

2.1 The self-sufficiency of the good life

Aristotle's remark about the political potential and tendency of human nature occurs in the course of his discussion of the different criteria that mark out the chief good, notably the requirements that it be chosen for itself, never for the sake of something else, and that it be something "self-sufficient" – that is to say, "what just on its own account makes life desirable and lacking in nothing" (*NE* I.7.1097b14–15). Here is how he introduces the section on self-sufficiency, again in Ross's (1925) translation:

> Now by self-sufficient we do not mean that which is sufficient for a man by himself, for one who lives a solitary life, but also for parents, children, wife, and in general for his friends and fellow citizens, since man is born for citizenship. But some limit must be set to this; for if we extend our requirement to ancestors and descendants and friends' friends we are in for an infinite series. Let us examine this question, however, on another occasion. (*NE* I.7.1097b8–13)

The thesis that man is born for citizenship – a version of a famous pronouncement of Aristotle's in the *Politics* (I.2.1253a2–3) that "man is by nature a political animal" – is here introduced as a premise. The premise supports the claim that self-sufficiency in this context means self-sufficiency for a person considered as a social being.

What Aristotle actually *says* is that it is self-sufficiency for his family, friends, and fellow citizens as well as him. But that cannot be quite what he has in mind – otherwise I could only achieve my good if all of them achieved theirs, or rather my good would simply become equivalent to the social good. What he must *mean* – as a passage in Book IX confirms (*NE* IX.9.1169b16–22) – is that the chief good has to be something which in and of itself satisfies the aspirations of someone who shares his life *with* the family that depends on him and with friends and fellow citizens, and satisfies them inasmuch as he does so. If the chief good then turns out to be happiness conceived as "activity of soul according with virtue or virtues," it follows that those virtues will have to be such as to enable a person in and of himself alone to behave as he should toward family members and toward friends and citizens, and to enjoy the life he shares with them to the full. They will have an inevitably social orientation.

Implicit in Aristotle's discussion of self-sufficiency here is the thought that whether a person attains his aspirations will be *affected* by what happens to his family and friends and the other citizens. The tragic loss or disfigurement of children, or the decimation of the population by war or disease, will make a difference. This is something we can infer from the reference to ancestors, descendants, and friends of friends. The point of wondering whether they are to be reckoned as members of our extended family or social circle can only be to flag as an issue the question whether what happens to *them* can affect the self-sufficiency of *our* lives – in the way (Aristotle seems to be presupposing) that it can be affected by what happens to our immediate family and friends and to the other citizens. He returns to that issue a bit later, so far as it relates to descendants and ancestors (in chapters 10 and 11 of Book I).

The *NE* makes it clear that the self-sufficiency of the good life – its success in satisfying our aspirations – is something primarily in our own hands: a matter of virtuous *activity*. That is what makes it *self*-sufficient. And that is why Aristotle thinks that the highest form of activity, philosophical reflection, is the most self-sufficient: because satisfying our potential for it is less dependent on anything external to reflection than is the case of any other activity (*NE* X.7.1177a27–b1). But a *life* devoted exclusively to reflection "would be above the human plane" (1177b26–7). "Insofar as he is a human being, and shares his life with others, he chooses to do what accords with virtue. So he will be in need of things external to himself if he is to live his humanity" (*NE* X.8.1178b5–7). There are different ways of thinking about what those needs consist in. In an earlier context, Aristotle is debating the feasibility of the popular idea that practical wisdom is a matter simply of trying to get what is good for yourself, without becoming involved in politics. On this he makes a wry observation: "Yet presumably one's own well-being is inseparable from the management of a household, and is dependent on a social and political system" (*NE* VI.8.1142a9–10).

So a self-sufficient human life is a life lived in a society, indeed in a *polis*, and is accordingly dependent on it. This is presumably not unconnected with Aristotle's treatment of self-sufficiency in the *Politics* as something primarily predicated of the city itself. The necessary conditions that need to be met if a community is to be positioned for achieving self-sufficiency are succinctly stated in Book VII:

> The first thing to be provided is food. The next is crafts; for many tools are needed for living. The third is arms: the members of the community must bear arms in

person, partly in order to maintain their rule over those who disobey, and partly to meet any threat of external aggression. Next is a supply of money and property, for both their own use and for the requirements of war. Fifth (but really first) religious cult, or (as it is called) priestcraft. Sixth in number, and most necessary of all, is a method of deciding what is in the public interest and where justice lies in people's dealings with each other. This list indicates the functions which every city may be said to need. For a city is not a casual collection of people. It is a body which, as we have said, is self-sufficient for life. If any of these things happens to be missing, it is impossible for this community to be truly self-sufficient. (*Pol.* VII.8.1328b5–19)

The conception of a self-sufficient community that emerges from this passage is of one that requires not only an adequate economy, with the functions needed to sustain it (here household management will have a major role to play), but a military capacity, proper provisions for religious observance, and rulers and judges able to enforce order and justice and to perceive and secure the common advantage. As Aristotle says early on in the *Politics* when discussing self-sufficiency, what is at stake here is not just living, but living the good life (*Pol.* I.2.1252b27–30). If (but only if) all these prerequisites are in place, citizens who have been properly brought up and educated will then be capable by their own virtuous activity alone (i.e. self-sufficiently) "of living happily and admirably," which is what a political community is ultimately there *for* (*Pol.* III.9.1280b39–1281a4).

2.2 The general virtue of justice

Justice, in Aristotle's scheme of things, comes in two varieties, one general, the other more specific or particular. The specific form is the virtue involved in justice as it is often understood nowadays. Aristotle distinguishes two main areas in which it operates: the rectification of wrongs committed by one individual or party against another (in other words, the justice dispensed by the courts or by arbitrators); and distributive justice (the fair division of benefits or rights in any relevant social context, including what he calls "political justice," the system determining participation in the government of a *polis*). Most of *NE* Book VI is devoted to discussion of justice so interpreted. But in its opening chapter, Aristotle offers a brief account of the *general* virtue of justice. Some examination of what he says here will help to advance our understanding of the political dimensions of virtue as he conceives it.

Aristotle's most striking claim about general justice comes at the start of his extended summing up:

This justice, then, is complete excellence, only not without qualification but in relation to another person. It is because of this that justice is often thought to be the mightiest of the excellences, so that "neither Evening Star nor Morning equals its wonder," and as the proverb says: "In justice is every virtue gathered." And it is complete excellence to the highest degree because it is the perfect activation of complete excellence; perfect, because the person who possesses it has the capacity to activate his excellence in relation to another person as well, and not just by himself. For many people are able to display their excellence in their own affairs, but incapable of doing so when it comes to dealing with another person. (*NE* V.1.1129b25– 1130a1, mostly in Christopher Rowe's translation [Broadie and Rowe 2002], adapted principally to accommodate the reading *aretēs teleia chrēsis* at 1129b31 proposed by Stewart [1892])

At first sight, it looks as though Aristotle is describing what we would call *altruism*. He seems to be talking of a general disposition to act out of consideration for others, not just ourselves. In fact, he goes on to remark – echoing Thrasymachus' words in Book I of the *Republic* – that "justice, alone of the virtues, is thought to be 'another's good', because it relates to another person: the just person does what is advantageous for someone else, whether someone in power or a person with whom he shares some form of association" (*NE* V.1.1130a3–5).

But Aristotle's justice has greater social density than our altruism. Indeed, *without* greater social density it would be something of a mystery why he would have called the disposition he has in mind *justice*. The way he indicates its social dimension is by appeal to the notion of law. As often, he starts by thinking about what constitutes a *failure* – here, a failure in justice. His answer: there are two sorts of person who get called unjust – the lawbreaker (corresponding to general justice) and the unfair person on the make (corresponding to particular justice). He infers that someone who is law-abiding, or alternatively someone who is fair, is what the just person is. The presupposition is that what is just is to be understood in one case as what is lawful, in the other as what is fair.

Following Aristotle's lead, we might ask: so what is *wrong* with breaking the law? And what makes that a form of behavior associated with moral vice, and compliance with law something morally virtuous? After his remarks about the identity of the unjust and the just person, Aristotle writes a passage which appears to be trying to deal with precisely this issue. His treatment of it has two components. (1) The first effectively consists in explaining why breaking the law is anti-social – indeed, more than anti-social, detrimental to the *polis*. The lawbreaker turns out to be unjust because he is an *anti-social threat to the well-being of the city*, rather as is argued by Plato in the *Crito* (50A–B). (2) The second spells out the way complying with the demands of the law (and therefore of justice) requires the exercise of the moral virtues, in the altruistic or other-regarding manner indicated in the passage quoted above.

(1) In articulating the social and political objectives of the legal system, Aristotle has recourse once more to the notion of the art of legislation. It is what the legislator specifies that counts as lawful and that we regard as just. The text continues:

Now the laws in their enactments on all subjects aim at the common advantage either of all or of the best or of those who hold power, or something of the sort; so that in one sense we call those acts just that tend to produce and preserve happiness and its components for the citizen community. (*NE* V.1.1129b14–19)

It is clear from the wording of the passage that Aristotle means his analysis to be valid for a wide range of political systems, whether more democratic or more aristocratic. He assumes that in *all* law-governed societies – as opposed, for example, to a lawless tyranny or an extreme democracy where mob rule prevails (as, in his jaundiced view, was true of contemporary Athens) – legislation will embody ideals analogous to those pursued by the true politician who has as his goal "the human good" (*NE* I.2.1094b7). Law-abiding behavior is to be considered just not on account of the mere fact that it is compliant with the law, but because it promotes or maintains the proper substantive *object* of law as determined by the legislator: *happiness for the community at large.*

(2) The virtue constituted by justice delineated here is not for Aristotle just one among the other virtues. It is a super-virtue or meta-excellence which requires the exercise of many other fundamental virtues. Aristotle explains how the provisions of the law itself make demands that can be met only by behaving in ways characteristic of the courageous person, the restrained person, the mild person, and so on:

> But the law also enjoins us to do what the courageous person does (e.g. not leaving one's post, or running away, or throwing down one's weapons), and what the restrained person does (e.g. not committing adultery, or rape), and what the mild person does (e.g. not throwing punches, or resorting to verbal abuse) – and similarly in accordance with the other excellences and the corresponding forms of badness, ordering us to do some things and forbidding others; correctly, if the law has been laid down correctly, but less well if it has been merely improvised. (*NE* V.1.1129b19–25)

This does *not* mean that justice has no identity of its own. As Richard Kraut (2002: 120) says, it would be a mistake to infer that justice "is nothing but a composite whose components are each a slice – the other-regarding slice – of the other ethical virtues." Justice has its own distinctive imperatives. Thus, for the good of the city, I may be required to fight as a hoplite in the line of battle, and to submit myself to the orders of my commander, who may issue the command not to retreat despite a fierce onslaught from the enemy. Meeting that requirement is my social and political duty, which I shall perform as such because I am in Aristotle's sense a just person: someone motivated to act out of regard for the interests of others (here, the community at large), not simply in my own interest. If I fail to enlist or if I disobey orders, I will be liable to punishment for breaking the law. But I will also be subject to moral criticism because in failing to play my part as a citizen I have behaved unjustly – I have failed to do what I should have done to promote the common advantage, the very thing the law exists to promote.

Of course, when the enemy attack, I need courage as well as justice to stand firm in the line. Acting justly in this instance rides on the back of courageous behavior. Justice may explain why on this occasion I am displaying my courage *on behalf of the city.* But as Aristotle sees it, acting justly is always likely to require the exercise of other more basic virtues, presumably because we are always having to cope with emotions and impulses – on the battlefield fear and daring – which the ordinary moral virtues enable us to handle appropriately. This indicates why justice is "complete excellence *to the highest degree.*" It is complete in the first instance because – as Aristotle implies in the passage just quoted – there is *no* basic virtue you may *not* be required to exercise in acting justly. Hence his endorsement of the saying: "In justice is every virtue gathered." It is complete in the highest degree because its exercise *perfects* each of the other virtues. Inasmuch as the good of the city is "greater and more complete" (*NE* I.2.1094b8) than the good of the individual, courage exercised in defense of the city will simply be a more admirable thing – courage at its very best – than courage in coping with life-threatening disease or the perils of seafaring. Book III confirms that death in battle is death in the circumstances of what is described as "the greatest and most admirable danger" (*NE* III.6.1115a30–31) – no doubt precisely because it is a sacrifice made for a whole community at risk, and so honored "in cities and by monarchs" (1115a32).

It might then come as a surprise that Aristotle distinguishes the true courage exhibited in death in battle from what he calls "civic" (*politikē*) courage. Here is his description of "civic" courage:

> Citizens are thought to withstand dangers facing them because of the penalties imposed by the laws and of people's reproaches, and because of the honors they win by such action. And so those peoples are thought to be most courageous who treat cowards with dishonor and hold the courageous in honor . . . This kind of courage has the greatest resemblance to the courage we described earlier, because it is due to virtue: to shame and desire for what is admirable (honor), and to escape reproach (as dishonorable). (*NE* III.8.1116a18–21, 27–9)

Why is that not real courage? Aristotle does not spell out an explanation. The point is presumably not that the citizens he speaks of do not have to cope with the fear of death – they behave as they do despite that. It must be that the motivations he mentions, while indeed admirable, and therefore virtuous, are not those that are most appropriate. Like the Christian citizens Rousseau imagines (who march without reluctance to war, confident that death will mean entry into paradise: *Le Contrat Social,* IV.8), those who withstand extreme danger for that sort of reason are not thinking primarily about the crucial thing: the good of the community. In fact, they are thinking primarily about themselves – of what might result for them as individuals, not of the interests of others. There is a certain sarcasm implicit in Aristotle's use of the word "civic" to characterize their disposition. Not for the only time in his ethical and political writings he is suggesting that the commitments of citizens to the ideals of the city are not what they should be or used to be (cf., for example, *Pol.* III.6.1279a8–16). Contrast those who face the possibility of death in battle because they accept that that is what the good of the community as interpreted by the *polis* requires. They recognize what it is that is greatest and most admirable about "the greatest and most admirable danger" – they see where the truest honor lies. Their behavior springs accordingly from a courage that is true because it is perfected by justice. That, as Aristotle says, is the really difficult achievement (*NE* V.1.1130a8).

The relationship between justice and a social excellence such as *megaloprepeia*, magnificence or grand style, must work in a rather different way from that between justice and virtues like courage and restraint, which simply as virtues are not defined in other-regarding terms. Whereas many practice other sorts of virtue in their own affairs but not with regard to others (*NE* V.1.1129b31–2), somebody who spends money only on himself does not count as virtuous at all: the person with a grand style "spends not on himself, but on public objects" (*NE* IV.2.1123a4–5). Although his house (for example) is likely to be an impressive structure, the more so the wealthier he happens to be, it is conceived as an ornament for the city rather than as a way of showing off his wealth.

Magnificent acts are hardly the sorts of thing required by the law; and presumably you do not need magnificence to be just. We might think of magnificence as a kind of supererogatory excellence that goes beyond justice, a form of liberality or open-handedness (discussed in the first chapter of *NE* Book IV) possible only for people who have great resources at their disposal. What it has in common with justice is a social orientation focused on the common good. The "greatest expenditures and those that carry most prestige" (IV.2.1122b35) are precisely those listed by Aristotle a little earlier:

> Magnificence is an attribute of expenditures of the kind we call honorific, e.g. those connected with the gods – votive offerings, ritual preparations, and sacrifices [i.e. supporting financially the principal institutions of civic religion] – and similarly with any being that is worshiped; and all those that are objects of public-spirited ambition, as when people think they ought to ensure the brilliant staging of a play or the fitting out of a trireme [i.e. contribute to the expenses associated with the major civic institution of the theater and with the city's naval capacity] or the provision of a feast for the city. (IV.2.1122b19–23)

On the other hand, it may be that Aristotle would have thought that an extremely wealthy person who did *not* spend lavishly on public objects was behaving unjustly insofar as he was not doing what the city properly *relies* on such persons to undertake in order to promote its well-being. Certainly he regards failures in liberality or open-handedness as wrongs, acts of injustice (*NE* V.2.1130a16–19). Here it is worth recalling Cicero's treatment of justice and liberality as intimately interconnected (*On Duties* I.20), so that sometimes liberality seems to be treated as a form of justice (I.42), sometimes both get subsumed under the general virtue of sociability (*communitas*, I.152; cf., for example, I.15–17; for discussion see Atkins 1990: 263–72).

2.3 Practical wisdom

In *NE* Book VI, Aristotle is keen to stress that practical wisdom (*phronēsis*) is a form of understanding which operates through deliberation about particulars triggering action. This immediately distinguishes it from theoretical understanding (*sophia*), which is focused on the universal and on what cannot be otherwise, and is accordingly an emphasis well suited to his tacit anti-Platonic agenda. Aristotle's commitment to that agenda is fierce and thoroughgoing in the central chapters of Book VI. It is as though his conviction of the wrong-headedness of Plato's undiscriminating epistemological obsession with the universal and the unchangeable impels him to insist – for one form of practical reasoning and judgment after another – that that is simply *not* what *they* are about: they "deal with what comes last, i.e. particulars," since their focus is on "what is to be done, and that is what comes last" (*NE* VI.11.1143a28–9, 1143a34–5; summarizing the upshot of *NE* VI.5–11 in general).

This emphasis has the effect of downplaying more architectonic uses of practical wisdom. It is not that Aristotle wishes to deny these. For example, at the very end of the chapter in which he works out in detail the contrast between theoretical and practical wisdom in the terms I have just mentioned, he allows that practical wisdom, too, may take an architectonic form, even if particular knowledge is ultimately more crucial for success in action (*NE* VI.7.1141b21–3). Moreover, his formal account of practical wisdom is appropriately neutral as between its exercise on more general and on more particular questions. It is "a true state of mind involving rational prescription, relating to action in the sphere of what is good and bad for human beings" (*NE* VI.5.1140b4–6; cf. 1140b20–21).

Aristotle's concession that there is also an architectonic form of practical wisdom is evidently prompted by recognition that he needs to square what he is arguing in Book VI with his treatment of political understanding as strategic elsewhere (notably at the beginning of Book I). He follows the concession with a paragraph in the first half of chapter 8 on political understanding and its relation to practical wisdom (*NE* VI.8.1141b23–1142a11). His first swift point is that they are in fact the same disposition or state of the mind, although they differ in essence (the idea doubtless being that political understanding is not to be *defined* as practical wisdom without further qualification, but as practical wisdom in its exercise in the political sphere). Having got that question out of the way, he then looks – still quite briefly, and indeed rather elliptically and unstraightforwardly – at two further issues: the contrast between a strategic and a more immediately practical form of politics and political understanding; and the popular tendency to identify practical wisdom as something concerned only with an individual's own preoccupations. I take it that the reason Aristotle says less on both issues than he might have done is because he is pulled in two opposite directions. On the one hand, he does not want to go back on his prominent claim at the beginning of Book I that the knowledge characteristic of politics is architectonic knowledge of the chief good, and as such the supremely authoritative form of knowledge in the realm of the practical (*NE* I.2.1094a26–8). On the other hand, he does not want to blunt the thrust of Book VI's argument that the *practical* orientation of practical reasoning and judgment dictates a focus on the particular, or to say anything that might impugn its reliance on examples drawn from the sphere of purely individual choice (such as one he has just invoked about the digestibility of light meats: *NE* VI.7.1141b18–21).

Nonetheless Aristotle does contrive – as much by implication as by express statement – to indicate (1) the limitations as well as the indispensability of a form of politics concerned solely with particular decisions, and (2) the implausibility of a conception of an individual's interests which insulates them from politics. As to (1), he points out in a passage already quoted (see p. 307 above) that, besides architectonic legislative understanding, political knowledge takes a form which "has to do with action and deliberation, for a resolution [i.e. of a council or an assembly], as the outcome of deliberation, is something requiring action" (*NE* VI.8.1141b26–8). And he notes, I think as something supporting the importance he attaches to political knowledge of this sort, that it tends to be what people ordinarily mean by "political understanding," and that they talk as though those who have it are the only people engaged in politics (which of course conflicts with his own view, as expressed in Book I, that the *true* politician is the legislator: *NE* I.13.1102a7–12). At the same time, he adds a comparison which indicates that there is something mistaken in the popular view. It is like treating artisans as the only people who actually *do* anything when a building is under construction (*NE* VI.8.1141b29). Perhaps they are. But the very mention of them reminds us of the existence of the master-builder. *He* it is who tells them *what* to do, and orchestrates their labors. As such he has the more important role in the process as a whole, thanks to his vision of the goal they are all trying – directly or indirectly – to achieve. Similarly (we infer) *mutatis mutandis* in politics.

As to (2), Aristotle allows that practical wisdom is generally taken to be something especially concerned with an individual's own interests (here one of the other possible translations of *phronēsis* – as "prudence" – comes to mind). He does not challenge the idea as such. The point he makes immediately (and very characteristically) is just that there are different ways in which one might be said to know what is in one's own interest. The implication is that some of them will be valid, some invalid – so someone who thinks that they have said anything true or helpful in asserting that practical wisdom is something focused on an individual's own interests will need to say a good deal more before we can tell whether they are right. And at the end of the passage, Aristotle raises a related question – not what, but how (*NE* VI.8.1142a10–11): "Again, *how* one should administer one's own affairs is unclear – it needs looking into."

Before then, most of his discussion is taken up with a tongue-in-cheek presentation of one popular *version* of the view that someone with practical wisdom is typically preoccupied with his own interests. This is a version that treats politicians as busybodies, in contrast to the sensible person who keeps a low profile and does not put himself to that kind of trouble – because he has his eye as he should on his *own* good (a quotation from Euripides is wheeled in to illustrate this outlook). We know from Aristotle's analysis of self-sufficiency in Book I that he would regard a conception of *my* good that treats me as a unit isolable from my fellow citizens and their interests, and for that reason not needing to get involved in politics, as reflecting a radically mistaken understanding of human nature. But here – in keeping with his generally understated handling of his material – he merely makes the mildly sarcastic comment (*NE* VI.8.1142a9–10, also quoted above): "Yet presumably one's own well-being is inseparable from the management of a household, and is dependent on a social and political system."

In the *Politics*, Aristotle goes much further than that. In effect, he there makes his treatment of practical wisdom follow through an implication of the dependence of a person's good on the social and political system. He advances the striking and (to a reader of *NE* Book VI) unexpected claim that practical wisdom is *the one virtue that can only be possessed by a ruler*, not by someone who is ruled by another (*Pol.* III.4.1277b25–30). No explanation is offered for this restrictive position. But the most plausible way of reconstructing an explanation looks as though it has to take the route I now sketch.

The reasoning needed to support Aristotle's claim must presumably go something like this. Since human beings are "born for citizenship," they will attain their good only in a political community designed to promote their happiness and well-being, and hence giving them opportunities to perform the admirable actions characteristic of courage and the other moral virtues in their highest forms. But citizenship – belonging to a political community – provides not only a framework for the good life, but is itself realized above all by *participation in the system of rule* by which a city is governed, and which in a *political* (as opposed to a monarchic) system will be a matter of taking one's turn at ruling as well as being ruled by others. Participation in rule is what accordingly enables someone to exercise the intellectual virtue of practical wisdom in the way that is most important and meaningful. For practical wisdom, as the *NE* says, is "directive" or "prescriptive" (*epitaktikē*) – "what one should do or not do": that is its goal (*NE* VI.10.1143a8–9). Participation in rule gives a person who possesses such wisdom the opportunity to help *determine* the way the city seeks to achieve the "greater and more complete good" (*NE* I.2.1094b8) of well-being for the community at large. Conversely, exclusion from rule means that people not only have no role in this, but are deprived in many consequential ways of the ability to direct their own lives to the degree they might. Most obviously, they will not be party to political decisions that will affect them and their family and friends in areas as diverse as war and peace, the proceedings of the courts, and the educational system, and will have a profound impact on their prospects for virtue and happiness.

It accordingly becomes intelligible why the *Politics* sets the bar of attainment so high where practical wisdom is concerned, and why it leaves those only subject to rule capable of nothing better than "true opinion" about what should be done (*Pol.* III.4.1277b28–9). Aristotle's thought must be that mere subjects – subjects of free status though they might be – have too little opportunity to develop properly the disposition enabling them to make important life choices which practical wisdom gives a person. They may to an extent be courageous and restrained: private individuals are thought to engage in decent behavior no less than despots – in fact, rather more so (*NE* X.8.1179a6–8). But they will not achieve the complete virtue of a truly good man. Only a citizen who participates in rule will be capable of the practical wisdom needed for that.

3 Conclusion

Self-sufficiency, moral virtue, practical wisdom: with respect to all these intimately related ingredients of the good life, Aristotle makes it plain enough that only by acting out his (one can hardly say her) citizenship in various ways will a human being achieve his potential. The passages in which he is most explicit about this are not very sustained, and not the occasion for his most powerful and intricate philosophical analyses in the *Nicomachean Ethics*. Even the most extensive of them – the discussion of justice in the first chapter of Book V – is only a preface, included because Aristotle wants to distinguish general justice clearly and sharply from the more specific justice that is to be his real subject (*NE* V.1.1130a4; cf. 2.1130b18– 20). What this indicates is not that the political dimensions of virtue and happiness are marginal to his ethical thought. Quite the contrary: in his final account of the best life for human beings considered as humans in chapter 8 of Book X, Aristotle continues to think of it as the *political* life, understood as a life involving active engagement in politics as well as other forms of activity on behalf of the city (*NE* X.8.1178a25–b3; cf. X.7.1177b6–15). The position is rather that the political dimensions of virtue are conceived as belonging to the overall framework of the good life, just as, in a different way, politics as a legislative project constitutes a framework for ethics – something Aristotle indicates (as we saw in section 1) by devoting the first and last chapters of the whole work to that topic.

References

Atkins, E. M. 1990: "'Domina et Regina Virtutum': Justice and *Societas* in *De Officiis*," *Phronesis* 35 (3): 258–89.

Broadie, S. and C. Rowe (eds) 2002: *Aristotle: Nicomachean Ethics*. Oxford: Oxford University Press.

Kraut, R. 2002: *Aristotle: Political Philosophy.* Oxford: Oxford University Press.

Ross, W. D. (trans.) 1925: *The Works of Aristotle Translated into English*, vol. 9: *Ethics.* Oxford: Clarendon Press.

Stewart, J. A. 1892: *Notes on the Nicomachean Ethics of Aristotle*, 2 vols. Oxford: Clarendon Press.

Further reading

Bodéüs, R. 1993: *The Political Dimensions of Aristotle's Ethics*, trans. J. E. Garrett. Albany, NY: State University of New York Press.

Cashdollar, S. 1973: "Aristotle's Politics of Morals," *Journal of the History of Philosophy* 11 (2): 145–60.

Fritz, K. von and Kapp, E. (eds) 1950: *Aristotle's Constitution of Athens and Related Texts.* New York: Hafner.

Kraut, R. 1989: *Aristotle on the Human Good.* Princeton, NJ: Princeton University Press.

Newman, W. L. 1887: *The Politics of Aristotle*, vol. II, appendix A. Oxford: Clarendon Press.

Roberts, J. 1989: "Political Animals in the *Nicomachean Ethics*," *Phronesis* 34 (2): 185–204.

15

Aquinas, Natural Law, and Aristotelian Eudaimonism

T. H. Irwin

I

Many students of Aristotle's *Nicomachean Ethics* recognize the value of comparisons between Aristotle and modern moralists. We are familiar with some of the ways in which reflection on Hume, Kant, Mill, Sidgwick, and more recent moral theorists can throw light on Aristotle. The light may come either from recognition of similarities or from a sharper awareness of differences. "Themes ancient and modern" is a familiar part of the contemporary study of Aristotle that needs no further commendation.[1]

Despite this interest in comparison, medieval moralists receive comparatively little attention; "themes ancient and modern" tend to omit 1500 years or so in the history of moral philosophy. And if one takes a broader view, one finds that the major modern commentaries on the *Nicomachean Ethics* in English have generally not exploited the abundant medieval commentaries on the *NE* and discussions of Aristotelian questions. The commentaries by Grant (1885), Stewart (1892), Burnet (1900), and Joachim (1951) do not suggest extensive acquaintance with Aquinas, let alone with less familiar medieval sources. This may partly reflect the long neglect of Scholasticism by philosophers in Great Britain from the eighteenth to the twentieth century.

One gets a different impression from French commentaries, especially the valuable work of Gauthier and Jolif (1970). But one may not be encouraged to follow them in studying Aquinas. For Gauthier has rather a low opinion of the commentary of Aquinas; his apparently authoritative verdict is unlikely to persuade readers that they ought to read Aquinas if they want to understand Aristotle better.[2]

If we do not include medieval reflections on Aristotle in our comparative studies, we miss a certain perspective that might help us to understand "themes ancient and modern." It should be useful to know whether, for instance, any contrasts that we find are contrasts between ancient-and-medieval and modern or contrasts between ancient and medieval-and-modern. If we know which sort of contrast we are considering, we may have a better prospect of explaining or understanding it. If, for instance, we try to explain an "ancient *vs* modern" contrast by appealing to distinctive features of the modern world or of modern thought, we may be barking up the wrong tree if we find that the "modern" view is also medieval.

For this purpose, I set aside two important questions that one might reasonably ask about Aquinas. (1) What has he to contribute to the exegesis of Aristotle? (2) What has he to contribute to moral philosophy? I will raise a different question. (3) What can we learn from Aquinas about Aristotle's moral philosophy? To answer the first question we would mainly need to concentrate on his commentary on the *Nicomachean Ethics*. To answer the second, we would need to consider his moral philosophy as a whole. To answer the third question, we need to consider the aspects of his moral philosophy that try to support, or to explain, or to develop, Aristotle's views. I want especially to consider some ways in which Aquinas develops Aristotle's views into views that cannot be found in Aristotle, but might reasonably be claimed to be derived from Aristotle and to go further in a direction in which Aristotle has already gone some distance. Admittedly, it is not always easy to decide whether a particular doctrine counts as a reasonable development of Aristotle, or as an innovation by Aquinas or by someone else. But I will try to see whether we can reach some decisions on this question.

One reason to doubt whether Aquinas (or any other medieval philosopher writing in Latin) has any light to throw on Aristotle rests on the obvious fact that he is a Christian theologian, and therefore committed to specific theological claims that are relevant to ethics. Even if we confined ourselves to Aquinas's commentary on the *NE*, which is not overtly presented as part of a theological system, we would not escape the theological influences. The theological influence is obvious if we turn to the work in which Aquinas reflects at length on Aristotelian ethics: the Second Part of the *Summa Theologiae*. "Aristotle baptized" might interest an historian interested in the absorption or adaptation of Aristotelian ethics within Christian moral theology. But does Aquinas offer more? Can we learn anything of use to the modern student of the *Nicomachean Ethics* as a part of moral philosophy?

I would like to sketch part of an answer to this question by considering one particular doctrine that might seem to separate Aquinas from Aristotle. His doctrine of natural law has no clear explicit basis in Aristotle, and it may well appear to introduce a basically un-Aristotelian element into his position. I will consider some reasons that support this view; then I will argue that nonetheless Aquinas's doctrine is a reasonable development of Aristotle rather than an un-Aristotelian innovation. Our discussion will lead us into several large issues about natural law, moral obligation, and ancient versus modern ethics. I will simply point to these issues and pass on. Though this treatment will be inconclusive, I hope it will be suggestive.

II

We might argue that an appeal to natural law introduces a basically legal conception of morality that is alien to Aristotle. This is the position of Anscombe's paper "Modern Moral Philosophy."[3] This paper was published over forty years ago, and has exerted considerable influence. It is one source of inspiration for recent "virtue ethics," which claims Aristotelian inspiration, and which reacts to a perceived shortcoming in the familiar versions of "modern" ethical theory. The author is an English Roman Catholic philosopher who knows both Aristotle and Aquinas well, and might therefore be expected to offer a reliable account of their similarities and differences. Since she argues that they differ fundamentally on a central element in ethical theory, someone who takes her view seriously will not be encouraged to look in Aquinas for a reasonable development of Aristotelian views.

In her view, the modern concepts of obligation, duty, and the moral ought are remnants of an earlier conception of ethics, and ought (as Anscombe puts it) to be abandoned.[4] This earlier conception of ethics is later than Aristotle; we can see this because we cannot find room for our concept of the moral in any accurate account of Aristotle. Indeed, the term "moral" itself "doesn't seem to fit, in its modern sense, into an account of Aristotelian ethics" (MMP 27).[5] Aristotle uses "should" and "ought" with reference to goodness and badness, but not in the special moral sense that these terms have now acquired.[6] In its moral sense, "ought" is equivalent to "is obliged" in a legal sense; it implies that some law obliges.[7] If a law obliges us, some legislator must command us. But we do not believe that any legislator commands us to do what we morally ought to do. Hence our use of the moral "ought" presupposes a conception of morality that we take to be false.

To explain why we, in contrast to Aristotle, use this moral "ought," Anscombe appeals to the influence of Christianity with its "*law* conception of ethics."[8] This historical background explains our modern use of "ought" in the moral sense.[9] Since Aristotle precedes the legal framework of Christianity, he does not use "ought" in the moral sense.[10] Since we are, in this respect, post-Christian, we use the term in the moral sense, but our use rests on presuppositions that have been generally abandoned.

Anscombe is not the first person to claim that legislative concepts have influenced the development and the presuppositions of modern ethics. Sidgwick, for instance, argues that modern ethics relies on "quasi-jural" notions that are largely foreign to Greek ethics.[11] He believes that the crucial element of modern ethics is foreshadowed in views that connect morality with the provisions of natural law; and in this connection he mentions the Stoics and Aquinas (Sidgwick 1902: 144, 160–62). Anscombe agrees with Schopenhauer[12] and Nietzsche[13] in offering a genealogical explanation, showing that a rationally indefensible practice is the residue of practices that relied on assumptions – now rejected – that made them defensible. Since modern philosophers have mostly discarded the outlook that would allow them to take the legal conception seriously, they cannot justify their reliance on the moral ought. Hence we ought to start ethics again where Aristotle started it, without any moral ought.[14]

If Anscombe is right, Aquinas will not help us to understand Aristotle on some central points. For he holds neither Aristotle's position, which lacks the moral ought, nor the modern position, which has the moral ought without belief in a lawgiver. Aquinas should exemplify the legal conception with the lawgiver. Hence Aristotle should lack the idea of moral obligation and Aquinas should have it, because Aquinas should have the legal conception of ethics that makes sense of moral obligation.

III

Aquinas's position seems to support Anscombe. For he gives a prominent place to natural law, which is almost absent from Aristotle.[15] He connects natural law with eternal law and divine law, and he takes the first principles of natural law to be the first principles of practical reason. We may suppose, therefore, that these are not only non-Aristotelian elements in Aquinas, but positively un-Aristotelian elements that mark him out as a Christian philosopher with a jural conception of morality.

Aquinas offers further apparent support for this interpretation; for he explains his view that there is a natural law by showing that it satisfies the necessary and sufficient conditions for a law. A law is a rule[16] that involves commands, moves agents to action, imposes obligation, and requires publication (*ST* 1–2 q90 a4). These features of a law easily suggest that a law essentially involves legislation and a legislator. Evidently, Aquinas believes that there is a divine legislator, and that natural law embodies eternal law, which is not independent of the mind of God. Hence he seems to agree with the Christian view (as Anscombe describes it) against the Aristotelian view, by treating morality as the product of legislation by a divine legislator.

This, however, is not Aquinas's position. In his view, the relevant features of law do not essentially involve legislation and a legislator; they can all be understood non-legislatively. He believes that natural law contains rules, commands, and action-guiding requirements, but he does not argue that law essentially consists in commands that are expressions of the will of a legislator. In his view, natural law follows from the goal-directed agency characteristic of human beings. Natural law is present in a rational creature insofar as one shares in divine providence by exercising foresight for oneself and for others.[17] Rational creatures share in divine reason, insofar as their own reason is naturally illuminated so that they can distinguish good from bad. This discrimination of good from bad, and this foresight for oneself and others, constitute natural law. Natural law includes commands that do not consist in expressions of the will of any external legislator. We find them in the principles discovered by practical reason as a result of deliberation about the final good; these principles, therefore, are precepts of natural law (1–2 q90 a1). Natural law imposes obligation that does not depend on the will of a legislator. We discover it by finding what is required by the principles discovered by deliberative practical reason.

Aquinas implies that the natural law in us is our disposition to deliberate with reference to our own ultimate end. The principle of voluntary movements is the "good in common" and the ultimate end, which corresponds to the first principles of demonstration in theoretical cases (1–2 q10 a1). All rational action, therefore, depends on the desire for the ultimate end, which is the basic principle that belongs to us through natural law.[18] Since natural law is a rational principle, it is guided by the first principle of practical reason, which directs us toward the ultimate end.[19] The first directing of our acts toward the end comes through natural law because that is how we exercise providence for ourselves. We are a law to ourselves, and we have natural law in ourselves because we are agents who direct our actions toward our happiness. Attention to natural law does not turn us away from the eudaemonist outlook that is characteristic of the *Summa*; it simply expresses this eudaemonist outlook.[20]

Aquinas's conception of natural law is reductive and deflationary, therefore, in one respect. He does not take our awareness of natural law to be a new source of moral insight distinct from reflection on our own happiness. He argues that, on a reasonable understanding of law, what he has said about the virtues and practical reason shows that we are aware of a natural law within us. Aquinas certainly believes in God as a legislator, but he does not take divine legislation to be essential to the existence of a natural law.

If this is the right way to understand Aquinas, his position counts against Anscombe's claims about moral requirements and legislation. In his view, the legal aspect of morality simply consists in the fact that moral principles are action-guiding rational principles of the sort that we discover by Aristotelian deliberation. Since, therefore, Anscombe believes that Aristotle does not accept a legislative conception of moral requirements, she ought to say the same about Aquinas.

IV

If, then, both Aristotle and Aquinas lack the moral ought as Anscombe understands it, she has not found a contrast between "ancient" and "post-ancient" views; nor has she found a contrast between pre-Christian and Christian views. Nor has she found a contrast between pre-modern and modern views. For some modern moralists agree with Aquinas's "naturalist" view that natural law, insofar as it expresses moral requirements, consists in facts about human nature that are independent of God's legislative will. Anscombe's thesis fits those moralists, often called "voluntarists," who reject Aquinas's naturalism.

To understand the dispute between voluntarists and their naturalist opponents, we need to distinguish two generally recognized elements of natural law. (1) One consists in "intrinsic" natural facts and properties: those that belong to nature in its own right, independently of God's legislative will. (2) The other depends on the exercise of God's legislative will in the issuing of commands. Theorists dispute about whether different features of natural law are intrinsic natural facts or products of divine legislation.

Their dispute is about independence of the legislative will of God, not about complete independence of the will of God. One might reasonably argue that no intrinsic natural facts that make essential reference to contingent particular beings are independent of the creative will of God.[21] But that does not settle the question about independence of God's legislative will.[22] Aquinas and other naturalists claim that the moral requirements of natural law are independent of God's legislative will.[23] According to voluntarists, God's legislative will is essential to moral requirements.[24] Pufendorf defends the voluntarist view by arguing that the will of a legislator, expressed in commands, is essential for obligations and, therefore, for moral requirements.

He recognizes that actions have natural goodness and badness apart from God's legislative will, but he affirms that this natural goodness and badness are insufficient for moral goodness or intrinsic rightness (*honestas*).[25] In his view, the only reasons that do not presuppose divine commands are reasons referring to the pleasant (*iucundum*) and the advantageous (*utile, commodum*). To recognize goodness as rightness (the *bonum honestum*) is to recognize that there are non-hedonic, non-instrumental ends, worth pursuing for their own sake; and to recognize actions as right is to recognize them as worth pursuing for their own sake, and not only for their instrumental advantage.

According to Pufendorf, this moral rightness requires divine legislation because natural goodness and badness do not support principles with the right content or the right stringency.[26] Natural goodness and badness provide reasons based on the pursuit of pleasure or advantage, which rest on inclination, whereas morality imposes requirements independent of inclination. Moral requirements override considerations of pleasure and advantage; they could not do this if they simply arose from natural goodness. They are the basis for praise, blame, and punishment; they could not be such a basis if they rested simply on natural goodness, since they would give me no reason to follow them independently of my inclination, and no reason to acknowledge that I deserved punishment from others simply for failing to follow considerations of my own pleasure and advantage.

According to Pufendorf, these features of morality imply that natural goodness and badness are insufficient for moral goodness and moral requirements. If we acknowledge that our actions sometimes deserve punishment, we must regard them as violations of laws expressed in commands. Only divine legislation, in his view, supports requirements with the peculiar stringency of morality. Anscombe agrees with him on the connection between oughts, obligations, and acts of legislation.

V

In response to this survey of the dispute between naturalists and voluntarists about natural law, one might reject Anscombe's claim that a legal conception of moral oughts is characteristic of pre-Reformation or early modern Christian thought. But would she be right to claim that it is characteristic of later modern moral philosophy? Do voluntarist arguments eliminate the naturalist position from serious consideration?

To see that naturalism is quite tenacious, we need only consider the series of early modern moralists writing in English who are naturalists about moral requirements and oughts.[27] Price agrees with the voluntarist claim that "right," "ought," and "obligation" imply one another.[28] But, contrary to the voluntarists and to Anscombe, he does not take "obligation" to explain the other terms; nor does he take obligation to require legislation and a legislator. He rejects this direction of explanation because he believes that rightness consists wholly in facts about objective properties of things that are independent of the will of any legislator.

Obligatoriness and rightness imply, in Price's view, some law binding us to do what is obligatory and right, but the existence of such a law does not imply any legislator. The law results simply from the fact that some things are right, and that therefore we ought to do them.[29] In speaking of moral oughts as containing an obligation and a law, we need not refer to any act of legislation by a legislator. The relevant type of law is an authoritative binding principle; we find such a principle where we find no rational alternative to acting as the principle prescribes. Rightness itself provides us with the relevant sort of principle. Price therefore considers a voluntarist and legislative analysis of the moral ought, and rejects it in favor of an analysis that appeals only to intrinsic rightness.

This survey suggests that we ought to agree with Anscombe's claim that Aristotle lacks the moral ought, as she conceives it. If we were to agree with Anscombe that the use of "ought" in a legislative sense is necessary for the moral ought and for the concept of morality, we would have to infer, as she sees, that Aristotle lacks the concept of morality. If her account of the moral ought were right, it would follow that Aquinas, Suarez, Price, and other non-voluntarists lack the moral ought as well.

But should we accept her account of the moral ought? She believes we can understand the overriding and obligatory character of moral requirements only if we connect them with presupposed acts of legislation; hence she infers that our use of "ought" is the residue of a past consensus about the truth of this presupposition. Our discussion, however, suggests that our present conception of moral requirements might express Price's view, that facts about intrinsic rightness and wrongness themselves generate the relevant requirements without reference to any act of legislation. We would be entitled to dismiss Price's view (expressing the view of his naturalist predecessors) only if it obviously failed to explain the features of morality that voluntarists claim to explain by reference to divine legislation. But Price's position is at least as plausible as Pufendorf's and Anscombe's voluntarism. Anscombe's view rests on the false claim that a voluntarist conception of moral requirements defines our concept of morality.

Our concept of moral obligation, therefore, does not divide us from Aristotle. Suarez's account of non-legislative morality and Price's account of obligation offer a plausible account of moral requirements that do not essentially involve legislation. It is not at all surprising that their account fits Aristotle quite well. For Suarez takes himself to be expounding the character of the morally good, the *honestum*. He uses the term that Latin philosophy uses to render Aristotle's term *kalon*, "fine," which marks a common feature of the virtues of character. This is the term that Aristotle uses to clarify the use of "ought" (*dein*) that is to be understood when we claim that virtuous people are angry or afraid or confident or willing to spend money to the extent that they ought (*NE* IV.1.1120b27–1121a4). He recognizes the fine as a goal distinct from the pleasant and the advantageous, and so he seems to commit himself to the sort of natural moral goodness that later naturalists treat as the basis of the moral ought.[30]

VI

So far I have argued, against Anscombe, that Aquinas does not differ from Aristotle about the moral ought. I have argued that his introduction of natural law does not alter the fundamentally eudaimonist basis of his moral theory. I now need to consider an argument that goes to the other extreme. If, in this case, Aquinas introduces nothing fundamentally un-Aristotelian, does he add anything to Aristotle that is worth our attention, or does he just serve the same Aristotelian wine in new bottles? Do his claims about natural law throw any new light on Aristotle's position?

It will help to focus on a specific question that arises from Pufendorf's attack on naturalism. One of his reasons for rejecting natural moral properties independent of legislation is his belief that without legislation we have reasons referring to pleasure and to advantage, but no reasons involving any other sort of goodness.[31] We might express one point in this claim by saying that all natural, non-legislative reasons are internal; we have reason to do what achieves the ends we already desire for their own sakes, or what produces means to these ends. Morality, however, presents us with external reasons – reasons that are not grounded in our antecedent desires.

This is a reasonable question to ask about Aristotelian eudaimonism, but we do not find much discussion of it in Aristotle. Though we might reasonably argue that he is committed to external reasons, his account of happiness does not make this completely clear.[32] On this point Aquinas has something to add.

VII

Though Aquinas expounds his doctrine of the final good in the first five questions of the *Prima Secundae* and does not reach natural law until question 90, these two doctrines are closely connected. Some of the main connections are these: (1) As I have already mentioned, he claims that the first principle of natural law is that good is to be done, and evil is to be avoided. This is not the claim that "good" is a prescriptive term, or that in taking something to be good we suppose it is to be done (cf. Grisez 1969). Aquinas relies on the account of goods that he has already presented; they are goods because they promote the ultimate good. Hence the first principle of natural law requires us to promote the ultimate good.[33] A natural law is present in human beings because they are rational agents; they are rational agents because they aim at their ultimate good. (2) The ultimate good for human beings is to fulfill their nature; in specifying the requirements of the ultimate good, we have to refer to the requirements of human nature. Hence the different virtues specify the precepts of natural law, since it prescribes action in accordance with nature.[34] What is natural for human beings expresses their nature as rational beings. Natural action is the sort of action toward which human beings have a natural inclination, which they form because of a natural judgment or "natural criterion of reason."[35] (3) These requirements of human nature include the requirements of social life, and therefore include friendship and justice between human beings. The highest precepts are immediately derived from the first principle, in accordance with the order of natural inclinations: "Therefore, according to the order of natural inclinations is the order of precepts of the law of nature" (1–2 q94 a2). Different natural inclinations rest on different aspects of our nature. (a) The inclination that results in precepts about self-preservation rests on the nature we share with all other natural substances. (b) The inclination that results in precepts about the satisfaction and control of bodily appetites rests on the nature we share with other animals. (c) The inclination that results in precepts about social life rests on our nature as rational animals (q94 a2, a4, q95 a4).

These different claims balance each other. The first two make it clear that the precepts of natural law are neither distinct from, nor prior to, the pursuit of the ultimate good. Equally they imply that the pursuit of the ultimate good does not commit us merely to a formal structure without definite content; the naturalist claim imposes a specific content on the human good and on the virtues. The third claim answers a familiar objection to Aristotelian eudaimonism, that it cannot support the interpersonal and impartial aspects of morality.

In stating these claims rather briefly and baldly, I have tried to make it clear that they are non-trivial and controversial. Rather than try to explain or to defend all three claims, I will pick out just one theme for discussion, to show how Aquinas adds something significant to Aristotle, and to show how it affects his exposition of the Aristotelian position.

VIII

Some of Aquinas's exposition of the final good is fairly familiar from Aristotle. But his account of happiness develops a point that is at most implicit in Aristotle.[36] He introduces happiness as "the ultimate perfection of a rational or intellectual nature" (1a q62 a1), and therefore a "state perfected by the collection of all goods" (1a q26 a1 ad1).[37] Perfection is the only thing that meets the conditions for being the ultimate end, and that all rational agents desire their perfection as the ultimate end (cf. 1a q60 a3).

He maintains that our aiming at perfection is the basis of our willing only one ultimate end, and of our willing everything we will for the sake of the one ultimate end (1–2 q1 a5–6). We have only one ultimate end because everything seeks its perfection, and therefore seeks an end that fulfills all its desires.[38] The desire for perfection is the desire for one's actualization.[39] This is common to all living creatures, since they are organized for the specific vital activities that constitute their actuality and end, specified by their form (see 1–2 q3 a2, q55 a1). The life that constitutes the healthy state of a creature is the one that actualizes its natural capacities. This connection between the good, completeness, and perfection commits Aquinas to a naturalist account of the good, resting on an essentialist claim about human beings. He identifies the good not simply with the systematic satisfaction of one's desires, but with the systematic application of rational activity to one's life, because this activity is the essential activity of a human being.[40]

To see the point of Aquinas's reference to perfection, we may consider why the ultimate end is not merely comprehensive. If all our reasons are internal, we may have a comprehensive ultimate end, but we cannot have a reason for having this comprehensive end resting on these preferences. For if all our reasons are based on preferences, we have exhausted our reasons in stating the ultimate preferences that determine our comprehensive end. When we confront alternatives to our total preferences, we must agree that we have no reason to prefer our preferences over the alternatives.

This attitude to our ultimate preferences fits our view of some of our ends. In some cases we regard our particular ends as a brute fact, a matter of taste, temperament, environment, and so on, and we recognize that we would not be worse off if we exchanged these ends for others, provided that our taste, temperament, and so on were adjusted to suit. Though I may prefer playing a violin to playing a trumpet, I need not think I would have suffered some major loss if I came to prefer the trumpet.

But this does not seem to be our view of all our ultimate ends. We normally assume that they cannot all be replaced without loss. I might be content to have my preference for one instrument replaced by my preference for another, but I would think myself worse off if my preference for music were replaced by a preference for gambling, even if I could afford to gamble, and even if I did not miss playing music; indeed, I might believe I would be even worse off if I did not regret the change. Similarly, though I might find that my concern for other people – family, colleagues, friends – imposes some irksome demands on me, I believe I would lose something significant if I no longer cared about these other people, and that I would lose even more if I did not regret my failure to care about them. If we treat our ends in this way, so that we believe we can assess them on their merits, not simply by their relation to our other desires and preferences, we assume that not all our reasons are based on preferences. We treat some of them as "external" to our preferences because they depend on the merits of different ends, and these merits are not exhausted by the relations of these ends to our desires and preferences.

Aquinas recognizes this feature of ends and reasons in his treatment of intellectual love. He distinguishes sensory love, belonging to the non-rational parts of the soul, from intellectual love, belonging to the will. It rests on a prior grasp by intellect (1a q27 a3 ad3), which grasps its object "under the common character of good," not simply as an object of some prior inclination (1a q82 a5). To be guided by intellectual love in the pursuit of ends that we take to constitute the ultimate end, we must recognize something good about them apart from our having some prior inclination toward them. Prior inclination belongs to the non-rational forms of love, but intellectual love is guided by the features of the object itself, not by their relation to some desire of ours.

The difference between intellectual and sensory love clarifies Aquinas's claim that we have a natural desire for the good. This may sound similar to the claim that we have a natural desire for sensory gratification or for revenge (objects of the non-rational parts). But this is not what he means. The desires of the non-rational parts aim at things that we recognize as actual objects of our desires (or means to achieving these objects). The desire of the rational part is directed to things whose properties merit their being desired, not to things that are already desired.

The doctrine of intellectual love shows, therefore, that Aquinas recognizes external reasons for preferring one set of ends to another. When we bring them under an ultimate end, we are not just guided by our preferences, and we do not treat the ultimate end as simply an ordered collection of objects of our basic preferences. We also treat it as including external reasons in support of our basic preferences.

Aquinas's appeal to human nature, therefore, does not rely on a conception of happiness as the fulfillment of one's desires. He argues that this is a mistaken conception of happiness because my ultimate end as a rational agent is not simply the satisfaction of my desires. I pursue my perfection, insofar as I seek to satisfy the desires that are worth satisfying. I do not want my ultimate ends to be things that I simply happen to prefer.

This makes a difference to how we understand the appeal to "natural inclinations." If we appeal to all unlearnt impulses or desires in anyone, some of these seem inappropriate to provide a moral norm or standard. Even if we appeal to the impulses that are statistically more widespread in the human species, we still seem to commit ourselves to morally doubtful conclusions. Aquinas believes that natural and widespread impulses are to be shaped and re-directed by the training that forms moral virtues; he could not reasonably take untrained natural impulses to set goals for morality.[41]

His claims about natural inclinations need to be interpreted in the light of his conception of agency. He thinks of human nature as essentially rational, and therefore as requiring the application of rational agency to choices.[42] This rational agency involves relations with others, and especially includes an inclination toward society.[43] We might think he refers to a natural desire for social life, and that the various principles of justice and so on seek to achieve this natural desire. This would be an insecure starting-point. For we might infer that the strength of my desire for the end determines the weight of my reason to pursue the means to the end, so that people who care less about social life have less reason to care about the good of others.

This is not Aquinas's argument. He means that a rational agent's perfection requires social life in which one is concerned about the good of others in the same way as one's own, and therefore for the sake of the others themselves.[44] Once we recognize that we care about perfection, not simply about the satisfaction of preferences, we also notice that my preferring this end – its being my end in particular – is not a sufficient reason for pursuing it. There must also be something to be said for it beyond the fact that I care about it.[45] In this sense, my desire for my happiness turns out not to be entirely self-centered, once I understand that happiness requires reasons that go beyond my preference.

The demand for reasons going beyond my preferences affects my adoption of one end over another, by accepting one conception of happiness over another. But it also affects my relations to other rational agents. To find a reason for preferring one end to another is to find a good that is good antecedently to my desiring it; my desire rests on an external reason that does not depend on my desires. External reasons are good reasons not because they seem good to me, but because they are good reasons that must seem good to a qualified judge who does not share my initial desires. This is how reason-based ends differ from preference-based ends.

In caring about my own perfection, therefore, and not simply about the satisfaction of my own preferences, I have to recognize other rational agents as agents who can recognize a good reason for preferring one end over another. Aquinas is right to suppose that my natural inclination – properly understood – toward my own good as a rational agent also implies an inclination toward social life. I have to respect the judgments of others to some degree, since I regard their judgments as being possibly relevant to my decisions about the ends it would be best for me to pursue. This kind of respect for others places us in a "community of reason" with them.

These arguments about the inclination to society indicate how one might connect Aquinas's claims about natural law with his conception of rational agency. Moreover, they are relevant to the claims that he presents more fully in his arguments for friendship and justice.

IX

I have followed a circuitous path in this chapter, but I hope it has been clear enough to suggest one way in which our reflections on Aristotle may benefit from Aquinas's development of an Aristotelian position. If we believed Anscombe, we would suppose that Aquinas differs sharply from Aristotle about the moral ought, but we ought not to believe her. If we believed Pufendorf's voluntarism (implicit in Anscombe), naturalists such as Aristotle and Aquinas cannot recognize a moral ought because they cannot recognize external reasons, but we ought not to believe him. We can see the place for external reasons within Aristotelian eudaimonism, if we notice the connections between Aquinas's views on natural law, perfection, and intellectual love.

I have not said enough to show that these connections between Aquinas's views allow him to present a defensible position. But I have suggested that he undertakes a task that an Aristotelian eudaimonist has good reason to undertake, and that his position deserves the attention of sympathetic students of Aristotle.

Notes

1 Some especially worthwhile examples of these comparative studies may be found in Annas (1993), Engstrom and Whiting (1996), and Sherman (1997). Finnis (1980) offers a useful contrast to the "ancient and modern" approach.
2 See Gauthier and Jolif (1970), I.1.130f (but note the qualification in 131 n140).
3 Anscombe (1958). I cite it as MMP. I have benefited from the discussion by Pigden (1988).
4 "the concepts of obligation and duty – *moral* obligation and *moral* duty, that is to say –and of what is *morally* right and wrong, and of the *moral* sense of 'ought,' ought to be jettisoned if this is psychologically possible; because they are survivals, or derivatives from survivals, from an earlier conception of ethics which no longer generally survives, and are only harmful without it" (MMP 26).
5 "If someone professes to be expounding Aristotle and talks in a modern fashion about 'moral' such-and-such, he must be very imperceptive if he does not constantly feel like someone whose jaws have somehow got out of alignment: the teeth don't come together in a proper bite" (MMP 26).
6 "[These terms] have now acquired a special so-called 'moral' sense – i.e., a sense in which they imply some absolute verdict (like one of guilty / not guilty on a man) on what is described in the 'ought' sentences used in certain types of context . . . The

ordinary (and quite indispensable) terms 'should,' 'needs,' 'ought,' 'must' – acquired this special sense by being equated in the relevant contexts with 'is obliged' or 'is bound' or 'is required to,' in the sense in which one can be obliged or bound by law, or something can be required by law" (MMP 29–30).

7   In a fuller discussion of these questions, it would be advisable to distinguish the moral "ought" from moral obligation. Following Anscombe, however, I will treat them as equivalent.

8   "How did this come about? The answer is in history: between Aristotle and us came Christianity, with its *law* conception of ethics . . . In consequence of the dominance of Christianity for many centuries, the concepts of being bound, permitted, or excused became deeply embedded in our language and thought" (MMP 30).

9   "so Hume discovered the situation in which the notion 'obligation' survived, and the word 'ought' was invested with that peculiar force having which it is said to be in a 'moral' sense, but in which the belief in divine law had long since been abandoned; for it was substantially given up among Protestants at the time of the Reformation. The situation, if I am right, was the interesting one of the survival of a concept outside the framework of thought that made it a really intelligible one" (MMP 30–31).

10 I will sometimes speak of "the moral ought" without inverted commas.

11 "it is possible to take a view of morality which at any rate leaves in the background the cognition of rule and restraint, the imperative, inhibitive, coercive effect of the moral ideal. We may consider the action to which the moral faculty prompts us intrinsically 'good'; so that the doing of it is in itself desirable, an end at which it is reasonable to aim. This . . . is the more ancient view of Ethics; it was taken exclusively by all the Greek schools of Moral Philosophy except the Stoics; and even with them 'Good' was the more fundamental conception, although in later Stoicism the quasi-jural aspect of good conduct came into prominence" (Sidgwick 1907: I.93). For related contrasts between ancient and modern ethics, see Brochard (1912: 492–3) and White (2002: ch. 3).

12 "In the centuries of Christianity, philosophical ethics has generally taken its form unconsciously from the theological. Now as theological ethics is essentially *dictatorial*, the philosophical has also appeared in the form of precept and moral obligation, in all innocence and without suspecting that for this, first another sanction is necessary" (Schopenhauer 1965: 54).

13 "It was in *this* sphere, then, the sphere of legal obligation, that the moral conceptual world of 'guilt,' 'conscience,' 'duty,' 'sacredness of duty' had its origins . . . And might one not add that, fundamentally, this world has never since lost a certain odour of blood and torture? (Not even in good old Kant; the categorical imperative smells of cruelty)" Nietzsche 1967: II.6.65).

14 In Anscombe's view, "we" presumably do not include Roman Catholics (or others who share her belief in the appropriate sort of divine legislator) addressing one another.

15 He relates it to Aristotle's views on natural justice, at *Commentary on NE* 1018.

16 *Summa Theologiae* (cited hereinafter without title) 1–2 q90 a1: "Law is some sort of (*quaedam*) rule and measure of acts, in accordance with which someone is led toward acting or is restrained from acting; for law (*lex*) is spoken of from binding (*ligare*) because it binds (*obligat*) one to acting."

17 "it is obvious that all things share in some way in the eternal law, namely to the extent that from its impression on them they have a tendency towards the acts and ends proper to them. Among other things, however, a rational creature is subject to divine providence in a more excellent way, to the extent that it itself acquires a share in providence, by exercising foresight [*providens*] for itself and others. Thus it shares in eternal reason, through which it has a natural inclination to the required [*debitum*] action and end. And in a rational creature this participation in the eternal law is called the natural law" (1–2 q91 a2).

18 "For all reasoning is derived from principles that are naturally known, and all desire of means to an end is derived from natural desire for the ultimate end. And so it is also necessary that the first directing of our acts towards the end comes about through natural law" (q91 a2 ad2).

19 "law belongs to that which is a principle of human acts, because it is a rule and measure. Now just as reason is a principle of human acts, so also in reason itself there is something which is a principle in respect of all the other things. Hence it is necessary that law belongs principally and most of all to this principle. Now the first principle in practical matters, which practical reason is about, is the ultimate end. Now the ultimate end of human life is happiness or blessedness, as stated above. Hence it is necessary that the law regards most of all the direction [*ordo*] towards happiness" (q90 a2).

20 The position I am disagreeing with here is stated by Schneewind (1997: 20): "But Thomas departs from Aristotle in holding that the laws of the virtues can be formulated and used in practical reasoning. There are laws containing precepts for all the virtues and thus providing rational guidance where we need it (1–2 q65 a3; cf. 1–2 q94 a3). Thomas does not invoke the Aristotelian insight of the virtuous agent as our final guide. For him the virtues are basically habits of obedience to laws." See also p. 287: "St Thomas subordinated the virtues to the laws of nature."

21 This clumsy formulation is intended to take some account of Suarez's views on essences (*Disputationes Metaphysicae* xxxi).

22 The different positions about morality and divine legislation may be described as "voluntarist" and "naturalist," and I will use these convenient terms. But the disputes we are concerned with do not raise all the issues that are raised by the medieval disputes that modern critics describe as disputes between voluntarism and naturalism. One might, for instance, dispute about whether facts about moral rightness are asymmetrically dependent on God's will. Either a voluntarist or a naturalist answer to that question would be consistent with the naturalist claim that rightness is fixed by natural facts independently of divine legislation; for one might hold that God's free act of creation, undetermined by any antecedent facts about what he ought to create, fixes the natural facts about rightness, independently of any legislation. Equally, one might claim that God's acts of creation and legislation are alike determined by antecedent facts about what he ought to create and how he ought to legislate, but still maintain that divine legislation is necessary for moral rightness.

23 This naturalist doctrine is accepted by (*inter alios*) Aquinas, and later by Suarez (1548–1617), and Grotius (1583–1645). For present purposes, I pass over differences in their views about the relation of natural law to morality and to divine commands.

24 Voluntarists (in this respect) among early modern philosophers include Cumberland (1632–1718) and Pufendorf (1632–94).

25 "[The naturalist view to be rejected]: that some things in themselves, apart from any imposition, are right [*honesta*] or wrong, and these constitute the object of natural and everlasting law [*ius*], whereas those things that are right are wrong because the legislator willed, come under the heading of positive laws [*leges*] . . ." (Pufendorf, *De iure naturae et gentium* [1934]: I.2.6).

26 "But this natural goodness and badness of actions in themselves does not at all place them in the area of morals" (Pufendorf 1934: I.2.6).

27 The naturalists include Cudworth (1617–88), Clarke (1675–1729), Balguy (1686–1748), Butler (1692–1752), and Price (1723–91).

28 "Obligation to action, and rightness of action, are plainly coincident and identical; so far so, that we cannot form a notion of the one, without taking in the other. This may appear to anyone upon considering, whether he can point out any difference between what is right, meet or fit to be done and what ought to be done. It is not indeed plainer, that figure implies something figured, solidity resistance, or an effect a cause, than it is that rightness implies oughtness (if I may be allowed this word) or obligatoriness" (Price 1974: 105).

29 "From the account given of obligation, it follows that rectitude is a law as well as a rule to us . . . Reason is the guide, the natural and authoritative guide of a rational being . . . But where he has this discernment, where moral good appears to him, and he cannot avoid pronouncing concerning an action that it is fit to be done, and evil to omit it; here he is tied in the most strict and absolute manner . . . That is properly a law to us, which we always and unavoidably feel and own ourselves obliged to obey . . . Rectitude, then, or virtue, is a law. And it is the first and supreme law, to which all other laws owe their force, on which they depend, and in virtue of which alone they oblige. It is an universal law" (Price 1974: 109).

30 Here I have raised a controversial issue about the interpretation of Aristotle's conception of the fine. For different views, see Rogers (1993), Cooper (1996), and Irwin (1998: 237).

31 "But to make these dictates of reason obtain the power and dignity of laws, it is necessary to call in a much higher principle to our assistance. For though their usefulness is by far the most obvious, still this alone could not fix a strong enough bond on human minds to prevent them from departing from it if it pleased someone to neglect his own advantage or he thought he could consult his advantage more by some other means" (Pufendorf 1934: II.3.20).

32 I have discussed some connected issues in Irwin (1988: 195–7).

33 See q90 a2, q91 a2 ad2 (quoted above nn 18, 19).

34 "If we speak of virtuous actions insofar as they are virtuous, in this way all virtuous actions belong to the law of nature. For it has been said that everything to which a human being is inclined in accordance with his nature belongs to the law of nature. Moreover, everything is naturally inclined to the activity that is suitable for it in accordance with its form, as fire, for instance, is inclined to heating. Hence, since rational animal is the form proper to a human being, every human being has a natural inclination towards action in accordance with reason. And this is action in accordance with virtue" (1–2 q94 a3).

35 I quote a few passages from the important chapter *Summa Contra Gentiles* III.129: "From what has been said, moreover, it is apparent that the things prescribed by divine

law have correctness not only because they are laid down by law, but also in accord with nature . . . Human beings by divine providence are allotted a natural criterion of reason [*naturale iudicatorium rationis*] as the principle of their proper activities. Now natural principles are directed to things that are naturally. Therefore there are activities naturally appropriate [*convenientes*] to a human being, which are in themselves correct, and not merely as being laid down by law . . . Wherever something is natural to a given subject, any other thing without which the first thing cannot be had must also be natural; for nature does not fail in necessities. Now it is natural to a human being to be a social animal; this is shown from the fact that one human being alone is not sufficient for all the things that are necessary for human life. Therefore the things without which human society cannot be preserved are naturally appropriate to a human being. Such things are securing to every person what is his own, and refraining from acts of injustice [*iniuriis*]. Some things, therefore, among human actions are naturally correct . . . In accordance with the natural direction [*ordo*], the body of a human being is because of the soul, and the lower powers of the soul are because of reason, just as in other things the matter is because of the form, and the instruments are because of the principal agent. Now from something that is directed to another thing, help, not hindrance, towards that other thing ought to come. It is therefore naturally correct for a human being to take care of his body and the lower powers of his soul so that as a result the action and the good of reason may not at all be hindered, but may rather be helped . . ."

36 At 1–2 q1 intro, happiness is introduced simply with *ponitur*. At q1 a7 sc, Aquinas cites Augustine, who says everyone agrees in seeking *ultimum finem, qui est beatitudo*. At q2 intro, Aquinas takes it for granted that the discussion has been about *beatitudo*.

37 Cf. 1–2 q3 a2 ad2, a3 ad2, q4 a7 ad2; *De Malo* 6.

38 "since everything seeks [*appetit*] its perfection, what someone seeks as ultimate end is what he seeks as a good that is perfect and that completes himself . . . It is necessary, therefore, that the ultimate end should so fulfill the whole of a human being's desire [*appetitus*] that nothing is left to be desired outside it. And this would not be possible if anything external to it were needed for his perfection" (1–2 q1 a5).

39 "The character of good consists in this, that something is desirable. Hence the Philosopher says 'Good is what all things desire.' Now it is clear that a thing is desirable only insofar as it is perfect; for all desire their own perfection. But everything is perfect so far as it is actual. Therefore it is clear that a thing is perfect so far as it exists; for it is existence that makes all things actual" (1a q5 a1; cf. q6 a1).

40 "Some activities are naturally appropriate [*convenientes*] to a human being, which are correct in themselves, and not merely as being laid down by law" (*Summa contra Gentiles* III.129.3).

41 I am not claiming that Aquinas always says what it would be reasonable for him to say on this point.

42 As Aquinas makes clear in speaking of the "order" of natural inclinations (q94 a2), the application of rational agency does not disregard the aspects of human beings that make them living organisms and make them animals.

43 "Thirdly, there is in man an inclination to good, according to the nature of his reason, which nature is proper to him: thus man has a natural inclination to know the truth

about God, and to live in society: and in this respect, whatever pertains to this inclination belongs to the natural law; for instance, to shun ignorance, to avoid offending those among whom one has to live, and other such things regarding the above inclination" (q94 a2).

44　"In the same way" is explained by "for their own sake." It does not imply "to the same degree" (cf. 2–2 q26 a4; *De Caritate* a9 ad9).

45　See *Scriptum super Sententiis* 2 d3 q4 a1 ad2; Finnis (1998: 111).

References

Annas, J. 1993: *The Morality of Happiness*. Oxford: Oxford University Press.

Anscombe, G. E. M. 1958: "Modern Moral Philosophy," *Philosophy* 33: 1–19; reprinted in *Collected Philosophical Papers*, vol. 3, pp. 26–42. Minneapolis, MN: University of Minnesota Press, 1981.

Aquinas, Thomas 1980: *Thomae Aquinatis Opera Omnia*, 4 vols, ed. R. Busa. Stuttgart: Frommann-Holzboog.

Brochard, V. 1912: *Études de philosophie ancienne et de philosophie moderne*. Paris: Alcan.

Burnet, John 1900: *The Ethics of Aristotle*. London: Methuen.

Cooper, J. M. 1996: "Reason, Moral Virtue, and Moral Value." In M. Frede and G. Striker (eds), *Rationality in Greek Thought*, pp. 81–114. Oxford: Oxford University Press.

Engstrom, S. and Whiting, J. (eds) 1996: *Rethinking Duty and Happiness: Aristotle, Kant, and the Stoics*. Cambridge: Cambridge University Press.

Finnis, J. M. 1980: *Natural Law and Natural Rights*. Oxford: Clarendon Press.

—1998: *Aquinas: Moral, Political, and Legal Theory*. Oxford: Oxford University Press.

Gauthier, R-A, and Jolif, J-Y. 1970: *Aristote: L'Éthique à Nicomaque*, 2nd edn, 4 vols. Louvain: Publications Universitaires.

Grant, Alexander 1885: *The Ethics of Aristotle*, 4th edn. London: Longmans, Green, and Co.

Grisez, G. G. 1969: "The First Principle of Natural Law." In A. J. P. Kenny (ed.), *Aquinas*, pp. 340–82. Garden City, NY: Doubleday.

Irwin, T. H. 1988: *Aristotle's First Principles*. Oxford: Clarendon Press.

Joachim, H. H. 1951: *Aristotle, The Nicomachean Ethics*, ed. D. A. Rees. Oxford: Clarendon Press.

Nietzsche, F. 1967: *Genealogy of Morals*, trans. W. Kaufmann. New York: Vintage.

Pigden, C. R. 1988: "Anscombe on 'Ought,'" *Philosophcal Quarterly* 38: 20–41.

Price, R. 1787: *A Review of the Principal Questions in Morals*, 3rd edn (first pub. 1758), ed. D. D. Raphael, 2nd edn. Oxford: Clarendon Press, 1974.

Pufendorf, S. 1934: *De iure naturae et gentium*, trans. C. H. Oldfather and W. A. Oldfather. Oxford: Clarendon Press.

Rogers, K. 1993: "Aristotle's Conception of *to kalon*," *Ancient Philosophy* 13: 355–71.

Schneewind, J. B. 1997: *The Invention of Autonomy*. Cambridge: Cambridge University Press.

Schopenhauer, A. 1965: *On the Basis of Morality*, trans. E. F. J. Payne. Indianapolis, IN: Bobbs-Merrill.

Sherman, N. 1997: *Making a Necessity out of Virtue*. Cambridge: Cambridge University Press.

Sidgwick, H.1902: *Outlines of the History of Ethics*, 4th edn. London: Macmillan.

— 1907: *The Methods of Ethics*, 7th edn. London: Macmillan.

Stewart, J. A. 1892: *Notes on the Nicomachean Ethics of Aristotle*. Oxford: Clarendon Press.

Suarez, F. 1866: *Opera Omnia*, ed. C. Berton, 28 vols. Paris: Vivès.

—1944: *Selections from Three Works*, 2 vols, trans. G. L. Williams et al. Oxford: Clarendon Press.

White, N. P. 2002: *Individual and Conflict in Greek Ethics*. Oxford: Oxford University Press.

Further reading

Bradley, D. J. M. 1997: *Aquinas on the Twofold Human Good*. Washington: CUA Press.

Doig, J. C. 2001: *Aquinas's Philosophical Commentary on Aristotle's Ethics*. Dordrecht: Kluwer.

MacDonald, S. C. 1990: "Egoistic Rationalism: Aquinas' Basis for Christian Morality." In M. D. Beaty (ed.), *Christian Theism and the Problems of Philosophy*. Notre Dame: University of Notre Dame Press.

—and Stump, E. S. (eds) 1998: *Aquinas's Moral Theory*. Ithaca, NY: Cornell University Press.

MacIntyre, A. C. 1988: *Whose Justice? Which Rationality?* London: Duckworth.

16

Aristotle and Contemporary Ethics

Sarah Broadie

In the twenty-three centuries of Western thinking since Aristotle, the subject called "ethics" has grown to embrace many more topics than Aristotle took account of under this or any title. Many of our own central preoccupations in ethics are with questions on which, for one or another reason, Aristotle has little or nothing to say. This is worth emphasizing. Because of Aristotle's pre-eminent greatness and the reach and power of his ancient authority, unwarned readers of his *Nicomachean Ethics* may simply take it for granted that in this or that important modern debate there is a theory of which Aristotle holds a version, or a side which he is recognizably on. Such assumptions are all the more easy to slip into because so much of what he *does* have to say in the *NE* continues to shape our own thinking on those particular matters, and so much of it comes in direct answer to questions whose universal relevance is as obvious in our day as it would have been in his.

What is more, because so much of what he has to say in the *NE* tends to seem to us extraordinarily sensible as well as illuminating, we can easily fail to absorb how unusual some of his presuppositions are by today's philosophical standards. In this chapter, I shall be bringing out some of the differences between Aristotle's concerns in ethics and contemporary concerns. However, there are parts of our Aristotelian legacy that we can wholeheartedly continue to endorse, and also parts from which we may be able to learn more than we have learned so far. Some of these, too, will be touched upon in this chapter.

Flourishing

Let us begin with a possession which it seems can hardly grow old: the great Aristotelian idea of human flourishing, or simple *flourishing* for short, since here we are setting aside the biological flourishing of plants and non-rational animals. To speak of flourishing in the human context is to speak, of course, of *eudaimonia*.

Yet it would be a mistake to propose "flourishing" as the preferred translation for *eudaimonia* in general. The word excellently captures the narrower idea of *human eudaimonia*, but – as Aristotle does not allow us to forget – *eudaimonia* was ascribed to the gods as well as to the best and most successful humans. The idea that gods and (some) human beings are alike subjects of *eudaimonia* is probably not an assumption we today require in order to reach ethical conclusions, even of an Aristotelian sort. But we have to allow to Aristotle this assumption, since on it rests his final argument in the *Nicomachean Ethics* identifying the most perfect form of human flourishing.

Now, it cannot be correct to speak of god or the gods as "flourishing." Why not? For exactly the reason why that word works so well for specifically human *eudaimonia*: what flourishes is what grows and dies and depends on an environment and can come to grief; all of which is true of humans. One does not need to believe in any god to feel the force of Aristotle's contrast, never far from the surface, between divine *eudaimonia* and the human kind which is the subject of the *NE*: in other words, to be constantly in mind of the universal human limitations and vulnerabilities, as well as potentialities. "Flourishing" alludes to all that. We *are* rational beings: but mortal, implanted in an environment, at its mercy through our bodies, born in thrall to the sensations and instinctual emotions necessary for bare survival, requiring constant care and replenishment, utterly dependent for our development on somewhat more mature versions of ourselves – that is, on beings with, at best, many of the same infirmities, and wielding no more than human capacities of understanding and protection. These conditions, and the resulting needs, longings, general patterns of relationship and authority, constitute the context for realizing any *eudaimonia* that might be open to humankind. Thus the concept of flourishing points both toward our highest aspirations and toward the mortal life-form in terms of which any of our aspirations are to be achieved.

So we have from Aristotle the seed – and more than just a seed – of a truly sound and fruitful approach to the question of human well-being. According to this approach, one starts by forming a systematic conception of the most significant features of the human animal. One forges an anthropological picture, partly empirical, partly a priori, which may even be quite detailed while maintaining universality. Such a picture is essential for well-informed, intelligent, discussion of what is involved, at any level, in human well-being – what it consists in and how it is to be realized. In a sense, the picture defines human well-being and its opposite, since it shows us the plexus of respects in which human life can go well or badly. List the respects and say: human well-being – or flourishing – is or entails being well off in *these*. Such a statement is not empty: it rules out some supposed possibilities as incoherent. But it only sets the stage for discussion of substantial options. A non-question-begging anthropological picture fails to generate a unique narrowly substantial account of the human good. In particular, it fails to justify the account for which Aristotle himself eventually settles: one that (a) equates flourishing with, predominantly, the activity of virtue, "virtue" being understood as meaning courage, moderation and the rest, and above all justice; and (b) interprets these qualities in the ordinary moralistic sense.

But there are those who "by any ethological standard of the bright eye and the gleaming coat [are] dangerously flourishing" (Williams 1985: 46): people who are ruthless and dishonest, but intelligent, well-organized, achievers of their goals, enjoying life. What about them? As contemporary ethicists, we wonder how Aristotle imagines he can get away with his equation. If, by a supposedly logical transition from "living [or functioning] well" (*eu*) to "living [or functioning] in accordance with virtue" (*kat'aretēn*), then the equation rests on an equivocation between the philosopher's formulaic sense of the virtue of an X – that whereby an X is or functions as a good one – and what the ordinary person understands by "virtue" as applied to human beings. A hedonist would or should argue that living or functioning well is living or functioning pleasantly, with "the (formulaic) virtue in accordance with which" understood as the capacity (or a set of capacities) for pleasure. Some hold that living well is living splendidly, which they identify perhaps with wielding power and the "triumph of the will"; or with the glamor of elegance and "cool"; the virtues, for them, correspond.

Reading Aristotle with a contemporary eye, and seeing clearly the absence of an analytic connection between "living well" (in the sense supplied by the anthropological picture) and living a life of ethical virtue, we can be easily drawn to conclude that Aristotle attaches flourishing to ethically virtuous activity in order to give us a needed motive toward the latter. Or we may conclude that Aristotle proposes flourishing as the "ultimate justification of morality"; that is to say, what makes it true that I ought to do what is morally right is that thereby I shall flourish.[1] But if doing what is right stands in need of justification, flourishing could provide this only if it is distinct from such ethically virtuous activity, whereas Aristotle all but identifies them. What is more, Aristotle knew that his equation was what we call a synthetic statement. As the style of his advocacy for it shows, he knew perfectly well that it was a contested position, and that both claim and counter-claim were logically intelligible. Aristotle, of course, thinks his equation well supported by reputable opinions; but an intellectually resourceful hedonist could have made a better case than Aristotle allows to appear, as could an intellectually resourceful adherent of "living splendidly" on one of the amoralist interpretations suggested above. No doubt Aristotle can defuse their cases by arguing that what is intuitively attractive about their candidates is in some satisfactory way provided, or the longing for it taken care of, by his own. However, one cannot help wondering whether a hedonist or a splendid life-ist as clever as Aristotle might not have turned the tables by showing ways in which what is intuitively attractive about virtuous (in the ordinary sense) activity is actually to be found, in some form or other, lurking within the folds of *their* ideals. Does Aristotle push ahead simply because no such clever other voice was raised?

Ethical Epistemology, Ethical Realism

No, Aristotle pushes ahead with the equation "flourishing is virtuous [in the ordinary sense] activity" because he is a person with a certain set of values (which he can defend up to a point, though there is no reason to believe *conclusively*), and he is addressing a likeminded audience or readership. The *Nicomachean Ethics* is meant for the "well-brought up." Only they have the right "starting-points" (*NE* I.4.1095b2–6). Of course, "well-brought up" can be interpreted in exactly as many ways as "living [or functioning] well" and as "virtue" in the abstract philosophical sense. What it amounts to, in the context of the reception of a certain ideal of life philosophically explicated, is a pre-philosophical preparedness, developed through living and practice, to resonate to that ideal. Thus whatever their articulated ideas may have been, Aristotle's audience (the one for which he hopes) have in fact been living or trying to live as if just, courageous, moderate and such like action is an absolutely precious thing in itself, and as if any pleasure, power, or splendor that could be got only by acting unjustly or in a cowardly or debauched way has no practical pull on them. The thought is not that they have been living as if those other values are of no interest (how, if so, could their culture have been one where debate about conflicting ethical ideals was such an engaging pastime?), but that when it came to a conflict they would put the morally good action first. Thus when Aristotle presents them – and himself – with his equation, he and they are immediately inclined to accept it. But the immediacy to them of its rightness or truth is an expression of their character, not of an analytic or conceptual connection between the left- and right-hand sides.

We today as philosophers may be inclined to feel that this is not a very satisfactory situation, epistemologically speaking. Or rather, we today as philosophers are divided into those who find the situation epistemologically unsatisfactory, and those who understand that dissatisfied response deeply and from within, but, by one path or another, have fought their way out of it intellectually, although they bear the scars and constantly tell the tale. In what follows, I shall largely ignore this very important difference between schools of "us today as philosophers." Aristotle and his audience, then, accept Aristotle's equation about flourishing as naturally and willingly as a carnivore accepts in a practical way the equation of food with flesh. (But the acceptance of the former is not, like that of the latter, mechanical or "knee-jerk," since it is forwarded by real, though not logically conclusive, argument.) If we today are in certain personal respects like the individuals in Aristotle's audience, then we too will resonate to the equation; we may feel it a very good thing that there are people who have the qualities in question; and we may be resolved to bring up our children to be the same. But as philosophers we are tempted to think that we do not *know* the truth of the equation, since there is no knock-down rational basis for it: that is, no basis that would render it compelling to all alert human beings regardless of their moral formation.

Aristotle might puzzle over what it is that we as philosophers think (or know what it is like to be tempted to think) we are *lacking* here. For not to have knowledge matters only if the not-having is a privation; indeed, if knowledge is supposed to be valuable, we do not want to call something "knowledge" unless we see the not-having as a privation. After all, none of the rival equations is analytically true either, so it is not as if in embracing ours we are missing something epistemologically better. Furthermore, it is not as if we need to be absolutely secure of our and Aristotle's equation in order to feel right about living as we do. For our living as we do, and feeling right about it, was there before we got the equation; that was what made us feel at home with it. The equation is just the ideological summary of the values we were already practicing. Being able to display the equation (or thinking we can display it) as an analytic truth certainly will not make us more practical in respect of those values. But now suppose that a logically compelling proof of the equation were produced (or, which is not completely impossible, that we have come to believe that there is, or even that we have, such a proof): then it can be shown that people with rival equations are wrong, and they can be led to see that they are wrong! But, by the above considerations, this will make no difference to their practice (cf. *NE* X.9.1179b5–18). What is more, to the extent that their actual practice fuels an ideology, it will continue to fuel an equation contrary to ours. Thus they will be tending to affirm the latter even at the same time (according to the hypothesis) as being in a position to acknowledge that it is analytically false. And by the same token they will still be tending to reject our equation even while in a position to acknowledge that it is analytically true. This is a very curious kind of "seeing themselves to be wrong!" In fact, the notion of analytic truth has been reduced to absurdity in this context. Thus Aristotle's equation lacks nothing by lacking it: its adherents can affirm in good epistemic conscience that their equation is everything it ought to be.

Most modern philosophers at this point are bound to want to say two things: (1) that adherents to rival equations can reach exactly the same position by the same steps with regard to their favored candidate; and (2) that consequently no side is entitled to consider their own equation as knowledge, or even as true. Aristotle, I believe, operates as if it is simply not his business that the situation envisaged in (1) can arise; hence as if it is not his business to go on and consider (2). (This is all the more easy in that rival equations probably represent minority opinions.)[2] That the situation envisaged in (1) can arise is not in itself going to alter our underlying practical commitments, and as long as they remain, our equation (which is the Aristotelian one, I am supposing) is in force. The modern philosopher may well want to insert a qualifier: our equation is in force *for us*. However, if it is *we* who are doing the talking here (we of the relevant practical commitments – and the modern philosopher who has just been mentioned is quite likely one of us when out of his study), "for us" is redundant or a weakener. Aristotle is addressing his *Nicomachean Ethics* to us as practical agents (see, for example, I.2.1094a22–6, 3.1095a1–11, X.9.1179a35–b2), and as practical agents we have no business to be trying to take up a standpoint in which we are no more committed to our own equation of flourishing than to any of the rivals, or to divide our individual selves into an unregenerate lower me_1 committed to the equation, and a higher, philosophical, me_2 who regards me_1's commitment as just one of many possible facts about human beings.

Thus the Aristotelian equation is in force; and explication of the term on the right-hand side is quite a large philosophical program. Aristotle's first task, as he sees it, is to get on with this.[3] Still, one can speculate on what he would have said if forced to give a general response to the fact that there might be rival equations of flourishing, each supported by a good stock of reputable opinions. He might have said that we have to argue each step of the way with each side (as, indeed, he does to a considerable extent in the NE), and one cannot know in advance how this would turn out. He might well have emphasized that the rivals, or anyway the plausible ones among them, in a way recognize the same values but accord them different priority. This means that the adherents on each side are not talking past each other: they have a common set of subject matters, and they cannot all be right. Finally, he would not have said that no one is closer to the truth than anyone else. Aristotle would have said that those who march under banners different from the one that defines him and his preferred audience are not seeing things straight: they are missing the truth or are purblind to it; and the fact that they cannot be logically prevented from saying the same about us is simply not something that should disturb our confidence in our own views and our scorn for theirs, any more than we should let our picture of the world waver just because we know that paranoiacs see us as seriously out of touch with reality. Remember, the adherents of rival equations are not simply persons who share "the moral point of view" with us but come down on the other side of some practical dilemma. They are persons who live by the belief that, in a conflict, getting pleasure or power, or maintaining "cool," is more important than refraining from an unjust or cowardly or debauched action: or, for that matter, than discouraging it in someone else. One does not in this sense count as adherent of a rival equation if one is simply pushing a rival equation in debate, with a view to getting, for example, Aristotle to defend and explicate his equation more fully, in the way Glaucon and Adimantus challenge Socrates to explain the intrinsic value of justice by arguing against their own unargued (and as yet unshaken) belief that it is more than a means to an end and matters in reality, not just on the level of appearance.

Contemporary theorists may be disappointed, or they may be put on their mettle, by the epistemological simplicity, or crudity, with which Aristotle sets up the basic proposition of the NE. In this respect, Aristotle is not, I think, a philosophical model that we in any straightforward way can follow. In this respect, he is a reminder of lost innocence, but not a leader back to it. There is, however, no shortage in the NE of philosophical refinement and dexterity once we are within the framework of Aristotle's basic proposition.

Having reached the issue of Aristotle's "moral realism," I now cease to focus on the "equation of flourishing," which is a universal philosophical statement, and turn instead to the question of ground-level practical judgments and feelings sparked in people by their particular situations. These include both judgments about particulars and the activations of various evaluative generalizations about persons, personal qualities, and behavior. Aristotle, as we all know, speaks of the virtuous person, the person of practical wisdom (*phronēsis*), as the ethical "yard-stick" of the particular situations he is presented with (*NE* III.4.1113a29–33). Aristotle is occasionally thought to mean by this that the say so of the *phronimos* determines, in the sense of actually constituting (or "constructing"), the truth about particular ethical questions. I do not think that this is Aristotle's view. He, of course, sees the *phronimos* as a good guide for the rest of us. To get the benefit of this guidance we do not (as is sometimes complained) need to be able to rec-ognize the *phronimos* independently. To be able to do that reliably we should have to be *phronimoi* ourselves, hence in no need of an external *phronimos*. But actually to get the benefit of the guidance of a *phronimos*, we only have to be lucky enough to be placed near one – one who takes an interest in us and whom we have been brought up to regard as a person to be listened to with respect.

However, Aristotle, I am sure, goes along with the *phronimos*'s personal experi-ence of forming ethical judgments, and with the experience of the less mature in getting his advice. To the *phronimos* in operation, considering how to respond in some particular situation, it seems as if he is looking for an answer which is in some sense "there"; or if he forms the judgment instantly, the discrimination, though obvious, presents itself as what would have been correct whether or not he had realized it. He sees himself as possibly making mistakes, and no doubt as having made them in the past. And the advice he gives others does not consist just of pre-scriptions but carries explanations: he gives reasons why this is better than that, and the recipients can see the reasons once they are pointed out, and can see in the light of those reasons that the prescribed action is appropriate. By such interaction they develop their own potential as *phronimoi*. (What they have to take on trust in these sessions is that the *phronimos* has considered all relevant factors.) Thus those who accept guidance by the *phronimos*, come to the answers as right ones which were "there," and which they might – and, on their own, would – have missed. Philosophers today have to *argue* themselves back into taking such experiences of objectivity at face value; for example: "If we take seriously the idea that there are not *two* criteria or sets of criteria for 'reality' – commonsense [or: human] criteria and philosophical criteria – but only one, then we are led naturally to the view that what demarcates 'reality' is something human . . ." (Putnam 1990: 247).

Aristotle, then, does not explain ethical truth as what the *phronimos* reliably apprehends: he explains the *phronimos* as reliably apprehending ethical truth. And he sometimes speaks of the apprehending as if it were a sort of perceptual access (for example, *NE* VI.12.1144a29–b1). A modern philosopher of not too long ago would have been impelled to ask: does this mean that Aristotle postulates a special faculty of ethical intuition, a moral sense? Well, if so, it would be a faculty developed through the right kind of habituation, but what could be the point of postulating a faculty in addition to the virtuous person's habituated qualities of character and practical intelligence? Presumably the idea of a special moral sense answers to an epistemological anxiety. Just as we justify many particular empirical claims by saying "I saw it with my own eyes," "I heard with my own ears," and so on, the philosopher wants us to be able to justify ethical claims analogously. But in fact we justify the ethical claims by pointing out or describing what we take to be the relevant facts in each case (often without explicitly invoking any principle of conduct). The philosophical anxiety, then, is that this sort of procedure, of which we all have an everyday understanding, is not good enough to deliver real ethical knowledge – or that its working is completely mysterious. The anxiety is bound up with the thought that if there is ethical knowledge, the properties and relations thereby known are metaphysically "queer" (Mackie 1977: 38–42). How can there really be such entities in the world, and how, if there are such, could they make their impact on us *just* in virtue of the fact that we have had a certain upbringing resulting in a certain kind of character?

The classic modern response to such worries has been to reject the whole idea of ethical truth: the appearance of ethical factuality is the "projection" by us of our attitudes or feelings on to objects which in themselves are devoid of ethical qualities. In the wake of this view come a variety of sophisticated efforts to hang on to the objectivity of ethical judgments while rejecting "queer" entities and the mysterious faculty of ethical knowledge. There are theories allowing for objectivity without truth, and there are "cognitive irrealist" theories allowing for truth without correspondence to realities. But how is it that Aristotle is so unperturbed by the worries which today drive us down these or similarly motivated routes? I do not mean to imply that he does not treat seriously various ancient arguments for ethical relativism (or anti-objectivism). But those arguments do not turn on the thought that there is something ontologically monstrous about, in particular, *ethical* realities (and would be even if all humans had one culture), so that our knowing *them* would be in principle mysterious: all this by comparison with some type of reality that philosophers feel to be non-"bizarre." This is an essentially modern thought. To try to diagnose it would be to enter a huge discussion. Here I shall only tender the familiar suggestion that the thought crystallizes inordinate respect for natural science. Ethical properties cannot be weighed, measured, physically analyzed, and so on by science. Nor are they reliable concomitants of the properties and relations that are weighed, measured, analyzed, and so on by science. Science rightly for its own purposes ignores ethical properties. But inordinate respect (an attitude of philosophers, not of scientists as such) sees the purposes of science as determining what is to count as regular, normal, metaphysically unsurprising, external-to-the-observer's-mind, reality. So it comes to seem that ethical properties and ethical facts either are unreal (projections of the observer's mind) or are realities of a strange unworldly kind.

Aristotle might have commented that regarding ethical properties as unreal because natural science does not take account of them is on a par with regarding physical change and physical matter as unreal because mathematics, that paradigm of knowledge in his day, abstracts from them. Plato, after all, in some of his writings might be accused of that mistake. Moreover, although Aristotle himself has great respect for the enterprise of physical science (and notwithstanding his teleology and his mainly non-quantitative approach, he, of course, is just as clear as we are that the subject matter of natural science is quite other than the subject matter of ethical judgments) – still, Western science at that time was still taking its first wobbling steps: it was not yet a mighty and prestigious institution.

A contemporary of Aristotle's, the great rhetorician Isocrates, who was without doubt one of the most cultivated men of the classical period, had so little sense of the seriousness of the business of theorizing about the universe that he dismissed all such discussions as amusements for the empty-headed.[4] There were no laboratories with state funding pouring into them, and there were few technological spin-offs, to counteract the picture of the natural philosopher as a wild-haired eccentric. In any case, the theories themselves were so speculative. Many people – educated ones like Isocrates – would have laughed at the idea that physics puts us in touch with "hard facts." To an ancient Greek (and surely to most people in any period) no theoretical claim in physics or medicine could have carried the same certainty as, for example: "Love is better than hate between close members of the same family, except under very strange circumstances – and such circumstances should be avoided like the plague." Why, then, when we compare, on the one hand, an ethical sensibility whose exercise in particular situations (including ones that are hearsay and ones that are fictional) delivers, reinforces, and perhaps gives more precise sense to the above generalization with, on the other hand, a scientific observer's (ethically) value-free focus on particulars that may confirm an hypothesis – why should we think the former less a source of respect-worthy knowledge than the latter? And if in each case the knowledge is respectable, why should we balk at admitting a known reality equally robust in each?

Deciding What is Right

From the topic of Aristotle's meta-ethical stance versus various modern positions, I now pass to comparisons under the heading of "normative ethics." What does Aristotle's *Nicomachean Ethics* tell us we should do, and what does the work offer by way of guidance in making decisions? To answer this, some exegesis is necessary.

Particularly in the *Nicomachean Ethics*, Aristotle deals with human objectives at two different levels. On the one hand, and most famously, there is that great objective the Good for Man, i.e. human *eudaimonia*. Aristotle sees this as the final goal of what he calls "political" thought and action. "Political" refers to a field where the job is to articulate and implement the best arrangements overall for life in human society. Thought and action on this level are "architectonic" (*NE* I.2.1094a27). Then, on the other hand, there is what we may call "ground-level" or "quotidian" activity.

The fundamental step in architectonic thinking is to set out a correct substantial account of flourishing with its ramifications: this will provide a "target" for "political" action (*NE* I.2.1094a22–6). The actions and decisions to be taken in its light will be what we can loosely call "big" ones. They will be concerned with life-shaping arrangements that are hard to reverse: those that make the context of everything else. It is distinctive of architectonic thinking that in its fundamental stage we take for granted no context other than the human condition itself. Obviously, as we move ahead to envisage implementations, we have to take account of unalterable or currently unalterable features of our specific context (for instance, geographical features, institutional features, material resources). But the thinking preserves its universal, philosophical, and architectonic character by reflecting on and evaluating these unalterable elements in terms of their effect on flourishing as spelled out at the first stage. What mainly distinguishes architectonic practical thinking from the ground-level kind is that the latter at any given moment accepts its particular set of circumstances with no more analysis than is necessary for deciding how best to manage from within them. In the light of this distinction, which brings out a generic difference between two kinds of practical thinking, it is superficial to draw a contrast between thinking on behalf of one, or a few, and thinking on behalf of many. This is why Aristotle calls the thinking "political" even when it is a case of individuals thinking out what path to follow in their individual lives (*NE* I.2.1094b7–11). It counts as "political" because it is architectonic.

Two more points should be made. The first, which may seem too obvious to mention, is that Aristotelian architectonic thinking figures in the *Nicomachean Ethics* from the very first line. The work starts with the famous assumption that there is a "highest good" functionally defined in terms of its endhood in relation to everything else, and it then proceeds (with arguments) to characterize this good substantially, by means of one of several logically possible equations of flourishing. The right-hand side of Aristotle's equation then gets detailed explication through portraits of the individual virtues. Here we are shown many examples of ground-level conduct, both good and bad. The account of the individual practical virtues reaches completion with a study of *phronēsis*, the kind of wisdom responsible for excellent ground-level or quotidian practical decision-making. It is in this central portion of Aristotle's entire ethical investigation – not earlier – that the question of excellent ground-level practical thinking comes to the fore. In short, the idea of this sort of thinking, the thinking of the *phronimos*, has quite a different place in the plan of the *NE* from the idea of architectonic thinking. Architectonic thinking engaged in by Aristotle is first and foremost what is producing the whole inquiry, and in so doing architectonic thinking occasionally refers to itself. But the thinking that typifies the *phronimos* figures only as one of the subject matters. It is not presented as directed toward the architectonic goal, whether to elucidate this goal philosophically or to work out large-scale arrangements for realizing it. Rather, the thinking of the *phronimos* is *part of* that goal as correctly elucidated.

The second point is that Aristotle's conception of the architectonic goal does not commit him to the view that we ought to be deliberately promoting it in all our plans and decisions. Clearly, it is not incumbent on human beings to be always engaging in architectonic thinking, even if it is foolish and unworthy to take no interest in it if one has the leisure to do it at all. Nor, in my view, does Aristotle see us as required at every juncture to be working to propagate the realization of the architectonic goal. He sees our lives as full of different obligations, interests, and commitments, and as requiring from us many immediate reactions to immediate circumstances.[5] This by and large is the nature of a human life, and his ideal is that we live such a life well, which for him means: mainly in terms of the virtues moralistically conceived.[6] It would fit in with this if Aristotle holds, as he surely does, not only that we need not always be working for the architectonic goal, but also that quotidian morality constrains architectonic practice. If I could promote the flourishing of many (on his interpretation of "flourishing"), but only by perpetrating flagrant acts of injustice against a few, would I be right to go ahead? There is no evidence that Aristotle, any more than common sense, thinks that I would be. What gives flourishing its status as the greatest of human ends is simply that it is the best of practicable goods. But this pre-eminence among goods does not confer on flourishing the right to make perpetual and absolute demands on our agency; nor does it confer the authority to justify any kind of action on its behalf.[7]

On one level, then, Aristotle gives a full, clear, and unitary answer to the question: "what should I do?" If the question is being asked from the architectonic perspective, the answer is in terms of a goal to be achieved, a good to be brought about – whether for one, few, or many persons, whether for oneself or others – and the portrait of that good is drawn in the *NE*. Architectonic performance, good or bad, right or wrong, must be judged against its goal, as medical performance against the goal of health. However, for the ground level of quotidian practicality, Aristotle attempts no general answer. He does not think that a useful one can be stated (see *NE* II.2.1104a1–10, quoted in the postscript to the next section). Apart from dividing the objects of practical interest into the advantageous, the pleasant, and the admirable (noble, fine) (*NE* II.3.1104b30–31), he does not, except in the sphere of special justice, try to elucidate principles of good action. He does not list rules of conduct, or rank them, or try to subsume some rules under others, or to reduce many rules to few or one. In short, on the quotidian level, except in the areas of distributive and corrective justice, Aristotle offers no theory at all to guide ethical decision-making.

He is not a consequentialist, and in particular not a eudaimonistic one. He has common-sense deontological leanings, but shows not the slightest interest in working them into a system. And his deontology, such as it is, involves no banging of the board against some alternative theory. Particular remarks make it clear that he does not "found the right on the good" (not even, as we have seen, on the highest good), but he never formulates this as a general position. He is not even, it has to be said, a modern-style "virtue-ethicist" if this means a philosopher who defines right or appropriate action as the action of the virtuous person (or the courageous or moderate or good-tempered or just and so on, depending on the case). On the contrary, Aristotle explains virtuousness and the virtues as dispositions for right or appropriate action and emotion (toward the appropriate people, at the appropriate moment, in the appropriate amount, and so on), but without ever being prompted to state a set of rules to which these responses would generally conform. Equally mythological is the view that, for example, the courageous agent according to Aristotle acts from a rule that goes: "Courage demands that one do so and so."

It is true that Aristotle does give a sort of classification of appropriate response when he divides life into the spheres of the virtues; this tells us that there are as many different kinds of appropriate response as there are spheres.[8] But this is not a taxonomy of specific rules or principles, nor does it entail any.[9]

Systematizing the Principles of Quotidian Conduct?

That Aristotle provides no ground-level normative ethics, and is apparently quite untroubled by any lack of a system here, gives us food for thought. He so blatantly fails to produce the kind of position that it is a modern tradition to expect as a main deliverance of philosophical ethics – and he is not wringing his hands! Of course, Aristotle was untouched by those historical influences that transformed philosophical ethics into, in large part, a "jural" business of formulating and justifying rules and principles. But while not disputing that true observation, let us think about what goes into forming a perspective from which a philosophical ethics *sans* codified principles of quotidian action could seem self-sufficient. In Aristotle's case, first and foremost is the fact that he is addressing "well-brought-up" persons. Such persons should know, or be able to work out, what to do in particular situations: and these judgments they, and anyone, may well be unable to make until immersed in the situation itself.[10]

Secondly, there is the fact that citizens are supposed to know the laws of their *polis*, and the laws enshrine values and principles of right and wrong: so much so that Aristotle regularly equates general injustice with disrespect for law (for example, *NE* V.1.1129b11ff). However, Aristotle cannot hope for hearers or readers who are uncritically acceptant of the laws and customs of their country, and of their own upbringing; on the contrary, he must hope for ones who will think afresh about such matters in the light of his own articulated ideal of flourishing.[11] So he assumes an intelligent, rationally responsive audience for ethics. Yet even for them he does not consider it the philosopher's job to deepen, by systematizing, their understanding of the rights and wrongs of quotidian conduct. True, no set of rules covers every situation, and rules do not interpret themselves, but philosophers who attempt to give us systems of rules are aware of that, and it does not stop them.

Aristotle's eccentricity here should perhaps make us curious to understand better the deeply entrenched modern assumption that a major, if not the central, task of philosophical ethics is to systematize the principles of ordinary personal conduct. And in thinking about the *raison* (or *raisons*) *d'être* of such systematics, one also naturally wonders whether Aristotelian ethics is better or worse for lacking that approach. In the present space, little more can be done than to advertise that question, but any discussion of it should observe two points. First, the question of the value of system must be separated from that of the goodness, rightness, or adequacy of the principles themselves. Obviously, there is the closest historical connection between the biblical origins of our inherited codifying approach, and the (in origin) Judeo-Christian values thereby standardly explicated. Even so, the type of approach and any specific content it targets are distinct issues. Hence we can register our moral alienhood from classical Greece's – and Aristotle's – lack of any ethic of universal respect for persons, and failure to recognize the virtue of compassion, without taking a stand on the value or point of systematics as such. There might conceivably have been a culture where universal respect and compassion were principles, and which made its laws of the land accordingly, but whose intellectual or spiritual leaders were no more disposed to organize normative ethics than is Aristotle.

Secondly, the point or value of systematization may be (a) intrinsic to the activity itself; or it may be that (b) system makes the targeted principles more normatively effective; or (c) the value may arise through extrinsic and variable circumstances. For example, the system-building might conceivably be engaged (a[i]) academically, just as an interesting theoretical exercise; or (a[ii]) because in doing it we are studying the unitary and harmonious will of God for man (even as the cosmologist studies a different aspect of the "mind of God"); or (a[iii]) because we are tracing the contours of universal and eternal ethical reality. Or (b[i]) it may be thought that by reducing the principles to a very abstract few, or ideally to one, we make them more "scientific" and epistemologically more secure: bringing out and thus reinforcing their true rational authority, so that the justifications they provide will be rationally compelling upon all rational beings as such. (Such an ambition could probably only arise in response to skeptical and sentimentalist onslaughts on the entire notion of practical reason.) More modestly, (b[ii]) it may be thought that systematizing the principles makes it easier to deal with hard cases and dilemmas (but could this motivation alone suffice?). Finally (c), system may be sought because of the historical circumstances: for example, things may have changed so that real-life justifications, in order to work between people, must now be allowed to depend less on trust and shared unspoken assumptions, and more on explicit endorsement of what others explicitly endorse.

These considerations (even if most of them could not have occurred to him) give us a sense of what Aristotle was not providing in not providing philosophical clarification of principles of conduct. I shall comment briefly on (b[i]), the Kantian program, and on the example under (c). As we have seen, Aristotle is untouched by any scientism that may be animating (b[i]). There is no pressure on him to feel that what is less scientific is therefore less rational or less epistemologically secure. Neither he nor any school of thought confronted by him divines grounds for worrying that practical right reason will turn out to be somehow less authoritative than we expect of it, unless we show that rejecting its decisions, or the reasons for them, traps one in some kind of logical inconsistency.

In general, nothing in Aristotle's dialectical scene makes it attractive to imagine that the authoritativeness of practical right reason depends on its formality or its abstractness or some other property with logico-aesthetic appeal. On the other hand, moral seriousness is no stranger to Aristotle. Thus, he would heartily endorse some of the Kantian associations of (b[i]), in particular the thought that the virtuous agent does what is right because it is right (or because of the reasons that render it right) and not because of some ulterior desiratum, as well as the thought that the virtuous agent honors and treasures *phronēsis* and the virtues for themselves, not for external results.[12] But these positions do not depend on conceiving of practical reason as "pure" in a rationalistic sense.

As for the case under (c): in multicultural societies, or in the context of a world community, less can safely be left implicit because different groups differ in many of their implicit assumptions. Fairness and mutual understanding require more formalization, and the philosopher may be ideal for this task. But it is not a task of purification or ratification that somehow confers authority on principles which they would otherwise intrinsically lack. It is a task of equipping practical agents with what they now need for ethical intercommunication when their previous, home-grown, resources in this regard are no longer adequate for all their interactions with others. Un-talked-over principles are fine in some communal situations, like that in which Aristotle lived by comparison with modern society. On the other hand, Aristotle as a practical philosopher might well have been willing to engage in a lot more ethical codification had he lived under different historical circumstances.

Postscript

So Aristotle refuses to offer rules for excellent quotidian conduct, and instead he hopes to promote it indirectly by emphasizing the importance of character and situational intelligence, and the role of upbringing in their formation. We may easily be left with the impression that Aristotle's philosophy holds out no practical assistance at all to the quotidian agent at the point of particular action. (Labeling the agent in that way is meant for the sake of contrast with (a) the architectonic or political agent, and (b) the excellent quotidian agent considered simply as the product of upbringing, i.e. as bearer of a set of ethical dispositions. The architectonic agent is helped by having the correct architectonic goal explained to him, and the product of upbringing will have gained from having been reared in the light of that goal.) Now, the above impression is inevitable if we assume that there is no way philosophy could be even imagined to help at the point of quotidian action otherwise than by providing philosophically burnished rules telling us what to do. On that assumption, whether or not we ourselves believe in the practical usefulness of such a set of rules, we shall construe Aristotle's statement that he has none to offer as showing that he regards philosophy as completely incapable of helping quotidian practice. We might well round this conclusion off with the thought that for Aristotle this is undisturbing, since he means to be addressing only people who, on the quotidian level, would anyway find themselves knowing what to do.

However, it turns out that this is not at all Aristotle's train of thought. Here is how he states the impossibility of giving rules:

> Since, then, the present undertaking is not for the sake of theory, as our others are (for we are not inquiring into what excellence is for the sake of knowing it, but for the sake of becoming good, since otherwise there would be no benefit in it at all), we need to inquire into the subjects relating to actions, i.e. to how one should act; for as we have said, our actions are also responsible for our coming to have dispositions of a certain sort. Now that one should act in accordance with the correct prescription [*kata ton orthon logon*] is a shared view – let it stand as a basic assumption; there will be a discussion about it later . . . But before that let it be agreed that everything one says about practical undertakings has to be said, not with precision, but in rough outline . . . things in the sphere of action and things that bring advantage have nothing stable about them, any more than things that bring health. But if what one says universally is like this, what one says about particulars is even more lacking in precision; for it does not fall under any expertise or under any set of rules – the agents themselves have to consider the circumstances relating to the occasion, just as happens in medicine, too, and in navigation. (*NE* II.2.1103b26–1104a11, trans. C. J. Rowe)

Aristotle next says: "But even though the present discussion is like this, *we must try to give some help.*" And then, straightaway, he propounds the idea of the ethical mean. In short, the idea of the ethical mean is something the philosopher can supply that would supposedly give some practical help in particular situations.

But how can it do that? Or how can Aristotle believe that it can – that knowing the adage that for every area of practical life there is a too much, a too little, and a right amount,[13] of some kind of feeling or action would help one to come up with appropriate particular responses? Presumably he thinks that bearing this constantly in mind in "real life" disposes one to monitor one's reactions in a way that tends to refine them, ethically speaking.[14] And this is surely true. It is plausible that, in any situation, being alive to the inherent tendency of the relevant feeling or urge to action to be "more" or "less" than is called for, makes me better at molding my response so that it is more as it should be. Only when the agent succeeds in determining the right response will he/she (or a bystander) be in a position to say what, in this case, "too much" and "too little" would have been more or less *than*. Thus the maxim to avoid "too much" and "too little" makes its practical contribution precisely by means of what is often called its "emptiness" – precisely through the fact that all it says is "avoid doing/feeling more and less than is right!" It cannot point toward what is right in the way in which a signpost does, or a commandment, but by imbuing my agency in particular situations with this maxim I make it more likely that I myself become pointed toward what is right.

No doubt the general idea of the ethical mean was not exactly news to Aristotle's ancient Greek audience (although they may not have realized before following his exposition the variety of areas in which it applies, and the number of not hitherto properly noticed ethical qualities it enables one to identify). But when the idea first appears in the *Nicomachean Ethics* it is not intended as information, or to make its full impact on the purely reflective level. Aristotle assumes, when he offers it as practical help, that the audience understands that this will be true of it only if they actively take it with them into particular practical situations. Perhaps the idea is a banality *now*, as we turn the pages of Aristotle, but we are not now in a practical situation where we are called upon to act and are not sure how. But *then*, for those who need the help, the adage will pay its way. The point is worth noting if only because it shows Aristotle doing abstract philosophical ethics in a way so different from how most of us do it today.

One Neglected Aristotelian Theme

Many topics descended from Aristotle's *Nicomachean Ethics* continue to be explored, exploited, adapted, and creatively transformed by philosophers today. Thus a vast amount of our contemporary discussion of well-being, practical reason, the virtues, situational intelligence, the ethical role of emotion, moral education, weakness of will, moral and legal responsibility makes of Aristotle a reference point, and sometimes an inspiration. But other veins too are still worth mining which do not receive the same attention. Here, I shall take just one example: the question of leisure. Aristotle's remarks about leisure are not copious, but the theme is a vitally important one for him. Most philosophers of ethics today regard as important the ethical matters that Aristotle regarded as important. Surprisingly, then, except for Josef Pieper's (1948) contribution, which is very much of the nature of a protreptic, there has been practically no modern ethical discussion of leisure. As can easily be verified, the topic does not appear in modern surveys and compendia of ethics.[15]

I can think of several reasons for this. First, leisure in Aristotle is associated with his notorious doctrine of the supremacy of the theoretical life, which in turn is based partly on a theological picture. And Pieper's (1948) essay, while often penetrating, ties leisure so closely to the sacred and the sacramental that there may seem not to be enough of a topic left over for non-religious philosophical reflection.[16] Secondly, a priori it may seem that even if there are philosophical questions about leisure, they are quite easy ones, presenting no professional challenge. Thirdly, philosophical discussion of leisure, especially in the footsteps of Aristotle and of Pieper, is sure to get on to the question of its proper uses, but to take that seriously may seem uncomfortably close to legislating about how people should use their leisure-time: "which is no one's business but their own." In response: first, there is plenty to be said humanistically about leisure. Secondly, even if the questions are easy, one can find this out only by engaging with them. Thirdly, if for a moment we allow ourselves the phrase "the purpose of leisure," why should that set us on the path of telling people what to do any more threateningly than a question about "the purpose of art" or, for that matter, "the purpose of morality?"

If we turn to existing views (the first stage of an Aristotelian investigation), Aristotle's main ones are these: leisure is in some sense the end of life; *eudaimonia* crucially depends on leisure; leisure is different from mere relaxation; hence leisure activities should not be trivial amusements; leisure is the space for "precious" (*timios*) as distinct from "necessary" activities; thus leisure activities, though "serious," should be quite different in kind from the labor that goes into building up the resources for leisure; leisure activities are valuable for their own sake; human beings need education for leisure activities; what to do in leisure is the most fundamental question of politics; the leisure activity *par excellence* is theoretical intellection (*Pol.* VII.14, VIII.3; *NE* X.6–8). An important modern view is that leisure is a sort of freedom. (The word comes from the Latin *licere*, which connotes having permission.)

Let us pass to the other Aristotelian initial stage of investigation: the raising of questions and problems. (a) One can point to an apparent contradiction between the Aristotelian emphasis on seriousness, which is restrictive, and the idea of leisure as "freedom." (b) How is leisure-freedom related to other senses of freedom studied by philosophers? It is not freedom from coercion, nor is it freedom from servitude to one's passions. More than anything, it is freedom from requirements, duties, and obligations. Can it be right, then, to think of leisure-freedom as immensely important if we are also impressed by the Kantian thought that the truest freedom is exercised when the moral agent acts from moral duty? (c) Here one touches on a question discussed by contemporary philosophers of ethics: are we ever free of requirements, duties, and obligations? (d) Leisure-freedom consists in the possibility of being active without any particular reference to circumstances and constraint, or only with reference to ones chosen or already laid down by oneself, and from which one can disengage at will. So "self-expression" is a key concept. Then can something be a good leisure activity if it necessarily involves doing something with others? (e) If the answer is "Yes," as it surely must be, does that suggest that the self being expressed is in some way corporate – and what can that mean? (f) Is there any sound basis for an argument that the self to be expressed in leisure activity is in some way "higher" than the self of ordinary work? (g) And if so, might there be any interesting analogy or other connection between this and that other possible "higher self," the subject of moral duty and practical reason? (h) In what way do leisure and leisure activities contribute to individuality? (i) What about the activities themselves: should we take Aristotelian theorizing as emblematic of the whole class, and, if so, which are its essential aspects, i.e. the aspects to be generalized? (j) Should the activities be worthwhile (or be thought so) because of their specific content or objects, or are they worthwhile just because they are free in the way sketched under (d) above? (k) If because of the specific contents, do those of different kinds of leisure activities have anything interesting in common? (l) Leisure seems to be the ideal opportunity for being perfectionist, and also for being adventurous. What do these hugely important motivations tell us about human nature? Is it only very rarely that they can be combined – do they tend to pull apart? (m) In areas where professionalism is possible, is leisure activity necessarily amateurish by comparison? (n) If we ought to look for non-trivial leisure activities, is this because of a duty (for want of a better word) to oneself, or is it also because a leisure activity should not make a mockery of the kind of efforts (individual, communal, even stretching back into the past) that went into building up the prosperity and other conditions needed for leisure?

Further exploration of this ground[17] might yield worthy additions to the tribute that continues to be paid to Aristotle in the form of contemporary work – not necessarily even work that mentions him much – on what were originally Aristotelian questions.

Notes

1 This proposal is the definition of "eudaimonism" according to *The Cambridge Dictionary of Philosophy* (Audi 1999). Prichard (1949: 2–17, esp. 13) is the *locus classicus* for the picture of Aristotle as eudaimonist in that sense. But in that sense, Aristotle was no eudaimonist.

2 They are not the moralities of "other cultures" (the equations of which may tend, abstracted from local coloring, to coincide with Aristotle's equation): they are rivals within the same culture.

3 His next task, as he sees it, is to discuss the political, social, educational, and such like arrangements that would best realize what is covered by the right-hand side of his equation. When that has been done, his work in ethics will be complete (*NE* X.9.1179a33ff, 1181b12–15).

4 Like most of his contemporaries, Isocrates believed that the serious work of life was political action, and above all effective political communication. He allowed a certain value to mathematics: it was useful for sharpening young men's minds. Beyond that, while he might not have frowned upon the occasional recreational use (he was aware of the attraction), his motto would have been: "Just say No to theoretical activity." The character Callicles in Plato's *Gorgias* takes the same line about fundamental discussions of ethics.

5 This is clear from the treatments of the individual character-virtues, and from the books on friendship.

6 It then becomes clear, but only at the end of the *Nicomachean Ethics*, that architectonic activity should include promoting the serious practice, under human conditions, of purely theoretical pursuits: this should become the distinctive quotidian activity of at least some citizens.

7 Thus the famous opening argument of the *NE* says that all *goods* are for the sake of the chief good, which is the architectonic goal. This does not imply that all ethically *right* actions as such are for the sake of that goal. At I.12.1102a2–4 he is likewise stating the relation of *eudaimonia* to the other *goods* (and the "we" in line 3 refers, in my view, to us as engaged in architectonic practice, not as engaged in practice in general).

8 Aristotle does not, however, think that there is a different kind of *phronēsis* for each sphere. *Phronēsis* is unitary.

9 But for more on this taxonomy, or the associated idea of the ethical "mean," see the end of the next section.

10 But we shall see later how they can get a bit of help from Aristotle's notion of the ethical mean.

11 Cf. the discussion at X.9.1180b28ff on what sort of person is a good legislator, and especially 1181b13–14.

12 However, at *EE* VIII.3 he makes a somewhat eccentric distinction between the good (virtuous) and the fine-and-good agent, whereby only the latter values virtue and virtuous activities for themselves.

13 "Too much" and "too little," of course, do duty for a host of ways in which a response can be misplaced.

14 Note that when he claims practical usefulness for the mean-idea, he is thinking of it as helping to elicit the responses that build good character (*NE* II.2.1104a12–b3). To the extent that the agent approximates toward fully formed virtue, the need for any such conscious mean-invoking self-monitoring lessens. The mean-idea is descriptively true of the responses of the formed virtuous agent, but presumably no longer plays its original part of consciously helping determine them.

15 The classic study of the theme in late fifth- and early fourth-century Greek literature is Solmsen (1964).

16 One does not have to be a non-believer to find off-putting such assertions as: "leisure . . . is not possible unless it has a durable and consequently living link with the *cultus*, with divine worship" (p. xiv), and "When separated from worship, leisure becomes toilsome and work becomes inhuman" (p. 54). Pieper also, following Aristotle, focuses too exclusively on intellectual and contemplative leisure activities. A conception of leisure that leaves no room for sport is defective, to put it mildly. One-sided, too, is Pieper's tendency to characterize leisure as *a state of mind*: a kind of serenity and receptiveness.

17 Which has just now sparked as many questions or groups of questions as there are books of Aristotle's *Metaphysics*.

References

Audi, Robert (ed.) 1999: *The Cambridge Dictionary of Philosophy*. Cambridge: Cambridge University Press.

Mackie, J. L. 1977: *Ethics: Inventing Right and Wrong*. Harmondsworth: Penguin.

Pieper, Josef 1948: *Musse und Kult*, trans. by Gerald Malsbary, with an introduction by Roger Scruton, as *Leisure the Basis of Culture*. South Bend: St Augustine Press, 1998.

Prichard, H. A. 1949: "Does Moral Philosophy Rest on a Mistake?" In *Moral Obligation*, pp. 2–17. Oxford: Oxford University Press.

Putnam, Hilary 1990: "James's Theory of Perception." In *Realism with a Human Face*. Cambridge, MA: Harvard University Press.

Solmsen, F. 1964: "Leisure and Play in Aristotle's Ideal State," *Rheinisches Museum für Philologie* 107: 193–220; reprinted in F. Solmsen, *Kleine Schriften*, Hildesheim, 1968.

Williams, Bernard 1985: *Ethics and the Limits of Philosophy*. Cambridge, MA: Harvard University Press.

Further reading

Broadie, Sarah 2002: "The Highest Human Good." In Sarah Broadie and Christopher Rowe (eds), *Aristotle: Nicomachean Ethics*, pp. 9–17. Oxford: Oxford University Press.

Louden, Robert 1991: "Aristotle's Practical Particularism." In J. P. Anton and A. Preus (eds), *Aristotle's Ethics: Essays in Ancient Greek Philosophy*, vol. 4, pp. 159–78. Albany, NY: State University of New York Press.

McDowell, John 1995: "Eudaimonism and Realism in Aristotle's Ethics." In Robert Heinaman (ed.), *Aristotle and Moral Realism*, pp. 201–18. Boulder, CO: Westview Press.

Nussbaum, Martha: "Non-relative Virtues: An Aristotelian Approach." In M. Nussbaum and A. Sen (eds), *The Quality of Life*, pp. 242–69. New York: Oxford University Press.

Simpson, Peter 1997: "Contemporary Virtue Ethics and Aristotle." In D. Statman (ed.), *Virtue Ethics: A Critical Reader*, pp. 245–59. Edinburgh: Edinburgh University Press.

Index of Passages
from Aristotle

Numbers in **bold** refer to page number.

General Index